Retirement and Estate Planning in Canada

Third Edition

(Revised Printing with Updates)

Coleen Clark

Captus Press

**Retirement and Estate Planning in Canada, Third Edition
(Revised Printing with Updates)**
© 2013–2016 by Coleen Clark and Captus Press Inc.

Captus Press Inc.
Units 14 & 15, 1600 Steeles Avenue West,
Concord, Ontario L4K 4M2
Telephone: (416) 736–5537
Fax: (416) 736–5793
Email: Info@captus.com
Internet: www.captus.com

Library and Archives Canada Cataloguing in Publication
Clark, Coleen, 1947–, author
    Retirement and estate planning in Canada / Coleen Clark. — Third edition.

Includes bibliographical references and index.
ISBN 978-1-55322-289-7 (pbk.)

1. Retirement income — Canada — Planning. 2. Estate planning — Canada. I. Title.

HG179.C63 2013   332.024'0140971   C2013-904807-3

 Canada

Financé par le gouvernement du Canada   Funded by the Government of Canada

0 9 8 7 6 5
Printed in Canada

Table of Contents

Table of Contents

Table of Contents

Preface

Financial planning as a field of study is a recent development, bringing together several well-established disciplines — tax planning, insurance, investments, retirement planning, and estate planning. Financial planners are generalists in the same way that a general practitioner (GP) is a generalist — someone having a very broad knowledge base without being a specialist in any one area. To continue the analogy, a financial planner is to a specialist in tax, investments, insurance, estate planning and retirement planning as a general practitioner is to a cardiologist, ophthalmologist, gynecologist, psychiatrist and dermatologist. In the same way that a GP can serve many, if not most, of our medical needs for expertise, a financial planner can attend to general financial matters for the client including short and long-term planning as well as general advice and guidance in various areas. However, again in the same way a GP refers patients to a specialist, there are times when it is appropriate for the planner to refer clients to an expert — to draw up a will, to invest in specific stocks, to buy a certain type of insurance policy — functions a financial planner is not licensed to perform.

A good financial planner knows enough to know when it is time to refer the client to a specialist — it is important to recognize what you don't know. A financial planner, therefore, must know enough about some topics to understand their complexity. This text acts as a survey course in the areas of retirement and estate planning, introducing many topics that are fundamental to the retirement and estate planning processes while not providing the depth and proficiency an expert has in any particular area.

The aim of this textbook is not only to meet external standards but to surpass them since the goal is not merely to train students, but also to educate them. As a result, topics are covered in a way that may not be part of a national examination but will ensure that the student understands both the topics and related calculations. We will study retirement planning without using a computerized financial planning package because it is important to understand the process and to know what to expect from the calculations. It has been our experience that the use of a retirement package can produce some serious errors because the program is making calculations using assumptions that are different from the assumptions the user is making. We want to encourage students of these topics to be the master of planning programs, not their slave.

Upon completing this course, the student will have a thorough knowledge of retirement and estate planning without being an expert in any area.

ACKNOWLEDGMENTS

In addition to thanking Ania Czyznielewski, Nici Chirita, Jason Wormald, and Pauline Lai at Captus Press, as well as the many anonymous reviewers for their valuable feedback and guidance, I wish to thank the 600 Ryerson University students of FIN 612 "Retirement and Estate Planning" from 2002 to 2005 for their patience, invaluable comments, copy editing and, most importantly, their candid requests for clarification. Thanks to Margot Danard, Stuart Mussells and their three daughters, my neighbours, for allowing me to take poetic licence with their lives. Thanks also to my friends and colleagues who put up with me over the long development period. In particular, thank you to Anne Peace and Judy Waalen who provided support when I was losing hope and advice when I floundered. Special thanks to Claudette Smith, whose support and encouragement went way beyond the requirements of a colleague and friend. And a second special thanks to Robert Halpern for his invaluable feedback both when he was a student in class using the first edition and his critical review of the second edition as it was in process. For this, the third edition, I must give special thanks to Carolyn Fallis for her on-going feedback throughout the book but in particular, her expertise and inspiration for revising Chapter 11, Taxation Issues. Thank you, Carolyn, I couldn't have done it without you!

Introduction

Planning for retirement involves deciding how much of the family's current and future income can be used to save for retirement. To do this, a family needs to set goals for retirement; for example, what lifestyle does the family want in retirement, where will they live (in the principal residence or will they downsize to free up some capital), do they want to travel. These goals are translated into specific objectives — when does the family expect to retire and how much annual income is needed to finance their retirement lifestyle. Then the family looks at how they will save for this retirement.

Estate planning looks at the process that distributes the family assets in a tax-efficient manner. The process involves determining what will be left to pass on to which beneficiaries and the various ways of transferring assets. This section will present details on wills, powers of attorney, taxation at death, trusts, and donating to charity.

PART 1. RETIREMENT PLANNING

Chapter 1 introduces the six-step retirement planning process, beginning with a general model and an example to provide an overview of the process. This is followed by a case to illustrate all the elements of this process.

Appendix 1A is a **review of time value of money** (TVM) calculations with examples because Chapters 1 to 12 require a good understanding of TVM. Students who need the review should refer to this chapter early in the course.

Chapter 2 discusses the **factors that affect retirement planning**: life expectancy or longevity, inflation, rates of return and personal income tax rates. This chapter also provides a **review of personal taxation** of regular income, dividends and capital gains as well as the calculation of average and marginal tax rates. The appendix provides the tax rates for all provinces and territories, although we will be using a generic provincial rate for ease of calculation.

Appendix 2A is a short review of **investment basics** — rates of return, measures of risk, and evaluating and comparing the risk of different asset classes.

Appendix 2B presents 2013 tax rates for all provinces and territories. Generic tax rates used in this text follow 2013 actual rates.

Chapter 3 presents **government-sponsored pension plans.** Since there is no guarantee that these plans will be available in their present form in the future, we can make allowances for them when doing long-term planning. The plans available now are the Canada Pension Plan (CPP), Quebec Pension Plan in Quebec (QPP), and Old Age Security (OAS) program. We can make an allowance for the future of these plans by assuming, for example, that the Old Age Security pension may become even more means-tested than it currently is and that, like the Guaranteed Income Supplement (GIS), it will only be available to very low-income seniors.

Chapters 4 and 5 look at **employer-sponsored pension plans.**

Chapter 4 presents the fundamentals of employer-sponsored Registered Pension Plans (RPP) along with their characteristics, who can join them, how they are funded, the benefit options, and when a pension plan member can retire. The Ontario Municipal Employees Retirement System (OMERS) is used as an illustration.

Chapter 5 continues with employer-sponsored **Registered Pension Plans (RPP)** beginning with the **pension adjustment (PA),** which puts limitations on annual tax-deductible retirement savings. While federal and provincial governments encourage saving for retirement, these tax sheltered savings reduce current tax revenues for these two levels of government. Since some employees are members of registered pension plans, while many employees and the self-employed are not, there are restrictions on the use of other tax-sheltered savings (such as Registered Retirement Savings Plans — RRSPs) for taxpayers who are members of RPPs. The chapter also illustrates various types of defined benefit pension plans.

Chapter 6 presents **Registered Retirement Savings Plans (RRSPs)** including investment restrictions and borrowing from the RRSP using the Home Buyers' Plan (HBP) and the Lifelong Learning Plan (LLP). The Registered Education Savings Plan (RESP) is also discussed since planning for the education of their children can be an important part of a family's savings goals. While the HBP, LLP and RESP are not part of retirement income, they can have a large impact on a family's ability to save for retirement. Many clients or potential clients who consult a financial planner may not have the resources to maximize all savings vehicles available to them while making mortgage payments, educating their children, etc. In addition, these topics are of personal interest to many students studying retirement planning. Chapter 6 also includes new plans — the Registered Disability Savings Plan and the Tax Free Savings Account.

Chapter 7 presents **retirement income options** for the registered plans described in Chapters 3 to 6. There are several options available, which can be quite confusing for retirees who have not had to make large financial decisions like this before.

At the end of Chapter 7, there is a **case assignment** for students.

PART 2.   ESTATE PLANNING

Chapter 8 discusses the **issues in estate planning** and continues the case presented in Chapter 1, taking Craig and Margot forward several years to the point where they are starting to think about estate planning issues.

Chapter 9 looks at **family law** and **power of attorney**, which can have an effect on retirement plans. While no one likes to imagine it, an untimely death or long illness of a major breadwinner can upset the best-made plans. Similarly, divorces do happen, even to couples who are currently getting along just fine. While we cannot necessarily avoid these changes, we can be aware of their implications when making plans.

Chapter 10 examines **wills** and the way they can help reduce taxes at death, what happens if you die without a will (called dying intestate), minimizing probate fees, the contents of a will and the duties of the executor.

Chapter 11 looks at **taxation issues** that can have an effect on long-term planning. These issues include income attribution (taxation on the income of gifts to non-arm's length people), passing on the family business, and taxation of Canadians living outside of Canada. We also look at the **final** or **terminal tax return** that is filed for the deceased after death. This chapter concludes with a look at **estate freezes** — locking in the value of family assets to minimize income tax on them.

Chapter 12 discusses the two kinds of **trusts** — testamentary (takes effect after death) and inter vivos (takes effect before death). Trusts can be a useful way to defer taxes on an estate. However, they involve administration charges and income taxes. There are rules for recognizing the capital gain on assets transferred into a trust and paying the tax on the gain. In addition, income left in a trust is subject to income tax. The chapter then covers the tax advantages of **donating to charity**. As part of estate planning, this is called "planned giving" and, again, can be used to minimize taxes over time both before and at death.

PART 3. APPENDICES

Acronyms, **formulas** and **tax rates** used are provided along with **glossaries** of retirement planning terms and estate planning terms.

This text assumes that the student has

- a solid knowledge of average and marginal tax rates on regular and interest income, dividend income, and capital gains,
- a good understanding of the time value of money,
- a basic understanding of Finance and Investments, and
- fluency with a financial calculator.

Tax basics are reviewed in Chapter 2. Part 3 includes two review chapters — time value of money and investment basics — which are critical to the understanding of this book.

MARGOT AND CRAIG AND OTHERS

Throughout this text, we are going to follow a family as they go through the retirement and estate planning processes. They are, in many ways, a typical family, albeit very much a middle-class family. They have a good income but they are by no means wealthy. So they must, like most families, allocate their funds to their various short and long-term goals. They have aging parents from whom they expect (and hope) to inherit.

Through Margot and Craig, readers will see issues and situations that they are likely to encounter and learn what they can do to minimize the minuses and optimize the pluses. Additional examples supplement the issues faced by Craig and Margot.

Part 1

Retirement Planning

Part 1: Retirement Planning

Margot, Craig, and their three daughters live in Kitchener, Ontario. Their neighbour, Francesca, is a Certified Financial Planner® (CFP®) and, over dinner now and again, has been chatting with them about retirement planning. Margot and Craig, now 44 and 43 respectively, have become aware that they should start planning for their retirement. Margot, an engineer, is willing to get professional advice but wants to understand the whys and wherefores of important decisions. She took a few business courses in university but finds her knowledge is not sufficient to answer all her questions. Also, they are both very busy and do not have time to become experts on their own. So, after dessert one evening, they get Francesca's business card with plans to can call and make an appointment to learn about the issues and to begin the retirement planning process.

Margot's mother is a widow living in Lunenburg, Nova Scotia, while Craig's parents live in Lethbridge, Alberta. Margot wants to be able to help them out on an informal basis. She knows she cannot give them expert advice, but she wants to know enough about the issues to be able to send them for professional help when appropriate. She thinks that while they should enjoy their money, her inheritance will be larger if she can send them in the right direction for advice when it is needed (Margot is nothing if not pragmatic).

For future reference, let's have a summary of Margot and Craig's plans now, in May 2009, as they begin the retirement planning process with Francesca. To simplify planning, let's assume that

- all **events happen** at the beginning of the year (before their birthdays),
- all retirement **savings happen** at the end of the year, and
- all retirement **spending happens** at the beginning of the year.

Ages of Margot and Craig

Year	Event	Margot	Craig
2014	They begin retirement planning	44	43
2031	Scenario I — they retire	61	60
2066	Both die	96	95

Their Planning Timeline

Year:	2014	2031	2066
Event:	**Start planning**	**They retire**	**Both die**
Time:	T_0	T_{17}	T_{52}
Timeline:			
Margot's age:	44	61	96
Craig's age:	43	60	95
Years **to** retirement:	17		
Years **in** retirement:		35	

1

The Retirement Planning Process

Learning Objectives

A. Understand the general model of the retirement planning process and review the role played by Time Value of Money concepts.

B. Demonstrate and explain the six-step retirement planning process.
- Gather current financial information.
- Prepare statements to reflect current financial situation:
  - the Statement of Financial Position (also called Statement of Net Worth or Balance Sheet), and
  - the Statement of Cash Flows.
- Quantify short- and long-term goals.
- Prepare short-term budgets and estimate retirement spending. These budgets have three purposes:
  - to help the client meet short-term goals
  - to ascertain how much the client will be able to save each year (and what adjustments, if any, must be made to the budget to meet retirement goals)
  - to estimate annual retirement spending.
- Calculate required retirement savings.
- Monitor results and make changes as needed.

INTRODUCTION

The retirement planning process for a family changes over time. Young families — single people, same-sex or opposite-sex married couples and partners, all with or without children — have many years of working before retirement. These families may go through changes in structure due to the arrival of children, divorce, death, and remarriage, all of which affect their family finances. In addition, family finances fluctuate with changing careers, buying houses, establishing lifestyles, etc. Young families will not be involved in retirement planning in a detailed way, as there are many demands on their budgets. As a family ages, however, mortgages consume less disposable income, children leave home, careers advance, and retirement is closer.

When planning for retirement, there are three aspects that most seriously affect the plan:

1. **The period of accumulation** — People often start to save later than they should to implement their retirement goals.
2. **The amount of annual savings required** — Many people underestimate how much they need to save each year and do not cut their expenses enough to meet retirement goals. Others do not estimate how much they will need to finance their retirement. As a result, they pick a number — for example, $1 million or $2 million — that turns out to be much more than their retirement goals would indicate is appropriate. They then make large sacrifices in terms of time spent working, travelling foregone, etc. in order to save for a retirement goal that they have not quantified.

3. **The rate of return** — By investing too conservatively, many people end up having to save more than they needed to had they been more aggressive in their investing. Alternatively, they cannot accumulate enough to retire when they plan to or with the lifestyle they would like.

The further off retirement is in the future, the more estimates will suffice. The closer one gets to retirement, the more the plan must be fine-tuned and specific decisions must be made: decisions such as when to start collecting the Canada Pension Plan (CPP) Retirement Pension and what retirement vehicles to use. In addition, retirement planning must be done in the context of all the other aspects of financial planning — insurance, investments, and tax and estate planning.

Since each family's situation is different, an effective financial planner, whether planning for personal needs or for others, must be able to provide advice that reflects a family's goals and objectives. Retirement planning needs to be done in detail, and is usually done in six steps:

Step 1   Gather current financial information.
Step 2   Prepare statements to reflect the current financial situation:
  • the Statement of Financial Position, and
  • the Statement of Cash Flows.
Step 3   Quantify short- and long-term goals.
Step 4   Prepare short-term budgets and estimate retirement spending. These budgets have three purposes:
  • to help the client meet short-term goals,
  • to ascertain how much the client will be able to save each year (and what adjustments, if any, must be made to the budget to meet retirement goals), and
  • to estimate annual retirement spending.
Step 5   Calculate required retirement savings.
Step 6   Monitor results and make changes as needed.

The first four-and-a-half steps of the retirement planning process are applicable to families of all ages as they quantify and plan for short- and long-term goals. For young families, retirement planning is a long-term goal to be kept in mind but is generally not a focus of attention. Families of all ages are saving for retirement as they make mandatory contributions to government and perhaps private pension plans. Families are also building retirement savings by making contributions to Registered Retirement Savings Plans (RRSPs) as funds are available.

We met Craig and Margot earlier. Their family can be summarized as:

> **Margot**, age 44, **Craig**, age 43, and their three daughters live in Kitchener, Ontario. Their neighbour, **Francesca** is a Certified Financial Planner® (CFP®) and is going to be working with them on retirement and estate planning. Margot's mother, a widow, lives in Lunenburg, Nova Scotia, while Craig's parents live in Lethbridge, Alberta.
>
> Craig wants to have an idea of what they are getting into. Francesca tells him that she will give them a general overview of the retirement planning process.

A. THE PLANNING MODEL

The **general model** for retirement planning requires that the amount available at retirement be equal to the amount of savings in place now, plus future savings each year until retirement, compounded at some reasonable rate of return.

Savings at retirement = Savings now + Savings each year in total

---

$$W_n = W_0(FVIF_{n,\,k}) + (E - C)_{EOY}(FVIFA_{n,\,k})$$

W_n	Savings at retirement
W_0	Savings now
$FVIF_{n,\,k}$	The value in the future of $1 today compounded for n periods at k%
n	Number of years to retirement
k	Rate of return earned on savings
E	Earnings each year
C	Consumption each year
E – C	Savings each year until retirement
EOY	End of year
$FVIFA_{n,\,k}$	The value in the future of $1 saved at the same time interval, for n time periods, compounded at some interest rate, k.

The amount available each year in retirement is based on the amount saved, expected investment returns in retirement, and an estimated age of death.

Savings at retirement = Annual retirement income in total until death

---

$$W_n = C_{BOY}(PVIFA_{n,\,k})$$

W_n	Savings at retirement to be consumed for n years of retirement
C	Consumption each year in retirement
BOY	Beginning of the year
$PVIFA_{n,\,k}$	The value at the beginning of retirement of the annual income to be received during retirement discounted at the discount rate k
n	Number of years in retirement
k	Rate of return earned on the savings while retired

The last equation assumes all assets are used up during retirement. If the retiree is planning on having an estate to leave to beneficiaries, this model will be modified to:

Savings at retirement = Total Annual Consumption until death + Estate

---

$$W_n = C(PVIFA_{n,\,k}) + Estate(PVIF_{n,\,k})$$

$PVIF_{n,\,k}$	The value, at retirement, of the amount of the estate at the end of retirement discounted for the period of retirement at some discount rate, k.

To make the equations balance, some of the variables may have to be changed — the date of retirement, annual savings, annual retirement expenditures, etc. Some changes reflect changes in taste, risk preferences, circumstances, etc. These factors will be explored as we proceed through the chapters.

Variables to Address in Retirement Planning

To expand the general model, the following variables need to be addressed in order to plan for retirement:

- **How much will you need** in retirement — that is, what will your retirement expenses be? Young people can use a percentage of current needs. However, as retirement planning becomes more focussed, annual retirement spending has to be calculated more carefully to reflect changes in lifestyle or circumstances, such as paying off the mortgage, having children complete their education, and planning retirement lifestyle.
- **What will you receive** from government pension programs, from current pension plans, and from current savings?
- Based on current savings rates and pension savings presently in place, **how much will you have** at retirement?
- What is the **shortfall** or **surplus**?
- If there is a shortfall, what changes can be made to meet the shortfall? Can the date of retirement be changed? Can annual savings be increased? Can more investment risk be taken on to increase the rate of return?

"Well, this is all very nice," says Craig, "but what exactly does it mean? And what is this present value, future value business?"

"I'll give you a short example," replies Francesca. "But before I do that, let me give you this little summary [Table 1.1] that I created for you. And here are some additional materials [Appendix 1A] that will give you a quick overview of the Time Value of Money, or TVM, which explains present and future value calculations. An understanding of TVM is crucial to understanding the long-term retirement planning process. Let's meet again next week so I can give you the example and go through it with you."

Time Value of Money

Money loses value over time. If we are saving for a new car or for the down payment on a house, the time frame is probably not all that long so we mostly don't worry about a dollar's loss of purchasing power. But in retirement planning, we plan for a few decades. The value of a dollar at the date of retirement can be quite different than the value of a dollar at the date of death if one lives in retirement for a long time. The change in the value happens, in part, based on levels of inflation. However, a dollar now has more value for most of us than the value of a dollar in the future even if there is no inflation.

For most people, given the option of receiving $1,000 now or $1,000 a year from now, they would choose to receive $1,000 now. Even if you offer $1,020 in a year to offset the effect of 2% inflation, most people would take $1,000 now. Why? Human nature. There are, however, other more "scientific" reasons. If you have the $1,000 today, you could put it in a savings account and earn interest that more than offsets inflation. Therefore, you will have more than $1,020 in a year. Or, if you have $1,000 today, you could buy a stereo and listen to it for a year rather than waiting for a year to begin your enjoyment. The fact is, the $1,000 you receive a year later does not have the same value as the $1,000 you have now, and vice versa. The worth of investments that offer you the same return but at different times, or the value of the same income you receive at different times are not the same. The difference is increased by higher levels of inflation, but waiting has a value — that is, **money loses value the longer you have to wait to get it or use it.** Therefore, it is important to understand how the time value of money works so that you can distinguish between "similar" investments and be able to find out how much you actually have at different times in your life. Table 1.1 summarizes the TVM formula and terminology that are used throughout this book.[1]

Table 1.1 Time Value of Money Formula and Terminology

Time value	Financial calculator	What is being done
FV	= PV (FVIF$_{n,k}$)	The future value of one amount of money.
FVA	= PMT (FVIFA$_{n,k}$)	The future value of a series of equal payments made at the end of the same, regular interval (an **ordinary annuity**).
PV	= FV (PVIF$_{n,k}$)	The present value (now at T_0) of one amount of money.
PVA	= PMT (PVIFA$_{n,k}$)	The present value of a series of equal payments made at the end of the same, regular interval (an **ordinary annuity**).

When the payments are made at the beginning of the period, it is called an **annuity due** and its value can be calculated by multiplying (1+k) to the interest factor for annuity (PVIFA or FVIFA).

Terms Used in TVM Formula

One amount of money		Annuities	
FV	Future value	FVA	Future value
PV	Present value	PVA	Present value
n	Number of *compounding periods*	n	Number of *payments**
i	Nominal interest rate	i	Nominal interest rate
k	Interest rate per *compounding period*	k	Interest rate per *payment* period*
EAR	Effective annual rate	EAR	Effective annual rate
		PMT	Amount of regular payment
		*The above formula assumes the PMT is at the end of the period.	

Let's see how Time Value of Money concepts are applicable to the retirement planning model presented earlier.

> The next time they meet, Francesca walks Margot and Craig through a simplified version of the calculation of the annual savings required to meet a rough estimate of their retirement needs.

Example 1   Suppose Craig and Margot decide they need to have $50,000 per year after tax in retirement. Francesca uses 2013 dollars to explain this concept — that is, she will not include any inflation so that the $50,000 per year has the same purchasing power in 2013 as when they are in retirement. Since the $50,000 per year has the same purchasing power every year, the $50,000 and the total are in **real dollars**. If Francesca were to include inflation, the $50,000 would increase every year to reflect inflation. These increasing amounts are called **nominal dollars**. Suppose further that Margot and Craig now have $98,700 in their RRSPs and they would like to retire in 17 years when Craig is 60. They imagine they will be retired for 35 years. They ask how much they will have to save each year from now until retirement in order to finance their retirement.

---

1.   For a more thorough review of the time value of money, refer to Appendix 1A.

We will first look at how much they need to have saved when they retire:

Savings at retirement = Annual retirement income in total

$W_n = C_{BOY}(PVIFA_{n,\,k})$

C Consumption each year in retirement
= $50,000 in real dollars at the beginning of the year = **$50,000$_{BOY}$**

BOY Beginning of the year[2]

$PVIFA_{n,\,k}$ The value at the beginning of the retirement of the income to be received during retirement discounted at the discount rate k

n Number of years in retirement = **35 years**

k Rate of return earned on the savings while retired
= **4% real return**$_{after\ tax}$ (without inflation)

W_n **Savings required at retirement,** to be consumed for 35 years of retirement:

$W_n = PVA =$ $50,000$_{BOY\ after\ tax}$ $(PVIFA_{35,\,4\%})$ = **$970,560$_{after\ tax}$**

"Ouch!" says Craig "How will we ever save that much?"

"First of all," says Francesca, "there are **government programs** that will provide you with some income. Let's estimate **$24,000** per year before tax for both of you from all government programs. For now, let's assume you will receive all retirement income equally — that is, you will *each* need $25,000 per year after tax. We can estimate your retirement taxes at 17% of income [we will go into this calculation further at another time]. That means you will receive **$19,920** [$24,000 × (1 − 0.17)] after tax in total, [or $9,960 *each*] from government plans in retirement. If we take the present value of this total, it reduces your required savings at retirement by:

$$W_n = \$19,920_{BOY\ after\ tax}\ (PVIFA_{35,\,4\%}) = \$386,671_{after\ tax}$$

So now you need to save **$583,889** [$970,560 − $386,671] after tax in total by the time you retire."

The wrinkles between Craig's eyebrows relax a bit, but not much.

"Now, let's look at your **present savings,**" says Francesca. "It is quite reasonable to assume you will earn a higher rate of return on your savings before retirement. At retirement, you do not have to reduce the risk on all of your savings significantly, but in general, we assume that one accepts less risk on savings in retirement. Less risk generally means a lower rate of return in retirement. But, let's still be conservative for now and assume a real (without inflation) rate of return before retirement of 6%."

Craig and Margot's current RRSP savings will grow to:

$$W_n = \$98,700\ (FVIF_{17,\,6\%}) \quad = \$265,777_{before\ tax}$$
$$= \$220,595_{after\ tax}\left[i.e.,\ \$265,777 \times (1 - 17\%)\right]$$

---

2   Throughout, we assume that all retirement cash flows happen at the begining of the year.

If we look at the whole equation, how much do Margot and Craig need to save each year to meet their retirement objectives? Assuming the savings happen at the end of the year (EOY), the equation now becomes:

$W_n =$ $\qquad$ $W_0(FVIF_{n, k})$ $\qquad$ $+ (E - C)(FVIFA_{n, k})$

$\$583,889 =$ $\qquad$ $\$220,595$ $\qquad$ $+$ Savings each year $(FVIFA_{17, 6\%})$

Savings each year$_{EOY}$ = $\qquad$ **$12,877, or about $13,000 a year**.

"Well," says Craig, "I am very surprised — that sounds do-able. How do we find out what we actually have to do? What are the steps in the retirement planning process?"

Overview of the Retirement-Planning Process

Francesca gives them a quick description of the six-step process and tells them to start by gathering the information she needs to determine their present financial position. Then, together, they will quantify Margot and Craig's goals — both short term and long term. The next step is to use their present financial position to prepare budgets for the next two or three years and also to take a first look at how much they will need each year in retirement to finance their desired retirement lifestyle. To see how much they need to save each year until their retirement, they will look at income from government plans as well as the value at retirement of whatever savings they have now. They will use all this information to determine whether or not their goals are realistic, making adjustments if necessary, and detailing what they need to do to meet their retirement objectives. As retirement draws closer, other factors will need to be considered more carefully.

"To plan at retirement, you must balance sheltered and unsheltered income in order to maximize your after-tax income," says Francesca. "**Sheltered savings** are payments into plans such as company pension plans and Registered Retirement Savings Plans whereby there is no tax paid *now* on contributions to these plans. Also, there is no tax paid on the income earned by these savings until the money is withdrawn from the plan. **Unsheltered savings** are savings such as investments in stocks and mutual funds that are purchased with tax-paid funds. Tax is paid annually on most income earned from non-sheltered savings, but there is less tax payable on these funds as they are liquidated, to be used in retirement. We will look at this more closely later.

In addition, there are other factors you have to plan for to prevent outliving the accumulated assets and to maximize the estate you would like to leave to your daughters," Francesca tells them. "Assuming you do not plan to consume all your assets in retirement, these factors include: how long you think you will live, future inflation rates, and tax rates, as well as projected returns on investments. We will look at these factors more closely at another time [in Chapter 2]."

Planning for retirement focuses on **two main goals** *during* retirement:

1. optimizing after-tax income during retirement, and
2. optimizing one's after-tax estate.

B.   IMPLEMENTING THE PROCESS

Francesca will now walk Margot and Craig through their financial plan. They will follow the six-step process described earlier.

Step 1	Gather current financial information.
	⇩
Step 2	Prepare statements to reflect current financial position.
	⇩
Step 3	Quantify short- and long-term goals.
	⇩
Step 4	Prepare short-term budgets and estimate retirement spending.
	⇩
Step 5	Calculate required retirement savings.
	⇩
Step 6*	Monitor and revise.

*We will not monitor and revise until Chapter 8. However, Margot and Craig will meet Francesca regularly — every two or three years — to monitor and revise their plans.

Step 1.   Gather Current Financial Information

Francesca tells them that the first step is to ascertain their financial position now. First they will set up a current Statement of Financial Position, their most recent annual Cash Flow Statement and a Budget for the next year or two. A "current" Cash Flow Statement will be for the year ended 2013 and a Statement of Financial Position at the end of 2013. They set up an appointment for Craig and Margot to return when they have gathered all the necessary information. They come in to see Francesca two weeks later with the following information.

Employment Information

Craig has worked as an architect in Kitchener for the past several years. His gross annual salary for 2013 was $90,000, which he expects will increase by only the cost of living since his company is bringing in a new pension plan in 2014. He pays $731 in long-term disability insurance premiums. Beginning in 2014, he and his employer will each contribute 6% of his salary (but not his taxable benefits) to this new **defined benefit pension plan** (DBPP),[3] which will pay him a pension of 2% a year for each year of service, based on his best three years' earnings. Craig has an employee benefits package that provides him with life insurance coverage for twice his annual salary, short- and long-term disability coverage, as well as extended health care for the family. His employer pays the premium of $125 a month for family coverage. These premiums are not a taxable benefit for Craig. However, the Ontario health tax will be paid by his employer, making it a taxable benefit for Craig. (Note: this detail is being added primarily to illustrate the effects of taxable benefits on tax. **The actual calculation of Craig's 2013 take-home pay is given in Chapter 2.**)

---

3   A defined benefit pension plan (DBPP) is an employer-sponsored pension plan that provides a pre-determined pension benefit. This topic will be discussed in detail in Chapters 4 and 5.

Margot works on an hourly basis for an engineering firm. Her annual gross income is generally about $60,000 per year from which no deductions are taken. As a self-employed person, she usually has tax deductions of about $800 per year. She has recently taken out disability insurance, which covers 66⅔% of her net/taxable income. The premium for this is $199.73 per month. **The calculation of her income after tax is covered in Chapter 3.**

General Tax Information: Craig and Margot have RRSP deduction limits of $35,600 and $28,000 respectively for 2013 according to the CRA *Notices of Assessment* that they each received in early May 2014. These limits include all the unused contribution room — RRSP contributions relating to prior years' income that they are eligible to make when they have the funds.

Assets

Financial Assets

Liquid Assets: Craig and Margot pay their household bills and everyday expenses from their joint chequing account, which has a current balance of $1,200. Craig and Margot have a savings account in Margot's name with a balance of $3,500. Margot also has $5,000 in regular interest Canada Savings Bonds (CSBs) as an emergency fund and earns 5% on these funds. The savings account, CSBs and, beginning in 2015, the Car Savings will be invested in Margot's name because her top tax rate is lower. When we look at Margot's tax calculation in Chapter 3, we will see that her marginal tax rate on interest income is 35.00%. Thus, this income will grow at an after-tax rate of 3.25% [5% × (1 − 0.3500)].

Non-registered Investment Assets: Craig has 200 Bartok preferred shares that his grandmother gave him when they got married. They cost $25 a share and are currently worth $8,000. Craig usually receives dividends of $320 per year. which are re-invested at a real (without inflation) after-tax rate of 3.30%. When we look at the calculation of Craig's take-home pay in Chapter 2, we will see that his marginal tax rate on dividend income is 17.45%. Just now, the shares are providing a before-tax rate of return of 4%, which is 3.30% after tax [4% × (1 − 0.1745)]. Craig does not consider these shares as part of his retirement savings because they are preferred shares, and he does not expect the market value to increase much. They have been included on the Statement of Financial Position, but they have not been included in Step 5, "Calculating required retirement savings." The amount is relatively small — let's treat it like a small cushion.

Craig's Registered Pension Plan (RPP): Craig has benefits from a plan with a previous employer. When he left the company and moved to his present position, he elected to leave the funds with his previous employer. He will receive non-indexed pension income of $10,800 per year if he begins receiving the pension at age 65, or non-indexed pension income of $8,100 per year if he begins receiving the pension at age 60.

> Francesca is not going to put this on their Statement of Financial Position because Craig cannot access this money until he collects it as retirement income, which is not until age 55 in most jurisdictions. Instead she is going to include it on the retirement income estimates when they get to that step.

Craig's RRSP Investment Assets: Craig currently has $59,700 in his personal RRSP, which is invested in a Canadian equity fund. He had a pre-authorized purchase plan at a local trust company and contributed $250 a month to his personal RRSP to the end of 2013. Now that the pension plan has started, he is not sure what he should do about his annual RRSP contributions. He is somewhat knowledgeable about investing and the score from his investor profile questionnaire categorizes him as a "moderately aggressive" investor.

Margot's RRSP Investment Assets: Margot has $39,000 in her RRSP, including her 2013 contribution of $3,000, which is invested in a Canadian dividend fund. She considers herself a relatively conservative investor, and the score from her investor profile questionnaire categorizes her as an "income and moderate growth" investor.

Income on their financial assets is not included in the Cash Flow Statement since this income is not used for annual spending but rather is left to accumulate. The accumulation is reflected in the increase in Financial Assets in the budgets prepared for Step 5. The income on the Registered Education Savings Plans (RESP) and RRSPs is calculated by multiplying 1 + the interest rate times the sum of the balances at the prior year-end for the accumulated contributions, income, and grants for the RESP. RESPs are presented in Chapter 6. The basics of RESPs are given at the end of "Expenses" below.

Personal Use Assets

Principal Residence: Their principal residence is valued at $300,000 and the house is held in joint tenancy. They have a mortgage, which is discussed in "Long-term Liabilities" below.

Household Contents: These are valued at $40,000.

Margot's Car: Margot has a seven-year-old automobile, which is worth approximately $6,000.

Craig's Van and Van Lease: Craig decided to get a van because the family goes on several camping trips each summer and skiing day trips in the winter. Since he bikes to work most days, he thought a van would best suit their needs. He has a three-year lease on his van. In November 2011, he made a down payment of $5,000 toward the lease and his monthly lease payments are $525. He can buy the van at the end of the lease for $9,265. The purchase price of the van was $30,000. The van is now worth about $21,000.

> At Francesca's request, Craig shows her the lease and she calculates that he is paying 6.18% interest on the van. (This scenario is covered in more detail with the timeline in Appendix 1A.) Francesca solves the following equation to find the interest rate:

Cost	=	down payment + present value of payments + present value of buyout
$30,000	=	$5,000 down + 525_{\text{BOM}}$ (PVIFA$_{36, \, k\%}$) + $9,265 (PVIF$_{36, \, k\%}$)
k	=	0.5151% per month or 6.18% per year.

At December 31, 2013, Craig has 10 payments remaining on the lease. So his liability or outstanding principal is:

PVA	=	525_{\text{BOM}}$ (PVIFA$_{10, \, 0.5151\%}$) + $9,265 (PVIF$_{10, \, 0.5151\%}$)
	=	$13,932, including the buyout.

Luxury Assets

Grand Piano and Loan: A few years ago, Margot decided she could not live without a grand piano on which she could play and on which the girls could practise (they take piano lessons from Carole, who lives just three doors away). The piano cost $19,000 and will hold its value well. She took out a bank loan for $16,000 at 7%, amortized over 48 months. Her monthly payments are $383.14. This loan is presented in detail with the timeline in Appendix 1A, Example 14.

Francesca shows Margot how the payments are calculated:

$19,000 = $3,000 down + PMT$_{EOM}$ (PVIFA$_{48, 0.5833\%}$)
PMT = $383.14

At December 31, 2013, Margot has 19 payments remaining on the loan. Her liability is:

PVA = 383.14_{EOM}$ (PVIFA$_{19, 0.5833\%}$)
PVA = $6,872

At December 31, 2014, her outstanding liability will be:

PVA = 383.14_{EOM}$ (PVIFA$_{7, 0.5833\%}$)
PVA = $2,620

Liabilities
Short-term Liabilities
Credit Cards: Margot and Craig each have a VISA card with an interest rate of 18.25% per year. They always pay off their monthly balances.

Line of Credit: If the couple require additional funds, they generally draw on their joint unsecured line of credit, which has a rate of prime plus 3%. The credit limit on the line of credit is $20,000 and they owe an amount of $5,000 at the end of 2013 after paying a fixed amount of $500 per month towards the line of credit during 2013.

Francesca estimates that at 7% interest (considering the prime at the moment is 4%) or so, they will pay $5,165 — $5,000 principal plus interest of $165 — and they will pay off the line of credit in 2014.

$5,000 = 500_{EOM}$ (PVIFA$_{n, 0.5833\%}$)
n = 10.33

During 2014, they will pay principal and interest of $5,165 (10.33 × $500) paying off the $5,000 balance at the end of 2013 and paying interest of $165 (total payments less the outstanding principal — $5,165 – 5,000).

Long-term Liabilities
Margot and Craig bought their house in January 2004 for $205,000 and put $51,250 down. The original mortgage at 7% was amortized over 25 years. They renewed the mortgage for another 5-year term at 7¼% in January 2009. In January 2014, they renewed their mortgage of $121,004 at 6.25% for another 5-year term. They make monthly mortgage payments of $1,032.26. They plan to pay off their mortgage in full before they retire. They have joint creditor life insurance on their mortgage, which is $474 per year.

Margot asks how they can figure out what their outstanding mortgage is at any time without having to call the bank. Francesca shows them.

In Canada, residential fixed-rate mortgages cannot compound more than two times a year. In the above calculations for the van and piano loans, the monthly rate was determined by dividing the APR by 12, which results in monthly compounding. However, since mortgages can compound only twice a year, finding the monthly rate is more complicated.

Step 1 Find the EAR

i.	Find the rate for six months	$0.0625 \div 2 = .03125$
ii.	(Add 1 and raise it to the power of 2) minus 1	$\left(1.03125^2\right) - 1 = 0.063476 = 6.3476\%$

Step 2 Find the Appropriate Interest Rate for Each Payment

monthly rate	Take the 12th root of (1 + EAR)	$(1.063476)^{1/12} - 1 = 0.005142 = 0.5142\%$
semi-monthly rate	Take the 24th root of (1 + EAR)	$(1.063476)^{1/24} - 1 = 0.002568 = 0.2568\%$
bi-weekly rate	Take the 26th root of (1 + EAR)	$(1.063476)^{1/26} - 1 = 0.002370 = 0.2370\%$
weekly rate	Take the 52nd root of (1 + EAR)	$(1.063476)^{1/52} - 1 = 0.001184 = 0.1184\%$

See Appendix 1a, Example 16 for a more detailed look at mortgages.

Since Margot and Craig pay their mortgage monthly, they will use the monthly interest rate to calculate the monthly payment:

$121,004 $\quad$ = $\quad$ PMT$_{EOM}$ (PVIFA$_{180, \ 0.5142\%}$)
PMT $\quad$ = $\quad$ $1,032.27

By 2013, the 25-year mortgage is reduced to 15 years, leaving 180 payments (15 years × 12 monthly payments) outstanding.

At December 31, 2014, they will have made 12 payments since they renewed. Now their outstanding principal (liability) will be:

PVA $\quad$ = $\quad$ $1,032.27$_{EOM}$ (PVIFA$_{168, \ 0.5142\%}$)
PVA $\quad$ = $\quad$ $115,942

Similarly:

At December 31, 2015: n = 156, PVA = $110,558
At December 31, 2016: n = 144, PVA = $104,832
At December 31, 2017: n = 132, PVA = $98,743

Expenses

Margot and Craig had the following annual expenses in 2013 in addition to those mentioned above: $2,812 for property tax; $1,587 in heating; $1,000 for hydro and water; $1,362 for telephone and Internet service; $1,509 for home maintenance; and $686 in home-insurance premiums. Food, wine, beer, and other household expenses were about $14,500. Transportation expenses were $2,206 for maintenance and licences, $2,820 for gas, and $2,384 for insurance premiums.

> Francesca asks about cable. Margot and Craig don't have cable or satellite service — they are so busy with all their day-to-day family activities, school events, camping and skiing, they don't watch much television.

They also spent $592 on books and newspapers, $3,932 on child care, $888 on the computer, and $1,687 at the veterinary clinic for the cat and the dog (it is usually this high). Donations were $2,125, and gifts were $2,956. Margot spent $846 on the garden, and the family spent $2,975 on clothes. In addition, Margot had to pay her income taxes and CPP, totalling $16,822.33 (tax of $12,614.83 and CPP of $4,204.50). Her CPP is double the amount of Craig's because for self-employment she has to pay both the employee and the employer's share of CPP. The employer's share is tax deductible while her employee's share is eligible for the non-refundable tax credit.

They spent $3,600 in 2013 on the family activities, camping and skiing fees, the girls' allowances, and the odd movie and night out. They also spent $1,777 for a new sound system. They took the whole family to Europe in 2013. It cost $8,450, but they wanted to go while the girls were still young enough to travel with them. They do not plan to take another large vacation like this in the foreseeable future.

Margot pays $173 per year for a 10-year term life insurance policy for $100,000 of coverage. Craig pays a total of $417 per year for two 10-year term life insurance policies, which are each for $100,000 of coverage (total of $200,000).

In 2013, they also put $4,000 into a Registered Education Savings Plan (RESP) for Louise, who is now 13. (RESPs are covered in Chapter 6.) Although there is no ceiling on the annual contribution, they would like to plan to save $4,000 a year for each child when they can. The federal government has a program which gives a grant called the Canada Education Savings Grant (CESG) of 25% of the contribution to a maximum of $500 p.a. for each child. The income is not taxed until the child withdraws the funds to go to school, at which time the child pays the tax, presumably at a lower rate than the contributor. They would like to maximize the grant, but are not sure how to go about this. They estimate that all three of their daughters will go to university, hopefully a local one — the University of Waterloo or Wilfrid Laurier or Guelph — that is not far away and would, perhaps, allow the girls to live at home to save money if necessary. Margot has an undergraduate degree in business — a subject she did not enjoy. It was her father's wish that she study business, and he was paying. She then put herself through graduate school to get an engineering degree, which was always her first choice. She does not want her daughters to face this kind of restriction and would like to plan for at least one of them to attend university that is further away and where room and board is an added expense. They estimate tuition and books may be $9,000 by the time Louise is ready to attend university in about six years' time. The other two will start university eight and ten years from now, respectively.

Step 2.   Prepare Statements to Reflect Current Financial Position

A financial plan begins by looking at the present financial position. The Statement of Financial Position provides a picture of where the family is now — what their assets are, their liabilities, and their net worth. The Statement of Annual Cash Flows provides information on their present spending. In some instances, it highlights problem areas, although not all families overspend. By structuring this statement to summarize annual spending, the planner and family can more easily see the broad categories of their spending. It also spells out how much might be available for saving if, for instance, certain loans were paid off. The Cash Flow Statement can then be rolled out into the future to produce spending and highlight areas of opportunity for savings for the family — it makes their future spending more concrete and real rather than abstract and vague. The Cash Flow Statement also provides the basis for deciding on required annual income in retirement, again to make this number concrete and not a vague statement like "We need a million dollars saved before we can retire."

Their current financial position is reflected in the following two statements:

• Statement of Financial Position
• Statement of Cash Flows

Francesca outlines how she will go about setting up Craig and Margot's Statement of Financial Position and Cash Flow Statement.

Statement of Financial Position
Assets

Financial: These assets both provide income in retirement and can be consumed in retirement. They are recorded at market value.

Personal Use: These assets are used in everyday life. They provide no income, since they are only consumed. The house and car are valued at market value. The rest are valued at replacement cost.

Luxury: These assets are used in everyday life, but they are marginal to the family's needs. While they are on the statement, they do not play a large part in retirement planning unless they will be sold in retirement.

Liabilities

Don't differentiate between **Current** and **Long-term** liabilities, since payments are usually monthly. Next year's Cash Flow Statement shows what must be paid that year, including living expenses and debt payments.

Net Worth

Net Worth = Assets – Liabilities.

Net worth may be negative in younger years. In planning for retirement, it must be positive by the planned retirement date. Also, if for instance, the mortgage will not be paid off, the potential retiree should generally plan to continue working until it is paid off.

Margot Daniels and Craig Stewart
Statement of Financial Position
as at December 31, 2013
in $2013

	Margot	Craig	Actual 2013
Financial assets			
Cash			$ 1,200
Savings — emergency	3,500		3,500
Savings — Canada Savings Bond (CSB)	5,000		5,000
RESP contributions			4,000
RESP grant			500
RRSP contributions	39,000	59,700	98,700
Preferred shares		8,000	8,000
			120,900
Personal use assets			
Clothing			20,000
Household			40,000
Car	6,000	21,000	27,000
House			300,000
			387,000
Luxury asset			
Grand piano			19,000
			$526,900
Liabilities			
Line of credit			$ 5,000
Car lease and buyout			13,932
Piano loan			6,872
Mortgage			121,003
			146,807
Net worth			380,093
			$526,900

Statement of Cash Flows
Expense Categories

A family *must* determine its own categories. "Dog," "Piano lessons," and "Garden" might be appropriate for one family, while "Entertainment," "Hair," and "Cleaning service" might be useful for another.

Debt Payments

Technically it is correct to separate debt payments into liabilities and interest expense. However, from a practical point of view, this is not very useful for budgeting purposes. It is better to include mortgage payments with shelter costs. This cash flow is discretionary in the long run, but since a family must live somewhere, it is more useful to treat the entire cost as an expense. The same is true of car payments — put the entire payment in Car expense. However, payments on credit cards or payments for one-time costs, such as a new dining room table or large-screen television, and, perhaps vacations, are more useful in discretionary spending at the end, since the family can more easily see what funds could be available for saving if these expenses were not there.

Step 3.   Quantify Short- and Long-term Goals

Francesca asks Margot and Craig about their short- and long-term goals. Margot says that they need to have more **liquid savings** in case of an emergency. Until recently, Margot did not have **disability insurance**. Since she has just taken it out, it is not reflected in their 2013 cash flows. In addition to **saving** in their RRSP, they want to save for their children's education using the RESP. They also want to start a regular savings program to buy a new car. They think $350 a month, or $4,200 a year, would be more than enough, since they are not car-proud — safety and reliability are more important to them.

They also wonder if they have enough **life insurance**. They think they probably do, since they got some when Margot took time off to be with the children when they were young. They don't want to be overinsured but … do they have enough? Francesca does a quick calculation. Margot has $100,000 of life insurance coverage. Her after-tax income is about $43,000 a year. Since their youngest daughter is nine years old, they should plan on needing Margot's salary for about 17 more years — until the earliest they might be able to retire. Discounting Margot's salary at a 3% real rate of return, Margot should have about:

$$
\begin{aligned}
PVA &= PMT_{BOY} (PVIFA_{n,\ k}) \\
&= \$42{,}378_{BOY} (PVIFA_{17,\ 3\%}) \\
&= \$574{,}688
\end{aligned}
$$

So Margot should take out more life insurance. While they were able to get by on Craig's salary alone while Margot was home with the children, if Margot were to die, there would be extra costs such as babysitting, meal preparation, etc.

Margot Daniels and Craig Stewart
Statement of Cash Flows
For the year ended December 31, 2013
in $2013

	Actual 2013
Revenue	
Craig — take-home pay	$61,171
Margot — net income	59,200
Margot — tax, CPP	(16,822)
	103,549
Shelter	
Mortgage	13,167
Mortgage insurance	474
Hydro, gas, etc.	2,587
House insurance	686
Realty taxes	2,812
Maintenance	1,509
	21,235
Car	
Lease payments	6,300
Insurance	2,384
Gas	2,820
Maintenance, licence	2,206
	13,710
Food, wine, beer	14,500
Other	
Books/newspapers	592
Child care	3,932
Clothes	2,975
Computer — misc.	888
Dog and cat	1,687
Donations	2,125
Family activities	3,600
Garden	846
Gifts	1,956
Insurance — life, disability	590
Telephone, Internet	1,362
	20,553
Total cash out	69,998
Net cash flow	33,551
Discretionary	
Line of credit	6,000
Piano loan	4,598
Vacation	9,450
Appliances, furniture	1,777
	21,825
Savings	
RESP contributions	4,000
RRSP contributions	6,000
RRSP tax @ marginal rate	(2,340)
	7,660
Net increase/(decrease)	$ 4,066

And Craig?

$$PVA = \$61,171_{BOY} \ (PVIFA_{17,\ 3\%})$$
$$= \$829,553$$

Craig has $200,000 of life insurance and is covered for $180,000 at work. So he too is underinsured.

Without going through the details of how the new total is calculated, Francesca tells them that their insurance expense will rise to $4,743 per year — the $590 already in place, plus $2,397 for Margot's disability insurance and $1,756 for more life insurance.

Step 4. Prepare Short-term Budgets and Estimate Retirement Spending

"We will now prepare a budget for your family for the next two or three years so you can get a better idea of what funds you will have available for saving for retirement after you have accomplished your shorter-term goals," says Francesca. "Then we will estimate your retirement expenses."

Like many people, Craig and Margot have some short-term debt that they need to attend to before they can begin to save seriously for retirement. They will now take a first look at what they will need to do to have the retirement they envision. Once they have finished the first draft with Francesca, the equations may not balance. Then they would have to take another look at:

• the age at which they will retire
• their estimated retirement lifestyle
• their planned savings for retirement, and
• the type of investments they can make to get the returns they require.

In **Step 5**, they will calculate:

• how much they need to have at the date of retirement to finance their retirement needs,
• how much they can reasonably expect to receive from government programs,
• how much they will have at retirement from their current savings.

"But," says Craig, "I have heard that we will need 60% to 70% of our pre-retirement income to finance our retirement. Why do we need to go through the bother of estimating our retirement needs?"

Francesca replies that "60% or 70% of pre-retirement income is an acceptable estimate for young couples who are just beginning to have children, are still in the early stages of their careers, and are probably still laden with student loans and household start-up expenses. But since you are in your mid-40s, you have a good handle on the spending requirements. Since your spending will be lower, it is very possible that you will both be in a lower tax bracket in retirement than you are now. This may mean that you will not need as much as you think you will to have the retirement you envision."

"Since you are paying me on an hourly basis," Francesca continues, "I have no vested interest in having you save, and therefore invest, more than you will actually need. This extra calculation does not take long and will allow you to have a much better idea of how much you have to give up today to have the retirement you want."

Some expenses will decrease in retirement, some will increase. In general, clothing expenses usually decrease, while medical expenses usually increase, especially now as governments continue to balance their budgets. The children don't live at home anymore, but often parents want to help them out rather than leave them an inheritance (give it to them now while they really need it). Transportation costs may drop, and debts should be paid off. Disability coverage is no longer needed, but there may be a need for new insurance policies to cover estate issues. In addition, there will be periodic expenses, such as a new car or a once-in-a-lifetime vacation.

Margot and Craig will look first at their budget for the next two to three years. Francesca will also prepare a Statement of Financial Position so that they can see how their spending is affecting their financial picture. Francesca will use these budgets to estimate their spending needs in retirement based on Craig and Margot's desired retirement lifestyle — more big vacations, more time to work on the garden, an increase in their donations, more funds for the newspapers and books they will finally have time to read, gifts for anticipated grandchildren.

On the **Statement of Cash Flows**, note in particular:

- Margot is self-employed. Her tax and CPP are deducted from her Net Income (from her consulting income) to arrive at the couple's net revenue.
- RRSP contributions are shown net of tax — the tax is *not* shown as an increase in revenue.
- No dividend or interest income is shown. Since they have no plans to use this income on a regular basis, this income is shown as an increase of the investments (see the Statement of Financial Position).
- The expense categories that work for Margot and Craig. Some families might prefer to have their children's costs in a separate category so that they know where they will stand when their children become self-sufficient.
- Craig's take-home pay drops by the after-tax amount of his pension contributions, which begin in 2014. This scenario is covered in Chapter 5.

Craig chuckles when he sees the numbers. "How on earth can you predict future costs? Do you have a crystal ball?" he asks.

"Not at all," replies Francesca. "First, remember everything is in 2013 dollars, so all the estimates have the same purchasing power. Also, we will review this statement every two or three years, but in the meantime we can make some educated guesses:

- "Hydro and gas have been going up, so unless you move into a smaller home, they will probably be higher in the future as resources become increasingly scarce.
- "You will probably need fewer clothes when you retire, since you won't have to dress for work.
- "Many people decide to increase their donations when they have extra cash. Remember, this is an estimate for planning purposes and we can easily revise the numbers.
- "You might decide to take up new interests that will involve taking courses, and you will possibly read more newspapers and magazines when you have more time.

Margot Daniels and Craig Stewart
Statement of Cash Flows
For the Year Ended December 31
in $2013

	Actual 2013	Budget 2014	Budget 2015	Budget 2016	In retirement
Revenue					
Craig — take-home pay	61,171	58,093	58,093	58,093	
Margot — net income	59,200	59,200	59,200	59,200	
Margot — tax, CPP	(16,822)	(16,822)	(16,822)	(16,822)	
	103,549	**100,471**	**100,471**	**100,471**	
Shelter					
Mortgage	13,167	12,387	12,387	12,387	0
Mortgage insurance	474	474	474	474	0
Hydro, gas, etc.	2,587	3,000	3,000	3,000	3,500
House insurance	686	700	700	700	700
Realty taxes	2,812	3,000	3,000	3,000	3,000
Maintenance	1,509	1,500	1,500	1,500	1,500
	21,235	21,061	21,061	21,061	8,700
Car					
Lease payments	6,300	14,515	0	0	1 car
Insurance	2,384	2,400	2,400	2,400	1,500
Gas	2,820	2,800	2,800	2,800	2,000
Maintenance, licence	2,206	2,200	2,200	2,200	1,500
	13,710	21,915	7,400	7,400	5,000
Food, wine, beer	14,500	14,500	14,500	14,500	12,300
Other					
Books, newspapers	592	600	600	600	1,400
Child care	3,932	4,000	4,000	4,000	0
Clothes	2,975	3,000	3,000	3,000	1,500
Computer — misc.	888	900	900	900	400
Dog and cat	1,687	1,600	1,600	1,600	1,600
Donations	2,125	2,100	2,100	2,100	5,000
Family activities	3,600	3,600	3,600	3,600	1,500
Garden	846	500	500	500	1,000
Gifts	1,956	2,000	2,000	2,000	5,000
Insurance — life, disability	590	4,743	4,700	4,700	0
Telephone, Internet	1,362	1,400	1,400	1,400	1,500
	20,553	24,443	24,400	24,400	18,900
Total cash out	69,998	81,919	67,361	67,361	44,900
Net cash flow	33,551	18,552	33,110	33,110	(44,900)
Discretionary					
Line of credit	6,000	5,167	0	0	0
Piano loan	4,598	2,682	0	0	
Vacation	9,450	0	0	0	5,000
Appliances, furniture	1,777	1,000	1,000	1,000	1,000
	21,825	8,848	1,000	1,000	6,000
Savings					
New car	0	0	4,200	4,200	0
RESP contributions	4,000	6,000	10,000	10,000	0
RRSP contributions	6,000	4,000	25,000	25,000	0
RRSP tax @ marg	(2,340)	(1,560)	(9,750)	(9,750)	0
	7,660	8,440	29,450	29,450	0
Net increase/(decrease)	**4,066**	**1,263**	**2,660**	**2,660**	**(50,900)**

- "With three daughters, you might have grandchildren for whom you would like to buy gifts.
- "Typically, car insurance goes down for older people, but the way insurance rates have been going up, let's assume an increase. It provides a cushion which, again, is subject to revision in the future.
- "Since you are not driving children to this and that, you might opt for a smaller car, and I am assuming only one car.

I don't have a crystal ball, but we have to start somewhere, so let's make these assumptions and review them regularly."

"Well, we sure were off the mark when we made the assumption we would need $64,000 after tax a year," says Margot. "We were told to estimate 60% to 70% of our pre-retirement income. That would be $96,600 [$138,000 × 70%]."

Francesca replies, "This is only the first round. You need to look at this again in two or three years to see how you are getting along with your short-term goals. Also, at this rate, you will have used up all your unused RRSP contribution room and we'll need to start looking at non-registered savings. I don't want to go into this in detail yet, but Margot can put about $10,300 [18% of her net income after expenses and CPP of $57,100] into an RRSP, and, Craig, with your new pension plan at work, you will be able to put only about $600 into an RRSP. And when the girls have finished school — granted, it will be a few years — you will have even more. You'll be able to firm up your retirement date. Let's look at the Statement of Financial Position."

On the **Statement of Financial Position**, note in particular:

- The growth in savings not recorded on the Statement of Cash Flows, as explained in the third bullet just before the Budgets for the Statement of Cash Flows on page 21.
- The non-growth in personal use assets. Margot and Craig are not counting on an increase in the market value of their house even though there is a strong possibility that this will happen. Since they plan to live in their house, they are not adding growth in its value to finance their retirement.
- Once they have paid off their car lease and consumer loans, they need about $65,000 a year for operating costs. Their **emergency savings** cover only about one-and-a-half months of day-to-day costs. This is not a lot, but they do have adequate disability insurance. Some of the operating costs can be deferred on a short-term basis if need be. The preferred shares return only 4% a year and could probably go in an emergency. Also, the savings accounts show year-end balances. Assuming they are saving monthly, they could use some of the funds set aside for saving during the year if required. They are not flush with emergency savings and may want to defer RRSP contributions to increase it.
- Both cars are decreasing in value to reflect annual depreciation.
- Registered assets grow at a before-tax rate, while non-registered assets grow at an after-tax rate. This issue is discussed in Chapter 2.
- The change in cash each year reflecting the net increase/(decrease) on the Statement of Cash Flows

  - 2014 cash balance:

+ 2013 Cash balance	$1,200	= December 31, 2013 Cash balance
+ 2014 Net Increase / (Decrease)	1,263	= from 2014 Statement of Cash Flow
= 2014 Cash balance	$ 2,463	= December 31, 2014 Cash balance

Margot Daniels and Craig Stewart
Statement of Financial Position
as at December 31
in $2013

	k real Before Tax	After Tax	Margot	Craig	Actual 2013	Budget 2014	Budget 2015	Budget 2016
Financial assets								
Cash					1,200	2,463	5,123	7,783
Savings — emergency	3.00%	1.95%	3,500		3,500	3,568	3,638	3,709
Savings — CSB	3.00%	1.95%	5,000		5,000	5,098	5,197	5,298
Savings — car	3.00%	1.95%			0	0	4,200	8,482
RESP contributions					4,000	10,000	20,000	30,000
RESP grant					500	1,700	3,200	4,700
RESP income @ 3% real	3.00%				0	135	490	1,201
RRSP contributions			39,000	59,700	98,700	102,700	127,700	152,700
RRSP income @ 6.8% real	6.80%					6,712	14,152	23,797
Preferred shares	4.00%	3.42%		8,000	8,000	8,273	8,556	8,848
					120,900	140,640	192,237	246,489
Personal use assets								
Clothing					20,000	20,000	20,000	20,000
Household					40,000	40,000	40,000	40,000
Car			6,000	21,000	27,000	22,000	17,000	12,000
House					300,000	300,000	300,000	300,000
					387,000	382,000	377,000	372,000
Luxury assets								
Grand piano					19,000	19,000	19,000	19,000
					526,800	541,640	588,237	637,489
Liabilities								
Line of credit					5,000	0	0	0
Car lease and buyout					13,932	0	0	0
Piano loan					6,872	2,620	0	0
Mortgage					121,003	115,941	110,557	104,832
					146,807	118,561	110,557	104,832
Net Worth					380,093	423,079	477,680	532,658
					526,900	541,640	588,237	637,489

Step 5.   Calculate Required Retirement Savings

"Now we will take a look at your savings requirements," says Francesca. "Since you are 20 years or so from retirement, we will not fine-tune them but just get an idea of what you might be facing. We must ask what you will receive from government programs, current pension plans, and current savings. Then we can start looking at your actual savings needs and how you will draw down your assets."

Conventional wisdom says to draw down assets in this order to minimize taxes on retirement income (ignoring annual taxes on non-registered assets held during retirement):

1. Non-registered assets of lower-income spouse
2. Non-registered assets of higher-income spouse
3. Registered assets of lower-income spouse
4. Registered assets of higher-income spouse

However, this approach does not take into account estate planning needs and taxes payable on assets remaining in the estate at death. It may be better to draw down all the registered assets before death if this can be done at less than the top marginal tax bracket, since one can leave cash to one's children (or whomever) without incurring taxes. For now, we will assume all RRSPs are drawn down between the date of retirement and death. Government and company pensions begin at retirement and end upon the death of the second spouse.

Calculating how much you need to save involves three steps:

1. The present value at retirement of retirement income required to finance the desired retirement lifestyle.
2. The present value at retirement of expected income from government plans.

The difference between steps 1 and 2 is the amount of savings needed at retirement.

3. The future value at retirement of current savings.

The difference is the amount of savings required between now and the date of retirement.

Retirement-Planning Information

Craig and Margot wonder if they can retire when Craig is aged 60 (Scenario I — retire in 18 years when Craig is 60 and Margot is 61). Alternatively, the couple may have to retire when Craig is aged 65 (Scenario II — retire in 23 years when Craig is 65 and Margot is 66).

Government Pensions

The federal government currently has two pension programs: the Canada Pension Plan (CPP) and the Old Age Security (OAS). Margot and Craig both expect to receive the maximum CPP retirement benefit, which stands at $12,150 in 2013, at age 65. We will be using a generic CPP retirement benefit of $11,500 for the full benefit at age 65 in addition to generic tax rates as shown in Appendix 2B. Both intend to begin receiving CPP when they retire (assuming they are eligible to receive the benefit, based on their ages). For now, they are not so sure about the OAS. They would rather leave it out of their planning.

Other Retirement-Planning Assumptions

They expect inflation to be 3% per year for the entire planning period and expect to earn an average rate of return of 10% per year on their investment assets *before* retirement. The couple expects to earn 7% per year on their investment assets *during* retirement. Craig does not want to include his Bartok shares (non-registered investments) as part of his retirement funds because the amount is quite small — these shares will provide a bit of cushion in their planning. They intend to remain in their present home during retirement and hope to leave the house as an inheritance to their children. They want to plan for an average retirement period of 30 years if they retire when Craig is aged 60 (Scenario I), or an average retirement period of 25 years if they retire when Craig is aged 65 (Scenario II). Assume they die at the same time.

The following table summarizes the before-tax rates of return we are using. Chapter 8 develops this model in much more detail. Here we are taking a first look at their planning needs.

Retirement	Before	During
k nominal, before tax	10.00%	7.00%
Inflation	3.00%	3.00%
k real, before tax	6.80%	3.88%
where real rate =	$\dfrac{1+\text{nominal rate}}{1+\text{inflation rate}} - 1$	

Craig and Margot — Retirement Savings Required

Margot and Craig estimate they will need $51,000 after tax per year in retirement. They would like to leave some room for contingencies and therefore would like to plan for $56,000 per year — $28,000 each.

How much is this before tax? To find out, we will use trial and error made much faster, but not easier, if the basic tax calculation is already in a spreadsheet. Essentially, you calculate the after-tax income for each amount until you come close to $28,000 after tax. For retirement income in this text book, in the non-refundable tax credits we will include the federal and provincial pension income amounts but not the age amount since it is means-tested. Without showing all the trials, the result, using generic tax rates shown at the end of Appendix 2B is:

Taxable Income		33,500.00
Federal tax: 15% × $33,500		5,025.00
Non-refundable tax credits:		
Basic personal amount	10,000.00	
Pension income amount	2,000.00	
	12,000.00	
× 15%		1,800.00
Basic Federal Tax (BFT)		3,225.00
Provincial tax: 8% × $33,500		2,680.00
Non-refundable tax credits:		
Basic personal amount	9,000.00	
Pension income amount	1,100.00	
	10,100.00	
× 8%		808.00
Basic Provincial Tax (BPT)		1,872.00
Total tax		5,097.00
Net after tax		28,403.00
× 2 incomes =		56,806
Average tax rate		16.72%

Note that through effective income splitting their combined average retirement tax rate is much lower than their pre-retirement tax rates:

	Income	Average tax rate	Total tax paid
Craig — Ch. 2	90,000	28.10%	
Margot — Ch. 3	59,200	21.02%	
In retirement — each	33,500	15.21%	5,097
In retirement — together	67,000	15.21%	10,194
In retirement — one income	67,000	21.72%	14,550
In retirement — tax saved by income splitting		6.51%	4,356

Retirement Income Needed

Begin by calculating the present value of their before-tax retirement income. *Always* draw a timeline first. Because some people think about their retirement income needs in before-tax amounts and some only look at after-tax requirements, we include both. Chapter 2 will illustrate that it doesn't matter to the calculation which one is used.

The Timeline

		T_0	T_1	...	T_{34}	T_{35}
Margot — age		61	62	...	94	95
Craig — age		60	61	...	93	94
Annual income before tax		67,000	67,000	...	67,000	67,000

The Calculations

Need in retirement:	n	k real	$BOY	Before tax	Tax	After Tax
					15.21%	
	35	3.88%	67,000	1,320,482	200,910	1,119,571

Retirement Income in Place

How much do Margot and Craig already have from government sources and from Craig's indexed pension? To be conservative, they leave out the Old Age Security (OAS) but include the full amount of the Canada Pension Plan (CPP) retirement income for which they will be eligible. If they do decide to retire when Craig turns 60, Margot will retire four years before reaching the maximum CPP of $11,500 — a generic rate. With the discount rate of 0.6% a month, she will collect only 71.2% of the full amount. Since Craig will retire five years before age 65, he can collect 64.0% of the full amount.[4]

Again, always begin by drawing the timeline. This information could have been included in the prior timeline. Notice that their indexed income is discounted at a real discount rate, while Craig's non-indexed pension income is discounted at a nominal discount rate. This is explained in Chapter 2.

		T_0	T_1	...	T_{34}	T_{35}
Margot — age		61	62	...	94	95
Craig — age		60	61	...	93	94
CPP — Margot		8,188	8,188	...	8,188	8,188
CPP — Craig		7,360	7,360	...	7,360	7,360
Indexed DB pension		28,080	28,080	...	28,080	28,080
Non-indexed pension		8,100	8,100	...	8,100	8,100

Have in place	n	k	$BOY	Before tax	Tax	After tax
					15.21%	
CPP — Margot			8,188			
CPP — Craig			7,360			
Craig's DP pension			28,080			
Indexed pensions	35	3.88%	43,628	859,850		
Non-indexed pension	35	7.00%	8,100	112,217		
				972,068	147,899	824,168

The calculation for Margot and Craig is quite straightforward because they are almost the same age and plan to live into their mid-90s. Planning becomes complicated when their ages are significantly different. It complicates the calculations, but not unduly as long as you draw the timelines and keep track of where you are going. Margot and Craig left out the OAS. Often it is included, but at only 40% or 50% of its current level.

---

4   CPP allows retirement pension to start from age 60 to age 70. The amount received will be discounted by 0.6% per month if you retire early (before age 65); or conversely, the amount will increase by 0.7% each month if you continue working beyond 65 (up to age 70). This is covered in Chapter 3.

RRSP Savings

So far Margot and Craig have figured out that they need $1,320,482 before-tax retirement income. They also know they have about $972,068 retirement income in place from the CPP and Craig's RPP. Therefore, they still need $348,414. How much of that amount will be covered by their RRSPs, based on the plan laid out so far:

- depositing $4,000 to their RRSPs at the end of 2014,
- depositing $25,000 a year at the end of 2015 to 2019 inclusive, and
- depositing $10,900 a year at the end of 2020 to 2028:

	End of Year (EOY)								BOY
	2013	2014	2015	...	2019	2020	...	2030	2031
	T_{-1}	T_0	T_1	...	T_5	T_6	...	T_{16}	T_{17}
Margot — age	43	44	45		49	50		60	61
Craig — age	42	43	46		48	49		59	60
RRSPs at end of 2013	98,700								FV?
$4,000 contribution		4,000							FV?
$25,000 contribution			25,000	...	25,000				FVA?
$10,900 contribution						10,900	...	10,900	FVA?

					Tax	
Savings EOY	n	k real	$EOY	Before tax	*15.21%*	After tax
RRSPs at end of 2013	17	6.80%	98,700	302,015		
RRSP contribution 2014	16	6.80%	4,000	11,460		
RRSP deposits 2015–2019	5	6.80%	25,000			
FVA of $25,000			143,196			
FV of $143,196	11	6.80%	143,196	295,267		
RRSP deposits 2020–2030	11	6.80%	10,900	170,229		
Balance EOY 16 = BOY 17				778,971	118,520	660,451

Summary of Margot and Craig

And where do they stand? We estimated they needed to save $348,414 before tax. This shows them having more than enough if they retire when Craig is 60. To summarize:

	Before tax	Tax	After tax
		15.21%	
Retirement income needed	1,320,482	200,910	1,119,571
Government and private pensions	972,068	147,899	824,168
Shortfall before RRSPs	348,414	53,011	295,403
RRSPs	778,971	118,520	660,451
Surplus/(Deficit)	430,557	65,509	365,048

Since they should have more than enough saved to retire when Craig is aged 60, we will not go through Scenario II — where they both retire when Craig is 65.

Step 6.   Monitoring Their Progress

Francesca will meet with Craig and Margot every two or three years to ensure they are on track and to fine-tune their planning as they get closer to retirement. There may be changes to their current financial situation, such as a job loss, a disability, a career change, a decision to send one or more of their children to a private school. They will need to monitor their actual rates of return on investments against planned returns, actual savings against planned savings, etc. Unless something major happens, meeting with Francesca every couple of years should suffice for the next several years. As they get closer to retirement, they will meet more often to firm up their retirement plans and make decisions about their retirement that will affect their financial situation during retirement.

SUMMARY

The retirement planning process involves saving funds from current income in order to provide income later in retirement. This process is somewhat imprecise because there are several unknown factors: how long retirement will last, what tax rates will be in effect during retirement, how much inflation will occur both before and during retirement, as well as what actual rates of return will be. As a result, several assumptions have be made, and must to be revisited to assess their appropriateness, with revisions made as required.

In addition, there are uncertainties in life that can affect a retirement plan, including the loss of a job, a decision to make a career change, the premature death of someone who affects your finances, and decisions to marry or have children. Retirement plans must be reviewed regularly, perhaps annually, and modified to reflect unexpected changes.

To conclude, retirement planning is a long-term project, and even after one actually retires, it is important that the planner and client stay on top of things to ensure that the client's goals are met.

Discounting and Compounding Rules Covered in Chapter 2

To discount or compound		Example	k
Retirement cash flows	Nominal	Non-indexed pension income	Nominal
	Real	Indexed pension income	Real
Retirement cash flows	Before tax		Before tax
	After tax		**Before tax**
Income from investments	Before tax	Registered investments (RRSP)	Before tax
	After tax	Non-registered investments (mutual funds, stocks, bonds, savings accounts, GICs)	After tax

Calculations Used in This Chapter

Time Value of Money	Ch. 1A
Mortgages	Ch. 1A
Leases and loans	Ch. 1A
Personal income taxes	Ch. 2
Craig's take-home pay	Ch. 2
Taxation on Craig's RPP contributions	Ch. 5
Margot's after-tax self-employed income	Ch. 3
Taxation on CPP contributions	Ch. 3
CPP income in retirement	Ch. 3
Registered Retirement Savings Plan (RRSP) contribution room	Ch. 6
Registered Education Savings Plan (RESP) and Grant (CESG)	Ch. 6

MARGOT AND CRAIG

Although Margot and Craig do not plan to retire for another 17 years, Francesca has taken them through the retirement planning process so they can maximize their savings during that time period. This process involves estimating annual spending in retirement in order to avoid either saving too little or sacrificing more in the present than they need to in order to have the retirement lifestyle they envision. In Chapter 8, "Monitoring the Process," we will look at Craig and Margot at retirement to see how their retirement savings plans worked out.

Craig and Margot are delighted to see that they may not be as far from their goals as they feared they would be. They enjoy their present lifestyle and plan to continue it, which means they can leave more of an estate for their children than they had planned. Or they might be able to help out their daughters more than just a little here and there when they are in their 20s and 30s.

Francesca tells them they can leave the plan as it is for now and think some more about how they want to spend their current income:

• Saving for their daughters' education using the RESP.
• Contributing less to their RRSPs in the next few years and perhaps travelling more while the girls are still willing to go with them.
• Buying a bigger house.

Francesca reminds them that they have not yet looked at Scenario II — retirement at age 66 (Margot) and 65 (Craig). If they retire five years later, they will:

• Receive the full CPP,
• Have five more years to save, and
• Have five less years of retirement to finance.

Margot and Craig will definitely be back to see Francesca in a couple of years to assess their progress and make adjustments to their plans to reflect any changes in their situation that might occur.

KEY TERMS

Canada Educational Savings Grant (CESG)	Old Age Security (OAS)
Canada Pension Plan (CPP)	Real dollars
General model	Real rate of return
Income tax rates	Registered Education Savings Plan (RESP)
Indexed	Registered Retirement Savings Plan (RRSP)
Mortgage payments	Retirement Planning Process
Nominal Dollars	Statement of Cash Flows
Nominal rate of return	Statement of Financial Position
Non-indexed	Time Value of Money (TVM)

See also:

Acronyms, Tax Rates and Time Value of Money Formula
Appendix 1A, Review of Time Value of Money

QUESTIONS AND PROBLEMS

1. What three factors affect the plan when planning for retirement?

2. What are the steps in the retirement planning process? (See Learning Objectives)

3. Does the possibility of leaving an estate for your children or other beneficiaries affect retirement planning?

4. What are five aspects of retirement income needs that have to be addressed in order to plan for retirement?

5. What are sheltered and unsheltered savings? What are the tax implications of each?

6. Planning for retirement focuses on two main goals during retirement. What are they?

7. Mary bought a car on January 1, 2013 costing $31,000. She made a down payment of $7,000 and arranged a four-year loan at 6% for the balance.
    (a) How much is her monthly payment if her payments are at the end of the month? (Answer: $563.64)
    (b) How much does she still owe on the car loan at December 31, 2013 and at December 31, 2014? (Answer: $18,527.45, $12,717.37)
    (c) How much interest did she pay in the first year? (Answer: $1,291.13)

8. Jim bought a boat on March 1, 2013 costing $35,000 and arranged a three-year lease at 5%. His lease called for a 20% down payment and a 20% buyout at the end of the lease. His lease payments are at the beginning of the month, and the buyout occurs at the end of the 36-month lease.
    (a) What is the monthly lease payment? (Answer: $655.82)
    (b) How much does he owe at December 31, 2014?

    > Note: The balance outstanding is the amount still owing after the December 1, 2014 payment plus the interest for the month of December, 2014).

    (Answer: $15,542.17)

9. Joan and Tim bought a house costing $150,000 and made a $38,000 down payment. The mortgage amortization period is 25 years, with a five-year locked-in term at 5%.
    (a) What is their monthly payment? (Answer: $651.40)
    (b) If the payment is weekly, what is it? (Answer: $150.07)
    (c) If mortgage rates do not change for the 25-year life of the mortgage, how much will they save by paying weekly instead of monthly? (Answer: $309.21 or $316 if payments are rounded)

10. What is the Canada Educational Savings Grant (CESG)? Are contributions tax deductible? Who pays the taxes when it is withdrawn?

11. Is it important to separate short-term liabilities on the family's Statement of Financial Position? Why or why not?

13. Cecil works as a computer analyst. His take-home pay is $75,000. He is the only breadwinner in the family. His wife, Jennifer, is a stay-at-home mom with their two children, Judy, 4, and John, 2. The only insurance the family has is the $200,000 life insurance Cecil has at his work. Taking this policy into account, roughly how much insurance do they need to buy if they decide that, to keep costs down, they will buy insurance for only 20 years, using a real discount rate of 3%? (Answer: $949,285 or $950,000)

12. Who should determine the categories for the Statement of Cash Flows? Is it more useful to a family to separate liability payments into the correct accounting categories of interest expense and principal payments, or is it more useful to put the entire payment under "Shelter costs"?

14. Is it more useful for a family to view a tax refund arising from contributions to an RRSP as part of "Revenue," or should it be considered a reduction of the cost of the contribution?

15. Simonetta's bank balance at December 31, 2013 was $728. During 2014, her net pay was $1,234 more than her spending. What was her bank balance on December 31, 2014? (Answer: $1,962)

16. To plan for retirement, Margot and Craig are using a nominal tax rate during retirement of 7% and a real tax rate (without inflation) of 3.88%. Which of these is used to discount retirement income that is indexed, and that is not indexed?

17. Tony and Brigid are 52 and expect to work until they are 63. They *each* have $110,000 in their RRSPs and expect to be able to contribute $13,000 *in total* per year to their RRSPs in the next 11 years. They think they will need $50,000 at the beginning of each year after tax in retirement. They are presently earning 6% real return on their RRSPs, and anticipate this will drop to 5% real return when they retire.
    (a) If they expect to live until age 90, what is the present value of their retirement income needs at age 63? (Answer: $768,759)
    (b) What is the value at age 63 of their current RRSP balances and future savings? Assume savings happen at the end of the year. (Answer: $612,257)
    (c) Ignoring government pensions, what can they do since they will not have saved enough?

Appendix 1A: Review of Time Value of Money

Learning Objectives

A.   Review the steps to follow when calculating the time value of money.

B.   Review various applications of time value of money concepts through 17 examples, covering:
   • basic calculations
   • assumptions implicit in an annuity formula
   • calculating the interest rate when the time period of the payments does not match the compounding period
   • the components of an interest rate
   • amortization table of loans and what they show
   • mortgages.

This appendix is intended to be a review of time value of money calculations and can be used as an aid for those students whose skills may be a little rusty. Several examples explain the concepts and provide full solutions. Examples 1 to 13 review basic time value of money calculations and applications. Examples 14 and 15 illustrate full amortization schedules to explain material presented in the Chapter 1 case of Margot and Craig. Example 16, the final example, illustrates the calculation of mortgages where the compounding rate does not match the payment schedule.

INTRODUCTION

Money loses value over time. If you are offered $1,000 today or $1,000 in five years, you will undoubtedly choose $1,000 today. To take the money in the future, you would want more than $1,000. You might, for instance, ask for $1,000 today but $1,276 in five years, even without inflation. Why? If you have to wait, you expect more.

   If you can earn 5% on your money, what amount in five years will have the same **value** to you as $1,000 today?

Year	Balance BOY		Interest earned	Balance EOY
1	1,000.00	× 1.05 =	50.00	1,050.00
2	1,050.00	× 1.05 =	52.50	1,102.50
3	1,102.50	× 1.05 =	55.13	1,157.63
4	1,157.63	× 1.05 =	57.88	1,215.51
5	1,215.51	× 1.05 =	60.78	1,276.28

BOY = beginning of the year
EOY = end of the year

There is an easier way to calculate the amount at the end of five years. You can use the "future value of a lump sum" formula to come to the same amount:

Future Value of One Amount

Using a financial calculator	or	Using a math formula
FV $= PV\ (FVIF_{n,\ k})$ $= \$1{,}000\ (FVIF_{5,\ 5\%})$ $= \$1{,}276.28$		FV $= PV\ [(1+k)^n]$ $= \$1{,}000\ [(1+0.05)^5]$ $= \$1{,}000\ (1.27628)$ $= \$1{,}276.28$

The formula on the right is the mathematical formula that was needed to calculate the amount before financial calculators became available. The four mathematical TMV formulas (shown below) are cumbersome and, using a financial calculator, no longer necessary. However, some texts still carry tables of factors for these four TMV formulas. The tables are the results of calculating the math formula for various time periods and for various interest rates. Try the calculation: $(1.05)^5$. You get the 1.276282 shown above on the right. This is the "factor", or **future value interest factor (FVIF)**, shown in the tables for 5% for five years when the present value is $1. This was repeated for several interest rates and for several years for each of the four TVM formulas. The invention and low cost of financial calculators means we no longer need to perform the mathematical calculations or use the tables of factors. So we will use the formulas on the left as a shorthand way of indicating which calculation we are performing

Time Value of Money Formulas and Terminology

Time value		Financial calculator	Math formula	What is being done
FV	$=$	$PV\ (FVIF_{n,k})$	$PV\ [(1+k)^n]$	The future value of one amount of money.
FVA	$=$	$PMT\ (FVIFA_{n,k})$	$PMT\left[\dfrac{(1+k)^n-1}{k}\right]$	The future value of a series of equal payments made at the end of the same, regular interval (an **ordinary annuity**).
PV	$=$	$FV\ (PVIF_{n,k})$	$FV\left[\dfrac{1}{(1+k)^n}\right]$	The present value (now at T_0) of one amount of money.
PVA	$=$	$PMT\ (PVIFA_{n,k})$	$\dfrac{PMT}{k}\left[1-\left(\dfrac{1}{\{1+k\}^n}\right)\right]$	The present value of a series of equal payments made at the end of the same regular interval (an **ordinary annuity**).

Note that both annuities (FVA and PVA) are **ordinary annuities**, meaning the equal payments occur at the *end* of the same, regular interval. If the payments are at the *beginning* of the period, the annuity is called an **annuity due,** and both the FVA and PVA formulas have to be adjusted by multiplying $(1 + k)$ at the end of the calculations. Or, more realistically, adjust your calculator to payments that are at the beginning (BGN) for annuity due calculations. These are illustrated in **Examples 4 and 6.**

One Amount of Money (Lump Sum)		Annuities	
FV	Future Value	FVA	Future Value
PV	Present Value	PVA	Present Value
n	Number of *compounding periods*	n	Number of *payments**
i	Nominal interest rate	i	Nominal interest rate
k	Interest rate per *compounding period*	k	Interest rate per *payment** period
EAR	Effective annual rate	EAR	Effective annual rate
		PMT	Amount of regular payment
		*Assumes PMT is at the *end* of the period	

Future Value Interest Factor (FVIF)

The future value interest factor (FVIF) is:

- the value in the future (the future value, FV)
- of $1.00 today (the present value, PV)
- for some number of time periods
- at some interest rate per time period.

For example, if we want to know the factor for $1.00 today compounded at 4% for five years, the TVM formula that we would write is FV = $1.00 (FVIF 5, 4%) and the factor that results is 1.21665. Thus the FV of:

- $1.00 is $1.22
- $1,00 = $1,21.17 ($100 × 1.21665), and
- $1,000 = $1,216.65 ($1,000 × 1.21665)

You do not actually have to calculate the factor since you are using a financial calculator. You would:

Write the formula	FV = 1,000 (FVIF 5, 4%)	
Enter the variables	1000	PV
	5	n
	4	i
	CPT	FV
Arrive at a FV of $1,216.65		

Present Value Interest Factor (PVIF)

The present value interest factor is the value today of $1.00 at some point in the future, discounted at some discount rate.

Calculating the *future value* uses an *interest rate*.
When the *present value* is calculated, the same rate is called a *discount rate*.

Future Value Interest Factor of an Annuity (FVIFA)

The future value interest factor of an annuity is the future value of $1.00 paid or received at the same time interval compounded at some interest rate.

Present Value Interest Factor of an Annuity (PVIFA)

The present value interest factor of an annuity is the value today (at time zero, or T_0) of a stream of payments made or received at the same time interval discounted at some discount rate.

Nominal Interest Rate

The **nominal interest rate** is also called:

- **APR**, or annual percentage rate; i.e., there is no compounding in the rate
- Stated rate
- Discount rate
- Required rate of return
- Opportunity cost
- Cost of capital
- Hurdle rate.

The nominal interest rate is the rate quoted in newspapers or on bank windows. This rate is *always* an annual rate unless specifically stated otherwise. If you see 5 1/4%, that means 5 1/4% APR, without compounding. If there is compounding, it may be stated 5% compounded quarterly, which means the effective annual rate (EAR) needs to be calculated in order to compare it to a rate of 5 1/4 compounded annually. This calculation is illustrated in **Example 5.**

The **effective annual rate (EAR)** reflects the effects of compounding, and will be illustrated in some of the following examples.

Decimal Places

Set the decimal place on your calculator for full or at least six decimal places. For small amounts, a significant difference can arise if too much rounding occurs during the calculation. A $100,000 mortgage at 7.02% amortized over 25 years (300 monthly payments) produces the following payments:

Number of decimal places	Interest rate %	Interest rate Decimal	Payment
6	0.5766%	0.005766	701.63
4	0.58%	0.0058	704.23
3	0.6%	0.006	719.59
2	1%	0.01	1,053.22

Round the final answer to dollars and cents.

HOW TO DO TVM CALCULATIONS

1. Draw the timeline including:
   - the dates
   - the "time" (i.e., T_1, T2, ... T_n)
   - amount(s) of money
   - the interest rates if it changes during the time of the timeline.
2. Write down what is given (i.e., PV, FV, PVA, FVA, PMT, n, and i).
3. Write the appropriate equation from the table on page 35. (i.e., the formula for PV, FV, PVA, or FVA)
4. Convert n and i to reflect the appropriate compounding, if required.
5. Write the equation with the numbers.
6. Solve for the unknown.

Drawing the timeline is extremely important. It is often tempting to dive into the calculations without taking the time to do this step. The timeline enables you to sort out the information. It is often not possible to get to the destination without a map to guide you. The timeline is the map.

Example 1   On July 1, 2014, you deposit $1,000 in Everfaithful Bank, which will pay you interest of 4¼% per annum (p.a.). How much will you have on July 1, 2018?

Rule 1	The interest rate given is always the APR — that is, compounded annually, unless specifically stated otherwise.

$$
\begin{array}{ccccc}
T_0 & T_1 & T_2 & T_3 & T_4 \\
\text{Jul 1/14} & & & & \text{Jul 1/18}
\end{array}
$$

$1,000   FV?

Appendix 1A: Review of Time Value of Money

$PV = \$1,000$
$n = 4$ years $= 4$ periods
$i = 4.25\%$ per year
$k = 4.25\%$/period

$FV = PV (FVIF_{n, k})$ or $FV = PV (1 + k)^n$
     $1,000 (FVIF_{4, 4.25\%})$ $1,000 (1.0425)^4$
     $1,181.15 $1,181.15

Example 2   You want to have $1,000 in four years time. If Everfaithful Bank pays you 4¼% on your savings, how much do you have to save today to have $1,000 in four years?

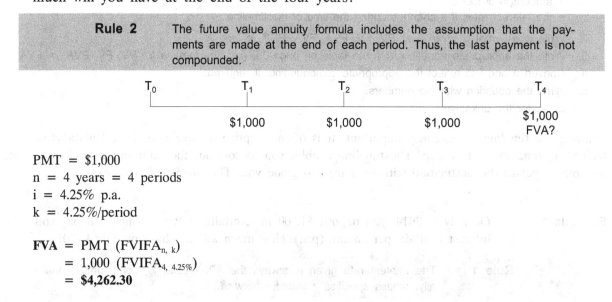

$FV = \$1,000$
$n = 4$ years $= 4$ periods
$i = 4.25\%$ p.a.
$k = 4.25\%$/period

$PV = FV (PVIF_{n, k})$
     $1,000 (PVIF_{4, 4.25\%})$
     $846.63

Example 3   You deposit $1,000 at the *end* of each of the next four years in Everfaithful Bank, which will pay you interest of 4¼% p.a. compounded annually. How much will you have at the end of the four years?

Rule 2	The future value annuity formula includes the assumption that the payments are made at the end of each period. Thus, the last payment is not compounded.

$PMT = \$1,000$
$n = 4$ years $= 4$ periods
$i = 4.25\%$ p.a.
$k = 4.25\%$/period

$FVA = PMT (FVIFA_{n, k})$
     $= 1,000 (FVIFA_{4, 4.25\%})$
     $= \mathbf{\$4,262.30}$

Example 4   You deposit $1,000 at the *beginning* of each of the next four years in Everfaithful Bank, which will pay you interest of 4 1/4% per year compounded annually. How much will you have at the end of the four years?

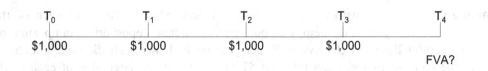

The payments in this question are made at the beginning of the year. Therefore, when you make the last payment, by the formula, you will be at T_3 (remember, the last payment receives no compounding). As a result, all of the payments will receive one more year of compounding than is in the formula. To add this year of compounding, multiply the answer from the formula by $(1 + k)$.

$PMT_{BOY} = \$1,000$
$n = 4$ payments $= 4$ years
$i = 4.25\%$ p.a.
$k = 4.25\%$/period

$FVA_{T3} = PMT\ (FVIFA_{n,\ k})$
$\quad\quad = 1,000\ (FVIFA_{4,\ 4.25\%})$
$\quad\quad = \$4,262.30$
$FVA_{T4} = \$4,262.30 \times 1.0425$
$\quad\quad = \mathbf{\$4,443.45}$

Alternatively, you can use the FVA formula, setting the payments on your calculator to "BEG" or "BGN" for the beginning of the year.

$FVA_{T4} = PMT_{BOY}\ (FVIFA_{n,\ k})$
$\quad\quad = 1,000_{BOY}\ (FVIFA_{4,\ 4.25\%})$
$\quad\quad = \mathbf{\$4,443.45}$

Rule 3	When you have used the formula, make sure you know where you are in time.

Example 5   Currently, Everfaithful Bank offers 4¼% p.a on your savings. How much do you need to put aside now in order to take out $1,000 a year at the *end* of each of the next four years?

Rule 4	The present value annuity formula assumes that the payments are made at the end of each period. The first payment is discounted one period.

$PMT = \$1,000$
$n = 4$ years $= 4$ periods
$i = k = 4.25\%$

$PVA = PMT\ (PVIFA_{n,\ k})$
$\quad\quad = 1,000\ (PVIFA_{4,\ 4.25\%})$
$\quad\quad = \mathbf{\$3,608.61}$

Appendix 1A: Review of Time Value of Money

Example 6   You worked out that you will need $1,000 a year for each of the next four years. To help you out, your grandma deposited a lump sum of money in Everfaithful Bank, which pays 4¼% per year on it. How much did your grandmother deposit in the bank so that you can take out $1,000 a year at the beginning of each of the next four years — $1,000 now and $1,000 for each of the next three years?

There are three ways to solves this.

1. Use the PVA formula for four payments and adjust the answer to T_0 (now)

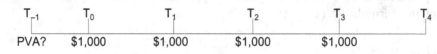

Where are you in time when your grandma deposited the money? Remember, that was last year. So you were at T_{-1}, which is one period (year) before now, T_0. With the ordinary annuity formula, the first payment is discounted by one period. As a result, all the payments have been discounted one period too many. To get to T_0, multiply the answer from the formula by $(1 + k)$.

PMT $= \$1,000$
n $= 4$ years $= 4$ periods
i $= k = 4.25\%$ p.a.

$$\begin{aligned}
\mathbf{PVA_{T\text{-}1}} &= \text{PMT } (\text{PVIFA}_{n,\,k}) \\
&= 1,000 \ (\text{PVIFA}_{4,\,4.25\%}) \\
&= \$3,608.61 \\
\mathbf{PVA_{T0}} &= \$3,608.61 \times 1.0425 \\
&= \mathbf{\$3,761.98}
\end{aligned}$$

2. Use the formula for the last three payments and add the first payment.

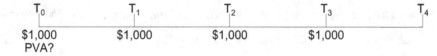

Since the first payment is not discounted, you can use the formula and discount all except the first payment. Then add the first payment.

PMT $= \$1,000$
n $= 3$ years $= 3$ periods
i $= k = 4.25\%$ p.a.

$$\begin{aligned}
\mathbf{PVA} &= \text{PMT } (\text{PVIFA}_{n,\,k}) \\
&= 1,000 + 1,000 \ (\text{PVIFA}_{3,\,4.25\%}) \\
&= 1,000 + 2,761.98 \\
&= \mathbf{\$3,761.98}
\end{aligned}$$

3. Use the PVA formula, setting the payments on your calculator to "BEG" or "BGN" for the beginning of the year.

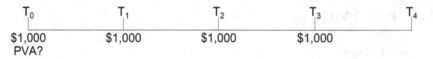

$$\begin{aligned} \mathbf{PVA} &= \mathrm{PMT_{BOY}}\ (\mathrm{PVIFA_{n,\ k}}) \\ &= 1{,}000_{\mathrm{BOY}}\ (\mathrm{PVIFA_{4,\ 4.25\%}}) \\ &= \mathbf{\$3{,}761.98} \end{aligned}$$

> Examples 3 and 5 illustrate annuities where the payment was at the end of the payment period (**ordinary annuities**). But many payments are at the beginning of the month, quarter, or year (**annuity due**). In Examples 4 and 6, the same formula is used, but with an adjustment for the payment at the beginning of the period.

Example 7   On July 1, 2014, you deposit $1,000 in Everfaithful Bank, which will pay you interest of 4 1/4% per year, compounded *quarterly*. How much will you have on July 1, 2018?

Rule 5	Always convert the interest rate to match the compounding or payment period.

Compounded quarterly means interest is calculated four times a year, so there will be 16 compounding periods in the four years. The interest rate of 4 1/4% p.a. is converted to a per period interest rate, "k" by dividing it by the number of compounding periods in a year — i.e., 4 1/4% ÷ 4 = 1.065% per quarter. The rate per quarter or month or week, etc. is also referred to as the **effective periodic rate (EPR)**.

> Generally, we do not use the features on a financial calculator that will convert the compounding from annually to quarterly for you. The reasons for this are:
>
> - Different calculators work differently. When calculating the yield on a bond, some calculators will automatically produce an APR, while other calculators may not reflect the fact that bond yields are always stated as APRs and thus will produce an EAR.
> - Students will have more than one kind of calculator throughout their careers.
> - It is important to understand the calculations. It is our experience that students run into trouble when they ask the calculator (or computer) to do the "knowing." Therefore, we encourage students to do the calculations the "long way." This long way breaks the steps down into small steps, so students need to figure out only one thing at a time.

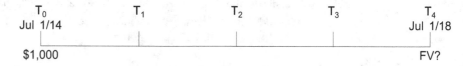

$$\begin{aligned} \mathrm{PV} &= \$1{,}000 \\ \mathrm{n} &= 4 \text{ years} = 16 \text{ periods} \\ \mathrm{i} &= 4.25\% \text{ p.a.} \\ \mathrm{k\ or\ PER} &= 1.0625\%/\text{period} \end{aligned}$$

$$\begin{aligned} \mathbf{FV} &= \mathrm{PV}\ (\mathrm{FVIF_{n,\ k}}) \\ &= 1{,}000\ (\mathrm{FVIF_{16,\ 1.0625\%}}) \\ &= \mathbf{\$1{,}184.24} \end{aligned}$$

Appendix 1A: Review of Time Value of Money

Example 8   You deposit $1,000 at the *end* of each of the next four years in Everfaithful Bank which will pay you interest of 4¼% p.a. compounded quarterly. How much will you have at the end of the four years?

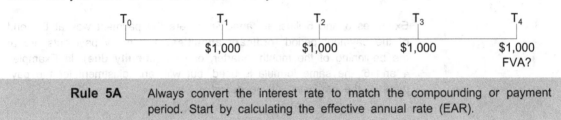

Rule 5A	Always convert the interest rate to match the compounding or payment period. Start by calculating the effective annual rate (EAR).

Compounded quarterly means interest is calculated four times a year.

- The interest rate used in the formula must be an annual rate because the deposits are being made annually.
- The annual rate must reflect the quarterly compounding.
- Calculate the **effective annual rate (EAR)**.

$$EAR = \left(1 + \frac{APR}{y}\right)^y - 1$$

where y is the number of compounding periods in a year.

$$EAR = \left(1 + \frac{.0425}{4}\right)^4 - 1 = 0.043182 = 4.3182\%$$

PMT = $1,000
n = 4 payments
i = 4.25% p.a.
k = EAR = 4.3182%/year

FVA = PMT (FVIFA$_{n, k}$)
     = 1,000 (FVIFA$_{4, 4.3182\%}$)
     = **$4,266.63**

Example 9   Eleanore is very confused. She can't sort out the APR from the EAR and when she should use what. Her friend Randy sums it up for her:

Rule 6	To get the monthly rate when given: • **APR**, divide the APR by 12: 9% APR ÷ 12 = 0.75% per month • **EAR**, add 1 to the EAR, take the 12th root, subtract 1 $(1.0938)^{1/12} - 1 = 0.75\%$ per month
Rule 7	Given a monthly rate, to get the: • **APR**, multiply by 12: 0.75% × 12 = 9.00% • **EAR**, add 1, raise it to the 12th power, subtract 1: $(1.0075)^{12} - 1 =$ 9.38%

The APR is used to calculate the appropriate periodic rate when the payment schedule matches the compounding schedule. Examples 14 and 15 are instances of loans with monthly payment schedules and monthly compounding. To calculate the monthly rate, just divide the APR by 12.

But in some loans, the payment schedule and compounding schedule are not on the same timetable. In this instance, one must first find the EAR, then, if necessary, take the appropriate root to arrive at the interest rate that matches the payment schedule.

- Example 8 has annual payments and the interest compounds quarterly.
- Example 10 has semi-annual payments while the interest compounds three times a year.
- Example 16 is a residential mortgage in which interest compounds twice a year but payments are monthly, semi-monthly, bi-weekly, or weekly.

Example 10   Jack and Virginia are getting a divorce. Two years ago, Virginia's father, Tom, lent Jack $30,000 to set up a carwash business. Neither Jack nor Tom knows much about the calculation of interest, although Tom knew how to make enough money to have it to lend and Jack knew enough to invest it in a successful business. At the time of the loan, Jack and Tom agreed that Jack would make semi-annual payments as large as Jack thought he could afford, and that the interest would be 6% compounded three times per year (don't laugh — this is a true story). Jack had paid Tom:

- $3,000 after 6 months
- $4,000 on the first anniversary of the loan, and
- $5,000 after 18 months

The second anniversary is coming up in three weeks. They turn to Francesca, Virginia's financial planner, to figure out how much is outstanding — principal and interest.

	T$_0$	T$_1$ 6 mo.	T$_2$ 1 yr.	T$_3$ 18 mo.	T$_4$ 2 yrs.
Loan	$30,000				
Payments		–$3,000	–$4,000	–$5,000	FV?

Step 1. What is the interest rate every six months? The interest rate is 6% a year compounded three times a year.

$$EAR = \left(1 + \frac{0.06}{3}\right)^3 - 1 = 0.061208 = 6.1208\%$$

$$k_{semi-annual} = (1.061208)^{1/2} - 1 = 0.030150\% = 3.0150\% \text{ per six months.}$$

Step 2. Carole sets up the following amortization schedule.

Time	Principal before Pmt	Payment			Principal after Pmt	
		Total	Interest 3.0150 %	Principal		Interest Calculation
6 months	30,000.00	3,000.00	904.50	2,095.50	27,904.50	0.30150 × 30,000.00
1 year	27,904.50	4,000.00	841.32	3,158.68	24,745.82	0.30150 × 27,904.50
18 moths	24,745.82	5,000.00	746.09	4,253.91	20,491.91	0.30150 × 24,745.82
2 years	20,491.91	21,109.74	617.83	20,491.91	0.00	0.30150 × 20,491.91

Jack should pay Tom $21,109.74. This amount will pay $20,491.91 of the outstanding principal and $617.83 interest for the six months.

Appendix 1A: Review of Time Value of Money

Example 11   Now it is Randy's turn to be confused. He notices that in Example 9, two different interest rates were used. He would like to know how one decides what interest rate to use. Francesca tells him there are many **components to interest rates.**

Pure, or **real, risk-free rates** reflect only the time value of money, which is typically is 2 – 4%.

Interest rates increase by:

- **Inflation**. The real risk-free rate plus inflation is called the **nominal** or **stated risk-free rate**. A Government of Canada treasury bill, which has no default risk, is generally used when a short-term risk-free rate is appropriate. The long-term Government of Canada bond rate is used for long-term risk-free rates.
- **Default risk** is the risk the debtor will not pay on the interest or principal when the payments are due. The buyer of the debt instrument requires a higher rate of return for accepting more risk. For example, second mortgages have a higher rate of interest than first mortgages if they are obtained at the same time, because the first mortgagor has first rights to the property in the event of a default.
- **Term to maturity** is the length of time before the debt instrument matures. Five-year mortgages usually, but not always, have a higher interest rate than one-year mortgages.

Rule 8	The formula for calculating the real interest rate (i.e., **taking inflation out of a nominal return**) is: $$\frac{(1+\text{nominal rate})}{(1+\text{inflation rate})}-1$$
Rule 9	The formula for calculating the nominal interest rate (i.e., **putting inflation back into a real rate**) is: $$\left[(1+\text{real rate})\times(1+\text{inflation rate})\right]-1$$

Rules 8 and 9 and their implications are explored in considerable detail in Chapter 2.

Example 12   You want to go back to school four years from today. You estimate you will need $6,000 p.a. at the *beginning* of each of the three years you will be at school. How much do you need to save at the *end* of each of the next four years if you can earn 5% per year compounded annually while you are in school and 6% compounded annually while you are saving?

Step 1: How much do you need to have when you go back to school?

Step 2: How much do you need to save each year to have the amount you need when you go back to school?

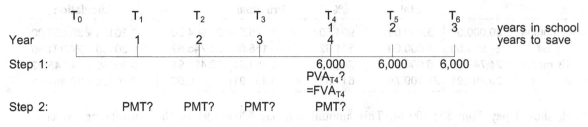

Step 1: Amount needed to save = present value of payments needed while in school

$$PVA_{T4} = 6{,}000 + 6{,}000 \ (PVIFA_{2,5\%})$$
$$= \mathbf{\$17{,}156.46}$$

Step 2: Amount to save each year = future value of annual savings

$$\$17{,}156.46_{T4} = PMT \ (FVIFA_{4,6\%})$$
$$PMT = \mathbf{\$3{,}921.82} \ \text{p.a.}$$

Example 13   Jake, age 83, has decided for several reasons that he would like to donate most of his net worth to an endowment fund at the university he attended: university was the best time of his life; he got an excellent education, which served him well; he doesn't believe in inherited wealth (like Bill Gates, he is willing to give his children what the rest of us would call a small fortune) so he will leave his children $1 million each and the rest, some $7.5 million, to the university. An endowment fund is a fund where only the income is paid out so the original donation remains unchanged. If the fund earns 8% a year, how much will the fund pay out each year? This is called a **perpetuity**.

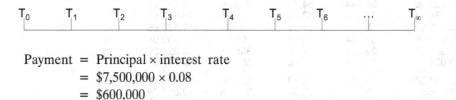

Payment = Principal × interest rate
= $7,500,000 × 0.08
= $600,000

Without touching the capital amount of $7.5 million, his university will have $600,000 a year to spend as long as the endowment funds earn 8%.

The following three examples are specific applications of the rules and uses of the time value of money. Examples 14 and 15 are loan amortization tables for Margot's piano loan and Craig's van, both of which are used in their Statement of Cash Flows and Budgets in Chapter 1. In both of these examples, the monthly interest rate matches the monthly payment, so the monthly interest rate is calculated by dividing the APR by 12. Example 16 deals with residential mortgages. This calculation is also used in Chapter 1 to determine the mortgage balances for Margot and Craig in the future for their Statement of Financial Position. Since residential mortgages compound twice a year, it is necessary to get a monthly payment by taking the 12th root of the EAR.

Amortization Tables — Personal Loans

In Chapter 1, we briefly discussed the two loans that Margot and Craig have. Here we will show the amortization tables that are used to work out the outstanding principal of their loans at different points in time. In the two personal loans presented here, by definition, the compounding is the same as the payment schedule, that is, if the payments are monthly, the compounding is monthly. Should we be making bi-weekly loan payments, by definition, the compounding would be bi-weekly. This is not true for residential mortgages as we shall see in Example 16.

Example 14   Margot wants more details on how Francesca figured out the balance on her **piano loan**. The piano cost $19,000 and Margot paid $3,000 down on it, leaving liability of $16,000. The APR is 7%, which results in a monthly rate of 0.5833%

Appendix 1A: Review of Time Value of Money

(APR ÷ 12 = 7% ÷ 12). There are 48 payments. To find the amount of the monthly payments, solve for PMT in: $16,000 = (\text{PVIFA}_{48,\ .5833\%})$.

Cost	19,000
Down Payment	−3,000
Loan	16,000
Payments EOM	−383.14 −383.14 −383.14 −383.14 ... −383.14 −383.14

With the monthly payment, Francesca prepares the following amortization table for Margot.

Pmt #	Principal before Pmt	Payment Total	Interest 0.5833%	Principal	Principal after Pmt	Pmts o/s	
	19,000.00	3,000.00		3,000.00	16,000.00		Aug. 1/11
1	16,000.00	383.14	93.33	289.81	15,710.19	47	
2	15,710.19	383.14	91.64	291.50	15,418.70	46	
3	15,418.70	383.14	89.94	293.20	15,125.50	45	
4	15,125.50	383.14	88.23	294.91	14,830.59	44	
5	14,830.59	383.14	86.51	296.63	14,533.96	43	Dec. 31/11
6	14,533.96	383.14	84.78	298.36	14,235.60	42	
7	14,235.60	383.14	83.04	300.10	13,935.50	41	
8	13,935.50	383.14	81.29	301.85	13,633.66	40	
9	13,633.66	383.14	79.53	303.61	13,330.04	39	
10	13,330.04	383.14	77.76	305.38	13,024.66	38	
11	13,024.66	383.14	75.98	307.16	12,717.50	37	
12	12,717.50	383.14	74.19	308.95	12,408.55	36	
13	12,408.55	383.14	72.38	310.76	12,097.79	35	
14	12,097.79	383.14	70.57	312.57	11,785.22	34	
15	11,785.22	383.14	68.75	314.39	11,470.83	33	
16	11,470.83	383.14	66.91	316.23	11,154.60	32	
17	11,154.60	383.14	65.07	318.07	10,836.53	31	Dec. 31/12
18	10,836.53	383.14	63.21	319.93	10,516.60	30	
19	10,516.60	383.14	61.35	321.79	10,194.81	29	
20	10,194.81	383.14	59.47	323.67	9,871.14	28	
21	9,871.14	383.14	57.58	325.56	9,45.58	27	
22	9,545.58	383.14	55.68	327.46	9,218.12	26	
23	9,218.12	383.14	53.77	329.37	8,888.75	25	
24	8,888.75	383.14	51.85	331.29	8,557.47	24	
25	8,557.47	383.14	49.92	333.22	8,224.24	23	
26	8,224.24	383.14	47.97	335.17	7,889.08	22	
27	7,889.08	383.14	46.02	337.12	7,551.96	21	
28	7,551.96	383.14	44.05	339.09	7,212.87	20	
29	7,212.87	383.14	42.08	341.06	6,871.81	19	Dec. 31/13
30	6,871.81	383.14	40.09	343.05	6,528.75	18	
31	6,528.75	383.14	38.08	345.06	6,183.70	17	
32	6,183.70	383.14	36.07	347.07	5,836.63	16	
33	5,836.63	383.14	34.05	349.09	5,487.54	15	
34	5,487.54	383.14	32.01	351.13	5,136.41	14	
35	5,136.41	383.14	29.96	353.18	4,783.23	13	
36	4,783.23	383.14	27.90	355.24	4,427.99	12	
37	4,427.99	383.14	25.83	357.31	4,070.68	11	
38	4,070.68	383.14	23.75	359.39	3,711.29	10	
39	3,711.29	383.14	21.65	361.49	3,349.80	9	
40	3,349.80	383.14	19.54	363.60	2,986.20	8	
41	2,986.20	383.14	17.42	365.72	2,620.48	7	Dec. 31/14
42	2,620.48	383.14	15.29	367.85	2,252.62	6	
43	2,252.62	383.14	13.14	370.00	1,882.62	5	
44	1,882.62	383.14	10.98	372.16	1,510.46	4	
45	1,510.46	383.14	8.81	374.33	1,136.13	3	
46	1,136.13	383.14	6.63	376.51	759.62	2	
47	759.62	383.14	4.43	378.71	380.91	1	
48	380.91	383.14	2.22	380.92	(0.00)	0	
		18,390.72	2,390.72	16,000.00			

Margot's loan payments equal $18,392.72, of which $2,390.72 is interest and $16,000 is principal. How much does Margot owe at:

- December 31, 2013: PVA = $383.14 (PVIFA$_{19, .5833\%}$) = $6,871.81
- December 31, 2014: PVA = $383.14 (PVIFA$_{7, .5833\%}$) = $2,620.48

Example 15 Craig asks about his van lease. Can Francesca do an amortization table for a lease? Craig's van cost $30,000, and he paid $5,000 down. His payments of $525.00 are at the beginning of the month. At the end of the 36-month lease, he can buy the van for $9,265.

	T$_0$	T$_1$	T$_2$	T$_3$	...	T$_{35}$	T$_{36}$
Cost	30,000						
Down payment	−5,000	0.4					
Loan	25,000						
Payment #	*1*	*2*	*3*	*4*	...	*36*	
Payment$_{BOM}$	525.00	525.00	525.00	525.00	...	525.00	
Buyout							9,265.00

Francesca finds the interest rate by solving for "k" in the following:

$25,000 = 525.00_{BOM}$ (PVIFA$_{36, k\%}$) + $9,265.00 (PVIF$_{36, k\%}$)

k = 0.51509% × 12 = 6.18% p.a.

Francesca points out:
- Payments are at the beginning of the month, so the first payment is 100% principal.
- The buyout is included at the end.
- The outstanding liability is the unpaid principal (same as Margot's loan) plus accrued interest for the month which is paid the next day. At December 31, 2013, the liability is $13,932 ($13,860.20 + $71.39).

Pmt #	Principal before Pmt	Payment — BOM			Principal after Pmt	Pmts o/s	o/s liab + accrued int	
		Total	Interest 0.51509%	Principal				
	30,000.00	5,000.00	0.00	5,000.00	25,000.00			
1	25,000.00	525.00	0.00	525.00	24,475.00	35		24,601.07
2	24,475.00	525.00	126.07	398.93	24,076.07	34	Dec 31/11	24,200.08
3	24,076.07	525.00	124.01	400.99	23,675.08	33		23,797.03
4	23,675.08	525.00	121.95	403.05	23,272.03	32		23,391.90
5	23,272.03	525.00	119.87	405.13	22,866.90	31		22,984.69
6	22,866.90	525.00	117.79	407.21	22,459.69	30		22,575.37
7	22,459.69	525.00	115.69	409.31	22,050.37	29		22,163.95
8	22,050.37	525.00	113.58	411.42	21,638.95	28		21,750.41
9	21,638.95	525.00	111.46	413.54	21,225.41	27		21,334.74
10	21,225.41	525.00	109.33	415.67	20,809.74	26		20,916.93
11	20,809.74	525.00	107.19	417.81	20,391.93	25		20,496.97
12	20,391.93	525.00	105.04	419.96	19,971.97	24		20,074.84
13	19,971.97	525.00	102.87	422.13	19,549.84	23		19,650.54
14	19,549.84	525.00	100.70	424.30	19,125.54	22	Dec 31/12	19,224.06
15	19,125.54	525.00	98.51	426.49	18,699.06	21		18,795.37
16	18,699.06	525.00	96.32	428.68	18,270.37	20		18,364.48
17	18,270.37	525.00	94.11	430.89	17,839.48	19		17,931.37
18	17,839.48	525.00	91.89	433.11	17,406.37	18		17,496.03
19	17,406.37	525.00	89.66	435.34	16,971.03	17		17,058.45
20	16,971.03	525.00	87.42	437.58	16,533.45	16		16,618.61

Continued.

Pmt #	Principal before Pmt	Payment — BOM			Principal after Pmt	Pmts o/s	o/s liab + accrued int
		Total	Interest 0.51509%	Principal			
21	16,533.45	525.00	85.16	439.84	16,093.61	15	16,176.50
22	16,093.61	525.00	82.90	442.10	15,651.50	14	15,732.12
23	15,651.50	525.00	80.62	444.38	15,207.12	13	15,285.45
24	15,207.12	525.00	78.33	446.67	14,760.45	12	14,836.48
25	14,760.45	525.00	76.03	448.97	14,311.48	11	14,385.20
26	14,311.48	525.00	73.72	451.28	13,860.20	10	Dec 31/13 **13,931.59**
27	13,860.20	525.00	71.39	453.61	13,406.59	9	13,475.65
28	13,406.59	525.00	69.06	455.94	12,950.65	8	13,017.36
29	12,950.65	525.00	66.71	458.29	12,492.36	7	12,556.70
30	12,492.36	525.00	64.35	460.65	12,031.70	6	12,093.68
31	12,031.70	525.00	61.97	463.03	11,568.68	5	11,628.27
32	11,568.68	525.00	59.59	465.41	11,103.27	4	11,160.46
33	11,103.27	525.00	57.19	467.81	10,635.46	3	10,690.24
34	10,635.46	525.00	54.78	470.22	10,165.24	2	10,217.60
35	10,165.24	525.00	52.36	472.64	9,692.60	1	9,742.53
36	9,692.60	525.00	49.93	475.07	9,217.53	0	9,265.01
Buyout	9,217.53	9,265.00	47.48	9,217.52	0.01		
		28,165.00	**3,165.01**	**24,999.99**			

Over the entire lease, Craig will make payments that total $28,165, of which $3,165 is interest and $25,000 is principal.

Mortgages

In Canada, residential fixed-rate mortgages cannot compound more than two times a year. In the above piano and van loan calculations, the monthly rate was arrived at by dividing the APR by 12, which results in monthly compounding. However, since mortgages can compound only twice a year, the monthly rate — or more precisely, the per-period rate — is more complicated.

First, calculate the EAR.

Then, to calculate:

- a monthly interest rate, take the 12th root of the EAR
- a semi-monthly rate, take the 24th root of the EAR
- a bi-weekly rate, take the 26th root of the EAR, and
- a weekly rate, take the 52nd root of the EAR.

Example 16 Margot and Craig have 15 years remaining on their mortgage. The interest rate is 6¼% for a five-year term (the term is the period for which the mortgage rate is locked in. This "term" has nothing to do with the calculation of anything). They owe $121,004 on the mortgage when they renew on January 1, 2014. How much are their monthly payments?

First, Francesca must calculate the monthly interest — monthly since they make monthly mortgage payments. As in Chapter 1, they worked out the various interest rates for different payment periods using this formula:

$$\text{Mortgage interest rate per period} = \left[\left(1+\frac{APR}{2}\right)^2\right]^{1/n} - 1 = \text{interest rate per period}$$

where n = # of payments in a year — for example, monthly (12), semi-monthly (24), bi-weekly (26), and weekly (52)

Specifically:

Step 1: Find the EAR

i.	Find the rate for 6 months	$0.0625 \div 2 = 0.03125$
ii.	(Add 1 and raise it to the power of 2) minus 1	$(1.03125^2) - 1 = 0.063476 = 6.3476\%$

Step 2: Find the appropriate interest rate for each payment

monthly rate	Take the 12th root of (1 + EAR)	$(1.063476)^{1/12} - 1 = 0.005142 = 0.5142\%$
semi-monthly rate	Take the 24th root of (1 + EAR)	$(1.063476)^{1/24} - 1 = 0.002568 = 0.2568\%$
bi-weekly rate	Take the 26th root of (1 + EAR)	$(1.063476)^{1/26} - 1 = 0.002370 = 0.2370\%$
weekly rate	Take the 52nd root of (1 + EAR)	$(1.063476)^{1/52} - 1 = 0.001184 = 0.1184\%$

With the interest rate per period calculated, they can find out their payment per period as well as their outstanding principal at any point in time. Let's see what will happen if Margot and Craig decide to make bi-weekly payments on their mortgage.

To calculate their bi-weekly payment:

$$\text{Mortgage outstanding} = \text{PMT}_{EOM} \, (\text{PVIFA}_{n,\, k\%})$$
$$\$121{,}004 = \text{PMT}_{EOM} \, (\text{PVIFA}_{390,\, .2370\%})$$
$$\text{PMT} = \$475.78 \text{ every 2 weeks}$$

where

n = # of payments outstanding on the mortgage
   = 15 years $\times$ 26 = 390

k = interest rate per payment period

$$= \left[1 + \left(\frac{0.0625}{2}\right)^2\right]^{1/26} - 1 = 0.002370 \text{ or } 0.2370\% \text{ bi-weekly}$$

At December 31, 2014, they would have made 26 payments since they renewed. Now their outstanding principal (liability) is:

$$\text{PVA} = \$475.78_{EOM} \, (\text{PVIFA}_{(364,\, 0.2370\%)}) = 115{,}942$$

Similarly:

At December 31, 2015: $n = 338$, PVA = $110,558
At December 31, 2016: $n = 312$, PVA = $104,832
At December 31, 2017: $n = 286$, PVA = $98,743

Let's compare these two, assuming that the remaining mortgage is paid either monthly or bi-weekly:

	Monthly	Bi-weekly
K per payment period	0.5142%	0.2370%
Number of payments — 15 years	180	390
Payments	1,032.27	475.78
Total payments	185,808.60	185,554.20
Outstanding mortgage	121,004.00	121,004.00
Total interest paid	64,804.60	64,550.20

By switching to bi-weekly payments, they will save $254.40 (64,804.60 – 64,550.20) over the 15 years or an average of $16.96 per year. Savings occur when making the *amount* of the semi-monthly payment and the payments are made bi-weekly (26 payments a year) instead of semi-monthly (24 payments a year). As demonstrated by this example, no significant amount of money is saved by merely making payments more frequently. The savings occur when the amount of each payment is increased with the extra amount being applied against the principal.

SUMMARY

This overview of calculations involving the Time Value of Money cannot replace an entire course. Computer programs definitely ease the burden of the calculations. However, this book is a learning text with an objective to teach principles, and retirement calculations can be done using a calculator, preferably a financial calculator. Doing the calculations manually using a calculator forces you to understand the concepts behind the calculations and enables you to "ballpark" the answer. A few years ago in an introductory financial planning course, some students submitted a project to me using a financial program that one of them had obtained from a parent. Unfortunately, there was a bug in the program and the inflation rate was not handled properly. The students cannot be faulted for using an available program. However, their lack of experience meant they were not able to look at the printouts and see that the result was completely unrealistic. By understanding the calculations, the students will not become dependent on a computer program, but will be able to use it appropriately.

SUMMARY OF THE TIME VALUE OF MONEY RULES

#	Rule
1.	The interest rate given is always the APR, i.e., compounded annually, unless specifically stated otherwise.
2.	The future value annuity formula includes the assumption that the payments are made at the end of each period. Thus, the last payment is not compounded.
3.	When you have used the formula, make sure you know where you are in time.
4.	The present value annuity formula assumes that the payments are made at the end of each period. The first payment is discounted one period.
5.	Always convert the interest rate to match the compounding or payment period.
6.	To get the monthly rate from the: • APR, divide the APR by 12: 9% APR ÷ 12 = 0.75% per month • EAR, add 1 to the EAR, take the 12th root, subtract 1 $(1.0938)^{1/12} - 1 = 0.75\%$ per month
7.	To get from a monthly rate to an: • APR, multiply by 12: 0.75% × 12 = 9.00% • EAR, add 1, raise it to the 12th power, subtract 1 $(1.0075)^{12} - 1 = 9.38\%$
8.	The formula for taking inflation out of a nominal return is: $$\frac{(1+\text{nominal rate})}{(1+\text{interest rate})} - 1 = \text{real rate}$$
9.	To put inflation back into a real rate: nominal rate = (1 + real rate) × (1 + inflation rate) − 1

KEY TERMS

Amortization table	Nominal interest rate
Annual percentage rate (APR)	Ordinary annuity
Annuity due	Perpetuity
Compounding	Pure interest rates
Compounding quarterly	Real interest rates
Default risk	Risk free interest rate
Effective annual rate (EAR)	Term to maturity
Holding period return (HPR)	

See also:
Acronyms, Tax Rates and Time Value of Money Formula

PROBLEMS

1. Mark wants to go to Italy in three years for the summer. His grandmother has just given him $1,000 for his 21st birthday, and Mark is willing to invest it rather than buy that fabulous leather jacket he saw last week. He can get 5% from a new bank if he is willing to lock the funds in for 3 years. After shopping around a bit, he realizes that this is a good deal with no risk. The interest is compounded annually.
   (a) How much will Mark have in three years? (Answer: $1,157.63)
   (b) If he adds $300 at the end of this year and the next two years, how much will he have in total in three years? (Answer: $2,103.38)

2. Mark's other grandmother has offered to give him $2,500 in five years. Or, he can take $1,800 now. Or, he can get $475 at the end of each of the next five years. However, he can have the money only if he does not spend it on his trip to Italy. If money is worth 5% compounded annually to Mark, which offer should he accept?

   > Hint: You could calculate the future value of these three options and arrive at the same conclusion. However, with questions like this (such as which of two settlement options one should choose when being downsized), the common practice is to take the present value, since that is where we are when making the decision.

   (Answer: PV = $1,958.82, PV = $1,800, PVA = $2,056.50)

3. If Craig's salary, $78,000 in 2014, increases by 2% a year until he is 65 (he is 43 now), what is his salary at age 65? (Answer: $120,586)

4. If Margot invests $1,000 a year at the beginning of each year for 10 years, how much does she have at the end of 10 years if her investments earn:
   (a) 9% (Answer: $16,560.29)
   (b) 9% compounded quarterly (Answer: $16,853.52)
   (c) 9% compounded monthly? (Answer: $16,923.11)

5. Margot wants to study botanical drawing. The program costs $3,000 a year and is a three-year, part-time program. If she can earn 5 1/2%, how much does she need to save at the end of each month for the next two years? Assume the compounding is the same during the time she saves and during the time she consumes her savings.

$(PVA = \$8,527.99)$

$(PMT_{EOM} = \$336.96)$

6. Frick borrowed $10,000 from Frack and agreed to make 11 quarterly payments of $1,000 each plus one other payment if required. The interest of 8% is compounded three times a year. Set up an amortization table to show the amortization of the loan. How much is the twelfth payment? (Answer: $265.47)

7. If Margot bought her piano for $19,000 on July 31, 2012, making a down payment of $6,000, and was paying an interest rate at the bank of 6% amortized over 36 months:
    (a) What are her monthly payments? (Answer: $395.49)
    (b) How much does she owe at December 31, 2013? (Answer: $7,151.30)
    (c) How much does she owe at December 31, 2014? (Answer: $2,713.85)
    (d) For the entire length of the loan, how much are the:
        i.   total payments (Answer: $14,237.47)
        ii. total principal (Answer: $13,000), and
        iii. total interest (Answer: $1,237.47)

8. On January 2, 2014, Craig and Margot renewed their mortgage of $121,004 for a five-year term with a 15-year amortization. They renewed at 8%.

    > Hint: Always assume residential mortgages are compounded semi-annually, and payments are made at the end of the period.

    (a) Complete the following table assuming interest rates remain the same. Round the interest rate to six decimal places.

Payments		Principal	
Frequency	Amount	Dec.31, 2014	Dec.31, 2021
Monthly	1,147.30	116,604.26	81,539.44
Semi-monthly	572.71	116,598.49	81,536.55
Bi-weekly	528.59	116,594.55	81,535.00

    (b) If, at January 2, 2014, Margot and Craig make the amount of the semi-monthly payment but make the payments bi-weekly:
        i. How many payments will they make?

        > Hint: Since they are following the payment schedule for bi-weekly payments, the interest rate is the rate used to calculate the bi-weekly payments.)

        (Answer: n = 337.20)
        ii. How much interest will they save by making the payments this way?

        > Hint: What is the difference in the total payments made using a bi-weekly schedule and bi-weekly amount compared to a bi-weekly schedule and the semi-monthly amount?

        (Answer: $13,031.25)

2

Factors Affecting Retirement Planning

Learning Objectives

Examine the factors that affect retirement planning, including:

A.   Learn about longevity, or life expectancy.

B.   Understand inflation and how we are going to deal with it in this text.

C.   Understand rates of return, measuring risk and choosing appropriate rates for planning.

D.   Learn about income tax rates now and in the future and their effect on retirement saving and consumption of assets during retirement. Using generic federal and provincial tax rates, calculate the tax, average tax rate, marginal tax rate and the use of these rates for interest and regular income, dividend income, and capital gains.

The Appendix shows the calculation of the tax, average tax rate, and marginal tax rate for interest/regular income for all provinces and territories for 2013.

INTRODUCTION

"Freedom 55." This slogan from an advertising campaign a few years ago has come to define our expectations: work hard, play hard, sacrifice a little now, invest wisely, and retire young enough to enjoy the "golden years." The little bit of sacrifice now turns out to be quite a bit of sacrifice if you take a hard look at the numbers. Mandatory retirement at age 65 or any age is being called into question by several provinces. In the United States, normal retirement age, the age when a person can first collect an unreduced Social Security pension, is being phased to move from age 65 to 67. In Canada, the same is happening with Old Age Security — the age when you can first collect it is being phased in over several years to increase it from age 65 to 67. The long bull market of the 1990s led many people who were inexperienced with the stock market to believe that double-digit rates of return on investments during periods of low inflation were inevitable.

History of Pensions

The Old Age Pension was set up in Canada in 1927 and provided a maximum of $20 a month. The Canada Pension Plan came into effect on January 1, 1966. Since the mid-1960s, average life expectancy has increased by about nine years. It has increased by 33 years since 1903, when average life expectancy was 49, and 57 years since 1003, when average life expectancy in the world was 25. The most important factor in this increase is the drop in infant and childhood mortality, but other factors are also important — clean water, sanitation, improved diets, access to adequate health care, and an improvement in surgical and medical procedures. Life expectancy is still lower in countries where infant mortality is high and these other factors are not present.

   The first universal pension was put in place by Bismarck and Emperor Wilhelm II in Germany in 1889. Retirement age was set at 70 — well beyond average life expectancy. In Europe, there had been intermittent pension provision, particularly for soldiers, since about 1600, but none was permanent. People were expected to have either land or children to support them in old age. Otherwise, they worked until they dropped. England enacted the Elizabethan Poor Law in 1601, which provided an allowance from the parish as long as the person was of good character and had worked until they no longer could. A census in 1570 in Norwich, a rich spinning centre in England, described three widows aged 74, 79, and 82 as "almost past work." Later in the 17th century, the parishes often made regular church attendance a qualification for poor relief. Parish decisions to withhold the allowance could be appealed to a magistrate but the applicants would only encounter the same criteria.

By 1740 in England, 10% of the population was over 60, while average life expectancy was less than 35 years due to high infant and childhood mortality. (In comparison, in 2007 in Canada, 19% of the population was over 60, while average life expectancy was 80.) So there were a lot of old people in England, many of whom had every reason to fear poverty in old age and thus had a strong motive to be deferential to the local gentry and parish authorities. In 1908, Britain introduced a non-contributory pension plan for all those over 70 who passed a means test.[1] The United States set up a national program in 1935, when the Social Security Act was implemented.

Future of Retirement

Canada's population had the following distribution:

Age	2008	2012
0–19	24%	22%
20–54	51%	50%
55–64	12%	13%
65+	13%	15%

Is Freedom 55 realistic? Is it realistic to expect to work for 35 years and then spend 25 years in retirement with only half of the population working? For some people, yes, it can be done. But not for most of us. The baby boomers — those born between 1946 and 1964, who are between the ages of 49 and 67 in 2013 — are now moving into retirement. There is an "echo baby boom", made up of those born between 1977 and 1994, who were aged between 19 and 36 in 2013. The years between 1964 and 1977 were years of reduced birth rates. How do the latter two groups feel about being the major taxpayers while boomers seek ways to minimize taxes in retirement as illustrated throughout this book? Not great.

There is some speculation that the baby boomers will not be as huge a consumer of the health care system as originally thought because they have looked after themselves and continue to eat well and be physically active. Perhaps, but they are predicted to be an ever-increasing proportion of the population for the next 30 years or so and this is reflected in the percentage in the above table.

Saving for retirement takes, among other things, real sacrifice now in order to finance retirement. Government plans provide some retirement income — not a lot, but a solid base. Fewer companies are providing private plans, and people are increasingly transient in jobs. It might be wise to seek less to retire early and seek more to enjoy one's work and to live and savour life while still working.

Conventional wisdom tells us that to achieve what we want, we need to plan ahead. But what do we need to know to plan for retirement?

To plan successfully for retirement, we need to understand that many factors will impact the outcome of a retirement plan. The better we understand how these factors affect retirement planning, the

---

1   A non-contributory pension is a pension plan to which employees do not make contributions. A means test is used to determine the amount received, which is less if your income is higher. These are explained in Chapter 4 and Chapter 3 respectively.

more likely it is that we will have the retirement that we envision. Some of these factors are controllable and some of them are not.

Controllable factors include:
• Date of retirement
• Planned retirement lifestyle
• Level of savings, and
• Investment decisions and asset allocation.

These factors will be examined as we progress through the chapters. Since they are controllable, they will vary to reflect changes in circumstances.

Uncontrollable factors include:
A. Life expectancy, or longevity
B. Inflation rates
C. Rates of return on investments, and
D. Income tax rates.

Although the outcome of some of these uncontrollable factors may be influenced by our decisions, adapting to them is the only appropriate response. Because they are uncontrollable, they are the cause of most imprecision in retirement planning, and we will examine them now.

A. LONGEVITY

While it is not possible to predict the age of death, retirees need to plan for a long life to avoid outliving their assets. As the old joke goes, "If I had known I was going to live this long, I would have taken better care of myself." As shown in Table 2.1, which illustrates the probabilities of men and women living to ages 60 and 65, women have a longer life expectancy than men. Combined with generally lower incomes, women run a greater risk of not having enough to live on in retirement, making proper retirement planning critical.

Table 2.1 Life Expectancy Rates

Probability of living to age	Male at age 60	Male at age 65	Female at age 60	Female at age 65
70	87%	92%	92%	95%
75	76%	80%	85%	87%
80	61%	65%	73%	76%
85	43%	45%	57%	59%
90	23%	24%	37%	38%
95	8%	9%	17%	17%

Source: Author's calculations are based on information provided in Life Tables, Canada, 2007 to 2009, Statistics Canada, Catalogue no. 84-537-X — No. 003.

B. INFLATION

Most of the time, we work in real dollars (adjusted to take out inflation; i.e., inflation is not included) rather than nominal dollars (not adjusted for inflation; i.e., past or future dollars that include inflation, or the actual dollars spent) for two reasons.

The **first reason** is that most people find it difficult to relate to future spending needs stated in nominal dollars. To say that a cup of coffee now costing $1.00 will cost $1.81 in 20 years sounds plausible — that is what a $1.00 cup of coffee will be if inflation is 3% a year. But what if it will cost $2.65 (i.e., the price if inflation is 5% a year)? To project required retirement savings of **$400,000** by saving $10,874 for 20 years and earning a 6% real return per year has a very different feel to people than telling them they must save **$1,061,319** in 20 years time because there is 5% inflation [FV of $400,000 in 20 years' adjusted to reflect 5% inflation: FV = $400,000 (FVIF$_{5\%, 20}$) = $1,061,319].

Table 2.2 $400,000 plus Inflation

Inflation @	In 10 years	In 20 years	In 30 years
0%	400,000	**400,000**	400,000
2%	487,598	594,379	724,545
4%	592,098	876,449	1,297,359
5%	651,558	**1,061,319**	1,728,777
6%	716,339	1,282,854	2,297,396
8%	863,570	1,864,383	4,025,063
10%	1,037,497	2,691,000	6,979,761

Tables such as 2.2 can also be used with clients to show them:

• The power of compounding, and
• The long-term difference of the effects of taking additional risk. Of course, taking additional risk does not guarantee a higher return; it just increases the probability of a higher return.

Here, $1,061,319 is what needs to be saved in 20 years to have the equivalent of $400,000 in today's dollars if inflation is 5% per year. But what if inflation is only 3%, or 2%? Some people will react to the $1 million figure by giving up. Others will start to save aggressively, putting more pressure on themselves than they need to.

This is not to downplay the valid need to save for retirement with inflation in mind. However, the goal must seem realistic if the client is to be able to do what is necessary to prepare financially for retirement.

The **second reason** for working in real dollars is that future inflation rates are impossible to predict or even estimate. As shown in Table 2A.2 in Appendix 2A, inflation can become very high. At the present time, considerable effort is put into keeping inflation rates low, close to the point it was at towards the end of the last recession. There was some speculation that the Bank of Canada was keeping inflation rates low at the cost of recovering from the recession. However, in the future, when the next generation of people (who have not lived with high inflation rates) are running the economy, they may change the focus and inflation could, once again, start increasing. Therefore, simply applying an estimated inflation rate in the projection of the required retirement savings does not necessarily result in better planning.

Good projections can be made while leaving out inflation as long as the client understands that, each year, inflation must be added to refine the projections. Example 1 demonstrates how actual inflation can be used to adjust projections made with an estimate of inflation to reflect actual returns.

Example 1   Andre's financial planner told him that, to meet his retirement goals, he needs to earn a *real* rate of return each year of 4%. In the year just ended, inflation jumped unexpectedly to 3½%. Andre's tax-sheltered retirement funds earned **7%**. Andre thought he had exceeded his required rate of return. What is his real rate of return?

$$k_{real} = \left(\frac{1 + \text{nominal rate}}{1 + \text{inflation rate}}\right) - 1 = \frac{(1.07)}{(1.035)} - 1 = 3.38\%$$

In order to meet his objectives, he should have earned **7.64%** $[(1.04 \times 1.035) - 1]$. As a result, Andre will have to either invest more aggressively next year or revise his retirement plans.

It does not matter to the final projections whether the planning is done in real or nominal dollars, as long as everyone involved clearly understands what the difference is. A planner using a financial-planning package could produce the plan both with and without different rates of inflation so that the client understands what future needs are if inflation turns out to be what is anticipated.

> Although Margot has quite a head for numbers, she does not see how it could make no difference to the outcome if the plan is done in real or nominal dollars. Francesca set up the following example to illustrate this point.

Example 2 shows that calculations with inflation are the same as calculations without inflation as long as the effect of inflation is taken into account at some point.

Example 2   Marjorie plans to save $5,000 a year for four years. Money will be put aside at the beginning of the year. She is only 49 years old, so she is willing to take some risk, but not a lot. Thus, she expects she can earn a nominal rate of return of 9% when inflation is 3%. Let's compare the future value calculated with and without inflation. We will then put inflation back into the "without inflation" calculation. The results should be the same.

With inflation: The amount that Marjorie will have to save each year will need to be increased by the amount of inflation. These amounts will then be compound at the nominal rate of return. If Marjorie saves at the beginning of each of the four years, by the end of the four years, she will have:

Year	Nominal savings$_{BOY}$		Growth in annual savings		
	Savings$_{\$ \, real}$ × FVIF	FV$_{\$ \, Nominal}$	Annual saving$_{\$ \, nominal}$		FV$_{EOY \, 4}$
1	5,000	5,000.00	FV$_{PMT \, 1}$ =	5,000.00 (FVIF$_{4, \, 9\%}$) =	7,057.91
2	5,000 × (FVIF$_{1, \, 3\%}$) =	5,150.00	FV$_{PMT \, 2}$ =	5,150.00 (FVIF$_{3, \, 9\%}$) =	6,669.40
3	5,000 × (FVIF$_{2, \, 3\%}$) =	5,304.50	FV$_{PMT \, 3}$ =	5,304.50 (FVIF$_{2, \, 9\%}$) =	6,302.28
4	5,000 × (FVIF$_{3, \, 3\%}$) =	5,463.64	FV$_{PMT \, 4}$ =	5,463.64 (FVIF$_{1, \, 9\%}$) =	5,955.37
					$25,984.96 nominal

Without inflation: The payments are not increased by inflation, which means they remain constant each year (i.e., this is an annuity). First, we must calculate the **real interest rate**. The formula is:

$$k_{real} = \left(\frac{1 + \text{nominal rate}}{1 + \text{inflation rate}}\right) - 1 = \left(\frac{1.09}{1.03}\right) - 1 = 5.825\%$$

$$FVA = 5,000_{BOY}\left(FVIFA_{4, \, 5.825\%}\right) = \textbf{\$23,087.15 real}$$

However, now we must put the inflation back in to find out what this amount is worth in nominal dollars. To put the inflation back in, inflate the real-dollar answer by 3% per year.

$$FV = 23,087.15 \, (FVIF_{4, \, 3\%}) = \textbf{\$25,984.79 nominal}$$

Many retirement cash flows are adjusted for inflation annually — they are called **indexed** cash flows. As we will see in the next, section, since the cash flows are increasing by inflation every year, we can use an uninflated cash flow which will be the same every year in real dollars, and discount it using a real rate of return.

However, some cash flows are not adjusted for inflation — they are called **non-indexed** cash flows. As a result, the purchasing power of the annual income decreases every year by the amount of inflation. These cash flows need to be discounted using a nominal interest rate, which reflects the effects of inflation.

Let's take a closer look at this concept and how it affects retirement income.

Income Indexed to Inflation

For income such as CPP, OAS, indexed pension income or an indexed annuity, the beginning amount can be used throughout, without inflation. In this case, the amount is in real dollars and will be discounted using a real discount rate.

Example 3 below shows that discounting indexed income using the real amount (the amount of the first payment) as the PMT in the PVA formula and a real discount rate produces the same result as discounting the nominal payments (payments increasing by inflation) using a nominal discount rate.

Example 3 Janine wants to estimate the value of her CPP retirement income of $9,300 at retirement. To discount, she will use a long-term Government of Canada bond rate of 7% at a time when inflation is 3%. We will first use nominal dollars and a nominal discount rate. Then we will use real dollars and a real discount rate. The answers should be the same. For simplicity, we will look only at five years.

Nominal income and nominal discount rate: First, the CPP retirement income is increased by the 3% rate of inflation to show nominal dollars for five years. Then these nominal dollars are discounted using a nominal discount rate.

	Nominal	2013	2014	2015	2016	2017
CPP income	$	9,300	9,579	9,866	10,162	10,467
PV at BOY 2013*	7.00%	9,300	8,952	8,618	8,296	7,985
PV — total		43,151				

*PV at BOY 2013: present value at beginning of the year 2013

Using only a calculator, it is a lot of work to first increase the income by inflation and then discount it at a nominal discount rate, let's say 20 years. Is it necessary to use a financial-planning package or a spreadsheet package? No. The calculation can be done without inflation and produces the same result.

Real income and real discount rate: Convert this income stream to **real dollars** and discount it using a **real discount rate of 3.88%** [(1.07 ÷ 1.03) − 1].

	Real	2013	2014	2015	2016	2017
CPP income	$	9,300	9,300	9,300	9,300	9,300
PV at BOY 2013	3.88%	9,300	8,952	8,618	8,296	7,985
PVA		**43,151**				

PVA = 9,300 $_{BOY}$ (PVIFA $_{3.88\%,\ 5}$) = 43,151

Although Janine's pension is indexed, only a financial calculator is needed to find the present value at retirement of this stream of income.

Income Not Indexed to Inflation

For income such as a non-indexed pension or a fixed annuity, the beginning amount will be used throughout, without inflation. The flat amount is in nominal dollars and will be discounted using a nominal discount rate.

Example 4 will demonstrate that discounting non-indexed income using the nominal amount (the amount of the first payment) as the PMT in the PVA formula and a nominal discount rate produces the same result as discounting the real payments (payments decreasing by inflation) using a real discount rate.

Example 4   Janine has a pension plan that will pay her $9,300 a year at the beginning of the year. However, this pension is not indexed. As a result, the income stream is in nominal dollars. What is its value at the beginning of 2013?

Non-indexed income and nominal discount rate: Because the amount of her pension income each year remains the same, the amount is a nominal amount — each year she will receive $9,300. So it is discounted using the nominal discount rate of 7% used in Example 3.

	Nominal	2013	2014	2015	2016	2017
Fixed annuity	$	9,300	9,300	9,300	9,300	9,300
PV at BOY 2013	7.00%	9,300	8,692	8,123	7,592	7,095
PVA		**40,801**				

PVA = 9,300 $_{BOY}$ (PVIFA $_{7\%,\ 5}$) = 40,801

Non-indexed income adjusted to real dollars and real discount rate: How do you know if the prior calculation is correct? Take the inflation out of the income stream to show it in real dollars and then calculate the present value using a real discount rate. Because the $9,300 is not indexed, if inflation is 3% a year, each year it loses purchasing power (by the amount of inflation). The real dollars are calculated by dividing the prior year's real income by 1+ Inflation rate.

	Real	2013	2014	2015	2016	2017
Fixed annuity	$	9,300	9,029	8,766	8,511	8,263
PV at BOY 2013	3.88%	9,300	8,692	8,123	7,592	7,095
PVA		**40,801**				

In Summary

Discount the **first amount** of:	
indexed income using a **real** discount rate	*Example 3*
non-indexed income using a **nominal** discount rate	*Example 4*

Inflation and Income Tax

Since future tax rates cannot be predicted, we must use current tax rates — average and marginal — as appropriate for planning (as we will see later in this chapter, taxes consume a large part of income). Taxes are paid on nominal income that has not been adjusted for inflation. At the present time, tax brackets are adjusted annually to reflect inflation. However, for several years in the recent past, these tax brackets did not change, resulting in **bracket creep**. Example 5 shows how bracket creep occurs. The tax rates used in Example 5 are the tax rates in effect in the year before the brackets started to be indexed again.

Example 5   For the past five years, Tom has received an annual raise of 3%, which reflected only the increase in the cost of living (i.e., inflation, as measured by the Consumer Price Index). However, the federal and provincial tax brackets and basic personal amount did not change, so Tom's taxes are increasing in real terms even though his salary is not, because the salary increases for inflation are pushing him into a higher tax bracket. To further illustrate how this affected Tom, note the following calculations using tax rates in effect for much of the 1990s and the provincial tax as a percentage of the federal tax (the method used to calculate provincial tax until 2001):

$Nominal T_0 = Salary now
$Nominal T_5 = Salary in five years increased by 3% inflation each year
          = FV = 58,000 (FVIF$_{5, 3\%}$) = \$67,238
$Real: T_0 @ T_5 = Salary in five years without inflation; that is, in today's dollars (T_0)

The third column, "$Real", is the present value of the second column "$Nominal T_5" discounted for five years at 3% to show that the amount of tax in $real is increasing because the tax brackets are not changing. So,

PV of \$67,238 is \$58,000 [PV = \$67,238 (PVIFA$_{3\%, 5}$) = \$58,000], and
PV of \$5,030 is \$4,339 [PV = \$5,030 (PVIFA$_{3\%, 5}$) = \$4,339], etc.

			$Nominal T_0		$Nominal T_5		$Real: T_0 @T$_5$	
			Average	Marginal	Average	Marginal	Average	Marginal
Salary			58,000.00	100.00	67,238.00	100.00	58,000.00	100.00
Federal tax:	17%	29,590	5,030.30		5,030.30		4,339.18	
	26%	29,590	7,386.60	26.00	7,693.40		6,636.39	
	29%				2,336.82	29.00	2,015.76	29.00
Total federal tax			12,416.90	26.00	15,060.52	29.00	12,991.33	29.00
NRTxCr	17%	6,700	1,139.00		1,139.00		982.51	
Basic federal tax			11,277.90	26.00	13,921.52	29.00	12,008.82	29.00
Provincial tax	43%	BFT	4,849.50	11.18	5,986.25	12.47	5,163.79	12.47
Total tax			16,127.40	37.18	19,907.77	41.47	17,172.61	41.47
Average tax rate			27.81%		29.61%		29.61%	
Marginal tax rate				37.18%		41.47%		41.47%

In the above table, notice the change in the average and marginal tax rates: both are increasing. Although Tom's salary was increasing, its increase reflects only inflation and there was no increase in his real income. With no inflation adjustment to the tax brackets, both the average and marginal tax rates for Tom increase — this is called **bracket creep**.

C. RATES OF RETURN

Income from investments such as stocks, bonds, mutual funds, savings accounts, and Guaranteed Investment Certificates (GICs) are taxed each year, as the income is earned if these investments are not in tax-sheltered retirement savings plans. As a result, the amount of annual earned income available to compound is decreased by the amount of the tax payable each year as the income is earned. When these assets are sold, tax is paid only on any capital gain — the principal amount invested was made from income that was already taxed — no further tax on the capital is required. However, the income on funds invested in registered plans such as Registered Pension Plans (RPPs) and Registered Retirement Savings Plans (RRSPs) is not taxed while the funds are still in the plan. These **tax-deferred,** or **tax-sheltered, savings** grow at a before-tax rate, so they grow faster because taxes are not paid on the income earned by the savings each year. As a result, the actual rate of return will be higher on registered assets. However, when these funds are received from the registered plan, the total amount is taxable, including the amount originally invested — it was tax deductible at the time it went into the registered plan.

In addition, the amount required to save for retirement is greatly affected by the rate of return that the savings earn. To plan for retirement, decisions have to be made about required rates of return and acceptable risk levels. Investments that earn higher rates of return usually come with more risk; hence, they may result in a rate of return that is less than expected. A review of investment basics is provided in Appendix 2A. In this chapter, we will concern ourselves with calculating real and nominal rates of return before and after tax on investments that are nominal and real.

Average Rate of Return (k)

An average rate of return is the average of the return for several years. Average rates of return are useful only if the standard deviation is also available. As shown in Table 2A.2, the rate of return can be misleading, as it may hide the asset's volatile nature. Historically, stocks provide a higher rate of return than bonds, bonds higher than funds whose return is guaranteed. As discussed in Appendix 2A, historically, higher returns are accompanied by higher volatility — the returns vary more from year to year as measured by the standard deviation.

Annual rates of return for investments such as those shown in Table 2A.2 can be found in the stocks section in most financial newspapers or on websites. To be useful, an average of several years with the corresponding standard deviation must be used when choosing a realistic rate of return on investments for clients. While standard deviations do not change much when converted to real dollars, nominal and real rates of return can change a great deal. A caveat is needed here: Published standard deviations are often calculated for only three years even when the rate of return is a 10-year average. This is not really long enough to see the real volatility in the return. The reader should try to get (or calculate) standard deviations based on returns for 10 years.

Rates of Return: Before Tax, Nominal, and Real

It is important to remember that reported rates of return are nominal returns — they include inflation. At the present time, the Bank of Canada is concerned with keeping inflation low because those of us who lived through high inflation in the 1970s know only too well the effects of high rates of inflation on our spending dollars. In the future, when the Bank of Canada and other financial institutions are being run by people who are now young and did not live through these times, the lesson of high inflation may be forgotten. An important component of interest rates (and therefore rates of return) is inflation. High rates of inflation distort actual returns, as shown in Table 2A.2.

The real returns in Table 2A.1 are calculated for *each year* with the data in Table 2A.2, using the following formula:

$$k_{real} = \left(\frac{1 + \text{nominal rate}}{1 + \text{inflation rate}} \right) - 1$$

For example, in 1981 T-bills had a nominal rate of return of 18.4%. However, inflation that year was 12.2% as measured by the Consumer Price Index. As a result, the real rate of return was only 5.5% — high for T-bills but nothing like 18.4%.

$$k_{real} = \left(\frac{1.184}{1.122} \right) - 1 = 0.055 = 5.5\%$$

Rates of Return: After Tax, Nominal, and Real

Since non-tax sheltered investments grow at an after-tax rate, we must be able to calculate the rate of return after tax. We will look at four scenarios.

Given the nominal rate of return before tax, we will calculate:

1. The nominal rate of return after tax (Example 6)
2. The real rate of return after tax (Example 7)

Given the purchase price, selling price, and annual cash flows for a five-year holding period, we will then calculate the Holding Period Return (HPR) and Effective Annual Rate (EAR, or average return). With that information we will then calculate:

3. The nominal return before and after tax (Example 8), and
4. The real return before and after tax. (We will not do this final calculation in detail.)

1. Nominal Rates of Return After Tax

These are fairly straightforward. After-tax rates of return are calculated using the following formula:

$$\text{Return} \times (1 - \text{marginal tax rate})$$

Example 6 calculates *nominal* rates of return after tax for interest and capital gain when the return is for *exactly one year*.

Example 6   Henry has received 6% interest on a GIC. His marginal tax rate is 48%. What is his after-tax rate of return? What is his after-tax return if the 6% return was a capital gain?

Nominal return, after tax on:
- Interest income of 6%: $[.06 \times (1 - 0.48)] = 3.12\%$

• Capital gain of 6%: $[.06 \times (1 - \{0.48 \times .5\})] = 4.56\%$

> Hint: A rate of return is *always*:
> • a **nominal** rate unless it is specifically stated that it is a real return,
> • an **annual percentage rate (APR)** without compounding unless it is specifically stated that is perhaps quarterly or compounded — that is, an effective annual rate of return (EAR). A commonly seen example would be the interest rate for savings offered by the banks. Listed as 10% compounded monthly would mean an EAR of 10.47%: $[1+(0.10 \div 12)]^{12} - 1 = 10.47\%$. Refer to Appendix 1A for a review of APR and EAR.

2. Real Rates of Return After Tax

These *must* be calculated in the following order:

Step 1   **Take off the tax** (i.e., calculate the after-tax rate of return).
Step 2   **Take out the inflation** (i.e., convert the after-tax nominal return to an after-tax real return).

Example 7 calculates the *real* rate of return after tax in Example 6.

Example 7   What is Henry's real after-tax rate of return if inflation is 3%?

Using $k_{real,\ AT} = \dfrac{1+k_{nom}(1-T)}{1+i} - 1$

Interest income of 6%: $k_{real,\ AT} = \dfrac{1+[0.06(1-0.48)]}{1.03} - 1 = 0.1165\%$

Capital gain of 6%: $k_{real,\ AT} = \dfrac{1+[0.06(1-0.24)]}{1.03} - 1 = 1.515\%$

> Craig still does not understand what difference it makes whether you take the tax off before or after the real return is calculated. Francesca gives him the following explanation.

Income on non-tax-sheltered assets is taxed as it is earned, except for capital gains, which are taxed when the return is realized (i.e., capital gains are taxed when the asset is sold). Thus, a portion of the income is used to pay tax each year and is *not* available for earning more income. In other words, income on non-tax-sheltered assets grows slower, at an after-tax rate. On the other hand, income on tax-sheltered assets is not taxed until it is withdrawn from the tax shelter. So tax-sheltered income grows at a before-tax rate of return.

3. Nominal Rates of Return Before and After Tax

We will now calculate the rate of return for a non-tax-sheltered investment held for five years. Example 8 shows the calculation of an average return as measured by the EAR for a non-tax sheltered investment that was held for five years. This investment paid quarterly dividends and produced a capital gain when it was sold. The capital gain is the difference between the purchase price and the selling price. Before-tax returns are calculated using before-tax cash flows, while after-tax returns are calculated using after-tax cash flows.

Example 8   Suppose Craig buys 100 8% $50 par value preferred shares that pay dividends quarterly. Thus, he receives $100 in dividends every three months. He buys the shares for $6,000 and sells them at the end of five years for $6,625. Assume his marginal tax rates are:

- 37.18% on regular income
- 18.59% (37.18% × 50%) on capital gain
- 22.64% on dividend income

What is his EAR before tax and after tax on these shares?

To find the EAR, they must first calculate Craig's **holding period return** (**HPR**) for the five years. Then they will calculate his **effective annual rate** (**EAR**) of return before tax and after tax on these shares.

Example 8–1   **HPR and EAR before tax**

Dividends not reinvested: Assume Craig and Margot took the dividends and went out for dinner four times a year — that is, they did not reinvest the dividends.

$$HPR = \left[\frac{\text{selling price} - \text{purchase price} + \text{income}}{\text{purchase price}} \right]$$

$$= \left[\frac{6,625 - 6,000 + (4 \times 100 \times 5)}{6,000} \right]$$

$$= 0.4375$$

$$= 43.75\%$$

$$EAR = (1.4375)^{1/5} - 1$$

$$= 0.07528$$

$$= 7.528\%$$

Dividends reinvested: If Craig had reinvested the dividends at 4%, at the end of each payment over the five years he would have, before tax:

$$FVA = 100 \, (FVIFA_{20, 1\%})$$

$$= \$2,201.90$$

Compound the before-tax dividends at the before-tax interest rate.

$$HPR = (625 + 2,201.90) \div 6,000$$

$$= 0.47115$$

$$= 47.115\%$$

$$EAR = (1.47115)^{1/5} - 1$$

$$= 0.080268$$

$$= 8.03\%$$

Example 8–2   HPR and EAR after tax

Assume the quarterly dividends were reinvested to earn interest income as they were received at a real return of 4% (1% a quarter). There are two ways of approaching this scenario, which we will call Method A and Method B. In **Method A**, the taxes on the dividends and interest are paid quarterly as the income is earned, while in **Method B**, the taxes on the dividends and interest are paid annually, which means there is a larger amount to compound until the taxes are paid at the end of the year. Generally, since Method B is much more complex, we will use Method A even though, in some circumstances, it would be less accurate.

The following table shows the difference in the above quarterly dividends *after one year*. In this example, the numbers are small so the difference is very small and can generally be ignored. However, the student needs to be aware of the assumptions being made about *when* the taxes are paid. In Method A, the dividends after tax are reinvested at 1% a quarter and compound at a quarterly after-tax rate, while in Method B, the income compounds for a year at the before-tax rate, the tax is paid, and then it compounds for four years at the after-tax rate.

Value at the End of One Year

Method A: Pay both taxes quarterly	Method B: Pay both taxes annually
	$FVA = 100 \ (FVIFA_{4,\ 1\%})$ $= 406.04$
$100(1 - 0.2264) \ [FVIFA_{4,\ 1\ (1 - 0.3718\%)}] = \$312.37$	$400(0.7736) + 6.04(0.6282)$ $= 309.44 + 3.79$
	$= \$313.23$

We will now calculate the EAR under each assumption.

Example 8-2a   Method A: Tax on both dividends and interest is paid quarterly.

Method A Example 8-2a Timeline

Cash flow for Step 1	k	T_0	T_1	T_2	T_3	T_4	T_5	...	T_{20}
Receive dividends $_{EOQ}$			+100.00	+100.00	+100.00	+100.00	+100.00	...	+100.00
Pay tax on dividends $_{EOQ}$	22.64%		−22.64	−22.64	−22.64	−22.64	−22.64	...	−22.64
Dividends after tax			77.36	77.36	77.36	77.36	77.36	...	77.36
Balance $_{BOQ}$			0.00	77.36	155.21	233.54	312.37		1,555.98
Interest income $_{EOQ}$	1.00%			+0.77	+1.55	+2.34	+3.12	...	+15.56
Pay tax on interest $_{EOQ}$	37.18%			−0.29	−0.58	−0.87	−1.16	...	−5.79
Balance $_{EOQ}$			77.36	155.21	233.54	312.37	391.69	...	1,643.11

Interest income is compounding each quarter at 0.6282% [1% × (1−.3718)]

BOQ = Beginning of quarter
EOQ = End of quarter

1. The after-tax value of the dividends after five years is:

$$FVA = 100(1 - 0.2264) \left[FVIFA_{20,\ 1(1 - 0.3718)\%} \right]$$

$$FVA = 77.36 \left[FVIFA_{20,\ 0.6282\%} \right]$$

$$FVA = \$1,643.11$$

Dividends are the after-tax amount. Interest compounds at the regular after-tax rate.

2. The amount of the capital gain after tax at the end of the fifth year when the investment is sold is:

Capital gain:
$$\text{Selling price} - \text{Purchase price}$$
$$\$6,625 - 6,000 = \$625$$

Tax on the capital gain: $\$116.19 \ (625 \times 0.1859)$

Capital gain after tax: **$\$508.81 \ (625.00 - 116.19)$**

3. HPR = (capital gain after tax + reinvested dividends) ÷ amount of investment
$$= (508.81 + 1,643.11) \div 6,000$$
$$= 35.8653\%$$

4. $\text{EAR} = (1.358653)^{1/5} - 1$

     $\text{EAR} = \textbf{6.3217\%}$

Example 8-2b   **Method B: Tax on both interest and dividend is paid annually, not quarterly.**

Method B Example 8-2b Timeline

Cash flow for Step 1	k	T_0	T_1	T_2	T_3	T_4	T_5	...	T_{20}
Receive dividends $_{EOQ}$			100.00	100.00	100.00	100.00	100.00	...	100.00
Pay tax on dividends $_{EOY}$	22.64%					−90.56		...	−90.56
Dividends $_{EOQ}$ after tax			100.00	100.00	100.00	9.44	100.00	...	9.44
Balance $_{EOQ}$			0.00	100.00	201.00	303.01	313.23	...	1,644.14
Interest income $_{EOQ}$	1.00%			1.00	2.01	3.03	3.13	...	16.44
Pay tax on interest $_{EOY}$	37.18%					−2.25		...	−21.90
Balance $_{EOQ}$			100.00	201.00	303.01	313.23	416.37	...	1,648.12
Interest income is compounding each year at 0.6282% [1−.3718]									
Taxable balances $_{EOQ}$									
Dividends			*100.00*	*200.00*	*300.00*	*400.00*	*100.00*		*400.00*
Interest			*0.00*	*1.00*	*3.01*	*6.04*	*3.13*		*62.12*

1a. The after-tax value of the dividends must be calculated in two steps.

At the end of *each* year, Craig would have
- before tax: FVA = 100 (FVIFA$_{4, 1\%}$) = 406.04
- after tax: 400(0.7736) + 6.04(0.6282) = 313.23
  Compound the dividends. Then pay the dividend tax on $400 and the regular tax on the interest income.

1b. Compound the after-tax annual dividends for five years at the after-tax reinvestment rate. Assume the reinvestment rate of 4% is compounded quarterly. The before-tax EAR used to compound is: 4.0604% [(1.01)^4 − 1]

EAR after tax = 4.0604% (1 − 0.3718)

EAR after tax = 2.5507%

FVA = 313.23 (FVIFA$_{5, 2.5507\%}$)

FVA = **$1,648.11**

2. The capital gain after tax is the same as in Method A: **$508.81**

3. HPR = (capital gain after tax + reinvested dividends) ÷ amount of investment
$$= (508.81 + 1,648.11) \div 6,000$$
$$= 35.9487\%$$

4. $EAR = (1.359487)^{1/5} - 1$

$\qquad = 6.3347\%$

The difference in this example is small because the amounts are small. However, the reader should note that Method B results in a higher return because the quarterly dividends and interest compound before tax during the year before the tax is paid.

	Total in Year 1		Total in Year 5	
	Method A	Method B	Method A	Method B
Dividends	400.00	400.00	400.00	400.00
Tax on dividends	90.56	90.56	90.56	90.56
Interest income	4.66	6.04	57.07	58.89
Tax on interest	1.73	2.25	21.22	21.90
EAR from HPR			6.3217%	6.3347%

4. Real Rates of Return

As with the prior rules, start by calculating the annual return after tax, as in Example 8. Then take out the inflation using an average inflation rate that covers the same time period.

In Summary

Discount or compound investment income, which is:		
before tax at a **before-tax** discount or interest rate	Registered plans	*Example 8–1b*
after tax using an **after-tax** discount or interest rate	Stocks, bonds, etc.	*Example 8–2*

D. INCOME TAX

We often hear tax experts describe tax rates on personal income as **average tax rates** or **marginal tax rates**. Similarly, in introductory personal financial-planning courses, students are frequently given the tax rates as "Martha's average tax rate is 37%" or "Mark's marginal tax rate is 47%." However, they must be able to calculate the average and marginal rates for their own province or territory when they start to plan for themselves, their relatives, or friends, or on the job. In addition, we will not use a formula to calculate tax rates because tax rates change frequently, making the formula outdated.

In the previous chapter, we touched on before-tax and after-tax amounts. The general model requires that savings at retirement be valued in after-tax dollars. Do we use average tax rates to work out the after-tax amount, or do we use marginal tax rates? It seems that we've been paying more tax than our parents, but the government says it is cutting taxes. How do we know what future tax rates to use in our planning?

Two aspects of personal taxation are designed to place a higher burden on higher income earners and also to encourage investments:

1. We have a progressive tax system whereby higher levels of income are taxed at a higher rate, and

2. Dividends from taxable Canadian Corporations and Capital Gains are taxed at lower rates.

Progressive Personal Income Tax System

Canada has a **progressive tax system** at both the federal and provincial levels — that is, the more taxable income a taxpayer has, the higher the tax rate. Retirement savings can be **tax sheltered** in registered plans, which means that these savings are not taxed when the income is earned — they are **tax-deferred savings**. These savings are taxed when they are withdrawn from the registered plans. Chapters 4, 5, and 6 look at these registered plans and the way in which personal income taxes can be deferred or even reduced by taking advantage of this progressive tax system.

Reduced Taxation of Dividend Income and Capital Gains

The **Canada Revenue Agency (CRA)** administers tax policy developed by the federal Department of Finance, which has created tax incentives to encourage Canadians to invest in Canadian companies. We will concern ourselves with only two basic incentives that are readily available to the average taxpayer — the dividend tax credit and capital gains inclusion rate.

The **dividend tax credit** is 15.0198% for 2013 for most, but not all, dividends received from taxable Canadian corporations. The effect of this dividend tax credit is that dividends are taxed at lower tax rates than salaried and interest income. There are two steps in calculating this credit. **Dividend income is grossed up by 38% to 138% of the amount received for 2013. This is the amount shown on a T5, T4PS, T3, or a T5013 form.**

Although federal tax is calculated on the grossed-up amount, the dividend tax credit is deducted from total federal tax, resulting in lower tax on the dividends received.

Capital gains are also, in effect, taxed at a lower rate because only part of the capital gain, called a **taxable capital gain**, is taxed at regular rates. A capital gain results when a taxpayer sells an asset for more than the cost (or the adjusted cost base [ACB] to be more accurate). In Canada, the principal residence is exempt from capital gains tax. But other assets, such as one's cottage, shares in a corporation, and bonds purchased at a discount, can result in a capital gains tax. Until 1972, capital gains were not taxed at all. These gains have been taxed at various rates over the years, and the calculation can be complex. Again, to be more accurate, a proportion of the gain is taxed at regular rates. The **inclusion rate**, currently 50%, indicates the portion of the capital gain realized that is subject to taxation.

At the beginning of the year 2000, the capital gains inclusion rate was 75%. In February 2000, the inclusion rate was decreased to 66⅔% and in October, 2000, it was dropped again to 50%, where it currently stands. The remaining 50% of the capital gain is not taxed. These changes in 2000 made the calculation of the taxable capital gain quite difficult for assets sold in the year 2000. Fortunately, we do not need to cover this aspect of the calculation in detail. However, it is important to understand how capital gains are taxed, since non-registered (non-tax-sheltered) savings may lead to this favourable taxation.

Note that these special savings are lost to the taxpayer if the funds are inside registered plans. The income is not taxed while in the plan, so no tax savings can be realized. When funds are withdrawn from registered plans, the income is 100% taxable, regardless of whether the funds withdrawn are from contributions or from income earned on the contributions.

Under a progressive tax system with reduced taxation on dividend income and capital gains, taxpayers pay different amounts of tax on their incomes. Consequently, the concepts of average and marginal tax rates are important because they change for an individual, depending on both the source of the income and the top tax bracket the taxpayer is in.

Provincial Taxes

Like federal tax rates, rates for all provinces and territories are progressive.[2] The calculation of taxes using actual tax rates for all the provinces and territories is shown in Appendix 2B. Rather than choosing one province's rates or inviting confusion by using rates for several provinces, we are going to use a **generic tax rate** as well as generic rates for the Canada Pension Plan (CPP), Old Age Security (OAS), and Employment Insurance (EI). These generic rates are on the last page of Appendix 2B and will be used throughout the rest of this textbook.

> "I don't understand," says Craig. "I thought progressive tax rates meant people with high incomes pay more tax on all their income. Are you telling me that's not the case?"
>
> "That's right," says Francesca. "Let me show you how taxes are calculated on your salary or on interest income — the calculation is the same for both as there are no special reductions in the method of taxing these."

Taxation of Interest and Regular Income

Federal tax rates are progressive; i.e., higher income is taxed at higher rates. Interest income is taxed like regular income. In the first example, all income is interest or salaried income. Using the generic tax rates found at the end of Appendix 2B, *all* tax payers pay:

- **15% federal tax** on the **first $39,500** of income (or total income, whichever is more)

Interest Income		30,000	80,000	130,000
Federal tax				
15% on the first	39,500	*4,500.00	5,925.00	5,925.00
*30,000 × 0.15 = 4,500.00				

- **22% federal tax** on the **next $39,500** (79,000 shown in the tax form minus 39,500)

Interest Income		30,000	80,000	130,000
Federal tax				
15% on the first	39,500	4,500.00	5,925.00	5,925.00
22% on the next	39,500		8,690.00	8,690.00

- **26% federal tax** on the **next $48,000** (127,000 − 39,500 − 39,500)

Interest Income		30,000	80,000	130,000
Federal tax				
15% on the first	39,500	4,500.00	5,925.00	5,925.00
22% on the next	39,500		8,690.00	8,690.00
26% on the next	48,000		260.00	12,480.00

---

2   Prior to January 1, 2001, provinces and territories used a **tax-on-tax** method in which the provincial tax was a percentage of the federal tax. Today, all provinces and territories are using the **Tax on Net Income (TONI)** method for calculating provincial tax, whereby they calculate their tax on taxable income in the same manner that federal tax is calculated. This new system allows each province and territory to customize its tax structure by setting its own tax rates and basic personal amount. However, it also complicates the calculation of the marginal rate, which is further complicated in provinces that have surtaxes (as the federal tax also had until 2001).

• **29% federal tax** on any income **over $127,000**

Interest Income		30,000	80,000	130,000
Federal tax				
15% on the first	39,500	4,500.00	5,925.00	5,925.00
22% on the next	39,500		8,690.00	8,690.00
26% on the next	48,000		260.00	12,480.00
29% over	127,000			870.00

Note that, although the tax return, T1 General "Forms" for all provinces and territories, shows calculations based on cumulative values, it is easier and faster to use the amounts for the individual brackets. Using the federal generic tax brackets and actual federal tax rates:

T1 General Tax Forms		Used in this Text	
15% of	39,500	15% on the first	39,500
5,925 + 22% of	79,500	22% on the next	39,500
14,615 + 26% of	127,000	26% on the next	48,000
27,095 + 29% of	127,000	29% over	127,000

• Subtract the **non-refundable tax credit (NRTxCr)** from the federal tax to arrive at the **basic federal tax (BFT)**. The non-refundable tax credit is calculated as 15% of the amount **available** for the non-refundable tax credit. In this example, the amount available is the generic federal basic personal amount of **$10,000**:

Interest Income		30,000	80,000	130,000
Federal tax				
15% on the first	39,500	4,500.00	5,925.00	5,925.00
22% on the next	39,500		8,690.00	8,690.00
26% on the next	48,000		260.00	12,480.00
29% over	127,000			870.00
Total federal tax		4,500.00	14,875.00	27,965.00
NRTxCr (1) — 15% of	10,000	1,500.00	1,500.00	1,500.00
Basic federal tax (BFT) (2)		3,000.00	13,375.00	26,465.00

(1) NRTxCr = Non-refundable tax credits: 15% × $10,000
(2) BFT = Basic federal tax: Total federal tax minus non-refundable tax credits

Repeat the entire process for the **provincial tax** and add the federal and provincial taxes together to arrive at Total tax payable.

Interest Income		30,000	80,000	130,000
Provincial tax				
8% on the first	38,000	2,400.00	3,040.00	3,040.00
13% on the next	38,000		4,940.00	4,940.00
17% on the next	76,000		680.00	9,180.00
Total provincial tax		2,400.00	8,660.00	17,160.00
NRTxCr — 8% of	9,000	720.00	720.00	720.00
Basic provincial tax (BPT)		1,680.00	7,940.00	16,440.00
Total tax		**4,680.00**	**21,315.00**	**42,905.00**
Income after tax		25,320.00	58,685.00	87,095.00

Average and Marginal Tax Rates

The **average tax** is total tax paid on total income *received* (or *earned* if including accrued). Its use is limited except to compare after-tax income at various levels of income before and after retirement and to compare tax rates between provinces and territories. Calculation of the average tax is often needed to calculate the marginal rate, which is much more useful. Calculation of marginal rates in provinces that have surtaxes (as the federal tax also had until 2001) can be particularly complicated. See the provincial examples in the appendix to this chapter.

Average Tax Rate

The **average tax rate** is the total tax divided by the total income **received.** For the prior calculations, the rates are:

Interest income received	30,000.00	80,000.00	130,000.00
Total tax	4,680.00	21,315.00	42,905.00
Average tax rate	*15.60%*	*26.64%*	*33.00%*

Marginal Tax Rate

The **marginal tax rate** is the tax paid on the next $1.00 of income or the tax saved on a $1.00 tax deduction. Because we have a progressive tax system, the marginal tax rate is different from the average tax rate. With a progressive tax system, tax-sheltered savings occur at each taxpayer's top marginal tax rate; i.e., taxes are not paid on funds put into registered plans. Therefore, this tax saving is at the individual's top tax rate. However, often in retirement, taxpayers will be in a lower tax bracket; i.e., their marginal rate is less than when they were saving for retirement. This scenario results not only in a **tax deferral** but also in **tax savings**, where some tax is never paid at all.

Example 9   In 2012, the year before he retired, Mark put $13,500 into his RRSP. His marginal tax rate was 47%, so he saved $6,345 ($13,500 × 0.47) in taxes. The first year of his retirement, he took the $13,500 out. However, his other taxable income had dropped significantly, so his marginal rate was now only 41%; that is, he paid $5,535 in taxes on the $13,500. Essentially, he arranged a tax deferral of $5,535 and tax savings of $810 ($6,345 – $5,535) — tax that he will never have to pay.

	Contribution to RRSP in 2012	Withdrawal from RRSP in 2013
Gross contribution/(withdrawn)	$13,500	($13,500)
Tax (saved)/paid	(6,345)	5,535
Net contribution/(withdrawal)	7,155	(7,965)
Tax deferred from 2012 to 2013	(5,535)	5,535
Tax not paid	(810)	

While the **marginal tax rate** is based on the next $1.00 of income. We will use $100.00 of income in our calculations only because it is important to carry enough decimal places. If the student prefers, the student may use $1.00 but must carry four decimal places when doing the calculation.

The question is: How much tax is paid on the **next $1.00 of interest income?**

- For the person making $30,000, another $1.00 of income takes this taxpayer to $30,001, so the next $1.00 will be taxed at 15% federal (although we will use $100.00 in the calculations instead of $1.00)
- For the person making $80,000, another $1.00 of income takes this taxpayer to $80,001, so the next $1.00 will be taxed at 26% federal
- The non-refundable tax credits have been used up — presumably there are no more non-refundable tax credits just because the taxpayer has another $1.00 of income.

		Average	Marginal	Average	Marginal	Average	Marginal
Interest income earned		30,000	**100.00**	80,000	**100.00**	130,000	**100.00**
Federal tax							
15% on the first	39,500	4,500.00	**15.00**	5,925.00		5,925.00	
22% on the next	39,500			8,690.00		8,690.00	
26% on the next	48,000			260.00	**26.00**	12,480.00	
29% over	127,000					870.00	**29.00**
Total federal tax		4,500.00	15.00	14,875.00	26.00	27,965.00	29.00
NRTxCr* — 15% of	10,000	1,500.00	**0.00**	1,500.00	**0.00**	1,500.00	**0.00**
Basic federal tax (BFT)		3,000.00	15.00	13,375.00	26.00	26,465.00	29.00
Provincial tax							
8% on the first	38,000	2,400.00	**8.00**	3,040.00		3,040.00	
13$ on the next	38,000			4,940.00		4,940.00	
17% over	76,000			680.00	**17.00**	9,180.00	**17.00**
Total provincial tax		2,400.00	8.00	8,660.00	17.00	17,160.00	17.00
NRTxCr — 8% of	9,000	720.00	**0.00**	720.00	**0.00**	720.00	**0.00**
Basic provincial tax (BPT)		1,680.00	8.00	7,940.00	17.00	16,440.00	17.00
Total tax		**4,680.00**	**23.00**	**21,315.00**	**43.00**	**42,905.00**	**46.00**
Income after tax		**25,320.00**	**77.00**	**58,685.00**	**57.00**	**87,095.00**	**54.00**
Average tax rate		*15.60%*		*26.64%*		*33.00%*	
Marginal tax rate			**23.00%**		**43.00%**		**46.00%**

* NRTxCr (Non-refundable tax credit):
- average $10,000 \times 0.15 = \$1,500.00$;
- marginal is $0 since an extra $1 of income does not increase the amount eligible for the non-refundable tax credit

Comparison of Tax Rates for Different Sources of Income

The following table illustrates the calculation of average and marginal tax rates on the three sources of income (the calculations in this example follow in the next section). Note that we calculate the:

- **average tax rate** by dividing the tax by the amount **received**, and
- **marginal tax rate** (the tax paid on the next $1.00 of income) on $100.00 because it is important to carry enough decimal places to keep the calculation accurate. The student can, if preferred, use $1.00 but must use four decimal places in the calculation.

Table 2.3 shows 100% of income coming from one source. This is not realistic or even desirable and is only being done to illustrate the tax rates on various sources of income. Table 2.4 later in this chapter adds these three sources of income to a basic salary.

Table 2.3 Comparison of Average and Marginal Rates for Different Sources of Income

$ Received:		Interest Average	Interest Marginal	Dividends Average	Dividends Marginal	Capital Gains Average	Capital Gains Marginal
Salary		0		0		0	
Interest		70,000	100.00				
Dividends				70,000	100.00		
Capital gains						70,000	100.00
Taxable income		70,000	100.00	101,500	145.00	35,000	50.00
Federal tax:							
15% on the first	39,500	5,925.00		5,925.00		5,250.00	**7.50**
22% on the next	39,500	6,710.00	**22.00**	8,690.00			
26% on the next	48,000			5,850.00	**37.70**		
29% over	127,000						
Total federal tax:		12,635.00	22.00	20,465.00	37.70	5,250.00	7.50
Dividend Tax Credit				19,249.98	27.50		
NRTxCr* — 15% of	10,000	1,500.00		1,500.00		1,500.00	
Basic federal tax (BFT)		**11,135.00**	**22.00**	**(284.98)**	**10.20**	**3,750.00**	**7.50**
Provincial tax							
8% on the first	38,000	3,040.00		3,040.00		2,800.00	4.00
13% on the next	38,000	4,160.00	13.00	4,940.00			
17% over	76,000			4,335.00	24.65		
Total provincial tax		7,200.00	13.00	12,315.00	24.65	2,800.00	4.00
Dividend Tax Credit				12,180.00	17.40		
NRTxCr* — 8% of	9,000	720.00		720.00		720.00	
Basic provincial tax (BPT)		**6,480.00**	**13.00**	**(585.00)**	**7.25**	**2,080.00**	**4.00**
Total Tax		**17,615.00**	**35.00**	**(869.98)**	**17.45**	**5,830.00**	**11.50**
Average tax rate		25.16%		−1.24%		8.33%	
Marginal tax rate			35.00%		17.45%		11.50%

*NRTxCr = non-refundable tax credit

Note: The non-refundable tax credits are non-refundable. So the tax and tax rates are not negative as shown above — they are reduced to the limit of the non-refundable tax credit until tax payable is zero.

Taxation of Dividend Income

Dividends from taxable Canadian corporations are subject to reduced taxes. Dividends are paid by a corporation out of after-tax net income; i.e., retained earnings contains all after-tax income that has not been paid out by the corporation. Until 1972, these dividends were not subject to personal taxation at all. However, as governments needed to increase revenues, this source of income became taxable, but at a reduced rate. The federal government uses tax rates to encourage certain types of investments. As a result, only dividends from taxable Canadian corporations are eligible for this reduced tax. **Dividends from other corporations** are taxed like interest income; i.e., they are taxed at full rates.

Calculating the Tax on Dividend Income

There are two types of dividends that individuals can receive from Canadian corporations (corporations are not eligible for this dividend tax credit), and the two types are handled differently. Most dividends are **Type A "Eligible" dividends**, and that is the type we will assume is being received throughout this text. Type A dividends came into being in 2006 — before 2006, there was only one type of dividend. However, the other kind, **Type B "Ineligible" Dividends**, are important to owners (shareholders) of private corporations and are handled the old way. We will use 2008 rate of 18.9655% and a gross-up of 45% as the generic rate for Type A eligible dividends.

Type A "Eligible" Dividends Gross-up 45%	Type B "Ineligible" Dividends Gross-up 25%
• 18.9655% of the **grossed-up amount**	• 13.3333% of the **grossed-up amount** • 16.6667% of the dividend received, or • 66.6667% or 2/3 of the gross-up

Type A dividends are from:
• Canadian public corporations,
• Canadian private corporations that are **not** Canadian controlled, or
• **Canadian Controlled Private Corporations (CCPC)** whose income is either:
  • business income taxed at the high corporate rates (no **Small Business Deduction [SBD]**), or
  • dividends received by the corporation that have been designated as Type A.

Type B dividends are from:
• CCPCs whose income is active business income and is taxed at lower corporate rates using the SBD,
• CCPCs with investment income (rent, interest, capital gains, dividends) and is designated as Type B, or
• CCPCs whose dividends received by the corporation have been designated as Type B.

A Canadian Controlled Private Corporation (CCPC), is:
• private (not listed on a stock exchange)
• not controlled by a non-resident or a public company
and qualifies for the Small Business Deduction (SBD) (which reduces federal and provincial corporate taxes) if at least 90% of the assets:
• were used to produce active business income (i.e., not passive investing), or
• were shares or debt of a connected corporation which itself qualifies.

This is the last you will hear of Type B dividends in this text. We will *always* assume that dividends received are Type A dividends received from public corporations.

Calculating the Tax on Type A Dividend Income

To calculate the tax, the **dividends received** are first grossed-up by 45% to arrive at **taxable dividends**, which are 145% of dividends received. When a taxpayer receives a T-5, T4PS, T3, or a T5013 form, the amount shown is already grossed-up. It is important to know if the dividends are dividends received or taxable dividends.

Dividends received	100%	30,000	80,000	130,000
Gross-up	45%	13,500	36,000	58,500
Taxable dividends	145%	43,500	116,000	188,500

Federal tax and provincial tax are calculated on the grossed-up amount, and the dividend tax credit is deducted from the total federal tax to arrive at the BFT. The dividend tax credit is:
• the actual federal rate of 18.9655% of the grossed-up amount, and
• the generic provincial rate of 12% of the grossed-up amount.

The total tax payable on dividend income is:

Dividends received	100%	30,000	80,000	130,000
Gross up	45%	13,500	36,000	58,500
Taxable dividends	**145%**	**43,500**	**116,000**	**188,500**
Federal tax				
15% on the first	39,500	5,925.00	5,925.00	5,925.00
22% on the next	39,500	880.00	8,690.00	8,690.00
26% on the next	48,000		9,620.00	12,480.00
29% over	127,000			17,835.00
Total federal tax		6,805.00	24,235.00	44,930.00
Dividend tax credit — 18.9655%				
of taxable dividends		**8,249.99**	**21,999.98**	**35,749.97**
NRTxCr — 15% of	10,000	1,500.00	1,500.00	1,500.00
Basic federal tax (BFT)		**(2,944.99)**	**735.02**	**7,680.03**
Provincial tax				
8% on the first	38,000	3,040.00	3,040.00	3,040.00
13% on the next	38,000	715.00	4,940.00	4,940.00
17% over	76,0000		19,720.00	21,045.00
Total provincial tax		3,755.00	27,700.00	40,025.00
Dividend tax credit — 12%		**5,220.00**	**13,920.00**	**22,620.00**
NRTxCr — 8% of	9,000	720.00	720.00	720.00
Basic provincial tax (BPT)		(2,185.00)	13,060.00	16,685.00
Total tax		**(5,129.99)**	**13,795.02**	**24,365.03**
Income after tax		**35,129.99**	**66,204.98**	**105,634.97**

In this illustration, for taxable dividends of $43,500, the BFT and BPT are negative. The non-refundable tax credits will be reduced to 0, and since no tax has been paid, no tax will be refunded if dividends are the only source of income. However, it is highly unlikely that dividends would be the only source of income, and tax paid on any other source of income such as salary or interest would be refunded. See Table 2.4, where the tax on income of $60,000 is *more than* the tax on $60,000 of salary plus $10,000 of dividends.

Average Tax Rate on Dividend Income

This is the total tax divided by the total dividend income **received**:

Average tax rate	−17.10%	17.24%	18.74%

Marginal Rate on Dividend Income

The **dividend tax credit** is available on the next $1.00 of dividend income received.

		Average	Marginal	Average	Marginal	Average	Marginal
Dividends received	100%	30,000	100.00	80,000	100.00	130,000	100.00
Gross up	45%	13,500	45.00	36,000	45.00	58,500	45.00
Taxable dividends	**145%**	**43,500**	**145.00**	**116,000**	**145.00**	**188,500**	**145.00**
Federal tax							
15% on the first	39,500	5,925.00		5,925.00		5,925.00	
22% on the next	39,500	880.00	**31.90**	8,690.00		8,690.00	
26% on the next	48,000			9,620.00	**37.70**	12,480.00	
29% over	127,000					17,835.00	**42.05**
Total federal tax		6,805.00	31.90	24,235.00	37.70	44,930.00	42.05
Dividend tax credit — 18.9655%		8,249.99	**27.50**	21,999.98	**27.50**	35,749.97	**27.50**
NRTxCr — 15% of	10,000	1,500.00		1,500.00		1,500.00	
Basic federal tax (BFT)		(2,944.99)*	4.40	735.02	10.20	7,680.03	14.55

Continued.

		Average	Marginal	Average	Marginal	Average	Marginal
Provincial tax							
8% on the first	38,000	3,040.00		3,040.00		3,040.00	
13% on the next	38,000	715.00	18.85	4,940.00		4,940.00	
17% over	76,000			19,720.00	24.65	32,045.00	24.65
Total provincial tax		3,755.00	18.85	27,700.00	24.65	40,025.00	24.65
Dividend tax credit — 12%		5,220.00	17.40	13,920.00	17.40	22,620.00	17.40
NRTxCr — 8% of	9,000	720.00		720.00		720.00	
Basic provincial tax (BPT)		(2,185.00)	1.45	13,060.00	7.25	16,685.00	7.25
Total tax		(5,129.99)	5.85	13,795.02	17.45	24,365.03	21.80
Income after tax		35,129.99	94.15	66,204.98	82.55	105,643.97	78.20
Average tax rate		-17.10%		17.24%		18.74%	
Marginal tax rate			5.85%		17.45%		21.80%

*See prior note about negative taxes on dividends.

Taxation of Capital Gains

Capital gains are not taxed until they are realized or received; i.e., until the asset has been sold. The **inclusion rate is 50%** — 50% of capital gains realized are included for taxation at regular rates:

Capital gains received		30,000	80,000	130,000
Taxable	50%	15,000	40,000	65,000
Federal tax				
15% on the first	39,500	2,250.00	5,925.00	5,925.00
22% on the next	39,500		110.00	5,610.00
26% on the next	48,000			
29% over	127,000			
Total federal tax:		2,250.00	6,035.00	11,535.00
NRTxCr — 15% of	10,000	1,500.00	1,500.00	1,500.00
Basic federal tax (BFT)		750.00	4,535.00	10,035.00
Provincial tax				
8% on the first	38,000	1,200.00	3,040.00	3,040.00
13% on the next	38,000		260.00	3,510.00
17% over	76,000			
Total provincial tax		1,200.00	3,300.00	6,550.00
NRTxCr — 8% of	9,000	720.00	720.00	720.00
Basic provincial tax (BPT)		480.00	2,580.00	5,830.00
Total tax		1,230.00	7,115.00	15,865.00
Income after tax		28,770.00	72,885.00	114,135.00
Average tax rate		4.10%	8.89%	12.20%

Again, the average tax rate is the total tax divided by capital gains income **received**.

The **marginal rate** on the next $1.00 (or $100.00 for ease of calculation) of **capital gain income *realized* (received)**:

		Average	Marginal	Average	Marginal	Average	Marginal
Capital gains received		30,000	100.00	80,000	100.00	130,000	100.00
Taxable	50%	15,000	50.00	40,000	50.00	65,000	50.00
Federal tax							
15% on the first	39,500	2,250.00	7.50	5,925.00		5,925.00	
22% on the next	39,500			110.00	11.00	5,610.00	11.00
26% on the next	48,000						
29% over	127,000						
Total federal tax		2,250.00	7.50	6,035.00	11.00	11,535.00	11.00
NRTxCr — 15% of	10,000	1,500.00	0.00	1,500.00	0.00	1,500.00	0.00
Basic federal tax (BFT)		750.00	7.50	4,535.00	11.00	10,035.00	11.00

Continued.

		Average	Marginal	Average	Marginal	Average	Marginal
Provincial tax							
8% on the first	38,000	1,200.00	**4.00**	3,040.00		3,040.00	
13% on the next	38,000			260.00	**6.50**	3,510.00	**6.50**
17% over	76,000						
Total provincial tax		1,200.00	4.00	3,300.00	6.50	6,550.00	6.50
NRTxCr — 8% of	9,000	720.00		720.00		720.00	
Basic provincial tax (BPT)		480.00	4.00	2,580.00	6.50	5,830.00	6.50
Total tax		**1,230.00**	**11.50**	**7,115.00**	**17.50**	**15,865.00**	**17.50**
Income after tax		28,770.00	88.50	72,885.00	82.50	114,135.00	82.50
Average tax rate		4.10%		8.89%		12.20%	
Marginal tax rate			11.50%		17.50%		17.50%

Comparison of Average and Marginal Tax Rates for Different Sources of Income Added to a Salary

In Table 2.3, we compared the tax rates on different sources of income assuming that the income for each was 100% interest or 100% dividends received or 100% capital gain realized. This is neither reasonable nor, in most cases, possible. So let's add the $10,000 of income from these three sources to a base salary of $60,000. This will be the reference for Problem 12, which is a **tax drill** (exercise) designed to give practice at calculating taxes. Notice that we are calculating the marginal rate on the *investment* income. It is not useful or even possible to calculate the marginal rate for dividends and capital gains together, for example, in the same calculation.

Table 2.4 Effect of Adding Different Sources to Salary

		Salary Only	Interest		Dividends		Capital Gains	
			Average	Marginal	Average	Marginal	Average	Marginal
Salary		60,000	60,000		60,000		60,000	
Interest			10,000	100.00				
Dividends					10,000	100.00		
Capital gains							10,000	100.00
Taxable income		60,000	70,000	100.00	74,500	145.00	65,000	100.00
Federal tax								
15% on the first	39,500	5,925.00	5,925.00		5,925.00		5,925.00	
22% on the next	39,500	4,510.00	6,710.00	22.00	7,700.00	31.90	5,610.00	11.00
26% on the next	48,000							
29% over	127,000							
Total federal tax		10,435.00	12,635.00	22.00	13,625.00	31.90	11,535.00	11.00
Dividend tax credit — 18.9655%					2,750.00	27.50		
NRTxCr — 15% of	10,000	1,500.00	1,500.00		1,500.00		1,500.00	
Basic federal tax (BFT)		**8,935.00**	**11,135.00**	**22.00**	**9,375.00**	**4.40**	**10,035.00**	**11.00**
Provincial tax								
8% on the first	38,000	3,040.00	3,040.00		3,040.00		3,040.00	
13% on the next	38,000	2,860.00	4,160.00	13.00	4,745.00	18.85	3,510.00	6.50
17% over	76,000							
Total provincial tax		5,900.00	7,200.00	13.00	7,785.00	18.85	6,550.00	6.50
Dividend tax credit — 12%					1,740.00	17.40		
NRTxCr — 8% of	9,000	720.00	720.00		720.00		720.00	
Basic provincial tax (BPT)		**5,180.00**	**6,480.00**	**13.00**	**5,325.00**	**1.45**	**5,830.00**	**6.50**
Total tax		**14,115.00**	**17,615.00**	**35.00**	**14,700.00**	**5.85**	**15,865.00**	**17.50**
Average tax rate on total income		23.53%	25.16%		21.00%		22.66%	
Marginal tax rate				35.00%		5.85%		17.50%

Use of Average and Marginal Tax Rates

"But what on earth am I supposed to do with average and marginal tax rates?" says Craig.

"Let me give you a couple of examples," says Francesca. "We will go into this more later, but for now... let's look at an example.

You estimate you will need $50,000 a year after tax in retirement. How much is this before tax? First, we assume that the two of you will save in such a way as to be able to have $25,000 after tax per year *each* in retirement. How much is this before tax? Let's see what the taxes on $30,000 are:

		Average	Marginal
Taxable income		30,000.00	100.00
Federal tax			
15% on the first	39,500	4,500.00	15.00
NRTxCr — 15% of	10,000	1,500.00	
Basic federal tax (BFT)		3,000.00	15.00
Provincial tax			
8% on the first	38,000	2,400.00	8.00
NRTxCr — 15% of	9,000	720.00	
Basic provincial tax (BPT)		1,680.00	8.00
Total tax		**4,680.00**	**23.00**
Income after tax		25,320.00	77.00
Average tax rate		*15.60%*	
Marginal tax rate			*23.00%*

"Since you need $25,000 after tax, we can use an estimated average tax rate of 15.60%. Let's use this rate to calculate your before-tax needs:

After-tax income=	Before-tax income × (1 – average-tax rate)
$25,000 =	Before-tax income (1 – 0.1560)
Before-tax income =	$29,620

"So you would need about $30,000 before tax in retirement. But the average rate changes with additional income, as you will see in the examples that follow. Nonetheless, the average tax rate is useful when we start calculating retirement income from various fully taxable sources. We will use the **average rate** to calculate your after-tax income in retirement. Otherwise, the average tax rate has limited use.

"Now, let's look at the use of the **marginal rate**. This tax rate is invaluable even though it is often just an estimate of additional after-tax income. Again, we will look at this in more detail later, but suppose you own a bond that pays regular interest of $900 a year, which you plan to invest. If this bond is being held outside of an RRSP, you will have to pay tax on the $900 each year before you can reinvest it. Since you have other income (let's assume you are still working and receiving a regular paycheque) the tax you will pay on this will be at the top tax rate — the $900 is added to your other income before the tax is calculated. If your salary is $37,000, your marginal tax rate is, and will remain, at 23.00% from the calculation below — it will not increase until the next $1.00 of income takes us into the next tax bracket. So you can estimate that the tax you will pay on this income will be $207.00 ($900 × 0.2300). Thus, you can *estimate* that you will receive $693.00 ($900.00 – $207.00) after tax from this investment each year. Let's do the calculation and see if it works. We can calculate the tax on $37,900 and then subtract it from the first calculation. Or we can use the marginal tax rate to get $693.00 after tax [$900.00 × (1 − .2300)].

Illustration of $900 Additional Bond Interest Income

				Difference	Marginal
Taxable income		37,000	37,900.00	900.00	100.00
Federal tax					
15% on the first	39,500	5,550.00	5,685.00	135.00	15.00
NRTxCr — 15% of	10,000	1,500.00	1,500.00	0.00	0.00
Basic federal fax (BFT)		4,050.00	4,185.00	135.00	15.00
Provincial tax					
8% on the first	38,000	2,960.00	3,032.00	72.00	8.00
NRTxCr — 8% of	9,000	720.00	720.00	0.00	0.00
Basic provincial tax (BPT)		2,240.00	2,312.00	72.00	8.00
Total tax		6,290.00	6,497.00	207.00	23.00
Income after tax		30,710.00	31,403.00	693.00	77.00
Average tax rate		*17.00%*	*17.14%*	*23.00%*	
Marginal tax rate					*23.00%*

The marginal tax rate is only an estimate of the tax on the next amount of income. For instance, if you are making $35,000 and receive a raise of $1,500, the marginal tax rate is useful for estimating how much your take-home pay will increase. The concept of the marginal tax rate is used to estimate the after-tax effects of various investment strategies. There is no absolute rule to know when the marginal rate is more appropriate than calculating the new tax from scratch. Generally, when you are looking at an RRSP contribution to see how much tax will be saved, the marginal tax rate is used. However, additional income or tax deductions can move you into a different tax bracket; that is, the top tax rate changes. Then your current marginal rate can be too much of an estimate to be useful.

"If, for instance, your bond earns $2,000 more, it would take you into the next tax bracket; that is, in this example, some income is taxed at 15% federal and 8% provincial and some at 22% federal and 13% provincial, as reflected in a change in the average tax rate from 23.00% in the prior example to 32.48% in the next example."

Illustration of $2,900 Additional Bond Interest Income

				Difference	Marginal
Taxable income		37,000.00	39,900.00	2,900.00	100.00
Federal tax					
15% on the first	39,500	5,500.00	5,925.00	375.00	
22% on the next	39,500		88.00	88.00	22.00
		5,500.00	6,013.00	463.00	22.00
NRTxCr — 15% of	10,000	1,500.00	1,500.00	0.00	0.00
Basic federal tax (BFT)		4,050.00	4,513.00	463.00	22.00
Provincial tax					
8% on the first	38,000	2,960.00	3,192.00	232.00	
13% on the next	38,000		247.00	247.00	13.00
Total provincial tax		2,960.00	3,439.00	479.00	13.00
NRTxCr — 8% of	9,000	720.00	720.00	0.00	0.00
Basic provincial tax (BPT)		2,240.00	2,719.00	479.00	13.00
Total tax		6,290.00	7,232.00	942.00	35.00
Income after tax		30,710.00	32,668.00	1,958.00	65.00
Average tax rate		*17.00%*	*18.13%*	*32.48%*	
Marginal tax rate					*35.00%*

"If the interest income is $2,900 instead of $900, the difference in tax is $735.00 ($942.00 – $207.00), which is 36.75% of the additional $2,000. Using the marginal tax rate on $39,900 would give us an estimate of $667.00 ($2,900.00 x 23.00%). You would underestimate the tax by $42.00. The marginal rate is not accurate when there is a change in tax bracket, but it serves as a quick and reasonable estimate of the after-tax amount for added income or an RRSP contribution."

Calculating Personal Income Tax

There are six basic steps for calculating tax payable (using the T1 General):

Step 1   Calculate **Total Income** (line 150), which includes (but is not limited to):
- Employment and commission income
- CPP benefits received
- Employment insurance benefits received
- Taxable amount of dividends from taxable Canadian corporations
- Interest and other investment income
- Registered Retirement Savings Plan income (includes all RRSP withdrawals)
- Self-employed income after expenses (net income)
- Workers' Compensation benefits received

Step 2   Calculate **Net Income** (line 236): reduce total income by payments which are **tax deductions** such as:
- Registered Retirement Savings Plan contributions
- Registered Pension Plan contributions
- Child-care expenses
- Union and professional dues
- Support payments made

Step 3   Calculate **Taxable Income** (line 260) and reduce net income by some deductions beyond the scope of this course. These deductions include:
- Employee home relocation loan deduction
- Non-capital losses of other years
- Net capital losses of other years
- Capital gain deduction

Note: For our purposes in this course, Net Income will equal Taxable Income.

Step 4   Calculate **Non-refundable Tax Credits** (line 350 on Schedule 1, Step 1). The amount *eligible* for the non-refundable tax credits includes (but is not limited to):
- Basic personal amount of $11,038 for 2013 (line 300)
- Canada Pension Plan contributions: maximum of $2,356.20 for 2013 (line 308)
- Employment Insurance (EI) premiums: maximum of $891.12 for 2013 (line 312)
- Pension income amount: maximum of $2,000 (line 314)
- Donations and gifts (line 349) for the estate planning part of the course.
  - The total amount *eligible* for non-refundable tax credits is multiplied by 15% for 2013 to arrive at the *amount* of the non-refundable tax credit.

Step 5   Calculate the **Federal Tax** on Schedule 1, Step 2.

Step 6   Calculate the **Basic Federal Tax (BFT)** by deducting the non-refundable tax credits and other tax credits such as the dividend tax credit from the amount of the federal tax. If the non-refundable tax credits deduction results in negative basic federal tax, there is no tax refund (hence "non-refundable tax credits").

Steps 4, 5, and 6 are then repeated to arrive at the **provincial tax**. The forms are included with the federal tax package (except for Quebec, which collects both the federal and Quebec taxes instead of the federal tax department collecting for both, as is the case for the others provinces), and there are different tax packages for each province and territory.

Note that **tax deductions** (Step 2) reduce taxable income, while **tax credits** (Step 5) reduce tax payable. This is illustrated in Chapter 3.

> It has been a while since Margot calculated her tax manually. She uses a tax package but admits she doesn't always know exactly what the package is doing. Francesca takes both Margot and Craig through the calculations.

Discounting Retirement Cash Flows Before and After Tax

When discounting retirement **cash flows** back to the date of retirement, it is necessary to use the before-tax discount rate on annual cash flows regardless of whether they are discounted before or after tax. Example 10 is a lengthy demonstration of this concept. In addition, this example expands Margot and Craig's situation from Chapter 1. Here, Laura and Stephen retire at the same time, but they do not die at the same time.

Example 10   Laura and Stephen are looking at their retirement-savings needs. They would like to retire when Laura is aged 63 and Stephen is aged 60. They begin by looking at sources of government income as well as Laura's employer pension plan, which will provide her with $30,000 a year and is not indexed. Since they are now in their early fifties, they assume the CPP will remain as it is now, with Laura collecting $10,120 and Stephen collecting $8,050. But they will plan on the OAS being only about $3,200 *each* which they can begin to collect at age 65. In addition, they will not include any survivor benefits. They estimate they will need about $64,000 after tax (or $32,000 each) in retirement. They want to plan on Laura living to age 90 (27 years of retirement), and Stephen living to only age 85 (25 years of retirement).

There are four steps to the solution:
1. Calculate average tax rate in retirement and income needed before tax
2. Draw the timeline
3. Calculate the present value (PV) of retirement income needed before and after tax
    Method I. Calculate the PV of income before tax, then deduct the tax
    Method II. Deduct the tax, then calculate the PV of income after tax
4. Calculate retirement income in place before and after tax
    Method 1. Find the PV before tax and then deduct the tax
    Method 2. Deduct the tax first and then take the PV.
    Method 3: Find the PV of each line of before-tax retirement income.
    All three methods produce the same result.

Step 1. Calculating Average Tax Rate in Retirement and Income Needed Before Tax

Since Laura and Stephen estimate they will need $64,000, or $32,000 after tax **each**, how much is the before-tax amount? Let's estimate that they will need $37,500 a year each. What are the taxes on $37,500? We will assume that this income is 100% taxable and use the generic basic personal amount and tax rates. In addition, we will omit the pension amount for this estimate, giving us a very conservative estimate.

Taxable income		37,500.00
Federal tax		
15% on the first	39,500	5,625.00
Total federal tax		5,625.00
NRTxCr — 15% of	10,000	1,500.00
Basic federal tax (BFT)		4,125.00
Provincial tax		
8% on the first	38,000	3,000.00
Total provincial tax		3,000.00
NRTxCr — 8% of	9,000	720.00
Basic provincial tax (BPT)		2,280.00
Total tax		6,405.00
Income after tax		31,095.00
Average tax rate		*17.08%*

Our estimate of $37,500 is somewhat low since the after-tax amount is about $900 too low for each of them. Since this calculation is quick, let's try $40,000.

		37,500	40,000
Taxable income			
Federal tax			
15% on the first	39,500	5.625.00	5,925.00
22% on the first	39,500		110.00
Total federal tax		5,625.00	6,035.00
NRTxCr — 15% of	10,000	1,500.00	1,500.00
Basic federal tax (BFT)		4,125.00	4,535.00
Provincial tax			
8% on the first	38,000	3,000.00	3,040.00
13% on the next	38,000		260.00
Total provincial tax		3,000.00	3,300.00
NRTxCr — 8% of	9,000	720.00	720.00
Basic provincial tax (BPT)		2,280.00	2,580.00
Total tax		6,405.00	7,115.00
Income after tax		31,095.00	**32,885.00**
Average tax rate		17.08%	17.79%

Forty thousand dollars each provides slightly higher than expected income, but we will use this figure, again in the name of being conservative. Further fine tuning is not really necessary as retirement is still several years away. Laura and Stephen's average tax rate is 17.79%.

Step 2. Draw the Timeline

By drawing the timeline, Laura and Stephen can see in one picture:
• Their before-tax needs
• What income they have in place

		T_0	T_1	T_2	T_3	T_4	T_5	T_6	...	T_{24}	T_{25}	T_{26}	T_{27}
Laura's age		63	64	65	66	67	68	69	...	87	88	89	90
Stephen's age		60	61	62	63	64	65	66	...	84	85		
Need (before tax)		80.0	80.0	80.0	80.0	80.0	80.0	80.0	...	80.0	70.0*	70.0	
In place													
Laura: not indexed		30.0	30.0	30.0	30.0	30.0	30.0	30.0	...	30.0	30.0	30.0	
Indexed													
L — CPP		10.1	10.1	10.1	10.1	10.1	10.1	10.1	...	10.1	10.1	10.1	
L — OAS				3.2	3.2	3.2	3.2	3.2	...	3.2	3.2	3.2	
S — CPP		8.1	8.1	8.1	8.1	8.1	8.1	8.1	...	8.1			
S — OAS							3.2	3.2	...	3.2			

*We have assumed Laura will need $10,000 a year less after Stephen has died.

When planning for retirement, we use *annual cash flows* for ease of calculation. The further away retirement is, the more an estimate using annual numbers (rather than monthly) will suffice. We assume all retirement cash flows happen at the *beginning of the year*.

Step 3. Calculating the Present Value of Retirement Income Needed Before and After Tax

Laura and Stephen will need $80,000 before tax a year for 25 years (i.e., until Laura is 88). Then, after Stephen dies, she will need $70,000 before tax per year for two years. We are using a 7% rate of return when inflation is 3%, which gives us a 3.88% real rate of return. We will calculate this two ways. First, we will take the present value of the before-tax cash flows and then deduct the tax. Second, we will begin by deducting the tax and then take the present value. The answer is the same either way. In both cases we use a before-tax discount rate.

Retirement Needs — Method I. Calculate PV of Income Before Tax, then Deduct the Tax

Laura's age:		**63, 64**	**65–67**	**68–87**	**88, 90**	**dies @ 90**
Stephen's age:		**60, 61**	**62–64**	**65–84**	**dies @ 85**	
Need before tax		80,000	80,000	80,000	70,000	
	$n =$	25			2	
	$k\ real =$	3.88%			3.88%	
PVA of each annuity		1,314,882			137,385	
Laura's age:		**63**	**65**	**68**	**88**	
	$n =$	0			25	
PV of each PVA		1,314,882			53,045	
Total PV before tax		**1,367,927**				
Taxes @ 17.79%		243,320				
PV after tax		**1,124,607**				

Retirement Needs — Method II. Deduct the Tax, then Calculate the PV of Income After Tax

		63, 64	65–67	68–87	88, 90	dies @ 90
Laura's age:		63, 64	65–67	68–87	88, 90	dies @ 90
Stephen's age:		60, 61	62–64	65–84	dies @ 85	
Need before tax		80,000	80,000	80,000	70,000	
Taxes @ 17.79%		14,230	14,230	14,230	12,451	
Need after tax		65,770	65,770	65,770	57,549	
	$n =$	25			2	
	$k\ real =$	3.88%			3.88%	
PVA of each annuity		1,080,997			112,948	
Laura's age:		**63**	**65**	**68**	**88**	
	$n =$	0			25	
PV of each PVA		1,080,997			43,609	
Total PV after tax		**1,124,607**				

This method does not contradict the earlier rule about using after-tax discount rates for after-tax income because in the prior rule we were talking about *investment income*, which is left to compound. Here we are discussing *cash flows*, which are being consumed.

Step 4. Calculating Retirement Income in Place Before and After Tax

There are several ways to calculate the value of the retirement income Laura and Stephen now have in place at the time they retire and how much they need to save, given the income from both private and government pension plans that they expect to receive (called **retirement income in place**). We could:

1. Find the present value, before tax, of pension income in place for:
    *   Indexed income
    *   Non-indexed income, then deduct the tax.
2. Deduct the tax from pension income, then find the present value of pension income in place for:
    *   Indexed income
    *   Non-indexed income
3. Find the present value of each line of retirement income before or after tax

We will show all three ways to illustrate that there are several approaches. For example, it will be easier to take it line by line where there is non-taxable capital being taken into income from non-registered investments. However, there are other instances where one of the first two methods will be much faster. Note that in the following examples, Laura and Stephen need to save $485,346 after tax for each of the following three methods.

Method 1

Here we will first calculate the present value of Stephen and Laura's income before tax at retirement. Then we will take off the tax. They have two sources of income: Laura's non-indexed pension of $30,000 p.a. and government benefits: Canada Pension Plan (CPP) of $10,120 for Laura and $8,050 for Stephen, as well as Old Age Security (OAS) at age 65. Both CPP and OAS are indexed.

Present Value of Laura's Before-tax, Non-Indexed Pension

Laura's age:		63–89 inclusive	Dies @ 90
Laura pension income		30,000	
	$n =$	27	
	k nominal =	7.00%	
PVA before tax		**384,773**	

Present Value of Before-tax, Indexed Government Retirement Benefits

Laura's age:		63, 64	65–67	68–87	88–89	Dies @ 90
Stephen's age:		60, 61	62–64	65–84	Dies @ 85	
Laura CPP		10,120	10,120	10,120	10,120	
Laura OAS			3,200	3,200	3,200	
Stephen CPP		8,050	8,050	8,050		
Stephen OAS				3,200		
BOY gross income		18,170	21,370	24,570	13,320	
	$n =$	2	3	20	2	
	k real =	3.88%	3.88%	3.88%	3.88%	
PVA of each annuity		35,661	61,745	350,585	26,142	
Laura's age:		63	65	68	88	
	$n =$	0	2	5	25	
PV of each PVA		35,661	57,219	289,824	10,094	
Total PV before tax		**392,798**				

Now, let's work out the total of both government and employer-sponsored pensions.

Retirement Income in Place Before and After Tax

Taxable income, non-indexed	384,773
Taxable income, indexed	392,798
	777,571
Taxes @ 17.79%	138,310
PV after tax	**639,261**

What is the effect of this pension income on the amount Laura and Stephen need to save for retirement?

Retirement Income to Save

	Before tax	Tax @ 17.79%	After tax
Retirement needs	**1,367,927**	243,320	**1,124,607**
Government retirement benefits	392,798	69,869	322,929
Laura's non-indexed pension	384,773	68,442	316,332
Have in place	777,571	138,310	639,261
Amount to save at retirement	**590,356**	**105,010**	**485,346**

At this point, we have calculated how much Laura and Stephen need to save but have not taken into account the amount they already have in RRSPs and non-registered savings.

Method 2

Would it make a difference if we took the tax off first? Let's find out. We will first deduct the tax from Laura and Stephen's retirement income needed and from retirement income in place. Then we will calculate the present value.

Present Value of Laura's After-tax, Non-Indexed Pension

Laura's age:		63–89
Laura pension income	Before tax	30,000
	Tax @ 17.79%	5,336
	After tax	24,664
$n =$		27
k nominal $=$		7.00%
PVA after tax		316,332

Present Value of After-tax, Indexed Government Retirement Benefits

Laura's age:	63, 64	65–67	68–87	88, 89
Stephen's age:	60, 61	62–64	65–84	
CPP, OAS	18,170	21,370	24,570	13,320
Taxes @ 17.79% each	3,232	3,801	4,370	2,369
Income after tax	14,938	17,569	20,200	10,951
$n =$	2	3	20	2
k real $=$	3.88%	3.88%	3.88%	3.88%
PVA	29,318	50,762	288,225	21,492
Laura's age:	**63**	**65**	**68**	**88**
$n =$	0	2	5	25
PV of PVA	29,318	47,041	238,271	8,298
PV after tax	**322,929**			

So, what is the total of both government and employer-sponsored pensions, after tax?

Retirement Income in Place After Tax

Non-indexed, after tax	316,332
Indexed, after tax	322,929
Total in place	**639,261**

This and the next calculation produce the same result as Method 1 where we took the present value at retirement and then deducted the tax.

Retirement Income to Save

	After tax
Retirement needs	1,124,607
Have in place	639,261
Amount to save at retirement	**485,346**

Method 3

This method will take the present value of each line of retirement income. The calculation can be done in two ways:

• Calculate the present value of before-tax incomes, add them up, and then deduct the tax.

- Deduct the tax, calculate the present value of the after-tax income, and then add them up. The results will be the same. We will show only the first calculation here. Students are invited to do the second method to confirm the result.

Present Value of Retirement Income in Place, Before Tax

Income	$	n	k	Formula	PVA	PV
Laura:						
Pension	30,000	27	7.00%	$PVA_{63} = 30,000_{BOY} (PVIFA_{27, 7\%})$	384,773	384,773
CPP	10,120	27	3.88%	$PVA_{63} = 10,120_{BOY} (PVIFA_{27, 3.88\%})$	174,001	174,001
OAS	3,200	25	3.88%	$PVA_{65} = 3,200_{BOY} (PVIFA_{25, 3.88\%})$	52,595	
		2	3.88%	$PV_{63} = 52,595_{BOY} (PVIF_{2, 3.88\%})$		48,740
Stephen:						
CPP	8,050	25	3.88%	$PVA_{60} = 8,050_{BOY} (PVIFA_{25, 3.88\%})$	132,310	132,310
OAS	3,200	20	3.88%	$PVA_{65} = 3,200_{BOY} (PVIFA_{20, 3.88\%})$	45,660	
		5	3.88%	$PV_{60} = 45,660_{BOY} (PVIF_{5, 3.88\%})$		37,747
Total						**777,571**

Retirement Income to Save

	Before tax	Tax @ 17.79%	After tax
Retirement needs	1,367,927	243,320	1,124,607
Have in place	777,571	138,310	639,261
Amount to save at retirement	590,356	105,010	485,346

In Summary

Discount cash flows that are:	
• **Before tax** using a **before-tax** discount rate	*Example 10, Methods 1 and 3*
• **After tax** using a **before-tax** discount rate	*Example 10, Method 2*

Craig's 2013 Take-home Pay

Craig asks Francesca how his net pay is calculated. While he is prepared to do his homework, he would like her to show him how the calculation is done using generic tax rates. Francesca tells him she will also calculate his average and marginal rates.

	Tax calculation	Net pay	Marginal on Interest	Dividends	RRSP
Dividends received				100.00	
Salary	90,000.00	90,000.00	100.00	**45%**	3,000.00
Taxable benefits	750.00				
Taxable dividends				145.00	
Gross amount		90,000.00			3,000.00
Taxable Income	90,750.00		100.00	145.00	
Federal tax					
15%	39,500	5,925.00			
22%	39,500	8,690.00			
26%	48,000	3,055.00	26.00	37.70	
29%	127,000				
		17,670.00	26.00	37.70	
Dividend tax credit	18.9655%			27.50	
Non-refundable tax credit:					
Basic personal amount	*10,000.00*				
CPP contributions	*2,103.75*		2,103.75		
EI premiums	*701.46*		701.46		
	12,805.21				
× 15%		1,920.72			
Basic federal tax (BFT)		15,749.22	26.00	10.20	
Provincial tax					
8%	38,000	3,040.00			
13%	38,000	4,940.00			
17%	76,000	2,507.50	17.00	24.65	
		10,487.50	17.00	24.65	
Dividend tax credit	12%			17.40	
Non-refundable tax credit					
Basic personal amount	*9,000.00*				
CPP contributions	*2,103.75*				
EI premiums	*701.46*				
	11,805.21				
× 8%		944.42			
Basic provincial tax (BPT)		9,543.08	17.00	7.25	43.00% =
Total tax		25,292.30 / 25,292.30	43.00	17.45	1,290.00
Disability		731.00			
Total deductions		28,828.51			
Net Pay		**61,171.49**	57.00	82.55	**1,710.00**
		67.97%			57.00%
Average tax rate		***28.10%***			
Marginal rate			*43.00%*	*17.45%*	

Craig's after-tax interest income can be calculated using the marginal tax rate. However, the dividend income must take into account the dividend tax credit. This calculation can be done by using his marginal tax rate on dividend income since he does not change tax brackets when the dividend income is added. Here, using a spreadsheet, we have simply calculated the tax on both the dividend income and the interest income "from scratch."

Using his marginal tax rate on:

- His salary, the after-tax amount of interest income is $71.90 [$100 × (1 − 0.2810)],
- Dividend income, the after-tax amount of dividend income is $82.55 [$100 × (1 − 0.1745)],
- His salary, the after-tax cost of his RRSP contribution is $1,710.00 [$3,000 × (1 − 0.4300)]. The tax saved because his RRSP contribution is tax deductible is $1,290.00 ($3,000 × 0.4300)

In Chapter 5, we will look at the effect of his 2014 RPP contributions on his pay. These contributions are also tax deductible and reduce his net pay by the after-tax amount.

SUMMARY

Statistically, if you live to age 60 or 65, you have a good chance of living for many years. It is important to plan for this possibility so as to not outlive your retirement savings. Inflation is presently quite low but may not always remain so. It is not necessary to assume future inflation rates in order to plan for retirement. However, it is important to check plans that have been adjusted for inflation rates against actual inflation to ascertain whether or not you are on track. Rates of return, before and after tax, depending on where they are invested, can get quite complicated. Again, we can plan using real discount rates but must check on a regular basis to see if actual nominal returns are achieving our objectives, even if those objectives were set using real dollars. This objective can be done by putting inflation back into the projections — an arduous task on a calculator, but not a difficult one when using retirement packages.

If there were no personal income taxes to consider, retirement and estate planning would be simple: You would use time value of money calculations to figure out how much you need to save for retirement and for your estate, and then save it. Personal income taxes complicate matters a great deal. In the following chapters that look at retirement incomes, we will find that they are usually taxed one way or another. We will also look at ways of saving for retirement, some of which are tax deductible at the time of the saving. Since we have a progressive tax system, higher levels of income are taxed at a higher rate — and these higher rates are high. While few Canadians will have $135,054, the bottom of the top tax bracket for 2013, of annual retirement income, the principle of progressive tax rates has implications for how to save for retirement as well as how to draw down assets in retirement.

The calculation of taxes can be complicated and time consuming. More important, students on the job will be using the latest financial-planning program to do tax calculations. Calculating taxes is therefore not the focus of this book.

> Margot will continue to use her tax program to do her annual taxes, but now that she understands how tax payable is calculated, she feels she will be better able to plan her annual income and RRSP contributions in order to minimize her taxes.

DISCOUNTING AND COMPOUNDING RULES

Discount the **first amount** of:	
• **indexed** income using a **real** discount rate	*Example 3*
• **non-indexed** income using a **nominal** discount rate	*Example 4*
Discount or compound **investment income** that is:	
• **before tax**, at a **before-tax** discount or interest rate	*Example 8*
• **after tax**, using an **after-tax** discount or interest rate	*Example 8*
Discount **cash flows** that are:	
• **before tax**, using a **before-tax** discount rate	*Example 10, Methods 1 and 3*
• **after tax**, using a **before-tax** discount rate	*Example 10, Method 2*

SOURCES — TAXATION

- Canada Revenue Agency <www.cra-arc.gc.ca>
- Revenu Quebec <www.revenu.gouv.qc.ca>

KEY TERMS

Average rate of return
Net income
Average tax rate
Basic federal tax (BFT)
Basic personal amount
Basic provincial tax (BPT)
Bracket creep
Canadian Controlled Private Corporation (CCPC)
Dividend tax credit
Effective Annual Rate (EAR)
Eligible dividends
Gross-up
Grossed-up
Guaranteed Investment Certificate (GIC)
Holding period return (HPR)
Inclusion rate of capital gains
Indexed cash flows
Life expectancy
Longevity
Marginal tax rate

Non-indexed cash flows
Non-refundable tax credits
Progressive tax system
Rates of return, before and after tax
Rates of return, nominal and real
Surtax
Tax credits
Tax deductions
Tax deferral
Tax saving
Tax sheltered
Taxable dividends
Taxable income
TONI — tax on net income
Total income
Type A "Eligible" Dividends
Type B "Ineligible" Dividends

See also:
Appendix 2A Review of Investment Basics
Appendix 2B Taxation for Provinces and Territories

QUESTIONS AND PROBLEMS

Note: The following answers were calculated in a spreadsheet package. Your results may vary *slightly* since rounding is not done in the spreadsheet.

A. Longevity

1. What is longevity? Why does it matter in the retirement planning process?

2. What is the probability of:
   (a) a 60-year-old man living to age 85? (Answer: 43%)
   (b) a 65-year-old man living to age 85? (Answer: 45%)

   > Note: These answers are different because some men die between the ages of 60 and 65. To reach the age of 85, a 60-year-old man must first live to age 85.

   (c) a 60-year-old woman living to age 80? (Answer: 73%)
   (d) a 65-year-old woman living to age 80? (Answer: 76%)

B. Inflation

3. What is the *value* in 30 years of $50,000 in 2013 dollars, if inflation is 2.5%? What is the *amount* in 30 years of $50,000 in $2043 if inflation is 2.5%? (Answer: $50,000, $104,878)

4. Jill will be receiving a pension at retirement of $35,000 a year. She expects to live to collect this pension for 30 years. The nominal discount rate is 7%, and inflation is expected to be 2%.
   (a) What is the real discount rate? (Answer: 4.9020%)
   (b) What is the present value at retirement of her pension if it is:
      i. Indexed? (Answer: $570,773)
      ii. Not indexed? (Answer: $464,719)

5. What is bracket creep?

6. Alice earned 9.2% on her RRSP investments this year, and inflation was 3.5%. Her investments are worth $150,000 and she wants to retire in 12 years.
   (a) What is the future value of her investment at the nominal rate of return? (Answer: $431,284)
   (b) What is the future value of her investments at the real rate of return?

      Hint: Use six decimal places for the real rate of return.

   (Answer: $285,415)
   (c) What is the value of part (b) if you add inflation back into the future value? (Answer: $431,284)

C. Rates of Return

7. Marshall's Guaranteed Investment Certificate (GIC) is earning 3% before tax, and his marginal tax rate is 44%.
   (a) What is his after-tax rate of return? (Answer: 1.68%)
   (b) If inflation is 2%, what is his real rate of return:
      i. Before tax? (Answer: 0.98%)
      ii. After tax? (Answer: −0.31%)

8. Mary earned 8% before tax on her investment. If her marginal tax rate is 44%, what is her after-tax return if her income was:
   (a) Interest income (Answer: 4.48%)
   (b) Capital gain (Answer: 6.24%)
   (c) If inflation is 2.5%, what is her real return after tax for the interest income and capital gain? (Answer: Interest 1.93%, Capital gain 3.65%)

9. Al earned 9.2% on his RRSP investments this year. He just read in the paper that inflation was 1.7% for the year ended March 31, 2013. His goal was to earn a 7.5% real rate of return.
   (a) What is Al's real rate of return? (Answer: 7.37%)
   (b) What should his rate of return have been? (Answer: 9.33%)
   (c) What would Al's real rate of return have been if inflation had been 4.2%? (Answer: 4.80%)
   (d) If inflation is 4.7%, what rate of return did Al need to achieve to have a 7.5% real rate of return? (Answer: 12.55%)

10. Bonnie has $10,000 in an RRSP earning 8% interest income. Since it is inside an RRSP, it compounds tax free because the tax is paid when the funds are withdrawn from the RRSP.

    (a) What will the $10,000 be worth in 12 years? (Answer: $25,181)

    (b) She also has $10,000 invested that is not in an RRSP. This investment yields a return of 8% a year. Her marginal tax rate is still 44%. Assuming she leaves the income to compound, how much will she have in 12 years? (Answer: $16,920)

11. Justin receives $6,000 of dividends a year, paid quarterly at the end of each quarter, from shares that cost him $100,000. His other income totals $130,000. As he receives the dividends, he puts them in a savings account earning 4.25% a year. He plans to renovate his basement next year, and he wants the funds ready to use.

    (a) If Justin does this for three years, how much will he have at the end of the three years, assuming he pays the income taxes when he receives the dividend?

> Hint: The marginal rates can be found in the tax drill below. Or they can be calculated from scratch.

    (Answer: $14,528.79)

    (b) If Justin sells the shares at the end of the three years for $109,000, what is his after-tax EAR? Assume he pays the income taxes when he receives the dividend. (Answer: HPR = 21.4588%, EAR = 6.69%)

D. Taxation

Throughout, we use generic tax rates and, except for Chapter 3 and the Case Assignment after Chapter 7, will **omit** Canada Pension Plan contributions and Employment Insurance premiums.

12. This is a **tax drill** whose purpose is to give students an opportunity to master the basic calculation of average and marginal tax on:

    (a) regular income at various levels of income

    (b) regular income plus dividend income

    (c) regular income plus a capital gain.

    For each of the following, calculate the total federal and provincial tax and the average and marginal tax rates using, Table 2.4 as a guideline.

    (a) On **salaried or interest income** of: $35,000, $66,000, $97,000, and $128,000.
        Answer:

	Average	Marginal	Average	Marginal	Average	Marginal	Average	Marginal
Salary or interest	35,000	100.00	66,000	100.00	97,000	100.00	128,000	100.00
Dividend received								
Capital gains received								
Basic federal tax (BFT)	3,750.00	15.00	10,255.00	22.00	17,795.00	26.00	25,885.00	29.00
Basic provincial tax (BPT)	2,080.00	8.00	5,960.00	13.00	10,830.00	17.00	16,100.00	17.00
Total tax	5,830.00	23.00	16,215.00	35.00	28,625.00	43.00	41,985.00	46.00
Average tax rate	16.66%		24.57%		29.51%		32.80%	
Marginal tax rate		23.00%		35.00%		43.00%		46.00%

    (b) **Dividend income.** For each level of salaried income in part (a), plus $1,300 in dividends *received* calculate:

      • the amount of tax,

      • the average tax rate on the total of these two sources of income, and

      • the marginal tax rate on the next $1.00 of dividend income received.
      Answer:

	Average	Marginal	Average	Marginal	Average	Marginal	Average	Marginal
Salary or interest	35,000		66,000		97,000		128,000	
Dividend received	1,300	100.00	1,300	100.00	1,300	100.00	1,300	100.00
Capital gains received								
Basic federal tax (BFT)	3,675.25	−5.75	10,312.20	4.40	17,927.60	10.20	26,074.15	14.55
Basic provincial tax (BPT)	2,004.60	−5.80	5,978.85	1.45	10,924.25	7.25	16,194.25	7.25
Total tax	5,679.86	−11.55	16,291.05	5.85	28,851.85	17.45	42,268.40	21.80
Average tax rate	15.65%		24.21%		29.35%		32.69%	
Marginal tax rate		−11.55%		5.85%		17.45%		21.80%

(c) **Capital gains.** For each level of salaried income in part (a), plus $3,000 in capital gains *received*, calculate:
- the amount of tax,
- the average tax rate on the total of these two sources of income, and
- the marginal tax rate on the next $1.00 of capital gains received.

Answer:

	Average	Marginal	Average	Marginal	Average	Marginal	Average	Marginal
Salary or interest	35,000		66,000		97,000		128,000	
Dividend received								
Capital gains received	3,000	100.00	3,000	100.00	3,000	100.00	3,000	100.00
Basic federal tax (BFT)	3,975.00	7.50	10,585.00	11.00	18,185.00	13.00	26,320.00	14.50
Basic provincial tax (BPT)	2,200.00	4.00	6,155.00	6.50	11,085.00	8.50	16,355.00	8.50
Total tax	6,175.00	11.50	16,740.00	17.50	29,270.00	21.50	42,675.00	23.00
Average tax rate	16.25%		24.26%		29.27%		32.58%	
Marginal tax rate		11.50%		17.50%		21.50%		23.00%

(d) **Dividends and capital gains** Repeat the above calculations adding dividends received of $1,300 and capital gains received of $3,000 to the salaries in part (a). The marginal rate is on the next $1.00 of *regular or interest income received*.

Answer:

	Average	Marginal	Average	Marginal	Average	Marginal	Average	Marginal
Salary or interest	35,000	100.00	66,000	100.00	97,000	100.00	128,000	100.00
Dividend received	1,300		1,300		1,300		1,300	
Capital gains received	3,000		3,000		3,000		3,000	
Basic federal tax (BFT)	3,900.25	15.00	10,642.20	22.00	18,317.60	26.00	26,509.15	29.00
Basic provincial tax (BPT)	2,143.85	13.00	6,173.85	13.00	11,179.25	17.00	16,449.25	17.00
Total tax	6,044.10	28.00	16,816.05	35.00	29,496.85	43.00	42,958.40	46.00
Average tax rate	15.38%		23.92%		29.12%		32.47%	
Marginal tax rate		28.00%		35.00%		43.00%		46.00%

13. Marco earns $67,000 a year in 2013.
    (a) How much will Marco pay in taxes in 2013? (Answer: $16,565.00)
    (b) If Marco gets a 4% raise every year for five years, but tax rates and tax brackets do not change,
        i. What will his income be in 2018? (Answer: $81,516)
        ii. How much will Marco pay in taxes in 2018? (Answer: $21,966.77)
    (c) What is his net pay as a percentage of his salary, average tax rate, and marginal tax rate for the two years? (Answer: 2013: 75.28%, 24.72%, 35.00%. 2018: 73.05%, 26.95%, 43.00%)

14. Marcia invested $5,000 in the common shares of You-Can't-Lose Inc. in 2002. In 2013, she sold the shares for $14,000. Her 2013 salary was $75,000.
    (a) What was her tax payable on her 2013 salary only? (Answer: $19,365.00)

(b) What is her 2013 marginal tax rate? (Answer: 35.00%)

(c) What is her tax payable on her salary and the capital gain? (Answer: $21,100.00)

(d) Using her marginal tax rate, how much tax would she pay on her capital gain? (Answer: $1,575.00)

(e) Using your answers to parts a and c, how much tax does she pay on the capital gain? (Answer: $1,735.00)

(f) Why are the two answers different?

15. Andrea is very excited. She has just received a big promotion that comes with a $10,000 a year raise. Her current salary is $75,000. She gets out her calculator to estimate how much extra take-home pay she will have a year. She estimates she will have $6,500.00 extra. She is very disappointed when she gets her next pay cheque to find that her annual take-home pay will go up by only $5,900.00.

(a) Calculate Andrea's current annual income after tax deducting only income tax using generic tax rates. Also calculate her average and marginal tax rate. (Answer: $55,635.00, average 25.82%, marginal 35.00%)

(b) Calculate Andrea's extra income after tax using the marginal rate from part (a). (Answer: $6,500.00)

(c) Calculate Andrea's new annual income after tax from scratch. Also calculate her new average and marginal tax rates. (Answer: $61,535.00, average 27.61%, marginal 43.00%)

(d) What is the difference between her estimate and the actual additional pay? (Answer: $600.00)

(e) Why are the calculations in part (b) and part (c) different?

16. After her raise, Andrea (from the prior question) puts $5,000 in her RRSP.

(a) How much tax does she save using:
   i. the difference between the actual tax, and
   ii. the marginal tax rate?

(b) Why can this calculation be done accurately using her new marginal tax rate while the marginal rate on her old income did not result in the correct answer in the prior problem?

Answer (a):

			(i)	(ii)
Using			**Actual**	**Marginal**
Taxable income	85,000.00	80,000.00	5,000.00	5,000.00
Total tax	23,465.00	21,315.00	2,150.00	2,150.00
Income after tax	61,535.00	58,685.00	2,850.00	2,850.00

Appendix 2A: Review of Investment Basics

Learning Objectives

When choosing or evaluating an investment for yourself or your client, you need to understand the following:[1]

A. average **rates of return (k)** for different kinds of assets (called *asset classes*)

B. **standard deviation** (σ) of each asset class. The standard deviation is one measure of the risk that each asset has demonstrated over several years

C. **coefficient of variation (CV),** which makes it possible to compare asset classes that have different levels of risk, and

D. **correlation coefficient (r),** which measures the way two investments move compared with each other.

The data on which these summaries are based is presented in Table 2A.2.

A. AVERAGE RATE OF RETURN (k)

Average rate of return for investments such as those shown in Table 2A.1 are useful when choosing a realistic rate of return on investments for clients. While the standard deviations do not show much change when converted to real dollars, nominal and real rates of return can change a great deal.

An average rate of return can be calculated from a few years or many years, as shown in Table 2A.1. The user must exercise judgement as to what reasonable time period would be useful. The long bull run of the 1990s would tend to increase expectations about what constitutes a reasonably good rate of return. High inflation as seen in the consumer price index (CPI) in the 1970s and early 1980s increases expectations about nominal rates of return, which can be rectified by looking at real rates of return from which inflation has been removed. Is a 50-year rate of return the answer? Only if you want to assume business conditions haven't changed over 50 years.

It would be gratifying if a rule could be stated that indicates the correct answer. Unfortunately, only judgement can be used to make the decision. The rates of return we are looking for are future returns. Historical returns provide a guideline about what we might expect from different asset classes in the future. This underscores the need to regularly review the progress of the financial plan to assess actual performance against expected performance based on assumptions made when creating the plan.

The real returns in Table 2A.1 are calculated for *each year*, using the data in Table 2A.2, which uses the formula:

$$k_{real} = \left(\frac{1 + \text{nominal rate}}{1 + \text{inflation rate}} \right) - 1$$

---

1   These concepts are provided as a reference when for deciding on appropriate types of investments. It is beyond the scope of this text to fully explain the concepts in this section. A complete explanation is covered in any Personal Financial Planning, Statistics, or Investments course.

In 1981, T-bills had a nominal rate of return of 17.9%. However, inflation that year was 12.2%, as measured by the CPI. As a result, the real rate of return was only 5.1% — high for T-bills, but nothing like 17.9%.

$$k_{real} = \left(\frac{1.179}{1.122} \right) - 1 = 0.051 = 5.1\%$$

B. STANDARD DEVIATION (σ)

The standard deviation is used as a measure of risk; i.e., the higher the standard deviation, the higher the variability of the rate of return. The standard deviation measures how far each rate of return is, on average, from the average rate of return. Many financial newspapers report three-year standard deviations. Looking at the variation in the rates of return in Table 2A.2, one can see that a three-year variation will probably not report the true variability in rates of return. *The Globe and Mail,* for instance, publishes a 15-year review of mutual funds three times a year (early November, February, and May). This and other sources provide the raw data for calculating standard deviation over a longer period of time (not difficult to do using a spreadsheet package). Sources such as these will also show how long the fund has existed. All rates of return are nominal in these reports.

The next table shows average rates of return and their standard deviations for the asset classes shown below. The results cover four different time periods to show how much the results can vary, depending on the time period chosen. The three time periods are:

- 61 years, from 1950 to 2010
- 10 years, from 1973 to 1982, when inflation was very high
- 10 years, from 1991 to 2000, when returns were very high but inflation was not high
- 10 years, from 2001 to 2010, only for more recent data

Table 2A.1 Average Returns and Standard Deviations of Asset Classes, 1950–2010

		Nominal						Real				
		CPI	T-bills	Bonds	TSX	S&P	World	T-bills	Bonds	TSX	S&P	World
Average	1950–2010	3.8	5.7	7.1	11.8	11.5	10.3	1.8	3.2	7.8	7.6	5.7
Returns	1973–1982	9.7	10.2	8.1	12.2	10.4	10.0	0.4	−1.3	2.4	0.8	0.4
	1991–2000	1.9	5.6	10.7	13.8	19.9	15.4	3.6	8.5	11.7	17.7	13.2
	2001–2010	2.0	2.7	6.3	8.7	−1.8	−0.2	0.8	4.3	6.6	−3.7	−2.1
Standard	1950–2010	3.2	3.7	8.1	17.2	16.0	16.2	2.9	8.4	16.8	15.9	15.8
Deviation	1973–1982	1.8	3.6	11.7	21.1	19.7	18.0	3.0	11.7	19.8	18.6	17.0
	1991–2000	1.0	1.5	8.1	12.6	12.6	11.1	1.2	7.5	12.2	12.7	11.3
	2001–2010	0.8	1.4	1.5	20.2	12.5	14.4	1.7	1.5	19.9	12.4	14.2

Source: Author's calculations are based on information provided in Ho and Robinson, *Personal Financial Planning, 5th edition*, Appendix D and E (Toronto: Captus Press, 2012).

CPI: Change in Canadian consumer price index

T-bills: Government of Canada 91-day treasury bills

Bonds: Scotia McLeod Long-term Bond Index (maturities longer than 10 years)

TSX: TSX 300 Index

S&P: Standard & Poor 500 Index (US shares) — in Canadian $

World: Morgan Stanley World Index — in Canadian $

What does the data in Table 2A.1 tell us? Looking at the real returns for 2001 to 2010, it tells us that T-bills provide a low return of only 0.8% but with a corresponding low risk (standard deviation) of only 1.7% Want a better return? You could have achieved an average real return on stocks of 6.6%, but it

Appendix 2A: Review of Investment Basics

comes with a higher risk factor — a standard deviation of 19.9%. The coefficient of variation and the correlation coefficient will help to compare and combine these asset classes in a portfolio of assets.

Table 2A.2 shows nominal and real rates of return for the 61-year time period from 1950 to 2010. Recessions are shaded. This data is provided so the student can understand:

1. Why the Bank of Canada works so hard to keep inflation low. People who have lived and worked though periods of high inflation know the negative effect it has on purchasing power and interest rates.
2. The great range of returns that can happen over time. The negative returns of the Standard and Poor Index in 1973 and 1974 was not regained for five years. An investor who was invested in an indexed fund in 1972 would have had to wait until 1980 to see a positive return on that 1972 investment. This is why a "buy and hold" strategy is recommended by many investment advisors.

Table 2A.2 Returns of Asset Classes 1950–2010

		Nominal % return						CPI*			Real % return				
		CPI	T-bills	Bonds	TSE	S&P	World				T-bills	Bonds	Equity	S&P	World
1.	1950	2.9	0.6	1.7	27.9	24.1		1.0			−2.3	−1.2	24.3	20.5	
2.	1951	10.6	0.8	−7.9	25.5	17.7		1.1			−8.8	−16.7	13.5	6.5	
3.	1952	2.4	1.1	5.0	1.2	7.3		1.1			−1.3	2.5	−1.2	4.7	
4.	1953	−0.9	1.7	5.0	−8.3	0.6		1.1			2.6	5.9	−7.5	1.5	
5.	1954	0.6	1.4	12.2	43.6	49.5		1.1			0.8	11.6	42.8	48.6	
6.	1955	0.2	1.6	0.1	24.1	29.4		1.1			1.5	0.0	23.9	29.2	
7.	1956	1.5	2.9	−8.9	8.8	4.2		1.1			1.4	−10.2	7.2	2.6	
8.	1957	1.7	3.8	3.8	7.9	-8.6		1.2			2.0	6.1	−22.0	−10.2	
9.	1958	2.8	2.3	4.9	30.7	36.2		1.2			-0.6	2.0	27.1	32.4	
10.	1959	1.1	4.8	−5.1	2.3	10.4		1.2			3.7	−6.1	1.2	9.2	
11.	1960	1.6	3.2	12.2	1.5	4.4		1.2			1.5	10.4	-0.1	2.7	
12.	1961	0.0	2.8	9.2	34.1	30.0		1.2			2.8	9.2	34.1	30.0	
13.	1962	1.6	4.1	9.0	−7.6	-3.1		1.3			2.4	7.3	-9.0	-4.6	
14.	1963	2.1	3.6	4.6	14.2	21.2		1.3			1.4	2.4	11.8	18.6	
15.	1964	2.1	3.8	6.2	24.7	15.0		1.3			1.7	4.0	22.2	12.7	
16.	1965	3.0	4.0	0.1	5.8	12.5		1.3			0.9	−2.9	2.6	9.1	
17.	1966	3.4	5.0	−1.1	−5.2	-9.0		1.4			1.5	−4.3	−8.4	−12.0	
18.	1967	3.8	4.6	−9.5	20.3	22.1		1.4			0.8	−12.8	15.9	17.6	
19.	1968	4.1	6.3	2.1	23.6	10.3		1.5			2.1	−1.9	18.7	5.9	
20.	1969	4.8	7.2	−2.9	−1.3	−8.4		1.6			2.3	−7.3	−5.9	−12.6	
21.	1970	1.3	6.0	15.4	−2.7	2.1	−4.8	1.6	1.0		4.7	14.0	−3.9	0.8	−6.0
22.	1971	5.0	3.3	14.8	11.3	13.0	17.7	1.7	1.1		−1.3	9.4	6.0	7.7	12.1
23.	1972	5.1	3.6	8.1	30.2	17.0	21.0	1.8	1.1		−1.5	2.8	23.8	11.3	15.1
24.	1973	9.4	5.5	2.0	−3.7	-14.2	−13.9	1.9	1.2		−3.6	−6.8	−12.0	−21.6	−21.2
25.	1974	12.3	7.8	−4.5	−27.0	-26.0	−24.3	2.2	1.4		−4.0	−15.0	−35.0	−34.1	−32.6
26.	1975	9.5	7.4	8.0	22.2	38.7	36.6	2.4	1.5		−1.9	−1.3	11.6	26.7	24.8
27.	1976	5.9	8.9	23.6	11.7	21.4	13.4	2.5	1.6		2.9	16.8	5.5	14.7	7.2
28.	1977	9.5	7.3	9.0	15.5	1.0	10.2	2.7	1.7		−2.0	−0.4	5.5	-7.8	0.7
29.	1978	8.4	8.7	4.1	29.4	15.7	26.1	3.0	1.9		0.3	−4.0	19.3	6.7	16.3
30.	1979	9.8	11.7	-2.8	50.6	15.6	10.6	3.3	2.0		1.8	−11.5	37.2	5.3	0.8
31.	1980	11.1	12.8	2.2	28.1	31.6	27.9	3.6	2.3	1.0	1.5	−8.0	15.2	18.5	15.1
32.	1981	12.2	17.9	4.2	−10.3	−4.6	−2.8	4.1	2.5	1.1	5.1	−7.1	−20.0	−14.9	−13.4
33.	1982	9.2	14.0	35.4	5.5	24.6	16.0	4.4	2.8	1.2	4.4	23.9	-3.4	14.1	6.2
34.	1983	4.6	9.3	11.5	35.5	22.3	22.7	4.7	2.9	1.3	4.4	6.6	29.5	16.9	17.3
35.	1984	3.7	11.1	14.7	−2.4	12.5	12.0	4.8	3.0	1.3	7.1	10.6	−5.9	8.5	8.0
36.	1985	4.4	9.5	21.2	25.1	35.8	42.8	5.0	3.2	1.4	4.9	16.1	19.8	30.1	36.8
37.	1986	4.2	9.1	14.7	9.0	17.0	36.5	5.2	3.3	1.4	4.7	10.1	4.6	12.3	31.0

Table 2A.2 Continued.

		Nominal % return						CPI*			Real % return				
		CPI	T-bills	Bonds	TSE	S&P	World				T-bills	Bonds	Equity	S&P	World
38.	1987	4.2	8.2	4.0	5.9	3.6	12.3	5.5	3.4	1.5	3.9	−0.1	1.7	−0.6	7.9
39.	1988	4.0	9.3	9.5	11.1	7.1	13.5	5.7	3.6	1.6	5.1	5.3	6.8	3.0	9.1
40.	1989	5.2	12.0	12.8	21.4	25.1	13.4	6.0	3.8	1.6	6.4	7.2	15.3	18.9	7.7
41.	1990	5.0	13.0	7.5	−14.8	−1.3	−13.9	6.3	3.9	1.7	7.6	2.4	−18.8	−6.0	−18.0
42.	1991	3.8	9.1	22.1	12.0	27.6	17.8	6.5	4.1	1.8	5.1	17.7	7.9	22.9	13.5
43.	1992	2.1	6.6	9.8	−1.4	17.4	5.2	6.7	4.2	1.8	4.3	7.5	-3.5	15.0	3.0
44.	1993	1.7	5.0	18.1	32.6	13.8	25.7	6.8	4.2	1.9	3.3	16.2	30.3	11.9	23.6
45.	1994	0.2	5.3	−4.3	−0.2	7.2	11.5	6.8	4.3	1.9	5.0	−4.5	−0.4	7.0	11.3
46.	1995	1.8	6.8	20.7	14.5	30.0	16.9	6.9	4.3	1.9	5.0	18.6	12.6	27.8	14.9
47.	1996	2.2	5.1	12.3	28.4	21.7	13.7	7.1	4.4	1.9	2.8	9.8	25.6	19.1	11.3
48.	1997	0.8	3.1	9.6	15.0	34.8	20.3	7.1	4.4	2.0	2.3	8.8	14.1	33.8	19.4
49.	1998	1.0	4.7	9.2	−1.6	37.7	33.7	7.2	4.5	2.0	3.7	8.1	−2.6	36.3	32.3
50.	1999	2.6	4.7	−1.1	31.7	14.2	18.2	7.4	4.6	2.0	2.0	−3.6	28.4	11.3	15.2
51.	2000	3.2	5.5	10.3	7.4	−5.5	−9.5	7.6	4.8	2.1	2.2	6.8	4.0	−8.5	−12.3
52.	2001	0.7	4.7	8.1	−12.6	-6.5	−11.4	7.7	4.8	2.1	4.0	7.3	−13.2	−7.1	−12.0
53.	2002	3.9	2.5	8.7	−12.4	−22.7	−20.2	7.9	5.0	2.2	−1.3	4.7	-15.7	−25.6	−23.2
54.	2003	2.0	2.9	6.7	26.7	5.3	9.4	8.1	5.1	2.2	0.9	4.6	24.2	3.2	7.3
55.	2004	2.1	2.3	7.2	14.5	3.3	7.3	8.3	5.2	2.3	0.2	4.9	12.1	1.1	5.1
56.	2005	2.1	2.6	6.5	24.1	1.6	6.6	8.4	5.3	2.3	0.5	4.3	21.6	−0.5	4.4
57.	2006	1.7	4.0	4.1	17.3	15.7	20.6	8.6	5.4	2.4	2.3	2.4	15.3	13.8	18.6
58.	2007	2.4	4.3	3.7	9.8	−10.6	−7.1	8.8	5.5	2.4	1.9	1.3	7.3	−12.6	−9.3
59.	2008	1.2	3.1	6.4	−33.0	−21.9	−26.1	8.9	5.6	2.5	1.9	5.2	−33.8	−22.8	−26.9
60.	2009	1.3	0.5	5.4	35.1	8.1	11.8	9.0	5.6	2.5	−0.8	4.0	33.3	6.7	10.3
61.	2010	2.4	0.4	6.7	17.6	9.4	6.8	9.2	5.8	2.5	−1.9	4.3	14.9	6.8	4.3

Shaded areas show years of recessions

Source: Ho and Robinson, *Personal Financial Planning*, 5th ed., Appendix D and E (Toronto: Captus Press, 2012; 3rd edition, 2000; and 2nd edition, 1996).

*The CPI in the centre of Table 2A.2 turns the CPI return into a purchasing-power index. For instance, a student loan of $10,000 in 1970 has an equivalent value in 2010 of $58,000. A house costing $20,000 in 1950 has an equivalent value of $184,000 in 2010.

C. COEFFICIENT OF VARIATION (CV)

How can these different asset classes be compared when the rates of return are different and also the standard deviation? Which one is the better deal?

One measure is one's own tolerance for risk, called **risk tolerance.** It is a fundamental assumption in investing that everyone prefers a better rate of return to a lesser rate of return for the same level of risk. As a result, as the risk increases, investors require a higher rate of return to compensate them for accepting the higher possibility of loss or a lower return. This is called the **risk/return tradeoff.** Some people will accept a lower return because higher possible returns also come with higher possibilities of losses. These people are called **risk averse.** Other people gladly accept more risk in order to have the potential of a higher return. They are called **risk takers.**

There is a way to measure the *relative* risk of investments. The **coefficient of variation** measures the *relative* risk of investments by indicating the amount of risk per unit of return — the higher the CV, the higher the risk for each 1% rate of return. The formula is:

standard deviation (σ) ÷ mean (k)

We can compare the 10-year real return (k real) and the standard deviation (σ) for 2001 to 2010 on the above asset classes using the Coefficient of Variation:

Table 2A.3 Coefficient of Variation

2001–2010	k_{real}	σ	CV
T-bills	0.8%	1.7%	2.26
Bonds	4.3%	1.5%	0.36
TSE	6.6%	19.9%	3.00
S&P	–3.7%	12.4%	–3.36
World	–2.7%	14.2%	–6.66

Source: Author's calculations are based on information in Table 2A.1.

The coefficient of variation measures the risk per unit of return. What if an investor wants a better return than T-bills can offer but wants to minimize risk? The TSX provided a higher return than bonds (6.6% vs. 4.3%) in that 10-year period, and the standard deviation was also higher (19.9% vs. 1.5%). How to choose? In this case it's rather obvious since the standard deviation on the TSX was so very much higher than for bonds. However, it is not always this clear cut. The CV for bonds is much less than the CV for the TSX (3.00 vs. 0.36) — the TSX had significantly more risk for each percentage of return than did bonds due to the much greater variation in returns for the TSX as measured by the standard deviation.

Using the same data, since approximately 68% of the returns falls within one standard deviation of the mean, one can expect the following range of real returns (calculated by $k_{real} +/-σ$):

Table 2A.4 Range of Returns

2000–2010	k_{real}	σ	Range of returns 2 years out of 3
T-bills	2.7%	1.4%	1.4% to 4.1%
Bonds	6.3%	1.5%	4.8% to 7.9%
TSX	8.7%	20.2%	11.5% to 28.9%
S&P	–1.8%	12.5%	14.3% to 10.6%
World	–0.2%	14.4%	14.6% to 14.1%

You can expect (but are not guaranteed) T-bills would provide a return of 1.4% to 4.1% two years out of three (with a probability of 68%).

Source: Author's calculations are based on information in Table 2A.1.

D. CORRELATION COEFFICIENT (r)

The correlation coefficient measures the covariance between two stocks or, in our examples, between two asset classes. The correlation coefficient tells us how two assets move relative to each other. Two stocks or asset classes or mutual funds can have a correlation coefficient that varies from a high of +1 to a low of –1.

If two classes are **perfectly positively correlated**, the correlation coefficient is +1, meaning they will move exactly the same way up and down. If one goes up by 15%, the other goes up by 15%. If two assets classes are **perfectly negatively correlated**, r is –1, when one moves up, the other moves down by the same amount. When the movement of two assets do not relate to each other, r is 0. A portfolio of assets with low correlation coefficients enables the investor to maintain returns of a portfolio while decreasing the risk (or standard deviation) of the portfolio.

The correlation coefficients shown in Table 2A.5 are included as a guide to building a balanced portfolio for clients. Coefficients that have a low or negative correlation are used to build a balanced portfolio.

Table 2A.5 Correlation Coefficients between Asset Classes

			Nominal				Real		
			Bonds	TSE	S&P		Bonds	TSE	S&P
1950–2010	61 years	T-bills	0.31	–0.11	0.04	T-bills	0.49	–0.11	0.19
		Bonds		0.02	0.29	Bonds		0.09	0.36
		TSE			0.68	TSE			0.69
1973–1982	10 years	T-bills	0.20	0.01	0.18	T-bills	0.49	0.22	0.43
		Bonds		–0.04	0.44	Bonds		0.06	0.50
		TSE			0.70	TSE			0.72
1991–2000	10 years	T-bills	0.54	–0.20	–0.01	T-bills	0.29	–0.49	0.22
		Bonds		0.18	0.37	Bonds		0.14	0.38
		TSE			–0.05	TSE			–0.04
2001–2010	10 years	T-bills	–0.16	0.44	–0.32	T-bills	0.14	–0.35	–0.09
		Bonds		–0.40	–0.39	Bonds		–0.40	–0.21
		TSE			0.83	TSE			0.83

Source: Ho and Robinson, *Personal Financial Planning*, 5th ed., Appendix D and E (Toronto: Captus Press, 2012; 3rd edition, 2000; and 2nd edition, 1996).

Example 1 illustrates how an investor can reduce risk by building a portfolio that takes the correlation coefficient into account. This example calculates the rate of return and standard deviation for a portfolio consisting of two funds that have different rates of return and different standard deviations.

Example 1   Let's assume an investor has a portfolio that consists of 30% bonds and 70% Canadian stocks. Again using 2001 to 2010 data, if the investor's portfolio were 100% bonds or 100% stocks, the investor could expect a real return and standard deviation as shown in the table below. The expected return of the portfolio is the weighted average return of the (only) *two* asset classes:

	% in Portfolio	k_{real}	σ
Bonds	30%	4.3%	1.5%
TSX	70%	6.6%	19.9%

The expected real rate of return is:

$$E(k)_p = wt_1E(r_1) + wt_2E(r_2)$$
$$= (.3 \times 4.3\%) + (.7 \times 6.6\%) = 5.9\%$$

The standard deviation is not the weighted average of the standard deviation of the two asset classes (which would give a standard deviation of 11.9%). It fails to take into account the **correlation coefficient** between the two, which is –0.40. Normally, they are positively correlated but in this volatile time, they are negatively correlated. The standard deviation for the portfolio is

σ =	$[wt_1^2\sigma_1^2 +$	$wt_2^2\sigma_2^2 +$	$2wt_1wt_2r_{1,2}\sigma_1\sigma_2]^{½}$
=	$[(.3 \times .3 \times .015 \times .015) +$	$(.7 \times .7 \times .199 \times .199) +$	$(2 \times .3 \times .7 \times -0.4 \times .015 \times .199)]^{½}$
=	$[.00002025 +$	$.01940449 +$	$-0.00050148]^{½}$
=			$0.01892326^{½}$
=			$0.13756184 = 13.8\%$

Note: If you do these calculations with a calculator, you will get a slightly different answer since all the percentages are not rounded in the spreadsheet.

This portfolio comprised of 30% bonds and 70% stocks can be expected to provide a real rate of return of 8.4% with a standard deviation of 11.3%

	% in Portfolio	k_{real}	σ
Bonds	30%	4.3%	1.5%
TSX	70%	6.6%	19.9%
Portfolio		5.9%	13.8%

This portfolio *decreases* the rate of return from the TSX by 11% [(5.9% − 6.6%) ÷ 6.6%] while *decreasing* the standard deviation by 31% [(13.8% − 19.9%) ÷ 19.9%]. By combining two asset classes that have a low correlation coefficient, this investor has decreased the return from the TSX somewhat, but has reduced the standard deviation by a lot more.

And if we look at the Correlation of Variation, the risk per unit of return has also decreased.

2001–2010	k_{real}	σ	CV
Bonds	4.3%	1.5%	0.35
TSE	6.6%	19.9%	3.02
Portfolio	5.9%	13.8%	2.33

Source: Author's calculations are based on information in Tables 2A.1 and 2A.4.

SUMMARY

Historical returns are used as a basis for choosing future rates of returns in order to build savings for retirement. Historical returns provide only a guideline — they are not a guarantee of future events. Nominal returns include the effects of inflation, which can be acknowledged by looking at real returns. This won't help when reviewing returns for abnormally long bull or bear markets. Knowledge of market conditions will always be needed when choosing projected returns.

The risk-return tradeoff states that higher expected returns are more volatile. The trade-off means that, in seeking higher returns, one must accept the greater possibility of both higher and lower returns from expected or desired returns. There are ways of assessing this volatility in order to compare asset classes but, again, this assessment of historical returns provides only guidelines, not guarantees, about future returns.

KEY TERMS

Asset classes

Average rate of return

Coefficient of variation (CV)

Correlation coefficient (r)

Negatively correlated

Nominal rate of return

Positively correlated

Real rate of return

Risk averse

Risk takers

Risk tolerance

Risk/return tradeoff

Standard deviation

QUESTIONS

1. The average rate of return on the TSX was 8.7% for the period 2001 to 2010, while the consumer price index was 2.0% for the same period.
    (a) Does 8.7% on the TSX include inflation? (Answer: Yes)
    (b) What is the nominal rate of return on the TSX for this period? (Answer: 8.7%)
    (c) Verify the real rate of return of 6.6% using the formula provided and the CPI.

2. For the period 1950–2010, bonds had a standard deviation of 8.1%, while equity (TSX) had a standard deviation of 17.2%.
    (a) Which is more risky? (Answer: TSX)
    (b) Does the comparative risk change when looking at the standard deviation based on real dollars? (Answer: No)

3. Using the coefficient of variation for 2001 to 2010, which is riskier — the TSE or T-bills? (Answer: TSX)

4. In a recession, will people probably eat more or less hamburger than steak? Is the consumption of hamburgers and steaks negatively or positively correlated?

5. After the fall in the stock market in the early 2000s due, in part, to the deep fall of tech stocks, would someone who is essentially risk averse, tend to buy bonds or stocks? (Bonds) What impact is this likely to have on the stock market in the short run?

6. Jason can choose between two equity mutual funds. In the past 10 years, Hare Fund earned 12.0% with a standard deviation of 16.8%. In the same time period, Tortoise Fund earned 8.0% with a standard deviation of 9.2%.
    (a) What range of returns can be expected on these two funds two years out of three? (Answer: Hare — 4.8% to 28.8%. Tortoise — 1.2% to 17.2%)
    (b) If Jason wants to minimize his risk, which fund should he choose; i.e., calculate the coefficient of variation for both funds. (Answer: Hare Fund CV = 1.4. Tortoise Fund CV = 1.15. Choose the Tortoise Fund).
    (c) What is the expected return and standard deviation on his portfolio if Jason's portfolio is 60% Hare and 40% Tortoise and:
        i.   these two funds have a correlation coefficient of +.3 (Answer: k = 10.4%, sd = 11.72%)
        ii. these two funds have a correlation coefficient of − .3. (Answer: k = 10.4%, sd = 9.64%)

Appendix 2B: Taxation for Provinces and Territories

Appendix 2B: Taxation for Provinces and Territories

The following is the actual tax calculation, using 2013 rates, of salaried or interest income for a single person with no dependants for each province and territory (in alphabetical order). Pay particular attention to the calculation of the marginal rate when there is a **provincial surtax**. There was a federal surtax for several years, which was discontinued in 2004. Surtaxes are "temporary" extra taxes on higher levels of income. The amounts eligible for the **non-refundable tax credit** for the provinces and territories can be different from the federal amounts. In these examples, only the basic personal amount is used for the non-refundable tax credit. Throughout this text, we will use a generic tax, which is shown at the end of this Appendix, after the Problems.

Provincial and Territorial Taxes and Tax Rates using 2013 Tax Rates

Taxable income	Average 30,000	Marginal 100.00	Average 80,000	Marginal 100.00	Average 130,000	Marginal 100.00
Taxes	$	$	$	$	$	$
Federal	2,844	15.00	15,210	26.00	31,258	29.00
Provincial						
Alberta	1,241	10.00	7,241	10.00	13,241	10.00
British Columbia	998	5.06	5,901	12.29	14,366	14.70
Manitoba	2,281	10.80	10,981	17.40	21,421	17.40
New Brunswick	1,876	9.10	8,903	12.40	16,787	14.30
Newfoundland	1,659	7.70	9,159	13.30	17,139	13.30
Northwest Territories	971	5.90	6,275	12.20	13,997	14.05
Nova Scotia	1,917	14.95	11,417	16.67	21,892	17.50
Nunavut	702	4.00	4,694	9.00	10,468	11.50
Ontario	1,032	5.05	7,049	17.41	17,494	17.41
Prince Edward Island	2,185	9.80	11,140	16.70	22,026	18.37
Quebec	2,561	16.00	14,430	24.00	29,705	25.75
Saskatchewan	1,623	11.00	9,165	13.00	17,514	15.00
Yukon	1,335	7.04	6,877	12.01	14,292	13.40
Tax rates						
Federal	9.48%	15.00%	16.90%	26.00%	20.84%	29.00%
Provincial						
Alberta	4.14%	10.00%	8.05%	10.00%	8.83%	10.00%
British Columbia	3.33%	5.06%	6.56%	12.29%	9.58%	14.70%
Manitoba	7.60%	10.80%	12.20%	17.40%	14.28%	17.40%
New Brunswick	6.25%	9.10%	9.89%	12.40%	11.19%	14.30%
Newfoundland	5.53%	7.70%	10.18%	13.30%	11.43%	13.30%
Northwest Territories	3.24%	5.90%	6.97%	12.20%	9.33%	14.05%
Nova Scotia	6.39%	14.95%	12.69%	16.67%	14.59%	17.50%
Nunavut	2.34%	4.00%	5.22%	9.00%	6.98%	11.50%
Ontario	3.44%	5.05%	7.83%	17.41%	11.66%	17.41%
Prince Edward Island	7.28%	9.80%	12.38%	16.70%	14.68%	18.37%
Quebec	6.97%	13.53%	13.24%	19.71%	16.36%	20.97%
Saskatchewan	5.41%	11.00%	10.18%	13.00%	11.68%	15.00%
Yukon	4.45%	7.04%	7.64%	12.01%	9.53%	13.40%

Sources: Canada Revenue Agency <www.cra-arc.gc.ca>; Federal tax rates, Provincial/territorial tax rates for 2013; TaxTips Canadian tax and Financial Information <www.taxtips.ca>; Ernst and Young Personal Tax Calculator for 2013 <www.ey.com>

Federal, using 2013 Rates

Salary/Interest Income		Average 30,000	Marginal 100.00	Average 90,000	Marginal 100.00	Average 150,000	Marginal 100.00
Federal tax							
15% on the first	43,561	4,500.00	15.00	6,534.15		6,534.15	
22% on the next	43,562			9,583.64		9,583.64	
26% on the next	47,931			748.02	26.00	12,462.06	
29% over	135,054					4,334.34	29.00
Total federal tax:		4,500.00	15.00	16,865.81	26.00	32,914.19	29.00
NRTxCr* — 15% of	11,038	1,655.70		1,655.70		1,655.70	
Basic federal tax (BFT)		**2,844.30**	**15.00**	**15,210.11**	**26.00**	**31,258.49**	**29.00**

* Non-refundable tax credit using only the "Basic personal amount"

Alberta, using 2013 Rates

Salary/Interest Income		Average 30,000	Marginal 100.00	Average 90,000	Marginal 100.00	Average 150,000	Marginal 100.00
Basic federal tax		2,844.30	15.00	15,210.11	26.00	31,258.49	29.00
Alberta tax							
10% of taxable income		3,000.00	10.00	9,000.00	10.00	15,000.00	10.00
		3,000.00	10.00	9,000.00	10.00	15,000.00	10.00
NRTxCr — 10% of	17,593	1,759.30		1,759.30		1,759.30	
Total Alberta tax		**1,240.70**	**10.00**	**7,240.70**	**10.00**	**13,240.70**	**10.00**
Total tax		4,085.00	25.00	22,450.81	36.00	44,499.19	39.00
Average tax rate		*13.62%*		*24.95%*		*29.67%*	
Marginal tax rate			*25.00%*		*36.00%*		*39.00%*

British Columbia, using 2013 Rates

Salary/Interest Income		Average 30,000	Marginal 100.00	Average 90,000	Marginal 100.00	Average 150,000	Marginal 100.00
Basic federal tax		2,844.30	15.00	15,210.11	26.00	31,258.49	29.00
B.C. tax							
5.06% on the first	37,568	1,518.00	5.06	1,900.94		1,900.94	
7.70% on the next	37,570			2,892.89		2,892.89	
10.50% on the next	11,130			1,168.65	12.29	1,168.65	
12.29 on the next	18,486			458.66		2,271.93	
14.70% over	104,754					6,651.16	14.70
		1,518.00	5.06	6,421.14	12.29	14,885.57	14.70
NRTxCr — 5.24% of	10,276	519.97		519.97		519.97	
Total B.C. tax		**998.03**	**5.06**	**5,901.18**	**12.29**	**14,365.61**	**14.70**
Total tax		3,842.33	20.06	21,111.29	38.29	45,624.10	43.70
Average tax rate		*12.81%*		*23.46%*		*30.42%*	
Marginal tax rate			*20.06%*		*38.29%*		*43.70%*

Manitoba, using 2013 Rates

Salary/Interest Income		Average 30,000	Marginal 100.00	Average 90,000	Marginal 100.00	Average 150,000	Marginal 100.00
Basic federal tax		2,844.30	15.00	15,210.11	26.00	31,258.49	29.00
Manitoba tax							
10.80% on the first	31,000	3,240.00	10.80	3,348.00		3,348.00	
12.75% on the next	36,000			4,590.00		4,590.00	
17.40% over	67,000			4,002.00	17.40	14,442.00	17.40
		3,240.00	10.80	11,940.00	17.40	22,380.00	17.40
NRTxCr — 10.80% of	8,884	959.47		959.47		959.47	
Total Manitoba tax		**2,280.53**	**10.80**	**10,980.53**	**17.40**	**21,420.53**	**17.40**
Total tax		5,124.83	25.80	26,190.64	43.40	52,679.02	46.40
Average tax rate		*17.08%*		*29.10%*		*35.12%*	
Marginal tax rate			*25.80%*		*43.40%*		*46.40%*

New Brunswick, using 2013 Rates

Salary/Interest Income		Average 30,000	Marginal 100.00	Average 90,000	Marginal 100.00	Average 150,000	Marginal 100.00
Basic federal tax		2,844.30	15.00	15,210.11	26.00	31,258.49	29.00
N.B. tax							
9.10% on the first	38,954	2,730.00	9.10	3,544.81		3,544.81	
12.10% on the next	38,954			4,713.43		4,713.43	
12.40% on the next	48,754			1,499.41	12.40	6,045.50	
14.30% over	126,662					3,337.33	14.30
		2,730.00	9.10	9,757.66	12.40	17,641.08	14.30
NRTxCr — 9.10% of	9,388	854.31		854.31		854.31	
Total N.B. tax		**1,875.69**	**9.10**	**8,903.35**	**12.40**	**16,786.77**	**14.30**
Total tax		4,719.99	24.10	24,113.46	38.40	48,045.26	43.30
Average tax rate		*15.73%*		*26.79%*		*32.03%*	
Marginal tax rate			*24.10%*		*38.40%*		*43.30%*

Newfoundland and Labrador, using 2013 Rates

Salary/Interest Income		Average 30,000	Marginal 100.00	Average 90,000	Marginal 100.00	Average 150,000	Marginal 100.00
Basic federal tax		2,844.30	15.00	15,210.11	26.00	31,258.49	29.00
Nfld. tax							
7.70% on the first	33,748	2,310.00	7.70	2,598.60		2,598.60	
12.50% on the next	33,748			4,218.50		4,218.50	
13.30% over	67,496			2,993.03	13.30	10,973.03	13.30
		2,310.00	7.70	9,810.13	13.30	17,790.13	13.30
NRTxCr — 7.70% of	8,451	650.73		650.73		650.73	
Total NL tax		**1,659.27**	**7.70**	**9,159.40**	**13.30**	**17,139.40**	**13.30**
Total tax		4,503.57	22.70	24,369.51	39.30	48,397.89	42.30
Average tax rate		*15.01%*		*27.08%*		*32.27%*	
Marginal tax rate			*22.70%*		*39.30%*		*42.30%*

Northwest Territories, using 2013 Rates

Salary/Interest Income		Average 30,000	Marginal 100.00	Average 90,000	Marginal 100.00	Average 150,000	Marginal 100.00
Basic federal tax		2,844.30	15.00	15,210.11	26.00	31,258.49	29.00
N.W.T. tax							
5.90% on the first	39,453	1,770.00	5.90	2,327.73		2,327.73	
8.60% on the next	39,455			3,393.13		3,393.13	
12.20% on the next	49,378			1,353.22	12.20	6,024.12	
14.05% over	128,286					3,050.82	14.05
		1,770.00	5.90	7,074.08	12.20	14,795.79	14.05
NRTxCr — 5.90% of	13,546	799.21		799.21		799.21	
Total N.W.T. tax		**970.79**	**5.90**	**6,274.87**	**12.20**	**13,996.58**	**14.05**
Total tax		3,815.09	20.90	21,484.98	38.20	45,255.07	43.05
Average tax rate		*12.72%*		*23.87%*		*30.17%*	
Marginal tax rate			*20.90%*		*38.20%*		*43.05%*

Nova Scotia, using 2013 Rates

Salary/Interest Income		Average 30,000	Marginal 100.00	Average 90,000	Marginal 100.00	Average 150,000	Marginal 100.00
Basic federal tax		2,844.30	15.00	15,210.11	26.00	31,258.49	29.00
N.S. tax							
8.79% on the first	29,590	2,600.96	14.95	2,600.96		2,600.96	
14.95% on the next	29,590	61.30		4,423.71		4,423.71	
16.67% on the next	33,820			5,137.69	16.67	5,637.79	
17.50% on the next	57,000					9,975.00	17.50
21.00% over	150,000						
		2,662.26	14.95	12,162.36	16.67	22,637.46	17.50
NRTxCr — 8.79% of	8,481	745.48		745.48		745.48	
Total NS tax		**1,916.78**	**14.95**	**11,416.88**	**16.67**	**21,891.98**	**17.50**
Total tax		4,761.08	29.95	26,626.99	42.67	53,150.47	46.50
Average tax rate		*15.87%*		*29.59%*		*35.43%*	
Marginal tax rate			*29.95%*		*42.67%*		*46.50%*

Nunavut, using 2013 Rates

Salary/Interest Income		Average 30,000	Marginal 100.00	Average 90,000	Marginal 100.00	Average 150,000	Marginal 100.00
Basic federal tax		2,844.30	15.00	15,210.11	26.00	31,258.49	29.00
Nunavut tax							
4.0% on the first	41,535	1,200.00	4.00	1,661.40		1,661.40	
7.0% on the next	41,535			2,907.45		2,907.45	
9.0 on the next	51,983			623.70	9.00	4,678.47	
11.5% over	135,054					1,718.79	11.50
		1,200.00	4.00	5,192.55	9.00	10,966.11	11.50
NRTxCr — 4.0% of	12,455	498.20		498.20		498.20	
Total Nunavut tax		**701.80**	**4.00**	**4,694.35**	**9.00**	**10,467.91**	**11.50**
Total tax		3,546.10	19.00	19,904.46	35.00	41,726.40	40.50
Average tax rate		*11.82%*		*22.12%*		*27.82%*	
Marginal tax rate			*19.00%*		*35.00%*		*40.50%*

Ontario, using 2013 Rates

Salary/Interest Income		Average 30,000	Marginal 100.00	Average 90,000	Marginal 100.00	Average 150,000	Marginal 100.00
Basic federal tax		2,844.30	15.00	15,210.11	26.00	31,258.49	29.00
Ontario tax							
5.05% on the first	39,723	1,515.00	5.05	2,006.01		2,006.01	
9.15% on the next	39,725			3,634.84		3,634.84	
11.16% over	429,552			1,177.60	11.16	7,873.60	11.16
13.16% over	509,000						
		1,515.00	5.05	6,818.45	11.16	13,514.45	11.16
NRTxCr — 6.05% of	8,681	483.49		483.49		483.49	
	(1)	1,031.51	5.05	6,334.97	11.16	13,030.97	11.16
Surtax: 20% of (1) over	4,162	0.00		409.19	2.23	1,748.39	2.23
Surtax: 36% of (1) over	5,249	0.00		304.55	4.02	2,715.11	4.02
Total Ontario tax		**1,031.51**	**5.05**	**7,048.71**	**17.41**	**17,494.47**	**17.41**
Total tax		3,875.81	20.05	22,258.82	43.41	48,752.96	46.41
Average tax rate		*12.92%*		*24.73%*		*32.50%*	
Marginal tax rate			*20.05%*		*43.41%*		*46.41%*

Prince Edward Island, using 2013 Rates

Salary/Interest Income		Average 30,000	Marginal 100.00	Average 90,000	Marginal 100.00	Average 150,000	Marginal 100.00
Basic federal tax		2,844.30	15.00	15,210.11	26.00	31,258.49	29.00
P.E.I. tax							
9.8% on the first	31,984	2,940.00	9.80	3,134.43		3,134.43	
13.8 on the next	31,985			4,413.93		4,413.93	
16.7% over	63,969			4,347.18	16.70	14,367.18	16.70
		2,940.00	9.80	11,895.54	16.70	21,915.54	16.70
NRTxCr — 9.8% of	7,708	755.38		755.38		755.38	
	(1)	2,184.62	9.80	11,140.16	16.70	21,160.16	16.70
Surtax: 10% of (1) over	12,500	0.00		0.00		866.02	1.67
Total P.E.I. tax		**2,184.62**	**9.80**	**11,140.16**	**16.70**	**22,026.17**	**18.37**
Total tax		5,028.92	24.80	26,350.27	42.70	53,284.66	47.37
Average tax rate		*16.76%*		*29.28%*		*35.52%*	
Marginal tax rate			*24.80%*		*42.70%*		*47.37%*

Quebec,* using 2013 Rates

Salary/Interest Income		Average 30,000	Marginal 100.00	Average 90,000	Marginal 100.00	Average 150,000	Marginal 100.00
Basic federal tax (BFT)		2,844.30	15.00	15,210.11	26.00	31,258.49	29.00
Refundable federal tax abatement of 16.5% of BFT		**469.31**	**2.48**	**2,509.67**	**4.29**	**5,157.65**	**4.79**
BFT – Net of abatement credit		**2,374.99**	**12.53**	**12,700.44**	**21.71**	**26,100.84**	**24.21**
Quebec tax							
16.00% on the first	41,095	4,800.00	16.00	6,575.20		6,575.20	
20.00% on the next	41,095			8,219.00		8,219.00	
24.00% over	17,810			1,874.40	24.00	4,274.40	
25.75% over	100,000					12,875.00	25.75
		4,800.00	16.00	16,668.60	24.00	31,943.60	25.75
NRTxCr — 20.00% of	11,195	2,239.00		2,239.00		2,239.00	
Total Quebec tax		**2,561.00**	**16.00**	**14,429.60**	**24.00**	**29,704.60**	**25.75**
Total tax		4,935.99	28.53	27,130.04	45.71	55,805.44	49.97
Average tax rate		*16.45%*		*30.14%*		*37.20%*	
Marginal tax rate			*28.53%*		*45.71%*		*49.97%*

*Quebec residents file a separate tax return for federal and provincial taxes.

Saskatchewan, using 2013 Rates

Salary/Interest Income		Average 30,000	Marginal 100.00	Average 90,000	Marginal 100.00	Average 150,000	Marginal 100.00
Basic federal tax		2,844.30	15.00	15,210.11	26.00	31,258.49	29.00
Sask. tax							
11% on the first	42,906	3,300.00	11.00	4,719.66		4,719.66	
13% on the next	79,683			6,122.22	13.00	10,358.79	
15% over	122,589					4,111.65	15.00
		3,300.00	11.00	10,841.88	13.00	19,190.10	15.00
NRTxCr — 11% of	15,241	1,676.51		1,676.51		1,676.51	
Total Sask. tax		**1,623.49**	**11.00**	**9,165.37**	**13.00**	**17,513.59**	**15.00**
Total tax		4,467.79	26.00	24,375.48	39.00	48,772.08	44.00
Average tax rate		*14.89%*		*27.08%*		*32.51%*	
Marginal tax rate			*26.00%*		*39.00%*		*44.00%*

Yukon, using 2013 Rates

Salary/Interest Income		Average 30,000	Marginal 100.00	Average 90,000	Marginal 100.00	Average 150,000	Marginal 100.00
Basic federal tax		2,844.30	15.00	15,210.11	26.00	31,258.49	29.00
Yukon tax							
7.04% on the first	43,561	2,112.00	7.04	3,066.69		3,066.69	
9.68 on the next	43,562			4,216.80		4,216.80	
11.44 on the next	47,931			329.13	11.44	5,483.31	
12.76% over	135,054					1,907.11	12.76
		2,112.00	7.04	7,612.62	11.44	14,673.91	12.76
NRTxCr — 7.04% of	11,038	777.08		777.08		777.08	
(1)		1,334.92	7.04	6,835.55	11.44	13,896.84	12.76
Surtax: 5% of (1) over	6,000	0.00		41.78	0.57	394.84	0.64
Total Yukon tax		**1,334.92**	**7.04**	**6,877.33**	**12.01**	**14,291.68**	**13.40**
Total tax		4,179.22	22.04	22,087.44	38.01	45,550.17	42.40
Average tax rate		13.93%		24.54%		30.37%	
Marginal tax rate			22.04%		38.01%		42.40%

Calculation of Marginal Rates with Surtaxes

If the surtax is not present in the average-tax calculation, it is not included in the marginal tax calculation. However, if the surtax is present in the average-tax calculation, it is included in the marginal tax calculation. The student needs to understand when the surtax is included in the marginal tax calculation. The federal surtax has, for the time being, been eliminated. However, several provinces still have surtaxes (supposedly temporary taxes, usually on higher income only), and the student must understand when to include the surtax in the calculation of the marginal rate. The surtaxes mean that one must calculate the average rate first to be able to calculate the marginal rate with the appropriate surtaxes.

PROBLEM

Gerry is thrilled. His new job gives him a salary increase of $20,000 — from $80,000 to $100,000. He does a quick calculation of his marginal tax rate on $80,000 and uses it to estimate his new take-home pay. Using 2013 actual tax rates and ignoring CPP and EI, calculate the total tax, average tax rate, and marginal tax rate for $80,000 and $100,000. Use the marginal tax rate on $80,000 to estimate his take-home pay for $100,000. What is the difference between this estimate and his actual increase in pay?

Answer:

Taxes	Average	Average	Increase in net pay using		
Taxable Income	80,000	100,000	Actual	Estimate	Difference
Federal	12,895	17,810			
Provincial					
Alberta	6,241	8,241	13,085	13,600	515
British Columbia	4,784	7,130	12,739	13,500	761
Manitoba	9,241	12,721	11,605	12,120	515
New Brunswick	7,663	10,143	12,605	13,120	515
Newfoundland	7,829	10,489	12,425	12,940	515
Northwest Territories	5,055	7,495	12,645	13,160	515
Nova Scotia	9,750	13,142	11,693	12,266	573
Nunavut	3,856	5,594	13,346	14,200	854
Ontario	5,405	8,790	11,700	12,922	1,221
Prince Edward Island	9,470	12,841	11,714	12,260	546
Quebec	12,117	16,830	11,184	12,326	1,142
Saskatchewan	7,865	10,465	12,485	13,000	515
Yukon	5,817	8,079	12,823	13,664	841

Tax Rates	Average	Marginal	Average	Marginal	Difference in Take-home Pay
Taxable Income	80,000	100.00	100,000	100.00	Estimate > Actual
Federal	16.12%	22.00%	17.81%	26.00%	
Provincial					
Alberta	7.80%	10.00%	8.24%	10.00%	2.58%
British Columbia	5.98%	10.50%	7.13%	12.29%	3.80%
Manitoba	11.55%	17.40%	12.72%	17.40%	2.58%
New Brunswick	9.58%	12.40%	10.14%	12.40%	2.58%
Newfoundland	9.79%	13.30%	10.49%	13.30%	2.58%
Northwest Territories	6.32%	12.20%	7.49%	12.20%	2.58%
Nova Scotia	12.19%	16.67%	13.14%	17.50%	2.87%
Nunavut	4.82%	7.00%	5.59%	9.00%	4.27%
Ontario	6.76%	13.39%	8.79%	17.41%	6.11%
Prince Edward Island	11.84%	16.70%	12.84%	18.37%	2.73%
Quebec	12.49%	16.37%	13.89%	19.71%	5.71%
Saskatchewan	9.83%	13.00%	10.47%	13.00%	2.58%
Yukon	7.27%	9.68%	8.08%	12.01%	4.20%

GENERIC TAX RATES

Salary/Interest Income		Average 30,000	Marginal 100.00	Average 80,000	Marginal 100.00	Average 130,000	Marginal 100.00
Federal Tax							
15% on the first	39,500	4,500.00	15.00	5,925.00		5,925.00	
22% on the next	39,500			8,690.00		8,690.00	
26% on the next	48,000			260.00	26.00	12,480.00	
29% over	127,000					870.00	29.00
Total federal tax		4,500.00	15.00	14,875.00		27,965.00	29.00
NRTxCr — 15% of	10,000	1,500.00		1,500.00	26.00	1,500.00	
Basic federal tax (BFT)		**3,000.00**	**15.00**	**13,375.00**	**26.00**	**26,465.00**	**29.00**
Provincial tax							
8% on the first	38,000	2,400.00	8.00	3,040.00		3,040.00	
13% on the next	38,000			4,940.00		4,940.00	
17% over	76,000			680.00	17.00	9,180.00	17.00
Total provincial tax		2,400.00	8.00	8,660.00	17.00	17,160.00	17.00
NRTxCr — 8% of	9,000	720.00		720.00		720.00	
Basic provincial tax (BPT)		**1,680.00**	**8.00**	**7,940.00**	**17.00**	**16,440.00**	**17.00**
Total tax		**4,680.00**	**23.00**	**21,315.00**	**43.00**	**42,905.00**	**46.00**
Average tax rate		15.60%		26.64%		33.00%	
Marginal tax rate			23.040		43.00%		46.00%

TAX CREDITS

	Federal		Provincial
	2008 Actual = Generic	2013	Generic
Dividend Gross-up	45%	38%	45%
Dividend Tax Credit	18.9655%	15.0198%	12%
Pension Amount	$2,000	$2,00	$1,000

CHAPTER 3: CPP, OAS AND EI

	Contribution Rates		Benefits	
Canada Pension Plan (CPP)	2013	Generic	2013	Generic
YMPE	51,100	**46,000**		
YBE	3,500	3,500		
Rate	4.95%	4.95%		
Maximum payable	2,356.20	2,103.75	12,150	**11,500**
5-year average YMPE (AYMPE)	48,600	44,000		
Old Age Security (OAS)	n/a	n/a	6,552,84	**6,400**
Clawback Threshold	70,954	68,000		
Employment Insurance (EI)				
Maximum insurable	47,400	**43,300**		
Rate	1.88%	1.62%		
Maximum amount	891.12	701.46		

CHAPTER 5: RATES FOR PENSIONS

	Money Purchase Limit	RRSP Dollar Limit	Defined Benefit Limit 1/9 of the Money Purchase Limit
2010	22,450	22,000	2,494.44
2011	22,970	22,450	2,552.22
2012	23,820	22,970	2,646.67
2013	24,270	23,820	2,696.67
2014		24,270	

3

Government
Pension Plans

Learning Objectives

A. Be aware of the magnitude of pension savings and pension plans in Canada.

B. For the Canada Pension Plan (CPP), understand
- the basis for
    - contributing to it, and
    - qualifying for various benefits
- the various benefits available from this program, including a retirement pension, disability benefits and survivor benefits.

C. For Old Age Security (OAS), understand
- the four benefits of this program: OAS pension, Guaranteed Income Supplement (GIS), Allowance and Allowance for Survivor
- the amount of benefits
- who is eligible for these benefits
- the special taxation of the OAS pension.

D. Understand the taxation of CPP contributions by employees and the self-employed and the taxation of CPP retirement income.

E. Calculate the present value at retirement of estimated CPP and OAS retirement pension and the effect of these benefits on retirement savings required.

Margot's mother, **Gloria**, is 64 and has been a widow for three years. Her husband was 65 when he died. She gets a cheque every month from the Canada Pension Plan but is not sure why. She owns her house and has some retirement savings but is concerned about what will happen to her when she can no longer work. Gloria works at the public library in Lunenburg, N.S., making $40,000 per year. The library does not have a pension plan, and Gloria would like to know what the government will pay her when she retires. She has worked at the library for forty-one years, taking only a few months off to have her children.

Margot asks what government pensions she and Craig might be able to expect when they retire. They have heard the CPP will not be able to give them anything. Can this be true after all the years they have paid into it? And what about Old Age Security? Craig's father was very happy when he and Craig's mother started receiving their OAS cheques. He wasn't quite so happy when he filed his first tax return that included the OAS and had to pay most of it back. Although he had not paid into the program, he felt he deserved to keep all of the OAS payments, even though his income from all sources was $83,000 a year. Craig thinks his father has plenty of income without the OAS but would like to be able to explain to him why he had to pay most of it back and now receives only a very small amount of OAS.

A. INTRODUCTION TO CANADA'S RETIREMENT INCOME SYSTEM

At the present time in Canada, there are three types of retirement-income programs: government sponsored programs, employer sponsored programs, and individual.

Retirement Income Programs in Canada

1.	Government sponsored plans	• Canada Pension Plan (CPP) and Quebec Pension Plan (QPP) • Old Age Security (OAS)
2.	Employer-sponsored registered plans	• Registered Pension Plan (RPP) • Deferred Profit Sharing Plan (DPSP) • Group Registered Retirement Savings Plan (GRRSP)
3.	Individual registered plans	• Registered Retirement Savings Plan (RRSP)

Table 3.1 below provides data on the number of Canadians participating in these plans as well as the total contributions for the years shown.

Table 3.1 Number of Contributors and Amount Contributed to Selected Retirement Income Programs

Type of program	Year	Contributions ($000,000)	Contributors (000)	Average contribution ($)
CPP, QPP	2010	47,215	16,517	2,859
RPP	2010	54,200	6,066	8,935
RRSP	2010	33,900	5,956	5,692
Total		135,315		

Sources: Various — Statistics Canada and Régime de rentes du Québec

By the end of 2010, the accumulated assets in these programs totalled $2.2 trillion.

Table 3.2 Market Value of Assets in Selected Retirement Programs December 31, 2010 ($000,000)

Type of program	$	% of total
CPP, QPP	173,897	8.0%
RPP	1,214,426	56.0%
RRSP	782,000	36.0%
Total	2,170,323	100.0%

Source: Statistic Canada, various tables.

As of January 1, 2011, there were 19,463 registered pension plans in Canada (Table 4.1), with total membership of 6,065,751 (Table 4.2) — just over 33% of the labour force. No employer is obligated to set up a pension plan.

In this chapter, we will look at the two government-administered programs: the Canada Pension Plan (CPP) and Old Age Security (OAS). These programs provide not only pensions to retirees, but also benefits to widowed spouses, orphaned children, and the disabled. The **Canada Pension Plan (CPP)** has no residency requirement — pensioners can live anywhere in the world and collect it. It is, however, a form of **social insurance,** meaning a pensioner must have contributed to it to collect it. The amount of the CPP benefit is prorated according to contributions made — the number of years worked and the amount of contributions made to CPP. In Quebec, the CPP is replaced by the **Quebec Pension Plan (QPP)**. The **Old Age Security (OAS)** program pays the OAS pension and also the **Guaranteed Income Supplement (GIS),** which is available to low-income seniors. The OAS program has some residency requirements — a pensioner must have lived in Canada for a certain number of years to collect these benefits. OAS and GIS are forms of **public assistance** and are available to all those who have lived in Canada, even if they have not worked here. OAS and GIS are paid out of general tax revenues, and no direct contributions are required. The OAS program began in 1927, while CPP was introduced in 1966.

B.   CANADA PENSION PLAN (CPP)

The Canada Pension Plan is a mandatory, contributory plan. The benefits received relate to earnings and contributions. *Mandatory* means that everyone who is eligible must contribute to the CPP. *Contributory* means that both employees and employers make contributions. CPP provides the following **benefits** for contributors:

- **Retirement pensions** are paid monthly to people aged 60 and up who have contributed to the CPP at least once. The amount of CPP retirement income to which pensioners are entitled depends on how much and for how long (the contributory period) they contributed to the plan. The age at which these pensioners choose to retire also affects the amount received.

- **Survivor benefits** are paid to the survivors if the contributor dies. Survivor benefits include:
  1. a Lump Sum Death Benefit paid to the estate of the contributor
  2. a Survivor Benefit payable to the surviving spouse
  3. a Children of Deceased Contributors Benefit.

- **Disability benefits** are payable if the contributor becomes disabled. It includes:
  1. a benefit payable to the disabled contributor
  2. a Children of Disabled Contributor Benefit payable to dependent children of contributors who are receiving CPP disability benefits.

Table 3.3 shows the maximum amounts of the various CPP benefits available for 2013. The percentages on the right are based on the pension benefits being 100% and are provided to give an indication of the scale of each benefit compared with the retirement pension. Current payment rates for CPP and OAS can, as of this writing, can be found on the Service Canada website <www.servicecanada.gc.ca>. The site is regularly updated and the paths can change. The fastest route is to Google "CPP benefits 2013." As with generic tax rates in earlier chapters, the generic rates in the table are the rates used in the examples.

   The second part of the table shows how Disability, Survivor, and the new Post-Retirement Benefit are calculated based on a fix amount for some and then some percentage of the Retirement Benefit.

Table 3.3 CPP Maximum Benefits for 2013

	Actual 2013 Rates			Generic per year
	$ per Month	$ per Year	%	$
Retirement (at age 65)	1,012.50	12,150.00	100.0%	11,500
Post-Retirement Benefit (at age 65)	25.31	303.72	2.5%	288
Disability	1,212.90	14,554.80	119.8%	14,000
Survivor (less than age 65)	556.64	6,679.68	55.0%	6,413
Survivor (age 65 and over)	604.50	7,254.00	59.7%	6,900
Children of disabled contributors	228.66	2,743.92	22.6%	2,714
Children of deceased contributors	228.66	2,743.92	22.6%	2,714
Survivor and retirement combined	1,012.50	12,150.00	100.0%	11,500
Survivor and disability combined	1,212.90	14,554.80	119.8%	14,000
Death benefit (one-time payment)	2,500.00			

Retirement benefit	25% of 5-year average YMPE			
	Earnings-related	Flat amount	Total/ Month	Total/ Year
Disability: Retirement × 75%	759.38	453.52	1,212.90	14,554.74
Survivor (< age 65): Retirement × 37.5%	379.69	176.95	556.64	6,679.65
Survivor (age 65 and over): Retirement × 60%	604.50		607.50	7,290.00
Post Retirement: Retirement × 1/40 (2.5%)	25.31		25.31	303.75

Source: <www.servicecanada.gc.ca>

The CPP retirement pension, for any year, is **fully taxable** and does not qualify for the pension credit in the non-refundable tax credits. In addition, all CPP benefits are **indexed**; i.e., they are increased each January to reflect increases in the cost of living for the prior year. A person can receive two CPP benefits at the same time. For instance, a widow(er) could receive both the retirement pension and a survivor benefit. In that case, there is a maximum amount of benefit that can be received from the combined benefits.

CPP Contributions

Everyone in Canada over the age of 18 who earns income must contribute to the CPP. **Earned income** for the CPP includes salary, self-employed income after operating expenses, and commissions. The employer matches the contribution made by the employee; i.e., the employer makes a contribution each month that is equal to that of the employee. Self-employed taxpayers pay both the employee and the employer's contribution.

Contributions stop when the employee:

- starts to receive a disability benefit
- is 65 or older and, even if working, chooses not to contribute
- reaches the age of 70.

The total period of time during which you must contribute is called your **contributory period**. The contributory period is one of the factors that determines the amount of the CPP benefit. Low-earning years can be omitted from the calculation to maximize the amount of the benefit. Low-earning years include:

- any month eligible for CPP disability pension
- periods at home raising children under the age of 7
- low income months after the age of 65
- sixteen percent, up to 7.5 years, of the lowest earning years in the contributory period. This moves to 17 percent, a maximum of eight years, in 2014.

The amount of the contributions is based on pensionable earnings and the contribution rate. **Pensionable earnings** are the amount of annual earnings on which the employee and the employer pay CPP contributions. There is a minimum and a maximum amount of pensionable earnings.

- The **minimum amount of pensionable earnings** is called the **Year's Basic Exemption (YBE)** and is the first amount of salary on which no one pays CPP contributions. It is $3,500 for 2013, which has been this amount for several years.
- The **maximum amount of pensionable earnings** is called the **Yearly Maximum Pensionable Earnings (YMPE)** and is the maximum amount of income on which one pays CPP contributions. This maximum changes every year and is $51,100 for 2013. We will use a generic earnings amount of $46,000.

The amount paid is called the **annual contribution**. It is calculated by multiplying the **contribution rate** by the pensionable earnings. Pensionable earnings is the *lesser of* YMPE and earned income minus YBE. For 2013, the annual maximum contribution is $2,356.20 [a contribution rate of 4.95% × (51,100 – 3,500)]. This $2,356.20 is paid both by the employer and the employee; i.e., the total maximum contribution for each employee is $4,712.40.

> Margot wants to see exactly how the calculations are done. She is self-employed and has net income (gross income minus operating expenses) of about $59,200 a year, while Craig earns $92,000 in salary.

Francesca gives them the following example using generic rates to illustrate how CPP contributions are calculated.

Example 1 Sonia, Craig's niece, makes $41,400 a year. She has told Craig that she thinks it is very strange that she has to pay almost as much in CPP contributions as Craig, who makes twice as much as she does.

	Margot	Craig	Sonia
Net income or salary	59,200	92,000	41,400
Pensionable income	46,000	46,000	41,400
Year's basic exemption (YBE)	3,500	3,500	3,500
Earnings subject to contribution	42,500	42,500	37,900
Contribution rate	4.95%	4.95%	4.95%
Contribution	2,103.75	2,103.75	1,876.05

When Sonia retires, if her salary and Craig's salary remain the same as they are now, Sonia will receive almost as much CPP retirement pension as Craig. This scenario will be illustrated in Example 2, where the benefits are described.

> Margot remembers the days when she was making a lot less, $40,000 per year, and wonders if she was paying the same CPP contribution rates then. And if the rates were lower, what effect do they have on her CPP pension when she collects it? Francesca tells her that the CPP pension is based on contributions that are indexed to inflation. So while Margot was paying a lot less 15 or 20 years ago, she can still collect the maximum if her CPP pensionable earnings remain higher than the YMPE.
>
> Francesca then shows Craig and Margot the following table, which shows the history of CPP contributions.

Craig understands that the CPP maximum should increase each year as a result of inflation. However, he is concerned that the contribution rate has been rising substantially in the past few years.

Table 3.4 History of CPP Contribution Rates and Pensionable Earnings

Year	Employee contribution rate %	Maximum pensionable earnings	Year's basic exemption	Employee contribution $	Self-employed contribution $
1966 to 1986	1.8%	5,000–25,800	600–2,500		
1987	1.9%	25,900	2,500	444.60	889.20
1988	2.0%	26,500	2,600	478.00	956.00
1989	2.1%	27,700	2,700	525.00	1,050.00
1900	2.2%	28,900	2,800	574.20	1,148.40
1991	2.3%	30,500	3,000	632.50	1,265.00
1992	2.4%	32,200	3,200	696.00	1,392.00
1993	2.5%	33,400	3,300	752.50	1,505.00
1994	2.6%	34,400	3,400	806.00	1,612.00
1995	2.7%	34,900	3,400	850.50	1,701.00
1996	2.8%	35,400	3,500	893.20	1,786.40
1997	3.0%	35,800	3,500	969.00	1,938.00
1998	3.2%	36,900	3,500	1,068.80	2,137.60
1999	3.5%	37,400	3,500	1,186.50	2,373.00
2000	3.9%	37,600	3,500	1,329.90	2,659.80
2001	4.3%	38,300	3,500	1,496.40	2,992.80
2002	4.7%	39,100	3,500	1,673.20	3,346.40
2003	4.95%*	39,900	3,500	1,801.80	3,603.60
2004	4.95%*	40,500	3,500	1,831.50	3,663.00
2005	4.95%*	41,100	3,500	1,861.20	3,722.40
2006	4.95%*	42,100	3,500	1,910.70	3,821.40
2007	4.95%*	43,700	3,500	1,989.90	3,979.80
2008	4.95%*	44,900	3,500	2,049.30	4,098.60
2009	4.95%*	46,300	3,500	2,118.60	4,237.20
2010	4.95%*	47,200	3,500	2,163.15	4,326.30
2011	4.95%*	48,300	3,500	2,217.60	4,435.20
2012	4.95%*	50,100	3,500	2,306.70	4,613.40
2013	4.95%*	51,100	3,500	2,356.20	4,712.40
Generic	4.95%*	46,000	3,500	2,103.75	4,207.50
5-year average 2009–2013 Actual		48,600			
5-year average Generic		46,200			

Source: <www.cra-arc.gc.ca>

*This is the **Steady-State Financing Rate** (4.95% × 2 = **9.9%**), described below.

Craig's concern was shared by many people who foresaw a smaller labour force having to finance the large number of "baby boomers." There were dire predictions of the next generation having a larger and larger burden to carry as this substantial proportion of the population lived longer and expected to live well. This situation has been addressed by what is called **steady-state financing**.

Steady-State Financing

The CPP was set up in 1966 as a "pay as you go," or unfunded pension plan — that is, a system that supports retiree benefits largely by the current year's contributions. It was expected that the combined employee and employer rates would never exceed 5.5% (2.75% each). Changing demographics, economic developments, and improved benefits have caused a significant increase in the contribution rate. With the CPP fund invested in low-yield, non-negotiable government securities, the federal and provincial finance ministers, in one of their five-times-yearly reviews in 1996, found the finances of the CPP in serious trouble. Not only were the combined contribution rates expected to rise to 10.1% by 2016 and 14.2% by 2030, but the CPP reserve fund was expected to be exhausted by 2015.

Consultations were conducted across the country, and changes were made effective April 1, 1998. The key change was the introduction of "steady-state" financing for CPP instead of "pay as you go." With steady-state financing, the contribution rate increased more rapidly in the short term to build up the reserve, and then stabilized. At the steady-state rate of 4.95% or a combined rate of 9.9%, as outlined in Bill C-2 in 1997, the plan will have a five-year benefit payout reserve; i.e., it will be 20% funded.

The legislation also brought a change in how the CPP funds are invested. Before Bill C-2, the funds were **passively invested** in a diversified portfolio of equity securities which replicated the TSE 300-stock composite index and a world market index. After Bill C-2, up to half of the domestic portfolio started to be invested by professional portfolios managers who expect to beat these index returns; i.e., up to half the fund is **actively managed**. The **Canada Pension Plan Investment Board (CPPIB)** was created by Parliament in 1997 to obtain a higher return than had been achieved by investing in bonds. It is estimated that, by 2016, the CPP portfolio of investments (called the **CPP Reserve Fund**, those funds not needed to pay current benefits) will grow to $250 billion, with half of that amount invested in the market. Although the government has detached itself from managing the fund, there is always some danger that future governments could appoint a compliant board willing to invest to create jobs in the short term to buy votes.

As of March 2008, there was a total of $122.8 billion in the CPP Reserve Fund invested in public and private equities, real estate, inflation-indexed bonds, infrastructure, and fixed income. About $65.1 billion is invested in Canada in a broadly diversified portfolio, while the remainder is invested globally. Information on the investments can be found at the board's website: <www.cppib.ca>.

Table 3.5 Asset Mix of CPP Investments as at March 31, 2013 ($ billions)

Assets	Total $	Total %
Public equities	59.0	32.2%
Private equities	32.7	17.8%
Fixed income	60.8	33.1%
Real estate	19.9	10.8%
Infrastructure	11.2	6.1%
	$183.5	**100.0%**

Source: <www.cppib.ca>

CPP Retirement Pension

This benefit is designed to replace approximately 25% of the five-year average YMPE adjusted for inflation. Pensionable earnings for 2013 are $47,600 (51,100 – 3,500), while the **full (or "maximum") pension for 2013 is $12,150,** which is 25.5% of $47,600.

The calculation of the pension depends on a number of factors, including:

• number of years the contribution were made
• number of years the contributions equalled the yearly maximum, and
• whether or not the contributions are still being made

Human Resources and Social Development Canada (HRSDC) can provide an estimate of the pension. It is also stated on the **Statement of Contributions**, which includes a history of:

• annual contributions
• when the contributions were based on the maximum pensionable earnings, and
• monthly benefit available now based on contributions made to date.

The Statement of Contributions also contains information on the amount of disability benefits and survivor benefits the taxpayer and the taxpayer's dependants could receive. It is mailed out to each taxpayer each year. To get an estimate of your own pension or to see a sample statement, go to Social Development Canada's website: <www.hrsdc.gc.ca>.

The CPP pension benefit ends when the pensioner dies. Since CPP benefits are paid at the beginning of the month, the last payment is in the month of death.

Example 2 shows the effect of the maximum CPP pensionable earnings on both the amount of CPP contributions and CPP retirement income.

Example 2   While Sonia's salary is less than half of Craig's, her earnings subject to contribution and her contributions are 89% of Craig's. As a result, she can expect to collect about 89% of the full CPP pension when she is retired.

From Example 1	Craig	Sonia
Net income or salary	92,000	41,400
	100.0%	45.0%
Earnings subject to contribution	42,500	37,900
Contributions	2,103.75	1,876.05
	100.0%	89.2%
Expected CPP retirement income	11,500	10,255
	100.0%	89.2%

You can apply for the pension at age 59 but payments must start no later than one year from the date of application. A retiree can collect a full or partial CPP pension if he or she has made at least one contribution to the plan and is at least 60 years old whether or not still working.

Early and Deferred Retirement

The full or maximum CPP pension is the amount that is paid when the retiree is age 65. However, a contributor can take the CPP pension as early as age 60. **Early retirement** results in a reduced CPP pension — it is reduced by 0.6% for each month before the sixty-fifth birthday. Thus, a CPP pension taken at age 60 will be reduced by 36% (60 months × 0.6%) and is not recalculated at age 65; i.e., the amount the retiree begins to receive before the age of 65 will *not* go up to 100% at age 65.

Similarly, a retiree can defer retirement and not collect this pension until age 70. The pension is increased by 0.7% each month for every month after the sixty-fifth birthday so that, at age 70, a retiree can collect 142% (100% at age 65 plus 60 months times 0.7%) of the maximum pension, which is $16,330 using the generic pension. The 0.6% decrease and 0.7% increase used to be 0.5%. The change is being phased in as shown in the following table. All of the examples and homework questions will assume the changes are fully implemented.

Table 3.6 Schedule for Phasing-in Changes to CPP Pension

Retire in	Early Retirement		Late Retirement	
	Decrease / month	Maximum decrease	Increase / month	Maximum increase
Old Rule	0.50%	30.00%	0.50%	30.00%
2011	0.50%	30.00%	0.57%	34.20%
2012	0.52%	31.20%	0.64%	38.40%
2013	0.54%	32.40%	0.70%	42.00%
2014	0.56%	33.60%		
2015	0.58%	34.80%		
2016	0.60%	36.00%		

Example 3 compares the value of taking a reduced pension at age 60 with taking the full pension at age 65. Notice that the pension at age 65 must be brought back to age 60 in order to compare the two options. According to time value of money principles, one cannot compare the present value of cash flows at age 60 with the present value of different cash flows at age 65 — both must be at either age 60 or age 65.

Example 3   Myra, aged 58, wonders if she should start collecting the CPP pension at 60 or wait until she is 65 or 70. If she waits until 65, she is eligible for $11,500 per year. We will use a real rate (without inflation) of return on bonds of 4% per year.

At Age 60

A woman aged 60 has a 51% chance of living to 85. What is the present value of her CPP pension at age 60 if she thinks she will live to age 85? The payments are received monthly at the beginning of the month, but we will use annual beginning-of-the year payments for this analysis. If she takes the CPP retirement pension at age 60, she will receive 64% (0.6% a month × 60 months less) of the full benefit she could receive at age 65.

The Data

Annual income	**PMT** = $11,500 × 64% (0.6 per month × 60 months = $7,360
Number of years	**n** = 25 years
Annual interest rate	**k** = 4%

The Timeline

T_0	T_1	T_2	T_3		T_{25}
60	61 yrs	62 yrs	63 yrs	...	85
7,360	7,360	7,360	7,360	...	7,360
PVA?					

The Calculation

$PVA_{age\ 60} = \$7,360_{BOM}\ (PVIFA_{25,\ 4\%}) = \mathbf{\$119,578}$ at age **60**.

At Age 65

Let us now compare this result to Myra taking the CPP pension at age 65 with no reduction.

The Data

Monthly income	**PMT** = $11,500
Number of years	**n** = 20 years
Annual interest rate	**k** = 4%

The Timeline

T_0	T_1		T_5	T_6		T_{25}
60	61 yrs	...	65 yrs	66 yrs	...	85
			11,500	11,500	...	11,500
PV?			PVA?			

The Calculations

$PVA_{age\ 65}$ = $11,500 ($PVIFA_{20,\ 4\%}$) = **$162,540** at age 65.

Now we will find the value at age 60 in order to be able to compare it to the first calculation. Since we used months in the first calculation, we must also use months in for the present value calculation.

$PVA_{age\ 60}$ = $162,540 ($PVIFA_{5,\ 4\%}$) = **$133,596** at age 65.

The following table summarizes the results of the two calculations above.

Take CPP at age:	60	65
Annual pension	7,360	11,500
Deduct 0.5% a month for each month before age 65	*64%*	*100%*
Number of years to age 85	25	20
Amount/year	7,360	11,500
Present value at age 65	n/a	162,540
Present value at age 60	**119,578**	**133,596**

If Myra lives to the age of 85, she will be better off taking the CPP at age 65 by $14,018 ($133,596 – $119,578) since the CPP is offering a rather large incentive for people to defer taking this retirement pension. Unfortunately, Myra does not know how long she will live.

Post-Retirement Benefit (PRB)

A person can take the CPP pension at age 60 while continuing to work full time. Their CPP pension will be reduced as described above. However, a CPP contributor can also take the CPP pension while continuing to work and contribute to the plan. As will be seen in Chapter 4, Registered Pension Plans do not allow you to both contribute to a RPP and receive a pension from that RPP at the same time but the CPP system now has a provision for contributing while receiving the retirement pension.

Table 3.7 Options for Contributing to and Collecting from the CPP

	Still Working		Not Working	
	Contribute to CPP	Take CPP Pension	Contribute to CPP	Take CPP Pension
Less than age 65	• must contribute	• can take	• cannot contribute	• can take
Age 65 to 69	• can contribute	• can take	• cannot contribute	• can take
Age 70 and over	• cannot contribute	• cant take	• cannot contribute	• can take

Contributors who are taking the CPP pension and continue to pay CPP contributions do not increase their CPP pension but rather earn the **Post-Retirement Benefit (PRB)**. The maximum amount of the PRB is 1/40 or 2.5% of the maximum pension amount. Each year of contributions creates a new PRB that is automatically paid the following year with any CPP pension; that is, the retiree does not have to apply for it. The first PRB is paid in 2013 based on 2012 income and maximum pensionable earnings. Each year's CPP contributions earn a PRB which is paid automatically the following year until the retiree dies. Each year, it increases by the amount of CPP contributions for the prior year. Note the following with regard to the PRB:

- It is mandatory to pay into it; that is, to make CPP contributions, if you are
  - under age 65,
  - working, and
  - receiving the CPP retirement pension.
- It is indexed annually.
- There is:
  - no disability or survivor coverage
  - no credit splitting or pension sharing
  - no retroactive contributions to buy back service prior to 2012
  - no increasing it by delaying it
  - no making partial contributions
  - no opting out if you are under age 65.

Example 4   A person, aged 65, making over the year's maximum pensionable earnings of $50,100 in 2012 will pay CPP contributions of $2,306.70 [($50,100 – 3,500) × 4.95%] and their 2013 PRB is $296.00 as shown in the following table.

$ nominal	2012	2013	2012	2013
	at age 65	at age 66	at age 68	at age 68
CPP Contributions — actual	2,306.70	2,356.20	2,306.70	2,356.20
CPP Pensionable earnings	50,100	51,100	50,100	51,100
YMPE — actual	50,100	51,100	50,100	51,100
PRB pays 1/40 of maximum CPP pension each year	2.5%	2.5%	2.5%	2.5%
Maximum CPP pension = 25% of pensionable earnings	25%	25%	25%	25%
MPEA — actual 5-year average YPME	47,360	48,600	47,360	48,600
AAF — adjustment for age	100.0%	100.0%	125.2%	125.2%
PRB the following year	**$296.00**	**$303.75**	**$370.59**	**$380.30**

The 2012 calculation
= (2012 pensionable earnings ÷ 2012 YMPE) × 2.5% x 25% × MPEA × AAF
= (50,100 ÷ 50,100) × 2.5% × 25% x 47,360 × 1.00

AAF = Actuarial Adjustment Factor = phased-in factor reflecting
- a 0.6% per month decrease before the age of 65 and
- a 0.7% increase after age 65

3 years = 36 months x .007/month = 25.2% increase

This table shows the calculation for the Post-Retirement Benefit for the following year, 2013 and the calculation of the PRB for someone taking CPP pension for the first time at the age of 68 and continuing to make CPP contributions.

How much is their total income from the two CPP plans in real dollars; that is without including the inflation adjustment for 2013 for both pensions (without including the adjustment for inflation in the second year)?

	2013	2014	2013	2014
PRB — Year 1	296	296	371	371
PRB — Year 2		304		380
Total	296	600	371	751
CPP Pension	11,500	11,500	14,398	14,392
Total	11,796	12,100	14,769	15,149

Cancelling CPP Retirement Pension

Retirees can change their mind and cancel the pension benefits up to six months after beginning to receive them. In this situation, benefits received must be paid back. If you were working while you received them, contributions made toward the Post-Retirement benefit are not refunded.

Pension Sharing or Assignment

This concept entails the sharing of CPP pension for spouses and common-law partners who are living together; i.e., not separated or divorced. A **spouse** is a person to whom one is legally married. A **common-law partner**, of either the same or opposite sex, is a person with whom one has had a conjugal relationship for at least one year. (The legislation on same-sex relationships is in a state of change, and rules that apply to the Income Tax Act do not necessarily apply to other legislation.) The amount of pension that can be shared is based on:

• the length of the contributory period, and
• the length of time of cohabitation.

Both spouses must be at least 60 years old and receiving the CPP pension if both contributed. If only one contributed, the CPP pension can also be shared. Example 5 shows the calculation of the amount to be shared between a married couple and the effect of the sharing on the CPP retirement income for each.

Example 5   Joanne and Pete have been married for 24 years. Joanne has contributed to the CPP for 40 years and can collect a full CPP pension of $11,500 per year. Pete has worked for 36 years and, if he retired now, could collect $9,000 per year (a fictitious amount). They have been careful to split their other taxable income in retirement and would like to also split their CPP pension.

How much can they split? Joanne can split 60% (24 ÷ 40) of her retirement pension with Pete. She can split $6,900 (11,500 × 0.6) equally with Pete and keep the remaining $4,600 (11,500 – 6,900). Pete can split 66.67% (24 ÷ 36) of his pension with Joanne. He can split $6,000 (9,000 × 0.6667) and keep the remaining $3,000 (9,000 – $6,000).

	Total	Joanne	Pete
Number of years contributed to CPP		40	36
Number of years married		24	24
% that can be shared		24 ÷ 40	24 ÷ 36
		60.00%	66.67%
CPP pension — total	**20,500**	**11,500**	**9,000**
CPP to split	12,900	6,900	6,000
50% of Joanne's to Pete	0	(3,450)	3,450
50% of Pete's to Joanne	0	3,000	(3,000)
Total each	12,900	6,450	6,450
Amount not split	7,600	4,600	3,000
Total taxable CPP pension	20,500	11,050	9,450

Credit Splitting

Couples who are divided by divorce or separation and former common-law partners can split the CPP pension credits they accrued while they were living together. Credit splitting is mandatory but not automatic — an application must be made. Each party can obtain a split even though one or the other may have remarried or if one spouse or partner did not work outside the home.

Late Applications

A retiree should apply for CPP retirement benefits six months before retiring. The pension starts the month after the application is received. Retirees over age 65 can receive up to 12 months back payments going back no further than the 65th birthday. If the retiree is under age 70, the back payments increase the monthly pension as outlined above; that is, by 0.7% a month, and the adjustment is permanent.

CPP Disability Benefits

Disability benefits are paid to contributors and to any dependent children they may have. There are **four qualifications** for this benefit:

1. The disability must be "severe and prolonged" and can be either mental or physical. **Severe** means one cannot work regularly at any job because of the disability. **Prolonged** means the condition either is long-term or will result in death.
2. The applicant contributed to the CPP
   - for at least four of the past six years, or
   - for at least 25 years and made valid contributions to the Plan during three of the past six years.
3. The applicant must be under the age of 65.
4. The applicant must apply in writing.

This is not permanent and will **stop**:

- when the beneficiary is able to go back to work (i.e., is no longer disabled)
- at age 65 when the CPP pension starts (or between ages 60 and 65 if early retirement is taken), or
- upon death.

Disability benefits can be received at the same time as survivor benefits.

A **Children's Benefit** is paid to dependent children of people receiving the CPP disability benefit. The child must be less than 18 years old, or between 18 and 25 and in school full time. The monthly benefit is indexed annually to inflation. For children under the age of 18, it is paid to the person with whom the child lives. The benefit is taxable. If the child is 18 to 25 and still in school, the benefit will be paid directly to the child.

CPP **disability benefits end** when a person turns 65. At that point, the person begins to collect the retirement pension. The drop in CPP benefits is more than offset by the receipt of Old Age Security benefits. Example 6 illustrates the effect on total government income when the CPP disability benefit ends and CPP retirement income and OAS pension begin.

Example 6   Ryan is 64 years of age. He is currently receiving the CPP disability benefit of $14,000 per year (a generic rate). Next year, when he turns 65, he will begin to receive the CPP pension and Old Age Security, but he will no longer receive the CPP disability benefit.

	Age 64	Age 65
CPP	14,000	11,500
OAS	0	6,400
Total	14,000	17,900

CPP Survivor Benefits

These benefits are paid to the deceased contributor's estate, spouse, or common-law partner, and to children. There are three types of survivor benefits:

1. The **survivor's benefit** is a monthly benefit paid to the contributor's surviving spouse or common-law partner. If the deceased contributor and the spouse were legally separated but not divorced and the deceased had no common-law partner, the surviving spouse may be able to collect this benefit. If the deceased died after January 1, 1998, a same-sex surviving partner may be eligible to collect.

   If the survivor is 65 years of age or older, the maximum pension is 60% of the deceased's pension. For spouses under the age of 65, the amount is reduced until, at age 35, a healthy surviving spouse who is not raising a dependent child would receive nothing until age 65 or until they became disabled. A healthy working spouse under the age of 35 who has dependent children can collect a flat amount plus 37.5% of the deceased's "calculated" retirement pension.

2. The **children's benefit** is a monthly benefit paid to the contributor's dependent children. The benefit is paid to the person with whom the child is living and is taxable.

3. The **death benefit** is a one-time payment. The benefit is six months of retirement pension, to a maximum amount of $2,500. The pension is the amount actually being paid or what it would have been had the contributor been 65 when death occurred.

For survivor benefits to be payable, the contributor must have made contributions for at least three years. If the contributory period is longer than nine years, the contributor must have paid into the CPP for the lesser of:

- at least 1/3 of the calendar years in the contributory period, or
- ten calendar years.

The survivor's benefit and children's benefit both continue even if the surviving spouse remarries. For the surviving spouse or partner over age 35, the survivor's benefit stops a month after the death of the survivor. The children's benefit stops when the child turns 18 unless the child is still in school full time. In that case, the children's benefit continues until the earliest of:

- the completion of school, or
- age 25.

C. OLD AGE SECURITY PROGRAM (OAS)

The Old Age Security (OAS) program was set up in 1952 to replace a 25-year old system whereby the federal and provincial governments together provided old-age benefits that were **means tested** (i.e., the more income you have, the less you get). The benefits paid out of this program continue to be means tested, although the program is now funded by the federal government alone out of general tax revenues.

All programs are **indexed** quarterly using the consumer price index to measure cost-of-living changes. The adjustment for inflation occurs four times a year, although it does not reduce the benefit if the cost of living falls. The four benefits provided are:

1. Old Age Security pension
2. Guaranteed Income Supplement (GIS)
3. Allowance, and
4. Allowance for the survivor

The following table summarizes the benefits available under the OAS program as well as the maximum amount of each benefit. Generic rates will be used in the Examples, Questions and Problems.

Table 3.8 OAS Maximum Benefits

	Quarter 1, 2013			Generic	
	Per month	Per year	Maximum income*	Per year	Maximum income
OAS pension	546.07	6,552.84	n/a	6,400	
GIS: single person	740.44	8,885.28	16,560	7,900	15,800
GIS: spouse/partner of a non-pensioner	740.44	8,885.28	39,696	7,900	37,880
GIS: spouse/partner of a pensioner	490.96	5,891.52	21,888	5,200	20,800
GIS: spouse/partner of an allowance recipient	490.96	5,891.52	39,696	5,200	37,880
Allowance	1,037.03	12,444.36	30,672	11,735	29,226
Allowance for the survivor	1,161.01	13,932.12	22,320	13,008	21,289
OAS threshold		70,954		68,000	

*See Example 11
Source: <www.servicecanada.gc.ca>

Old Age Security Pension

This pension is available at the age of 65 to people who are or were Canadian citizens or legal residents of Canada. The following table shows the criteria for determining whether or not a person is eligible for a full or partial OAS pension. The age of 65 is being phased out over the six years starting in 2023 so that by January 2029, the age will be 67. Related OAS programs will also be increased by two years changing from ages 60 to 64 to ages 62 to 66. For this edition, we will continue to use age 65.

Table 3.9 Eligibility for Full or Partial OAS Pension

Now Living	Age	Legal resident of Canada or Canadian citizen when:	Lived in Canada after age 18 for at least:
In Canada	65 or older	OAS was approved	10 years
Outside Canada	65 or older	You stopped living in Canada	20 years

Source: <www.servicecanada.gc.ca>

People who are not in either of these two categories may still qualify for an OAS pension since Canada has **social security agreements** with several countries. A meaningful discussion of this topic is beyond the scope of this introductory course. The list of countries is available at the Service Canada website: <www.servicecanada.gc.ca>.

Benefits can continue to be received outside of Canada if:

- the recipient lived in Canada for at least 20 years after reaching age 18, **or**
- the residency requirement is met by living or working in another country with which Canada has a social security agreement.

If **neither** of these conditions is met, the benefits will continue for the departure month plus six more months. Benefit payments will start again when residency in Canada is resumed. Benefits do not stop until the recipient dies, except in the case that the recipient leaves the country.

Full OAS Pension

The following table shows the various criteria that must be met to receive a full OAS pension.

Table 3.10 Eligibility to Receive a Full Pension

1.	Lived in Canada 40 years between ages **18 and 65**
or	
2.	Lived in Canada sometime after turning **18** and before **July 1, 1977,** and was born before July 1, 1952
and	Lived in Canada immediately before the OAS was approved for:
2a.	10 years
	or
2b.	1 year, **and**
	• before the past 10 years
	• at least **3 times as long** as the total absences in the past 10 years
	• after turning 18

Source: <www.servicecanada.gc.ca>

Example 7 shows how someone who was not born in Canada and lived here for a total of only 14 years, 12 of them immediately before retiring here, can qualify for a full OAS pension.

Example 7   Maurice was born in France in 1948. He lived in Canada for two years, between March 1980 and April 1982. At that time, he moved to Hong Kong and returned to Canada in 2001. Since Maurice meets criterion 2a above, he qualifies for a full OAS pension, even though he has lived in Canada for only fourteen years by the time he turned 65 in 2013.

Partial OAS Pension

A partial pension is available to people who have lived in Canada after age 18 and do not meet the criteria for a full OAS pension. For each year of residence, the recipient receives 1/40 of the full pension. This portion is determined when the application is made and never increases (except for the cost-of-living adjustment). Example 8 takes the information from Example 7 and has Maurice living in Canada for 10 years before July 1, 1977, but for only six months before applying for the OAS pension.

Example 8   Assume Maurice lived in Canada for 10 years before July 1, 1977, left for more than 30 years, and returned to Canada six months before he applied for the OAS pension. He would be eligible for 25% (10 ÷ 40) of the OAS.

Deferred Applications

The federal government wishes to encourage people to defer the OAS. As a result, beginning on July 1, 2013, the OAS will increase 0.6% for every month beyond age 65 that the citizen defers the application for OAS.

Late Applications

Late applicants can receive up to one year of retroactive payments. In addition, OAS benefits can be stopped and reinstated later, although no retroactive payments are available in this case.

Taxation of OAS Income

The OAS pension is considered **taxable income**. In addition, it is subject to a special tax referred to as a **clawback**. This tax is 15% of OAS pension income over $68,000 (the generic **threshold amount**) until, at total income of $110,667 [($6,400 OAS pension ÷ 15%) + $68,000], the entire OAS pension benefit is clawed back. Example 9 shows the calculation of the OAS clawback.

Example 9   Martha's total income will be $71,400 including $6,400 OAS pension. Because Martha's income is above the OAS threshold, she must repay 15% of her OAS income over $68,000. For Martha, the clawback will be $510, leaving her with an OAS of $5,890 ($6,400 – $510) and taxable income of $70,890.

Income		
OAS (maximum)		6,400
CPP (maximum)		11,500
Taxable dividend income		1,500
Pension		52,000
		71,400
Clawback calculation		
Taxable income	71,400	
minus threshold	68,000	
She must repay 15% of:	3,400	
Amount to pay back		510
Taxable income		70,890

Effect of the Clawback on People Who Retire at Age 65 or Later

The OAS clawback is based on income received in the prior 6 to 18 months. Thus, income received in 2012 is the basis for the clawback for the second half of 2013 (July to December) and the first half of 2014 (January to June).

Total Income For	Affects the Clawback for:	
	July–December	January–June
2012	2013	2014
2013	2014	2015
2014	2015	2016
2015	2016	2017
2016	2017	2018

Example 10A Dennis retired on June 30, 2013 having turned 63 on June 28, 2013. His income for 2012 was $140,000 while his annual pension income is $65,000, CPP is 11,500 and OAS is 6,400 when he begins to collect it. What effect does the clawback have on his OAS income when he begins to collect it?

Dennis is not eligible to collect OAS until he turns 65, two years after he retires. His income for the year before he begins to collect it will be $65,000 plus CPP of $11,500 and OAS of $6,400. As a result, his OAS will be clawed back by $2,235 (65,000 + 11,500 + 6,400 minus the threshold of 68,000 = 14,900 × 15%).

Example 10B Let's assume Dennis turned 65 on June 28, 2013. Now he is eligible to collect the OAS pension as soon as he retires and is, without the clawback eligible to receive OAS pension of $3,200 in 2013 and $6,400 in 2014 and 2015. How will the clawback affect him now?

OAS before clawback	Clawback for July–Dec.	Clawback for Jan.–June	Clawback is based on income for	Salary	Pension	CPP	OAS	Total	OAS After Clawback
3,200	2013		2012	140,000	0	0	0	140,000	0
3,200		2014							0
3,200	2014		2013	70,000	32,500	5,750	3,200	111,450	0
3,200		2015							0
3,200	2015		2014	0	65,000	11,500	6,400	82,900	2,083
3,200		2016							2,083

Since Dennis' OAS is being completely clawed back for the first 24 months of his retirement, he should not take the OAS when he retires. If he waits for two years until July 1, 2015, his OAS will increase by 14.4% (0.6% a month for 24 months) from $6,400 to $7,321.60.

Guaranteed Income Supplement (GIS)

The GIS is available to low-income seniors who are collecting the OAS. The amount received is based on the prior year's income. Individuals must apply for it every year, either automatically by filing a tax return or by filling in an actual application. Many people fail to reapply and thus fail to continue to receive it. They may not receive it one year due to a large RRSP withdrawal the prior year but are eligible the following year if income drops again. It is available to both single individuals and those who are married or living in common-law relationships (both same-sex and opposite-sex). If one of the people in a marriage or common-law relationship begins to live in a hospital or nursing home, each can be considered a single person if that will result in a higher benefit. If the couple separates for any other reason, each will be considered a single person, and that may affect the amount of the benefits.

The GIS is paid when total "other income," including any income that does not come from the OAS program, falls below the threshold shown in **Table 3.6**. **Other income includes:**
- CPP or QPP pension benefits
- Private pension income
- RRSPs cashed in
- Employment insurance benefits
- Interest income
- Capital gains
- Dividend income
- Income from rental properties
- Employment income
- Other sources (e.g., workers' compensation benefits, alimony, etc.).

Other income does **not** include:
- OAS pension
- GIS income
- Allowance income from the OAS program.

The first $3,500 of employment income does not affect the amount of GIS a person can receive. The GIS is intended to assist low-income seniors living in Canada. Thus, payments will continue for only the month of departure and for six more months after leaving the country. It can be started again by reapplying. Benefits also stop:
- if the recipient's income gets too high
- if the recipient fails to reapply each April, or
- if the recipient dies.

GIS is **not taxable income,** although it is reported on the income tax return.

The **maximum GIS is reduced** by $1 for every $2 of "other income" received so that, at $15,800 (the generic maximum income), the GIS is reduced to $0. It is reduced $1 for every $4 for the combined income of a couple. Example 11 illustrates the calculation of the GIS for someone whose total income without the GIS is $16,400.

Example 11   Mrs. Thomas received $16,400, including the OAS. She is eligible for GIS of $2,900. The following table shows how much GIS she will be able to collect based on her "other income."

	Total income	Other income
CPP retirement benefits	5,700	5,700
CPP survivor benefits	1,100	1,100
OAS	6,400	
GIS		
Deceased husband's pension	3,200	3,200
	16,400	10,000
GIS — maximum		7,900
less $1 reduction for every $2 other income		5,000
GIS available to Mrs. Thomas		**2,900**

This table shows how much Mrs. Thomas will receive if her "Other Income" increases.

Total "Other income"	10,000	12,500	15,000
Maximum income	15,800	15,800	15,800
Amount of other income she can earn before			
becoming ineligible for the GIS	5,800	3,300	800
GIS — maximum	7,900	7,900	7,900
Less $1 reduction for every $2 other income	5,000	6,250	7,500
GIS available to Mrs. Thomas	2,900	1,650	400

Suppose Mr. and Mrs. Thomas are both receiving the OAS pension and their combined "other income" is $10,000 The second example assumes their combined "other income" is $15,000. How much GIS could they collect?

	Each	Together	Each	Together
Total "Other Income"	5,000	10,000	7,500	15,000
GIS — maximum	5,200	10,400	5,200	10,400
Less $1 reduction for every				
$4 other income	1,250	2,500	1,875	3,750
GIS available to them	3,950	7,900	3,325	6,650

Allowance

The OAS Allowance is available to spouses or partners of low-income seniors who meet *all* of the following criteria:

• the spouse or partner receives or could receive the OAS pension and the GIS
• they are aged 60 to 64 (at 65, Allowance recipients become eligible for the OAS pension and GIS)
• they are Canadian citizens or legal residents of Canada, and
• they have lived in Canada for at least 10 years since age 18 or come from a country with whom Canada has a social security agreement.

Benefits are based on the combined income for the prior year of the recipient and the recipient's spouse or partner. Income here has the same definition as income for the GIS. The benefit can begin the month following the sixtieth birthday of the recipient. Late applications are eligible for up to 12 months retroactive benefits, including the month of application. Benefits will cease when:

• combined income is too high
• recipient leaves Canada for more than six months
• recipient fails to reapply
• spouse or partner dies (see "Allowance for the Survivor" below)
• relationship breaks down and the couple is no longer living together; the payments will end three months later, **or**
• recipient dies.

The Allowance is **not taxable,** although it must be reported on the income tax return.

Allowance for the Survivor

This OAS benefit is available to seniors who meet the following criteria:

• they are 60 to 64 years of age
• they are Canadian citizens or legal residents when application is approved or when they last lived in Canada
• their spouse or partner has died
• they have lived in Canada for at least 10 years since age 18 or have lived in a country that has a social security agreement with Canada.

Income is the same as for GIS benefits. The benefits cease if the recipient remarries or lives in a common-law relationship for at least one year. Benefits end when any of the following occurs:

- income is more than the maximum allowed
- residence in Canada ceases for more than six months
- the recipient fails to reapply
- a new cohabitation relationship is established, **or**
- the recipient dies.

This benefit ends at age 65, when it is automatically changed to the OAS pension. At that point, the pensioner may be eligible for the GIS. This benefit is not taxable, although it must be reported on the income tax return.

D. TAXATION OF CPP CONTRIBUTIONS AND RETIREMENT PENSION

> Craig thinks there should be lower tax rates after retirement, or tax breaks, or something. "After all," he says, "you have worked so hard to get to retirement. Why shouldn't there be some tax breaks in retirement?"
>
> "What if your retirement income is $100,000 a year? Would you like retirement tax breaks then?" asks Francesca.
>
> Craig laughs. "I don't think I'm going to have to worry about taxes on that kind of income in my retirement." Francesca offers to show him an example of the difference between the taxation of pension income and salaried income.

Employment Insurance (EI)

Employee CPP contributions and Employment Insurance (EI) premiums are both eligible for the non-refundable tax credit. CPP contribution rates are given earlier in this chapter. Employment insurance premiums are a certain percentage of maximum insurable earnings, as shown in Table 3.11.

Table 3.11 Employment Insurance Rates

	2013	Generic
Maximum insurable earnings	47,400	43,300
Rate	1.88%	1.62%
EI premium	891.12	701.46

As we will see in Part D of this chapter, employers pay CPP contributions that are the same as employees. However, employers pay 1.4 times what employees pay in EI premiums. Up-to-date rates for both CPP and EI can be found on the Canada Revenue Agency website: <www.cra-arc.gc.ca>.

Income from pension plans is eligible for the $2,000 **federal pension income amount**, which is also part of the non-refundable tax credit. The amount for provincial pension income amount in the non-refundable tax credits varies by province so we will use a generic rate of $1,100. We will compare salaried income before retirement with pension income to see the effect on after-tax, or take-home, pay. Example 12 shows the difference in after-tax income between someone working and someone who is retired.

Example 12   Judy and her grandmother both receive $50,000 a year in income — Judy from her job, her grandmother from various sources of pension income. Because her grandmother does not have to pay CPP contributions and EI premiums, her grandmother's net after deductions is 6.8% higher than Judy's.

	Salary	Pension	Difference
Income	**50,000.00**	**50,000.00**	**0.00**
Federal tax	8,235.00	8,235.00	0.00
Non-refundable tax credits:			
Basic personal amount	10,000.00	10,000.00	0.00
CPP contributions	2,103.75		2,103.75
EI premiums	701.46		701.46
Pension amount		2,000.00	(2,000.00)
	12,805.21	12,000.00	805.21
× 15%	1,920.78	1,800.00	120.78
Basic federal tax (BFT)	6,314.22	6,435.00	(120.78)
Provincial tax	4,600.00	4,600.00	0.00
Non-refundable tax credits			
Basic personal amount	9,000.00	9,000.00	0.00
CPP contributions	2,103.75		2,103.75
EI premiums	701.46		701.46
Pension amount		1,100.00	(1,100.00)
	11,805.21	10,100.00	1,705.21
× 8%	944.42	808.00	136.42
Basic provincial tax (BPT)	3,655.58	3,792.00	(136.42)
Total tax	9,969.80	10,227.00	(257.20)
CPP and EI deductions	2,805.21	0.00	2,805.21
Total deductions	12,775.01	10,227.00	2,548.01
Net after deductions	37,224.99	39,773.00	(2,548.01)
Net as % of income	*74.45%*	*79.55%*	

In addition, for tax years ending after 2000, 50% of CPP contributions on self-employed income is eligible for the non-refundable tax credits (and is thus deducted as a **tax credit**), while the other 50% is deducted as a **tax deduction**. Example 13 shows the difference in after-tax income for self-employed net income and a salary.

Example 13   Judy wants to know how she would be taxed differently if her $50,000 was self-employed income after operating expenses, rather than a salary.

	Salary	Net Income	Difference
Income	50,000.00	50,000.00	0.00
CPP contributions		2,103.75	2,103.75
Taxable income	**50,000.00**	47,896.25	(2,103.75)
Federal tax	8,235.00	7,772.18	(462.82)
Non-refundable tax credits			
Basic personal amount	10,000.00	10,000.00	0.00
CPP — employer contributions	2,103.75	2,103.75	0.00
EI premiums	701.46		(701.46)
Pension amount			0.00
	12,805.21	12,103.75	(701.46)
× 15%	1,920.78	1,815.56	(105.22)
Basic federal tax (BFT)	6,314.22	5,956.61	(357.61)
Provincial tax	4,600.00	4,326.51	(273.49)
Non-refundable tax credits			
Basic personal amount	9,000.00	9,000.00	
CPP — employee contributions	2,103.75	2,103.75	
EI premiums	701.46		(701.46)
Pension amount			0.00
	11,805.21	11,103.75	(701.46)
× 8%	944.42	888.30	(56.12)
Basic provincial tax (BPT)	3,655.58	3,438.21	(217.37)
Total tax	9,969.80	9,394.83	(574.98)
CPP — total contributions	2,103.75	4,207.50	2,103.75
EI premiums	701.46		(701.46)
Total deductions	12,775.01	13,602.33	827.31
Net after deductions	37,224.99	36,397.68	(827.31)
Net as % of income	*74.45%*	*72.80%*	

Margot uses a tax package and does not know exactly how her tax calculations work. Francesca offers to show her the calculation.

In Chapter 1, we looked at the calculation of Craig's take-home pay. Since Margot is self-employed, the calculation of her pay is different because:

• She can deduct work-related expenses (in this case, $800)
• She does not pay Employment Insurance premiums
• She must pay the employer's share of CPP contributions. These are deducted as expenses to arrive at her taxable income.

Like Craig's, Margot's employee CPP contributions are included as part of the non-refundable tax credits.

Margot — Tax Calculations

	Tax Calculation	Income after Tax	Marginal Rate
Gross income	60,000.00	60,000.00	100.00
CPP — Employer's contribution	(2,103.75)		
Miscellaneous expenses	(800.00)	800.00	
Taxable/Net Income	57,096.25	59,200.00	100.00
Federal tax			
15% on the first 39,500	5,925.00		
22% on the next 39,500	3,871.18		22.00
	9,796.18		
Non-refundable tax credits			
Basic personal amount	*10,000.00*		
CPP — Employee's contributions	*2,103.75*	2,103.75	
	12,103.75		
× 15%	1,815.56		
Basic federal tax (BFT)	**7,980.61**		
Provincial tax			
8% on the first 38,000	3,040.00		
13% on the next 38,000	2,482.51		13.00
	5,522.51		
Non-refundable tax credits			
Basic personal amount	*9,000.00*		
CPP contributions	*2,103.75*		
	11,103.75		
× 8%	888.30		
Basic provincial tax (BPT)	**4,634.21**		
Total tax	12,614.83	12,614.83	
CPP — Employer's contributions		2,103.75	
Total deductions		16,822.33	35.00
Net pay		**42,377.68**	65.00
Net pay as % of net income		**71.58%**	
Average tax rate on gross income		*21.02%*	
Marginal tax rate on gross income			*35.00%*

E. EFFECT OF GOVERNMENT PENSIONS ON RETIREMENT SAVINGS REQUIRED

Margot wants to know how the CPP pension and OAS pension will affect their retirement savings needs.

In Chapter 1, we saw that Margot and Craig will need to have total after-tax income of $56,000 — $28,000 each. The following table shows the present value at retirement of:

+ their retirement-spending needs
– what they have in place
= what they need to save by retirement.

From Chapter 1:

	2014	2031–2066				
Margot's age	44	61–96	dies @ 96			
Craig's age	43	60–95	dies @ 95			

	n	k	$ BOY	Before tax	Tax @ 15.21	After tax
Need in retirement	35	3.88%	67,000	1,320,482	200,910	1,119,571
Have in place						
CPP — Margot			8,188			
CPP — Craig			7,360			
Craig's DB pension			28,080			
Total indexed pensions	35	3.88%	43,628	859,850		
Non-indexed pension	35	7.00%	8,100	112,217		
				972,068	147,899	824,168
Shortfall before RRSPs				348,414	53,011	294,403

Let's take a closer look at the CPP calculation from Chapter 1.

Present Value at Retirement of Combined CPP Retirement Pension

	T_0	T_1	...	T_{34}	T_{35}
Margot — age	61	62	...	94	95
Craig — age	60	61	...	93	94
CPP — Margot	8,188	8,188	...	8,188	8,188
CPP — Craig	7,360	7,360	...	7,360	7,360
	15,548	15,548	...	15,548	15,548
	PVA?				

$$\textbf{PVA} = \$15,548_{BOY} \ (\text{PVIFA}_{35 \ years, \ 3.88\%}) = \textbf{\$306,431}$$

The calculation for Margot and Craig is quite straightforward because they are almost the same age and want to plan on living into their mid-90s. Also, they are not including the OAS, which begins at age 65.

Let's change the assumptions:

• They will each collect $3,200 OAS (50% of the full OAS pension) at age 65
• Craig retires at age 60 to catch up on all the books he has been buying but has not had time to read
• Margot continues to work until she is age 67; her CPP will be $13,432 (11,500 × 1.168)
• Craig is not optimistic about his life expectancy and expects to live only until age 84
• Margot thinks she can easily live to age 98
• Since Craig is sitting around reading books while Margot continues to work, they decide they must have all their retirement savings in place by the time Craig retires — they do not want to save any more after Craig retires (this simplifies the calculation: if Margot is still working, her earned income during these years generates RRSP contribution room, and she can continue to contribute to her RRSP).

We will look only at the effect of these changes on the calculations of their government pension income. To make it more interesting, we use a 9% discount rate when inflation is 4%, giving us a real rate of return of 4.81%.

Present Value at Retirement of Combined CPP and OAS Retirement Pension

What is the present value at retirement of their CPP and OAS retirement benefits if Craig retires at age 60 and Margot retires at age 67?

1. The Timeline

	T_0	T_1	...	T_4	T_5	T_6	...	T_{24}	...	T_{36}	T_{37}
Craig's age	60	61	...	64	65	66	...	84			
Margot's age	61	62	...	65	66	67	...	85	...	97	98
CPP — Craig	7,360	7,360	...	7,360	7,360	7,360	...	Dies			
CPP — Margot						13,432	...	13,432	...	13,432	Dies
OAS — Craig					3,200	3,200	...	Dies			
OAS — Margot				3,200	3,200	3,200	...	3,200	...	3,200	
	7,360	7,360	...	10,560	13,760	27,192	...	16,632	...	16,632	
	PV?										

Let's put this information in a table. Margot and Craig will receive $7,360 for four years. Then they will receive $10,560 for one year. And so on.

To find the present value of these cash flows at the date of Craig's retirement:

i. Take the present value of each annuity (for amounts they will receive for more than one year) and for each single amount of government income. Each of these PVAs or PVs is the amount at the beginning of the year(s) for which it was calculated.

ii. Take each of the PVAs and PVs back to Craig's age 60.

iii. Add up all the PVs at Craig's age 60.

2. The Calculation: PV of Total Annual Income

| | | Craig's Age | 60 | 64 | 65 | 66 | 84 | |
		Margot's Age	61	65	66	67	85	98
	CPP — Craig		7,360	7,360	7,360	7,360	Dies	
	CPP — Margot					13,432	13,432	Dies
	OAS — Craig				3,200	3,200		
	OAS — Margot			3,200	3,200	3,200	3,200	
			87,360	10,560	13,760	27,192	16,632	
i.	n 1		4	1	1	18	13	
	k real		4.81%					
	PV or PVA		27,475	10,560	13,760	338,154	165,638	
ii.	n 2		0	4	5	6	24	
	PV of PV(A)		27,475	8,751	10,879	255,093	53,641	
iii.	Total PV		355,838					

n 1 = Number of years of each income stream. When Craig retires at age 60, there will be four years to wait before Margot can begin to collect the OAS. Once Margot begins to collect the CPP, they will both collect both pensions for 18 years before Craig dies. After Craig dies, Margot will continue to receive the CPP and OAS for 13 years.

n 2 = Number of years to discount the present value of each income stream back to Craig's retirement date. For instance, Craig dies at age 84 and Margot lives for another 13 years. The present value of Margot's government income at her age 85 is $165,638. Now we must bring it back 24 years to her age 61.

Alternately, we could calculate the present value at Craig's retirement of each income stream.

2. Alternate Calculation: PV of Each Source of Income

Income	$ BOY	n	k	Formula	PVA	PV
Craig — CPP	7,360	24	4.81%	$PVA_{60} = 7,360_{BOY} (PVIFA_{24,\,4.81\%})$	108,438	108,439
Craig — OAS	3,200	19	4.81%	$PVA_{65} = 3,200_{BOY} (PVIFA_{19,\,4.81\%})$	41,168	
		5	4.81%	$PV_{60} = 41,168 (PVIF_{5,\,4.81\%})$		32,550
Margot — CPP	13,432	31	4.81%	$PVA_{67} = 13,432_{BOY} (PVIFA_{31,\,4.81\%})$	224,463	
		6	4.81%	$PV_{61} = 224,463 (PVIF_{6,\,4.81\%})$		169,328
Margot — OAS	3,200	33	4.81%	$PVA_{65} = 3,200_{BOY} (PVIFA_{33,\,4.81\%})$	54,933	
		4	4.81%	$PV_{61} = 54,933 (PVIF_{4,\,4.81\%})$		45,522
Total						**355,838**

The second method of calculating this present value looks easier but, in fact, it is more difficult to calculate correctly — the problem is with the "n". However, some students may find this method clearer.

SUMMARY

Government pension plans provide a modest but important basis for retirement income. The Canada Pension Plan is based on contributions made throughout one's working life, while Old Age Security is based on residency in Canada. The Guaranteed Income Supplement provides a supplement for seniors whose income is very low. As part of the OAS program, it is based on the number of years and timing of the years one has lived in Canada.

CPP contributions are large enough to have a significant impact on savings for retirement income. In addition, while the CPP and OAS pension benefits are not huge, they do make a significant contribution to the amount of savings required for retirement.

The CPP is a pension plan and contributions to this plan are deducted as part of the non-refundable tax credits for employees and as tax deductions for employers and the self-employed. In following chapters, we will see that contributions to employer-sponsored pension plans and to registered retirement savings plans are tax deductible for everyone concerned.

> Margot's mom, Gloria, is greatly relieved to see that there are options available for her — that after working all her life, she will be able to retire, if not in great comfort, at least above the poverty line. She has her house, which she is prepared to sell if she needs to. She could also turn it into a bed and breakfast in the summer tourist season, at least until she is too old to look after such an enterprise.
>
> As for Craig, he now knows how to explain to his father why he is not "entitled" to keep the entire OAS — he doesn't need it and it is not intended to help make the well-off better off.

SOURCES

- Canada Pension Plan Investment Board <www.cppib.ca>
- Canada Revenue Agency <www.cra-arc.gc.ca>
- Service Canada <www.servicecanada.gc.ca>

KEY TERMS

Actively managed	Means tested
Actuarial Adjustment Factor (AAF)	OAS allowance
Allowance, OAS	Old Age Security (OAS) maximum benefits
Allowance for the Survivor, OAS	Old Age Security (OAS) pension
Assignment	Old Age Security program
Children's benefit	Partial pension, OAS
Clawback	Passively invested
Contribution rate	Pension assignment
Contributory period	Pension income amount
CPP contributions	Pension sharing
CPP disability benefits	Pensionable earnings, CPP
CPP maximum benefits	Post-Retirement Benefits (PRB)
CPP survivor benefits	Public assistance
Credit splitting	Retirement pension, CPP
Death benefit	Social insurance
Disability benefits, CPP	Statement of Contributions
Early retirement	Steady-State Financing
Earned income	Survivor benefits, CPP
Employment insurance (EI) premiums	Tax credit
Full pension, OAS	Tax deduction
Full retirement pension, CPP	Threshold Amount
Guaranteed Income Supplement (GIS)	Yearly Maximum Pensionable Earnings (YMPE)
Maximum GIS	Year's Basic Exemption (YBE)

QUESTIONS AND PROBLEMS

Use generic rates unless the question provides specific actual rates.

CPP Contributions

1. Is sit possible for someone to opt out of making CPP contributions?

2. Is the CPP retirement pension taxable? Indexed?

3. Does earned income for CPP contributions include dividend income?

4. Can you contribute to the CPP at age 70 if you are still working?

5. What is the maximum pensionable earnings using the generic rate? (See Table 3.3)

6. What is the steady-state financing rate for:
   (a) 2003?
   (b) 2005?
   (c) 2013? (See Table 3.4)

7. Up to what percentage of CPP investments can be actively managed?

8. What is the amount of Jamie's CPP contribution using generic rates if his earned income is:
   (a) $48,000 (Answer: $2,103.75)

(b) $32,000 (Answer: $1,410.75)

9. If Jamie's earned income were $48,000 and the year's basic exemption was at 2013 levels, how much will Jamie's CPP contribution be in:
   (a) 2002? (Answer: $1,673.20)
   (b) 2007? (Answer: $1,989.90)
   (c) 2013? (Answer: $2,356.20)

CPP Retirement Pension

10. CPP contributions are based on "pensionable earnings." The pension benefit is intended to be about what percentage of five-year average Yearly Maximum Pensionable Earnings?

11. If a taxpayer has paid the maximum for the required number of years, at what age does he or she qualify for the full (maximum) pension, whether or not still earning a substantial income?

12. Calculate the present value at age 60 of Myra taking the CPP at age 60 and age 65, assuming she lives to age 80. Use a discount rate of 4% a year.

	Age 60	Age 65
Number of years to age 80	20	15
Present value at age 60	104,026	109,297

Post-Retirement Benefit (PRB)

13. If you are collecting the CPP pension and still working, are you required to make CPP contributions if you are:
    (a) less than 65 years old?
    (b) 65 or older?

14. How much is the contribution to the PRB compared to CPP contributions?

15. Does the PRB have all the supplementary benefits such as Survivor benefit and Disability benefit that are part of the CPP program?

16. Diana's salary is $45,000 a year. She is 63 years old and has decided to take her CPP pension.
    (a) Can she elect not to pay into the PRB plan? (Answer: No)
    (b) How much are her;
        i.   pensionable earnings (Answer: $45,000)
        ii. contributions for age 63 in 2012 and age 64 in 2013 if her salary remains the same? (Answer: $2,054.25)
    (c) How much is her AAF — Actuarial Adjustment Factor for her age? (Answer: 85.6%)
    (d) How much is her PRB earned for each year? (Answer: $227.58, $228.97)
    (e) Calculate her total CPP and PRB pension for 2013 and 2014 by completing the following table. (Answer: $10,071.58, $10,300.55)

			2012	**2013**
			at age 63	at age 64
(a)	ii	CPP Contribution		
(b)	i	CPP Pensionable earnings		
		YMPE — actual	50,100	51,100
		PRB pays 1/40 of maximum CPP pension each year	2.5%	2.5%
		Maximum CPP pension = 25% of 5-year average pensionable earnings	25%	25%
		MPEA — 5-year average YMPE	47,360	48,600
(c)		AAF — adjustment for age	85.6%	85.6%
(d)		PRB the following year	$227.58	$228.97

			2013	**2014**
		PRB — year 1	227.58	227.58
		PRB — year 2		228.97
		Total	227.58	456.55
		CPP pension		
(e)		Total		

CPP Pension Sharing

17. Janet is 62, and has worked all of her adult life. She has had several contract positions drafting legislation and implementing new government programs such as Pay Equity and the Office of the Ombudsman. However, she is now finding it increasingly difficult to find work, so she is considering retirement. She might then look for some part-time work, and live off that and her RRSPs and government pensions.
    (a) If Janet qualifies for a full CPP pension at age 65, what percentage and what dollar amount would she receive if she took the CPP pension on her:
        i. 62nd birthday? (Answer: 78.4%, $9,016)
        ii. 69th? (Answer: 133.6%, $15,364)
    (b) If she takes the pension now, will it go up when she turns 65?
    (c) How long does Janet have to change her mind and stop her CPP pension if she should get a job?
    (d) How can Janet find out how much CPP pension she would get?
    (e) Janet's husband is receiving a partial CPP pension, and she can give him part of her CPP pension, since hers is more. What is this called?
    (f) If Janet's partner is a woman, could she share her pension?
    (g) Janet's husband is not yet collecting the CPP pension because he is still working full-time. Would she want to share her pension with him to reduce her taxes?
    (h) If Janet has been married for 1/3 of her contributory period, how much of her pension can she share? If her pension is $9,800, while her husband's is $8,600 (for a total of $18,400), and he has been married for 36% of his contributory period, how much would each receive? (Answer: Janet $9,714.67, husband $8,685.33)

CPP Disability Benefits

18. Mary is 64 and currently receiving the maximum CPP disability benefit.
    (a) How much does she receive annually? (Table 3.3)

(b) If Mary has a son who is 23 and attending university full-time, how much will he receive annually?

(c) What and how much will she receive when she turns 65, including OAS? (Answer: $17,900)

CPP Survivor Benefits

19. Mark and Grace are 66 and retired. Grace dies, leaving Mark frantic as to how he will get along financially without her. Grace was receiving the maximum CPP pension, while Mark is collecting 90% and the OAS (but not GIS — they have rental income).

   (a) If Mark were eligible to receive the full survivor benefit, how much would it be, and what percentage is it of the retirement pension? (Table 3.3)

   (b) How much survivor benefit can Mark collect, given that he is receiving 90% of the full CPP pension? (Answer: $1,150)

   (c) Mark will also receive another benefit upon her death. What is it, and how much is the maximum?

   (d) If Mark marries Theresa, can he continue to receive the survivor benefit?

Old Age Security Pension

20. Is the OAS pension indexed to inflation? How does this work?

21. Randy's grandmother, age 62, came to Canada from Europe 50 years ago and has not ever left. She never worked "outside of the home for money." Can she collect the full OAS pension? (Answer: Yes)

22. Is the OAS taxable?

23. How much OAS do you keep as taxable income if your total income before the clawback is $76,000? (Answer: $5,200)

Guaranteed Income Supplement

24. Lucy's grandmother, Camilla, is 65, and has worked for the past 50 years. Ever since the Canada Pension Plan was introduced in 1966, she has earned slightly more than the CPP pensionable earnings but, as a widow, was not able to save any money. As a result, she is getting the maximum CPP benefit and the maximum OAS.

   (a) How much GIS can Camilla collect? (Answer: $2,150.00)

   (b) Lucy's mother gives Camilla $300 cash a month as a gift to help out. Is this part of Camilla's "income"?

   (c) Is the CPP benefit part of "other monthly" income?

   (d) Camilla is thinking about moving to Vienna for a couple of years. What effect would this have on her GIS?

25. What events (or non-events) will cause the GIS to end?

26. Is the GIS taxable? Reportable?

OAS Allowance

27. Anne is 65 and has just started receiving the full OAS and some GIS. Frank, her husband, is 63. They both worked all their lives at low-paying jobs. They collect CPP pension benefits, but their combined income is below the GIS maximum. Their health is not good, so they work very little now.

    (a) What four criteria must Frank meet to collect the Allowance?

    (b) If they had been living common-law all these years, would this affect his OAS Allowance?

    (c) What will Frank receive annually if he gets the maximum Allowance? (Answer: $11,735)

    (d) What happens to Frank's Allowance if they separate?

    (e) Will Frank continue to get the Allowance when he turns 65?

28. What events would cause the Allowance to stop?

29. Is the Allowance indexed to inflation?

30. Is the Allowance taxable? Reportable on your tax return?

Allowance for the Survivor

31. Anne (from Question 26) dies before Frank turns 65. The Spouse's Allowance stops.

    (a) Does he meet the criteria for the "Allowance for the survivor"? What are the criteria? (Answer: Yes)

    (b) What happens if Frank remarries or lives common-law with someone?

    (c) What events would cause the benefits to stop?

32. Is this benefit taxable? Is it reportable on his tax return?

Marginal Tax Rate with and Without CPP and EI

33. Jason's current salary is $42,000.

    (a) What are Jason's average and marginal tax rates? Calculate his marginal tax rate with and without CPP contributions and EI premiums. (Answer: 17.19%, with 33.49%, without 35.00%)

> Hint: Generally, we do not concern ourselves with the increase in CPP contributions and EI premiums. However, since Jason is below the maximum for both of these, he will pay more CPP and EI, which increase his non-refundable tax credits which, in turn, decrease his taxes. This point is brought up to illustrate marginal tax rates. In reality, it is unlikely (but not impossible) that someone who makes $42,000 would be seeking advice from a financial planner. Once income is over the maximum pensionable earnings and maximum insurable earnings, this issue disappears since both CPP contributions and EI premiums are at their maximums.

    (b) Jason's grandfather has pension income of $42,000. Including the "pension amount", how much does he have after tax? (Answer: $34,573.00) Why is his net income more than Jason's take-home pay? Calculate the difference for each line to see where the differences are.

    (c) Calculate Jason's net pay after tax and CPP contributions if he earns net income of $42,000 from being self-employed. (Answer: $31,478.84) Calculate the difference for each line to see where the differences are.

34. Margot is self-employed. Calculate Margot's tax and CPP payable, average and marginal tax rates on Net income (calculate marginal without CPP in the non-refundable tax credits) if her net income before Employer's CPP contribution is:

	Net Income	Total Tax	Total CPP	Average	Marginal
(a)	40,000	6,158.56	3,613.50	15.40%	28.00%
(b)	60,000	12,894.86	4,207.50	21.49%	35.00%
(c)	80,000	19,970.68	4,207.50	24.96%	39.00%

After-tax Amount of RRSP Contribution

35. For each of the above, assume that Margot makes an RRSP contribution of 18% of her net income. This contribution is tax deductible — her taxable income is reduced by the amount of the RRSP contribution.

    (a) Using the marginal tax rates from the prior question, what is her estimated RRSP contribution after tax?

    > Hint: Use RRSP contribution × (1 − marginal tax rate)] See chart after part b below.

    (b) What is the actual after-tax cost of the RRSP contribution? Calculate the tax from scratch, deducting the RRSP contribution from taxable income.

Net Income	Taxable Income	RRSP after tax	
		Estimate	Actual
40,000	30,993.25	5,184.00	5,534.34
60,000	47,096.25	7,020.00	7,020.00
80,000	63,496.25	8,784.00	9,284.15

    (c) Why are they different?

Present Value of Government Pensions at Retirement

36. Craig and Margot think they will be able to collect the maximum CPP, and estimate they will collect $3,200 OAS each. If they live to ages 89 and 90, respectively, and using a discount rate of 8% when inflation is 3.5%, what is the present value before tax at retirement of their government pensions if they retire when Margot is 61 and Craig is 60? Use annual, beginning of the year cash flows. (Answer: $346,693)

37. Re-do the previous question, assuming that Margot will live to age 95 and Craig will live to age 90, and that they retire when Margot is 64 and Craig is 63. (Answer: $448,309)

RRSP Savings Needed at Retirement

38. Melvyn, age 47, is starting to think about retirement. He does not want to plan on the OAS, so he will make his estimate based on receiving only the CPP pension. He plans to retire at age 62. He estimates he will need $60,000 before tax in retirement to give him the lifestyle he

wants. His father died at 92, so he is going to base his estimate on dying at age 92. He estimates his indexed pension will pay him about $35,000 p.a. Assuming he can save all he needs in an RRSP, and that he currently has $30,000 in an RRSP, how much does he need to save each year from now until retirement to meet his retirement objectives?

Assume:

1. Annual cash flows.
2. All savings are at the end of the year.
3. Retirement consumption occurs at the beginning of the year.
4. He can earn 6% real return on his savings before retirement, and 4% real return is an appropriate discount rate after retirement.

Steps:

1. Draw the timeline.
2. What is the present value of his income needs at retirement? (Answer: $1,079,023)
3a. What is the present value at retirement of his CPP income? (Answer: $162,141)
3b. What is the present value at retirement of his pension? (Answer: $629,430)
4. What is the future value at retirement of his current savings? (Answer: $71,897)
5. How much does he need to save each year to meet his retirement needs? (Answer: $9,261)

39. Re-do the previous problem, assuming that his pension is not indexed and that inflation is 2.5%.

Step 1.   same timeline
Step 2.   no change
Step 3a. no change
Step 3b. non-indexed pension (Answer: $482,210)
Step 4.   no change
Step 5.   PMT = $15,586

4

Registered Pension Plans (RPPs)

Learning Objectives

A. Understand the basic similarities and differences between the two kinds of registered pension plans: Defined Contribution Pension Plans (DCPPs) and Defined Benefit Pension Plans (DBPPs).

B. Know the fundamental requirements of setting up Registered Pension Plans (RPPs).

C. Learn the features of RPPs.

D. Understand the benefits available from RPPs.

E. Understand the requirements for beginning to collect a pension.

F. Examine details of the Ontario Municipal Employees Retirement System (OMERS), which is the third-largest pension plan in Canada.

Craig is an architect. The company he works for has decided to set up a pension plan. Craig and Margot have not managed to save much in their RRSPs because they have been paying their mortgage (unfortunately, they bought at the top of the market so their mortgage is quite high) and Margot took time off work when each of their daughters was born. Therefore, the idea of a pension plan sounds good to them, although they do understand that the pension plan is a form of deferred compensation and that Craig's raises in the future may be less in order to finance the plan. A pension consultant has come to the company to explain the various features available in a pension plan. Craig thought he understood the options when they were presented, but he is having difficulty explaining everything to Margot.

They already have another appointment set up with Francesca, but Margot gives her a call to tell her that they need information on pensions to help them understand the options presented at Craig's company.

INTRODUCTION

As pointed out in the previous chapter, aside from the two government-administered pension plans, there are other types of pension plans that individuals can use to save for retirement. There are Registered Pension Plans (RPPs), which are mostly employer sponsored, and Registered Retirement Savings Plans (RRSPs) for individuals.

The primary differences between employer-sponsored pension plans (RPPs) and registered retirement savings plans (RRSPs) are:

1. RPPs are managed by professional pension fund mangers, while the contributor actively participates in the investment decisions for an RRSP.
2. Funds in an RPP are locked-in; i.e., they cannot be accessed until retirement, while funds in an RRSP can be withdrawn at any time (unless they are in a locked-in RRSP).

High-income owners-managers have specialized vehicles for tax-deferred retirement savings other than RRSPs. There are also ways an employer can provide additional pension savings for key personnel. These means are described in the next chapter. Because the federal and provincial governments want to encourage Canadians to save for retirement, they offer tax incentives for doing so. As a result, these plans all centre around deferring taxation on employment income until the funds are withdrawn from the plan. This is the equivalent of saying that a pension is a form of **deferred compensation** — that is, it is employment income that is not received until retirement. Since registered retirement savings generate tax savings now, there are mechanisms in place to limit contributions (called the **Money Purchase Limit**) and to provide equality between those who are members of registered pension plans and those who are not (called the **Pension Adjustment**). These will be explained in the next chapter. In this chapter, we will focus on the more commonly seen RPPs. Although the focus of this book is retirement planning, information on topics such as registration of the plan, use of excess surplus, and investment restrictions is provided to give students general information about how RPPs are formed and managed.

A. TYPES OF REGISTERED PENSION PLANS

There are two basic types of RPPs:

1. Defined Contribution Pension Plan
2. Defined Benefit Pension Plan

A **Defined Contribution Pension Plan (DCPP)** defines the contribution levels for the employer and the employees but not the level of pension received at retirement. Instead, it provides a pension that is based on contributions made to the plan and the growth of these contributions while the money is in the pension plan. Thus, in a DCPP, *employees* take the investment risk, as the amount of an employee's pension depends on the balance in the fund at the date of retirement.

Technically, a **DCPP** covers *both*:

- a **Money Purchase Plan (MPP)**, whose contribution rates are defined, and
- a **Deferred Profit Sharing Plan (DPSP)**, whose contributions are based on profits

since the amount of the benefit for both plans is determined by the contributions and the income earned on those contributions. However, a money purchase plan is more commonly known as a DCPP, while a deferred profit sharing plan is always referred to as a DPSP. Canada Revenue Agency (CRA) refers only to money purchase plans and defined benefit plans when discussing pension plans (CRA makes this distinction in its Guides). We shall use the term *defined contribution pension plan* to refer to the money purchase pension plan.

Unlike a DCPP, where the pension benefits are undefined, a **Defined Benefit Pension Plan (DBPP)** specifies the amount of the pension benefit using a definite formula that is typically based on the number of years of service as well as being related to earnings during the last few years of employment. In DBPPs, *employers* take the investment risk. Although both employers and employees also have defined contribution levels, it is the employer who must ensure that the plan is funded well enough to pay for the benefits established in the plan.

Most, but not all, private sector plans are defined contribution plans, while most, but not all, public sector plans are defined benefit plans. Table 4.1 below is a summary of Table 4.1a. These tables show the number of plans by type of plan in both the private and public sectors.

Table 4.1 Summary of the Number of RPPs, by Type of Plan, at January 1, 2011

Types of plans	Total plans		Public sector		Private sector		Total plans 1992	Change 2011 > 1992	
	#	%	#	%	#	%		#	%
% in each sector									
Defined contribution	6,826	100.0%	861	12.6%	5,965	87.4%			
Defined benefit	11,975	100.0%	410	3.4%	11,565	96.6%			
Composite/combined	662	100.0%	33	5.0%	629	95.0%			
	19,463	100.0%	1,304	6.7%	18,159	93.3%			
% Type of plan									
Defined contribution	6,826	35.1%	861	66.0%	5,965	32.8%	9,901	–3,075	–31.1%
Defined benefit	11,975	61.5%	410	31.4%	11,565	63.7%	7,870	4,105	52.2%
Composite/combined	662	3.4%	33	2.5%	629	3.5%	257	405	157.6%
	19,463	100.0%	1,304	100.0%	18,159	100.0%	18,028	1,435	8.0%

Source: Statistics Canada Table 280-0016, Registered pension plans (RPPs), members and market value of assets, by type of plan, sector and contributory status

Most plans are in the private sector in part because public sector plans can be very large. Notice also that the number of DC plans has decreased 31.1% from 1992 while the number of DB plans has increased by 52.2%. From January 1, 2003 to January 1, 2007, nearly 3,400 small RPPs were added that are mainly for specified individuals, that is, individuals in Individual Pension Plans (IPPs) for self-employed people, such as doctors, lawyers, and owner-managers, or for "connected persons", such as executives. Without these 3,400 additions for small plans, DBPP increased by only 9.0% and total plans fell by 10.9%. These 3,400 small plans represent less than 0.1% of the total membership. These IPPs and other specialized DBPPs are also known as **designated plans** and are covered in Chapter 5.

Table 4.1a Number of RPPs, by Type of Plan, at January 1, 2011

Types of plans	Total plans			Public sector			Private sector		
	#	% of		#	% of		#	% of	
		Total	Each		Total	Each		Total	Each
Defined contribution									
Money purchase	6,775	34.8%	99.3%	861	66.0%	100.0%	5,914	32.6%	99.1%
Profit sharing	51	0.3%	0.7%	0	0.0%	0.0%	51	0.3%	0.9%
	6,826	35.1%	100.0%	861	66.0%	100.0%	5,965	32.8%	100.0%
Defined benefit									
Final/average	5,784	29.7%	48.3%	337	25.8%	82.2%	5,447	30.0%	47.1%
Career average	5,575	28.6%	46.6%	73	5.6%	17.8%	5,502	30.3%	47.6%
Flat benefit	616	3.2%	5.1%	0	0.0%	0.0%	616	3.4%	5.3%
	11,975	61.5%	100.0%	410	31.4%	100.0%	11,565	63.7%	100.0%
Composite/combined	662	3.4%		33	2.5%		629	3.5%	
	19,463	100.0%		1,304	100.0%		18,159	100.0%	

Source: Statistics Canada Table 280-0016, Registered pension plans (RPPs), members and market value of assets, by type of plan, sector and contributory status

Table 4.2 below is a summary of Table 4.2a. It shows the number of members by type plan in the private and public sectors.

Table 4.2 Summary of the Number of Members of RPPs, at January 1, 2011

Types of plans	Total members		Public sector		Private sector		Total plans 1992	Change 2011> 1992	
	#	%	#	%	#	%		#	% chg
% each sector									
Defined contribution	969,207	100.0%	151,562	15.6%	817,645	84.4%			
Defined benefit	4,484,011	100.0%	2,953,976	65.9%	1,530,035	34.1%			
Composite/combined	612,533	100.0%	35,427	5.8%	577,106	94.2%			
Total	6,065,751	100.0%	3,140,965	51.8%	2,924,786	48.2%			
% type of plan									
Defined contribution	969,207	16.0%	151,562	4.8%	817,645	28.0%	469,144	500,063	106.6%
Defined benefit	4,484,011	73.9%	2,953,976	94.0%	1,530,035	52.3%	4,775,543	−291,532	−6.1%
Composite/combined	612,533	10.1%	35,427	1.1%	577,106	19.7%	73,403	539,130	734.5%
Total	6,065,751	100.0%	3,140,965	100.0%	2,924,786	100.0%	5,318,090	747,661	14.1%

Source: Statistics Canada Table 280-0016, Registered pension plans (RPPs), members and market value of assets, by type of plan, sector and contributory status, 1974 to 2007.

Slightly more members are in the public sector, and most members are in defined benefit plans. Membership in DBPPs is down 6.1% from 1992, while membership in DCPPs has more than doubled. From the detailed Table 4.2a, we can see that the number of members who are in plans providing a pension that is a composite or a combination of DCPP and DBPP has more than doubled between 1992 and 2011 as organizations top up DBPP with DCPP in order to move some of the investment risk from the employer (DBPP) to the employee (DCPP). This hybrid plan is described later in the chapter under "Types of Benefits" while the types of defined benefit plans are discussed in the next chapter.

Table 4.2a Number of Members of RPPs, by Type of Plan, at January 1, 2011

Types of plans	Total members			Public sector			Private sector		
	#	% of Total	% of Each	#	% of Total	% of Each	#	% of Total	% of Each
Defined contribution									
Money purchase	963,294	15.9%	99.4%	151,562	4.8%	100.0%	811,732	27.8%	99.3%
Profit sharing	5,913	0.1%	0.6%	0	0.0%	0.0%	5,913	0.2%	0.7%
	969,207	16.0%	100.0%	151,562	4.8%	100.0%	817,645	28.0%	100.0%
Defined benefit									
Final/average	3,521,311	58.1%	78.5%	2,910,122	92.7%	98.5%	611,189	20.9%	39.9%
Career average	213,391	3.5%	4.8%	43,854	1.4%	1.5%	169,537	5.8%	11.1%
Flat benefit	749,309	12.4%	16.7%	0	0.0%	0.0%	749,309	25.6%	49.0%
	4,484,011	73.9%	100.0%	2,953,976	94.0%	100.0%	1,530,035	52.3%	100.0%
Composite/combined	612,533	10.1%		35,427	1.1%		577,106	19.7%	
	6,065,751	100.0%		3,140,965	100.0%		2,924,786	100.0%	

Source: Statistics Canada Table 280-0016, Registered pension plans (RPPs), members and market value of assets, by type of plan, sector and contributory status

Table 4.3 shows some of the largest RPPs in Canada, including the top 10. Their assets are in millions of dollars. In fact, the Ontario Teachers' Pension Plan Board, the largest RPP, has assets of $116 billion and is the nineteenth largest RPP in the world. For the two columns on the right, "Public" is the public sector while "Private" is the private sector.

Table 4.3 Pension Fund Assets, December 31 2011 ($ millions)

Rank		Defined benefit	Defined contribution	Public	Private
	Canada Pension Plan Investment Board	161,245			Private*
1	Ontario Teachers' Pension Plan Board	116,258		Public	
2	Ontario Municipal Employees Retirement System	55,802		Public	
3	Public Service Pension Plan (Federal)	42,310		Public	
4	Quebec Government and Public Employees Retirement Plan	41,982		Public	
5	Healthcare of Ontario Pension Plan	40,000		Public	
6	B.C. Municipal Pension Fund	27,998		Public	
7	Alberta Local Authorities Pension Plan	19,617		Public	
8	B.C. Public Service Pension Fund	18,635		Public	
9	Ontario Pension Board	18,521		Public	
10	B.C. Teachers' Pension Fund	16,886		Public	
14	Canadian National Railways	14,574			Private
16	Quebec Construction Industry		13,143		Private
21	Nova Scotia Pension Agency		8,208	Public	
22	Royal Bank of Canada		7,541		Private
24	Telus Corp. Pension Plan	6,751			Private
27	Province of Newfoundland & Labrador	5,992		Public	
31	New Brunswick Public Service Superannuation	5,041		Public	
39	Winnipeg Civic Employees'/Police Pension Program	4,380		Public	
55	Bombardier		3,369		Private
58	IBM Canada Ltd		3,219		Private
60	Co-operative Superannuation Society Pension Plan		3,083		Private

Note: Some plans are a combination of defined benefit and defined contribution. This occurred when plans merged. Since the larger plan was defined contribution, they are designated as defined contribution since the defined benefit portion tends to be small.

Source: Benefits Canada <www.benefitscanada.com>
* CPPIB is listed here as a private plan because all employees and all employers in all sectors must contribute.

B. SETTING UP A REGISTERED PENSION PLAN

Registered pension plans can be set up by an employer, a group of employers (in which case they are called multi-employer pension plans or MEPPs[1]), or a union, but employers are not obligated to set up pension plans. An RPP must be set up with the primary purpose to provide a life annuity to retired employees, and an employer must be a contributor if a pension plan is to be registered.

To apply for registration, an Application for Registration of Employees Pension Plan (510), along with a copy of the relevant insurance contract or trust agreement, is sent to the CRA for approval. In addition, the plan must be registered with appropriate federal or provincial pension jurisdiction before deductions become tax-deductible. Any later revision must also go through this approval process.

Contributory or Non-contributory

RPPs can be contributory or non-contributory. In a **non-contributory plan**, employees do not make contributions; only the employer makes contributions to the pension fund. However, in a **contributory plan**, both employees and employers make contributions. Table 4.4 shows that in the public sector, 97.4% of pension *plans* are contributory, while in the private sector, 65.0% are non-contributory. Additionally, between 2002 and 2007, the number of non-contributory plans in the private sector increased by 4,895 due, in large part, to the 3,400 new plans mentioned above for specified individuals.

Tables 4.4 and 4.4a show the same numbers but are set up differently to show different percentages.

---

1   Under a multi-employer pension plan, no more than 95% of active plan members will work for one participating employer. Specified Multi-employer Pension Plans (SMEPPs) is a type of MEPP with at least 15 participating employers, or 10% or more of the active members who are employed by more than one participating employer, whose employer contributions and the benefit level are established by a collective agreement. The International Brotherhood of Electrical Workers Pension Plan is an example of SMEPP and whose members are employed for a particular job as opposed to being hired by a particular employer on an indefinite basis.

Table 4.4 Number of RPPs, by Contributory Status, at January 1, 2011

	Total Plans		Contributory		Non-contributory		Total Plans 1992	
	#	%	#	%	#	%	#	%
Public sector	1,304	100.0%	1,270	97.4%	34	2.6%	1,260	96.6%
Private sector	18,159	100.0%	6,355	35.0%	11,804	65.0%	12,601	69.4%
	19,463	100.0%	7,625	39.2%	11,838	60.8%	13,861	71.2%
Defined contribution	6,826	100.0%	5,488	80.4%	1,338	19.6%	9,901	145.0%
Defined benefit	11,975	100.0%	1,669	13.9%	10,306	86.1%	7,870	65.7%
Other	662	100.0%	468	70.7%	194	29.3%	257	38.8%
	19,463	100.0%	7,625	39.2%	11,838	60.8%	18,028	92.6%

Sources: Statistics Canada , Table 280-0016, Registered pension plans (RPPs), members and market value of assets, by type of plan, sector and contributory status,

Statistics Canada, Table 280-0012, Registered pension plans (RPPs), members and market value of assets, by type of organization, type of plan and contributory status.

Table 4.4a Number of RPPs, by Contributory Status, at January 1, 2011

	Total Plans		Public Sector		Private Sector		Total Plans 1992	
	#	%	#	%	#	%	#	%
Contributory	7,625	100.0%	1,270	16.7%	6,355	83.3%	10,264	134.6%
Non-contributory	11,838	100.0%	34	0.3%	11,804	99.7%	7,764	65.6%
	19,463	100.0%	1,304	6.7%	18,159	93.3%	18,028	92.6%
			Defined Contribution		Defined Benefit		Other	
Contributory	7,625	100.0%	5,488	72.0%	1,669	21.9%	468	6.1%
Non-contributory	11,838	100.0%	1,338	11.3%	10,306	87.1%	194	1.6%
	19,463	100.0%	6,826	35.1%	11,975	61.5%	662	3.4%

Tables 4.5 and 4.5a show that, in the public sector, most *members* of pension plans are in contributory plans while in the private sector, 64% of members are in contributory plans.

Table 4.5 Number of Members, by Contributory Status, at January 1, 2011

	Total Members		Contributory		Non-contributory		Total Plans 1992	
	#	%	#	%	#	%	#	%
Public sector	3,140,965	100.0%	3,134,379	99.8%	6,586	0.2%	1,260	0.0%
Private sector	2,924,786	100.0%	1,961,186	67.1%	963,600	32.9%	12,601	0.4%
	6,065,751	100.0%	5,095,565	84.0%	970,186	16.0%	13,861	0.2%
Defined contribution	969,207	100.0%	785,031	81.0%	184,176	19.0%	9,901	1.0%
Defined benefit	4,484,011	100.0%	3,818,296	85.2%	665,715	14.8%	7,870	0.2%
Other	612,533	100.0%	492,238	80.4%	120,295	19.6%	257	0.0%
	6,065,751	100.0%	5,095,565	84.0%	970,186	16.0%	18,028	0.3%

Sources: Statistics Canada, Table 280-0016, Statistics Canada, Table 280-0012.

Table 4.5a Number of Members, by Contributory Status, at January 1, 2011

	Total Members		Public Sector		Private Sector		Total Plans 1992	
	#	%	#	%	#	%	#	%
Contributory	5,095,565	100.0%	3,134,379	61.5%	1,961,186	38.5%	10,264	0.2%
Non-contributory	970,186	100.0%	6,586	0.7%	963,600	99.3%	7,764	0.8%
	6,065,751	100.0%	3,140,965	51.8%	2,924,786	48.2%	18,028	0.3%
			Defined Contribution		Defined Benefit		Other	
Contributory	5,095,565	100.0%	785,031	15.4%	3,818,296	74.9%	492,238	9.7%
Non-contributory	970,186	100.0%	184,176	19.0%	665,715	68.6%	120,295	12.4%
	6,065,751	100.0%	969,207	16.0%	4,484,011	73.9%	612,533	10.1%

Contributions to an RPP must continue on a regular basis; i.e., there can be no interruption in contributions except when the pension fund has generated a surplus, which can be used to make the contributions. A **surplus** in a pension plan is generated when the investment income grows so much that the assets needed to pay the future liability to retirees is overfunded. There are other circumstances under which individual employees are allowed to suspend contributions for up to two years. However, the intent is not for individuals to stop and start contributions at will. Furthermore, contributions made to the plan can be withdrawn only to provide the retiree with retirement income.

Who Is Covered by the Plan

An RPP must state which class of employees it covers, what the eligibility requirements are, and whether or not participation is compulsory. Since RPP pension benefits are provided as payment for services rendered by the employee, payment of benefits is restricted to employees who are members of the plan, their beneficiaries, or their estates.

Funding the Pension Plan

By law, the pension-plan obligations must be funded through one of the following:

1. an insurance contract with a life insurance company authorized to conduct business in Canada
2. a trust in Canada that has a written trust agreement and whose trustees are either:
   (a) a trust company, or
   (b) individuals of whom:
       • at least three live in Canada, and
       • one is independent to the extent that they are not a significant shareholder, partner, proprietor, or employee of the participating employer.
3. a pension corporation
4. an arrangement administered by the federal or provincial government or agent
5. a combination of the above

Foreign Pension Plans

Foreign employees' pension plans with foreign fund administrators are permitted if:

• the plan is for foreign employees working outside Canada for the Canadian employer, and
• the benefits in the foreign plan are no more beneficial than a Canadian plan could provide.

Taxation

Contributions made by both employers and employees towards a registered plan are tax deductible.

Employee pension contributions are deducted from Net Income (line 150 on the 2013 tax return) on line 207 to arrive at taxable income. The amount of benefit earned for defined benefit plans, the pension adjustment, is reported on line 206 but is not part of the tax payable calculations. The pension adjustment is used to calculate the amount of RRSP contribution room available to the employee for the following year.

RPP pension benefits received are 100% taxable when received. They are eligible for the **pension income amount** (a maximum of $2,000 federal) — a **tax credit** that is part of the non-refundable tax credits. (Remember that tax credits reduce the amount of taxes payable, while **tax deductions** reduce the amount of income on which taxes are calculated.)

Overview of Features, Types and Eligibility

In the next three sections, we will look at various aspects of employer-sponsored pension plans. (Table 4.6 provides a summary of these features.) Table 4.6 offers a summary of:

C. Features of Registered Pension Plans
D. Types of Benefits, and
E. Eligibility for Retirement

Table 4.6 Comparison of Features of Defined Benefit Pension Plans and Defined Contribution Pension Plans

C. Features of Registered Pension Plans

	Defined benefit	Defined contribution
Contributions — employers	Must contribute	Same (as Defined Benefit)
• Minimum contribution	None	1% of employee remuneration
• Additional voluntary contributions (AVC)	Not allowed except to buy past service credits	Allowed
• AVC re: purchase of past service*	Employee required to pay all	Not allowed
Eligible earnings	Salary, wages, etc.	Same
• Prescribed compensation for eligible services	Employees and employers pay premiums to buy years of reduced or no service	Same
• Eligibility	Only employees; i.e., not people on contract or acting as consultants	Same
Investments	Rules to safeguard assets	Same
Loans to employees	Not allowed	Same
• Assignments	Pension benefits may not be used as collateral on a loan	Same
Vesting	Age or service requirements before employer contribution belong to employee	Same
Portability	Vested benefits stay with employee when they change jobs	Same
Use of excess surplus	1. Refund as taxable income 2. Contribution holiday 3. Improve pension benefits	Does not generate excess surplus

D. Types of Benefits

	Defined benefit	Defined contribution
Pension benefits	Calculation known in advance	Depends on the return on investment
• Who bears the investment risk	Employer must ensure there is enough money in the pension-plan fund to pay the pre-determined benefits.	Employee receives a pension based on the value of the pension-plan fund at retirement
• Guaranteed number of years	Life of member	Maximum when paid as a life annuity is the lesser of: 15 years or retirement date to day before 86th birthday
• Indexed to provide inflation protection	Can be built in by means of indexed benefits	Depends on type of income (discussed in Chapter 7)
Maximum benefit		
• Per year of service	Defined benefit limit — $2,696.67 for 2013	None
• Number of years	No legislated maximum after 1991 — was 35 years before 1992 and many plans still have this limit	None
• Annual pension	Defined benefit limit × maximum in plan	None

D. Types of Benefits Continued.

	Defined benefit	Defined contribution
Type of retirement income	Life income, perhaps with annual increases for inflation	Various (discussed in Chapter 7)
Commutation payment**	Allowed with restrictions	Same
Death benefits	Allowed	Same
Life insurance	Part of the contribution may be a life insurance premium	Same
Termination benefits	Paid in various ways	Same

E. Eligibility for Retirement

	Defined benefit	Defined contribution
Normal retirement age (NRA)	Between month of 60th birthday and day before 71st birthday	Same
Early retirement	Before NRA is permitted, with restrictions	Same
• early retirement for disability	Included in some plans	Same

Source: Author's compilation

*A plan which is primarily for the benefit of significant shareholders cannot allow contributions for past-service.

**Commutation payment is a lump sum payment

C. FEATURES OF REGISTERED PENSION PLANS

Contributions

Employers are required to make contributions; in some plans, employees may make optional additional contributions.

Required Contributions

Registered pension plans can be contributory or non-contributory. Employers are always required to contribute to each type, while employees are not required to contribute to non-contributory plans. Contribution levels are normally established by the plan, and for a **DCPP**, the **minimum required** employer contribution is 1% of employee remuneration for the year.

Additional Voluntary Contributions (AVC)

Additional voluntary contributions (AVCs) are permitted in most DCPPs. AVCs made by the member to increase the pension benefit must take into account contributions to earlier pension plans with which the current pension plan has a reciprocal or portability agreement; i.e., a member and/or the employer can contribute to one pension plan for 10 years, transfer the pension or the pension rights to a second employer, and then contribute to a second plan for 25 years. But the member cannot then make an AVC to the second plan if it would exceed the amount of the total tax deduction permitted for a 35-year limit.

If a member has made AVCs to one plan, and these contributions are transferred to a second plan, these AVCs will continue to be counted as AVCs unless the member chooses to use them to make contributions in the new plan. The status of the contributions as AVCs or as required payments can affect the maximum pension (see "Types of Benefits", below).

Members of a DBPP cannot make AVCs to their DBPP although some, such as OMERS discussed later in this chapter, have set up AVCs for pension members. These AVCs are similar to group RRSPs, allowing members to save more in a registered plan, and have the funds grow before tax. However, the AVCs do not increase their DBPP entitlements. In addition, members of DBPP can elect to buy past-service benefits and, in doing so, will probably have to make additional contributions. These contributions are required contributions, *not* additional voluntary contributions. This is discussed in Chapter 5 under "Past Service Pension Adjustment".

The **Co-operative Superannuation Society Pension Plan (CSSPP)** began in Saskatchewan and was incorporated in 1943 as a pension plan for credit union organizations and their employees. It provides retirement services to more than 530 co-operatives and credit unions across Canada. It is also a defined contribution plan. Its Rules and Regulations state:[2]

> Member Employee:
> (a) (i) The required rate of member employee contributions, ranging from 0 to nine (9) percent shall be established by the member employer for each designated unit. Such amount shall be deducted from the salary, wages, or as the case may be, compensation of each member employee at the end of each established pay period and remitted to the Plan.
>
> (ii) A member may contribute in excess of the required rate. Such additional contributions shall be treated as additional voluntary contributions.
>
> Member Employer:
> ... The member employer may contribute at a rate in excess of the required rate as provided (above) on behalf of a member employee. Such contribution shall be designated as an employer unmatched contribution.

However, the CSSPP "Plan Summary" states things somewhat differently and is definitely easier to read:

> The Pension Plan recommends that contributions to the Plan be matched at 5% of salary (5% from the employee and 5% from the employer) up to the annual Canada Pension Plan Year's Maximum Pensionable Earnings (CPP YMPE), and 6% of salary in excess of the CPP YMPE. However, member employers are free to set a greater or lesser contribution rate. Also, both the employer and the employee members may make additional contributions up to the Revenue Canada maximums. Additional employee contributions are not affected by pension legislation and may be withdrawn at termination of employment or retirement or used to provide more monthly income.

Eligible Earnings

Eligible earnings include salary, wages, bonuses, vacation pay, honorariums, commissions, taxable allowances, taxable benefits, and directors and officers' fees.

The **Saskatchewan Public Employees Pension Plan (PEPP)**[3] states:

> ... Your regular earnings include bonuses (such as signing bonuses or performance payments), but does not include overtime pay or payment for temporary assignment of higher duties.

---

2   All information on the CSSPP was obtained from Co-operative Superannuation Society Pension Plan: (1) Frequently Asked Questions <www.csspen.com/faq>; (2) Plan — Rules and Regulations <www.csspen.com/rules>; and (3) The Plan in a Nut-Shell <www.csspen.com/plansummary>.

3   All PEPP information is derived from the Public Employees Pension Plan Member Booklet, available at <www.peba.gov.sk.ca/PEPP>.

Prescribed Compensation

Prescribed compensation defines the level of contributions that can be made during **periods of reduced service** without violating **pension adjustment limits (PAs)**, which will be discussed in detail in the next chapter. Pension adjustments put a limit on total contributions to RPPs, RRSPs and DPSPs. The limit, called the **money purchase limit**, is 18% of compensation to a maximum of $20,000 in 2007, $21,000 in 2008, and $22,000 in 2009, after which it will be indexed. Failing to respect pension-adjustment limits can cause the plan to be revoked.

Prescribed compensation is a notional amount of remuneration that can be included in an individual's compensation during a period when a person's pay is less than usual — often because of disability, reduced services or periods of temporary absence, such as periods of parenting. During such periods, employers are allowed to continue making contributions to the employee's pension plan, and benefits under defined benefit provisions can continue to accrue without exceeding the PA restriction. In contributory plans, employees must also make their contributions. The periods of eligible reduced or no service are described below under "Eligible service."

Eligible Service

Pension regulations define **eligible service** as service with an employer that carries on all or part of its business in Canada. Under prescribed compensation, eligible service may also be expanded to include the following if the plan permits:

1. A reciprocal agreement with another employer to accept prior service with the other employer as eligible service.

> **Example 1**   Tony taught music at Young University for eight years. After attaining tenure, Tony obtained a tenured position at Ancient University. Ancient has a reciprocal agreement with Young so that, at Ancient, Tony was able to have credit in the pension plan for the eight years he taught at Young.

2. Three years or less of service with a company that is affiliated with the participating employer.

3. Periods of paid or unpaid sabbatical leaves, education leaves, and maternity, paternity, and adoption leaves, can be counted as eligible service. In addition, disability leaves and periods of active service in the Canadian Armed Forces or with allied forces during World War II and the Korean War count as eligible service.

4. Eligible service can also include:
   • Work with a federal or provincial government, committee, or commission, or
   • A loan to a union, educational institute, or charitable organization
   where an appointment:
   • does not provide accrued benefits under another pension plan
   • is for a period not to exceed three years
   • is paid or unpaid.

5. Up to two years of other unpaid leave, including layoff.

The **Saskatchewan Public Employees Pension Plan (PEPP)** handbook states:

> If you take an unpaid leave of absence from your employer (e.g., education leave, maternity leave or parental leave), you may choose whether you want to make contributions to

the Plan for the period of the leave. You have 90 days from the date you return to work to make your decision.

If you elect to contribute for the period of your leave, your contributions will be based on the salary you were earning before you went on leave. You may choose one of the following methods of paying for your contributions:
• a lump sum payment by personal cheque ..., or
• a lump sum payment by payroll deduction, or
• making double contributions to the Plan by payroll deduction for a period of time equal to the length of the leave taken, or
• a transfer from your RRSP ...

If you do not complete and return the form within 90 days, you may not contribute for the period of leave or purchase the service at a later date. Since the Public Employees Pension Plan is a defined contribution plan, the Income Tax Act (Canada) does not permit the purchase of past service.

Subject to any other agreement between you and your employer, if you decide to contribute to the period of leave, your employer is required to make contributions to the Plan in the same manner you choose (e.g., if you contribute for the period of leave in a lump sum, your employer must contribute in a lump sum as well).

Investments

RPPs place limitations on the plan's investment options.

> The administrator of the plan must establish and adopt a written statement of investment policies and goals for the plan ... the selection of investments must be made with consideration given to the overall context of the investment portfolio without undue risk of loss or impairment and with a reasonable expectation of fair return or appreciation given the nature of the investment.[4]

There is a long list of rules and restrictions whose goal is to safeguard the assets. As shown in Table 4.3 above, pension funds are very large and require professional management, and there is legislation that sets parameters for pension fund managers. Table 4.7 summarizes pension-plan assets in Canada for 2002 by market value.

Table 4.7 Pension Plan Assets in Canada, December 31, 2012, $ Nominal ($ millions)

Market value	Total		Public sector		Private sector		March 1993	Change 2012 > 1993	
	$	%	$	%	$	%	$	$	% chg
Bonds	443,295	37.1%	294,605	36.3%	148,690	38.9%	113,591	329,704	290.3%
Stocks	372,930	31.2%	247,436	30.5%	125,494	32.8%	96,544	276,386	286.3%
Mortgages	12,994	1.1%	9,090	1.1%	3,904	1.0%	8,253	4,741	57.4%
Real estate	95,786	8.0%	85,659	10.6%	10,127	2.6%	8,590	87,196	1015.1%
Short-term	41,502	3.5%	28,338	3.5%	13,164	3.4%	19,816	21,686	109.4%
Other	219,500	18.4%	145,724	18.0%	73,776	19.3%	16,468	203,032	1232.9%
> $10 million	7,438	0.6%	178	0.0%	7,260	1.9%	2,258	5,180	229.4%
	1,193,445	100.0%	811,030	100.0%	382,415	100.0%	265,520	927,925	349.5%

---

4   Pension Benefits Act, Revised Statutes of Ontario, 1990, Chapter P.8, as amended by: 1997, Chapter 28, ss. 190–224 and the following Regulations (as amended): General (R.R.) 1990, Reg. 909, February 26, 1999. Printed by the Queen's Printer for Ontario.

Table 4.7 Continued

Book value	Total		Public sector		Private sector		March 1993	Change 2012 > 1993	
	$	%	$	%	$	%	$	$	% chg
Bonds	398,948	37.0%	263,678	36.3%	135,270	38.6%	109,013	289,935	266.0%
Stocks	343,870	31.9%	227,709	31.3%	116,161	33.2%	86,541	257,329	297.3%
Mortgages	12,975	1.2%	9,437	1.3%	3,538	1.0%	8,064	4,911	60.9%
Real estate	69,192	6.4%	62,964	8.7%	6,228	1.8%	9,190	60,002	652.9%
Short-term	41,435	3.8%	28,346	3.9%	13,089	3.7%	20,599	20,836	101.2%
Other	204,006	18.9%	134,887	18.5%	69,119	19.7%	14,970	189,036	1262.8%
> $10 million	6,768	0.6%	158	0.0%	6,610	1.9%	2,061	4,707	228.4%
	1,077,194	100.0%	727,179	100.0%	350,015	100.0%	250,438	826,756	330.1%
Market > Book	116,251		83,851		32,400		15,082		

Source: Statistics Canada Table 280-0002 Trusteed pension funds, market and book value of assets, by private and public sector category

In defined contribution plans, employees often have some choice about how their contributions are invested. For example, the **Saskatchewan Public Employees Pension Plan** states:

> All contributions are forwarded to the Public Employees Pension Plan for deposit into your choice of one or more of the investment funds of the Public Employees Pension Plan. Currently, PEPP has two investment funds: the Balanced Fund and the Short-term Bond Fund.
>
> Your contributions and the employer contributions made on your behalf are directed to the Balanced Fund unless You specify otherwise (default). If you wish, you may direct all or a portion of your contributions and your employer's contributions on your behalf to the Short-term Bond Fund. You may also elect to transfer money from one investment to another.

Loans and Assignments

As the sole purpose of an RPP is to provide pension to retired employees, pension benefits, including those arising from voluntary contributions, may *not* be used as collateral on a loan. A pension plan *cannot* loan money to members except if the plan invests in mortgages and a plan member is one of the mortgagors. Generally, plan trustees cannot borrow money on behalf of the fund except:

- to pay current benefits and avoid the distress sale of assets, and
- to make additional investments although the fund assets cannot be used as collateral and the total amount borrowed cannot total more than the combination of
  - current-services contributions for the next 12 months, and
  - investment income for the next 12 months.

Benefits may be assigned only as a result of a marriage breakdown, where the pension credits are split under a separation agreement or in accordance with a decree or order of judgment by a competent tribunal.

Vesting

Retirement benefits become vested when the employer's contributions belong to the employee. Benefits are vested when the employee has met age or service requirements (e.g., under the federal Pensions Benefit Act, an employee must be a member of a pension plan for two years before the employer's contributions are vested). The **Saskatchewan Public Employees Pension Plan** handbook states:

You become vested and all required contributions become locked in on the earliest date in which you meet one of the following criteria:
- you have been a PEPP member for one year, or
- you have been employed by a participating employer for two continuous years.

Portability

When an employee quits a job to go to another job, pension benefits earned at the first job are portable; if the **benefits are vested**, the employee can move the pension credits to an RRSP or to the new RPP.

If the benefits arising from the employer's contribution are **not vested**, the employee can:

- take their own contributions in a taxable lump sum
- transfer the contribution to:
  - a Locked-in RRSP (LRSP — federal) or a Locked-in Retirement Account (LIRA — provincial), as discussed in Chapter 7, or
  - a new RPP.

Use of Fund Surplus

Defined contribution plans do not generate surpluses. Strong growth in the pension fund simply means retirees receive larger pensions. **Defined benefit plans** can, however, generate pension surpluses. RPPs provide tax-deferred savings. Regular reviews, required by regulations, are made by actuaries to check whether or not there are sufficient funds in the plan to pay future liabilities. If the fund does not have sufficient funds, the employer is required to make additional contributions to pay pensions to present retirees. Contributions for current employees can also be increased but if the across-the-board increase is not sufficient (because some plan members are close to retirement), the employer must make up the difference.

Pension-fund surpluses are generally the result of high return of investment; for example, the long bull market in the late 1990s generated large surpluses in many pension funds. A **surplus**, as certified by an actuary, is the excess value of the assets in the fund over the value of the pension liabilities. The pension liability is the present value of the future benefits that will be paid out.

An **excess surplus** is a surplus greater than a certain minimum level of surplus. The calculations are not important for our purposes and the following information on the calculation of excess surplus is provided for general interest only. An excess surplus is the *least* of:

(a) The Going Concern Surplus, which is the Actuarial Value of Assets (book value plus the average five-year difference between market and book value) minus Accrued Actuarial Liabilities (amount due if the plan was terminated on the valuation date)

(b) 20% of accrued liabilities

(c) The greater of:
   i. 10% of accrued liabilities
   ii. the normal contributions required for the next 24 months.

Since the contributions are made from before-tax income (i.e., the pension contributions are tax deductible), CRA requires that an excess surplus be eliminated to prevent excess contributions, which grow on a tax-deferred basis. An excess surplus can be:

- refunded to the employer and the employees as taxable income
- used to pay employer and/or employees contributions for current and future eligible service (referred to as a **contribution holiday**), or

• used to improve pension benefits (pension benefits do not include improving a employer-sponsored disability plan or improvements to medical benefits for retirees).

The Ontario Municipal Employees Retirement System (OMERS) was established in 1962 as a multi-employer pension plan for employees of local government in Ontario. Its purpose is to guarantee the retirement income of more than 270,000 active and retired members. The plan description states:

> OMERS is a defined benefit plan fully funded by equal contributions from employers and employees and by the investment earnings of the OMERS Fund. ... Members and employers are currently enjoying a full contribution holiday. From the pay period that included August 1, 1998 to the present (May 2002), member and employer contribution rates are 0%.[5]

Table 4.8 Source of Pension Surplus, Excess Surplus, and Deficit

	Year 1	Year 2	Year 3
	Surplus	Excess surplus	Deficit
Assets			
BOY	1,000	1,038	1,158
Rate of return	4%	4%	4%
Income	40	42	46
Unrealized change in market value	0	80	(200)
Paid to retirees	(21)	(21)	(21)
Contributions	20	20	20
Expenses	(1)	(1)	(1)
EOY	1,038	1,158	1,002
Less Accrued liabilities			
BOY	996	1,000	1,004
Paid to retirees	(21)	(21)	(21)
Owed for current contributions	25	25	25
EOY	1,000	1,004	1,008
Surplus/(deficit)	38	154	(6)
Excess surplus = surplus greater than the least of:			
Going concern surplus	**38**	154	**(6)**
20% of accrued liabilities	200	201	202
Greater of:			
10% of accrued liabilities	100	**100**	101
2 years' contributions	40	40	40
Excess surplus	none	54	none
Deficit to fund			**(6)**

Other DBPPs that have had an excess surplus have improved benefits, which are payable to retirees as well as future retirees, reflecting that the excess surplus arises, in part, from retiree contributions.

Table 4.8 illustrates the differences in the Statement of Financial Position for the above situations. The value of the assets is an average of the prior few years' market value of the assets. This value increases each year by means of:

• contributions made to the plan
• income earned by the assets
• gains in the current year's market value.

---

5   From OMERS website <www.omers.ca>

The asset value decreases by:

- payments to retirees
- administrative expenses
- losses in the current year's market value.

The table gives a simplistic and somewhat unrealistic example intended to illustrate a surplus in year 1, an excess surplus in year 2, and a deficit in year 3. It is unrealistic because it is highly unlikely that a deficit could be created in the year immediately following an excess surplus. While we are not covering this topic in detail, it is important to understand the concepts in theory, since employers are required to top up any deficits and an excess surplus must be used up. The long bull market in late 1990s created excess surpluses for many pension funds such as the OMERS described above. However, the more recent market downturn has created deficits which the employer must finance.

D. TYPES OF BENEFITS

Although the purpose of all pension plans is to save and invest money to provide pension benefits in retirement, most pension plans provide other benefits for eligible employees. This section will describe the most common benefits that can be found in RPPs.

Pension Benefits

The purpose of all pension plans is to save and invest money for retirement. The amount of pension benefits provided by these plans varies, since it is based on different formulae.

1. Defined Contribution Plan

In a DCPP (or money purchase plan), each employee has an individual account administered by the pension plan. The pension benefit is based on the contributions plus the income the contributions have earned and accumulated till retirement. While employees take the investment risk, there is no maximum for pension payments. See Focus Box 4–1 for an example of a DCP.

2. Defined Benefit Plan

In a DBPP, there is a specific formula that provides an annuity for life at retirement. The most common types of benefit formulae are based on (a) final earnings and career average earnings, or (b) a flat benefit. Some plans are integrated with the CPP and cover more than one employer (i.e., multi-employer plans).

Since the amount of the benefit is defined, the *employer* must ensure that the plan is funded well enough to provide these benefits. In other words, the employer takes the investment risk.

The pension benefit in the form of a life annuity must be payable in equal periodic (usually monthly) amounts at least for life *except* when:

1. The annuity would be no more than 4% of the year's Maximum Pensionable Earnings. In this instance, a lump-sum **commutation payment** is permitted.
2. The plan member has only a short time to live as evidenced by a doctor's statement. Also, in this instance, a lump-sum commutation payment is permitted.
3. A lump sum derived from additional voluntary contributions is paid.
4. The pension payments are integrated with the Canada Pension Plan.

Focus Box 4–1   The Saskatchewan Public Employees Pension Plan (PEPP)

The **Saskatchewan PEPP** is a DCP, and its handbook states:

> *When you are eligible to retire, you may use your PEPP account balance to provide an immediate or a deferred retirement benefit.*
>
> *If you want to begin receiving retirement income as soon as your employment with a participating employer ceases, you may elect one or more of the following options:*
> * *purchase a life annuity;*
> * *transfer your account to a registered Locked-in Retirement Income Fund (LRIF); or*
> * *transfer your account balance to a registered Life Income Fund (LIF).**

For example, assume Derek has $237,628 in his DCPP when he retires. He elects a non-indexed annuity for a period of 25 years. Using a nominal interest rate of 7%, he will receive a pension of $1,669.76 per month [$237,628 = PMT_{BOM} $(PVIFA_{25 \times 12, \ 7 \div 12\%})$].

* These payout options will be discussed in detail in Chapter 7.

5. The pension payments are paid as a variable or escalating annuity for life.
6. A joint-and-last-survivor annuity pays an amount equal to or less than the amount that was being paid to the member.
7. The commuted value may be transferred to a locked-in registered retirement savings plan which will eventually pay a pension to the member in the form of a life annuity.

Focus Box 4–2 provides an example of a defined benefit plan (the Ontario Municipal Employees Retirement System, OMERS).

3. Hybrid Plan

Commonly categorized as defined benefit plans, hybrid plans combine both defined benefit and defined contribution plans.

The University of Manitoba Pension Plan (1993) provides eligible employees of the university with retirement, termination, and death benefits. This is a hybrid pension plan, with retirement benefits calculated using two different methods. The first method calculates an annuity that uses a pension factor established by the university's actuary and is paid from the plan. The second method calculates a defined benefit pension based on a formula involving a member's years of service and highest average earnings. If the second method is greater than the first, the difference, known as the **supplementary pension**, is paid from the plan.[6]

Guaranteed Number of Years

A **defined benefit pension** is paid as a **life benefit (life annuity)**: that is, it is paid until the pensioner dies, at which point a surviving spouse or financially dependent child or grandchild can collect at least

---

6   See the University of Manitoba 1993 Pension Plan homepage: <www.umanitoba.ca/admin/human_resources/staff_benefits/pension_plans/1993_Plan>.

60% of the pensioner's benefit (as described under "Death Benefit", below). For a **defined contribution pension**, the maximum number of years that can be guaranteed when it is paid as a **life annuity** is the lesser of:

- fifteen years, or
- date of retirement to the day before the member's 86th birthday

If the member dies before reaching the end of the guaranteed period, the unpaid pension will be paid as a lump-sum commutation payment or as continued annuity payments to the estate or beneficiary. In a joint-and-last-survivor annuity, if the beneficiary dies before the end of the guarantee period, the payments stop unless the guaranteed period on the original member's life still has not expired; that is, there is no guarantee on the second life.

Indexed Payment

A **defined benefit plan** might include a regular increase to reflect an increase in the cost of living. This increase is called a **supplementary pension benefit**. The increase can be based on:

- changes to the consumer price index, or
- the **excess earnings approach** in which the plan must specify:
  - what the base rate is
  - the formula for determining the earnings rate, and
  - a reasonable allocation of the earnings (the earnings rate can be related to the earnings on fund investments or to some external index).

A **defined contribution plan** can also use the excess earnings approach to provide increases to reflect changes in the cost of living.

Maximum Benefit Limit

Defined contribution plans have no maximums.

Defined benefit plans and **hybrid/combination plans** have several legislated limits on the annual pension benefit.

1. A pension cannot be more than 2% per year of pensionable earnings.
2. The amount of pension for each year of service cannot be more than the **defined benefit limit,** which is the *greater* of:
   (a) the overriding provision under the Maximum Pension Rule, which is $1,722.22 after 1994 ($1,715 before 1995), and
   (b) 1/9 of the **Money Purchase Limit**, which is the maximum a taxpayer can contribute to all registered plans in any year. It is $24,270 for 2013, making the maximum per year $2,696.67 ($24,270 ÷ 9).
3. Until 1992, an RPP could not pay a pension on more than 35 years of service. This restriction was removed in 1992. However pension plans generally had this maximum included in the plan and many plans have not been revised to remove this **35-year limit**.

As a result of these restrictions, the maximum pension *was* $60,278 ($1,722.22 × 35 years) and the maximum pensionable earnings *was* $86,111 ($1,722.22 ÷ 0.02). A plan can provide a pension that is less than these limits such as 1.75% of the applicable earnings. In this case, the maximum pensionable earnings before 2004 would be $98,413 ($1,722.22 ÷ 0.0175), and the maximum pension for this plan if it had a 35-year ceiling would be $60,278 if pensionable earnings were more than $98,413. This concept is discussed in greater detail in the next chapter.

Example 2   Jason retired at the end of 2013 with average earnings for the previous three years of $130,000. He has worked for Ever-Faithful Bank for 38 years, but his plan has a maximum of 35 years. His pension is:
- 2,696.67 $(1/9 \times 24,270) \times 35$ years = **$94,383**

These rules do not apply:

- if the annual pension is $300 a year or less, or
- to that portion of a pension that is a result of **voluntary contributions,** as long as this portion of the pension is based on a **defined contribution plan**.

    Jason might be able to increase his pension by making voluntary contributions to a money purchase plan. If he made these voluntary contributions, he could collect a pension based on the combination of his mandatory and voluntary contributions and the income earned on both of these contributions.

The plan is required to set a **reasonable minimum pension benefit** after 10 years of eligible service; $300 a month is considered a reasonable minimum amount.

Commutation Payment

This is a lump-sum payment of a pension to the pension plan member. It equals the present value of the expected future annuity payments (the calculation is covered in more detail in Chapter 7). Commutation **may occur** in various situations:

1. As in the seven examples stated earlier in the section on defined benefit plans under "Pension Benefits — Defined Benefit Plan"
2. On or after death
3. Upon termination of employment
4. Upon termination of the plan before the plan member retires, or
5. When the pension benefits are transferred to a member's spouse as a result of a written agreement, decree, order, or judgment following marriage breakdown.

Most important, commutation **may not occur**:

1. When employment terminates because of retirement
2. If the member changes jobs and will continue to be a member of the same pension plan.

Example 3   Jane, a nurse, quit the Woodstock General Hospital to work at the Sudbury Community Hospital. Assuming both hospitals are members of HOOPP (Healthcare of Ontario Pension Plan), Jane would not be able to take a commutation payment.

3. If the member accepts another job in the same organization and the new position does not permit membership in the plan
4. If a member voluntarily quits a plan in which membership is not compulsory.

In two instances, the commuted value may be **rolled over** into an RRSP while the member is still employed by the plan employer:

1. An employee makes a one-time withdrawal of voluntary contributions at a time when the plan is amended to deny voluntary contributions, and

2. An employee makes a one-time withdrawal of required contributions at a time when the plan is amended to delete contributions by members and to require the employer to make all the contributions.

The CRA places a limit on the amount of the commuted value that can be transferred into another registered plan. This is covered in Chapter 7.

Death Benefits

Death benefits can be paid if the member **dies before retirement**. The maximum amount that can be paid as a lump-sum may not exceed the greater of:

• Accrued entitlement, or
• Total contributions plus income earned.

If a pensioner **dies after retirement, dependants' pension benefits** may be paid to the spouse, including a common-law spouse, or to a parent, sister, brother, or child who was financially dependent on the plan member at the time of death. The pension must be a reasonable minimum pension: e.g., 60% of the member's pension is the legislated amount for all provinces and federal pension plans except for Manitoba, where it is 66 2/3%. In several provinces, there are pension plans that have to be adjusted because the provision is for only 50%.

The death benefit can be paid as a lump sum, an immediate annuity for life, a deferred annuity for life beginning before the beneficiary turns 65, in immediate instalments, or an annuity certain commencing immediately. All amounts are taxable when received.

Life Insurance Benefits

An RPP may have a provision for life insurance to be paid should the member die before retirement. The contribution must be apportioned between the life insurance benefits and the pension benefits and recorded separately in the books of the employer. Any life insurance paid out is not a pension benefit and is taxed as life insurance, not as pension income.

Termination Benefits

Termination benefits are paid when an employee terminates employment before retirement, or if the plan is terminated. Benefits can be paid to the plan member:

1. In a lump sum if the contributions are net yet vested
2. By instalments or by an annuity certain beginning no later than the earliest date a pension could be payable under the plan
3. As an annuity for life maturing before the plan member turns 71, or
4. Any combination of these.

In addition, the commuted value of the benefits can be transferred to:

• Another registered pension plan, or
• A registered retirement savings plan.

The value of these benefits is subject to the maximum pension payment rules.

E. ELIGIBILITY FOR RETIREMENT

Eligibility for retirement in an RPP is normally determined by the employee's age and years of service, the regulations for which are established in the plan. Although there is no law in Canada that requires retirement at a particular age, many workplaces mandate retirement at age 65, even if an employee still wants to work.[7] Mandatory retirement may be part of a collective agreement negotiated between the employer and union or contained in an employer's personnel policies. However, most pension plans allow employees some flexibility as to when they will retire. As a result, plans may have age requirements for early, normal, and late retirement.

Normal Retirement Age (NRA)

Normal retirement age is the age at which a plan member can retire and receive an **unreduced pension**, which means the retiree collects the full formula amount for each year of service. By regulation, the NRA should be defined between the month the member turns 60 and the day before the member's 71st birthday. If the plan is insured and retirement is based on the anniversary date, then retirement can occur up to 183 days before the member's 60th birthday. A normal retirement age after age 71 is acceptable only when a person is retiring immediately after joining the plan.

Before the age of 65, the member must have actually retired to collect pension benefits. After a member turns 65, a member can be deemed retired and collect a full or partial pension even though that member is still employed. A member who has reached the normal retirement age, is less than 65 years old, and is still working can collect a whole or partial pension if:

- The pension is compensating for reduced earnings, or
- Further delay would result in a basic pension that exceeds the maximum defined amount by the Income Tax Regulations (see above under "Maximum Benefit Limit").

No further benefits can accrue for a member who:

- Is receiving a full or partial pension **and**
- Remains employed **or**
- Returns to employment after a break.

A member of a pension plan cannot receive a pension and contribute to that pension plan at the same time.

A member can continue employment after his or her 71st birthday while receiving pension benefits. A member who continues to work and does not collect a pension cannot have further benefits accrue after age 71, although this time can count for eligibility for coverage.

Normal retirement age can be less than 60 if retirement depends on having at least:

- 30 years' service, **or**
- a combination of age and years of service of 80 or more.

The plan can contain a clause that requires retirement for long-time employees because of:

- Automation, or
- Inability to keep knowledge up-to-date with advances in technology.

In these instances, even though the employee may retire earlier than the set NRA, the pension might not be reduced due to early retirement; i.e., the member might be deemed to have reached the normal retirement age if the additional pension is reasonable.

The **Co-operative Superannuation Society Pension Plan (CSSPP)** Rules and Regulations state:

---

7   Mandatory retirement may be a thing of the past as many provinces, such as Manitoba, New Bruswick, Ontario, and Quebec (and countries such as Australia and New Zealand) have already banned mandatory retirement.

The normal retirement age for plan participants shall be 60 years of age.

Plan participants may elect to retire with retirement benefits at the earliest of age 50 or when age plus years of continuous service equal a factor of 75 or more.

This is a defined contribution plan, and early retirement means both less time to save and longer to collect the pension after retirement. And in a defined contribution plan, the amount of income is dependent on the balance in the retiree's account at the date of retirement.

Early Retirement

Early retirement is one of the three possible retirement dates in a pension plan. Both the Co-operative Superannuation Society Pension Plan and the Saskatchewan PEPP cited earlier allow early retirement at age 50, regardless of how long the employee has been a member of the plan. Both of these plans are defined contribution plans.

In a defined benefit plan, early retirement other than for disability can occur before the NRA, but the present value of the pension payments must not be more than the **maximum value** of a pension outlined earlier (see "Maximum Benefit Limits"), which is paid as either:

- A single life annuity guaranteed for 10 years, or
- A 60% joint-and-last-survivor annuity and begins at the earliest of:
  - age 60
  - normal retirement age, or
  - age at the date of disability.

Early Retirement for Disability

Some pension plans allow unreduced early retirement pensions for employees who have to retire early because of permanent disability. In this case, years of service will include years of service and years of disability up to the normal retirement age. A smaller disability pension might be paid to someone who can return to work but at a job that pays less than the one held before the disability. The total of such disability pension and the salary must not be more than the amount of disability pension that would have been received if the member were totally disabled. A member receiving a disability pension is deemed retired with regard to the pension plan. No more pension benefits can accrue to that member since a member of a pension plan cannot receive a pension and contribute to that pension.

SUMMARY

During the long bull market of the 1990s, if given a choice, many people would have switched their pension plans from defined benefit to defined contribution. Rates of return in the stock market were very high, and the guaranteed pension offered by a defined benefit plan looked very modest in comparison. People who made this switch did not understand two things:

1. Stock markets go up in the long run, but they go up and down a lot along the way.
2. In defined benefit plans, it is the employer who takes the investment risk: i.e., the employer has to fund the pension plan and to ensure sufficient funds are available to pay all pension liabilities. In defined contribution plans, it is the employee who takes the investment risk. It makes no difference to the employer how the pension plan performs — the employer must

Focus Box 4–2   Ontario Municipal Employees Retirement System (OMERS)

The OMERS pension fund is one of the largest pension funds in Canada. Information on the plan is available at their website: <www.omers.ca>. Although it is applicable to Ontario only, it is presented here as an example of a **defined benefit pension plan**.

The normal retirement age (NRA) at OMERS is 65 except for police and firefighters, who have an NRA of 60.

Contributions

The OMERS plan is integrated with the Canada Pension Plan. Integration with CPP is discussed in the next chapter. However, this integration means that the contribution rates are different below and above the Year's Maximum Pensionable Earnings (YMPE) for CPP.

Both employees' and employers' 2013 contribution rates are:	for NRA* 65	for NRA* 60
Contributory earnings up to YMPE	9.0%	9.3%
Contributory earnings above YMPE	14.6%	15.9%

The YMPE for 2013 is $51,100, and the 2013 5-year average YMPE (AYMPE) is $48,600.

*NRA = Normal Retirement Age

Jeremy, an administrator in Sudbury, earns a salary $72,000 a year. Using generic rates, his pension contribution is:

46,000 YMPE × 9% =	4,140.00
26,000 (72,000 − 46,000 × 14.6% =	3,796.00
	7,936.00

While OMERS employers and members enjoyed a contribution holiday from 1998 to 2003 paying contributions out of the excess surplus generated by strong stock market returns, the 2008 downturn in the market from which world economies have not fully recovered has forced a significant increase in contribution rates. Beginning in 2011, over three years, contribution rates increased between 38% and 52%. NRA 65 was 6.5% and 9.6% while NRA 60 was 7.9% and 10.7%.

Benefits

Since OMERS is a defined benefit plan, the benefit must be defined. Because it is an integrated plan, the benefit reflects CPP retirement income. The benefit formula is:

2%	× the highest 60 consecutive months of contributory earnings (× 12 for an annual pension)	×	credited service (maximum 35 years)

less the CPP offset (at age 65 or earlier if disabled):

0.675%	× the lesser of: • 5-year average YMPE • pensionable earnings	×	credited service from January 1, 1966 to a maximum 35 years

The CPP offset is called a **Bridge Benefit** because it doesn't start until age 65 even if the retiree takes a reduced CPP benefit before age 65 since an OMERS member can still receive a reduced CPP pension as early as age 60. In this case, a retiree would receive the OMERS pension without the offset until age 65 plus the reduced CPP pension. At age 65, the CPP offset would being to reduce the OMERS pension.

Focus Box 4–2 (continued)

For example, Jeremy, age 65, retires after 45 years of service. His highest 60 consecutive month's salary average $68,000. Jeremy's pension in the first year is:

2.0%	×	$68,000		×	35 years =	**47,600.00**
0.675%	×	the lesser of:				
		44,000 generic AYMPE	×		35 years =	**−10,395.00**
		68,000				**−16,065.00**
						$37,205.00

Jeremy will receive $37,205 from his OMERS pension and $11,500 generic CPP retirement benefits (Jeremy will also receive the OAS, which is not part of this calculation).

If Jeremy had retired at age 62 with 42 years of service, he would have received $47,600 until he turned 65 regardless of whether or not he took his CPP pension when he retired. At age 65, he will begin to receive $37,205 from OMERS.

Early Retirement

Employees can take early retirement if they are within 10 years if their normal retirement date but must meet certain requirements in order to obtain an unreduced pension, which is also called early retirement without penalty. Note that in pension language, this unreduced pension is referred to as a **full pension**, meaning there is no reduction for early retirement and the pension is based on the actual number of years of service.

Early retirement *without penalty* is available for OMERS members if they meet certain criteria.

They must be within 10 years of NRA (Normal Retirement Age) **and**	
have the least of:	30 years of service
	or
	for NRA 65 a 90 factor
	for NRA 60 an 85 factor
factor = age + years of service	

For example, Jane, Jeremy's wife, is 58 and would like to retire with him. She has worked in the Sudbury municipal office for 33 years. She can retire on an unreduced pension since her factor totals 91 (58 + 33). She can receive an unreduced pension based on her 33 years of service. If her best consecutive 60 months of salary averages $39,000, she can collect:

$$2\% \times \$39,000 \times 33 \text{ years} = \mathbf{\$21,780}$$

When she reaches the age of 65, her OMERS pension will be reduced by:

$$0.675\% \times \$39,000 \times 33 \text{ years} = \mathbf{\$8,687.25}$$

In addition, she can collect a reduced CPP retirement benefit at age 60 or wait and collect the full benefit at age 65.

Early retirement *with a penalty* is also available to OMERS members if they do not meet the above criteria but are within 10 years of the NRA. Also called a **reduced pension**, this pension provides retirees with a smaller proportion of the formula times the actual number of years of service. OMERS members who take early retirement have their pension reduced by a penalty based on the *least* of the number of years short in each of the following categories.

Focus Box 4–2 (continued)

	NRA 65	NRA 60
Must be at least age:	**55**	**50**
Penalty = 5% × number of years short of the *least* of:		
• normal retirement age	65	60
• number of years of credited service	30	30
• factor	90	85

To calculate the penalty, multiply 5% times the number short in each of the above three categories. The penalty is the least of the three amounts.

For example, Elaine, Jeremy's colleague, is 50 years old and wants to retire after 27 years on the police force. Her penalty is the least of:

	Elaine	NRA 60	Penalty = the least of
Must be at least age:	50	50	
Penalty = 5% × number of years short of the *least* of:			
• normal retirement age	50	60	10 × 5% = 50%
• number of years of credited service	27	30	3 × 5% = 15%
• a factor of	77	85	8 × 5% = 40%

Elaine can retire and take a pension that is reduced by 15%.

guarantee nothing, and the employee's pension income is dependent on both contributions to the plan and rates of return generated in the pension plan.

The factor that offsets the investment risk in DCPPs is the absence of a ceiling on annual pensions. These plans are subject to the same overall contribution limits, but if investment returns are strong enough, they can provide a higher pension than a DBPP can.

Pension plans are a form of deferred compensation on which the taxes are also deferred. As a result, they are highly regulated both to protect contributions to them and to prevent abuses of them. Since the goal of a plan is to provide income throughout retirement, there are minimum age and service requirements to meet before the funds can be withdrawn as retirement income.

Craig and Margot are relieved to find out that the issues are not as complex as they had feared. They now understand that as far as investments go, a defined benefit pension plan is one of the most secure. They know that some of their teacher friends had a pension plan but assumed it was necessary to be a "lifer" at one place of employment to be able to collect a pension. Craig has been at this job for 17 years and has no plans to move on, but is reassured to find out that if he does change employers, he will not have to walk away from the pension benefits he has accumulated at his current

Focus Box 4–3   Pensions for Members of Parliament

Federal members of parliament receive pension benefits that are greater than the benefits available to other Canadians. The justification is that many of them leave behind their former work life to serve their constituents and cannot easily return to that former life if they fail to be re-elected (possibly through no fault of their own). The issue is the size of the pension compared to their salary and years of service.

The Canadian Taxpayers Federation has prepared a report on MP pensions that includes estimates of the pension for each member.

How MP Pension are Calculated

Defeated or retired MPs can collect a pension at age 55 if they have served at least six years in the House of Commons. These pensions are fully indexed at age 60. The formula for calculating their pension is:

> (Best 5-year average salary x 3% x number of years of service) to a maximum of 75% of their salary.

If they have additional roles, such as party leader or committee chair, extra accrual is obtained at the rate of 3% a year meaning their pensions accrue at a rate of 3% to 6%. Since CRA stipulates that no pension shall accrue at more than 2% a year, the MP's pension is split in two, one part being an RCA as described in Chapter 5.

MP Pension Contributions

MPs contribute 7% of their salaries — someone earning $150,000 contributes $10,500 a year to earn a pension benefit of 3% per year of service. A person in OMERS would contribute $19,038 [(51,100 × 9%) + (98,900 × 14.6%)] assuming the entire $150,000 is pensionable to earn a benefit of 1.325% a year at age 65.

Rates of Return

This is an unfunded pension plan, something that is not allowed in RPPs. The rate of return is notional (it isn't actually invested each year) and is determined by government legislation and regulation, not the market. The dictated rate of return is 2.5% a quarter — a 10.4% EAR. The report points out the following returns:

	10-year return	2008 return
Parliamentary pension plan	10.40%	10.40%
CPP	6.50%	−18.60%
Ontario Teachers Pension Plan	7.30%	− 0.18%
S&P / TSX	8.70%	− 0.33%

Taxpayers in 2009–10 contributed $248,668 for every MP — $90,939 higher than a backbench MP's basic salary of $157,731.

Source: CTF Report on MP Pensions: A Taxpayers' Indictment <taxpayers.com>

place of employment. Many of his friends had advised going into a money purchase plan, but Craig now understands that this was a result of the long bull market, which provided higher than normal returns for a few years. He likes the idea of his pension plan having a professional manager whose job it is to look after the pension fund for the long run.

SOURCES

- Canada Revenue Agency: <www.cra-arc.gc.ca>
  - Registered Plans
    - IC72-13R8 Employees' Pension Plans
    - IC98-2 Information Circular
    - Registered Plans Directorate Newsletter, no. 92-11, November 20, 1992
- Draft Amendments to the Income Tax Regulations Relating to Retirement Savings, 1995 Budget Measures Relating to Retirement Savings <www.fin.gc.ca>
- Bill C-28, part 84(1) paragraph (g) to (j) of the definition "money purchase limit" in subsection 147.1(1) of the Act: <www.parl.gc.ca>
- Ontario Municipal Employees Retirement System <www.omers.ca>
- Statistics Canada <www.statcan.ca>
- Co-operative Superannuation Society Pension Plan <www.csspen.com>
- Saskatchewan Public Employees Pension Plan <www.peba.gov.sk.ca>

KEY TERMS

Additional voluntary contributions (AVC)	Government administered pension plans
Assignments	Guaranteed number of years
Bridge benefit	Hybrid plan
Commutation payment	Life annuity
Contribution holiday	Life benefit
Contribution limit, RRSP	Maximum benefit limit
Contributory plan	Maximum pensionable earnings
Death benefit	Money purchase limit
Deferred compensation	Money purchase plan (MPP)
Deferred profit sharing plan (DPSP)	Multi-employer pension plan (MEPP)
Defined benefit limit	Non-contributory plan
Defined benefit pension plan (DBPP or DB)	Normal retirement age (NRA)
Defined contribution pension plan (DCPP or DC)	Overriding provision
Dependants' pension benefit	Pension adjustment (PA)
Early retirement	Portability
Early retirement for disability	Prescribed compensation
Early retirement with a penalty	Reasonable minimum pension
Early retirement without penalty	Reduced pension
Eligible earnings	RRSP contribution limit
Eligible service	Specified multi-employer pension plan (SMEPP)
Eligibility for participation in the plan	Supplementary pension benefit
Eligibility for retirement	Surplus
Employer-sponsored registered plans	Termination benefits
Excess earnings approach	Unreduced pension
Excess surplus	Vesting
Foreign pension plan	Voluntary contributions

QUESTIONS

1. What are the three sources of retirement income programs?

2. Why is a pension plan considered to be deferred compensation?

Types of Registered Pension Plans

3. What is a defined contribution plan? A defined benefit plan? A money purchase plan? A deferred profit sharing plan?

4. What percentage of RPPs are in the private sector and the public sector, respectively? What percentage of members of RPPs are in the public sector and the private sector, respectively? (Tables 4.1 and 4.2)

5. What type of plan is:
   (a) the Saskatchewan Public Employees Superannuation Plan — defined benefit or defined contribution?
   (b) Telus Corp.? (Table 4.3)

Setting up a Registered Pension Plan

6. Can a trade union set up a pension plan for its members?

7. Are the following allowed?
   (a) Only the employer makes contributions — the employee does not contribute.
   (b) Only the employee makes contributions — the employer does not contribute.

8. Can a trade union set up a pension plan for its members whereby only the members make contributions?

9. What percentage of RPP are contributory, and what percentage are non-contributory? What percentage of members of RPP are in contributory and non-contributory plans? (Table 4.4 and 4.5)

10. Is it possible for a Registered Pension Plan (RPP) to work like an RRSP whereby the employee can make contributions, and also can make withdrawals before retirement as needed?

11. Is it possible for an employee to take a contribution holiday if he or she has just bought a new house and money is tight?

12. Which of the following financial institutions can be the funding medium for a pension plan?
    (a) a life insurance company
    (b) a trust company; e.g., Canada Trust or Royal Trust
    (c) a pension corporation; e.g., Ontario Municipal Employees Retirement System

Features of Registered Pension Plans

13. Magnum Inc. has a total payroll of $5 million a year, and a defined contribution pension plan. What is the minimum required contribution to the pension plan that Magnum must make? (Answer: $50,000)

14. Claudia, age 55, now regrets that, many years ago, she did not leave her pension contributions with her former employer. Taking advantage of the rules in place at that time, she withdrew her contributions and paid off her credit card and went on a small but very pleasant vacation — she never dreamt that one day she would prefer a pension to faded memories of a great long weekend.
    (a) She now works for a company that has a defined contribution pension plan. If the plan permits, can she make additional voluntary contributions to increase her pension in a belated attempt to offset her foolish decision many years ago to take her money and play?
    (b) Can she make AVC to the plan if it is a defined benefit plan?

15. Arthur was paid a bonus at the end of 2013. Is this bonus part of his RPP eligible earnings?

16. Does "eligible earnings" include the value of taxable benefits?

17. Christian does work for ABC Company. He sends in an invoice each month for the hours he worked and receives the gross amount of the invoice. Can Cristian be a member of ABC Company's pension plan?

18. Can an owner-manager make contributions to his company's pension plan for his wife who does not work for the company?

19. Which of the following might count as eligible service:
    (a) sabbatical or maternity leave
    (b) taking a leave from work to fight in the Canadian army during a war
    (c) a two-year appointment to a Royal Commission on Children and Poverty.

20. Arthur was seconded to an affiliated company for 18 months to help sort out their management reporting. The affiliate does not have a pension plan. Can Arthur's company make pension contributions based on his salary while he is at the affiliate?

21. Referring to Table 4.7:
    (a) What is the total market value and book value of pension fund assets at January 1, 2013?
    (b) Which sector invests a larger *proportion* of its pension fund assets in:
        i. Bonds
        ii. Stocks
        iii. Real estate
    (c) Which sector has the larger *investment* in:
        i. Bonds
        ii. Stocks
        iii. Real estate

22. Can a plan member borrow from his or her pension plan to buy a house or to go back to school?

23. Can a pension be paid to a bank because the pension was used as collateral for a loan and the person in question died before the loan was paid back?

24. Many years ago, Claudia worked for a large primary manufacturer as a financial analyst. After five years, she moved on to bigger and better things and received her contributions plus income in a cash refund. At that time, she could either take the refund or leave her pension with the manufacturer. The rules have changed since then. What effect do current portability and vesting rules have on her options now?

25. Due to superlative investing decisions by the pension fund manager, the pension fund for Acme Inc. has built up a large surplus, some of which is considered to be excess surplus.
    (a) What is an excess surplus?
    (b) Can Acme just ignore this excess surplus, continuing to let it grow?
    (c) What are Acme's options?

Types of Benefits

26. What is the maximum pension that can be paid from a defined contribution plan?

27. If you are retired, 67 and dying, can you take out more than the usual amount from your DBPP?

28. Rose and Randy are 67, in terrific health, and about to retire. They believe in living life now, and elect to use their DCPP to buy a guaranteed annuity in order to get more money now. What is the maximum number of years they can elect to receive this guaranteed pension?

29. Antoinette has worked for Haggis for 47 years, and her best three years of income average $110,000. Her plan pays 2% for every year of service to a maximum of 35 years.
    (a) What is the maximum number of years she can use to calculate her pension? (Answer: 35 years)
    (b) What is the maximum pension she can receive using:
        i.   the 2013 money purchase limit of $24,270? (Answer: $94,383)
        ii. her actual salary? (Answer: 77,000)
    (c) How much pension will she receive? (Answer: $77,000)

30. Eleanor is a member of the Saskatchewan Employees Pension Plan. She moves from Regina to Moose Jaw. Although she has a new job, she will continue to be a member of this pension plan. Can she take a commutation payment?

31. If Lulu dies shortly after retiring, what RPP benefit might her spouse be entitled to?

32. Anne is retired and lives with her physically-handicapped niece, who has never been able to work. What is a reasonable percentage of her pension that may be paid to her niece?

33. Jill and her employer each pay $250 a month toward her pension. This includes life insurance benefits should she die before she retires. If the insurance would cost $47 a month, how much are they contributing to the pension plan each month? (Answer: $453)

Eligibility for Retirement

34. What are the youngest and oldest ages that can be defined as "Normal Retirement Age"?

35. If Adam is 66 and still working, can he receive a pension?

36. Adrian is 55 and has been working at Freedom Insurance Company for 32 years. Assuming his plan permits, can he retire under the "Normal Retirement Age" requirement? (Answer: Yes)

37. Andrew is 57 and has worked for 20 years at We Love Our Employees Inc. Try as he might, he has been completely unable to master the new computer package his job requires. Is it possible for him to retire with a full pension? (Answer: Yes)

38. Hank is 73. He loves his job, and is alert and lively, thanks to the ballroom dancing he and his wife enjoy. His salary of $75,000 is more than enough for their needs, so he is not collecting his pension yet.

    (a) If he retires at 75, can he collect a pension and contribute to the pension plan at the same time?

    (b) Will he continue to accumulate pension credits after age 70?

The OMERS Plan

39. What is the normal retirement age for a firefighter?

40. What is the Year's Maximum Pensionable Earnings (YMPE) for Pete, a firefighter in 2013 using the 2013 CPP rates? (Answer: $51,100)

41. If Pete earns $75,000 a year, how much would he contribute to the pension plan in 2013 using the generic YMPE? (Answer: $8,889.00)

42. Pete retired at age 58, with 36 years of service, and his earnings had been:

    | 2013 | $75,000 |
    | 2012 | $73,000 |
    | 2011 | $71,000 |
    | 2010 | $69,000 |
    | 2009 | $67,000 |
    | Average | $71,000 |

    (a) What annual pension would Pete receive when he retires using the generic AYMPE? Check to see if he receives a full pension or a reduced pension. (Answer: Full, $49,700)

    (b) How much will Pete's pension be reduced when he turns 65, using generic AYPME and ignoring his annual inflation increases? (Answer: $10,395.00).

    (c) If Pete waits until age 65 to collect the CPP retirement benefit, by how much will his pension income increase (without OAS and using generic CPP rates)? (Answer: $1,105.00)

	Question 42	Question 43	Question 44	for NRA 60
Minimum Age				50
Normal retirement age	58	51	53	60
Years of service	36	29	28	30
Factor	94	80	81	85

43. A few years ago, Pete was seriously injured on the job. He made a full recovery, but wondered if he was getting too old and thought that perhaps he should retire early. He was 51 at the time. By what percentage would his pension for the 29 years of service he had at that time have been reduced if he had retired then? (Answer: 5%)

44. Joe, a police officer, is 53, and wishes to retire. He has 28 years of service. How much will his pension be reduced if he takes early retirement? (Answer: 10%)

5

Pension Adjustment (PA) and Other Pension Plans

Learning Objectives

A. Understand the Pension Adjustment (PA):
   - Be able to calculate it for Defined Contribution Plans (DCPPs), Defined Benefit Plans (DBPPs), and Deferred Profit Sharing Plans (DPSPs),
   - Know the effect of the pension adjustment on RRSP contribution room for various types of defined benefit plans
   - Know what Past Service Pension Adjustment (PSPA) means for an employee buying credits for past service
   - Understand Pension Adjustment Reversal (PAR), which occurs when an employee terminates employment before vesting or possibly when an employee leaves a plan.

B. Know the various types of profit-sharing plans:
   - Cash profit-sharing plan
   - Employee profit-sharing plan
   - Deferred Profit-Sharing Plan (DPSP).

C. Learn about special types of retirement plans:
   - Plans for significant shareholders
   - Individual Pension Plans (IPPs)
   - Supplemental Retirement Arrangements (SRAs)
   - Supplemental Employee Retirement Plans (SERPs)
   - Capital Accumulation Plan (CAP)

D. Understand the effect of RPP contributions on current taxes.

> Craig's company has decided on a defined benefit pension plan, perhaps to be supplemented by a deferred profit sharing plan when company profits are particularly strong. The pension administrator has outlined several different possibilities for the payment of the retirement benefit, and Craig and Margot want to know the effect this development will have on his ability to contribute to his RRSP. In addition, there is a possibility that the company will arrange for pension contributions for years prior to setting up this plan. They understand this may also affect their RRSP contributions in the future and are wondering what would happen if Craig decided to leave the company.

INTRODUCTION

In order to promote a level playing field, the Income Tax Act places restrictions on the amount an individual can contribute to tax-sheltered retirement savings. The mechanism for enacting this level playing field is the **Pension Adjustment (PA),** which reduces RRSP contribution room for people who have employer-sponsored pension plans. In addition, employees in defined benefit plans are sometimes given an opportunity to purchase pension benefits for past service. These additional pension credits require a compensating reduction in RRSP contribution room, called the **Past Service Pension Adjustment (PSPA).** Lastly, when a person terminates employment after pension benefits are vested, the amount of benefits they can transfer may be less than the amount of their pension adjustment in respect of those contributions. The **Pension Adjustment Reversal (PAR)** restores RRSP contribution room to the individual to compensate them for the loss in pension benefits.

Profit-sharing plans allow employees to participate in company profits. In addition, owner-managers and high-income employees also have vehicles for tax-deferred retirement savings other than RRSPs. These vehicles include plans for significant shareholders (small companies with few non-family employees), Individual Pension Plans (IPPs), and plans that supplement pensions for high-income employees, specifically Supplemental Retirement Arrangements (SRAs) and Supplemental Employee Retirement Plans (SERPs).

A. PENSION ADJUSTMENT AND ITS EFFECT ON RRSP CONTRIBUTIONS

The Income Tax Act places restrictions on the amount an individual can contribute to tax-sheltered retirement savings since all tax-sheltered retirement savings plans defer taxes. They can also reduce taxes, as illustrated in Chapter 2, Example 2, where Mark was able not only to defer taxes when he saved but was also able to save taxes because he was in a lower tax bracket when he withdrew the funds. It is unfair to allow everyone the same level of RRSP contribution when, as pointed out in Chapter 3, one-third of the Canadian labour force is already covered by a registered pension plan. To even out the pension-saving playing field for all Canadians, the pension adjustment (PA) was introduced. The PA is an amount that reduces the RRSP deduction limit for people who are in company-sponsored registered pension plans.

Pension Adjustment (PA)

A pension adjustment calculation is required of all employers who provide their employees with either a registered pension plan (RPP) and/or a deferred profit sharing plan (DPSP). The purpose of the pension adjustment is to put a limit on the annual RRSP contribution that an employee can make when that employee is a member of one of these registered plans. The maximum annual amount an employee can contribute to the combination of a registered retirement savings plan (RRSP), registered pension plan (RPP), and a deferred profit-sharing plan (DPSP) for the *current* year is called the **RRSP maximum dollar limit** and is the *lesser* of:

- 18% of *prior* year's total compensation, or
- the **money purchase limit** for the *prior* year. (See Table 5.1.)

Failure to respect the PA limits can result in the pension plan being revoked or terminated.

The PA is the total of a member's **pension credits** from all pension plans in which the member's employer participated during a calendar year. A **pension credit** is a measure of the value of the benefit the member earned or accrued during the calendar year under a DPSP, a DBPP and a DCPP. RRSPs do not generate pension credits. An individual's PA for a year is the *total pension credits* from:

- a defined contribution pension plan
- a defined benefit pension plan
- a deferred profit-sharing plan

- **Forfeited amounts**, or amounts to which a member no longer has a right, arise mostly from non-vested contributions by the employer: that is, an employee has left a job before these contributions have vested. The benefits arising from the employer's contributions are lost to the departed employee and are distributed to other employees as forfeited amounts.
- Additional voluntary contributions (AVCs).

The PA for a year reduces the amount that a member can contribute to an RRSP in the *following year*. The first year an employer had to calculate a PA was 1990 — there are no PAs for earlier years. Thus, the first year in which RRSP deduction room was reduced by PAs was 1991.

In 2014, RRSP contribution room (RRSP maximum dollar limit) is the lesser of:

- 18% of 2013 earned income less 2013 PA, and
- 2013 money purchase limit less 2013 PA (see Exhibit 5.1).

Table 5.1 Money Purchase Limit and RRSP Maximum Dollar Limit

Money Purchase Limit		RRSP Maximum Dollar Limit	
1990	11,500		
1991–92	12,500	1991	11,500
1993	13,500	1992–93	12,500
1994	14,500	1994	13,500
1995	15,500	1995	14,500
1996–2002	13,500	1996	15,500
2003	15,500	1997–2003	13,500
2004	16,500	2004	15,500
2005	18,000	2005	16,500
2006	19,000	2006	18,000
2007	20,000	2007	19,000
2008	21,000	2008	20,000
2009	22,000	2009	21,000
2010	22,450	2010	22,000
2011	22,970	2011	22,450
2012	23,820	2012	22,970
2013	24,270	2013	23,820
2014 and onward	The greater of:	2014	24,270

- $24,270 × (average wage* for the year ÷ average wage for 2013) rounded to the closest $10 and rounded up if halfway between to multiples of 10, and
- the money purchase limit for the previous year.

*The average wage is available from Statistics Canada.

Source: T4084(E) Rev. 08 Pension Adjustment Guide <www.cra-arc.gc.ca> Glossary, p 5.

Calculating the Pension Adjustment

The PA must be calculated for:

1. Defined contribution plans (DCPPs) and deferred profit sharing plans (DPSPs), both based on contributions, and
2. Defined benefit plans (DBPPs) based on benefit earned.

and includes any forfeited amounts and additional voluntary payments where AVCs are permitted.

Contributions to these plans must be such that the PA for a year is not greater than the money purchase limit of the following year because the money purchase limit is the maximum amount of contributions or benefit earned that can be made to *all* registered plans.

Therefore, the pension adjustment for *2013* is the total of the pension credits for:

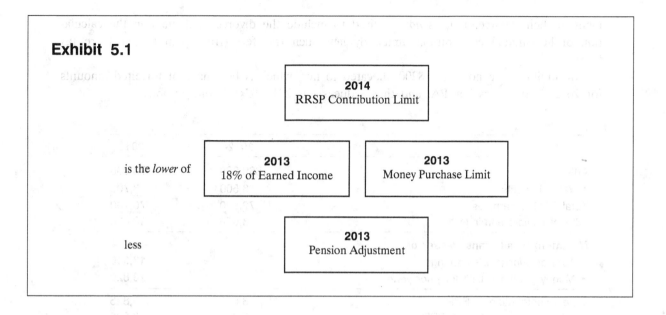

Exhibit 5.1

1. Registered Pension Plans (DBP or DCP) in *2013*
2. Deferred Profit Sharing Plans (DPSP) in *2013*
3. Forfeited Amounts for all plans (DBP, DCP, and DPSP) in *2013*, and
4. Additional Voluntary Contributions made in *2013* (for defined contribution plans).

to a maximum of the money purchase limit for *2013*, which is $24,270.

In other words, the *2013* pension adjustment limits the *2014* RRSP contribution room (and, again, the 2014 RRSP maximum dollar limit is the 2013 money purchase limit). There are various types of pension plans, and the pension-adjustment calculation is different for each type.

Defined Contribution Pension Plan (DCPP)

As discussed previously, a DCPP is one in which the pension benefit depends on the amount in the fund at the time of retirement. The RPP pension adjustment for an employee who is a member of a DCPP equals the total amount of the employee and employer contributions in the year. Example 1 illustrates the calculation of a PA for a DCPP and its effect on RRSP contribution limits.

Example 1   Jane is a member of a DCPP. She and her employer each contribute 5% of her eligible earnings each year. As she is starting to think about filing her 2013 tax return (due by April 30, 2014), she wants to know how much she can contribute to her RRSP for 2013 (the contribution deadline is February 28, 2014). The money purchase limit for 2013 is $24,270 and, for 2012, is $23,820. She has been told that she will not receive her T4 for 2013 until the end of February, 2014, and she is worried that she might miss the 2013 RRSP contribution deadline. However, Jane does notice that her previous year's T4 (2012) lists a PA amount. It is her 2012 PA from her *2012* T4 that affects her 2013 RRSP contribution, meaning she has had the information she needs to maximize her 2013 RRSP contribution for nearly a year.

Jane is uncertain if she should include the $20,000 transferred to her plan as her share of her ex-husband's pension. The amount was allocated to Jane as part of the final settlement in their divorce. Jane is *not* required to include the divorce settlement in the calculation of her annual contribution limits. By law, such transfers (from plan to plan) are tax free.

In addition, she notes the $200 allocated to her, which is her share of forfeited amounts for 2012. It increases her PA, and thus reduces her 2013 RRSP contributions.

	2012	2013
Salary	$69,000	$73,000
Taxable benefits	3,500	3,700
Total eligible earnings	72,500	76,700
18% of eligible earnings	**13,050**	13,806
Maximum to all plans: *lesser of*:		
• 18% of *prior year's* earnings		**13,050**
• Money purchase limit for *prior year*		23,820
Jane's contribution to RPP	3,625	3,835
Employer's contribution to RPP	3,625	3,835
Forfeited amount	200	
Pension adjustment for current year	**7,450**	**7,670**
Maximum to all plans for 2013		13,050
PA for *prior year* from 2012 T4		7,450
Amount Jane can contribute to her RRSP for 2013		5,600

Deferred Profit Sharing Plan (DPSP)

A DPSP is a defined contribution pension plan whereby the contributions are based on a formula that is based on profits. The pension adjustment for the *current* year for the employee with regard to all DPSPs to which the employee might belong is the total of:

• all employer contributions (employees do not make contributions), and
• any forfeited amounts

to a maximum of the *lesser* of:

• 1/2 of the money purchase limit for the *current year,* or
• 18% of earnings for the *current* year before the DPSP contribution.

Example 2 illustrates the maximum amount that can be contributed to a DPSP when there is no RPP but there is a DPSP forfeited amount.

Example 2   Mark's salary in 2013 is $65,000. His company has no RPP but it has a DPSP and Mark participates in it. The plan can compensate Mark for 3% of the company's net income, which is expected to be $500,000 this year. Mark's colleague, Andre, left the plan in 2013 after 18 months, and Mark's share of Andre's forfeited contributions to the DPSP is $900.

What is the maximum his employer can contribute to the DPSP in 2013 on his behalf without contravening the legislative limit?

Employer contribution

Maximum contribution is the *lesser of*:
• 1/2 of 2013 money purchase limit	24,270 × 0.50	=	12,135
• 18% of 2013 salary	65,000 × 0.18	=	**11,700**
minus forfeited amount =			900
Maximum possible contribution to DPSP in 2013			**10,800**

Assuming Mark's employer makes the maximum possible contribution to his DPSP, the PA for the DPSP appearing on Mark's 2013 T4 will be $11,700 ($10,800 for the DPSP + $900 for the forfeited amount). His 2014 RRSP contribution room will be:

2014 RRSP contribution limit

Maximum RRSP for the year is the *lesser* of:
• money purchase limit for 2013		24,270
• 18% of 2013 earnings	65,000 × 18% =	**11,700**
minus total PA of all registered plans		11,700
Maximum to RRSP		0

If the employee is also a member of an RPP or another DPSP, the employer's contribution to the DPSP must not be so high that causes the PA to be greater than the *lesser* of:

- 18% of earned income, or
- the money purchase limit.

Defined Benefit Pension Plan (DBPP)

As stated before, a defined benefit plan is an RPP that specifies the pension benefit for plan members, with the employer having full responsibility for ensuring that there are sufficient funds in the plan to pay the defined benefits. Calculating the PA for a DBPP is much more complex than calculating the PA for a defined contribution plan. It entails two steps.

Step 1.   Calculate the **benefit earned** for the year. The benefit earned is the accrued amount of a member's pension benefit during the year. It is the *lowest* of:

1. The plan formula — for example, 1.5% (an arbitrary number) × earnings for the PA year
2. 2% of earnings up to the maximum pensionable earnings for the PA year, which is $134,833 for 2013 (2% × $134,833 = $2,696.67 for 2013), and
3. The **defined benefit limit** for the PA year, which places an upper limit on the annual benefit earned. The defined benefit limit is the *greater* of:
   i. The legislated **overriding provision**, which is the maximum amount of annual benefit earned under the **Maximum Pension Rule**. It is **$1,722.22 as of 1995.** (Note: A plan can stipulate an overriding provision that is less than the legislation allows.), and
   ii. 1/9 of the money purchase limit

   except for 1990 to 1994 inclusively, when the benefit earned was restricted to 1/9 of the money purchase limit (called the **dollar limit** for these five years). In the calculations in Table 5.2 below, the dollar limit is indicated with an asterisk.

Step 2.   Apply the **Pension Credit Formula**, which is:

$$(9 \times \text{benefit earned}) - \text{PA offset}$$

where the **Pension Adjustment (PA) offset** is $600 as of 1997 and was $1,000 from 1990 to 1996 (the figure used when recalculating the pension credit for these years).

Table 5.2 Determining Defined Benefit Limit

Year	Money purchase limit	1/9 of money purchase limit	Overriding provision	Defined benefit limit	Maximum pensionable earnings**
1	2	3	4	5	6
		column 2 ÷ 9		greater of 3 or 4 except for 1990–1994	column 5 ÷ 2%
1990	11,500	1,277.78*	1,715.00	1,277.78*	63,889
1991–2	12,500	1,388.89*	1,715.00	1,388.89*	69,445
1993	13,500	1,500.00*	1,715.00	1,500.00*	75,000
1994	14,500	1,611.11*	1,715.00	1,611.11*	80,556
1995	15,500	1,722.22	1,722.22	1,722.22	86,111
1996–2002	13,500	1,500.00	1,722.22	1,722.22	86,111
2003	15,500	1,722.22	1,722.22	1,722.22	86,111
2004	16,500	1,833.33	1,722.22	1,833.33	91,667
2005	18,000	2,000.00	1,722.22	2,000.00	100,000
2006	19,000	2,111.11	1,722.22	2,111.11	105,556
2007	20,000	2,222.22	1,722.22	2,222.22	111,111
2008	21,000	2,333.33	1,722.22	2,333.33	116,667
2009	22,000	2,444.44	1,722.22	2,444.44	122,222
2010	22,450	2,494.44	1,722.22	2,494.44	124,722
2011	22,970	2,552.22	1,722.22	2,552.22	127,611
2012	23,820	2,646.67	1,722.22	2,646.67	132,333
2013	24,270	2,696.67	1,722.22	2,696.67	134,833
After 2013	indexed		1,722.22	indexed	indexed

*The **dollar limit**
**This is the maximum pensionable earnings for a plan that pays 2% for each year of service — divide the defined benefit limit by 2%. Examples 7 and 9 illustrate the maximum pensionable earnings for plans that pay less than 2%.

The **pension credit** is the *lesser* of:

• the result from the Pension Credit Formula, and
• the money purchase limit.

The pension credit can be zero but is never negative.

These limits reflect only the legislative limits. Actual defined benefit pension plans may have limits that are more restrictive. As stated earlier, the pension adjustment is the total of the pension credits from all sources.

Illustrations of the calculation of the pension adjustment for defined benefit plans is found in Example 3a, and Example 3b then calculates the DPSP contribution and pension credit when there is a defined benefit plan.

Example 3a   Mary's salary is $65,000 in 2013. Her company has a defined benefit pension plan that entitles her to 2% of the average of her last five years' salary. How much can Mary contribute to her RRSP in 2014?

Pension formula	2% of the average of the last five years' earnings	
2013 Earnings	**65,000**	
Pension credit for RPP		
Benefit earned for 2013 is the *lesser* of:		
• plan formula	2% × 65,000 =	**1,300.00**
• 2% of earnings	2% × 65,000 =	**1,300.00**
• defined benefit limit for 2013	2% × 134,833 =	2,696.67
Pension credit for RPP	(9 × 1,300) − 600 =	**11,100**
2014 RRSP contribution limit is the *lesser* of:		
• money purchase limit for 2013		24,270
• 18% of 2013 salary	65,000 × 18% =	**11,700**
minus PA for RPP		11,100
2014 RRSP contribution room		600

Example 3b   The company also has a profit sharing plan that can compensate Mary for 3% of the company's net income, which is expected to be $500,000 this year. What is the maximum her employer can contribute to the DPSP in 2013 on her behalf without contravening the legislative limit. Also, what will Mary's RRSP contribution limit be for 2014?

Pension formula	2% of the average of the last five years' earnings	
2013 Earnings before DPSP	**65,000**	
1. **Pension credit for RPP** (from Example 3a)		11,100
2. Maximum possible PA for all registered plans is the *lesser* of:		
• money purchase limit for 2013		24,270
• 18% of 2013 salary	65,000 × 18% =	**11,700**
3. Maximum possible pension credit for DPSP is the *lesser* of:		
• 1/2 of money purchase limit for 2013	24,270 × 50% =	12,135
• 18% of 2013 salary	65,000 × 18% =	**11,700**
Pension credit available for DPSP = Maximum possible PA minus pension credit for DBPP	11,700 − 11,100	**600**
Pension adjustment for both plans	11,100 + 600 =	11,700
4. RRSP contribution limit for 2014 is the *lesser* of:		
• money purchase limit for 2013		24,270
• 18% of 2013 salary	65,000 × 18% =	**11,700**
minus total PA of all registered plans		11,700
2014 RRSP contribution room		0

Note: The **pension formula** states how much will be paid for each year of eligible service and is the basis for calculating:

1. The **pension adjustment**, which is based on only the current year's earnings — *one year only*.

2. The **pension benefit**, which often uses the *average of several years' earnings* and the number of years of pensionable service.

The following examples will illustrate

• the most common defined benefit provisions
• the pension benefit that will result from the pension formula, and
• the effect of the 2013 PA on the 2014 RRSP contribution limit.

Types of Defined Benefit Pension Plans

There are several types of defined benefit provisions, as shown in Tables 4.1a and 4.2a:

- final earnings (48% of DBPPs and 79% of plan members),
- career average earnings (47% of DBPP and 5% of plan members), and
- flat benefit (5% of DBPPs and 17% of plan members).

In addition, some plans:

- are integrated with the Canada Pension Plan, and
- cover more than one member (multi-employer plans).

1. Final or Best Average Earnings

Pension formulas under this provision will calculate the pension benefit based on some percentage (perhaps 2% or 1.75%) of the average of "x" number of years of service, where "x" can be any predetermined number of years such as three or five years.

Final or best average earnings uses a pre-determined number of years for "x", such as three years or five years.

Career average earnings are calculated the same way as "final earnings", except that they use the average earnings of that member's entire career, instead of the final or best years.

In Example 4, Janet, who is considering retiring, will find out her pension amount (if she retires this year) and her RRSP contribution with or without a DPSP.

Example 4a   Janet is a member of a pension plan that provides a pension using the following pension formula.

Pension formula: 1.75 % of the average of the best three years' of earnings

Janet's best three years of earnings were $56,000, $58,300, and $60,000, giving her an average of $58,100 if she retires now. She has 27 years of eligible service with this employer, and her pension benefit is calculated:

Pension benefit: Pension formula × number of years of eligible service

$$1.75\% \times \$58,100 \times 27 \text{ years} = \$27,452.25$$

If Janet has made contributions to only the RPP in 2013, her RRSP contribution room for 2014 is:

2013 Earnings		60,000
2013 Pension adjustment for RPP		
1. Benefit earned is the *lesser* of:		
• plan formula	1.75% × 60,000 =	**1,050.00**
• 2% of earnings	2 × 60,000 =	1,200.00
• defined benefit limit for 2013		2,696.67
2. PA = Pension credit for 2013	(9 × $1,050.00) − 600 =	**8,850.00**
2014 RRSP contribution limit is the *lesser* of:		
• 2013 money purchase limit		24,270
• 18% of 2013 earnings	60,000 × 18% =	**10,800**
less 2013 PA		8,850
2014 RRSP contribution room		**1,950**

Note: Janet can make this 2014 RRSP contribution even if she is retired for all of 2014. This is discussed further in Chapter 6.

Example 4b shows the effect on 2014 RRSP contributions in Example 4a if Janet also has a deferred profit sharing plan.

Example 4b   Janet's company has a DPSP. What is the maximum her employer can contribute to the DPSP on her behalf? If her employer contributed $1,500 to the DPSP on her behalf, what is her 2014 RRSP contribution room?

2013 Earnings before DPSP	**60,000**	
Maximum possible pension credit for DPSP is the *lesser* of:		
• 1/2 of the 2013 money purchase limit	24,270 × 0.50 =	12,135
• 18% of 2013 income	60,000 × 0.18 =	**10,800**
2014 RRSP contribution limit	Calculated in 4a above	10,800
minus pension credit for RPP	Calculated in 4a above	8,850
Pension credit available for DPSP		**1,950**
Employer contribution to DPSP in 2013		1,500
2014 RRSP contribution room		**450**

2. Flat Rate

Flat-rate pensions are based on a flat amount multiplied by the number of months or years worked, with or without fractions of a year. Example 5 shows both Jean's pension in 2014 and her 2014 RRSP contribution room based on her 2013 salary of $60,000.

Example 5   Jean's company provides the following DBPP.

Pension formula: $100 a month for each full month worked

By the end of 2013, Jean has 27 years (324 months) of eligible service with this employer. Her pension benefit when she retires in January 2014 is:

Pension benefit: $100 × 324 months = $32,400

If Jean has made contributions to only her RPP in 2013, her RRSP contribution room for 2014 is:

Pension formula	$100 a month for each full year worked	
2013 Earnings	60,000	
2013 pension adjustment		
1. Benefit earned is the *lesser* of:		
• plan formula	100 × 12 =	**1,200.00**
• 2% of salary	60,000 × 2% =	1,200.00
• defined benefit limit for 2013		2,696.67
2. PA = Pension credit for 2013	(9 × $1,200.00) − 600 =	**10,200**
2014 RRSP contribution limit is the *lesser* of:		
• 2013 money purchase limit		24,270
• 18% of 2013 earnings	60,000 × 18% =	**10,800**
less 2013 PA		10,200
2014 RRSP contribution room		**600**

3. Integrated Formula

Some pension plans are integrated with the benefits provided by the CPP or OAS. The benefit earned is reduced by a factor that takes into account an estimate of the amount the employee will collect from CPP. One method was illustrated in the OMERS plan outlined in Chapter 4. Both the pension contribution and the pension benefit are adjusted to reflect the CPP Offset. Since this offset does not take effect until age 65, the OMERS plan provides a bridge benefit for those members who retire before age 65. Example 6 and 7 provide two different formula for integrating the CPP.

Example 6 shows the calculation for the first year of Jane's integrated pension in 2014, based on the average of her best 3 years of earnings of $58,300 and her 2014 RRSP contribution based on her 2013 salary of $60,000.

Example 6   Jane's company pension plan provides her pension using the following pension formula:

Pension formula: 2% × average earnings of the best three years *minus*
[(1 ÷ 35) × actual CPP pension]

Jane's best three years' average earnings is $58,300, and she will receive $8,135 in CPP pension (she is not receiving the maximum possible CPP). She has 33 years of service.

Pension benefit: 2% × average earnings of the best three years *minus*
(1 ÷ 35) × actual CPP pension × number of years of RPP service

The first year she is retired she will collect:

From her pension plan		
2% × average earnings of the best three years	58,300 × 2% =	1,166.00
minus CPP offset	8,135 × 1/35 =	232.43
Amount for each year of service		933.57
RPP income	933.57 × 33 years =	30,807.81
CPP retirement benefits		8,135.00
Total pension income		38,942.81

Jane's 2013 pension adjustment and 2014 RRSP contribution room are:

Pension formula	2% × best 3 years' earnings *minus* (1 ÷ 35) × actual CPP benefits	
2013 Earnings	**60,000**	
2013 YMPE (Year's Maximum Pensionable Earnings for CPP)	46,000 (generic rate)	
CPP offset[1]	25% × 46,000 × (1 ÷ 35) =	328.57
2013 Pension adjustment		
1. Benefit earned is the *lesser* of:		
• plan formula	(60,000 × 2%) − 328.57 =	**871.43**
• 2% of earnings	2% × 60,000 =	1,200.00
• defined benefit limit for 2013		2,696.67
2. PA = Pension credit for 2013	(9 × $871.43) − 600 =	**7,242.86**
2014 RRSP contribution limit is the *lesser* of:		
• 2013 money purchase limit		24,270.00
• 18% of 2013 earnings	60,000 × 18% =	**10,800.00**
less 2013 PA		7,242.86
2014 RRSP contribution room		**3,557.14**

---

1   In Chapter 3, we stated that CPP retirement income is approximately 25% of the year's maximum pension earnings. So the CPP offset for this plan is the YMPE × 25%. Another example of the CPP offset was also given in Chapter 4 in the OMERS illustration.

Example 7 illustrates another possible integrated formula whereby contributions to and benefits from the pension plan are stepped to take into account CPP retirement benefits, similar to the OMERS example in Chapter 4. In this example, the pension benefit is based on the best five-year average earnings and the five-year average year's maximum pensionable earnings (AYMPE).

Example 7   Janice's company pension plan provides pension benefits using the following pension formula:

Pension formula: (1.2% × average of the best five years' earnings up to the AYMPE)
+ (2% × average of the best five years' earnings over the AYMPE)

Janice retires at the end of 2013 with 32 years of service, and the average of her best five years' earnings is $58,300. She is eligible to receive a CPP retirement benefit of $11,500 (generic rate). The *generic* average YMPE (AYMPE) is $44,000. For each year of service, she will receive a pension of:

Rate	On	$ per year of service
1.2%	$44,000	525.00
2.0%	$14,300 (58,300 − 44,000)	286.00
		814.00

Pension benefit: Pension formula × number of years of service

With 32 years of service, her pension income in 2014 will be:

RPP income	814.00 × 32 =	26,048.00
CPP retirement benefits		11,500.00
Total pension income		**37,548.00**

If Janice's pension is indexed, RPP income will increase the following year by some amount to reflect all or part of inflation. We know that the CPP retirement benefit is indexed and will increase.

Janice checks the CRA website and finds that the money purchase limit for 2013 is $24,270. Her PA for 2013 and her 2014 RRSP contribution room are:

Pension formula	(1.2% × best five years' earnings up to YMPE) + (2% × best five years' earnings over YMPE)	
2013 Earnings	60,000	
2013 YMPE	46,000 generic rate	
five years' AYMPE	44,000 generic rate	
2013 Pension adjustment		
1. Benefit earned is the *lesser* of:		
• plan formula	552.00 (1.2% × 46,000) +	
	280.00 (2% × (60,000 − 46,000))	**832.00**
• 2% of earnings	2% × 60,000 =	1,200.00
• defined benefit limit for 2013		2,696.67
2. **2013 PA = Pension credit**	(9 × $832.00) − $600 =	**6,888.00**
2014 RRSP contribution limit is the *lesser* of:		
• 2013 money purchase limit		24,270.00
• 18% of 2013 earnings	60,000 × 18% =	**10,800.00**
less 2013 PA		6,888.00
2014 RRSP contribution room		**3,912.00**

Janice's company pension plan is a contributory plan. According to the pension plan contract, with the year's basic exemption (YBE) at $3,500, her contributions are:

8.0% for earnings below the YBE
plus 6.2% for earnings between the YBE and the YMPE
plus 8.0% for earnings in excess of the YMPE up to a maximum pensionable earning of $140,622

Because the pension formula is integrated with the CPP YMPE, the maximum pensionable earnings is higher than the $134,833 shown in Table 5.2 for 2013.

Maximum limit on benefit earned for 2013	2,696.67
less 1.2% × 46,000 (generic YMPE)	−552.00
Amount of benefit earned available for 2%	2,144.67
Additional salary pensionable at 2% (2,144.67 ÷ .02)	107,234
Add YMPE (pensionable @ 1.2%)	46,000
Total pensionable earnings	**153,234**

Since Janice earned only $60,000 in 2013, she will make the following contributions to her DBPP:

Rate	Applied to	Contribution per year
8.0%	3,500	280.00
6.2%	42,500 (46,000 − 3,500)	2,635.00
8.0%	14,000 (60,000 − 46,000)	1,120.00
		4,035.00

Notice that her tax-deductible contribution is $4,035.00, while her pension adjustment, calculated above, is $6,888.00.

4. Multi-Employer Plan (MEP)

A multi-employer plan (MEP) can have several employers and thousands of members. If the employee works for more than one employer and each provides a pension plan, all the employers have to calculate the pension adjustment. Example 8 shows the calculation of the pension adjustment for a member under a multi-employer plan who worked for each employer for part of a year.

Example 8   John was Assistant Director of Human Resources for the Woodstock General Hospital for many years. He quit as of May 31, 2013, to move to the Stratford Regional Health Centre, where he became the Assistant Vice-President of Human Resources. He earned $33,750 for the five months he worked in Woodstock and $52,500 for the seven months he worked in Stratford. The hospitals are both members of the We'll Help You Retire Pension Plan, a DBPP that pays 2% for each year of service up to the legislated maximum.

	Woodstock		Stratford	
Annualized earnings	(33,750 ÷ 5) × 12 = $81,000		(52,500 ÷ 7) × 12 = $90,000	
Benefit earned — *lesser* of:				
• pension formula	2% × 81,000 =	**1,620.00**	2% × 90,000 =	**1,800.00**
• 2% of earnings	2% × 81,000 =	**2,696.67**	2% × 90,000 =	**1,800.00**
• defined benefit limit for 2013		2,696.67		2,696.67
Pension credit *lesser* of				
• Pension credit formula	(9 × 1,620) − 600 =	**13,980**	(9 × 1,800) − 600 =	**15,600**
• 2013 money purchase limit		24,270		24,270
Pro-rated PA	13,980 × (5 ÷ 12) =	5,825	15,600 × (7 ÷ 12) =	9,100

John's pension adjustment will be $14,925 [5,825 + 9,100].

5. Member with a High Salary

Example 9 illustrates the PA calculation for a member with a high salary.

Example 9   Arthur earned an average of $160,000 a year for the past three years —
$140,000 in 2011, $155,000 in 2012, and $185,000 in 2013. He has a DBPP at
work that will pay 1.75% of the average of his last three years' earnings to a maximum of
35 years of pensionable service.

Pension formula: 1.75% of the average of the last three years' earnings

The defined benefit limit is the maximum per year that a pension can pay. Because his pension formula is less than 2%, his maximum pensionable earnings are more than those shown in Table 5.2. Let's compare the 2013 maximum earnings at a pension of 2% and 1.75%.

2013 defined benefit limit	Rate		Maximum earnings
2,696.67	÷ 2.00%	=	134,833
6,696.67	÷ 1.75%	=	154,095

We need to calculate the maximum pensionable earnings for all three years, since Arthur's income is higher than the maximum pensionable earnings for all three years.

Year	Defined benefit limit	Maximum pensionable earnings (defined benefit limit ÷ 1.75%)
2011	2,552.22	145,841
2012	2,646.67	151,238
2013	2,696.67	154,095
Average	2,631.85	150,391

If Arthur retires at the end of 2013 with 40 years of service, he will receive a pension of:

Pension benefit is the *lesser* of:
- Pension formula   160,000 × 1.75% × 35 years = $98,000
- Maximum pensionable earnings   150,391 × 1.75% × 35 years =   **$92,114**

His 2013 pension adjustment and 2014 RRSP contribution room are:

Pension formula	1.75% of last three years' earnings	
2013 Earnings	**185,000**	
2013 Pension adjustment		
1. Benefit earned is the *lesser* of:		
• plan formula	185,000 × 0.0175 =	3,237.50
• 2% of pensionable earnings	154,095 × 0.02 =	3,081.90
• defined benefit limit for 2013		**2,696.67**
2. 2013 PA = Pension credit	(9 × $2,696.67) − 600 =	23,670
2014 RRSP contribution limit the *lesser* of:		
• money purchase limit for 2013		**24,270**
• 18% of 2013 earnings	185,000 × 0.18 =	33,300
less 2013 PA		23,670
2014 RRSP contribution room		**600**

Note: Except when the DPSP uses all available RRSP contribution room, the "− 600" in the pension credit formula means the plan member can always deposit at least $600 to an RRSP.

As shown by these examples, the calculation of PAs can be quite complex. Fortunately, the PA for the year 2013 is shown on the 2013 T4, which employees receive in February 2014. The 2013 PA affects RRSP contributions for the following year — in this case 2014 — and these RRSP contributions do not have to be made until February 28, 2015.

Effect of Contribution Holidays on PA

CRA requires that any excess surplus in a pension plan be eliminated to prevent excess contributions that grow on a tax-deferred basis. When an excess surplus is used to pay employer and/or employee contributions, it is referred to as a **contribution holiday.** Contribution holidays can only be given if the employer's actuary confirms that there is an excess surplus and that the financial health of the plan will not be weakened by the holiday. Also, contribution holidays apply only to a defined benefit plan, since the pension adjustment is based on the benefit earned, not on the contributions made. Defined contribution plans can never have a pension surplus; thus, they never have contribution holidays. Because DBPP members continue to accrue pension benefits during a contribution holiday, the pension adjustment is not affected. The long bull market of the 1990s produced surpluses for many DBPPs, and several plans gave their members contribution holidays. More recently, there have been few surpluses large enough to merit a contribution holiday. Example 10 illustrates the possible consequences of failing to understand the basis for calculating the pension adjustment.

Example 10   Rosa teaches philosophy at a large university. Her defined benefit plan is administered by OMERS, which had been enjoying superlative investing results. As a result, the faculty at her university received a contribution holiday between 1998 and 2000. Rosa knows a great deal about philosophy but not a great deal about pensions. In 2001, on the advice of her accountant, who also does not understand pensions, she contributed $13,500, the maximum money purchase limit for the year, to her RRSP for 2000. She was very surprised to receive a notice from CRA stating that she had over-contributed to her RRSP by $11,500 and would be subject to a penalty.

Rosa and her accountant did not understand that the pension adjustment reflects her benefits earned, not contributions made. Since the surplus in her pension plan was paying the pension contributions, her PA was calculated in the same manner as it would have been if she and her employer had made the contributions. A detailed example of this scenario is provided in Chapter 6.

Double Dipping

This term refers to extra RRSP contributions that can be made in the year a company sets up a registered plan. Since RRSP contributions are based on the prior year's pension contributions, in the year a pension plan is set up, an employee could contribute the maximum money purchase limit for that year to an RRSP in addition to the pension contributions made through the company.

A **connected person** is someone who is closely connected to the corporation or a related corporation, such as:

- someone who directly or indirectly owns 10% or more of the shares of the employer or any related corporation, or
- someone who does not deal at arm's length with the employer.

If the employee is a connected person after 1989, his or her allowable contribution is reduced by the **prescribed amount**, which is the lesser of:

• 18% of the connected person's 1990 earned income for RRSP purposes, and
• $11,500.

Past Service Pension Adjustment (PSPA)

A past service pension adjustment (PSPA) is a pension adjustment for additional benefits received during years of previous service in a defined benefit plan. A PSPA arises out of benefit improvements that are related to a member's past service after 1989. They can be:

• benefits that are improved retroactively
• an additional period of past service that is credited to the member, or
• a retroactive change to the way in which a member's benefits are determined.

There cannot be past-service benefits for a money purchase plan or a deferred profit-sharing plan. A PSPA is equal to the additional pension credits that would have been included in the member's PA if the upgraded benefits or additional service had actually been provided in those previous years. Similar to a PA, a PSPA reduces the amount that a member can contribute to an RRSP in the current year (the year of the past service event)[2] and, perhaps, in following years. There are two types of PSPA: exempt PSPAs and certifiable PSPAs. An **exempt PSPA** usually occurs when all or almost all plan members receive past service benefit upgrades. A **certifiable PSPA** usually occurs if an RPP plan member decides to buy a period of past service that is pensionable service under the plan. In the latter case, approval by CRA is required before the employee can receive the benefits under the plan.

The employee can fund the past-service benefits either by writing a cheque or by transferring funds from an RRSP, as illustrated in the next example.

Example 11   Omar was recently given the opportunity to buy back three years of service he accrued while working for his current employer as a contract employee. Since he will have only 28 years of service when he retires, this option is attractive to him. It is not an attractive option to his colleague, John, who has already worked for their company for 36 years and will not retire for another four years. Since their plan has a maximum of 35 years of service, and John has already reached the maximum, he is not interested in this opportunity.

Because the rules about the tax deductibility of these contributions are complex and involve

• pre-1990 service while not a contributor,
• pre-1990 service while a contributor, and
• post-1989 service,

that are beyond the scope of this book, we will ignore the tax impact of the past service buyback in this discussion.

To make this past-service purchase, Omar must have or create sufficient RRSP contribution room because the purchase will earn him pension credits that will reduce his RRSP contribution room. This reduction is referred to as the past service pension adjustment (PSPA).

---

2   A past service event is defined as any transaction, event, or circumstance that causes a member's post-1989 benefits to increase.

If Omar *has sufficient RRSP contribution room*, he can simply write a cheque to pay for this purchase, or he can transfer some or all of the required amount from his RRSP. The CRA must approve the contribution, which will reduce available RRSP contribution room in the year the contribution is made.

If Omar *does not have sufficient RRSP contribution room* available, he can only transfer funds from his RRSP to his RPP to pay for this past service. This purchase may also use up future contribution room, since the PSPA will be greater than his contribution.

The plan actuaries tell Omar it will cost him $28,109 to buy this three years of service. The estimated PSPA will be $12,162. Is it worth it?

Several assumptions must be made. (This scenario is provided as an example only. A benefits specialist must be involved in this evaluation.) Omar is now 55 years old. If Omar:

- retires at age 65 (10 years from now),
- has pensionable earnings of $90,000 when he retires,
- has a plan whereby his benefit is 2% of earnings (paid at the beginning of the year), and
- lives to age 90,

he will receive an extra $5,400 a year (2% × $90,000 × 3 years) for each of the 25 years that he is retired. The offer from this plan states some assumptions about its future earnings:

- The pension fund will earn a rate of return of 7.5% a year.
- Inflation will be 2.5%.
- His salary will increase by 4.5% a year.

Timeline of Additional Income

	T_0	...	T_{10}	...	T_{35}
Annual increase in pension			5,400	...	5,400
PVA at retirement			PVA?		
PV now	PV?				

Omar's pension benefit is indexed, so we use a real rate of return of 4.88% [(1.075 ÷ 1.025) − 1] to analyze this offer. The present value at retirement of the additional benefit discounted at 4.88% is:

$$PVA_{65} = \$5,400_{BOY}(PVIFA_{25,\,4.88\%}) = \$80,790$$

And the value now of this $80,790?

$$PV_{55} = \$80,790\,(PVIF_{10,\,4.88\%}) = \$50,168$$

The cost to Omar is a total of $40,271 — $28,109 cash plus $12,162 in RRSP contribution room. It appears that Omar would be better off by buying back these years. In addition, Omar is married. If he should die before his wife, she can receive 60% of his pension.

Pension Adjustment Reversal (PAR)

A **pension adjustment reversal (PAR)** restores an individual's RRSP contribution room in situations where the individual terminates membership in a registered pension plan either by terminating employment or by terminating participation in the plan. The PAR restores RRSP contribution room when the amount received on termination is less than the accumulated PAs and PSPAs that have been calculated with respect to the benefit. The PAR applies to people who leave a plan before retirement after 1996 and is retroactive to 1991.

In a **defined contribution plan**, either a money purchase plan or a DPSP, a PAR occurs only if the employers' contributions are not vested. The amount of the PAR equals the amount of the contributions lost. The PAR does *not include* interest earned while the contributions were still in the plan.

The PAR *includes* forfeited amounts that had been allocated to the individual while that individual remained a member of the plan.

The PAR *does not include* the individual's own contributions:

- taken in cash as a lump-sum payment because this satisfies the individual's rights to benefits under the plan, or
- transferred to another plan.

For a **defined benefit plan**, the calculation is more complicated. In general, a PAR is issued when the contributions were less than the benefit earned. The PAR is:

+	the pension credit or money purchase limit, whichever is lower
+	pension credits received under a PSPA
–	benefits transferred to another plan or to a locked-in RRSP

The actual calculations can be quite complicated since the new plan may be different from the old plan. Reviewing the possible variations is beyond the scope of this book. Example 12 illustrates a PAR when DBPP benefits were not vested and the employee's contributions and income earned on those contributions are transferred to a DCPP.

Example 12   Andre left his company on January 15, 2014, after working there for two years (he works in a province where vesting does not occur until after three years of service). In 2012, he and his employer each made pension contributions of $4,200 (7% of his $60,000-per-year salary), while in 2013, his contributions were $4,550 (7% × $65,000). When he left, he transferred his contributions to the defined contribution plan at his new company and lost the benefits from the employer's contributions since they were not vested. His termination benefits include his contributions and interest earned on these contributions. His defined benefit pension plan would have paid a benefit of 2% on the average of his best three years' earnings.

Line #		2012	2013
1	Salary	60,000	65,000
2	Contribution to pension by Andre	4,200	4,550
	PA and PAR for the RRSP year:	**2013**	**2014**
	Maximum RRSP contribution room for the following year:		
3	• 18% × salary	**10,800**	**11,700**
4	Benefit earned (2% × salary)	1,200	1,300
5	Pension adjustment: (9 × benefit earned) – $600	**10,200**	**11,100**
6	RRSP contribution room the next year	**600**	**600**
7	Original pension adjustment (line 5)	10,200	11,100
	less: Value of pension transferred		
8	• His contributions to the defined benefit plan	(4,200)	(4,550)
9	• Income earned on his contributions	(460)	(180)
10	**Pension adjustment reversal** (PAR)	**5,540**	**6,370**
11	Original RRSP contribution room (line 6)	600	600
12	PAR	5,540	6,370
13	RRSP contribution room after PAR	**6,140**	**6,970**
14	PAR occurs in 2014 (6,140 + 6,970)		13,110

$13,110 will be added back to Andre's 2014 RRSP contribution room.

B. PROFIT SHARING PLANS

Profit sharing is an effective way to motivate employees in small- and medium-sized businesses, which are growing and require financial flexibility. Its goal is to make employees feel that they are valued partners in the company, improve employee loyalty and retention, increase productivity and profit, and build a congruent company culture. There are three types of profit-sharing plans:

1. Cash Profit Sharing Plans
2. Employee Profit Sharing Plans (EPSPs)
3. Deferred Profit Sharing Plans (DPSPs)

1. Cash Profit Sharing Plans

In these plans, cash profits are paid out as a lump sum once or twice a year. The payment can be related to:

*   minimum revenue or profit
*   an employee's salary
*   service or merit.

In effect, cash profit sharing plans are bonuses. They are fully taxable to the employee and fully tax deductible to the employer. Thus, there is no pension adjustment on these plans.

2. Employee Profit Sharing Plans (EPSP)

These plans are based on some percentage of profits with no maximum. They are used to increase employee compensation over the limits of deferred profit-sharing plans. The contributions are made to a trustee who allocates all contributions, income generated, and any forfeited amounts to all participants. The amount of each allocation is included in the employee's taxable income for the year. If the plan is filed with CRA, the employer contributions are tax deductible to the employer and taxable to the employee in the year of the contribution. Employees may also make contributions, on which there is no maximum but their contributions are not tax deductible. However, when the benefits are paid out to the employee, they are received tax free since tax has already been paid by the employee. There are no restrictions on the plan's investment, and these plans are often used as an investment vehicle for the company's own stock. Most contributions vest (almost) immediately, and there tends to be penalties on withdrawals to discourage frivolous withdrawals. There is no pension adjustment on these plans.

3. Deferred Profit Sharing Plans (DPSPs)

Deferred profit sharing plans are *registered money purchase plans* with contributions that are made out of profits. They are subject to rules and limitations in the same way as other registered pension plans. Like other plans, funds cannot be withdrawn. They are not very popular as the sole source of pension income, for two reasons:

1. the date of retirement, depends on company profits — the employee cannot retire until the plan holds sufficient funds, and
2. the annual contribution maximums are lower (one-half of the money purchase limit for the year — $12,135 in 2013).

DPSP contributions are paid by employers to a registered trust on behalf of some or all employees. Contributions by employees are not permitted. Contributions are based on profits of the current or prior years. If there are no profits, there might be no contributions. In other words, there is no minimum required contribution. Furthermore, effective after 1990, contributions can be made contingent on a condition such as employee performance, or at the employer's discretion. The pension credit equals the amount of the contribution.

There are investment restrictions on the trust funds, including but not limited to:

- The fund may not loan money to:
  - the company
  - an affiliate of the company
  - employees of the company making the contributions, or
  - to employees.
- The fund cannot be invested in notes, bonds, or debentures of the employer making the contributions, or in a corporation with which the employer does not deal at arm's length.
- The trustee must allocate all income received, capital gains made and losses incurred by the trust within 90 days of the trust's year-end; the funds are allocated to the beneficiaries of the plan.

Contributions are vested after two years' membership in the plan. Vested amounts are payable to the employee or the employee's beneficiary within 90 days after the earliest of:

(a)   the death of the employee
(b)   the day on which an employee ceases to be employed by the contributing employer
(c)   the day on which the employee turns 71 years old, and
(d)   the winding up of the plan.

Once payable, the funds can be paid out:

- at regular intervals not longer than 10 years, or
- as an annuity that must begin before the employees 71st birthday; any guaranteed term must not exceed 15 years.

A DPSP can usually be transferred to another registered plan (an RPP, RRSP, or another DPSP) if:

- the amount transferred is a lump sum,
- the amount transferred is on behalf of the employee or former employee or the employee's spouse (including a common-law spouse), and
- the benefits are part of the (former) employee's benefits from the plan.

C.   OTHER TYPES OF PLANS

For most Canadians, their registered retirement savings are a combination of employer-sponsored registered pension plans (DBPPs, DCPPs, and DPSPs) and personal Registered Retirement Savings Plans (RRSPs). However, self-employed professionals (e.g., doctors, lawyers, accountants, consultants), small business owners, and senior executives are often high-income earners and have income that can support a more aggressive tax-deferral arrangement. The usual employer-sponsored plans are insufficient or inappropriate. The following plans meet some of their needs:

- Plans for Significant Shareholders,
- Individual Pension Plans (IPP), and
- Supplemental Retirement Arrangements (SRA) and Supplemental Employee Retirement Plans (SERP).

In addition to these plans, Capital Accumulation Plans (CAP) can be set up to assist employees in making investment decisions in tax-assisted savings plans sponsored by employers.

Plans for Significant Shareholders

Many Canadian businesses are small businesses run by partners, proprietors, spouses, and/or family members. There are restrictions on pension plans for these small businesses based on the expected pension benefit by significant shareholders compared with the benefit by the total workforce of the small business.

A **significant shareholder** is defined as a person who, alone or together with a related person (parent, spouse, child, or sibling) owns or has an indirect or direct beneficial interest in 10% or more of the voting shares. A pension plan has been **set up primarily for the benefit of significant shareholders** and/or related persons if the present value of the benefits for the significant shareholders and/or related persons is more than 50% of the present value of all the benefits in the plan.

A **defined benefit plan** must *not* have been set up primarily for the benefit of significant shareholders; i.e., the pension benefits for the significant shareholders must not be more than 50% of the total pension benefits. A **defined contribution plan** that has been set up primarily for significant shareholders or persons related to them who are also employees faces contribution limits. The maximum the employer can contribute for each significant shareholder/employee is the *lesser of*:

- $3,500, or
- 20% of the employee's remuneration for the year in question,

and the maximum the employee can contribute is the same. If the significant shareholder belongs to more than one pension, the above limits apply to the total contributions.

Example 13   Liz owns a company that manufactures toys for cats. She owns 80% of the company while her daughter, Larissa owns 20%. Liz's salary is $80,000 per year. She has two employees who make $35,000 each, and Larissa makes $15,000 working for Liz in the summers (Larissa has three undergraduate degrees, one master's and is currently in her second year of a PhD program).

Liz *cannot* set up a **defined benefit pension plan.** The problem is not that Liz and Larissa own more than 10% of the company. The problem is that, between them, they make up 57.5% [($80,000 + 15,000) ÷ (80,000 + 15,000 + 35,000 + 35,000)] of the salaries — their pension benefits would probably be 57.5% of the total pension benefits. If Liz were to set up a pension plan with the benefit based on a flat rate multiplied by the years of service — it would be a defined benefit plan — but she is not interested in such a plan.

Liz *could* set up a defined benefit plan *if* salaries equalled total remuneration, and:

- Liz owned all the voting shares and Larissa was hired as just another employee. Liz's salary (and presumably her pension benefit) would then be 48.5% of the total remuneration. This scenario assumes that Larissa would have neither a direct nor an indirect interest in the voting shares. In other words, Larissa would have no beneficial interest in the company except as just another employee — an unlikely assumption; or
- Liz had a third employee who also earned $35,000. Then Liz and Larissa's salaries and pension benefits would be 47.5% of the total.

Liz *could also* set up a **defined contribution pension plan.** In this case, Liz's contributions for herself would be limited to *the lesser of*:

- $3,500, or
- $16,000 (20% of her salary: $80,000 × 20%)

and Larissa's contributions are limited to the *lesser of*:

- $3,500, and
- $3,000 ($15,000 × 20%).

If Liz wants her daughter and her employees to have a defined contribution pension plan, she might consider setting up a defined contribution plan whereby the total employee and employer contributions are a maximum of 4.375% of their salaries (since Liz is limited to $3,500, or 4.375% of her salary, presumably all would be restricted to 4.375%). The employee contributions would be:

Individual	Salary	Contributions	% each contribution
Liz	80,000	3,500.00	48.5%
Larissa	15,000	656.25	9.1%
Employee 1	35,000	1,531.25	21.2%
Employee 2	35,000	1,531.25	21.2%
	165,000	7,218.75	100.0%

Individual Pension Plans (IPPs)

An IPP is a defined benefit pension plan that benefits one individual or a group of employees. IPPs were first allowed in 1991 for self-employed, incorporated individuals who are significant shareholders (now, essentially, "connected persons"). They are also appropriate for executives.

Since is classified as a DBPP, the pension benefits are restricted to the defined benefit limit for each year of pensionable service. There is no minimum age or level of annual income, but generally it is most attractive to individuals between 45 and 71 years of age making at least $100,000 per year. Since the IPP is intended to provide a predetermined amount of pension income, it has to reach a certain value by the date of retirement. The older the planholder, the higher the required contributions which are generally higher than the RRSP contribution limit and are fully tax deductible to the corporation. Unlike RRSPs, all expenses associated with IPPs are also tax deductible to the corporation.

The required contributions are based on age, gender, years of service with the company, and the performance of the investments in the plan since the plan must have a certain value by the date of retirement. As a result, the older the employee, the higher the tax-deductible contributions, which are not limited to 18% of the employee's income. That is the attraction. In addition, when the plan is set up, the employer can make an additional contribution to fund years of past service. The PSPA takes into account any RRSP contributions made during the period of past service as well as unused RRSP contribution room. The individual must transfer an amount from their RRSP to the IPP equal to the PSPA. Any shortfall can be made up by the employer; i.e., the individual might have to clean out their RRSP in exchange for helping to fund a predetermined pension benefit. This transfer is tax free. The corporation can fund the past service over 15 years, and the contributions are fully tax deductible. For a 50-year-old, the cost could be as much as $88,000 for past service, and for a 60-year-old, as much as $144,000.[3]

The plan must be approved by the CRA and must be set up primarily to provide pension income. CRA does not allow an IPP to be set up for the purpose of receiving registered funds from other plans, although these transfers are permitted.

Like other pension plans, IPP contributions are made over time, and like a DBPP, an IPP must be reviewed by an actuary every three years to ensure that there is enough money in the plan to fund the predetermined retirement benefit. In addition, additional contributions can be required if the investment returns fall below expectations.

---

3   Individual Pension Plans, Phillips, Hager & North Investment Management Inc., May 2004: <www.phn.com/pdfs/featured_articles/individual_pension_plan>.

Advantages of IPPs

IPPs have the following advantages:

- Tax-deductible contributions can be significantly higher than RRSP deduction limits
- Investments held in the plan grow and compound tax free until their withdrawal at retirement.
- Contributions are treated as non-taxable benefits to the employee.
- Contributions and expenses (set-up fees, maintenance fees, as well as interest on a loan to top up the plan) are tax deductible to the plan sponsor (i.e., the employer).
- IPPs can be terminally funded (a one-time cost to make up for a fund shortage) for early retirement situations.
- There is flexibility at retirement, allowing members various payout options:
  - continuation of the plan, receiving the defined benefit; the tri-annual actuarial review continues and any underfunding must be financed by the employer who might also be the planholder.
  - purchase of an annuity with a joint-and-survivor benefit in which the annuity provider takes the investment risk — however, annual payments will be lower.
  - transfer to an RRSP and RRIF, which is then subject to restrictions (Chapter 7), or
  - transfer to the RPP of a new employer.
- The plan is protected from creditors, unlike most RRSPs (depending on the province).
- If the PA is small enough, RRSP contributions can be made.

Disadvantages of IPPs

IPPs have the following disadvantages:

- The required rate of return is predetermined by the CRA.
- No single equity position can exceed 10%.
- Funds are locked in while RRSP funds can be accessed.
- Administration costs can be high: $5,000 to set up, $500 for annual administration, and $1,500 for each tri-annual actuarial review.
- Contributions are mandatory.
- No income splitting (like a spousal RRSP) is permitted, although the spouse can participate if he or she is also an employee.
- If the CRA deems that the IPP was not set up in good faith — that is, not set up primarily to provide pension income — the registration can be cancelled and all the accumulated funds become fully taxable.

Supplemental Retirement Arrangements (SRAs) and Supplemental Employee Retirement Plans (SERPs)

The CRA sets a maximum on pension income from a defined benefit pension plan for each year of service. In addition, before January 1, 1992, the maximum number of years of pensionable service was 35, and many plans still have this stipulation. As a result, the defined benefit limit of $1,722.22 until 2003 restricted pension income based on 35 years to $60,278 ($1,722.22 × 35 years). Although the defined benefit limit has been increased (see Table 5.2), pension income from registered plans continues to be restricted. While there are no pension benefit limits on defined contribution plans, there are limits on contributions. Since the pension benefit is dependent on the amount of contributions, the rates of returns generated by the funds, and interest rates on annuities at the time of retirement, the amount of pension income from a defined contribution plan, while not limited by law, is restricted. For both types of pension plan, the retirement pensions from an RPP will not be representative of the pre-retirement income level of an increasing number of planholders. Since many of these planholders are crucial employees to the employer, it is in the employer's interest to address this income gap to retain those employees.

Supplemental Retirement Arrangements (SRAs) fall under the CRA definition of "Specified Retirement Arrangements." Universities call these plans SRAs, but in the private sector they are called Supplemental Employee Retirement Plans (SERPs). These are non-registered plans that allow employers to provide pension benefits over and above the limits imposed by the CRA. Most supplemental plans use the same pension formula as the underlying registered plan, but some provide an enhanced level of benefits. Most plans have vesting provisions that are the same as the underlying pension plan, although some have rules that are more restrictive — meaning the pension benefits are forfeited if the member terminates employment before the benefits have vested. It is also possible to deny benefits if the employee is fired for just cause or resigns, but this must be clearly spelled out in the SERP or SRA contract, as the underlying RPP is *required* to pay out all vested benefits regardless of the reason for the termination of employment. In addition, SERPs can contain non-compete clauses. Hence, they can be a kind of "golden handcuff," serving to keep key personnel, in addition to providing extra benefits not allowed by CRA to all personnel.

Example 14   Randy retired in 2013, and his best 5-year average pensionable salary was $80,000, which entitled him to a defined benefit of $56,000 ($80,000 × 2% × 35 years) from his employer's pension plan. Pauline also retired in 2013, and her best 5-year average pensionable salary was $160,000, which would have given her an annual pension of $112,000 ($160,000 × 2% × 35 years). However, the maximum pension payable from the registered pension plan was $94,383 ($2,696.67 × 35) because of the CRA restriction — a difference of $17,617 annually. If the employer has a SERP, that employer will pay the difference.

Funding of SRAs and SERPs

These plans can be fully funded, partially funded, or unfunded. In **funded plans,** employees do not usually contribute — that is, only employers contribute and their contributions are tax deductible. Employee contribution are also tax deductible if the contributions are both required and do not exceed the contributions of the employer. Plans can be funded with a **Retirement Compensation Arrangement (RCA)** or a **Line of Credit (LOC)** both of which provide creditor protection for the employee.

Unfunded plans do not provide a secure benefit in the private sector, particularly in the event of a takeover, a merger, a change in management, or a downturn in the financial fortunes of the company. In addition, while the employee has a contract to receive the benefits, the plan can be very expensive to finance after the member has retired since the employee could very well live for 30 years or more after retiring.

A 2008 survey[4] by Aon Consulting and FEI Canada found that 36% of the SERPs in the survey were funded with an RCA, 20% were funded with a letter of credit, and 44% were unsecured. It has been estimated that, by 2005, perhaps 25% of members of DBPPs will have some of their retirement benefits in supplemental plans.

The University of Toronto Proposal for Supplemental Retirement Arrangement[5] states:

> (viii) The University will accumulate funds outside the University Pension Plan in respect of the obligations under the SRA, but such funds will not be irrevocably earmarked for

4   Canadian Pension Plan Survey, Aon Consulting and FEI Canada, Summer 2008.
5   University of Toronto Proposal for Supplemental Retirement Arrangement: <www.mcmaster.ca/mufa/oft.htm>.

pension obligations. The SRA will not be considered a Retirement Compensation Arrangements ("RCA") under the ITA, provided the funds:

(a) do not constitute trust property;
(b) will be available to satisfy the claims of the University's creditors, if necessary;
(c) may be applied to any other purpose that the university may determine from time to time;
(d) will be commingled with other assets of the University; and
(e) will not be subject to direct claim of any members of the SRA.

(ix) Provided there is a sufficient surplus in the University Pension Plan, the University intends to set aside in University funds part of all of the University current service cost not made to the University Pension Plan, subject to the treatment of such funds as described above, and shall continue to do so, until the funds (including related investment income) equal the past service liability of the SRA, as certified by the actuary.

The plan at the University of Toronto was set up in 1996, when many pension plans were generating large surpluses. In early 2004, the university announced a new pension strategy, which requires full regular contributions from both the university and employees, as both the main RPP and the SRA were in a deficit position.

Retirement Compensation Arrangement (RCA)

An RCA is a trust that holds funds until a member retires. The contribution is tax deductible for both the employer and employee (if any) at the time of the contribution. However, 50% of the total contributions made by both the employer and the employee must be deposited in a refundable tax account with the CRA until the employee begins to collect the pension. At that time, $1 is refunded to the trust for every $2 the employee collects. This system has the effect of eliminating the difference in timing between the time when the contribution is made and when the employee receives the benefit, thereby maintaining the spirit of the maximum pension rule. In addition, 50% of all income earned (interest income, dividend income without the gross-up, and 100% of capital gains) must also be deposited with the CRA in the refundable tax account.

The trust can be managed by either a trustee or a custodian (a trust company or insurance company). There are few restrictions on the investment of the funds, although they are typically invested in stocks, bonds, mutual funds, T-bills and GICs. The funds can also be used to purchased an exempt life insurance policy, usually a Universal Life Policy, where part of the proceeds pays the premium on the policy and the rest is invested to produce income that is not taxable until is it withdrawn and is, therefore, not subject to the refundable tax.

Letter of Credit (LOC)

In lieu of funding, the RCA trust can hold an irrevocable letter of credit, which provides the trustee with access to the bank's funds to pay the benefit if the employer is unable or unwilling to pay it — even in the case of bankruptcy. The LOC fee varies from .25% to 1.5% of the employer's contribution. To fund a contribution of $100,000 with an RCA, an employer would have to contribute $200,000 to provide for the 50% refundable tax, while with an LOC, the employer would contribute only $3,000 – $1,500 to pay the LOC fee and $1,500 going to CRA. The LOC must not be secured by specific assets.

Capital Accumulation Plan (CAP)

A CAP is a tax-assisted investment or savings plan that allows its members to make investment decisions from not less than two options. Examples of CAPs include a DCPP, a DPSP, a Group RRSP and a Group RESP (the latter two are covered in Chapter 6). CAPs can be set up by employers, trade unions, associations, or a combination and are called the **plan sponsor.** The plan sponsor will often use **service providers** who provide legal and investment advice. Sponsors have a responsibility to ensure that members are educated to understand their options regarding investment choices and contribution rates and their implications for retirement planning.

The sponsor has to decide on the objectives and rules of the plan and communicate these to its members. These include:

- whether or not participation is compulsory
- eligibility rules
- vesting rules
- contribution rates when there is a choice
- investment options with information on how investments work, investment types and risk, etc.
- the policy if a member fails to make an investment decision
- fees, expenses and any penalties that might be incurred by the plan and by members
- how often members can make transfers among investment options and how much to charge for each transfer, and
- the extent to which the employer will match employee contributions when there is a choice.

D. TAXATION

Pension contributions are tax deductible; i.e., they are deducted from net income to arrive at taxable income. In addition, the pension adjustment is reported on the tax return each year in order to calculate RRSP contribution room, which is included in the Notice of Assessment that is sent out after the tax return is filed. The Notice of Assessment details the calculation of tax and also indicates changes to RRSP contribution room for the taxation year following the year of the tax return.

Craig's RRSP Contribution Room

Craig asks Francesca to look at his RRSP contribution room. Now that Craig has a pension at work, he has almost no new RRSP contribution room. Francesca advises him to put his unused RRSP contributions into a spousal RRSP since he will be receiving pension income from his company's pension plan. In calculating his contribution room for 2015, Francesca decides to leave out double dipping since they have quite a bit of unused contribution room.

Craig's 2015 RRSP Contribution Room with His PA

Pension formula	2% of last five years' earnings
2014 Earnings	90,000
2014 Pension adjustment	
1. Benefit earned is *the lesser of:*	
• plan formula (2%)	$90,000 × 2% = **1,800.00**
• 2% of earnings	$90,000 × 2% = **1,800.00**
• defined benefit limit for 2014 (using 2013)	2,696.67
2. 2014 PA = Pension credit	(9 × $1,800) − 600 = **15,600**
2015 RRSP contribution limit the *lesser* of:	
• money purchase limit for 2014 (using 2013)	24,270
• 18% of 2014 earnings	**16,200**
less 2014 PA	15,600
2015 RRSP contribution room	**600**

Earlier, we learned that Craig's salary was $90,000 in 2013 and that his company implemented a pension plan in 2014. What effect does this have on his pay? (We will continue to use generic tax rates and exemptions.)

Craig's Net (Take-home) Pay

The following table provides the calculations of Craig's net (take-home) pay for:
- 2013 with no RPP contributions, and
- 2014 with RPP contributions

		Calculation of 2013		Calculation of 2014		Difference in	
		Tax	Pay	Tax	Pay	Tax	Pay
Salary		90,000.00	90,000.00	90,000.00	90,000.00	0.00	0.00
Taxable benefits		750.00		750.00		0.00	0.00
			90,000.00		90,000.00		0.00
RPP contributions 6%			0.00	(5,400.00)	5,400.00	(5,400.00)	5,400.00
Disability			731.00		731.00		0.00
Taxable income		90,750.00		85,350.00		(5,400.00)	
Federal tax							
15% of	39,500	5,925.00		5,925.00		0.00	
22% of	39,500	8,690.00		8,690.00		0.00	
26% of	11,750	3,055.00		1,651.00		(1,404.00)	
		17,670.00		16,266.00		(1,404.00)	
Non-refundable tax credits:							
Basic personal amount		*10,000.00*					
CPP contributions		*2,103.75*	2,103.75		2,103.75		0.00
EI premiums		*701.46*	701.46		701.46		0.00
		12,805.21					
× 15%		1,920.78		1,920.78		0.00	
Basic federal tax (BFT)		15,749.22		14,345.22		(1,404.00)	
Provincial tax							
8% of	38,000	3,040.00		3,040.00		0.00	
13% of	38,000	4,940.00		4,940.00		0.00	
17% of	14,000	2,507.50		1,589.50		(918.00)	
		10,487.50		9,569.50		(918.00)	
Non-refundable tax credits:							
Basic personal amount		*9,000.00*					
CPP contributions		*2,103.75*					
EI premiums		*701.46*					
		11,805.21					
× 8%		944.42		944.42		0.00	
Basic provincial tax (BPT)		9,543.08		8,625.08		(918.00)	
Total tax		25,292.30	25,292.30	22,970.30	22,970.30	(2,322.00)	(2,322.00)
Total deductions			28,828.51		31,906.51		3,078.00
Net			**61,171.49**		**58,093.49**		**(3,078.00)**
Net as percentage of gross pay			67.97%		64.55%		−3.42%
Average tax rate			*28.10%*		*25.52%*		−2.58%
Marginal rate (calculation not shown)			*43.00%*		*43.00%*		

($xxx) = decrease, $xxx = increase

Comparing his 2014 pay with his 2013 pay, the average tax rate for Craig has gone down because the RPP contributions are tax deductible. However, his marginal tax rate has not changed because his top tax bracket has not changed. Craig's take-home pay is decreased by the after-tax amount of his RPP contribution, which can be calculated by using his marginal tax rate since it did not change:

$$\$3,078.00 = \$5,400 \times (1 - 0.43)$$

The employer's contribution to the company RPP for 2014 does not affect Craig's taxes. The employer's contributions are deferred compensation — the taxes will be paid by Craig when he receives the pension income in retirement. The employer's contributions are tax deductible for the 2014 tax year.

SUMMARY

To level the retirement-saving capacity for all Canadians, there are regulations reducing RRSP contribution rooms for taxpayers who are under an RPP: the pension adjustment (PA) and the past-service pension adjustment. Calculating the PA can become quite complex for some defined benefit pension plans. It is straightforward for defined contribution plans — both money purchase plans and deferred profit sharing plans — equals the total contributions of both the employer and employee. Where an employee in a DBPP can purchase pension benefits for past service, the purchase generates a past service pension adjustment (PSPA). While the amount can be large, it is usually a good idea since the employer shoulders the investment risk. While both the PA and the PSPA reduce RRSP contribution room, the pension adjustment reversal (PAR) restores RRSP contribution room to an employee if employment terminates before the employer's contributions vest.

Profit-sharing plans allow employers to compensate some or all employees who helped generate profits for the company. However, only deferred profit sharing plans are registered plans. In addition to DBPPs, DCPPs, and DPSPs, there are also special plans for both small business owners and high-income earners whom an employer wants to retain.

As all these registered plans are forms of deferred compensation, contributions are tax deductible. Taxes are paid when the employee receives the retirement benefit.

Margot and Craig came away from this meeting with Francesca feeling that they would just as soon worry about some of the "what ifs" when, and if, they happen! And Craig came away feeling very content that his company is probably going to opt for a five-years' best earnings pension plan. They were, nonetheless, glad to know the implications for their RRSPs. Margot does not have a pension plan at work, and her RRSP savings will not be affected by the new plan at Craig's company. In addition, they will be able to top up their retirement savings if Craig's plan does not turn out to maximize their retirement-savings possibilities.

SOURCES

Canada Revenue Agency: <www.cra-arc.gc.ca>
- T4084 Pension Adjustment Guide
- IC77-1R4 Deferred Profit Sharing Plans
- T4104(E) Past Service Pension Adjustment Guide
- RC4137(e) Pension Adjustment Reversal Guide
- T4041(E) Rev.03 Retirement compensation Agreements Guide
Guidelines for Capital Accumulation Plans <www.jointform-formjoint.ca>

KEY TERMS

Average Year's Maximum Pensionable Earnings (AYMPE)

Benefit earned	Money purchase limit
Best average earnings	Multi-employer plans
Capital Accumulation Plan (CAP)	Overriding provision
Career average earnings	Past service pension adjustment (PSPA)
Cash profit sharing plan	Pension adjustment (PA)
Connected person	Pension adjustment offset
Contribution holiday	Pension adjustment reversal (PAR)
Deferred profit sharing plan (DPSP)	Pension benefit
Defined benefit limit	Pension credit
Dollar limit	Pension credit formula
Double dipping	Pension formula
Employee profit sharing plan	Prescribed amount
Final average earnings	Profit sharing plans
Flat rate	Retirement Compensation Arrangement (RCA)
Forfeited amount	RRSP contribution limit
Funded plans (SRAs and SERPs)	RRSP contribution room
Individual pension plan (IPP)	Significant shareholder
Integrated formula	Specified retirement arrangements (SRA)
Letter of credit (LOC)	Supplemental employee retirement plans (SERP)
Maximum pension rule	Supplemental retirement arrangements (SRA)
Maximum pensionable salaries	Unfunded plans (SRAs and SERPs)
Member with a high salary	

QUESTIONS

Pension Adjustment (PA)

1. What is the money-purchase limit and how much is it for 2012 and 2013?

2. Michelle has a pension credit from her RPP of $6,300 and a pension credit from her deferred profit sharing plan of $2,100. What is her pension adjustment? (Answer: $8,400)

3. What is a forfeited amount? What effect does it have on RRSP contribution room?

4. For the current taxation year, Andy has a pension credit from his RPP of $5,500 and a forfeited amount of $700. His corresponding salary is $55,000.
    (a) What is the maximum he could contribute to all registered plans? (Answer: $9,900)
    (b) How much is his pension adjustment? (Answer: $6,200)
    (c) What is the maximum he could contribute to his RRSP? (Answer: $3,700)
    (d) Andy's RPP allows him to make additional voluntary contributions, so he contributed an extra $2,200 to his RPP. How much can he contribute to his RRSP? (Answer: $1,500)

5. The pension adjustment for 2013 is based on earnings for what year? What effect does it have on:
    (a) 2013 RRSP contribution room?
    (b) 2014 RRSP contribution room?

6. In a defined contribution pension plan, how is the pension credit for the year's contribution calculated?

7. Ross and his employer each contributed $5,000 to his defined contribution pension plan. In addition, his employer contributed $2,000 on his behalf to a deferred profit sharing plan. What was the amount of Ross' pension adjustment? (Answer: $12,000)

8. Alison earned $120,000 in 2013 working for Joe Schmoe Unlimited.
    (a) What is her benefit earned using only:
        i. the plan formula if Schmoe's pension plan formula is 1.95%. (Answer: $2,340)
        ii. 2% of her maximum pensionable earnings. (Answer: $2,400.00)
        iii. the defined benefit limit:
            1. overriding provision. (Answer: $1,722.22)
            2. 1/9 of the money purchase limit. (Answer: $2,696.67)
    (b) What is her benefit earned using all the criteria? (Answer: $2,340.00)
    (c) What is her pension credit for 2013? (Answer: $20,460)

9. Marcia's employer has a defined benefit pension plan and a deferred profit sharing plan. Marcia's annual salary for 2013 is $78,000, and her pension credit for the DBPP for 2013 is $9,000.
    (a) What is the maximum contribution her employer can make to the deferred profit sharing plan? (Answer: $5,040)
    (b) If Marcia's company had no RPP, what is the maximum contribution her employer could make to the DPSP in 2013? (Answer: $12,135)

10. In a flat benefit plan, if two people earn $25,000 and $35,000 p.a., who will earn more pension credits?

11. Using Example 6:
    (a) What is Jane's pension adjustment and RRSP contribution limit if her salary is $50,000 using the CPP generic rate? (Answer: $5,442.86, $3,557.14)
    (b) What is Jane's pension income from her RPP and CPP if her best three year's earnings average $48,500? (Answer: $32,474.86)

12. Using Example 7:
    (a) What is Janice's PA and RRSP contribution limit if her salary is $50,000? (Answer: $5,088.00, $3,912.00)
    (b) What are Janice's annual contributions to her RPP? (Answer: $3,235.00)
    (c) What is Janice's pension income from her RPP and CPP if her best five-year's earnings average $48,500? (Answer: $31,276.00)

13. Claudette had the following earnings for the seven years she worked at her company.
    (a) The defined benefit pension plan is 2% of earnings. What is her pension credit for each of the following years if earnings is defined as (1) final three years, (2) best five-year's average and (3) career average?

Year	Earnings	Answer		
		Final 3 average	Best 5 average	Career average
2013	78,000	13,440	13,440	13,440
2012	75,000	12,900	12,900	12,900
2011	72,000	12,360	12,360	12,360
2010	36,000	5,880	5,880	5,880
2009	36,000	5,880	5,880	5,880
2008	70,000	12,000	12,000	12,000
2007	68,000	11,640	11,640	11,640

(b) For each of the three pension formulas, what is her pension benefit if she retires at the end of 2009?

Year	Earnings	Answer		
		Final 3 average	Best 5 average	Career average
2013	78,000	10,500	10,164	8,700
2012	75,000			
2011	72,000			
2010	36,000			
2009	36,000			
2008	70,000			
2007	68,000			

14. Elinor was a senior administrator with the Kitchener-Waterloo City Police Force. During 2009, she left that job to take a better job with the Guelph Regional Police Force. She earned $25,000 in the 2 1/2 months she worked in K/W. She earned $109,000 during the 9 1/2 months she worked in Guelph. She is in the same pension plan in both positions, which will provide her with a pension of 2% a year for every year of service. See Example 8.
    (a) What is her PA from Kitchener/Waterloo? (Answer: $4,375)
    (b) What is her PA from Guelph? (Answer: $18,739)
    (c) What is her total PA? (Answer: $23,114)

15. Sandra is a connected person of Running with the Poodles Unlimited. In 2013, Poodles introduced an RPP for all employees. Her earned income in 2012 and 2013 was $77,000 while her income in 1990 was $36,000. She expects her pension credit for 2013 will be about $12,000. What is the maximum she can contribute to an RRSP in 2014? (Answer: $7,380)

16. If Sandra were not a connected person, how much could she contribute to her RRSP? (Answer: $13,860)

Past Service Pension Adjustment (PSPA)

17. Conrad, age 45, can buy back seven years of service with his company. These were the years when he worked on contract. His current salary is $60,000, and he will retire in 20 years at the age of 65. He thinks his salary will increase by 3% a year, on average, above the rate of inflation. His company has a defined benefit plan that pays a pension of 2% based on the average of the last three years of earnings.
    (a) Assume that the calculation is based on Conrad living to age 90, and that the real discount rate is 5%.
        i. What will Conrad's real income be in years 18, 19, and 20? (Answer: $102,146, $105,210, $108,367)
        ii. By how much will this past service increase his annual pension? (Answer: $14,734)
        iii. What is the present value at age 65 of this increased income? (Answer: $218,039)
        iv. What is the present value now of this increased pension? (Answer: $82,177)
        v. What is the most Conrad should pay to buy back this increase? (Answer: $82,177)
    (b) When the actuaries completed their calculations, they told Conrad it would cost him $78,029.32 to buy back these years of service, and that the purchase will use up RRSP contribution room of $34,000. Conrad has $77,000 of unused contribution room in his RRSP, and $62,000 in his RRSPs. What are the ways he can pay for this buyback if he decides it is worth it?

Pension Adjustment Reversal (PAR)

18. Michelle was fired on January 2, 2014 after working for Jones Ltd. for one year. She and her employer each paid contributions of 6% of her salary, which was $75,000. When she left, she transferred the amount of her contributions plus 5% interest on the average balance of her contributions for the year (use 2½% of her contributions for the year to calculate the interest income on her contributions) to her RRSP. Her employer's share was not vested, and she lost it.
    (a) If Jones Ltd. had a defined contribution plan:
        i.   How much was her PA for 2013? (Answer: $9,000)
        ii. How much did Michelle transfer? (Answer: $4,612.50)
        iii. How much is her PAR? (Answer: $4,500)
    (b) If Jones Ltd. had a defined benefit plan that would pay her 2% of her best five-year's earnings times the number of years of service:
        i. How much was her PA for 2013? (Answer: $12,900)
        ii. How much was her PAR? (Answer: $8,287.50)

Deferred Profit Sharing Plans (DPSP)

19. Andre earns $70,000 p.a., and there is no RPP at his company.
    (a) How much can his company contribute to a DPSP on his behalf if the money purchase limit is $24,270? (Answer: $12,135)
    (b) How much can he contribute to this DPSP? (Answer: $0)
    (c) If his employer contributes the maximum possible to his DPSP, how much can he contribute to his RRSP next year if he has no other RPP? (Answer: $465)

20. John wants to set up a DPSP for 5 key employees. They are not necessarily the highest paid, but they would be hard to replace.
    (a) Can John set up a DPSP for some, but not all, of his employees?
    (b) The earnings of John's company are very volatile. Can he designate funds for DPSP in the years when he has a net loss by defining profits as "retained profits", not "current year's profits"?
    (c) To sweeten the deal, can John tell these select employees that they can borrow from the DPSP?
    (d) One of John's valued long-time employees quit to become a Tai Chi teacher. To how much of the DPSP is this individual entitled?
    (e) The Tai Chi teacher wanted to transfer all of the benefits in the DPSP directly to an RRSP. Is this allowed?

Plans for Significant Shareholders

21. Daphne owns 40% of the shares of Haggis Inc. She works for Haggis full time, and there are two people who work there two days a week each.
    (a) Is she a significant shareholder?
    (b) Can Haggis set up a defined benefit plan?
    (c) If Haggis sets up a defined contribution plan, and Daphne's earnings are $90,000 a year while the other employees earn a total of $24,000, what is the maximum Haggis can contribute on her behalf? (Answer: $3,500)

22. Matt, John, Tom, and Dick each own 25% of the shares of Dog Biscuits Unlimited. Matt and John work for Dog Biscuits, while Tom and Dick are partners in a small C.A. firm, and do not work for Dog Biscuit.
    (a) Which of the owners may participate in a defined benefit pension plan if there are no other employees? (Answer: None)
    (b) Which owners can participate if Dog Biscuits has 20 employees whose salaries total $560,000 p.a. and Matt's, John's and Martha's salaries total $185,000? Martha is Tom's wife and she works part-time at Dog Biscuit developing new recipes. Assume pension benefits are in direct proportion to their salaries. (Answer: Matt and John)
    (c) If Martha bills on an hourly basis as a consultant, not as an employee, can she be a member?

23. Re-do the previous question, assuming it is a defined contribution plan.
    (a) Which of the owners may participate in a defined contribution pension plan if there are no other employees? (Answer: Matt and John)
    (b) Which owners can participate if Dog Biscuits has 20 employees whose salaries total $560,000 p.a. and Matt's, John's and Martha's salaries total $185,000? Martha is Tom's wife, and she works part-time at Dog Biscuit developing new recipes. Assume pension benefits are in direct proportion to their salaries. (Answer: Matt and John)
    (c) If Martha bills on an hourly basis as a consultant, not as an employee, can she be a member?

Individual Pension Plans (IPP)

24. What kind of pension plan is an IPP?

25. Is the maximum amount of pension credit higher for an IPP than for other DBPPs?

26. If the employer must contribute $35,000 to fund the pension benefits for 2013, how much of the $35,000 is tax deductible to the employer? (Answer: $35,000)

SRAs and SERPs

27. Would a company that has a DCPP set up a SERP? Why or why not?

28. What is the disadvantage to an employee of an unfunded SERP?

29. Articles in the popular press discuss the tax on retirement compensation arrangements (RCAs), and use this tax to calculate the after-tax cost of the RCA. Is this treatment of the deposit with CRA appropriate?

CAPs

30. Why would someone who is a member of a Group RRSP want to participate in a CAP when they could choose their own investment?

Take-Home Pay and Pension Adjustment

31. Roger earns $52,500 a year in 2013, and has taxable benefits of $700, which are paid for by his employer. He and his employer each make RPP contributions of 5% of his income, including

taxable benefits. The DBPP will pay a pension of 2% of his best 3 years earnings, including taxable benefits. He pays $45 a month in union dues and $40 a month for disability insurance premiums. The disability premiums are not tax deductible for Roger: that is, if he collects disability benefit, he will receive these benefits tax free. In addition, his employer contributed $500 to a DPSP on Roger's behalf.

(a) How much is Roger's taxable income? (Answer: $50,000)

(b) Roger pays CPP contributions of $2,103.75, EI premiums of $701.46, and income tax of $9,889.80. What is his take-home pay? (Answer: $36,124.99)

(c) What is Roger's pension adjustment? (Answer: $9,476)

(d) How much can he contribute to his RRSP in 2014? (Answer: $100)

6

Registered Retirement Savings Plans and Other Savings Plans

Learning Objectives

A. Know the features of RRSPs, and the basis for contributing to them; the features of spousal RRSPs; the consequences of overcontributing; and investment options for RRSP funds.

B. Learn the rules for borrowing from and making repayments to an RRSP using the:
    • Home Buyers' Plan (HBP)
    • Lifelong Learning Plan (LLP).

C. Find out how to use an RRSP to give yourself a mortgage.

D. Understand the rules for contributions to and tax implications of withdrawals from a Registered Education Savings Plan (RESP).

E. Learn about the Tax-Free Savings Account (TFSA).

F. Understand the effect of taxes on sheltered and non-sheltered investments.

G. Understand the fundamentals of the Registered Disability Savings Plan (RDSP).

Margot and Craig assume their three daughters — Louise, 13; Susan, 11; and Elaine, 9 — will all go on to further their education after they finish high school since they all enjoy school and do well. Margot and Craig have seen the ads for the Registered Education Savings Plan (RESP) and would like to know if it is as useful as advertised for helping them save for their children's education. They contributed $4,000 to an RESP this year, but they wonder if they would be better off saving for their retirement. Louise will be in university in five years — she just turned 13 in the summer of 2013. Although she loves her job, Margot is also thinking of going back to school when the children are a bit older. She enjoys sewing (when she has time) and has always wanted to study fashion design. She thinks this might make a fun second career. Margot and Craig have heard of a program whereby, in addition to being able to borrow from one's RRSP to buy a home (the Home Buyers' Plan), RRSP holders can also borrow to go back to school (the Lifelong Learning Plan). They have heard that RRSP holders can use their RRSP to give themselves a mortgage. They like the idea of making their mortgage payments to themselves.

Margot, who is 44 years old, worked for several years before she and Craig, age 43, had children. For Louise and Susan, Margot took six months off work. After Elaine was born, Margot and Craig agreed that Margot would stay home for a few years to raise their daughters.

Margot has unused RRSP contribution room of $28,000, and Craig has unused RRSP contribution room of $35,600. Margot lost some of the unused RRSP contribution room she had before Louise was born, although since 1990, this unused contribution room can be carried forward forever. She took two maternity leaves and then was out of the workforce for four years. She has returned to work as an engineer three days a week. She is paid on an hourly basis and makes about $60,000 a year working three days a week.

They also have one last question (they have started making a list of their questions because there are so many): The pension consultant at work told Craig about something called "double-dipping", which would give him extra contribution room for the year his company sets up a pension plan.

They go to Francesca's office for their next appointment with their list of questions in hand.

INTRODUCTION

For 67% of Canadians, Registered Retirement Saving Plans (RRSPs) are their only retirement-saving vehicle other than the Canada Pension Plan (CPP) — about 33% of the labour force has a Registered Pension Plan (RPP). CPP and Old Age Security (OAS) benefits have never been extravagant, but the threat to them in the 1990s drew many people's attention to the need to provide for their own retirements:

> When it comes to retirement assets, Statistics Canada reports that Canadians had about $1.51 trillion stashed away at the end of the 2001 tax year (the most current available statistics). About 69 per cent of that money was in employer-sponsored pension plans and eight per cent in government pension plans. A further 25 per cent, or $292.5 billion, was held in RRSPs. That's more than double in 1991, when Canadians had $131.8 billion tucked away. *Jim Middlemiss, "RRSPs pave the road to retirement" for ING Direct, posted 12 December, 2004, <www.bankrate.com>.*

As shown in Table 3.2, retirement savings total $2.17 trillion at the beginning of 2011, with 56% ($54.2 billion) in RPPs, 36% ($782 billion) in RRSPs and 8% in the CPP and QPP. This is a large increase from both 1991 and 2004, but not nearly enough to adequately finance of the retirement of the baby boomers who are turning 65 in 2013 and will continue to enter retirement for the next 20 years or so.

The maximum contribution per year to an RRSP is 18% of earned income to a current maximum of $24,270 (the 2013 money purchase limit) minus any pension adjustment for contributions made to RPPs and deferred profit-sharing plans. The popular financial press regularly complains about this low contribution limit. However, the Toronto-based Canadian Association of Retired Persons (CARP) states:

> Only about 40% of Canadians contribute to their RRSPs, because [the rest] can't afford to do so. And most of those who do contribute only contribute a small amount annually ... at the same time, employee pension plans are disappearing. *The Globe and Mail, 15 December, 2001.*

Table 6.1 shows details of unused contribution room for 2012, which is based on 2011 earned income.

Table 6.1 Unused RRSP Contribution Room at December 31, 2012

	$ (000)				# of people	
Unused room since 1991	683,560,310	88.5%	57%	With unused room	21,415,440	94.2%
New room*	88,932,550	11.5%		With only new room	1,329,920	5.8%
Total	772,492,860	100.0%		With RRSP room	22,745,360	100.0%
2011 RRSP contributions	34,401,410	4.5%				
Total new room since 1991**	$1.2 trillion		100%			

* New room for 2012 is 18% of 2011 income minus any PA and PSPA and available for contributions in 2012.

** New room without room based on 2011 earnings which is not available to be used until 2012.

Source: Registered Retirement Savings Plan (RRSP) room, annual, Statistics Canada, Table 111-0040 and Registered Retirement Savings Plan (RRSP) contributions, by contributor characteristics, annual, Statistics Canada Table 111-0039.

While many young people and non-unionized, low-income earners make up a significant portion of those who are not eligible to contribute, there is also a sizable number of people who are not able to maximize their contributions because they cannot afford to.

Table 6.2 shows that a significant portion of contributors and contributions are made by those aged 45 to 54. It is also noteworthy that 33% of contributors earn less than $40,000 a year although their contributions total only 15% of total contributions.

Table 6.2 RRSP Contributors and Contributions for 2011

	Tax filers	Contributors			RRSP contributions
		#	Age	Income	
Total	24,841,630	5,953,370			$34,401,410,000
Average					$5,778
By age		3%	0–24		1%
		19%	25–34		12%
		23%	35–44		20%
		30%	45–54		32%
		21%	55–64		28%
		4%	65+		7%
		100%			100%
By income		5%		<$20,000	2%
		20%		$20,000–$39,999	8%
		27%		$40,000–$59,999	16%
		19%		$60,000–$79,999	17%
		29%		>$80,000	57%
		100%			100%

Source: Registered Retirement Savings Plan (RRSP) contributions, by contributor characteristics, annual, Table 111-0039.

A. FEATURES OF RRSPS

Most people who have RRSPs know that any money withdrawn is taxable, but many do not understand exactly how it is taxed. In addition, unlike other investment tools, the following expenses are *not* **tax deductible**:

- Interest paid on funds borrowed to make an RRSP contribution
- Administrative charges on self-directed RRSPs, and
- Brokerage fees paid to buy and sell securities in a self-directed RRSP.

Withdrawal before Retirement

RRSPs are intended to be a tax-deferred way for individuals to save for retirement. However, unless funds have been transferred to a locked-in plan from an RPP or DPSP, funds can be withdrawn at any time. Many people find they need funds for other uses before retirement, and an RRSP can be an effective way to save for a low-income year or two, or it can be used as an emergency fund. However, when funds are taken out of an RRSP, the withdrawal is added to income and is taxable at the full or marginal rate. In addition, the contribution room used to make the original contribution is *not* recoverable when funds are withdrawn from a RRSP — the contribution room is lost. Example 1 illustrates the tax consequences of withdrawing funds from an RRSP before retirement.

Example 1   Alice and John have decided that they would like to take their children to France for a month. They have been making regular contributions to their RRSPs and have decided that this once-in-a-lifetime trip is worth taking some of these funds out to help finance the trip. They decided that they will each withdraw $4,000 from their respective RRSPs. They are both in a 48% marginal tax bracket.

- The $4,000 represents $22,222 of earned income for each of them ($4,000 ÷ .18)
- In making this withdrawal, the $4,000 is 100% taxable; i.e., each of them will pay $1,920 tax on the $4,000 ($4,000 × 0.48)
- When they make their withdrawal, they do not receive the full $4,000 because there is a **withholding tax** on funds withdrawn from RRSPs before retirement. Withholding taxes are:
  - 10% (5% in Quebec) on the first $5,000 or less
  - 20% (10% in Quebec) on the *next* $10,000 (if the withdrawal is between $5,001 and $15,000)
  - 30% (15% in Quebec) on any amount over $15,000 if the withdrawal is more than $15,000.

When Alice and John make their withdrawal, they will receive only $3,600 ($4,000 – $400 withholding tax). When they get their T4RSP in early March the following year, it will show the $4,000, which must be added to their other income. It will also show that $400 of tax has been paid. They will still owe taxes of $1,520 on the $4,000 ($1,920 taxes payable minus $400 taxes withheld and remitted to CRA by the trust company or bank).

If they want $8,000 ($4,000 each) to make the trip, they will have to withdraw $4,444 each ($4,000 ÷ 90%) – ($4,444 – $444 withholding tax) gives them $4,000.

If they decide to put the $4,000 back into their RRSPs, they will have to use new earned income to provide the contribution room. This means they will end up with the $4,000 in their RRSP but will have used up the $22,222 ($4,000 ÷ 18%) allowable earnings twice.

Earned Income

As stated earlier, an individual's maximum contribution to all registered plans per year is the *lesser* of: *18%* of the prior year's earned income or the prior year's money purchase limit, which is set by the federal government.

In addition, RRSP contribution room for a taxation year is based on earned income of the *prior year* minus any pension adjustment from the *prior year*. **Earned income** is:

+   Employment, commission and other income (lines 101 and 104 on the T1 general tax return)
     – royalties (line 104)
     – net research grants (line 104)
     – profits from profit-sharing plans (line 104)
     – unemployment benefits received (line 104)
–   Union, professional, or other dues (line 212)

- Employment expenses (line 229)
+ Disability payments received from CPP and QPP and other taxable sources
+/- **Net** income/loss from a business earned as a sole proprietor or partner
  - taxable portion of gain on disposal of eligible capital property
+/- **Net** rental income/loss from real property
+/- Taxable support payments received/paid

Earned income does **not** include:

• Investment income
• Pension benefits, including amounts received from an RRSP or DPSP
• Retiring allowances
• Severance pay
• Death benefits
• Business income earned as a limited partner.

Example 2 shows what is not considered earned income for RRSP contribution room.

Example 2   Khan is self-employed and had gross income of $85,000 last year. His business expenses totalled $15,000, giving him net income of $70,000. He also received $3,000 in dividends from his Bank of Nova Scotia shares. In addition, he sold his Bank of Montreal shares, which gave him a capital gain of $10,000. His RRSP contribution room this year will be based on:

	Taxable income	Earned income for RRSP contribution room
Employment income	$70,000	$70,000
Taxable dividends	4,350	0
Taxable capital gain	5,000	0
	$79,350	$70,000

Contribution Limit and Contribution Room

Contributions to RRSPs for any taxation year can be made from January of that year to 60 days after the end of the next year — for example, from January 1, 2014 to March 1, 2015 (if the next year is a leap year — a year evenly divisible by 4 — the deadline is February 29). In this example, the maximum deduction limit for 2014 is 18% of 2013 earned income, to a maximum of the 2013 money purchase limit of $24,270 minus any 2013 pension adjustment for contributions made to RPPs and DPSPs. Example 3 illustrates the calculation of:

• **New contribution room** (for the taxation year),
• **Unused contribution room** (from prior years), and
• **Contribution limit** (for the current year, which is the total of new contribution room and unused contribution room).

Example 3   Janice earned $40,000 in 2013 and has no pension at work. She can contribute a maximum of $7,200 ($40,000 × 0.18) to her RRSP in 2014. In fact, she contributed only $3,000 because she recently bought a house and was not able to save more than $3,000.

In 2014, Janice earned $43,000. For the 2015 taxation year, she will have a **contribution limit** of $11,940:

- $4,200 ($7,200 – $3,000) **unused contribution room** from 2014, and
- $7,740 ($43,000 × 0.18) **new contribution room** for 2015 based on her 2014 earned income.

This deduction limit will appear on her 2015 Notice of Assessment (or Reassessment), which she receives each year from the **Canada Revenue Agency (CRA)**.

Until 1990, the unused contribution room could be carried forward for only seven years and was then lost. This unused contribution room can now be carried forward forever (to be more accurate, until the year the taxpayer turns 71, when the RRSP must be transferred to a retirement income plan to be drawn down as retirement income). However, there is always the possibility that a limit will be set on the carryforward in the future.

Taxpayers start gathering contribution room as soon as they start filing tax returns. This means that teenagers should file a tax return even for baby-sitting income. They will not pay any tax on the first $10,000 or so of income (the amount covered by the basic personal amount). Even if they cannot make an RRSP contribution, they can carry forward the contribution room.

Transfers and Contributions That Do Not Affect Contribution Room

Some amounts can be transferred to an RRSP without affecting the contribution room:

1. Transfers can be made directly from a registered plan to an RRSP. In addition to not having an effect on the contribution room, these transfers are also not subject to tax. (Details will be discussed in Chapter 7.) These transfers include:
    - Transfers from other **unmatured RRSPs** (RRSPs that are not paying out retirement income) for the same individual
    - Transfers from an RPP, DPSP, or an RRSP commutation payment, and an excess amount from a Registered Retirement Income Fund (RRIF)
    - Transfers from a deceased's RRSP to the spouse's RRSP on the death of the taxpayer (this transfer is called a **spousal rollover**).
2. Persons receiving a **retiring allowance** and/or **severance pay** when leaving employment can use these funds to make extra contributions to their RRSPs. The extra contribution is based on the number of years of service with the employer and is limited to:
    - $2,000 for each full or part-year of service before 1996, plus
    - $1,500 for each full or part-year of service before 1989, as long as the employee did not earn any pension benefits from an RPP or a DPSP from contributions made by the employer.

Example 4 illustrates additional contribution room generated by someone who has lost his job.

Example 4   Tom lost his job in November 2013 due to a restructuring after a takeover by another company. His company had implemented a pension plan in June 1985. Tom had worked for this company since July 12, 1983. His 2013 earned income was $72,000. He received severance pay of $45,000. Of this $45,000, he can put the following amount into an RRSP in 2013:

Source		Calculations
$2,000	26,000	13 years — 1983 to 1995, inclusive
$1,500	4,500	3 years — 1983 to 1985, inclusive
Total from severance	30,500	
2013 earned income	12,960	$72,000 × 18%
RRSP contribution room		
from 2013 income and severance	43,460	

Pension Income Splitting

Beginning in 2007, Canadian residents can split up to one-half of their pension income with their married or common-law spouse if they were living together and both were resident in Canada on December 31 or were resident in Canada on the date of death or bankruptcy during the year. Generally the person receiving the pension must be over 65 years of age, although someone under 65 can split income with the spouse if the payments are from a lifetime annuity payment from an RPP or as a result of the death of the original annuitant. Both must sign a form with CRA (form T1032) agreeing to both the splitting and the percentage that is split. The percentage can change each year.

Eligible income includes most pension income including lifetime annuity payments from RRSPs, RPPs, DPSPs, Registered Retirement Income Funds (RRIFs) and Life Income Funds (LIFs). OAS and CPPs pension income do not qualify. Each person will be able to claim the $2,000 federal pension amount.

RRSP *withdrawals*, such as those in Example 5, cannot be split, although lifetime annuity payments from RRSPs can be split.

Spousal RRSPs

A taxpayer can make a contribution to their own RRSP as well as to their spouse's. A spouse includes a married partner, an opposite-sex partner, or a same-sex partner, with whom the contributor is living. The total contribution cannot exceed the taxpayer's total contribution room. Contributions to a spousal RRSP must remain in the RRSP for at least two tax (i.e., calendar) years before the calendar year of a **withdrawal by the spouse** in order for the withdrawal to be taxed in the hands of the spouse. Earlier withdrawals are subject to **income attribution rules** of the Income Tax Act, which cause the income to be taxed in the hands of the contributing spouse.

The spousal RRSP is less important than it used to be, since spouses can now divide their pension income equally for tax purposes. However, the way they have saved in their non-registered savings may still make this attractive. Also, the scenario described in Example 5 is possible only with a Spousal RRSP.

Example 5 shows the taxes payable, and by whom, when funds are withdrawn from a spousal RRSP at various times: the year of the last contribution (Example 5a), the year after the last contribution (Example 5b), and two and three years after the last contribution (Examples 5c and 5d, respectively).

Example 5   Andrea made $90,000 in 2013. She has a defined contribution pension plan at work, to which she and her employer each contributed $4,500 in 2013, giving her a PA of $9,000 for 2013. Her spouse, Joe, does not have earned income because he stays home, to take care of their 18-month-old triplets. The total contribution that Andrea could make to registered pension plans in 2014 is $16,200, which is the *lesser* of:

- **$16,200** (18% of earned income)
- $24,270 (the 2013 money purchase limit).

In 2014, Andrea could contribute a maximum of $7,200 ($16,200 – 9,000) to:
- her own RRSP
- a spousal RRSP for Joe (and none to her own RRSP), or
- some combination of her plan and Joe's plan, as long as the total contributions do not exceed $7,200.

Andrea makes the following contributions to a spousal RRSP for Joe and deducts the contribution for the tax year in which the contribution was made:

2014	$ 4,300
2015	4,100
2016	3,900
	$12,300

In November 2016, Andrea and Joe consider the possibility of withdrawing $5,000 from Joe's RRSP to buy some badly needed furniture for the triplets. They would withdraw it from Joe's spousal RRSP because he has no other income and would be in a significantly lower tax bracket than Andrea. The contributions must remain in the spousal RRSP for the two calendar years prior to the year of the withdrawal in order for Joe to pay all the tax.

If Joe makes this **withdrawal in 2016,** Andrea will pay tax on the entire $5,000 and Joe will pay no tax because the funds have not been in the RRSP for two calendar years — Andrea made spousal contributions for 2015 and 2016. Andrea would have to include $5,000 in her 2016 income, the **lesser of**:

- the total of the deposits for the year of withdrawal and the two prior years — $12,300
- the amount withdrawn — $5,000.

As the following chart illustrates, Joe would have to wait until 2019 to withdraw the $5,000 in order to be the one to pay the associated tax — if, and only if, Andrea made no contributions to his spousal RRSP in 2017, 2018, and 2019 (see Example 5d). In the first and second examples, there are no years between the year of the contribution and the withdrawal. As a result, Andrea will pay tax on the entire $5,000 — this income is **attributed** to Andrea. In the third example, there is only one year between the contribution and the withdrawal. Thus, Andrea will have to pay tax on $3,900, and Joe will pay tax on $1,100, which is from the $4,100 contributed in 2015, leaving two years between the contribution and the withdrawal.

	Example 5a		Example 5b		Example 5c		Example 5d	
	Deposit	**Withdrawal**	**Deposit**	**Withdrawal**	**Deposit**	**Withdrawal**	**Deposit**	**Withdrawal**
2014	4,300		4,300		4,300		4,300	
2015	4,100		4,100		4,100		4,100	
2016	3,900	5,000	3,900		3,900		3,900	
2017			0	5,000	0		0	
2018				0	0	5,000	0	
2019							0	5,000
Total*	12,300		8,000		3,900		0	

*Total = Total deposits in the year of the withdrawal and the two prior calendar years

Andrea pays tax on:

2016	5,000		
2017		5,000	
2018			3,900
2019				0

Joe pays tax on:

2016	0		
2017		0	
2018			1,100
2019				5,000

The income attribution rule on spousal RRSPs applies to any contributions to, and withdrawals from, any plan; i.e., one cannot have three spousal plans in order to rotate contributions and withdrawals to get around this rule.[1]

There are exceptions to this attribution rule. For instance, if the couple is living separately because of a breakdown in the relationship or if they are non-residents at the time of the withdrawal, the rules do not apply.

Contributions after Death

The last year that a person can contribute to an RRSP is the year in which they turn 71. In the case of a spousal RRSP, the last year of contributions is the year the spouse turns 71.

No contributions may be made to a deceased's RRSP after the date of death. However, a contribution can still be made to a spousal RRSP in the year of the deceased's death or up to 60 days after the year of death, as long as the spouse is less than 72 years old. Example 6 illustrates the contribution to a spousal RRSP after someone dies before they had made a contribution to an RRSP in the year of death.

Example 6   John died unexpectedly on August 12, 2014. He had not made a contribution to either his RRSP or a spousal RRSP. In January, his executor and his widow agreed to contribute the entire amount of his unused contribution room of $12,600 to a spousal RRSP. After John's death, it is not possible to contribute to *his* RRSP.

Overcontributing to RRSPs

Because the RRSP is a tax-deferred savings vehicle, there is a yearly limit on the contribution. A taxpayer may contribute up to $2,000 more than the RRSP deduction limit without penalty. If more than the lifetime contribution of $2,000 is contributed, there is usually a penalty of 1% a month on the excess. (There are a few exceptions, which are more appropriately covered in a tax course.) The entire overcontribution is *not* tax deductible. If the 1% penalty is payable, the penalty must be paid no later than 90 days after the end of the year in which the overcontribution exists. Example 7 shows the calculation of the penalty for an RRSP overcontribution that is left in the RRSP for the year of the overcontribution and the year following. The years used in Example 7 reflect the years that many pension plans were producing excess surpluses, as described in Chapter 4 and were, as a result, having contribution holidays.

---

1   This is implied, but not clearly stated in "Interpretation Bulletin IT-307R3 — Spousal Registered Retirement Savings Plans": <www.cra-arc.gc.ca>.

Example 7   Ralph earned $70,000 in 2001 and $80,000 in 2002. Due to a large surplus in his defined benefit pension plan, Ralph enjoyed the benefit of a contribution holiday and did not make any contributions to his RPP in 2002 and 2003. Normally, he makes a contribution of 7% of his earned income each year. As a result, Ralph thought he was free to contribute the maximum to his RRSP in 2002. Wanting to maximize the power of before-tax compounding, Ralph took out a bank loan to make a **contribution of $12,600** [($70,000 × 18%) – $0 contributions] in mid-January 2002 with the intention of deducting it from his 2001 tax return.

He was very surprised when he received a Notice of Assessment from the CRA informing him that he had an **overcontributed by $11,685**, an amount on which he had to pay a penalty of 1% a month for the overcontribution in excess of $2,000. Had he thought to look, his pension adjustment for 2001 was on his 2001 T4 and was $11,685.

Ralph could have withdrawn his overcontribution to avoid the penalty. However, he decided to leave the overcontribution in his RRSP, thinking the penalty after tax would be more or less offset by the after-tax interest. He did not know that he could deduct neither the penalty nor the interest on the bank loan.

Ralph's pension adjustment for 2002 was $13,440, based on his 2002 earned income and benefit earned. As a result, he still had an overcontribution subject to penalty of $9,625 at the end of 2003. Ralph is beginning to get the point that, as a member of an RPP, he is earning pension benefits whether or not he is making contributions. And he is better off taking the overcontribution out of his RRSP because it isn't going to go away for several years.

He owed a penalty for 2002 of $1,162.00 ($96.85 × 12 months), which was due to CRA 90 days after the year in which the overcontribution existed.

The interest on the bank loan is not tax deductible. Having learned his lesson, Ralph withdrew the overcontribution at the beginning of 2004.

	2001	2002	2003	2004
Earned income	70,000	80,000	90,000	
RPP contributions — 7%	4,900	0	0	
PA current year				
Benefit earned is the *lesser* of:				
• plan formula 1.95% of salary	**1,365**	**1,560**	1,755	
• defined benefit limit	1,722	1,722	**1,722**	
• 2% of earned income to $86,111	1,400	1,600	**1,722**	
Pension credit = PA current year	**11,685**	**13,440**	**14,900**	
RRSP contribution limit for current year:				
(1) the lesser of:				
money purchase limit for prior year*		13,500	**13,500**	**15,500**
18% of prior year's earned income		**12,600**	14,400	16,200
(2) less PA for prior year		**11,685**	**13,440**	**14,900**
RRSP contribution room available		915	60	600
RRSP contribution made		12,600	0	
Overcontribution		11,685		
– $2,000 allowed once		(2,000)		
Amount subject to penalty carried forward			9,685	
Amount subject to penalty		9,685	9,625	
Penalty @ 1% a month		96.85	96.25	
Penalty for 12 months		**1,162**	**1,155**	

*These are the money purchase limits in place at the time of the overcontribution; they were revised by Bill C-28 in 2003

As we can see from Ralph's case, an unintentional overcontribution can be costly. However, there is an instance in which a taxpayer can **deliberately make an overcontribution**. An RRSP must be wound up by the end of the year in which the taxpayer turns 71. However, if the taxpayer has earned income in that year, the taxpayer could make an overcontribution in December before winding up the RRSP at the end of December. The RRSP contribution could then be deducted in the next tax year. Example 8 shows the effects of overcontributing in the year one retires.

Example 8   Marcia turned 71 in June 2014. She decided it was time to retire completely and stop the part-time consulting she had been doing for the past seven years. She cannot make an RRSP contribution in 2015 because she has to wind up her RRSP by December 31 in the year she turns 71, which for her is 2014.

However, Marcia can take advantage of the fact that the new RRSP contribution room is based on the prior year's earned income. Since her income was $50,000 in 2013 and $52,000 in 2014, Marcia makes an RRSP contribution of $18,360 ($9,000 + $9,360) in December 2014, giving her an overcontribution of $9,360 for 2014. She will deduct $9,000 ($50,000 × 0.18) in 2014 and $9,360 ($52,000 × 0.18) in 2015. She will pay a penalty on **$7,360 (the amount in excess of $2,000)** for the month of December, but the overcontribution disappears in January 2015 and can be deducted in 2015, even though she no longer has an RRSP.

	2013	2014	2015
Earned income	50,000	52,000	0
Retirement income			40,000
RRSP contribution room		9,000	9,360
Contribution made			
for 2013		9,000	
for 2014 = overcontribution		9,360	
Total contribution made		18,360	
Deductible contribution		9,000	9,360
Overcontribution subject to penalty		7,360	
Penalty = 1% for December 2014		73.60	

Winding Up an RRSP

An RRSP must be wound up by the end of the year the taxpayer turns 71. Retirees can:

- cash in their RRSP and withdraw the savings, though this is not recommended because they will have to pay tax on the whole amount, and they don't normally need the RRSP funds immediately or all at once
- select a retirement income option for their RRSP savings:
  - buy a life or term-certain annuity
  - transfer the entire amount to a Registered Retirement Income Fund (RRIF) or, in some provinces, a Locked-in Retirement Income Fund (LRIF)
- a combination of the available options.

Retirees can pick the option that best suits their income needs at retirement.

Payments from an RRSP

The purpose of an RRSP is to provide retirement income. An RRSP that has not yet started to pay retirement income is called an **unmatured RRSP**. Unlike RPPs, taxpayers can withdraw funds from their RRSPs at any time (except for locked-in RRSPs), as Alice and John did in Example 1.

A **matured RRSP** is an RRSP that is paying an annuity to the RRSP holder or beneficiary if the holder or annuitant has died. This amount is fully taxable as regular income and may be eligible for the **pension income amount**. The federal pension income amount is a maximum $2,000, which is part of the non-refundable tax credits on the personal tax return. Only pension income, annuity income, RRIF income, and RRSP annuity income qualify for the pension income amount. To use this tax credit, a taxpayer must be 65 years old or be receiving the payments because the spouse has died. Benefits such as OAS and CPP are not eligible.

Investment Options

Unlike non-registered investments, there are restrictions on the investment options for RRSPs.

Eligible Investments

An RRSP can hold a variety of investments, but they must be qualified investments as defined in the Income Tax Act (See Focus Box 6–1). The purchase of non-qualified investments causes any taxable capital gains that result from these investments to be included in taxable income.

Property such as stocks and bonds can be transferred into an RRSP at fair market value (FMV), leading to a **deemed disposition**, meaning the property is considered to have been sold even though there has not been an actual sale. As a result, any:

• capital gain is taxable (at the 50% inclusion rate), while
• capital loss is deemed to be zero and is not deductible — it is lost forever.

Example 9 illustrates the tax consequences when shares are transferred to a RRSP and generate first a capital gain and, second, a capital loss.

Example 9   David wants to transfer his Bank of Montreal (BOM) shares into his RRSP. They have a current market value of $6,000 and an adjusted cost base (ACB — cost plus purchasing expenses) of $2,400. He also has some shares in Gooseberry. which he would also like to transfer. He bought these shares for $12,000. Although they now have a FMV of $3,200, he believes they will increase in value and wants to keep them. He will use up the rest of his current contribution room, which is $13,140, with cash. He asks Francesca for advice.

	FMV	ACB	Capital gain/ (loss)	Taxable capital gain/ (allowable capital loss)
BOM shares	6,000	2,400	3,600	1,800
Gooseberry shares	3,200	12,000	(8,800)	0
Cash	3,940			
	13,140			

Francesca advises David to transfer the BOM shares but not the Gooseberry shares. When he transfers the BOM shares, he will have a taxable capital gain of $1,800 ($3,600 × 50%).

Focus Box 6–1   Eligible Investments for an RRSP

The eligible investments for an RRSP include:

1. Cash in Canadian dollars, Guaranteed Investment Certificates (GICs), and deposits with Canadian banks, trust companies, and credit unions
2. Shares of:
    (a) public companies listed on a prescribed stock exchange in or outside of Canada
    (b) small business corporations
    (c) eligible corporations — a specified holding corporation, a venture capital corporation, or a taxable Canadian corporation (the latter with conditions)
    (d) investment corporations (closed-end mutual funds) and mutual funds that qualify under the Income Tax Act
    (e) income trusts, royalty units and partnership units listed on a prescribed stock exchange
    (f) investment-grade gold and silver bullion and coins
3. Bonds, debentures, and notes issued by:
    (a) Canadian public companies
    (b) federal, provincial, and municipal governments, including debts guaranteed by them
    (c) co-operative corporations or credit unions that meet the requirements of the Income Tax Act
    (d) foreign governments that have an investment grade rating from a bond-rating agency, such as the Dominion Bond Rating Service
    (e) foreign companies, if their shares qualify
4. Mortgages:
    (a) that are insured under the National Housing Act or by the Mortgage Insurance Corporation of Canada
    (b) on the investor's own home
5. Warrants or rights listed on Canadian stock exchanges, which entitle holders to RRSP-qualified securities
6. Some life annuities and certain life insurance policies
7. Limited partnership units listed on a Canadian exchange

Source: Canadian Revenue Agency, Qualified Investments — Trusts Governed by Registered Retirement Savings Plans, Registered Education Savings Plans and Registered Retirement Income Funds. IT-320R3.

The following investments are not eligible for an RRSP:

1. Gold, silver and other precious metals
2. Gems and other precious stones
3. Commodity futures or contracts
4. Listed Personal Property such as works of art and antiques
5. Land
6. Employee options to purchase stock
7. Mortgages on commercial properties owned by you or a family member
8. Small business investments
9. Puts and uncovered call options
10. Bonds where the issuer is a wholly-owned subsidiary and the shares of its parent are not listed on a Canadian stock exchange.
11. Bonds or debentures of a company whose shares are listed only on a prescribed foreign stock exchange, even though the company's shares may be qualified

Source: Investopedia <http://www.investopedia.com/university/rrsp/rrsp5.asp> whose source is Canada Revenue Agency.

But if he transfers the Gooseberry shares, he will have an allowable taxable loss of $0. If he is convinced the Gooseberry shares will go up, he can:

* first sell the Gooseberry shares, which will give him an allowable capital loss of $4,400 ($8,800 × 50%) that he can deduct from the capital gains received from the sale of the BOM shares (furthermore, the loss can be carried back three years, and forward indefinity).
* then contribute cash to his RRSP and buy the shares with his RRSP funds.

Francesca thinks David should not just walk away from a $4,400 allowable capital loss he would have on the Gooseberry shares by transferring them into his RRSP.

B. BORROWING FROM AN RRSP

Withdrawals from RRSPs are taxed as regular income at full rates. However, individuals can borrow from their RRSPs to buy their first home or go back to school without paying tax on the withdrawals and without paying interest on the "loan" from the RRSP.

There are two plans for borrowing from an RRSP:

1. the **Home Buyers' Plan (HBP)** — to help individuals buy a first home
2. the **Lifelong Learning Plan (LLP)** — to help individuals go to school

The popular financial press often frowns on these loans because the funds are not in the RRSP to compound. While this is true, the loss must be evaluated against the tax-free growth in value that a home can experience over the long run. Also, investing in one's human capital may offset the growth lost in the RRSP. An investment in one's human capital may not provide the same monetary rewards as the compounded return in an RRSP, but it may improve one's quality of life — and that, after all, is one of the uses of money.

1. Home Buyers' Plan (HBP)

First introduced in 1992, the Home Buyers' Plan program was created to help Canadians buy or build homes for themselves. By participating in the plan, taxpayers may borrow up to $25,000 each from their RRSPs to buy or build a "qualifying" home. These funds are not taxable when withdrawn but must be repaid in no more than 15 years. The withdrawals are non-interest-bearing, and there is no withholding tax on them. RRSPs such as locked-in RRSPs and group RRSPs do not allow this withdrawal. Funds may also be withdrawn to acquire a qualifying home for a related disabled person or to provide funds to a related disabled person to make their home more accessible to them. The rules for related disabled persons can be found in the HBP guide available on the CRA website.

To meet the tax-free status of the withdrawal, certain requirements must be met before, when, and after the funds are withdrawn.

Before the withdrawal, the taxpayer must:

* have signed a written agreement to buy or build a "qualifying" home
* plan to live in the home as the principal residence
* be considered a "first-time buyer"
* have an HBP balance at the beginning of the year of purchase of zero if the taxpayer has participated in this plan before.

A **qualifying home** must be:

* located in Canada

- a single-family dwelling; a semi-detached home; a townhouse; a mobile home; a condominium unit; a share of the equity in a co-op; or an apartment in a duplex, triplex, fourplex or an apartment building

The taxpayer *must intend to move into* the home within 12 months of the withdrawal. However, there is no minimum occupancy period.

A **first-time buyer** is someone who, with or without a spouse, or common-law partner, did not own a home and occupy it as a principal residence during the time period beginning January 1 of the fourth year before the year of the withdrawal and ending 31 days before the withdrawal. If the taxpayer lived in an owner-occupied home for only part of this time period with a spouse, one or the other *may* qualify as a first-time buyer. Example 10 illustrates the eligibility rules of the HBP.

Example 10   Pete and Cindy separated in June 2009. Pete moved out of the matrimonial home, and Cindy bought out his share in late 2009. Pete was not sure what he wanted to do, so he has been renting an apartment since the divorce. Now in March 2014, Pete is buying a house with Linda — they plan to marry and move into the house in June 2014. Linda is in the process of selling the house she has lived in since 2004. She will use the net proceeds as her share of the investment in the house with Pete.

Pete has not owned a house for four years (2010 to 2013 inclusively) since his divorce from Cindy, and he has not lived with Linda in her house as a spouse. Thus, he is considered a first-time buyer and is eligible for the HBP as long as he makes his withdrawal within 30 days of buying the house.

Linda is not eligible for the HBP — she already owns a house. In addition, for Pete to remain eligible for the HBP, she must not own the new house for more than 30 days before Pete makes his withdrawal. It is important that they are not already married before Pete makes his withdrawal. Since Linda does not qualify, if they were already married, neither would qualify. Since Pete and Linda have never participated in the HBP before, they both meet the requirement that the **HBP balance must be zero** on January 1 of the year of withdrawal.

At the time of the withdrawal, the taxpayer and spouse must:

1. not have owned the home for more than 30 days before the first withdrawal; i.e., they must make the first withdrawal within 30 days of buying the home
2. be residents in Canada
3. fill in form T1036
4. receive all the withdrawals in the same year
5. not withdraw more than $25,000 **each** (if there is a spouse and both spouses qualify); any amount over $25,000 is taxable income in the year withdrawn

After the withdrawal, the taxpayer must buy or build the qualifying home before October 1 of the year after the withdrawal. A home is built when it becomes habitable. If the taxpayer does not buy or build by this date, they will still be considered to have met the deadline if *either* of the **following two situations** exists.

The **first situation** requires that the taxpayer:

1. has had in place a written agreement to buy by the deadline
2. purchased the home by October 1 of the second year following the withdrawal
3. be a Canadian resident at the time of purchase

In the **second situation**, the taxpayer must have paid an amount at least equal to the withdrawal to the builders or suppliers of the home before October 31 of the year following the withdrawal. The transaction with the builder or supplier must be one at arm's length.

Example 11 illustrates the occupancy requirements when someone does not move in immediately after the purchase.

Example 11   Joan bought a unit in a co-op and made a withdrawal on November 12, 2013, to make the down payment. She completed the purchase on March 31, 2014. However, there was a tenant in the unit whose lease did not end until October 31, so Joan could not move in until November 1, 2014.

This purchase remains qualified because Joan fits the first situation, where she:

- Had an agreement to buy the home before October 1, 2014
- Bought it on March 31, 2014 before October 1, 2015, and
- Was a Canadian resident at the time of the purchase

Example 12 illustrates the occupancy requirements when a home is purchased before it is ready for occupancy.

Example 12   Alan withdrew $15,000 from his RRSP on September 17, 2013, to pay the contractor as a commitment to purchase a townhouse that was being built. He also paid the contractor:

- $10,000 on September 27, 2013
- $10,000 on August 4, 2014
- $18,000 on November 30, 2014

As a result of a fire on September 18, 2014, Alan was not able to move in until August 12, 2015.

This home purchase remains qualified because Alan fits the second situation, where the amount he withdrew, $15,000, is less than the total of $35,000 ($15,000 + $10,000 + $10,000) he had paid to the builder by October 1, 2014. He had paid an amount at least equal to the withdrawal to the builders or suppliers of the home before October 31 of the year following the withdrawal. Also, Alan's transaction was at arm's length to the builder.

Repayments

Under the Home Buyers' Plan, repayments of withdrawals from the RRSP are spread equally over 15 years. The taxpayer can pay it back faster, but no less than 1/15 of the borrowed amount must be paid each year. Even if the taxpayer declares bankruptcy, the loan must be repaid to avoid being taxed. The repayments start the second year following the year of the withdrawal. Repayments are not RRSP contributions and are therefore not tax-deductible. The unpaid balance becomes due if the HBP participant dies, becomes a non-resident, or turns 71 years of age:

- At death, any HBP balance must be included on the participant's final tax return as taxable income unless the surviving spouse elects to make the repayment in lieu of the participant.
- If the borrower becomes a non-resident, the unpaid balance must be paid within 60 days of becoming a non-resident. Any unpaid balance is included in taxable income in the year the person became a non-resident.

- Since contributions cannot be made to an RRSP after the year in which a taxpayer turns 71, the outstanding repayments are included in income in each year that they would have been due.

Taxpayers can start to repay earlier than required. Lump-sum payments that are larger than the required payment reduce the amount to be repaid each year in the future. Example 13 shows two effects on subsequent payments of a lump-sum payment.

Example 13   Anne withdrew $15,000 from her RRSP under the HBP in May 2009. She was required to pay $1,000 a year beginning in 2011. Anne received an unexpected bonus of $800 in December 2010 and immediately used it towards her 2011 repayment, which was thus reduced to $200 ($1,000 – $800).

By December 2014, Anne had made four payments totalling $4,000, leaving $11,000 outstanding to be paid over 11 years. In January 2015, Anne's favourite aunt died and left her $5,000. She immediately applied it to her HBP repayments, leaving *$6,000 outstanding*. This lump-sum repayment reduces her future (including 2015) minimum payments to $545.45 a year ($6,000 ÷ 11 years outstanding).

Withdrawals from an RRSP under the HBP are not taxable only if the HBP participants repay their yearly amount in full and on time. If any of the repayments are less than the required amount, the **shortfall is considered taxable income**. However, once the shortfall is accounted for as taxable income, it does not have to be repaid. In addition, **contributions to RRSPs** are applied first to the repayment outstanding for the current year and are not tax-deductible as an RRSP contribution. Example 14 shows two tax effects of failing to repay the required amount while making an RRSP contribution.

Example 14   Cathy withdrew $15,000 from her RRSP under the HBP in May 2013. She is required to pay $1,000 a year, beginning in 2015. Cathy did not make the payment and put $700 into her RRSP for 2015. This amount cannot be deducted as an RRSP contribution and is applied as part of the HBP repayment for 2015. Furthermore, Cathy will still have to pay tax on the $300 repayment she did not make.

Effect on Contribution Room

Any RRSP deduction for a contribution made 89 days before the first withdrawal can affect RRSP contributions. If the withdrawal reduces the fair market value of the RRSP balance to less than an RRSP contribution made within 89 days before the withdrawal, the excess of the contribution over the market value of the RRSP after the withdrawal is not tax deductible. Example 15 explains the result of withdrawing funds from an RRSP for the HBP within 89 days of making an RRSP contribution.

Example 15   Janet had $7,000 in her RRSP before she made a $6,000 RRSP contribution on February 28, 2014. On May 15, 76 days later, she withdrew $9,000 to help make the down payment on a new home. She forgot that she had planned to take the funds out on May 29, which would have been 90 days after the RRSP contribution. She is upset to learn that her oversight has cost her almost $2,000 worth of deductions.

RRSP balance as of January 1, 2014	7,000
RRSP contribution made on February 28, 2014, for 2013	6,000
Income earned in RRSP between January 1, 2014 and May 14, 2014	325
HBP withdrawal on May 15, 2014	(9,000)
RRSP balance after withdrawal — market value	4,325
Maximum RRSP deduction for 2013 = market value of RRSP	4,325
Contribution disallowed for 2013 ($6,000 − $4,325)	1,675

As long as you follow all the rules, you can use the funds withdrawn under the HBP for any purpose. In addition, you can participate in the HBP if you have not fully repaid funds withdrawn from your RRSP under the Lifelong Learning Plan (LLP), and the reverse is also true.

2. Lifelong Learning Plan (LLP)

The Lifelong Learning Plan was introduced by the federal government in 1999 to help taxpayers who want to return to school to further their education by allowing interest-free loans from their own RRSPs. The LLP allows RRSP holders to borrow up to $10,000 a year (the **annual LLP limit**) to a maximum of $20,000 (the **total LLP limit**) from their RRSPs to finance *full-time* training or education for themselves or their spouse, but not their children. Disabled students can be enrolled on a part-time basis.

Both spouses or partners can withdraw from their RRSPs under the LLP at the same time. In addition, in the year after the LLP withdrawal has been repaid and has a balance of $0, funds can be withdrawn to participate in the LLP program again. The withdrawal can also be cancelled by repaying the amount withdrawn.

Withdrawals can be made over four years and up to January of the 4th year after the first withdrawal. There is no withholding tax on the withdrawals, and the amounts are non-interest-bearing. However, if more than $10,000 is withdrawn in a year, the excess amount must be included in taxable income and is not considered part of the LLP interest-free loan from the RRSP. The withdrawn amounts are repayable over 10 years. Example 16 demonstrates the withdrawal requirements for the LLP.

Example 16   After several years of working in dead-end jobs, Rosie decided to go back to school. She started in September 2013 and withdrew $4,000 to help pay her tuition. Although she enrolled in a four-year program, she wanted to keep a reserve in case she ran out of funds or did not graduate according to her original plan. She withdrew $4,000 in September of 2014, 2015, and 2016. If Rosie wants to withdraw the balance of the allowed $20,000 — that is, $4,000 — she must do so in January 2017, which is the fourth year after her first withdrawal.

To participate in the LLP, the individual must be under the age of 71 and enrolled in a **qualifying educational program** at a **designated educational institute**, which is a university, college, or other educational institute that qualifies for the education tax credit in the non-refundable tax-credit portion of the tax return. The program must last three months, and the student must be in class or at work at least 10 hours per week. Courses and work include lectures, practical training, labs, and research, but does not include study time.

As with the HBP, if the withdrawal reduces the RRSP balance to less than an RRSP contribution made within 89 days before the withdrawal, the excess of the contribution over the market value of the RRSP after the withdrawal is not tax deductible. See Example 15 in the previous section for an illustration.

Repayments

Repayments are 1/10 of the total amount taken out and can start as late as the fifth year after the year of the first withdrawal, on the condition that the student is in school. If the student finishes school; i.e., there is no "Tuition and education amounts" for at least three months on the student's tax return for two years in a row, the repayments start in the second of the two years. The same rules for failing to make the minimum payments to the HBP apply here also. Example 17 demonstrates the years of required repayments.

Example 17   After working for a few years, Jason decided to go back to school to complete his M.B.A. He withdrew $10,000 in September 2013 and September 2014 to help pay his school expenses. He completed his M.B.A. in May 2015. Therefore, he must start repaying his withdrawals in 2017. While 2017 is only the fourth year after the first withdrawal, because he has completed his education and will not be in school in 2016 and 2017, he must start the repayments in the second of the two years — 2017.

C. USING YOUR RRSP TO GIVE YOURSELF A MORTGAGE

It is possible for an RRSP holder to give themselves a mortgage using funds in an RRSP. This transaction is subject to several limitations. The funds have to be in a self-directed RRSP on which the financial institution may charge a fee, generally $100 to $200 a year, that is *not* tax deductible. There are also set-up costs of about $200 plus the annual administration fee. Other costs, such as legal fees, may also apply. Thus, even though paying mortgage interest to oneself can be very attractive, anyone who is interested needs to take a close look at the costs. The rule of thumb is that it is not worthwhile unless the mortgage is at least $50,000. In addition, before investing in one's own mortgage, the RRSP holder should investigate the returns, after annual management fees, offered on similar investment options, such as mortgage mutual funds, since lending to yourself is only one of the mortgage-investment options if you want to invest in personal mortgages.

Financial institutions do not promote this possibility, in part because they prefer that RRSP holders invest in the institution's own mutual funds or other investments. It would also cut into their own mortgage business. Investment options offered by financial institutions may not normally carry a direct charge, but the financial institution would have reduced investment returns to provide itself with the required compensation.

To use one's RRSP for a mortgage, the mortgage must:

1.   Be insured through a mortgage insurance corporation or under the National Housing Act
2.   Be administered by an approved lender, such as a bank or a trust company
3.   Charge an interest rate that is within 2% of the posted market rates, with terms that are normally available from conventional lenders

If the RRSP holder defaults on the payments, the financial institution will foreclose on the property in the same way it would if the mortgage was with the institution directly. The mortgage does not have to be the only mortgage on the home.

There are downsides to using RRSP funds to finance a mortgage:

- If the home is sold, it might not be desirable to have the new purchaser assume the mortgage (although taking over the mortgage is an option available to the seller, not a requirement).
- If market conditions change, the funds are tied up and not available for other investments (although this might also be true for funds invested in a mutual fund that has a back-end load, which decreases the longer the fund is held).
- Having all or most of one's funds invested in the family home. This is the most important consideration. For many families, a home is the largest investment they will make. Holding one's own mortgage does not diversify one's investments.

D. REGISTERED EDUCATION SAVINGS PLAN (RESP)

The Registered Education Savings Plan (RESP) is sponsored by the federal government to provide an incentive for taxpayers to save for their children's post-secondary education. Unlike RRSPs, contributions made to an RESP are not tax deductible. However, the contributions grow tax-free within the plan, and the income earned on the contributions is not taxable until funds are paid out to a beneficiary, who is typically taxed at a very low rate, if at all. There is no annual contribution limit, and the lifetime contribution limit is $50,000. A penalty of 1% a month is levied by the Canada Revenue Agency if the total contributions exceed the $50,000 lifetime limit. This penalty continues until the overcontribution is withdrawn and is pro-rated between all contributors, based on their contributions. The RESP can be open for a maximum of 36 years.

Each plan is a contract that involves three parties:

1. **the subscriber,** who opens the RESP and makes the contributions
2. **the promoter,** a financial institution such as a bank or credit union or group plan dealer and financial service provider. Human Resources and Social Development Canada (HRSDC) publishes a list of providers and the services each provides,[2] and
3. **the beneficiary,** who receives the capital and income upon enrollment in a **qualifying educational program** at a **qualifying institution**

The RESP contract is between the subscriber and the promoter and is registered with Canada Revenue Agency.

To be a **qualifying educational program**, the program must be at the post-secondary level — a trade school, CEGEP in Quebec, a college, or university — and can include apprenticeships. The student can be attending either full- or part-time. A full-time program is one which:

- requires students to spend 10 hours or more per week on courses or work in the program, and
- will last three weeks in a row (at least 13 weeks if the program is outside Canada)

Part-time programs must include at least 12 hours a month spent on courses. A program does not qualify if the student is receiving employment income other than from part-time or temporary work to finance their studies.

Qualifying educational institutions include:

- all universities, colleges, or other designated educational institutions in Canada or outside of Canada that offer courses at the post-secondary school level and the course in which the student is enrolled, asts at least 13 weeks
- educational institutions in Canada that are certified by the Minister of Social Development as offering non-credit courses to develop or improve skills for an occupation

2   Available from <www.hrsdc.gc.ca/en/ > Home > Learning > Saving for Education> Registered Education Savings Plan > RESP provider

For RESPs that started after 1997, the **original subscriber** can be replaced only if:

* the original subscriber dies
* the new subscriber is the former spouse or common-law partner of the original subscriber, and the rights were obtained under a divorce decree or a written agreement dividing the property upon separation

The estate of a deceased original subscriber can also become the subscriber.

Types of Plans

A child can be a member of more than one plan, and the lifetime maximum contribution of $50,000 applies to each child. There are three types of plans:

* **Individual Plans** are for one person who does not have to be related to the subscriber and can be for the subscriber or another adult since there are no age limits. There is one subscriber which can include child care agencies or joint subscribers who are married or have a common-law relationship. If the contract permits, a replacement beneficiary can be named. Contributions can be made for 21 years after the plan was opened. The subscriber makes the investment decisions.

* **Family Plans** have one or more children as beneficiaries. The children must be related to the subscriber — children (including adopted children), grandchildren, brothers, or sisters. The funds for all the children in *each* Family Plan are pooled for investment purposes. The lifetime contribution limit and Canada Education Savings Grant (CESG) limits apply to *each* child. Contributions must stop before the beneficiary turns 21. The subscriber decides how to invest the money. The funds do not have to be shared equally.

* **Group Plans** (also called **Group Scholarship Plans**, **Group Scholarship Trust Plans**, and **Education Funds**) pool the savings for each age group and the amount each child receives depends on how much money is in the pool and on the total number of children who are the same age and are in school that year. Each Group Plan is a collection of individual plans — there is a Group Plan for *each* beneficiary. They usually require regular contributions over a defined period of time. Only one child can be named as beneficiary, and the child does not have to be related to the subscriber. The Group Plan dealer makes the investment decision, usually choosing low-risk investments. These plans usually charge very high up-front fees, and if subscribers withdraw their contributions early, the subscriber can end up with less money than they contributed. In addition, subscribers do not receive the income that their contributions have earned if the contributions are withdrawn early or if the plan is terminated by the promoter. In 2006, 15,387 or 1.9%[3] of Group Plans were closed by the group providers, mostly because the subscriber was not able to keep up with the required minimum payments. Their eligibility rules for payments can be much more restrictive than the legislated rules.

The subscriber can withdraw contributions at any time. However, if the child is not enrolled in a qualifying educational program and is therefore not eligible to receive an educational assistance payment from the RESP, any incentives (CESG, CLB and/or ACESPG described below) on the withdrawn contributions will have to be returned. Some plans charge a penalty for early withdrawals. Some RESPs are invested in mutual funds, which sometimes charge very high annual management expense ratios (MERs), which are not charged on other investment choices such as GICs or by all financial institutions. The subscriber is not required to have a bank account with the financial institution that holds their RESP, so it pays to shop around.

---

3   For source, see the report in footnote 4

A few years ago, Human Resources and Social Development Canada commissioned a review of RESP Industry practices.[4] The 50-page report, released in August, 2008, describes in detail the practices and problems that consumers have encountered with RESP providers.

HRSDC suggests you ask potential RESP providers the following questions[5] before signing up with a provider:

- Does it cost anything to open an RESP?
- Once I have opened an RESP, will I have to pay any fees? If so, what are they for and how much will I have to pay?
- Do I have to put a minimum amount of money into an RESP?
- Do I have to make regular payments?
- What happens if I cannot make regular payments?
- What are my investment choices? What are the benefits of each choice? Can the value of my investment go down?
- Can I withdraw money if I need it? Are there any fees or penalties for withdrawing money early?
- Can I transfer the RESP to another person, or to another RESP provider? What is the cost to transfer?
- What will happen to my savings in the RESP if the recipient of the RESP does not continue his or her education after high school?
- Does the RESP provider limit the types of qualified educational programs for which I can use my RESP?
- What happens if I close my RESP early?
- What if my child decides to go to school part-time?

Contribution Limits

Until January 1, 2007, there was an annual limit on the contribution. Overcontributions were charged a penalty of 1% a month until the overcontribution was withdrawn. If more than one subscriber created the overcontribution, the penalty was pro-rated according to their respective contributions. The same applies to contributions over the current lifetime maximum of $50,000.

Canada Education Savings Grant (CESG)

While families have many competing demands on their finances and must set their own priorities, the importance of higher education to the future of the nation is undeniable. In his 1998 budget speech, then Finance Minister Paul Martin said, "We believe that RESPs will soon come to be considered as essential for future planning as RRSPs are now." To encourage Canadians to contribute to RESPs, the federal government introduced the Canada Education Savings Grant (CESG) the same year.

This grant is available to all eligible RESPs of a qualifying beneficiary who is *less than 18 years old*. The grant is:

- 40% or $200 on the first $500 of annual contributions if net family income is $43,561 or less,
- 30% or $150 on the first $500 if net family income is between $43,561 and $87,123 for 2013,
- 20% or $100 on the first $500 for net family income more than $87,123, and

---

4   *Review of Registered Education Savings Plan Industry Practices.* Report prepared for Human Resources and Social Development Canada by Informetrica Limited. Final Report August, 2008. Prepared by: Bill Knight, Bert Waslander and Arlene Wortsman and reviewed by Michael C. McCracken. <www.servicecanada.gc.ca> search for "RESP industry practices".

5   <www.hrsdc.gc.ca/en> Home > Learning > Saving for Education> Registered Education Savings Plan > Booklet > RESPs: Special Savings Plans for Education.

• 20% or a maximum of $400 for contributions over $500 to a maximum of $2,500

to a lifetime maximum for each beneficiary of **$7,200.** Lifetime means from birth to the end of the year the child turns 17 with minimum required contributions for children aged 15 to 17. The grant is paid to the trustee of the plan.

Unused grant room can be carried forward and used in future years (maximum $400 a year in CESG from 1998 to 2006 and $500 beginning in 2007).

Example 18   Because he was on disability benefits this year, earning only $35,000 a year, Terry was able to make a deposit of only $1,500 to his son's RESP. The RESP received the CESG of $400 and has unused grant room of $200 — 20% of the unused $1,000. The next year, he's back at work earning $45,000 a year. If he can make a contribution of $3,500 next year, his son's RESP will receive a grant of $750.

			This Year		Next Year	
Income			35,000		45,000	
Contribution			1,500		3,500	
Unused CESG carried forward			1,000			
CESG on first $500	40%	200	40% × 500			
CESG on first $500	30%				150	30% × 500
CESG on contributions $500 to $2,500	20%	200	20% × 1,000		600	20% × 3,000
Total CESG		400			750	

Because the purpose of the CESG is to encourage savings for higher education, the grant and the earnings generated by the grant are paid only to the beneficiary as part of the **educational assistance payment (EAP)**, which is taxable income to the beneficiary. The CESG grant is a loan in the sense that, if the child does not use it to go to school, the grant and the income earned on it are forfeited. When the grant and its income are withdrawn from the RESP to go to school, they are taxable income to the beneficiary. In the following examples, contributions are made and grants are received at the end of the year. Example 19 illustrates the effects on total grants received as well as on the total amount available for withdrawal by making contributions of $10,000 a year for 5 years compared to $2,600 a year for 14 years and then contributions of $3,400 for four years.

Example 19   Joyce wants to save for her son Robin's education. She has a good lifestyle and does not find it difficult to contribute $10,000 a year for 5 years, totalling $50,000. Joyce will receive the $2,500 CESG.

Contribution			Grants		
$	#	Total	$	#	Total
10,000	5	50,000	500	5	2,500

Joyce's sister, Janice, also has a beloved son, Elliott, and she would like to save for his education. Unfortunately, Janice does not have as much money as Joyce and can save only $2,600 a year for 14 years and then $3,400 a year for each of the last four years. Janice will receive the maximum CESG of $7,200. Joyce earns more than the amount required to qualify for either 30% or 40% on the first $500 of her contribution. Even if she did qualify for these additional amounts, the maximum lifetime CESG Elliott can receive is still $7,200.

	Contribution			Grants		
$	#	Total		$	#	Total
2,600	14	36,400		500	14	7.000
3,400	4	13,600		200	1	200
		50,000				7,200

The following table shows the accumulation and drawdown of these funds, assuming both Robin and Elliott go to university for four years beginning in the 19th year, T_{19} (which is also the end of the 18th year). Assume all savings and income occur at the end of the year, while the funds are taken out at the beginning of each of the four years. Also assume a *real* interest rate of 3%.

Robin

	T_0	T_1	...	T_5	T_6	...	...	T_{19}	T_{20}	T_{21}	T_{22}
Contributions$_{EOY}$		10.0	...	10.0	...	...	...	FVA?			
Grants$_{EOY}$		0.5		0.5				FVA?			
Withdrawals$_{BOY}$								PMT	PMT	PMT	PMT

Elliott

	T_0	T_1	...	T_{14}	T_{15}	...	T_{18}	T_{19}	T_{20}	T_{21}	T_{22}
Contributions$_{EOY}$		2.6	...	2.6	3.4	...	3.4	FVA?			
Grants$_{EOY}$		0.5		0.5	0.2			FVA?			
Withdrawals$_{BOY}$								PMT	PMT	PMT	PMT

Janice will be making her last deposit at the end of the 18th year, which will also be the beginning of the 19th year, when Elliott begins university.

Robin	Total	Calculations	
Contributions	50,000	$FVA_{EOY5} = 10,000_{EOY} (FVIFA_{5,\ 3\%}) = 53,091$ $FV_{EOY18} = 53,091_{EOY5} (FVIF_{13,\ 3\%})$	77,966
Grants	2,500	$FVA_{EOY5} = 500 (FVIFA_{5,\ 3\%}) = \$2,655$ $FV_{EOY18} = 2,655 (FVIF_{13,\ 3\%})$	3,898
Total$_{EOY18}$	52,500		**81,864**
Withdrawals	$_{BOY19}$	$81,864_{BOY19} = PMT_{BOY} (PVIFA_{4,\ 3\%})$	21,382

Elliott	Total	Calculations	
Contributions	36,400	$FVA_{EOY14} = 2,600 (FVIFA_{14,\ 3\%}) = \$44,424$ $FV_{EOY18} = 44,424_{EOY14} (FVIF_{4,\ 3\%})$	50,000
	13,600	$FVA_{EOY18} = 3,400 (FVIFA_{4,\ 3\%})$	14,224
Grants	7,200	$FVA_{EOY14} = 500 (FVIFA_{14,\ 3\%}) = \$8,543$ $FV_{EOY18} = 8,543_{EOY14} (FVIF_{4,\ 3\%})$ $FV_{EOY18} = 200 (FVIF_{3,\ 3\%})$	9,615 219
Total$_{EOY18}$	57,200		**74,058**
Withdrawals	$_{BOY19}$	$74,058_{BOY19} = PMT_{BOY} (PVIFA_{4,\ 3\%})$	19,343

They both contribute $50,000. However, Janice is eligible for more grants because she will be making more annual contributions than Joyce. Even though her contributions are lower, each of them is enough to receive the maximum CESG available for the year. Janice will be able to collect 14 grants of $500 each and one grant of $200, while Joyce will be able to collect only 5 grants of $500 each. Since Joyce is able to contribute more to the RESP in the early years, with the advantage of the before-tax growth on the contributions and grants, her RESP will grow at a greater rate to become a larger amount even though her total grant is less.

Canada Learning Bond (CLB)

The CLB is available to a child born after December 31, 2003, if the parent or guardian receives the National Child Benefit Supplement as part of the Canada Child Tax Benefit (commonly known as "family allowance"). Usually this means net family income is $43,561 (for 2013) or less per year.

The first deposit is $500 plus $25 to help cover the cost of setting up the plan. After the first deposit, the CLB pays $100 a year to a lifetime maximum of $2,000. The deposits continue to the child's age of 15 as long as the family continues to receive the family allowance. The subscriber does not have to contribute to the RESP, the child must be a beneficiary under an RESP and the Government of Canada deposits the funds directly into the child's RESP. The bond and income on the bond are taxed the same way as the CESG — the beneficiary pays the tax when the funds are withdrawn.

If the child does not continue education after high school, the CLB is returned to the government and cannot be transferred to another child.

Alberta Centennial Education Savings Plan Grant (ACESPG)

ACES will contribute an initial grant of $500 to the RESP of every child born to Alberta residents after 2005. In addition, grants of $100 are available to children who turn 8, 11, and 14 after 2004 if the children are attending school. The total possible grants are $800 — the initial $500 plus three grants of $100 each. To receive the $100 grant, the subscriber must contribute a minimum of $100 to the RESP within one year before applying for the grant.

Payments from an RESP

There are four ways the funds can be paid out of an RESP.[6]

1. Contributions

The original contributions of the RESP can be paid to the subscriber at any time or to the beneficiary when the beneficiary is enrolled in a qualifying educational program **tax-free,** since the contributions were made with after-tax dollars.

---

6   The most complete source of information about RESPs is the 282-page guide for promoters. It is available at <www.hrsdc.gc.ca>. Canada Education Savings Program, Registered Education Savings Plan Provider User Guide, March 31, 2013.

2. Educational Assistance Payments (EAPs)

The CESG plus the income earned on both the contributions and the CESG can be disbursed, as **educational assistance payments (EAPs)**, to beneficiaries who are enrolled in a qualifying educational program. The maximum amount that will be paid as soon as the beneficiary is qualified is $5,000 ($2,500 for part-time enrollment). After 13 weeks in the program, there is no limit to the amount that can be paid. If the student leaves school for 12 consecutive months, the $5,000, 13-week rule will apply again. The student must not be receiving regular full-time employment income, although part-time or temporary income is permitted. The EAP is considered **taxable income** to the student. Example 20 shows the tax paid by the children in Example 19 when they withdraw the funds from their RESPs.

Example 20   In the prior example, the students will pay tax on a total of:

Robin	$31,864 ($81,864 – $50,000 in contributions)
Elliott	$24,058 ($74,058 – $50,000 in contributions)

The tax will be spread over the four years of the withdrawals.

3. Payments to a Designated Educational Institution in Canada

Funds from an RESP can be paid to a designated educational institution in Canada on behalf of the beneficiary if:

- the beneficiary is no longer eligible for an EAP
- grants and bonds have been repaid, and
- the subscriber does not qualify for an AIP

The payments are a gift and do not qualify as charitable donations. They are **taxed** in the same manner as EAPs.

4. Accumulated Income Payments (AIPs)

RESP funds can also be paid out as **accumulated income payments (AIPs)**, usually to the subscriber. These payments are the income from the contributions, *not* the grants and bond (CESG, CLB, and ACESPG) and *not* the income earned by the grants and bond (the contributions can be paid to the subscriber as tax-free contributions). These payments are allowed if *all* of the following conditions are met:

- The recipient is a resident of Canada.
- The recipient is the subscriber, unless the subscriber has died.
- Each beneficiary has died or is 21 or older and is not eligible to receive EAPs.
- The RESP has existed for at least 10 years.

The last two conditions may be waived if the beneficiary now suffers from a severe and prolonged mental impairment.
   AIPs are subject to two taxes:

1. Regular tax on income when AIPs are added to other taxable income
2. An additional tax of 20% (12% for Quebec residents) to be paid by the same date the recipient's regular income tax is due, usually April 30 of the following year

The amount of AIP subject to tax can be reduced if *all* of the following conditions are met:

1. The recipient of the AIP is the subscriber or spouse or common-law partner of a deceased subscriber. The AIP tax cannot be reduced if the recipient is the subscriber because the original subscriber has died and the recipient is someone other than the spouse or common-law partner.
2. The recipient deposits an amount not greater than the AIP to an RRSP or spousal RRSP to a lifetime maximum of $50,000 of AIPs. The deposit to the RRSP must be in the same taxation year as the AIP was received or within 60 days of the following year.
3. The recipient has enough unused contribution room to absorb all of the AIPs deposited.

Example 21 illustrates the growth in the RESP set up by Harry and Betsy.

Example 21   When Harry's first child was born on May 31, 2014, both Harry and his mother-in-law, Betsy, immediately set up an RESP for Harry Jr. Both Harry and Betsy are dismayed to learn, 18 years later, that Harry, Jr., now 18 years old, is not interested in going to university or college. He has a great talent in carpentry and studied it at every opportunity while he was in high school. Friends of relatives are already hiring him to build custom-made garden furniture and small outdoor buildings. As a result, the funds in his RESP are of no use to him.

They had each contributed $1,400 per year for 17 years and $1,200 for one year to the RESPs. These funds had earned a modest 3% real rate of return and now there is $39,975 in each account (see "Robin" in Example 19 above for the calculation). In addition, Harry and Betsy must wait until Harry Jr. is 21 years old before they can take AIPs. Let's assume that all the funds remain in the RESP until Harry Jr. is 21.

	RESP		
	Total	Harry	Betsy
Contributions	50,000	25,000	25,000
+ Income on the contributions	19,206	9,603	9,603
= FV of contributions @ age 21	69,206	34,603	34,603
CESG received	7,200	3,600	3,600
+ Income on the grants	3,546	1,773	1,773
= FV of CESG @ age 21	10,746	5,373	5,373
Balance in the RESP	79,951	39,975	39,975

Now that Harry, Jr. does not want to go to college or university (or anything else), what can Harry and Betsy salvage from this investment?

The CRA does not want the RESP and its grants to become a tax-free investing tool for the subscriber. Since the contributions were not tax deductible, Betsy and Harry can get them back without any tax implications. However, they are not entitled to the grants or to the income the grants generated. Both Betsy and Harry can collect the income on the contributions. But what are the tax implications?

If Harry has unused RRSP contribution room that is more than the $9,603 the RESP earned on his contributions, he can transfer the entire $9,603 to his RRSP using up $9,603 of his unused contribution room. He must include the AIP in taxable income but the tax effect is offset by a deduction for the amount transferred to his RRSP. Also, he does not have to pay the additional 20% tax as long as the amount of the AIP received in this and previous years does not exceed $50,000.

If Betsy has no RRSP contribution room, she must count the income on the contributions into her taxable income. She will pay a tax on:

- the $9,603 at her marginal rate, plus
- $1,920.60 ($9,603 income on the contributions × 20%)

E. TAX-FREE SAVINGS ACCOUNT (TFSA)

Tax-Free Savings Accounts (more accurately called **Tax-Free Savings Plan**) became available on January 2, 2009. The maximum annual contribution was $5,000 from 2009 to 2012 and is $5,500 beginning in 2013. This maximum will be indexed annually and rounded to the nearest $500 annually. They are offered by the same financial institutions that issue RRSPs: banks, credit unions, trust companies, and life insurance companies. They are savings accounts whose earnings are never taxed. Any unused contribution room can be carried forward indefinitely to future years, and any withdrawals can be replaced later; that is, the contribution room is not lost when funds are withdrawn. Anyone over the age of 18 except a trust can open a TFSA, and a person can hold more than one TFSA.

Contribution room begins to accumulate when a person turns 18. It is available in any year for people who have lived in Canada for at least one day. There is no income attribution on funds given to a spouse or common-law partner to make a contribution. Generally, if a person holding a TFSA dies, the balance in the fund can be transferred tax-free to a surviving spouse.

Withdrawals can be used for anything and, since withdrawals are not taxable income, do not affect income-tested benefits, such as the Canada Child Tax Benefit,[7] the Working Income Tax Benefit,[8] the goods and services tax credit, the age credit, Old Age Security, Guaranteed Income Supplement and Employment Insurance benefits. Contribution room for withdrawals is added back to contribution room at the beginning of the year following the withdrawal.

Example 22   Andrew deposited the maximum each year to his TFSA. By early, 2014, he had deposited $31,000 ($5,000 for four years and $5,500 for 2013 and 2014). He had taken a big risk which, fortunately for him, had provided him with a large capital gain with the result that his TFSA had a balance of $39,206 on November 7, 2014. He withdraw the entire amount to help finance the purchase of his first condo knowing that his beloved grandmother's estate would be settled in late December. How much contribution room will Andrew have on January 2, 2015?

Andrew will have $44,705 contribution room on January 2, 2015 — the $39,206 that he withdrew plus the new contribution room for 2015 of $5,500.

Excess contributions are subject to a penalty of 1% a month as long as the excess remains in the plan. Americans who are resident in Canada have to pay tax on their worldwide income and receive a tax credit for taxes paid in Canada. However, unlike RRSPS, the TFSA is not part of the Canada-United States tax treaty and will likely be subject to American income taxes (which are generally lower than Canadian and can, therefore, offer some tax relief).

While the TSFA is ideal for short-term savings, such as saving for a car, a down payment, a renovation, a cottage, additional education savings, emergency savings, a dream vacation, or to start a new business, people are also using it to save for retirement for both workers and non-working spouses. Companies are looking at adding group plans to their benefits as a way of attracting and retaining em-

---

7   The Canada Child Tax Benefit (CCTB) is a means-tested, non-taxable amount paid to low-income families resident in Canada to help raise children under the age of 18. It can include the Child Disability Benefit (CDB) and the National Child Benefit Supplement (NCBS).

8   The Working Income Tax Benefit (WITB) is a refundable tax credit available to low-income individuals and families. The WITB pays up to $500 for individuals whose income is more than $3,000 and less than $17,824 for 2013 and up to $1,000 for an individual with eligible spouse and/or children whose income is more than $3,000 and less than $27,489. There is an additional supplement available for low-income people with disabilities who work.

ployees as well as keeping their benefits packages competitive. An evaluation[9] of the TFSA by the federal Department of Finance finds that:

- Individuals across all income levels are saving using the TFSA, that individuals with incomes below $80,000 account for 80% of TFSA contributors and contributions in 2011.
- 30% of adult tax filers had a TFSA in 2011. Participation rates are stable between ages 25 and 49, and increases with age.
- Low-income seniors hold TFSA. GIS recipients represent 6% of TFSA holders, and their participation rate was 23% — 3% higher than that of low-income individuals in general.

Qualified investments are the same as arms-length RRSP qualified investments.

The following table summarizes the similarities and differences between the three plans.

F. TAXES ON SHELTERED AND NON-SHELTERED SAVINGS

Part of the appeal of registered pension plans is their ability to have investments grow tax-free. However, **sheltered savings** lose some of their tax advantage when funds are withdrawn from the plan since

Table 6.3 Comparison of RRSP, RESP, and TFSA

	RRSP	RESP	TFSA
• Contributions are tax deductible.	Yes	No	No
• Contributions are based on earned income.	Yes	No	No
• Withdrawals are taxable (and thus increase taxable income).	Yes	No	No
• Income earned is taxable while in the plan.	No	No	No
• Funds withdrawn from the plan can be replaced later without using new contribution room.	No	No	Yes
• Income earned is fully taxable when withdrawn from the plan.	Yes	Yes	No
• Interest on money borrowed to invest is tax deductible.	No	No	No
• Administration fees are tax deductible.	No	No	No
• Incentives are available (grants, bond).	No	Yes	No
• Funds in the plan can be used as security for a loan.	No	No^	Yes
• Funds given to spouse, common-law partner or child over the age of 18 to take advantage of their contribution room are subject to income attribution (income attribution is covered in Chapter 11).	Yes	No	No
• Employer contributions are a taxable benefit.	Yes*	Yes+	Yes+

^ It is the financial institution, a bank for instance, that makes this decision, not Canada Revenue Agency. It is likely that a bank would not accept an RESP as security for a loan since the RESP would have to be cashed-in for the bank to collect its money if the borrower defaults.

* RRSP contributions made by an employer are taxable to the employee, who can then also deduct both employer and employee contributions.

+ Employer contributions are subject to normal payroll taxes (CPP, EI) for lower-income employees and are taxable for employees.

---

9   Tax Expenditures and Evaluations 2012: Part 2 – Tax-Free Savings Accounts: A Profile of Account Holders, Department of Finance <www.fin.gc.ca>

all funds received from sheltered plans are taxed at 100%. Example 23 shows the tax advantage lost on a capital gain generated in an RRSP, as well as the tax advantage of the TFSA.

Example 23   Sharon invested in shares using a self-directed RRSP. She bought the shares for $10,000 and sold them for $25,000 several years later. Since the capital gain is inside her RRSP, when she withdraws the funds from her RRSP she will pay tax on the entire $25,000. The original investment of $10,000 has already provided her with a tax deduction when the funds were contributed to her RRSP.

The Tax Free Savings Account is also tax-sheltered. While the contributions are tax deductible, the income is never taxed.

Non-sheltered savings — investments or savings outside RRSPs and RPPs — usually generate annual income that is taxed when the income is earned. As mentioned in Chapter 2, tax rates differ, depending on the source of the income. Example 24 shows the after-tax rate of return when cashing in an investment that generates only a **capital gain**. The first investment is in an RRSP, the second in a TFSA, while the third is not sheltered. Note in particular the calculation of the capital gain — only the gain is taxed, not the original investment.

Example 24   Sharon decided to collapse her RRSP and use the $25,000 to go on a trip to see the Hermitage Museum in St. Petersburg, Russia. Her marginal tax rate is 45%. The following table illustrates the after-tax effects of investing inside and outside an RRSP. Outside an RRSP, the growth is taxed as a **capital gain**. As a result, there is no annual income to compound either before or after tax. Consequently, the after-tax amounts are very different, reflecting the primary advantage of tax-sheltered savings — the savings compound tax-free. Of course, if she withdraws the funds from her TFSA, she can put the amount back in later.

	RRSP	TFSA	Non-sheltered
Amount invested	10,000	10,000	10,000
Tax refund on RRSP contribution	4,500	0	0
Net investment	5,500	10,000	10,000
n	20	20	20
k	4.69%	4.69%	4.69%
Proceeds	25,000	25,000	25,000
Cost	10,000	10,000	10,000
Capital gain	15,000	15,000	15,000
Taxable amount	25,000	0	7,500
Tax @ 45%	11,250	0	3,375
Net proceeds after tax	13,750	25,000	21,625
Net return after tax	8,250	15,000	11,625
Rate of return after tax on net investment	150%	150%	116%

Example 24a provides a higher rate of return, 9.37%, reflecting either some degree of luck for accepting more risk or a higher rate of inflation, or some combination of both.

Example 24a   Let's redo the calculation for Sharon, assuming the selling price is $60,000 instead of $25,000. Since this is a capital gain and capital gains are not taxed until they are sold (for non-sheltered assets) or sold and withdrawn (for sheltered assets), the growth rate does not depend on the annual income being before or after tax.

	RRSP	TFSA	Non-sheltered
Amount invested	10,000	10,000	10,000
Tax refund on RRSP contribution	4,500	0	0
Net investment	**5,500**	**10,000**	**10,000**
n	*20*	*20*	*20*
k	*9.37%*	*9.37%*	*9.37%*
Proceeds	60,000	60,000	60,000
Cost	10,000	10,000	10,000
Capital gain	50,000	50,000	50,000
Taxable amount	60,000	0	25,000
Tax @ 45%	27,000	0	11,250
Net proceeds after tax	**33,000**	**60,000**	**48,750**
Net return after tax	**27,500**	**50,000**	**38,750**
Rate of return after tax on net investment	500%	500%	387%

Margot would like to see an example using **interest income**. She is somewhat sceptical that the power of compounding before taxes is all that significant, since the funds are taxed when they come out of the registered plan anyway.

Francesca produces the following example to show the effects of investments that grow before and after tax.

Example 25 also shows the after-tax rate of return from cashing in an investment. However, this time the income generated is **interest income**, not a capital gain.

Example 25 Margot has $10,000 to invest for 20 years. She can either:

1. Contribute the $10,000 to her RRSP and then make her investments
2. Contribute the $10,000 to her TFSA, or
3. Invest the $10,000 in a non-sheltered investment.

Her investment will earn interest income — no capital gain at all. The nominal rate of return is 4.69% before tax and 2.58% (4.69% × 0.55) after tax. Non-sheltered assets grow at the after-tax rate of return since taxes are paid on the interest each year and the amount of the tax is not available to earn interest over the 20 years of the investment.

	RRSP	TFSA	Non-sheltered
Amount invested	10,000	10,000	10,000
Tax refund on RRSP contribution	4,500	0	0
Net investment	**5,500**	**10,000**	**10,000**
n	*20*	*20*	*20*
k	*4.69%*	*4.69%*	*2.58%*
Proceeds	25,000	25,000	16,639
Cost	10,000	10,000	10,000
Interest earned	15,000	15,000	6,639
% subject to tax at maturity	*100%**	*0%+*	*0%^*
Taxable amount	25,000	0	0
Tax @ 45%	11,250	0	0
Net proceeds after tax	**13,750**	**25,000**	**16,639**
Net return after tax	**8,250**	**15,000**	**6,639**
Rate of return after tax on net investment	150%	150%	66%

* 100% of funds withdrawn from an RRSP are subject to regular tax.

\+ The TFSA is not taxed — ever.

^ Interest income, non-registered, is taxed as regular income in the year the income is earned, so only the after-tax amount is available to grow.

Example 25a repeats Example 25 but uses a higher rate of inflation, which increases the growth rate.

Example 25a To see the effects of inflation, let's repeat the previous example using 9.37% before-tax growth rate instead of 4.69%.

	RRSP	TFSA	Non-sheltered
Amount invested	10,000	10,000	10,000
Tax refund on RRSP contribution	4,500	0	0
Net investment	**5,500**	**10,000**	**10,000**
n	*20*	*20*	*20*
k	*9.37%*	*9.37%*	*5.15%*
Proceeds	60,000	60,000	27,326
Cost	10,000	10,000	10,000
Interest earned	**50,000**	**50,000**	**17,326**
% subject to tax at maturity	*100%*	*0%*	*0%*
Taxable amount	60,000	0	0
Tax @ 45%	27,000	0	0
Net proceeds after tax	**33,000**	**60,000**	**27,326**
Net return after tax	**27,500**	**50,000**	**17,326**
Rate of return after tax on net investment	500%	500%	173%

Increased rates of return due to inflation greatly increase the future value, after tax, of investments.

G. PENSION REFORM

As illustrated in Table 6.1, Canadians are not taking advantage of all opportunities available to them to save for retirement and, as a result, they are not saving enough. In addition to low savings rates, savings plans have to contend with low interest rates, unstable capital markets, and longer life expectancy that is creating an aging population. One advantage of RPPs is that, if the employer has an RPP in place, it is generally mandatory for employees to participate. One option that is being explored is expanding the Canada Pension Plan system — increasing the contribution limits and therefore, the benefit limits. Small businesses in particular object to being required to finance more retirement savings for their employees. The self-employed who must pay both the employee and the employer's share of CPP contributions also find the prospect daunting. Some provinces have passed legislation that allows Pooled Registered Pension Plans in which employers do not have to participate and employees can participate even if the employer does not.

If this issue is to find resolution, everyone — the federal government, employers, and the labour force — must come to terms with the need to save today in order to not work during retirement. Someone has to pay for it and we have to ask: Is it fair to ask the next generation to pay for our retirement since we couldn't save enough? The CPP has a captive audience — it is mandatory for all employers and employees to participate and, bottom line, it is likely the best route for financing future retirement income for those who do not have a mandatory RPP since the CPP is mandatory.

Pooled Registered Pension Plan (PRPP)

The is a DCPP offered by a financial institution such as a bank or insurance company. The goal is that employee contributions can be pooled together in order to reduce administration costs and to attain better investment returns through economies of scale. Group RRSPs require more administration on the part of the employer and are not available to the self-employed.

An employer can choose to participate and their employees are automatically enrolled although they can opt out. If the employer does not participate, an employee or a self-employed person can enrol directly with the financial institution. Investment options are similar to those for other registered plans and employees would have a choice of funds with varying levels of risk. Since it is a registered plan, RRSP contribution limits apply.

Like RPP and the CPP, funds are locked in until retirement. Some plans are expected to allow flexible contributions, meaning an employee can increase or suspend contributions depending on their current financial circumstances.

Table 6.4 Comparison of PRPP, RRSP, CPP and DCPP

	PRPP	RRSP	CPP	DCPP
• It is mandatory for the employer	No	No	Yes	No
• If the employer participates, it is mandatory for the employee.	No	No	Yes	Yes
• If the employer does not participate, the employee can participate.	Yes	Yes	n/a	No
• Contributions are pooled for investing.	Yes	No	Yes	Yes
• Employee contributions are tax deductible.	Yes	Yes	No	Yes
• Employee contributions are eligible for a non-refundable tax credit.	No	No	Yes	No
• You can take funds out before retirement; i.e., they are not locked in until age 55, 60 or perhaps age 65.	No	Yes	No	No

Saskatchewan Pension Plan (SPP)

This registered saving plan is available to all Canadians age 18 to 71. The maximum annual contribution is $2,500 and you can transfer an additional $10,000 to it from an existing RRSP or RRIF. Contributions are flexible and come out of RRSP contribution room. It offers professional management and some choice of investments for those who do not have access to an RPP. The expense ratio is about 1%, much lower than many management expense ratios on mutual funds. You can set it up online and make contributions online or through the mail using a credit card, automatic debit or a cheque.

Shared-Risk Pension

New Brunswick has introduced a shared-risk pension model that is intended to address the issues being faced by DBPP. This shared-risk plan is asking that employees and employers share equally in the investment risk. Currently, employers take all the investment risk for DBPP and employees take all the investment risk for DCPP. With a shared-risk pension, a current DBPP is converted into a new shared-risk pension plan that has been used in some north European countries including The Netherlands for about 15 years.

Benefits earned at the date of conversion are part of the member's "base benefit" and the new benefit formula is essentially a target benefit based on an enhanced career-average earnings formula instead of, for example the best five-years formula. This means it will use actual salary each year adjusted for inflation (COLA — cost of living allowance) when the member reaches retirement. Indexing of pensions will depend on investment returns and, when granted, will apply to the base benefit for all members — active and retired.

Phased-in Retirement

In phased-in retirement, older employees can reduce their working hours and begin to draw some portion of their DBPP while continuing to make contributions on their reduced earnings. Most pension plans do not allow this and would have to be revised. Some plans currently allow employees with a pre-determined number of years of service or age (like age 65) to work part-time, receiving part of their salary and all of their pension. However, their plan requires that they must take all of their pension and cannot make contributions which would increase future pension benefits.

In 2007, the Income Tax Act (ITA) was revised to allow people to collect monthly pension benefits while still working and contributing to their plan. Quebec had been allowing this since 1997, Alberta since 2000 and had gotten around the ITA prohibition against it by paying a lump-sum pension benefit once a year.

H. REGISTERED DISABILITY SAVINGS PLAN (RDSP)

The Registered Disability Savings Plan became law on December 14, 2007. It is similar to an RESP in that contributions are not tax-deductible, income earned in the plan is not taxed, and tax on payments is paid by the beneficiary. It can be set up by an individual eligible for the disability tax credit (DTC), their parent or other legal representative and contributions can be made by anyone — the beneficiary, parents, other relatives, friends, and community groups. The DTC-eligible individual is the plan beneficiary.

There is no **annual contribution limit**, and the **lifetime contribution limit is $200,000**. Contributions are permitted until the end of the year in which the beneficiary turns 59. Contributors cannot receive a refund of contributions. Parents and grandparents of a financially dependent child or grandchild can transfer some or all of the balance of their registered savings — RRSPs, RRIFs or RPPs — tax-free to the RDSP when they die. To be financially dependent, the child or grandchild's net income must be less than the basic personal amount and the disability credit of the previous year. This rollover is included in the $200,000 lifetime maximum.

Disability assistance payments from the RDSP can be made as soon as the RDSP is established and are required beginning the year the beneficiary turns 60. Each plan must specify when the plan is set up whether payments that are not lifetime payments are allowed or not. These payments can trigger a required repayment of some of the grant and the bond. Required withdrawals, called **lifetime disability assistance payments**, are subject to an annual maximum based on the life expectancy of the beneficiary and the fair market value of the property in the plan. Once lifetime payments are initiated, they must be made every year. Ad hoc payments (encroachments) for a special purpose or situation from the RDSP are permitted. Payments do not affect and are not affected by income from Old Age Security and Employment Insurance benefits. Payments from the plan can be used for any purpose.

Income from the plan, the Disability Savings Grant and Bond and the income from them are taxed in the hands of the beneficiary when the funds are withdrawn from the plan. Every payment is part taxable, part non taxable and there is a formula for determining this based on contributions, grants, bonds and income earned.

Some provinces exempt RDSP assets and income from calculations for provincial social assistance.

Canada Disability Savings Grant (CDSG)

The Canada Disability Savings Grant matches contributions at a rate of 100%, 200%, or 300%, based on net family income to a lifetime maximum of $70,000. The CDSG can be received until the beneficiary turns 50. The beneficiary must then wait 10 years after receiving the CDSG (and the bond) before withdrawing the grant to avoid penalties. The grant matching rates for 2013 are:

2013 Family income	
Up to $87,123	$87,123 and over
300% on 1st $500 200% on next $1,000 to a maximum grant of $3,500	100% on the 1st $1,000 to a maximum grant of $1,000

Family income for the grant and the bond is the family of original while the beneficiary is less than 19 years old. The year in which the beneficiary turns 19, family income is that of the beneficiary.

Canada Disability Savings Bond (CDSB)

The Canada Disability Savings Bond of up to $1,000 a year is available to low-income families to a lifetime maximum of $20,000. Contributions to the RDSP do *not* have to be made to receive it. An RDSP can receive the CDSB until the end of the year the beneficiary turns 49, and the beneficiary cannot withdraw the bond for 10 years without facing penalties.

2013 Family income	
Up to $25,356	$25,356 to $43,561
$1,000	$500

Example 26   Jillian, age 16, was thrown from her horse at her riding lesson a couple of years ago. Extensive rehabilitation has helped but she will remain disabled and qualifies for the Disability Tax Credit. She lives with her parents, Stan, a high school teacher, and Maria, an accountant, whose combined income is about $175,000 a year. Maria's mother died recently and Maria was the beneficiary on her RRIF. Maria would like to transfer some of the RRSP funds directly into Jillian's RDSP.

This year Stan and Maria opened an RDSP for Jillian and deposited $10,000. They plan to continue to this until the $200,000 maximum is reached. They have the following questions for Francesca.

1. Can Maria transfer her inheritance directly into the RDSP on a tax-deferred basis?
   - The answer is "no" because Jillian was not financially dependent on her grandmother at the time of her grandmother's death. If Jillian had been financially dependent, the funds could have rolled over into the RDSP tax-free as a contribution on which Jillian would have paid tax when she withdrew the funds in the future. Regular contributions are not taxable as withdrawn since they were not tax-deductible when contributed.

2. How much CDSG will Jillian receive?

- For the next three years, she will receive a grant of $1,000 a year since her family income is well above $87,123.
- In the year that Jillian turns 19, if her income is less than $87,123, she will receive $3,500 if the contribution is at least $1,500. She receives $1,500 which is 300% of the first $500 contributed and then she receives $2,000 which is 200% on the next $1,000 deposited.

3. How much CDSB will Jillian receive?
   - For the next three years, she will receive nothing as the bond is based on her parent's income.
   - In the year she turns 19, if her income is less than $25,356, she will receive $1,000 even if she does not make a contribution to the RDSP. If her income is more than $25,356 but less than $43,562, she will receive $500, again with no contributions.

MARGOT AND CRAIG

Margot and Craig want to start planning how to use up their unused RRSP contribution room ($28,000 for Craig and $35,600 for Margot at the end of 2013). Now that Craig's company has a defined benefit pension plan, he has RRSP contribution room each year of $600. He is thinking that he could use up his existing and future RRSP contribution room in a spousal RRSP in order to split his income in retirement, although the implementing of pension sharing in 2007 makes this less urgent. Margot's net income of $57,096 generates RRSP contribution room of $10,277 per year and, with the introduction of the DBPP at work, Craig has $600 a year of contribution room. Margot wonders how long it will take to use up the unused contribution room if they can afford to make the following RRSP contribution and RESP contributions. She also wonders if the following RESP contributions will be enough.

	RRSP	RESP
2013	6,000	4,000
2014	4,000	6,000
2015	25,000	10,000
2016	25,000	10,000
2017	25,000	10,000
2018	???	10,000
2019	???	10,000
2020	???	10,000
2021	???	10,000

It will take them several years to use up their unused RRSP contribution room. If they are able to continue contributing $25,000 per year, they will not use up all the contribution room until 2019:

Margot and Craig — RRSP contributions	2014	2015	2016	2017	2018	2019
o/s room — BOY	63.6	70.5	56.4	42.3	28.2	14.1
Contributions	−4.0	−25.0	−25.0	−25.0	−25.0	−25.0
New room	10.9	10.9	10.9	10.9	10.9	10.9
	70.5	56.4	42.3	28.2	14.1	0.0

RESP Savings

Louise age		13	14	15	16	17	18				
Susan age		11	12	13	14	15	16	17	18		
Elaine age		9	10	11	12	13	14	15	16	17	18
	2013 T_{-1}	2014 T_0	2015 T_1	2016 T_2	2017 T_3	2018 T_4	2019 T_5	2020 T_6	2021 T_7	2022 T_8	2023 T_9
Contributions	4.0	6.0	10.0	10.0	10.0	10.0	10.0	10.0	10.0	3.6	3.6
Grants	0.5	1.2	1.5	1.5	1.5	1.5	1.5	1.0	1.0	0.5	0.5
Total	4.5	7.2	11.5	11.5	11.5	11.5	11.5	11.0	11.0	4.1	4.1
PVA for each?											

Notice that the grants drop in 2020 when they are no longer contributing for Louise, who would be at university.

What does it cost to send each child to school if they estimate the yearly cost will be $9,000 in real dollars with a real interest rate of 3%? Since the time frame is quite long, we will not concern ourselves with part-years for this calculation.

$$PVA = 9,000_{BOY} (PVIFA_{4, 3\%}) = \$34,458$$

The value now, at T_0, the beginning of 2014?

Louise   PV = 34,458 $(PVIF_{5, 3\%})$ =   29,723
Susan   PV = 34,458 $(PVIF_{7, 3\%})$ =   28,017
Elaine   PV = 34,458 $(PVIF_{9, 3\%})$ =   <u>26,409</u>
                                                   <u>84,149</u>

The present value now, at T_0, of the contributions and CESG made at the end of the year, assuming the deposits and grants are made at the end of the year:

	Amount	Calculation	Value at T_0
T_{-1}	4,500		4,500
T_0	7,200	$(PVIF_{1, 3\%})$ =	6,990
T_1 to T_5	11,500	$(PVIFA_{5, 3\%})$ = 52,667 52,667 $(PVIF_{2, 3\%})$ =	49,643
T_6 to T_7	11,000	$(PVIF_{2, 3\%})$ = 21,048 21,048 $(PVIF_{7, 3\%})$ =	17,114
T_8 to T_9	4,100	$(PVIF_{2, 3\%})$ = 7,845 7,845 $(PVIF_{9, 3\%})$ =	<u>6,013</u>
			<u>84,260</u>

So, at the present rate of contributions, Margot and Craig are on-target in their savings needs to finance their children's education if their assumption about $9,000 is correct. They can revisit this after they have done the calculations for their retirement. In 2019, they will have used up all of their prior unused RRSP contribution room and will be in a better position to contribute more to their daughters' education fund, although not to the RESP. Or perhaps they should contribute less to the RRSP in the next few years and contribute more to the RESP. They do not have to make this decision now. They can certainly wait until they have taken a look at their retirement savings needs. Or they can change their mind at any time in the next few years while they have an opportunity to see how their financial position unfolds.

SUMMARY

Registered Retirement Savings Plans, or RRSPs, are designed to provide individuals with a tax-sheltered way to save for retirement in addition to RPPs and DPSPs. However, unlike RPPs, individuals can withdraw the funds before retiring, although they have to pay tax on the funds at their marginal tax rate and cannot recover the contribution room. Recognizing that some individuals may need access to these retirement funds before retirement, there are provisions for borrowing from RRSPs in two instances: one for first-time homebuyers and one for individuals going back to school. There is another way of personally using RRSP savings without being taxed. It is possible to give oneself a mortgage on one's own home or cottage, since a mortgage is an eligible RRSP investment.

While not tax deductible, the Registered Education Savings Plan (RESP) can be an effective way to save for children's education and income split the earnings generated by the savings, as the tax will be paid by the child when withdrawn; presumably the child is in a lower tax bracket than the parent. As an incentive to encourage people to save for their children's education, a grant (the CESG) is offered to match contributions within certain limits.

The Tax-Free Savings Account (TFSA) provides an incentive for Canadians to increase their savings rates since the income is never taxed and contributors can replace any savings they withdraw without using up contribution room. The Registered Disability Savings Plan (RDSP) provides support to help families who care for children with disabilities.

The Pooled Registered Pension Plan (PRPP) has been adopted by some jurisdictions in order to encourage people to save for retirement at their place of employment without setting up a formal RPP.

> Margot and Craig are relieved to find that they can "borrow" from their RRSP if they need to, and the contribution room will be there even if they cannot afford to use up all their of contribution room right away. As they ponder all this new information, they speculate that they will probably never borrow from their RRSPs — but they could, for the two very specific plans (HBP and LLP), if they needed to.
>
> They will definitely continue contributing to the RESPs for their daughters. There seems to be no downside to this plan that they can see. And they both communicate regularly with their in-laws, so they shouldn't be in danger of inadvertently overcontributing.
>
> They might consider using their RRSPs to give themselves a mortgage if they ever buy the cottage they have been thinking of buying. But, then, will all their eggs will be in one basket? Maybe not.

SOURCES

Canada Revenue Agency: <www.cra-arc.gc.ca>
- Registered Plans
  - T4040(E) Rev. 07 RRSPs and Other Registered Plans for Retirement 2007
  - IT—320R3 Qualified Investments—Trusts Governed by Registered Retirement Savings Plans, Registered Education Savings Plans and Registered Retirement Income Funds.
  - IT-307R3 Spousal Registered Retirement Savings Plans
  - RC4135(E) Rev. 07 Home Buyers' Plan (HBP)
  - RC4112(E) Rev. 07 Lifelong Learning Plan (LLP)
  - RC4092(E) Rev. 08 Registered Education Savings Plans (RESPs)
  - RC4064 Medical and Disability-Related Information

• Pooled Registered Pension Plans (PRPP) — Questions and answers for employers
Saskatchewan Pension Plan <www.saskpension.com>
Tax-Free Savings Account — Frequently Asked Questions — Canada Revenue Agency

KEY TERMS

Accumulated income payments (AIP)	Named beneficiary
Alberta Centennial Education Savings Plan Grant (ACESPG)	National Child Benefit Supplement (NCBS)
	New contribution room, RRSP
Beneficiary, RESP	Non-sheltered savings
Canada Child Tax Benefit (CCTB)	Original subscriber
Canada Disability Savings Bond (CDSB)	Overcontribution to RRSP
Canada Disability Savings Grant (CDSG)	Pension income splitting
Canada Education Savings Grant (CESG)	Pooled Registered Savings Plan (PRPP)
Canada Learning Bond (CLB)	Promoter
Child Disability Benefit (CDB)	Qualifying educational institution
Contribution limit, RESP	Qualifying educational program
Contribution limit, RRSP	Qualifying home
Designated educational institute	Registered Disability Savings Plan (RDSP)
Disability assistance payments	Registered Education Savings Plan (RESP)
Earned income for RRSP	Repayments
Education Funds	Retiring allowance
Educational assistance payments (EAP)	RRSP contributions
Eligible investments, RRSP	Saskatchewan Savings Plan (SPP)
Fair Market Value (FMV)	Self-directed RRSP
Family plans	Sheltered savings
First time buyer	Severance pay
Group plans	Spousal rollover
Group scholarship plans	Spousal RRSP
Group scholarship trust plans	Spouse
Home Buyers' Plan (HBP)	Subscriber
Income attribution rules	Tax-Free Savings Account (TFSA)
Individual plans	Unmatured RRSP
Lifelong Learning Plan (LLP)	Unused grant room
Lifetime disability assistance payments	Unused RRSP contribution room
Matured RRSP	Withholding tax
	Working Income Tax Benefit (WITB)

QUESTIONS AND PROBLEMS
Registered Retirement Savings Plans

1. RRSP contribution rules underwent a major reform that became effective January 1, 1991. Before that date, contribution room was lost if it was unused after 7 years. Now it can be carried forward forever. What percentage of total contribution room at the end of 2012 is unused room for the period 1991 to 2012? What percentage of total contribution room at the end of

2012 is new room for 2012? What is the amount of RRSP contributions made in 2011? (Answer: 88.5%, 11.5%, $34,401,410)

2. Using Table 6.2, in the year 2011:
   (a) what percentage of tax filers contributed to their RRSPs? (Answer: 24.0%)
   (b) which age group had the highest percentage of:
       i. contributors?
       ii. RRSP contributions?
   (c) which income group had the highest percentage of:
       i. contributors?
       ii. RRSP contributions?

3. Can you deduct administration and brokerage fees for RRSP transactions?

4. Can you deduct interest on a loan obtained to "top up" (i.e., use up unused contribution room) your RRSP?

5. If Alice in Example 1 takes $10,000 out of her RRSP:
   (a) How much earned income has she used up that cannot be recovered? (Answer: $55,556)
   (b) How much of the $10,000 is taxable? (Answer: 100%)
   (c) How much will she receive after the withholding tax? (Answer: $8,500)
   (d) If they live in British Columbia, and Alice earns $80,000 a year, how much tax will she owe on the withdrawal? Assume a marginal tax rate of 36.50% (Answer: $2,150)

6. Which of the following are "earned income" for calculating RRSP contribution room?
   (a) Royalties on a hit record
   (b) Employment insurance benefits received while between jobs
   (c) Net income from renting out an extra bedroom to students
   (d) Bonus for completing a project on time and under budget
   (e) Dividends received
   (f) Severance pay received when the company downsized
   (g) Commissions earned by a Toyota sales person

7. John earned $50,000 in 2013 and $55,000 in 2014. For the first time he did not make an RRSP contribution in 2014.
   (a) What is his new contribution room for 2015? (Answer: $9,900)
   (b) What is his unused contribution room in 2015? (Answer: $9,000)
   (c) What is his contribution limit for 2015? (Answer: $18,900)

8. What is the maximum age at which you can contribute to an RRSP?

9. Eleanor earned $70,000 in 2013 and $75,000 in 2014.
   (a) What is the maximum she can contribute to her RRSP for 2014? (Answer: $12,600)
   (b) Eleanor has a pension adjustment for 2013 of $7,500. What is her RRSP contribution limit for 2014? (Answer: $5,100)

10. Jennifer's husband died shortly after he retired. Jennifer transferred the commuted value of his RPP to her RPP. What effect does this have on her RRSP contribution room; i.e., does she receive a pension adjustment for this that would reduce her current and future RRSP contributions?

11. When Janet and Steve divorced, Steve was awarded 24% of Janet's RPP. Steve transferred the commuted value of this pension to his RPP. Does this affect his RRSP contribution room?

12. Cathy worked for an interesting but poverty-stricken national magazine. She was terminated after 17 years of service (from June, 1987 to August, 2013). She received a severance equal to $40,000.

    (a) If the magazine had a pension plan, how much is she entitled to transfer to an RRSP? (Answer: $18,000)

    (b) If the magazine had no pension plan, how much could she transfer to an RRSP? (Answer: $21,000)

    (c) What effect would (a) and (b) have on Cathy's RRSP contribution room?

13 When Henry died on November 12, he had not made a contribution to his RRSP for the current year.

    (a) Can his executor and/or wife make the contribution on his behalf?

    (b) How can this contribution room be used?

    (c) What is the latest this contribution can be made?

14. For a spousal RRSP, which of the following qualifies as a spouse?

    (a) A common-law partner of the opposite sex

    (b) A husband or wife

    (c) A same-sex partner

15. Tom is a successful consultant and has been contributing $6,500 a year to a spousal RRSP for several years. In 2014, Tom and his wife decide to take $10,000 a year for four years out of the spousal RRSP to send one of their daughters to a private school. Marsha, Tom's wife, works three days a week earning $25,000 a year, while Tom makes $100,000 a year. Tom's last contribution to the spousal RRSP was in 2013. Tom does not plan to make any more deposits to the spousal RRSP until their daughter is finished school. For each of the withdrawals, in whose hands is it taxable?

    Hint: The withdrawals are done on a LIFO basis — last in, first out. When the first withdrawal is made, from which RRSP contribution does it come?

Year	Deposits	Withdrawals	Tom	Marsha
2010	6,500			
2011	6,500			
2012	6,500			
2013	6,500			
2014	0	10,000	10,000	
2015	0	10,000		10,000
2016	0	10,000		10,000
2017	0	10,000		10,000

16. Because Marlene has a pension at work, she was not sure how much she could contribute to her RRSP. She made her 2013 contribution on November 1, 2013. It turns out that she overcontributed by $5,000.

    (a) On how much will she have to pay a penalty? (Answer: $3,000)

    (b) How much will the penalty be? (Answer: $60)

    (c) The overcontribution may end on January 1, 2014. Under what circumstances does the overcontribution end at that time?

17. Using Example 7, Ralph, re-do the calculation of the penalty assuming the pension holiday was applied to only 40% of his annual contributions. How is his contribution room affected by the

40% holiday? (It isn't.) If he makes a contribution in 2002 of $8,100 (60% of $13,500), what is the penalty he will pay in 2002 and 2003? (Answer: $622.20, $615.00)

> Hint: 1. The calculation is the same to the end of the line "RRSP contribution room available 915, 60, 600." 2. The money purchase limits were revised in June 2003. The example uses the money purchase limits as they were in 2002 and the beginning of 2003, before the revision.

18. Andy turned 72 on August 12, 2014. During 2013, he contributed $13,500, the maximum possible, to his RRSP (before he made the transfer to his RRIF) and deducted $7,000 from his 2013 income. Can he deduct the remaining $6,500 on his 2014 return?

19. Allison had earned income of $70,000 in 2013 and 2014. She contributed $25,200 to her RRSP on December 3, 2014. She turned 71 years old on December 28, 2014, and retired as of December 31, 2014. On December 31, 2014, she also transferred the balance in her RRSP to an RRIF.
    (a) How much penalty will she pay? (Answer: $106)
    (b) How much can she deduct from taxable income in:
        i. 2013? (Answer: $12,600)
        ii. 2014? (Answer: $12,600)

20. What is an "unmatured RRSP"?

21. What is a "matured RRSP"?

22. Which of the following can you hold in an RRSP?
    (a) Canada Savings Bonds
    (b) Your grandmother's very old, very precious engagement ring
    (c) A GIC with the Bank of Nova Scotia
    (d) Your cottage
    (e) The mortgage on your cottage
    (f) Shares of American corporations listed on a Canadian stock exchange
    (g) Shares of American corporations not listed on a Canadian stock exchange
    (h) Shares of the new company your friend Theresa set up

23. Anne wants to transfer her shares in Rebus Inc. and Bombardier to her RRSP. She bought the Rebus shares for a total of $7,000, and they now have a market value of $5,000. She bought the Bombardier shares for $4,000, and they now have a market value of $10,000. If she transfers both shares in the same tax year, how much tax will she owe? She lives in PEI, and earns $80,000. Her marginal tax rate is 42.70% (Answer: $1,281.00)

24. Maureen bought shares worth $8,000 in Hi-growth Inc. These shares are expected to grow by $12% a year, paying no dividends, for the next 10 years, at which time she will sell them. Inflation is expected to be 2% a year during the next 10 years. Maureen lives in Regina, Saskatchewan and earns $80,000 a year. Her marginal tax rate is 39.00%
    (a) What is the value in 10 years of these shares:
        i. in $ nominal (Answer: $24,847)
        ii. in $ real (Answer: $20,383)
    (b) If the shares are a non-registered investment:
        i. How much will she have after tax in 10 years if she sells the shares? (Answer: $17,968).

> Hint: Since tax brackets are expected to increase by inflation in the next 10 years, use the real, not nominal future value to calculate the after-tax amount.

      ii.   What is her holding period return and EAR after tax based on her after-tax initial investment? (Answer: HPR 124.60% EAR 8.43%)

    (c) If the shares are invested using her RRSP and she withdraws all the funds in a lump sum in 10 years:

      i.   How much will she have after tax? (Answer: $12,434)

      ii.   What is her initial investment after tax? (Answer: $4,880)

      iii.   What is her holding period return and EAR after tax based on her after-tax initial investment? (Answer: HPR 154.79%, EAR 9.80%)

Home Buyers' Plan (HBP)

25. Candice has been contributing to a spousal RRSP for her husband, Arthur, who is raising their year-old triplets.

    (a) Can Candice withdraw funds from this spousal RRSP for the HBP? (Answer: No)

    (b) Can Arthur withdraw these funds? (Answer: Yes)

    (c) Candice and Arthur have found their dream home, but they can't afford it. On March 15, their offer on a good-enough and affordable house was accepted. The closing date is in two months, on May 5, 2014.

      i.   Can they withdraw the funds now? (Answer: Yes)

      ii.   What is the latest date they can make an HBP withdrawal? (Answer: April 14)

    (d) To help their cash flows, they are considering renting out the house for a year before they move in. Is this allowed under the HBP?

    (e) Candice owned a house with her ex-husband from August 2004 to July 2009. Arthur owned a mobile trailer with his brother from September, 2001 to December, 2009. Do they qualify as first-time buyers?

    (f) Arthur wonders if they could buy a nice mobile home and live on it under the HBP. He envisions living there with the triplets, two dogs, the cat, and the gerbil.

26. What is the maximum withdrawal?

27. How much do you have to repay each year?

28. When do the repayments start?

29. Can you get rid of the obligation to repay by declaring bankruptcy?

30. In 2013, Mark withdrew $11,500 from his RRSP using the HBP. He paid $1,000 in 2014 and $1,100 in 2015. In 2016, he lost his job, so he skipped the payment. On how much will he have to pay tax? (Answer: $671.42).

Lifelong Learning Plan (LLP)

31. What is the maximum that can be withdrawn in one year?

32. What is the maximum that can be withdrawn in total?

33. Can the funds be used for a spouse? For children?

34. Max withdrew $5,000 on September 1, 2012, 2013, and 2014. What is the date by which Max must withdraw the balance? (Answer: January 2015)

35. When do the repayments for Max start? (Answer: 2017)

36. Is there interest on the funds withdrawn?

37. What is the maximum number of years over which the repayment can be amortized?

Using an RRSP to Give Yourself a Mortgage

38. What is the biggest disadvantage to this?

39. What happens if you default on the mortgage; i.e., if you fail to make the payments?

Registered Education Savings Plan (RESP)

40. Which type of RESP plan would be best for someone who wants to make regular, monthly payments and does not want to make investment decisions?

41. Michelle, a single mother with a daughter named Riley who turned six this year, lives in Alberta. Although she makes only $35,000 a year, Michelle is extremely good at saving money.
    (a) If Michelle deposits $2,000 into an RESP, as she does every year, what is the maximum annual incentive she can receive for:
        i.   Canada Education Savings Grant (CESG) (Answer: $500 to a $7,200 lifetime maximum)
        ii. Canada Leaning Bond (CLB) (Answer: $525 for the first year, then $100 a year, to a $2,000 lifetime maximum)
        iii. Alberta Centennial Education Savings Plan Grant (ACESPG) (Answer: $100)
    (b) If Riley does not go to university or college, can Michelle keep the grants, the bond, and the income earned on the grants and bond?
    (c) Michelle takes all the money out of the RESP when Riley is 22 and determined to pursue a modelling career. Since Michelle is such a good saver, she has no unused RRSP contribution room. She has contributed a total of $36,000 to the RESP, and these contributions have earned income of $10,900. How much tax will she pay on the withdrawal of $46,900 if her marginal tax rate is 27%? (Answer: $5,123)

Tax-Free Savings Account (TFSA)

42. Mike put $5,000 in his TFSA every year for 15 years. The account now has a balance of $107,900. Now he wants to start a new business and takes out $50,000.
    (a) How much tax has he paid on the annual income?
    (b) How much tax does he owe on the annual income when he takes out the $50,000?
    (c) Can he use the $57,900 in the TFSA as collateral on a loan?
    (d) How much tax does he owe on the $50,000 if his marginal tax rate is $40%?
    (e) His business is successful beyond his wildest dreams, and two years later he is in a position to put the $50,000 back into his TFSA. He has not made any deposits during the past two years. What is the maximum he can contribute to his TFSA now that he has the money and the contribution limit is $5,500?

Pension Reform

43. In a Pooled Registered Pension Plan (PRPP):
    (a) Is the employer required to set it up?
    (b) If the employer sets one up, it is mandatory for the employee to participate?
    (c) Can a self-employed person join one? If yes, how?

44. With regard to the Saskatchewan Pension Plan (SPP):
    (a) Can any Canadian join?
    (b) Do you have to join in person or can you sign up online?
    (c) What is the maximum contribution per year?
    (d) How much can you transfer to it from your RRSP each year to take advantage of the professional management and low fees?

45. Who takes the investment risk in a shared-risk pension – the employer or employees?

46. What aspect of a phased-in retirement plan makes it unique?

Registered Disability Savings Plan (RDSP)

47. Virginia, Robin's mother, just inherited $100,000 after tax. She puts the entire amount into a new RDSP with Robin as the beneficiary. Robin is now 37 years old, and his annual income is $40,000.
    (a) When can Robin start taking disability assistance payments from the plan?
    (b) Robin applies for a Canada Disability Savings Grant. How much will he get? (Answer: $3,500)
    (c) If he begins to take disability assistance payments when he is 45 years old, can he keep all the grant?
    (d) If he begins to take the payments when he is 60 years old, will he pay tax on the contribution, grant, and all income earned?
    (e) Is Robin eligible for the Canada Disability Savings Bond?

Problem

48. Roger and Gail, Margot and Craig's neighbours, want to make contributions to their RRSP as well as to RESPs for their three boys, Adam, age 14; Nathan, 12; and Lucas, 10. They realize they are late getting started, but they were too busy paying off their mortgage to be able to think about their children's RESPs. Roger (Question 31 in Chapter 5) can contribute $100 a year to his RRSP. Gail owns and manages a café, so she is self-employed. Her net income from the business in 2013 was $29,000.
    (a) How much can Gail contribute to her RRSP in 2014? (Answer: $5,220)
    (b) They think they will be able to contribute $8,000 a year to RESPs for their children. They are estimating that the children will go to a college or university at age 18 — they have four years to save before Adam *starts*. They are not sure how to allocate the saving to maximize the grants, and they propose the following.

	T0	T1	T2	T3	T4	T5	T6	T7	T8	Total
Adam					x	x	x	x	x	
Nathan							x	x	x	
Lucas									x	

RESP — EOY

	T0	T1	T2	T3	T4	T5	T6	T7	T8	Total
Adam	4,000	4,000	4,000	4,000	0	0	0	0	0	16,000
Nathan	2,500	2,500	2,500	2,500	5,500	5,500	0	0	0	21,000
Lucas	1,500	1,500	1,500	1,500	2,500	2,500	8,000	8,000	0	27,000
	8,000	8,000	8,000	8,000	8,000	8,000	8,000	8,000	0	

CESG — EOY

	T0	T1	T2	T3	T4	T5	T6	T7	T8	Total
Adam	500	500	500	500	0	0	0	0	0	2,000
Nathan	500	500	500	500	500	500	0	0	0	3,000
Lucas	300	300	300	300	500	500	500	500	0	3,200
	1,300	1,300	1,300	1,300	1,000	1,000	500	500	0	

Total

	T0	T1	T2	T3	T4	T5	T6	T7	T8	Total
Adam	4,500	4,500	4,500	4,500	0	0	0	0	0	18,000
Nathan	3,000	3,000	3,000	3,000	6,000	6,000	0	0	0	24,000
Lucas	1,800	1,800	1,800	1,800	3,000	3,000	8,500	8,500	0	30,200
	9,300	9,300	9,300	9,300	9,000	9,000	8,500	8,500	0	

What is the present value now of these savings for each child, using a real interest rate of 3%? (Answer: Adam $16,727, Nathan $21,352, Lucas $25,412)

(c) Gail and Roger are hoping that tuition and books will not be higher than about $6,500 a year in the future, and they will insist that the boys go to a local university or college so that they can live at home.

  i. What is the present value when they start their post-secondary education of four years of tuition and books? (Answer: $24,886)

  ii. What is the present value today for each of the boys? (Answer: Adam $22,111; Nathan $20,842; Lucas $19,645)

(d) Can you think of a better way to do this analysis?

(e) If Roger and Gail put less in her RRSP and more into the RESPs:

  i. What are the benefits?

  ii. What is the cost?

7

Retirement Income Options

Learning Objectives

A. Be able to identify which registered plans are to be transferred and what the transfer options are, both before and at retirement.

B. For **registered funds:**
- Know what options are available at retirement
- Recognize which plans have maximums placed on the annual withdrawal and be able to calculate these maximums
- Calculate minimum required withdrawals from registered income funds at various interest rates
- Understand the tax implications of Spousal Registered Retirement Income Funds
- Know the various types of annuities and the factors which affect the amount of income from them.

C. For **non-registered savings:**
- Know how to use the systematic withdrawal plan to draw down non-registered assets
- Appreciate the positive and negative aspects of reverse mortgages.

D. Know the implications of demutualization of insurance companies on taxable income.

E. Calculate the tax on annuity income.

Craig and Margot arrive for their next appointment with Francesca. Margot used the Internet to look up some of the options for RRSPs at retirement: RRIFs, LIFs, LRIFs, LIRAs, minimum withdrawals, excess amounts, more income attribution. She would like to know why there are so many confusing options. Francesca calms the couple down by assuring them that there are not really all that many options, and each option has various advantages and disadvantages.

The various options that are available for retirees vary in terms of:

- Guaranteed income
- Guaranteed term
- Control over investments, even in retirement
- Decisions about how much to withdraw each year (within some limitations)

Francesca will start by summarizing the options for transferring registered funds. Since the purpose of registered plans is to provide retirement income, there are rules for forcing the contents of the plans into taxable income as the retiree ages and for receiving retirement income from registered plans until death.

INTRODUCTION

The three types of registered plans (RPPs, RRSPs, and DPSPs) are tax-sheltered forms of retirement savings. As a result, when the funds are withdrawn, they are considered income and are fully taxable. Since the intent of these plans is to provide retirement income, there are rules to ensure that the income will continue until the retiree's death. There are also other rules to ensure that the income is not deferred indefinitely and that the retiree receives some taxable income each year. We will discuss these rules in this chapter.

A. TRANSFER OF REGISTERED PLANS

Since the purpose of registered plans is to provide retirement income, there are rules about when and to what funds can be or must be transferred to provide retirement income. While there are exceptions, the rules can be generalized as:

* Funds contributed to registered plans are **locked in** (except for RRSPs) until the person is within 10 years of normal retirement age (NRA), which is 55 in most provinces but can be as low as age 50. This means that registered funds cannot begin to pay pension income until the age of 55 (except for RRIFs, which have no minimum age).
* Funds in registered plans must start paying pension income in the year the individual turns 72.
* There are minimum annual withdrawal requirements for registered retirement funds and some plans also have maximum annual restrictions to ensure the retiree does not run out of retirement income.

Retirement Savings at Retirement

When a person in a registered pension plan leaves employment before retirement, one option available to them is to transfer accrued pension benefits to an RRSP, which is locked-in until retirement. These locked-in accounts are called **Locked-in Retirement Accounts (LIRAs)** for provincially regulated pension plans and **Locked-in RRSP (LRSPs)** for federally regulated pension plans. LIRAs and LRSPs are interim accounts whose function is to hold funds until retirement income is needed — they do not allow withdrawals. When the plan holder retires, funds in a LIRA or an LRSP are first transferred to a retirement-income vehicle from which retirement income is withdrawn.

At retirement or by the end of the year the planholder turns 71, all RRSPs, DPSPs, LIRAs, and LRSPs must be transferred to a fund that will pay out retirement income. The individual is then required to begin receiving retirement income no later than the following year — the year the person turns 72. RPPs are also required to begin paying pension income no later than the year the retiree turns 72. At retirement (at maturity), the funds in an RRSP or a DPSP can be taken as a lump-sum withdrawal. Since the entire amount would be taxable, this avenue is seldom taken but it is an option not available with other registered savings. The effect is that all registered plans, including RPPs, must begin paying retirement income in the year the individual turns 72.

Prior to age 71, funds in registered savings plans can be transferred among themselves (if the plan allows) or to a LIRA or LRSP. **Contributions** *can be made* to RPPs, RRSPs, and DPSPs. Contributions *cannot be made* to LIRAs/LRSPs, RRIFs, LRIFs, LIFs, and annuities since they can only receive transfers from other plans.

The following table summarizes all options for retirement savings and retirement income plans.

Table 7.1 Summary of Transfer Options and Restrictions

From:	To:						
	Before retirement				At retirement		
	RPP	RRSP	DPSP	LIRA/ LRSP	RRIF or LRIF	LIF or LRIF	Annuity
RPP DC	Yes	Yes	Yes	Yes	Yes	Yes	Yes
RPP DB	Yes	Yes		Yes	Yes	Yes[1]	Yes
Unmatured RRSP	Yes	Yes			Yes		No
Matured RRSP	No	Yes			Yes		Yes
DPSP	Yes	Yes	Yes	No	No	No	No
LIRA/LRSP					Yes	Yes	Yes
RRIF	No	No			Yes		Yes
RRIF of deceased spouse	No	Yes			Yes		Yes
LRIF							Yes
LIF[3]							Must at 80[2]
Life annuity							
Pays out funds before retirement	No	Yes	Yes	No		1	
Pays out funds in retirement	Yes	No	No	No	Yes	Yes	Yes
Individual controls investment	No	Yes	Yes	Yes	Yes	Yes	No
Minimum withdrawals		No	No		Yes	Yes	
Maximum withdrawals		No	No		No	Yes	
Must transfer at age 71		Yes	Yes	Yes	No		
Can purchase an annuity		Yes	Yes	Yes	Yes	Yes	
Must transfer to life annuity at age 80						LIF Maybe,[2] LRIF No	
Can take cash lump sum	No	Yes	Yes[4]	No	No	No	No

LIRA: Locked-in Retirement Account (provincial) = LRSP

LRSP: Locked-in RRSP (federal) = LIRA

RRIF: Registered Retirement Income Fund

LIF: Life Income Fund

LRIF: Locked-in Retirement Income Fund (= locked-in RRIF)

This table does not include permitted transfers due to breakdown of marriage or relationship, nor does it include transfers for non-residents of Canada. See T4079 T4RSP and T4RIF Guide.

1 Where plan permits.

2 Federal legislation requires that LIFs be converted to an annuity at age 80; some provinces and territories also require this and some do not require this at all.

3 In some instances, funds in LIFs can be accessed before retirement, as explained in the section on LIFs.

4 Can take as a cash withdrawal over not more than 10 years; in effect, an annuity over 10 years.

Options vary according to the jurisdiction of the plan and the financial institution

Options for Retirement Savings Plans
1. Registered Pension Plan (RPP)

Participation in this plan is often mandatory and, as mentioned previously, may be contributory or non-contributory. If the employee leaves their job for another job, the funds in these plans can be transferred to other plans, either to hold funds until retirement or to pay out retirement income.

When an employee leaves the company *before retirement*, and

1. before pension contributions are locked in, the employer's contributions become forfeited amounts to be distributed to the employees still in the plan. The employee can receive their own contributions as a cash refund or can transfer the funds to another plan (an RRSP or a new RPP).

2. after pension contributions are locked in, the employee has several options:
    (a) leave the pension benefits with the **old employer** to be received as pension in retirement, or
    (b) transfer the **commuted value** (the present value of the future benefits) of vested pension benefits directly, without paying any tax to another registered plan, depending on their age:
        i. If the employee is less than age 54 or is age 55 and still working, the funds can be transferred to:
            (1) a **new employer's RPP**, if the new employer's plan permits,
            (2) a **locked-in RRSP (LRSP)** or a **locked-in retirement account (LIRA)**, which are the same thing but called by different names in different jurisdictions. See Table 7.4.
        ii. If the employee is age 54 and can begin to receive retirement income (in most provinces and territories at age 55, but at age 50 in some jurisdictions), the funds can be transferred to:
            (1) a **Life Income Fund (LIF)**
            (2) a **Locked-in Retirement Income Fund (LRIF)**, or
            (3) a **carrier** for the purchase of a **Life Annuity** (a carrier is an insurance company, a Canadian trust company, or an institution that is licensed to carry on annuities business).

RPP pension benefits can also be transferred to:

1. the former spouse under a divorce decree or separation agreement
2. a spouse on the death of the annuitant.

Under these same two circumstances, RRSPs can also be transferred to the spouse or former spouse's:

• RPP
• locked-in RRSP or LIRA
• locked-in RRIF.

Transferring the Commuted Value of a DBPP to Another Registered Plan

When an employee leaves one job for another and is not old enough to receive a pension, they must make a decision about accrued pension benefits as outlined above. One of the options for DBPP pension credits is to transfer the **commuted value** of future pension benefits to another registered plan. However, CRA limits the amount that can be transferred to the *lesser* of:

• **Prescribed amount** which is the maximum transfer value calculated by multiplying the annual pension by a present value factor that is adjusted for the age of the employee at the time of the calculation (called Attained Age Present Value Factor)
    • the table for "Attained Age Present Value Factor" begins at 9.0 for age 50 and under. The factor, maximizes at 12.4 at age 64/65 and then declines to include age "96 and over". (Income Tax Regulation 8517)

Under 50	9.0	54	10.2	59	11.3	64	12.4
50	9.4	55	10.4	60	11.5	65	12.4
51	9.6	56	10.6	61	11.7	66	12.0
52	9.8	57	10.8	62	12.0	67	11.7
53	10.0	58	11.0	63	12.2	68	11.3

- **Commuted value** which is the amount that is required to provide a lifetime pension and this equals the present value of the lifetime pension benefits. This actuarial calculation takes into account several factors such as:
  - age at the time of the calculation
  - age it is assumed the pension will begin
  - adjustments for any guarantees such as indexing for inflation, spousal benefit after the death of the pensioner, and/or health and dental benefits in retirement
  - long-term Government of Canada bond yields

Any excess amount must be taken in cash, is subject to withholding tax and if fully taxable.

Example 1   Emily, age 51, has just given her notice to her employer that she will be leaving at the end of the month. She has been with her employer for 17 years and has earned pension credits in her DBPP that will provide her with a pension of $3,000 a month at age 65, based on her 17 years of service. The prescribed amount is $345,600 ($3,000 × 12 months × 9.6 factor) while the commuted value provided by the actuaries is $215,000.

   Thus Emily can transfer $215,000 to a locked-in registered plan. She must, however, take $130,600 (345,600 – 215,000) in cash — an amount that is taxable and subject to withholding tax (outlined in Chapter 6, Example 1) of $37,180. She will receive a net of $93,420 (130,600 – 37,180). Note that she owes tax at her marginal tax rate on the $130,600 and the withholding tax of $37,180 will be applied against this tax owing.

What should she do? It depends on several factors, some of which are subjective:
- How is her health and that of her parents; that is, will she live a long time? If the answer is yes, take the guaranteed pension.
- Is the old company healthy and likely to remain so? Not sure? Take the commuted value. Remember the now defunct Nortel and the court battle pensioners are having in order to get some portion of their pensions.
- Do you want to manage the money? If not, take the pension plan having professional managers.
- Is your pension indexed? Yes? Take the pension and reduce your exposure to inflation.
- Does your pension include benefits? If yes, that's worth perhaps $1,000 a year or more.

2. Deferred Profit Sharing Plan (DPSP)
By law, all funds must be withdrawn from a DPSP within 90 days of the earliest of:

1. retirement or termination of employment
2. the year in which the employee turns 71
3. employee's death
4. termination of the plan.

A DPSP can be transferred to:

- an RPP (if allowed by the plan)
- an RRSP, and
- another DPSP with at least five beneficiaries

or it can be taken as cash over not more than 10 years — in effect, a 10-year annuity.

3. Registered Retirement Savings Plan (RRSP)

RRSPs are also tax-sheltered savings that allow taxpayers to save for retirement on a tax-deferred basis. Sometimes companies contribute to RRSPs for employees; employees may or may not be required to match the contribution. The employer's contribution is a taxable benefit but is added to the RRSP tax deduction for the individual. In addition, employer contributions are subject to CPP contributions and EI premiums. Unlike other registered plans, RRSPs are not locked in — the funds can be withdrawn at any time and are included in taxable income when withdrawn.

Unmatured RRSPs are RRSPs that are not paying retirement income. They can be transferred directly on a tax-free basis to:

1. **Another RRSP** for the same individual (who is called the **annuitant,** even though the plan is not yet paying an annuity)
2. **An RRIF** for the same annuitant
3. **An RPP** for the benefit of the individual.

Matured RRSPs are RRSPs that are paying retirement income and cannot be transferred on a tax-free basis. However, there is a tax deduction equal to the amount of the transfer if the amount is transferred directly to:

- **Another RRSP** for the same individual
- **An RRIF** for the same annuitant
- **A carrier** to buy an annuity.

4. Locked-in Retirement Account (LIRA)

As indicated above, funds can be transferred from a registered pension plan if an employee leaves the company before retirement. They allow the individual to make the investment decisions. It does not pay retirement income and, by the end of the year the individual turns 71, the LIRA *must* be transferred to:

- purchase a life annuity,
- a Life Income Fund (LIF), or
- a Locked-in Retirement Income Fund (LRIF).

LIRAs can also be transferred to another LIRA before the end of the year in which the individual turns 71.

Table 7.2 Summary of Transfer Options for Registered Assets at Maturity — No Later than the Year in Which the Individual Turns 71

	Can be transferred to:	Which can further be transferred to:
RRSP	1. Withdraw and pay tax 2. RRIF 3. Annuity — life or term-certain	Annuity — Life or Term Certain *can* be purchased
DPSP	Take as cash over a maximum of 10 years	
LIRA/LRSP	1. LIF 2. LRIF where available 3. Life annuity	Life annuity *must* be purchased by age 80 in some jurisdictions and not at all in others Life annuity *can* be purchased at any time

Death of an RRSP Annuitant

When the owner of an RRSP dies, the RRSP ends and the fair market value of the RRSP must be included in the deceased's income on the final tax return. However, if the beneficiary is the spouse, common-law partner, or a financially dependent child or grandchild, the RRSP is treated as a **refund of premiums,** which offsets the amount declared as income. The refund of premiums can be:

- taken as cash by the beneficiary and is taxable in the hands of the beneficiary, or
- transferred tax free to an RRSP of the beneficiary without affecting the beneficiary's RRSP contribution room.

If the deceased had unused tax losses, the executor might include some of the RRSP in the deceased's income; this portion is not part of the refund of premiums, is not taxable to the beneficiary, and cannot be transferred to a beneficiary's RRSP tax-free. The Income Tax Act provides a formula [ITA s. 146(8.9)] for calculating the maximum amount that can be designated as a refund of premiums.

If the annuitant was receiving annuity income from the RRSP, a beneficiary listed in the previous paragraph can become the successor annuitant, paying tax on the income as it is received.

When an annuitant dies, the recipient of a tax-free amount from an RRSP is jointly and severally liable with the deceased annuitant for a portion of the deceased's additional tax payable on this RRSP income. The liability is pro-rated according to the amount received as a proportion of the total RRSP. If the estate is the beneficiary, it is liable, but the beneficiaries of the estate are not.

A single or lump-sum payment out of an RRSP is not an annuity payment and does not fall within the definition of "pension income" whether the RRSP is registered or was registered and is no longer. Thus, a refund of premiums or a commutation payment received by the beneficiary is neither "qualified pension income" nor "pension income" for the purposes of the non-refundable tax credit for eligible pension income.

Pension Income Amount

The federal $2,000 pension income amount and varying amounts for the provinces and territories in the non-refundable tax credits can be used with only certain pension income.[1] In addition, there are age restrictions for some types of income. It is available to:
- Tax payers of any age receiving:
  - Annuity income from a pension plan (also sometimes called superannuation plan)
  - RRSP, DPSP and RRIF income received as a result of the death of a spouse or common-law partner
- Retirees 65 years old or older at December 31 who receive:
  - RRIF income
  - LIF income
  - LRIF income
  - RRSP annuity payments
  - DPSP annuity payments
- It cannot be used with:
  - OAS benefits
  - CPP or QPP benefits
  - RRSP withdrawals
  - Death benefits
  - Retiring allowances
  - Excess amounts from a RRIF transferred to an RRSP, another RRIF or annuity
  - Amounts received from a retirement compensation arrangement

---

1   Canada Revenue Agency:
     - General Income Tax and Benefit Guide, Line 115 — Other pensions or superannuation, Line 116 — Elected split-pension amount, Line 129 – RRSP income, and Line 314 — Pension income amount <www.cra.gc.ca>
     - Federal Worksheet, Line 314 — Pension income amount

B. RETIREMENT FUND OPTIONS

The Canada Revenue Agency requires that RRSPs, LIRAs, and LRSPs be transferred to a retirement income fund by December 31 of the year the individual turns 71. The options were summarized in Table 7.1. They differ in the amount of control the retiree has over the amount of withdrawals, as well as the options for investing the funds. The options are presented in the following table.

Table 7.3 Summary of the Characteristics of the Transfer Options

Holds funds	Pays out funds	Allow control of investment	Transfer to	Minimum withdrawals	Maximum withdrawals
Life annuity	Yes	No	n/a	n/a	n/a
LIF	Yes	Yes	Must transfer to life annuity at age 80 if federally regulated; though not in all provinces and territories	Yes	Yes
LRIF	Yes	Yes	Can transfer to life annuity any time	Yes	Yes
RRIF	Yes	Yes	Annuity — life or term-certain any time	Yes	No

LIF: Life Income Fund
LRIF: Locked-in Retirement Income Fund — a locked-in RRIF
RRIF: Registered Retirement Income Fund

Table 7.4 shows the variation in pension options by jurisdiction. Remember, pension regulations change regularly!

Table 7.4 Pension Options by Jurisdiction

	Before retirement		After retirement			
	LRSP	LIRA	LIF	LRIF	PRIF	Life Annuity Minimum Survivor Benefit
			Convert at Age		(See note below)	
Federally regulated	Yes		Yes 80	No		60%
Alberta		Yes	Yes 80	Yes		60%
British Columbia	Yes		Yes None	No		60%
Manitoba		Yes	Yes None	Yes	Yes	66.67%
New Brunswick		Yes	Yes None	No		60%
Newfoundland		Yes	Yes 80	Yes		60%
Northwest Territories	Yes		Yes 80	No		60%
Nova Scotia		Yes	Yes None	No		60%
Nunavut	Yes		Yes 80	No		60%
Ontario		Yes	Yes 80	Yes		60%
Prince Edward Island	Yes		No n/a	No		60%
Quebec		Yes	Yes None	No		60%
Saskatchewan			No n/a	No	Yes	60%
Yukon	Yes		Yes 80	No		60%

Note: Prescribed Retirement Income Funds (PRIF)
PRIFs have minimum required withdrawals but no maximums. In addition Spouses are automatically the designated beneficiary and must sign a waiver allowing a different beneficiary.

- Manitoba allows a one-time transfer of up to 50% of the assets in a LIF or LRIF to a PRIF, which can be cashed-out, transferred to another PRIF or to a life annuity contract.
- Saskatchewan allows transfer of 100% of the assets in a locked-in pension account subject to spousal consent.

Investment Options

By and large, the investment options for the income funds that receive and hold registered funds are the same as the investment options for RRSPs. Except for RRIFs, these funds cannot be invested in a self-directed mortgage unless the mortgage was set up in the RRSP.

Life Annuity

Life annuities pay income until the individual dies, at which point it stops if there is no surviving spouse or a surviving spouse has waived his or her right to a survivor benefit. Annuity payments can also be guaranteed for a certain period so that if the annuitant dies before the guaranteed period ends, the beneficiary receives the annuity payments until the end of the guaranteed period. The beneficiary can receive the amounts as a taxable lump sum, or it can be transferred to a RRIF. Most provinces allow purchase of an annuity from a registered plan at age 55; some allow it at age 50; and, in some provinces, there is no minimum age (assuming the registered plan allows it).

Life Income Fund (LIF) and Locked-in Retirement Fund (LRIF)

Both funds have minimum and maximum withdrawal requirements and both allow the retiree to decide on the investments. A LIF *sometimes requires* the retiree to buy a life annuity by age 80, while a LRIF *allows* the purchase of a life annuity at any time or not at all. In addition, for a LRIF, the maximum is based on the investment income from the prior year meaning income can vary from year-to-year. If the permitted maximum is not withdrawn, the unused amount can be carried forward to future years. Most provincial plans restrict transfer to these options to within 10 years of normal retirement — age 55 in most provinces — while most federal plans have no minimum age restriction. As shown in Table 7.4, most provinces and territories have LIFs, while only a few have LRIFs.

Both LIFs and LRIFs pay out retirement income with a minimum withdrawal requirement, as well as a limit on the maximum withdrawal. The withdrawal ceiling for a LIF is based on the balance in the fund and the retiree's age, while the LRIF also incorporates investment income earned, even if unrealized, in the prior year.

Minimum and Maximum Withdrawals

Tax-sheltered savings encourage taxpayers to save for their retirement by tax-sheltering the deposits to registered plans. However, the funds in these plans are intended to be consumed in retirement (barring death). As a result, there is a requirement that a minimum amount be withdrawn each year as taxable income. In addition, both LIF and LRIF place a maximum on the amount the retiree can withdraw from the fund while RRIFs have no annual maximum.

Minimum Withdrawals

The minimum required withdrawal is all retirement income plans except annuities. Because these options are intended to fund one's retirement, income earned inside the plans remains tax-sheltered. Some plans may also have a limit on the maximum that can be withdrawn so as to maintain sufficient capital in the plan to generate income. The minimum withdrawals from a RRIF, LIF, and LRIF are the same. **There are no minimum withdrawals required in the year the RRIF, LIF, or LRIF is set up.**

Maximum Withdrawals for LIFS and LRIFs

A maximum withdrawal ensures that the retiree will be able to buy a life annuity at age 80 if he or she is required to do so and the retiree does not live in a province where a LRIF is available.

Maximum Withdrawal from a LIF

The **formula for the maximum withdrawal from a LIF** is:

Balance at the beginning of the year

÷

Present value of $1 paid at the beginning of the year from current age to age 90

Using an interest rate that can be either:

- 6% for the entire term, or
- The CANSIM[2] rate, which is 2.27% at December 2012; the CANSIM rate is used for federal pensions, while a 6% CANSIM rate is used in most other jurisdictions.

Example 2 calculates the maximum withdrawal from a LIF using a 6% CANSIM interest rate.

Example 2   Noreen turned 67 on October 23. When she retired from her full-time job at age 63, she transferred the balance in her money purchase pension plan to a LIRA because she continued to work on a consulting basis. Now, at age 67, she decides to retire full-time and transfer the funds, $300,000, out of the LIRA and to an **LIF** because she expects to live a long time and wants to be sure she has an income after age 80, since she lives in a province where she must buy an annuity at age 80.

The **minimum amount** she must withdraw and bring into taxable income uses the same formula as for a RRIF and is described below.

Using the above formula for the maximum withdrawal with a 6% interest rate, her **maximum withdrawal for the first year** is:

| $300,000 ÷ $1.00_BOY (PVIFA$_{6\%, (90-67)}$) = 13.0416 | = $23,003 |

$$\frac{\$300{,}000}{\$1.00_{BOY}\ (PVIFA_{6\%,\ (90-67)}) = 13.0416} = \$23{,}003$$

Noreen makes the maximum withdrawal at the beginning of each year.

---

2   Canada Socio-Economic Information Management System series V122487 compiled by Statistics Canada and available on the website maintained by the Bank of Canada.

1	2	3	4	5	6	7	8
Age BOY	Balance BOY	90 – Age	PVA of $1 to Age 90	Maximum withdrawal	Balance after withdrawal	Income @ 5.00%	Balance EOY
				$(2) \div (4)$	$(2) - (5)$	$(6) \times 5\%$	$(6) + (7)$
67	300,000	23	13.0416	–23,003	276,997	13,850	290,846
68	290,846	22	12.7641	–22,786	268,060	13,403	281,463
69	281,463	21	12.4699	–22,571	258,892	12,945	271,836
70	271,836	20	12.1581	–22,358	249,478	12,474	261,952
71	261,952	19	11.8276	–22,148	239,804	11,990	251,795
72	251,795	18	11.4773	–21,939	229,856	11,493	241,349
73	241,349	17	11.1059	–21,732	219,617	10,981	230,598
74	230,598	16	10.7122	–21,527	209,071	10,454	219,525
75	219,525	15	10.2950	–21,323	198,202	9,910	208,112
76	208,112	14	9.8527	–21,122	186,989	9,349	196,339
77	196,339	13	9.3838	–20,923	175,416	8,771	184,187
78	184,187	12	8.8869	–20,726	163,461	8,173	171,634
79	171,634	11	8.3601	–20,530	151,104	7,555	158,659
80	158,659	10	7.8017	–20,336	138,322	6,916	145,239

If Noreen takes out the maximum each year, she will have $145,239 with which she must buy a life annuity by December 31 of the year she turns 80 (because she lives in a province that requires this). In this example. Noreen is earning 5% on the balance while withdrawing the maximum based on 6%. The calculation isn't shown here but Noreen makes the maximum withdrawal of $18,674 at age 89; she has a balance in the LIF of $0. Let's hope she's on good terms with her children if she is still alive.

Maximum Withdrawal from a LRIF

The **formula for the maximum withdrawal from a Locked-in Retirement Income Fund (LRIF)** is much more complicated. There are several ways to calculate the possible maximum, and we will show somewhat simplified example, since one of the options is based on the income earned in the prior year including unrealized capital gains. There is no minimum required withdrawal the year the LRIF is set up but we will assume that Noreen takes out the maximum possible.

The maximum withdrawal from a LRIF is the greatest of:

1. the minimum required withdrawal,
2. in the first two years, 6% of the value of the fund at the beginning of the year,
3. market value at the beginning of the year minus the net value of transfers in and out of the fund without withdrawals, (in Example 3, this equals the FMV at the beginning of the year minus $300,000), and
4. investment income earned during the prior year, including unrealized capital gains.

Example 3 illustrates the possible fluctuation in annual income for a LRIF due to fluctuations in stock market returns. This example assumes that Noreen transfers the funds into a LRIF instead of a LIF. Further, Noreen is invested in an Index Fund. The following table show the rate of return using the S&P/TSX (Standard and Poor and Toronto Stock Exchange) Composite Index as at November 15. Another possible calculation is the minimum withdrawal which is the same calculation as for the RRIF, which is shown in the next section.

S&P/TSX at November 15

Year	Index	Change
2000	8,820	
2001	7,426	−15.8%
2002	6,570	−11.5%
2003	7,859	19.6%
2004	9,030	14.9%
2005	10,824	19.9%
2006	12,752	17.8%
2007	13,689	7.3%
2008	9,056	−33.8%

Example 3 Noreen transferred the funds into a LRIF in 2005 and took out the maximum at the beginning of each year. Instead of investing in an instrument that would pay a steady 5%, she invested in an Index Fund. The first four columns correspond to the four criteria for determining the maximum, which is shown in bold.

	1	2	3	4	5	6	7	8	9	10
	Maximum				RRIF				S&P/TSX	
Age	Minimum 6%	Yr 1 or 2: 6%	FMV − Tsf In	Return prior year	FMV$_{BOY}$	Withdrawals BOY	FMV$_{BOY}$ after withdrawal	Income	Annual returns	
67	0	**18,000**		0	300,000	−18,000	282,000	56,028	2005	19.9%
68	15,365	20,282	38,028	**56,028**	338,028	−56,028	282,000	50,236	2006	17.8%
69	15,821		32,236	**50,236**	332,236	−50,236	282,000	20,715	2007	7.3%
70	15,136		2,715	**20,715**	302,715	−20,715	282,000	−95,444	2008	−33.8%
71	**9,819**		−113,444	−95,444	186,556	−9,819	176,737	???	2009	

The calculations are accurate if you want to check them but are not important since LRIFs have many more rules that are beyond the scope of this textbook. What is important is to notice the great variation in Noreen's annual income from the LRIF.

Additional Withdrawal Options for LIFs and Locked-in RRSPs

Federally regulated LIF and LRSP contracts entered into after May 8, 2008, pension benefit credits in some circumstances, and some provincially regulated LIRAs can make additional withdrawals through the following provisions:

Age	Name	Maximum
For those aged 55 and older	One-Time Unlocking	50%
	Small Balance Unlocking	100%
At any age	Non-Resident Unlocking	100%
	Shortened Life Expectancy Unlocking	100%
Financial hardship at any age	Low Income Unlocking	50% of YMPE
	Medical or Disability-related Expenditures	50% of YMPE

People making these transfers must attest in writing that they understand that unlocked funds:

- lose creditor-protection,
- are taxable if taken into income, and
- they should get professional advice about the legal and financial implications.

In addition the transfer requires attestation as to expected income, written consent by a spouse or common-law partner and certification by a licensed Canadian physician for medical or disability-related expenditures.

One-Time Unlocking — 50%

Individuals age 55 or older can transfer, only once, up to 100% of the balance of a LIF, a locked-in RRSP and, in certain circumstances, pension benefits credits to a Restricted Life Income Fund (RLIF). A RLIF is a locked-in fund that allows holders to transfer up to 50% of the balance in the RLIF to several tax-deferred vehicles.

- an RRSP or RRIF which do not have maximum annual withdrawal limits. The transfer must happen with 60 days of the set-up of the RLIF, or the old LIF minimum and maximum rules apply,
- another RLIF,
- a Life Annuity, or
- a **Restricted Locked-in Savings Plan (RLSP)** that is a new vehicle for receiving funds from a RLIF.

RLIF funds cannot be transferred back to a LIF or to a locked-in RRSP. The latter allows the holder to decide not to receive a steady source of income at that point in time. Funds in the RLSP can be transferred to:

- another RLSP,
- a RLIF,
- a Life Annuity, or
- a RPP if the plan permits it.

Small Balance Unlocking — 100%

Individuals age 55 or older whose holdings in the total of LIFs, locked-in RRSPs, RLIFs, and RLSPs is $25,550 (50% of the year's maximum pensionable earnings, YMPE, $51,100 for 2013) or less will be able to wind up 100% of the LIFs, RLIFs, and RLSPs (but not locked-in RRSPs). They can either take the cash (and pay taxes on it) or convert it to a tax-deferred savings vehicle such as an RRSP or a RRIF. The threshold will be indexed annually.

The small balance unlocking and one-time unlocking can be combined.

Non-Resident Unlocking — 100%

Locked-in plan holders who are non-residents, that is who have not lived in Canada for at least two calendar years, can unlock 100% of their existing (pre-May 8, 2008) and future LIFs and locked-in RRSPs. In addition, a RPP member who is retired and is also a non-resident can unlock pension benefits. For this and the following transfer:

- there is no minimum age requirement, and
- they have been in place for many years.

Shortened Life Expectancy Unlocking — 100%

Locked-in plan holders whose expectancy is shortened, often defined as less than two years, can unlock 100% of locked-in assets.

Financial Hardship Unlocking

These mechanisms have been in place for many years. People of any age can unlock up to 50% of the YMPE or $25,550 for 2013 from any combination of federally-regulated LIFs, locked-in RRSPs, RLIFs and RLSPs annually within a calendar year as long as all withdrawals from all plans are done within 30 days. This is available to people who are experiencing financial hardship due to:

* low income for which the low income limit is 75% of the YMPE or $38,325 for 2013, or
* medical expenditures and/or disability expenditures that are more than 20% of their annual income.

Low Income

They can convert up to 50% of the YMPE minus 2/3 of expected annual income. Expected annual income does not include amounts withdrawn as a result of the financial hardship withdrawals.

Medical or Disability-Related Expenditures

People who spend more than 20% of their annual income on medical treatment, assistive technology, or other expenses related to a condition or disability can recover up to 50% of the YMPE for their expected expenditures in any year.

Registered Retirement Income Fund (RRIF)

RRIFs can be established only by transferring funds from an RRSP, an RPP if the plan permits, or another RRIF. A taxpayer cannot deposit funds directly into a RRIF. In addition, amounts from a matured RRSP or RPP can be transferred to the RRIF of a former spouse if the transfer is made as a settlement or decree resulted from a relationship breakdown.

If a taxpayer dies, amounts from their matured RRSPs, RRIFs, and/or a lump sum from an RPP can be transferred to the RRIF of a surviving spouse or **financially dependent child or grandchild**. The latter is someone who, at the time of the taxpayer's death:

* is mentally or physically infirm
* normally resides with the annuitant
* earns less than $18,368 for 2013 — the sum of the basic personal amount, $10,822, and the disability credit, $7,546, of the previous year, 2012.

Minimum Withdrawals

There is a requirement that beginning in the *year following* the establishment of the RRIF, a **minimum amount** must be withdrawn from a RRIF.

Minimum withdrawals from RRIFs, LIFs, and LRIFs are based on:

* The *age* (in whole numbers) of the individual at the *beginning of the year* (or the age they would have been had they been alive at the beginning of the year). The age of the spouse can also be

used. This option would have appeal if the spouse is younger since the younger the age, the lower is the required withdrawal. If this option is selected, it cannot be changed later.

• The *fair market value* of the RRIF at the *beginning of the year*.

Withdrawals from the RRIF *must* start the *year after* the RRIF was established but can be anytime during that year — at the beginning of the year, each month or at the end of the year. The advantage of having an end-of-year withdrawal is that the funds can continue to compound tax-free until with-drawn. The minimum amount is in effect until the taxpayer's death.

A taxpayer can elect to withdraw more than the minimum amount each or any year. This amount is called an **excess amount** and is also fully taxable in the year of the withdrawal. In addition, this **excess amount is subject to withholding tax**, which varies from 10% to 30%, as discussed in Chapter 6.

There are **two types of RRIFs**, and they have different required minimum withdrawals. They are:

1. **Qualifying RRIFs**, which:
   • were entered into before 1993, and
   • have not had any property transferred into them after 1992, except property from another qualifying RRIF.
2. **Non-qualifying RRIFs**, which:
   • were entered into after 1992, **or**
   • were entered into before 1993, **and**
   • had property transferred into them after 1993. This transferred property was any property not from a qualifying RRIF.

The CRA has designated minimum withdrawal rates for all RRIFs. These rates were changed at the end of 1992 to make newer RRIFs (i.e., non-qualified RRIFs) draw down the funds faster up to the age of 78. A factor based on the formula $[1 \div (90 - age)]$ is used to determine the minimum with-drawal from both qualifying RRIFs until the annuitant reaches the age of 78 and non-qualifying RRIFs before age 71. After age 78, the required withdrawals for both RRIFs are based on the same rates provided by the CRA. Table 7.5 shows the difference in rates for both RRIFs, with the factors for qualifying RRIFs calculated and shown as qualifying equivalents. This table begins with age 69 to show that the rates are the same before the age of 71, even though withdrawals from a RRIF are not re-quired until the year the individual turns 72.

Table 7.5 CRA-Designated Minimum RRIF Withdrawal Rates

Age @ beginning of year	Qualifying RRIF before 1993	Qualifying equivalent	Non-qualifying RRIF after 1992	Difference
69	$1 \div (90 - age)$	0.0476	$1 \div (90 - age)$	0.0000
70	$1 \div (90 - age)$	0.0500	$1 \div (90 - age)$	0.0000
71	$1 \div (90 - age)$	0.0526	0.0738	**0.0212**
72	$1 \div (90 - age)$	0.0556	0.0748	**0.0192**
73	$1 \div (90 - age)$	0.0588	0.0759	**0.0171**
74	$1 \div (90 - age)$	0.0625	0.0771	**0.0146**
75	$1 \div (90 - age)$	0.0667	0.0785	**0.0118**

Table 7.5 Continued.

Age @ beginning of year	Qualifying RRIF before 1993	Qualifying equivalent	Non-qualifying RRIF after 1992	Difference
76	1 ÷ (90 – age)	0.0714	0.0799	**0.0085**
77	1 ÷ (90 – age)	0.0769	0.0815	**0.0046**
78	1 ÷ (90 – age)	0.0833	0.0833	0.0000
79	0.0853		0.0853	0.0000
80	0.0875		0.0875	0.0000
81	0.0899		0.0899	0.0000
82	0.0927		0.0927	0.0000
83	0.0958		0.0958	0.0000
84	0.0993		0.0993	0.0000
85	0.1033		0.1033	0.0000
86	0.1079		0.1079	0.0000
87	0.1133		0.1133	0.0000
88	0.1196		0.1196	0.0000
89	0.1271		0.1271	0.0000
90	0.1362		0.1362	0.0000
91	0.1473		0.1473	0.0000
92	0.1612		0.1612	0.0000
93	0.1792		0.1792	0.0000
94 and after	0.2000		0.2000	0.0000

Sources: 1. IC78-18R5 Registered Retirement Income Funds. Minimum Amount, parts 7 and 8, available at <www.cra-arc.gc.ca>

2. T4RSP and T4RIF Guides Appendix D, available at <www.cra-arc.gc.ca>

Notice that the factors for the qualifying RRIF before age 74 and for the non-qualifying RRIF before age 71 are less than 6%. This means that, for an RRIF set up before these ages (and after age 55), the RRIF balance would continue to grow above the amount transferred in if the RRIF balance earns 6%. Examples 4, 5 and 6 use a rate of return of 6%.

Notice also that the old RRIFs, the qualifying RRIFs, require less minimum withdrawals until age 77, which leaves a larger balance to earn income if only the minimum required amount is withdrawn. This is illustrated in Example 4.

Craig wonders about the difference between a qualifying and a non-qualifying RRIF, even though he and Margot will never have a qualifying RRIF.

To show Craig the difference, Francesca compares the required minimum withdrawals from a qualifying RRIF and those from a non-qualifying RRIF, using a 6% rate of return.

Example 4   Assume that there are two RRIFs: one is a qualifying RRIF established in 1992, with no funds transferred in since; the other is a non-qualifying RRIF started in 1993. Both RRIFs will have a 6% interest rate and started with a RRSP rollover at age 71. The effect of increasing the minimum withdrawal factor below age 78 is to increase the withdrawal below age 78. The result is more capital withdrawn and taxed sooner.

Difference in Minimum Withdrawals for a Qualifying and Non-qualifying RRIF @ 6%

| | Minimum withdrawal | | | | Balance | | |
Age	Qualifying	Non-qualifying	Difference	Cumulative difference	Qualifying	Non-qualifying	Difference
71	15,789	22,140	6,351	6,351	301,263	294,532	6,732
72	16,737	22,031	5,294	11,645	301,598	288,851	12,747
73	17,741	21,924	4,183	15,827	300,888	282,943	17,946
74	18,806	21,815	3,009	18,837	299,008	276,795	22,212
75	19,934	21,728	1,795	20,631	295,818	270,371	25,447
76	21,130	21,603	473	21,104	291,170	263,694	27,475
77	22,398	21,491	(907)	20,197	284,898	256,735	28,163
78	23,742	21,386	(2,355)	17,842	276,826	249,470	27,356
79	23,613	21,280	(2,333)	15,509	268,406	241,882	26,524
80	23,486	21,165	(2,321)	13,188	259,615	233,960	25,655
90	21,899	19,735	(2,164)	(9,208)	147,221	132,672	14,548
100	7,656	6,899	(757)	(24,730)	32,460	29,252	3,208
	587,080	537,620	(24,730)				

The comparison clearly shows the effect of increasing the withdrawal factor below age 78 for the non-qualifying RRIF. The result is more capital withdrawn and taxed sooner and lower total minimum required withdrawals.

Non-Qualifying RRIFs

The following RRIF examples use these assumptions:

(a) Withdrawals begin at age 71, the year after the RRIF is set up

(b) The individual's birthday is *not* January 1 (so the individual is still 71 for calculating the minimum withdrawal)

(c) There is one withdrawal a year at the beginning of the year (BOY); in fact, the withdrawals would probably be monthly, but to simplify the examples, we will use annual withdrawals

(d) The income earned by the RRIF is:
  i. interest income
  ii. based on the end-of-the-year balance after a beginning-of-the-year withdrawal.

Example 5 shows the minimum required withdrawals from a non-qualifying RRIF that was set up after 1992. The example assumes that only the minimum amount is withdrawn — if more than the minimum amount is withdrawn, the minimum required withdrawal for the following years will decrease, as the opening balance will be less.

Example 5   Alice turned 71 on September 23 and set up an RRIF in December of that year. The RRIF earns **6%** a year. At the end of the year that she transferred the RRSP to the RRIF, the RRSP had a balance of $300,000. Since the RRIF was set up after 1992, it is a **non-qualifying RRIF.** The required withdrawals in the first two years are less than the income Alice earns on the outstanding balance. As a result, the balance in the RRIF increases for two years. After that, the withdrawals exceed the income, and the capital is drawn down each year. The withdrawals are 100% taxable in the year of the withdrawal.

Minimum Withdrawal from a Non-qualifying RRIF — Balance Earns 6%

Age	Balance BOY	Required withdrawal		Balance after withdrawal	Interest @ 6%	Balance EOY
		Formula	BOY $			
71	0					300,000
71	300,000	0.0738	22,140	277,860	16,672	294,532
72	294,532	0.0748	22,031	272,501	16,350	288,851
73	288,851	0.0759	21,924	266,927	16,016	282,943
74	282,943	0.0771	21,815	261,128	15,668	276,795
75	276795	0.0785	21,728	255,067	15,304	270,371
76	270,371	0.0799	21,603	248,768	14,926	263,694
77	263,694	0.0815	21,491	242,203	14,532	256,735
78	256,735	0.0833	21,386	235,349	14,121	249,470
79	249,470	0.0853	21,280	228,191	13,691	241,882
80	241882	0.0875	21,165	220,717	13,243	233,960
81	233,960	0.0899	21,033	212,927	12,776	225,703
82	225,703	0.0927	20,923	204,780	12,287	217,067
83	217,067	0.0958	20,795	196,272	11,776	208,048
84	208,048	0.0993	20,659	187,389	11,243	198,633
85	198,633	0.1033	20,519	178,114	10,687	188,801
86	188,801	0.1079	20,372	168,429	10,106	178,535
87	178,535	0.1133	20,228	158,307	9,498	167,805
88	167,805	0.1196	20,070	147,736	8,864	156,600
89	156,600	0.1271	19,904	136,696	8,202	144,898
90	144898	0.1362	19,735	125,163	7,510	132,672
91	132,672	0.1473	19,543	113,130	6,788	119,918
92	119,918	0.1612	19,331	100,587	6,035	106,622
93	106,622	0.1792	19,107	87,515	5,251	92,766
94	92,766	0.2000	18,553	74,213	4,453	78,666
95	78,666	0.2000	15,733	62,933	3,776	66,709
96	66,709	0.2000	13,342	53,367	3,202	56,569
97	56,569	0.2000	11,314	45,255	2,715	47,970
98	47,970	0.2000	9,594	38,376	2,303	40,679
99	40,679	0.2000	8,136	32,543	1,953	34,496
100	34,496	0.2000	6,899	27,597	1.656	29,252
			562,350		291,602	

The total withdrawals for Example 5 equal:

Initial capital	+	300,000
Income on capital balance	+	291,602
Total withdrawals	−	562,350
Capital remaining at age 100	=	29,252

Margot asks what would have happened to Alice's annual income if she had been able to earn only **4%** on the capital in her RRIF instead of 6%? And what if she had earned **8%** a year?

Margot asks Francesca to provide a summary to make the annual income at the three different interest rates easier to compare.

Comparison of Minimum Withdrawal from a Non-qualifying RRIF, Example 5 — Balance Earns 4%, 6%, and 8%

Age	4%	Difference 6%–4%	6%	Difference 8%–6%	8%	Difference 8%–4%
71	22,140	0	22,140	0	22,140	0
72	21,615	416	22,031	416	22,447	831
80	17,830	3,334	21,165	3,878	25,042	7,212
90	13,742	5,993	19,735	8,415	28,150	14,408
100	3,971	2,928	6,899	4,964	11,864	7,893
Total	445,046	117,304	562,350	161,467	723,817	278,771

Craig and Margot wonder what would happen to the annual income if Alice had been able to save the same $300,000 so she could **retire at 55 instead of 71**.

In Example 6, Francesca compares the withdrawals from two non-qualifying RRIFS: one set up at age 55 and the other set up age 71.

Example 6 Let's compare the minimum withdrawals of two non-qualifying RRIFs for Alice: one set up at age 55 and the other at age 71, both with a beginning balance of $300,000 and a 6% interest rate. The required withdrawal for persons under the age of 71 for both RRIFs is based on the factor formula [1 ÷ (90 – age)]. For persons over the age of 70, the rates required by CRA are used.

Comparison of Minimum Withdrawal at Age 55 with Age 71 — RRIF Earns 6%

	Age 55					Age 71	
Age	Balance BOY	Withdrawal BOY	Balance after withdrawal	Interest @ 6%	Balance EOY	Withdrawal	Balance EOY
55	0				300,000		
55	300,000	8,571	291,429	17,486	308,914		
56	308,914	9,086	299,829	17,990	317,818		
57	317,818	9,631	308,187	18,491	326,679		
58	326,679	10,209	316,470	18,988	335,458		
59	335,458	10,821	324,637	19,478	344,115		
60	344,115	11,471	332,645	19,959	352,603		
65	383,753	15,350	368,403	22,104	390,507		
70	410,839	20,542	390,297	23,418	**413,714**	age 71	300,000
71	413,714	30,946	382,769	22,966	405,735	22,140	294,532
72	405,735	30,795	374,939	22,496	397,436	22,031	288,851
80	328,633	29,544	299,089	17,945	317,034	21,165	233,960
81	317,034	29,389	287,645	17,259	304,904	21,033	225,703
82	304,904	29,210	275,694	16,542	**292,236**	20,923	217,067
90	186,359	27,451	158,908	9,534	168,442	19,735	132,672
100	41,089	8,218	32,872	1,972	**34,844**	6,899	**29,252**
		987,075		721,919		562,350	

Notice that the balance in the RRIF taken at age 55 continues to grow until age 70, at which point the factor for the minimum withdrawal is more than the 6% the RRIF is earning. Notice also that the balance does not drop below the original $300,000 until age 82, whereas the balance after the first withdrawal for the RRIF set up at age 71 is below $300,000 in the first year, since the minimum withdrawal is more than the income earned at 6%.

When the interest rate is **6%**, the total withdrawals in Example 6 equal:

		Age 55	Age 71
Initial capital	+	300,000	300,000
Income on capital balance	+	721,919	291,602
Total withdrawals	–	987,075	562,350
Capital remaining at age 100	=	34,844	29,252
Number of years retired		46	30
Average withdrawal per year		21,458	18,745

"What am I working for?" says Craig, laughing. "Of course, Alice would have 16 fewer years to save for her retirement if she retired at 55 instead of 71. And she would have to save more each year. Furthermore $21,000 a year is not a lot of income, so we would probably want more than $300,000. But, still, it is interesting to see that you actually have more annual income. Is the result the same if she earns less than 6%?"

Francesca offers to show them a summary of the difference using 4% instead of 6%.

The comparison shows that the average income is significantly lower with an interest rate of 4% for both RRIFs, and even more so for the RRIF set up at age 55.

Example 6 Summary

Age	RRIF at age 55			RRIF at age 71		
	4%	6%	Difference	4%	6%	Difference
Initial capital	300,000	300,000		300,000	300,000	
+ Income	351,463	721,919	(370,456)	161,565	291,602	(130,037)
– Total withdrawals	636,956	987,075	(350,120)	445,046	562,350	(117,304)
= Capital	14,507	34,844	(20,336)	16,519	29,252	(12,733)
Number of years retired	46	46		30	30	
Average withdrawal per year	13,847	21,458	(7,611)	14,835	18,745	(3,910)

A RRIF can pay out for the entire retirement or it can be used to purchase a life annuity or a fixed-term annuity. If the annuity has a guaranteed term or is a fixed-term annuity, the term cannot be more than **90 minus the age** of the annuitant or the annuitant's spouse at the time the annuity is purchased. The annuity must begin to make payments no later than one year after it is purchased.

Effect of Changes in Market Value on Beginning of the Year Balance

In the prior examples, it was always assumed that the rate of return was fixed. However, this will be the case only if the RRIF is invested in an instrument that provides a fixed rate of return — not a very realistic assumption in most cases. Example 7 shows the effect of a large drop in the expected rate of return in a RRIF.

Example 7   Donna, age 54, was a psychologist with the Ministry of Correctional Services.
      Her defined contribution pension plan (DCPP) was earning only 4% a year. She was tired of her job and had been learning about the stock market. Because the returns on her investments in her non-registered savings had been much better than 4%, she decided to take early retirement. Her DCPP had a provision that she could move it into a locked-in retirement account (LIRA) if she retired before the age of 55.

At age 54, Donna retired and had the $250,000 commuted value of her DCPP trans-ferred to a LIRA. She did not retire immediately. Instead, she chose to consult for a few years before transferring the balance to a RRIF, where she would be required to withdraw a minimum amount each year.

Always an early riser, Donna would get up at 5 a.m. each morning to work on her port-folio. She quickly came to see that investing is a job that requires constant vigilance. How-ever, she was willing to accept a lot of investment risk. She also put her psychology to work and was able to second guess the market very successfully — after three years, Donna's port-folio was worth $800,000. Most of her investments were in high-tech stocks, which seemed to have no ceiling on their upward trend. (Don't laugh, this example is based on a true story!)

Since getting consulting clients is more difficult than it looks, Donna decided that it was time for semi-retirement. She transferred the funds in her LIRA to a RRIF about six months before the bottom fell out of tech stocks. The following table shows Donna's expected cash flows to age 70. She had decided to be conservative and assume her stocks would grow by only 15% a year in the future and not the 47% she had seen in the three years since she set up the LIRA.

Expected Cash Flow to Age 70

Age	Balance BOY		Required withdrawal		Balance after withdrawal	Growth @ 47.36%	Balance EOY
			Formula	$			
57	0						250,000
58	250,000	LIRA			250,000	118,400	368,400
59	368,400	LIRA			368,400	174,474	542,874
60	542,874	LIRA			542,874	257,105	799,979
						15.00%	
61	799,979	RRIF	1 ÷ (90 − age)	27,585	772,394	115,859	888,253
62	888,253	RRIF	1 ÷ (90 − age)	31,723	856,530	128,479	985,009
63	985,009	RRIF	1 ÷ (90 − age)	36,482	948,527	142,279	1,090,807
64	1,090,807	RRIF	1 ÷ (90 − age)	41,954	1,048,852	157,328	1,206,180
65	1,206,180	RRIF	1 ÷ (90 − age)	48,247	1,157,933	173,690	1,331,623
66	1,331,623	RRIF	1 ÷ (90 − age)	55,484	1,276,139	191,421	1,467,560
67	1,467,560	RRIF	1 ÷ (90 − age)	63,807	1,403,753	210,563	1,614,315
68	1,614,315	RRIF	1 ÷ (90 − age)	73,378	1,540,938	231,141	1,772,078
69	1,772,078	RRIF	1 ÷ (90 − age)	84,385	1,687,693	253,154	1,940,847
70	1,940,847	RRIF	1 ÷ (90 − age)	97,042	1,843,805	276,571	2,120,376

The following table shows Donna's actual position after two years, when her portfolio (not diversified) lost 48% a year, on average.

Actual Cash Flow for Age 61 and 62

Age	Balance BOY		Required withdrawal		Balance after withdrawal	Growth @ 47.35%	Balance EOY
			Formula	$			
57	0						250,000
58	250,000	LIRA			250,000	118,400	368,400
59	368,400	LIRA			368,400	174,474	542,874
60	542,874	LIRA			542,874	257,105	799,979
						−48.00%	
61	799,979	RRIF	1 ÷ (90 − age)	27,585	772,394	(370,749)	401,645
62	401,645	RRIF	1 ÷ (90 − age)	14,344	387,300	(185,904)	201,396

Donna has renewed her interest in consulting.

This example may seem extreme as Donna had already rolled her LIRA into a RRIF. However, it shows the painful effect of declines in the stock market on retirement savings. It illustrates the dire consequences for employees who work in the United States for companies such as Enron and had all their retirement savings in 401(k)s[3] invested totally in company stock.. This is the way in which their retirement savings shrank.

Spousal RRIFs

When a Spousal RRSP is rolled over into a RRIF, it is considered a spousal RRIF. **Income attribution** rules remain in effect and apply to any *excess amount* withdrawn from a spousal RRIF but not to the minimum required withdrawal. In addition, as with RRIFs, **withholding tax** is applied to the *excess amount*.

Example 8 illustrates the effect of income attribution rules on a spousal RRIF. It also shows the effects on the minimum required withdrawals for future years when more than the minimum required amount is withdrawn. The following compares with the minimum required withdrawals shown in Example 3.

Example 8   Refer to Example 3 above, where Alice transferred her $300,000 RRSP to a RRIF in the year she turned 71. Let's change Alice's RRSP to a spousal RRSP to which Alice had been contributing for her husband, Alex, also age 71 on September 23. The RRSP had been earning 6%. But now let's assume that Alice had been depositing $12,000 a year into the spousal RRSP up to and including the year the RRIF was set up. The RRSP contributions were made at the end of the year, while the RRIF withdrawals were made at the beginning of the year. Let's further assume that Alex will withdraw $30,000 a year, which will be more than the minimum required withdrawal. The minimum withdrawals for the first four years and the related taxes are shown below.

---

3   A 401(K) is a defined contribution pension plan but functions more like a RRSP where the employee makes the investment decision.

Tax Paid on Withdrawals from a Spousal RRIF

| Age BOY | Spousal RRIF | | | | | | Example 3 |
	Minimum withdrawal	Actual withdrawal	Excess amount	Contributions	Taxable to Alice	Taxable to Alex	Minimum withdrawal
68				12,000			
69				12,000			
70				12,000			
71	22,140	30,000	7,860		7,860	22,140	22,140
72	21,408	30,000	8,592		4,140	25,860	22,031
73	20,612	30,000	9,388		0	30,000	21,924
74	19,743	30,000	10,257		0	30,000	21,815

Alex's withdrawals, which are higher than the minimum, change the minimum required withdrawals after the first year (see highlighted areas). This is a result of having less capital in the account at the beginning of each year to earn interest. Because Alice had made contributions to the spousal RRSP in the three years before it was rolled over into a spousal RRIF, she will pay the tax on the excess amount incurred in the first two withdrawals.

Annuities

As shown in Table 7.1, all retirement-income options can eventually convert into an annuity. An annuity is an investment contract between a financial institution and the annuitant. The annuitant pays the institution a lump sum or a series of contributions. In return, they will receive a stream of income (interest plus a portion of the invested capital) over a period of time. Annuities are always based on a specified interest rate, which determines the interest portion of the payment and is usually fixed for the life of the annuity contract.

There are many types of annuities available, and their options can have great impact on the amount of monthly income. In general, the longer the period the income is guaranteed, the smaller the monthly payout will be. Given the high probability of at least one spouse living past the age of 90 (as shown in Table 2.1), the selection of an appropriate annuity can be extremely important.

Generally, annuities can be categorized as:

1. **Term-certain annuities** (also called **fixed-term annuities**, or **annuity certain**), which pay a fixed amount for a specific time period, such as 5 years, 10 years, or to a specific age, such as age 85, specified at the time of purchase
2. **Life annuities**, also called **ordinary life annuities**, which pay until the annuitant dies and then cease immediately; this is the least expensive plan, and the regular payments are the highest.

Annuities can also be categorized as:

• **Fixed**, where the insurance company takes the investment risk and pays the same amount for the life of the annuity, or
• **Variable**, where the amount paid depends on the investment return after expenses. In this type, the annuitant take the investment risk.

Within these categories, there are many variations. The following are some of the options available:

• **Cashable annuities** can be cashed in to buy another annuity if interest rates have increased a lot — however, a penalty will be charged.
• **Contingent annuities** pay until the second spouse dies.

- **Deferred annuities** do not begin making payments to the annuitant until a later date, normally less than 10 years from the date of purchase. The latest the payments can be deferred for a registered annuity is January of the year the annuitant turns 72. While the funds are in the annuity waiting to be paid out, they are earning income. Therefore, the longer the payments can be deferred, the higher the payments will be.
- **Guaranteed-term annuities** pay for a particular number of years or up to a particular age — for instance, to age 90. If the annuitant dies before the end of the guaranteed term, the estate or beneficiary will receive the remaining payments or the commuted value of the payments.
- **Immediate annuities** begin to pay one time period, usually one month, after the annuity is purchased.
- **Income-reducing annuities** decrease the amount of the payment when the original annuitant dies and the annuity payment is paid to the surviving spouse.
- **Indexed annuities** increase on a regular basis to compensate for increases in the cost of living.
- **Insured annuities** consist of two contracts: a life annuity and a permanent insurance policy — for example, a whole life policy (not a term policy unless it is Term-to-100) — in which a portion of the regular cash flow is used to pay the premium on the insurance policy. When the annuitant dies, the capital is preserved through the insurance policy. As the policy is locked in for life — that is, the annuitant cannot cash in the policy to receive its **cash surrender value**[4] — it is more appropriate for older people who face fewer cash crunches.
- **Integrated annuities**, also called **reducing annuities**, pay more until age 60 and then decrease when the annuitant can start taking the CPP pension.
- **Joint-and-survivor annuities** pay some amount, — perhaps 100%, perhaps less — to the surviving spouse when the annuitant dies.
- **Joint-and-survivor, guaranteed 5, 10, or 15 years** annuities pay a guaranteed number of payments. If both spouses dies before the minimum number of payments have been made, the remaining payments are commuted and paid as a death benefit to the estate.
- **Life annuities with a guaranteed term** provide payments for the duration of the annuitant's life and also for a guaranteed period of time even if the annuitant dies. — that is, payments will be made for the guaranteed period even if the annuitant dies one year into the contract.

Prescribed annuities allow the annuitant to spread the interest evenly over the life of the annuity for up to 15 years so that the same amount of interest is taxable in every year instead of the early years being more heavily taxed since they are comprised of more interest. The amortization of prescribed annuities and regular annuities is covered under "Taxation of Annuities" later in this chapter.

Exhibit 7.1 provides sample monthly incomes for various types of annuities bought for $100,000. For comparison, the single life annuity is 100% and the rest are shown as a percentage of single life. These amounts are examples used only for comparison.

Retirees purchase annuities for two reasons:

1. Annuities can offer income for a guaranteed period of time and/or for a surviving spouse.
2. Annuities do not have to be managed by the annuitant. This is a particularly important characteristic for retirees who do not have much knowledge of investments. However, since annuities are based on a specified interest rate, which affects the interest portion of the payment, retirees should be aware that interest rates at the time the annuity is purchased can have a major impact on their future annuity income.

Example 9 shows the calculation of the amount received per month from a life annuity when the annuity is based on both a 12% rate of return and a 4½% rate of return.

---

4   The cash surrender value (CSV) is the amount of cash a permanent insurance policy accumulates in the savings portion of the policy. Permanent insurance includes whole life and universal life. If the annuity holder surrenders the policy (terminates the policy), the policyholder receives the amount of the accumulated savings and interest.

Exhibit 7.1 Sample Monthly Income for Various Types of Annuities

Form of annuity	$	%
Single life	$734	100.0%
Single life guaranteed for 5 years	725	98.8%
Single life guaranteed for 10 years	701	95.5%
Joint-and-survivor reducing to 60%	648	88.3%
Joint-and-survivor reducing to 75%	629	85.7%
Joint-and-survivor not reducing	600	81.7%
Joint-and-survivor not reducing, guaranteed for 10 years	599	81.6%

Example 9   Several years ago, Andy bought a life annuity when inflation was about 8%.

As a result, he was able to get an annuity based on a **12%** rate of return. He had $200,000 in his RRIF when he bought a 15-year annuity. He receives **$2,376.57 per month**:

$$\$200,000 = PMT_{BOM} (PVIFA_{1\%, \ 180})$$

$$PMT = \$2,376.57$$

Inflation is now about 1% and Andy wonders how much he would receive if he were buying an annuity now. He finds out that an estimate of his annuity would be based on an interest rate of approximately 4½%. If Andy were the same age as when he bought the original annuity, he would now receive **$1,524.27 per month**:

$$\$200,000 = PMT_{BOM} (PVIFA_{.375\%, \ 180})$$

$$PMT = \$1,524.27$$

The drop in interest rates from 12% to 4½% reduces his payments by 36% [(2,376.57 – 1,524.27) ÷ 2,376.57].

C.   NON-REGISTERED INVESTMENTS

For many Canadians, government pension plans and registered savings plans are their only saving vehicles and sources of retirement income. There are Canadians, however, who can save more than the maximum that tax-sheltered savings plans allows. These people can save only in non-registered investments. Unlike registered income funds, which can provide regular income over a period of time, investments in non-registered assets must be sold to provide retirement income. If they sold these non-registered investments all at once, the transaction would normally result in a large lump sum, which is both not required and can generate a large capital gain. To overcome this obstacle, retirees can purchase an annuity that provides regular monthly income or participate in a systematic withdrawal plan that sells part of the investment at regular intervals. In addition, some seniors need retirement income over and above what they have been able to save. In this case, if they own a home, they can create a reverse mortgage based on the net investment in their family home. A reverse mortgage pays the owner either a lump sum or a regular amount as long as the owner continues to own the home.

Annuities

Retirees who choose to purchase an annuity with non-registered funds no longer have the responsibility of managing the investment. They also know how much regular income they will receive in the future and will pay taxes on only the interest portion of their annuity payment. In return, they give up any possibility of future growth in their investment because annuities are normally locked in with a fixed interest rate that cannot be renegotiated.

Systematic Withdrawal Plans (SWPs)

For retirees who are knowledgeable investors and want to keep control over their retirement income, Systematic Withdrawal Plans (SWPs) better suit their needs. Also called **Automatic Withdrawal Plans (AWPs)**, these are repeat redemption orders that enable investors to liquidate small portions of their units from non-registered mutual fund portfolios on a regular basis — monthly, quarterly, or annually. The capital can remain invested while income is received from selling small portions of the units. These small portions are made up of some of the after-tax capital invested as well as unrealized capital gains. The withdrawals can be altered or discontinued at any time. Some companies have a minimum fund requirement, such as $25,000, to implement SWPs. However, there is then no minimum withdrawal.

Example 10 calculates the after-tax amount received from non-registered his SWP.

Example 10   Steve set up a SWP for XYZ Mutual Fund, which is not a tax-sheltered fund.

His fund account was worth $150,000 when he set up the SWP. He had bought the units for $80,000. He wants to liquidate $900 a month. He has a 40% marginal tax rate.

As Steve liquidates his fund units, he will have a taxable capital gain. The gain will vary depending on the price of the fund at the time of sale. He will receive (before transaction costs):

	Tax	Net proceeds
Proceeds	900	900
Cost* (80 ÷150) × 900	480	
Capital gain	420	
Taxable capital gain at 50% inclusion rate	210	
Tax at 40%	84	84
Proceeds after tax		816

*The amount of his cost will change as the value of the fund increases and decreases, changing the number of units that must be sold to generate the $900.

If this mutual fund were held in a registered plan, he would have $540 after tax [(900 × (1 − 0.4)]. Of course, his initial investment in a registered plan would have cost less because of the tax reduction it generated.

Reverse Mortgages

At the time they retire, many people own a home, which may also be the largest asset they own. Owning a home appears to be a *necessity* in many people's lives. They invest in their home before considering other investments (registered or non-registered). Although this choice results in non-diversification of investments, it often makes sense because the principal residence is exempt from capital gains tax.

295

The Canadian Home Income Plan (CHIP) was introduced in 1986 by a private company called Canadian Home Income Plan Incorporation in Vancouver B.C., which now has its head office in Toronto, Ontario. Reverse mortgages are widely accepted today as an alternative source of retirement income, and the CHIP reverse mortgage plan is available across Canada through national chartered banks, credit unions, mortgage brokers, and investment and financial planning firms.

A reverse mortgage is a loan against the accumulated home equity. It offers homeowners that age 55 or older loans that range from 10% to 40% of the appraised value of their principal residence, less any borrowing secured by it. The proceeds can be received tax-free as a cash lump sum, guaranteed monthly payments, or a combination of the two. There are no restrictions on the use of the money. The interest portion of annuity income from a reverse mortgage is not taxable in the same way the original mortgage interest paid was not tax deductible. If, instead of an annuity, the homeowner uses the proceeds from the reverse mortgage to invest, the resulting income is taxable. However, the interest portion of the reverse mortgage is tax deductible against this investment income. Furthermore, the proceeds will not affect the homeowner's eligibility for income-tested government benefits such as old age security, the guaranteed income supplement or veteran's income supplement.

Repayment is not required for as long as the homeowner or their spouse lives in the home although the home can be rented out for short periods of time. The mortgage (principal plus interest) is due for payment only when the homeowner as well as their spouse dies or sells the home. Reverse mortgages, like regular mortgages, can be transferred to a new home if the homeowner so chooses. The reverse mortgage continues to grow while it is in place, but the amount to be repaid is guaranteed not to be more than the home's value at the time the loan is to be repaid; i.e., if the mortgage is higher than the value of the home, the lender will not recover the excess.

Exhibit 7.2 provides two examples of the maximum amount of loan that can be obtained from a reverse mortgage taken at age 62 and age 70 when current mortgage rates are 6% and 8%. The maximum loan can be taken as a lump sum or as an annuity.

In effect, the reverse mortgage gives a mortgage that can grow to a maximum of 75% of the estimated future value of the home at age 90. The interest charge on reverse mortgages can consume the equity in a short period of time.

Exhibit 7.2 Reverse Mortgage Loan

	Current age of homeowner			
	62		70	
Fair market value (FMV) of home today (PV)	250,000		250,000	
Expected FMV at age 90:				
Increase per year (k)	3%		3%	
Years to age 90 (n)	28		20	
Future value (FV)	571,982		451,528	
75% of FV	428,986		338,646	
Present value (PV) of 75% of FV discounted @ current mortgage rates:				
Current mortgage rates	8.0%	6.0%	8.0%	6.0%
Years from age 90	28	28	20	20
PV = **maximum loan**	49,725	83,923	72,656	105,591
% of home's current value	19.9%	33.6%	29.1%	42.2%

As shown in Example 11, reverse mortgages are useful for people who have only a very few years to live or for people who think they will live a very long time. The problem is that the interest rate on the mortgage is probably higher than the growth rate of the home. This means the mortgage is growing faster than the value of the home. A short-term reverse mortgage still leaves equity. A long-term reverse mortgage will probably consume all the equity and then some. This result is acceptable only if the retiree does not plan to leave the home to anyone or is not counting on the proceeds to finance the very last years of life.

Example 11 shows the effect on the equity in a home of taking a reverse mortgage.

Example 11   Roberta owns her home, which is now worth $250,000. She can get a reverse mortgage for $49,725, as shown in Exhibit 7.2. Should she do it? It depends on how long she thinks she will live, how long she wants to live in the house, and whether or not she wants to leave her home as an estate to her heirs.

The following table shows the net equity if Roberta lives to ages 68, 83, and 98, presuming the assumptions about future growth in housing prices are certain — the home grows in value at 3% and the mortgage grows at 8% nominal or 4.85% real.

Live to age:				68	83	98
	@ age 62	k	n =	6	21	36
$ Nominal						
Current value	250,000	3%		298,513	465,074	724,570
Reverse mortgage	49,725	8%		78,907	250,307	794,017
Equity after reverse mortgage	200,275			219,606	214,767	(69,447)
Change in equity				19,331	14,492	(269,722)
$ Real						
Current value	250,000	0.00%		250,000	250,000	250,000
Reverse mortgage	49,725	4.85%		66,067	134,435	273,551
Equity after reverse mortgage	200,275			183,933	115,565	(23,551)
Change in equity				(16,342)	(84,710)	(223,826)

Since the mortgage rate is larger than the increase in the price of Roberta's house, even in real dollars, the equity will decrease even if she lives for only one year. But if she lives for 21 years, the value of the equity is greatly eroded. If she lives for 36 years and remains in the home, her estate and/or heir(s) are not obligated to pay the negative equity.

The Financial Consumer Agency of Canada at <www.fcac-acfc.gc.ca> summarized the advantages and disadvantages outlined above and adds some tips to keep in mind. With regards to disadvantages, they point out that:
• the interest rate on the reverse mortgage is higher than other types of mortgages
• the costs can bef quite high and can include a home appraisal fee, application fee, or closing fee
• a repayment penalty if you sell your house within three years of obtaining the reverse mortgage, and
• legal fees for independent advice.

D.   DEMUTUALIZATION AND GOVERNMENT PENSIONS

Insurance companies can be either *mutual insurers* or *stock insurers*. Mutual insurers raise capital through profitable operations and surplus notes, which are similar to corporate bonds. **Stock insurers** can raise capital through profitable operations but also by issuing shares or bonds. Recently, many mutual insurers have been demutualizing — that is, changing their structure so they can sell shares and issue bonds.

To make this change, the total value of the company must be distributed to voting policyholders in exchange for their rights and interest in the company. As a result, several insurance companies have recently offered policyholders a choice of a lump-sum payment or shares in the stock company. The way a policyholder chooses to take their new shares (called demutualization) can affect the amount of taxable income a retiree has.

Cash payments are treated as dividend income in the year received. These dividends are treated like regular dividends for tax purposes and generate a gross-up and the dividend tax credit. **Shares received** will probably generate a capital gain in the future when the shares are sold. This capital gain will be subject to the current inclusion rate (50% in 2013), which is taxed at regular rates. Both options can have an effect on taxable income and, thus, can have an effect on OAS pension, GIS, and allowance, which are subject to a means test.

E. TAXATION OF ANNUITIES

Since many retirees receive their retirement income in the form of an annuity, it is important to understand how an annuity payment is taxed. An annuity provides its annuitant with a regular stream of predetermined income payments consisting of principal and interest. Life insurance proceeds taken as an annuity also generate taxable income.

Retirement Income

The source of annuity income in retirement determines how it is taxed. Annuity income in retirement can be received from either registered or non-registered sources.

Registered Plans

Taxation on annuity income from registered funds is straightforward. The whole amount is fully taxable as received since it is being withdrawn from a tax-deferred registered plan whose funds were granted tax relief when the contribution was made.

Non-registered Plans

Annuity income from non-registered funds is more complex. Because the annuity is bought with after-tax dollars, only the interest portion is taxable. This interest income is taxable on an accrual basis or, in a prescribed annuity, on an interest-as-a-percentage-of-total-received basis. In **accrual annuities**, higher taxes are paid in the earlier years when interest is higher — the same way interest is a larger part of the early payments on a mortgage. The interest is higher in the early years because the principal is larger. In **prescribed annuities**, payments are calculated based on life expectancy, but the annual taxable interest income is not based on the outstanding principal. Rather, the interest in each payment is a fixed percentage based on the total amount of interest paid divided by the total payments for the life of the annuity. This method spreads the tax impact equally over the duration of the annuity by keeping the taxable interest portion at the same level throughout the life of the annuity. Example 12 illustrates the present value of the after-tax amount of a prescribed annuity and an accrual annuity.

Example 12   When Jerry retired, he bought a $100,000 15-year term annuity using a GIC. He elected to have the annuity treated as a prescribed annuity. We will use annual income to simplify the example.

$$\$100,000 = \text{PMT}_{\text{BOY}} \ (\text{PVIFA}_{15, \ 7.0\%})$$

Annual payment = \$10,261.18

The total payments are $153,918 ($10,261.18 × 15 years).

For a **prescribed annuity**, the payment will be calculated as:

Line		Total $	Total %	Each payment $	
1	Total payment(s)	153,918	100.0%	**10,261**	
2	– Principal	–100,000	65.0%	–6,667	**Not taxable**
3	= Interest	53,918	35.0%	3,594	**Taxable**
4	Tax on interest at 30%	16,175		1,078	
	Payment after tax (line 1 – 4)	137,743		9,183	

What is the present value of the after-tax payments?

$$\text{PVA} = \$9,183 \ _{\text{BOY}} \ (\text{PVIFA}_{15, \ 7.00\%})$$

PVA = \$89,493

If Jerry had elected to take an **accrual annuity**, he would have the following income after tax. The present value is **$88,699**. This PV is less because taxes are higher in the early years, resulting in a smaller amount being received in the early years, which are discounted less. The total tax paid is the same as in the prescribed annuity — it is paid at a different time.

Year	Principal BOY	Payment_BOY			Principal EOY	Tax %	Received after Tax	PV
		Total	Interest 7.00%	Principal		30%		7.00%
1	100,000	10,261	0	10,261	89,739	0	10,261	10,261
2	89,739	10,261	6,282	3,979	85,759	1,885	8,377	7,829
3	85,759	10,261	6,003	4,258	81,501	1,801	8,460	7,389
4	81,501	10,261	5,705	4,556	76,945	1,712	8,550	6,979
5	76,945	10,261	5,386	4,875	72,070	1,616	8,645	6,595
6	72,070	10,261	5,045	5,216	66,854	1,513	8,748	6,237
7	66,854	10,261	4,680	5,581	61,273	1,404	8,857	5,902
8	61,273	10,261	4,289	5,972	55,300	1,287	8,974	5,589
9	55,300	10,261	3,871	6,390	48,910	1,161	9,100	5,296
10	48,910	10,261	3,424	6,837	42,073	1,027	9,234	5,023
11	42,073	10,261	2,945	7,316	34,757	884	9,378	4,767
12	34,757	10,261	2,433	7,828	26,929	730	9,531	4,528
13	26,929	10,261	1,885	8,376	18,552	566	9,696	4,305
14	18,552	10,261	1,299	8,963	9,590	390	9,872	4,096
15	9,590	10,261	671	9,590	0	201	10,060	3,901
		153,918	53,918	100,000		16,175	137,742	88,699

If the annuitant dies before the prescribed annuity is fully paid out, the annuity ends and there is no refund of the unpaid portion of the annuity unless it is a joint-and-last-survivor contract. In this case, the annuitant can only be a spouse or sibling. Furthermore, age plus guarantee period cannot exceed 91.

Life Insurance Proceeds

The taxation of the proceeds from life insurance depends on how the proceeds are received — as a lump sum or as an annuity.

Lump Sum Payment

The proceeds received from life insurance (e.g., on the death of a spouse) as a **lump sum** are not taxable. These tax-free proceeds can be used to provide for the surviving spouse or to pay taxes on the estate at death.

Annuity Payments

The interest portion of life insurance proceeds received in **periodic payments** is taxable on an accrual basis. Example 13 shows the present value of the after-tax amount of a regular annuity set up from the proceeds of a life insurance policy.

Example 13   Mina's husband, Lorne, died. He had a **term life insurance policy** in force, which had a face value of $100,000. Mina can receive the $100,000 as a lump sum or as an annuity. If she takes the funds out as a lump sum, this amount is not taxed. She elects to take the funds as an annuity, receiving one payment at the beginning of each year over a 15-year period. (We have chosen annual payments to shorten the calculation. In reality, she would probably receive monthly payments, which would be about $882 a month.)

Year	Principal BOY	Payment BOY Total	Taxable Interest 7.00%	Principal	Principal EOY
1	100,000	10,261	0	10,261	89,739
2	89,739	10,261	6,282	3,979	85,759
3	85,759	10,261	6,003	4,258	81,501
4	81,501	10,261	5,705	4,556	76,945
5	76,945	10,261	5,386	4,875	72,070
6	72,070	10,261	5,045	5,216	66,854
7	66,854	10,261	4,680	5,581	61,273
8	61,273	10,261	4,289	5,972	55,300
9	55,300	10,261	3,871	6,390	48,910
10	48,910	10,261	3,424	6,837	42,073
11	42,073	10,261	2,945	7,316	34,757
12	34,757	10,261	2,433	7,828	26,929
13	26,929	10,261	1,885	8,376	18,552
14	18,552	10,261	1,299	8,963	9,590
15	9,590	10,261	671	9,590	0
		153,918	53,918	100,000	

The total cash flow in nominal dollars and taxable interest in this example is the same as in the prior example since all the variables are the same.

Mina could also have chosen a prescribed annuity to minimize her taxes. However, since she is the survivor, she might not choose this option as the annuity will end when she dies.

CRAIG AND MARGOT

Craig and Margot are very surprised to find that the options for retirement are not as complicated as they had thought. They can see what each of the options is trying to achieve. They had not realized the extent to which interest rates at retirement could have an effect on income throughout retirement if the funds are locked in.

They also found the calculation of savings for retirement very enlightening. They had assumed that they would need a million dollars to have a decent retirement. That seemed like such a large amount to save that they had put the whole issue on the back burner because they couldn't imagine being able to save enough. Roger and Gail, who live next door, have been scrimping and saving for their retirement because they were terrified that without a million dollars or so, they would end up on the street (although Gail always claimed she was going to make her sons look after her in retirement).

As we learned from Francesca's calculations in Chapter 1, Margot and Craig have a surplus. Their planned annual saving is more than enough to meet their goals. They could, of course, save less each year. We will look at their actual results in Chapter 8, when they come to Francesca to look at their actual financial situation as they begin retirement.

SUMMARY

Both federal and provincial governments encourage people to save for retirement by providing a tax deduction for contributions to registered savings plans. While people can withdraw funds from RRSPs before retiring, contributions to employer-sponsored plans are locked in until they are withdrawn as retirement income. In addition, the tax has been deferred and, at retirement, governments want to start collecting the tax. There are requirements for both the latest possible age to begin withdrawing the funds as fully taxable income and the minimum amounts that must be withdrawn.

People who are comfortable with investments can continue to manage their retirement funds. Others can buy an annuity and leave the investment managing to someone else.

Although the amount provided by the government pensions is not great, the aggregate, especially for a couple, adds up to a considerable sum that reduces the amount each individual needs to save for retirement. There is always a fear that these plans will not be there by the time we retire. In reality, these plans will probably remain although they may be subject to increased taxation by, for example, lowering the threshold amount for the OAS or, as has just incurred, increasing the age for OAS to 67. It is entirely reasonable to expect that the age at which one may collect the full CPP retirement benefit will increase from 65 to perhaps 67 or 69. This will provide more years of contributions and fewer years of collecting.

SOURCES

Canada Revenue Agency: <www.cra-arc.gc.ca>
• IT528 Transfers of Funds Between Registered Plans
• P119(e) Rev. 07 When You Retire
• Circular 78-18R6 Registered Retirement Income Funds

Department of Finance, Canada: <www.fin.gc.ca>
• Regulatory Changes Related to Federally Regulated Life Income Funds and Licked-in Registered Retirement Savings Plans, Effective May. 2008

Financial Consumer Agency of Canada at <www.fcac-acfc.gc.ca>
CHIP Home Income Plan <www.chip.ca>

KEY TERMS

Accrual annuity
Annuitant
Annuities
CANSIM
Carrier
Cash surrender value
Cashable annuity
CRA designated
Commuted value
Contingent annuity
Deferred annuity
Demutualization
Expected annual income
Excess amount
Financial hardship unlocking
Financially dependent child or grandchild
Fixed-term annuity
Guaranteed term annuity
Immediate annuity
Income attribution rules
Income reducing annuity
Indexed annuity
Insured annuity
Integrated annuity
Joint and survivor annuity
Life annuity
Life annuity with a guaranteed term
Life income fund (LIF)
Life insurance proceeds

Locked-in retirement account (LIRA)
Locked-in retirement income fund (LRIF)
Locked-in RRSP (LRSP)
Low income limit
Low income unlocking
Matured RRSP
Maximum withdrawals
Medical/Disability unlocking
Minimum withdrawals
Non-qualifying RRIF
Non-resident unlocking
One-time unlocking
Prescribed annuity
Prescribed Retirement Income Funds (PRIF)
Qualifying RRIF
Reducing annuity
Refund of premiums
Term certain annuity
Registered retirement income fund (RRIF)
Restricted Life Income Fund (RLIF)
Restricted Locked-in Savings Plan (RLSP)
Reverse mortgage
Shortened life expectancy unlocking
Small balance unlocking
Spousal RRIF
Systematic withdrawal plan (SWP)
Unmatured RRSP
Variable annuity
Withholding tax

QUESTIONS AND PROBLEM
Registered Plans

1. To what kind of RRSP can an RPP be transferred if you change jobs at age 38?

2. Marta, age 47, left her job of 12 years to take a better position at another firm in her industry. She had been contributing to a DCPP. The commuted value of her pension benefits is $78,032. What can she do with this commuted value?

3. With respect to an RPP, under what two circumstances can an amount be transferred from an individual's RPP to a spouse or former spouse?

4. To what can a DPSP be transferred? Under what circumstances would the transfer be made, and when?

5. What are the three options for an unmatured RRSP by the end of the year in which the annuitant turns 71?

6. To whose RRSP can the RRSP of a deceased person be transferred without paying tax at the time of the transfer?

7. What circumstance causes a LIRA to be set up?

Retirement Funds

8. In which of the following does the retiree control the investment decisions: Life Annuity? LIF? LRIF? RRIF?

9. Which province requires that the Survivor Benefit for a Life Annuity be something other than 60%? What is the requirement in that province?

10. Federally-regulated LIFs require that LIFs buy a life annuity at age 80. Do all provinces and territories also require this? Does British Columbia require this?

11. Saskatchewan and Manitoba have a special kind of RRIF. What is it called?

12. How are the investment options for retirement funds different from investment options for RRSPs?

13. With regard to LIFs, LRIFs and RRIFs withdrawals:
    (a) Which:
        i. has a maximum withdrawal?
        ii. has a minimum required withdrawal?
    (b) Are all the minimums calculated the same way?
    (c) Are all the maximums calculated the same way?

14. One of the ways the annual maximum required withdrawal from a LRIF is calculated is using "Market Value at the beginning of the calendar year". Does "Market Value" include unrealized capital gains?

15. Jill worked for Unlimited Computers Support in their head office accounting department for 22 years. She resigned five years ago at the age of 43, transferred her pension to a locked-in RRSP, and set up a consulting business. To access the funds, she will first have to transfer the locked-in RRSP to a Locked-in Retirement Income Fund (LRIF). The following scenarios are independent of each other. For each of the following, what is the name of the appropriate LRIF unlocking provision for Jill and how much of the LRIF can she unlock?
    (a) Finding that she was getting more and more work in Switzerland, she moved there to live permanently three years ago. She now wants to semi-retire using some of her LIRA funds.
    (b) Jill consulted for 16 years and has now been offered a permanent part-time job. She would like to access some of her locked-in funds so she can semi-retire.
    (c) Jill, now age 47, was diagnosed with Parkinson's Disease at age 47. She finds she is spending about 25% of her income on medical treatment and other assistance that is not covered by her provincial plan.
    (d) Jill, now age 49 has just been diagnosed with Multiple System Atrophy (MSA) which will slowly take away her ability to walk and talk and from which she will die within six to nine years. She wants to quit work and live life while she can.

16. Joanne, age 42, quit her job after seven years of service to go to another job. She had accumulated $50,000 in the company RPP.

(a) She would like to go back to school for eight months before starting the new job (assume this is OK with the new employer).

    i. Can she take the $50,000 out in cash (and, of course, pay the appropriate income taxes)?

    ii. If she first transfers the $50,000 to a Locked-In Retirement Account (LIRA) could she then take the funds out to go back to school?

    iii. Is it required that she transfer the funds to a LIRA when she leaves the first job?

    iv. If Joanne's husband dies, can she transfer the funds from his locked-in RPP into her LIRA?

    v. If Joanne and her husband divorce and she receives part of his RPP in the divorce settlement, can these funds be transferred to her LIRA?

(b) Joanne can transfer the funds to a LIRA and from there she can purchase a life annuity.

    i. What is the major advantage of a life annuity?

    ii. What is the minimum age (in most provinces) at which you can buy a life annuity?

(c) Joanne transferred the funds to a Locked-in Retirement Income Fund (LRIF = locked-in RRIF).

    i. Does she have to take money out of the LRIF now, i.e., before she retires at age 65?

    ii. Is there a minimum she must withdraw the year after the fund is set up?

    iii. Can she take as much as she likes?

(d) If Joanne transferred the funds to a life income fund (LIF), does she have to take money out now or can she defer it for a year?

    i. Does she have to transfer the funds before she can start withdrawing from the LIF?

    ii. Is there a minimum she must withdraw the first year after the fund is set up?

    iii. Can she take as much as she likes?

    iv. In what major way is an LIF different from an LRIF?

Registered Retirement Income Funds (RRIF)

17. When a RRIF is set up, when must the individual start withdrawing the minimum amount?

18. What is a qualifying RRIF? A non-qualifying RRIF?

19. Anne transferred $200,000 from her RRSP to a RRIF on November 30, 2013, when she was 62 (her birthday is April 23). She takes her first withdrawal, the minimum requirement amount, the following year at the beginning of the year. Her RRIF earns 5% a year. Complete the following table. What are the total withdrawals? (Answer: $94,299) What is her total income? (Answer: $99,049)

Age BOY	Balance BOY	Factor	Required Formula	Withdrawal $ BOY	Balance after withdrawal	Interest @ 5%	Balance EOY
							200,000
62							
63							
64							
65							
66							
67							
68							
69							
70							
71							204,750

20. After Anne, made 72 as the elected age for her RRIF, she realized she could have elected Jim's age for her RRIF. Jim is 67.
    (a) Can she elect Jim's age now?
    (b) Can she change her mind (before she dies)?

Spousal RRIF

21. Why does determining the excess amount matter?

22. Laura made the following deposits to a spousal RRSP, and her husband, Marco made the following withdrawals after the RRSP was transferred to a RRIF. Who pays the tax on how much if Marco was 63 when he began to make withdrawals?

Withdrawal			Contributions	Total taxable to:	
Minimum	Actual	Excess		Laura	Marco
			10,000 .		
			10,000		
			10,000		
7,407	17,000	9,593		9,593	7,407
7,390	17,500	10,110		407	17,093
7,335	18,000	10,665		0	18,000
7,235	18,500	11,265		0	18,500

Annuities

23. Name five types of annuities.

24. On what does the amount of the annuity depend?

25. What are the investment restrictions of a life annuity; i.e., in what way can the rate of return change once you have made your selection?

26. Can you change your mind about the kind of annuity once you are receiving payments?

Systematic Withdrawal Plans (SWPs)

27. Howard wants to withdraw the funds from his non-registered mutual funds using a SWP. The fund has a current value of $80 a unit, while the adjusted cost base (ACB) is $30 a unit. His marginal tax rate is 35%.
    (a) How many units will be sold to give him an income of $2,000 the first month? (Answer: 25)
    (b) How much will he receive after tax from the $2,000? (Answer: $1,781.25)
    (c) The unit price falls to $66.67 a unit. How many units will be sold now to give him an income of $2,000 a month? (Answer: 30)
    (d) How much will he receive after tax from the $2,000? (Answer: $1,807.49)

Reverse Mortgages

28. Charles, age 76, wants to use a reverse mortgage to have some money to take a cruise. He has always wanted to go around the Mediterranean to see all the places he read about as a boy in his studies of Greek mythology. The cruise would cost $9,500 for 2 weeks.

(a) Can Charles use the money for a cruise?

(b) Can Charles take the loan in a lump sum cash payment?

(c) His condo is now worth $180,000. If mortgage rates are 7% and condo prices are expected to increase by 2% a year, how much can Charles get from the reverse mortgage? (Answer: $69,082)

Demutualization and Your Pension

29. Linda has a life insurance policy with Monolife which is now becoming a stock company instead of being a policyholder company. As a result, she is eligible to receive $2,400 in a lump-sum cash payment or she can take the amount in shares in the new company.

(a) If she takes the cash now, what effect does this have on her taxable income now? Later?

(b) If she takes the shares, what effect does this have on her taxable income now? Later?

Taxation of Annuities

30. In comparing the total tax paid by Jerry in Example 12, how much is the total tax paid by Jerry if it is a prescribed annuity? (Answer: $16,175) An accrual annuity? (Answer: $16,175) Since the tax paid is the same, why would Jerry bother with a prescribed annuity? What is the present value of the after-tax payments if he elects a prescribed annuity? (Answer: $89,493) An accrual annuity? (Answer: $88,699)

Problem

31. Hillary (age 57) and David (age 60) think they will have enough to be able to retire part-time in three years. They plan to be semi-retired for seven years or so and then retire completely. They currently earn $80,000 a year each and want to cut back to three days a week, earning $50,000 for seven years until they retire completely. They estimate that they will need $75,000 after tax a year to travel the way they want — they want to take a major trip every year for maybe 15 years. At that point, they believe they will have been everywhere they want to go. Besides, they will be getting on and probably won't be able to travel as much. But just in case, they want to be able to save for a major trip every three or four years. So when Hillary is 75 and David is 78, they expect that $60,000 after tax a year will be sufficient. When David dies at age 95, they expect Hillary's income could drop to $45,000 a year until she dies at age 95. Since they have no children, they are not concerned about leaving an estate.

They are using an interest rate of 7.0% before full retirement and 5.0% during full retirement when inflation is 2.0%. Include CPP contributions, EI premiums, and the pension income amount for these calculations wherever appropriate.

The following timeline is provided to help the student organize the material in this question.

Hillary's age	57	60–66	67–74	75–91	92–94	dies @ 95
David's age	60	63–69	70–77	78–94		dies @ 95
n		7	8	17	3	35

(a) What is the present value at Hillary's age 67 of their retirement needs after tax? (Answer: $1,254,817)

(b) Calculate income after tax and other deductions for the following:
 i. $80,000 average and marginal tax rates (Answer: $56,525, 25.84%, 43.00%)
 ii. $50,000 average and marginal tax rates (Answer: $37,225, 19.94%, 35.00%)

(c) What gross income in retirement will give them approximately $37,500 each, and what is the average tax rate? (Answer: $46,300, 19.03%)

(d) From now until they semi-retire, David and Hillary want to make the maximum contribution to their RRSPs. They do no want to use their retirement savings during the period they are semi-retired, although they realize they may not be able to contribute the maximum possible to their RRSPs during their semi-retirement.
 i. Using the marginal tax rates above, what do the RRSPs cost them after tax if they contribute the maximum possible until they retire? (Answer: $8,208, $5,850)
 ii. What is their total annual net cash flow before and during semi-retirement? (Answer: $96,634, $62,750)

(e) Can they take the CPP retirement income when they semi-retire?
 i. Assume they decide they will not take CPP retirement benefits until they are fully retired. Using generic rates, how much do they each get per year? (Answer: Hillary $12,880, David $14,950)
 ii. They are not going to count on the OAS, so they will leave it out of their plans. If they do get the OAS, they will save it for another trip. What is the present value at Hillary's age 67 of their CPP retirement income before and after tax? Use annual beginning-of-the-year cash flows (Answer: $520,337, $421,313)

(f) David worked for the local library for many years. It will give him a non-indexed pension of $25,000 whenever he retires. What is the present value of this before and after tax at his age 70? (Answer: $369,966, $299,559)

(g) Hillary now has $225,000 in her RRSP, while David has $87,000. What is the future value of this before and after tax and of the RRSP contributions from Hillary's age 57 to 66 at Hillary's age 67? (Answer: $776,408, $682,652)

(h) Can they retire and semi-retire according to plan? Prepare a table summarizing the present value of their needs and cash flows. At this point, you have not calculated their before-tax income needs. Calculate it using: Income after tax ÷ (1 – tax rate). Answer:

PV at Hillary's age 67	PVA before tax	Tax @ 19.03%	PVA after tax
Retirement needs	1,549,744	294,927	1,254,817
CPP income	520,337	99,024	421,313
David's pension	369,966	70,407	299,559
RRSPs	776,408	147,756	628,652
	1,666,711	317,187	1,349,524
Surplus / (deficit)	116,967	22,260	94,708

(i) They are showing a somewhat modest surplus — 7.5% of their before-tax needs. As they get closer to retirement, if they decide they should have more funds, what can they do?

(j) One last question, just for fun. Assume that all the RRSPs are held in the name of either David or Hillary. If he or she withdraws all the RRSP income at the date of full retirement, how much tax would be payable? (Answer: $436,664 using the pension income amount). Compare this with the amount of tax payable and the average tax rate if the RRSP is drawn down over the 25 years of their full retirement (above).

Retirement Planning Case Assignment

We have completed the review of the elements in the retirement planning process. We will conclude Part I with a case assignment, which requires students to apply what they have learned so far. It would be beneficial for students to revisit Chapter 1, where the retirement planning process is presented through Margot and Craig's story. In addition, in Chapter 8, Francesca provides an overview of the entire retirement planning process in "C. Margot and Craig: Accumulating Assets".

Chapter 1 shows how the savings needs of Margot and Craig were identified, and how Francesca, the advisor, estimated their total retirement savings needs, and how much they would need to save each year. To do so, Francesca did a number of calculations:

1. How much they need after tax
2. How much this amount is before tax given they are able to split their retirement income perfectly (this calculation also provides their average tax rate in retirement)
3. The present value, at retirement, of their annual retirement income
4. The present value, at retirement, of government and employer-sponsored pension plans
5. The future value, at retirement, of their present RRSP balances
6. The future value, at retirement, of the amount they plan to save each year.

Having completed Chapters 2 to 7, students are now ready to prepare their own financial plan.

THE CASE — JOHN AND RACHEL WHITNEY

You have recently been awarded the CFP designation after having worked for Francesca as an assistant planner for four years. Francesca has decided that you are ready to work independently and has given you your first assignment: John and Rachel Whitney.

Background Information

John Whitney (age 49) and his wife, **Rachel (age 42),** have been married for 14 years. They live in Waterloo, Ontario. This is John's second marriage and Rachel's first marriage. John's daughter, **Marianne (age 20)**, is in her third year at university. John and Rachel have two children, **Mark (age 11)** and **Virginia (age 8)**. The Whitneys come to see you in early January 2014 and provide you with the following information.

Employment Information

John has worked as a planner for the city of Waterloo for six years. His gross annual salary for 2013 was $93,000. John expects his salary to remain the same in real terms until retirement. He and his employer each contribute 7% of his salary to a defined contribution pension plan (DCPP). John has an employee benefits package that provides him with life insurance coverage for twice his annual salary, short-term disability coverage, as well as extended health care for the family. His employer pays the premium of $130 a month for family coverage. In addition, John pays, at work, $659 in long-term disability insurance premiums, which would provide him with two-thirds of his salary should he become disabled. Because John pays the premiums, the two-thirds would be received as non-taxable income.

Rachel works as an administrative assistant for a small firm in Waterloo's twin city, Kitchener. Her gross annual salary for 2013 was $42,000. She also expects her salary to remain unchanged in real terms until retirement. Rachel has no group insurance, but her employer does provide a group RRSP (GRRSP). Rachel contributes 6% of her salary to the GRRSP, and her employer matches her contribution to a maximum of 6% of her salary. The employer's contribution is added to her taxable income, but she can deduct both the employer's and her own contributions to the GRRSP.

Assets and Liabilities
Liquid Assets

The Whitneys pay their household bills and everyday expenses from their joint chequing account, which has a current balance of $700. They opened Tax Free Savings Accounts at the beginning of 2012 for each of the following two savings accounts which earned 2% each. Since they want to keep these funds liquid, they expect the 2% to continue in the future.

- They had $10,000 after tax in a joint savings account for emergencies which they transferred to a TFSA at the beginning of 2012. It now has a balance of $10,099.
- They have been saving about $600 a year in order to be able to get financial planning advice. They currently have $3,000, which they estimate they will spend now, in early 2014, on financial planning advice. They plan to save $500 a year in a TFSA so that every four or five years in the future, they can return to their financial planner to assess their position.

> Hint: They will spend about $3,000 this year for their first comprehensive financial plan. They have saved for this event and will use their financial-planning savings to pay for it. Do not show the amount as coming from their cash flows — their financial-planning savings will be used up and at the end of 2014; they will save $500 for future advice.

Beginning in 2015, after the car lease is paid, they plan to save $350 a month so they can pay cash for their next new car. This account will also be liquid, earning 2% a year.

They have not yet used their TFSA contribution room of $5,500 each for 2013. Altogether, to the end of 2013, together they have $51,000 of TFSA contribution room and have used only $35,000.

As emergency funds, at December 31, 2013, John has $7,000 in Canada Savings Bonds (CSBs) which earn 3% before tax and Rachel has $5,000 invested in a Guaranteed Investment Certificate (GIC) that earns 4%. They plan to reinvest these funds when they mature and expect to make the same return. These two accounts are also in a TFSA — the annual income is not taxable. They do not consider these emergency funds to be part of "Non-Registered Investments".

> Hint: Remember to work in real dollars. Also, all non-registered funds grow after tax. Refer to Chapter 1 **"Margot and Craig," "Statement of Financial Position"** and **"Statement of Cash Flows"** which include their budgets for the next few years.

Non Registered Investment Assets

In January 2012, John transferred shares they owned to their TFSAs using all the contribution room for 2012. The shares are $10 par value, 6% preferred shares of Big Deal Unlimited, which have an adjusted cost base (ACB) of $10 per share and are currently worth $10 a share. The dividends are paid quarterly and are reinvested in Big Deal shares. At December 31, 2013, they have 546 shares each.

When they have prepared their budgets for the years until retirement, any excess funds not invested in the long-term TFSA will be invested in a Balanced Mutual Fund in Rachel's name since she is in the lower tax bracket. John is going to assume that he will be able to earn 6.5% rate of return on both of the long-term accounts.

John's Registered Pension Plans (RPPs)

These assets include the two pensions plans to which John belongs: a defined contribution pension plan (DCPP) with his current employer and a defined benefit pension plan (DBPP) with his former employer. The DCPP is valued at $72,500 and is invested in funds that, despite the recent market turmoil, are expected to return 7% a year, on average, when inflation is expected to be about 1.5% a year. John and his employer each contributes 7.0% of his annual salary to the DCPP. John was a member of a DBPP with a former employer for 12 years. When he left the company and moved to his present employer, he elected to leave the funds with this previous employer and take a pension at retirement. He will receive *non-indexed* pension income of $10,400 per year beginning at age 65. If he dies before Rachel, Rachel will receive 60% of John's pension.

John's RRSP Investment Assets

John currently has $30,400 in his personal RRSP, which is invested in a Canadian equity fund. He has a pre-authorized purchase plan (PPP) and contributes the maximum possible each year on a monthly basis to his personal RRSP. He is fairly knowledgeable about investing, and the score on his investor profile questionnaire categorizes him as an "aggressive growth" investor. Until the downturn in the market a few years ago, John was earning double-digit real returns. He has revised his expectations and now aims to earn an average of 7.0% per year instead.

Rachel's RRSP Investment Assets

Rachel considers herself a relatively conservative investor, and the score on her investor profile questionnaire categorizes her as an "income and moderate growth" investor. She has $47,200 in her group RRSP (GRRSP), which is invested in a Canadian dividend fund earning 4.5% a year. In addition, she has $18,400 in her personal RRSP, which also earns a 4.5% a year. She also has a PPP and contributes the maximum possible towards her personal RRSP.

Personal Use Assets

The family's **principal residence** is valued at $220,000, and the house is held in joint tenancy by John and Rachel. **Household contents** are valued at $55,000, while their clothes are estimated to be worth $25,000. Rachel has a four-year-old **automobile**, which is worth approximately $9,000. On March 31, 2012, John signed a three-year **lease** on his car. The car cost $26,000 and he made a 20% down payment towards the lease; his lease payments are made at the beginning of the month. He is paying interest of 6.0% on the lease and plans to buy the car for the 20% buyout when the lease expires. The car has a current market value of $16,000.

> Hint: Refer to Chapter 1, **"Margot and Craig"**, **"Personal Use Assets"** for the equation to calculate the monthly payment.

Short-term Liabilities

In addition to the car lease, John and Rachel each have a VISA card with an interest rate of 17.25% per year. They currently have a balance of $2,102 and made payments of $6,537 in 2013. You suggest that they pay this debt off as soon as possible in order to avoid the high interest charges. Although John and Rachel could take out a bank loan to save interest, they are nervous about having zero balance on their credit card — they might run it up again. You advise them that, in this case, they should just keep plugging away and pay off the balance as fast as possible. Rachel and John think they could reasonably pay it all off in 2014. They will then have this money to contribute to either non-registered savings or RESPs for their children.

Long-term Liabilities

Rachel and John bought their house at the end of June 1998, making their first **mortgage payment** on July 15, 1998. The **house** cost $150,000 and they put 25% down. The interest rate has always been 7.00%. They renewed for a 5-year term in June 2013. The mortgage has been amortized over 25 years, and they make semi-monthly, end-of-period mortgage payments. The couple hopes to pay off their mortgage in full before they retire. They have joint creditor life insurance on their mortgage, which is $427 per year.

> Hint: Refer to "Appendix 1A: Review of Time Value of Money, Mortgages, Example 16".

Expenses

John and Rachel have the following expenses, in addition to those mentioned above. **House-related** expenses in 2013 were: $2,889 for property taxes; $2,957 for heat, hydro, and water; $762 in home insurance premiums; and $1,223 for home maintenance.

In addition to the lease payments, **transportation** expenses were $1,490 for automobile maintenance and licence, $1,580 for gas and oil, and $2,604 per year for insurance premiums.

Food, pet food, personal care, beer and wine are currently about $12,000. John and Rachel go out to the occasional movie but most of their entertainment activities are family affairs and with friends at home, so their entertainment expenses are included in the $12,000.

Rachel pays $185 per year for a 10-year term **life insurance** policy for $100,000 of coverage. John pays $420 a year for a 10-year term life insurance policy worth $200,000. They spend $83 a month for the maximum possible long-term disability insurance for Rachel. They currently pay $8,000 a year towards **Marianne's university costs,** based on John's divorce agreement (see Education Funding, below). Marianne has one more year of university.

They spent about $1,800 in 2013 on family recreational activities and allowances for their children, $1,300 for gifts, and $1,500 for charitable donations, while clothing cost $4,325. Other costs were $400 on the garden; $372 on a *Globe and Mail* subscription; $1,567 for telephone, Internet service and cable; $1,100 for veterinary costs for the dog and cat, and $500 for miscellaneous computer expenses. Child-care expenses for the children were $2,432 in 2013. They estimate that when the child-care expenses begin to decrease, they will be offset by additional costs for their teenage children. They anticipate these expenses will last until 2020, when their children will be old enough to have summer jobs.

The family spent $4,000 on a **vacation** this year. Rachel's parents live in Victoria, B.C., while John's parents live in St. John, New Brunswick. Rachel and John try to visit each set of parents every other year. In 2013, they spent $1,209 on small furniture and appliances. They also spent $5,000 for a new furnace when the old one died in the middle of February. They do not expect to have to replace it for several years.

In response to your question about priorities, they say their current level of spending reflects their family's priorities and lifestyle choices. They are not, for instance, willing to get rid of their pets or decrease their donations in order to save more for their retirement.

> Hint: As stated earlier, you, as a financial planner, must respect your clients' priorities unless, after drafting their financial plan, you have very good reason to encourage them to cut back somewhere.

John and Rachel make contributions to their respective RRSPs using all their available contribution room. They received $1,600 and $882 respectively, in May 2013 as refunds from the Canada Revenue Agency for their contributions to their 2012 RRSPs of $3,720 and $2,520. According to the Revenue Canada *Notice of Assessment* each received in May 2013, neither had unused contribution room.

> Hint: Refer to Chapter 1:
> - **Craig's 2013 tax calculation** for taxable income and handling of deductions
> - Margot and Craig's **"Statement of Cash Flows"** and **"Statement of Financial Position"** for handling of investment income, RRSPs, and tax consequences of RRSP contributions
> - You will need the marginal tax rates for interest income for both John and Rachel to calculate $k_{real\ after\ tax}$

In order to simplify this case, do not adjust their income taxes to reflect their donations and child-care expenses.

Retirement Planning Information

Rachel and John hope to retire when John turns 65 and Rachel 58. They have read in the "Report on Business" in *The Globe and Mail* that financial advisors estimate a couple will need 60 to 70% of their current gross annual salaries *during* retirement to meet their retirement expenses on a before-tax basis.

Government Pensions

John expects to receive the maximum CPP retirement benefit at age 65. However, Rachel earns less than John, and worked part-time when the children were very young. She will collect the CPP at age 60. They estimate that she will receive about 85% of the maximum amount anyone can collect at age 60 (i.e., she will collect 85% of 70%). Rachel and John will each be eligible to receive an OAS pension. However, to be conservative, the couple only wants to include about $3,200 each for OAS benefits in their retirement plan.

Other Retirement Planning Assumptions

Again, based on the "Report on Business", they estimate their tax rate in retirement to be about 30%.

> Hint: You will need to check this rate. See Chapter 2, **"Discounting Retirement Cash Flows before and after Tax," Step 1.**

They expect inflation to be 1.5% per year for the entire planning period. Since John is a more aggressive investor than Rachel, *before retirement*, he expects his investments will earn 7.0% while Rachel expects to earn 4.5%. *During retirement*, John will drop his expectations to 5.5% while Rachel's returns will drop to an estimated 3.0%. They want to continue their present "cash" investments (savings account, CSB, and GIC) but do not consider them to be part of their retirement savings since these funds provide the security they need to sleep at night. They intend to remain in their present home during retirement and hope to leave the house as an inheritance for their children. Rachel thinks she would probably move into a condominium if John dies first.

John has expressed concern about Rachel's having enough to live on after he dies. His concern is based on several factors:

(a) John is seven years older than Rachel.
(b) Women's life expectancy is several years longer than men's.
(c) John's grandparents died in their 70s. His parents, now in their late 70s, are not in good health. John thinks it is reasonable that he will not live past his 85th birthday.
(d) Rachel's grandparents died in their mid-80s. Her parents, now in their late 60s, are in excellent health and are very active. Rachel and John agree that they should plan on Rachel living to her 95th birthday.

Education Funding for the Children

They will continue to contribute $8,000 a year to Marianne's tuition for the next year. As well, John and Rachel want to make provision for their children's education funding, taking maximum advantage of the Canada Education Savings Grant (CESG). They estimate the cost of a four-year university program, which includes fees for tuition and books, will increase to $10,000 per year in real dollars when Mark and Virginia begin university. They expect the children to complete their educations at one of the two local universities. Since they are funding tuition costs for Marianne, John feels strongly that they need to fund the $10,000 in tuition for Virginia and Mark. They have six years to save for Mark and nine years to save for Virginia. (Note: Taking maximum advantage of the CESG does not mean making the maximum contribution each year.) In 2013, they made a $2,000 RESP contribution for Mark, receiving $400 in CESG.

Assignment

You have been asked by Francesca to prepare a financial plan for John and Rachel Whitney together with covering letters.

Several hours will be required to review the case and to develop the financial plan. Your analysis for the financial plan should address the issues listed below. Francesca will be reviewing the file — make it easy for her to do so. She expects your presentation, while perhaps not identical to hers, will be up to the standards she has set for her financial-planning practice.

Covering Letters

Write two covering letters addressed to Joan and Rachel Whitney:

• The first for Part 1 summarizes what you will be doing for them, their short- and long-term goals and objectives as you understand them and your findings so far.
• The second for Part 2 summarizes your key recommendations, together with a suggested action plan.

Action Plan

Answer the following questions for the couple. **State any assumptions and show all calculations.** Your covering letters and action plan should reference the calculations so your report can easily be read by John and Rachel after they leave your office. Again, Francesca will review the file — make it easy for her to do so.

The Case: Retirement Planning Case Assignment

Part 1

1. **Goals and objectives.** Determine their financial goals and prioritized objectives.
2. **Current position.** Construct the following two statements to ascertain the couple's current financial position:
   i. Statement of Financial Position as at December 31, 2013, and
   ii. Cash Flow Statement for 2013.
      - For both CPP and EI, use salary only.
      - Rachel's group RRSP is deducted from her pay, so treat it as a deduction from her employment income.
      - Craig's net pay with a pension plan is shown in Chapter 5; use it as a reference.
      - Use generic rates for tax, CPP, and EI or the most recently-available tax year as indicated by your Professor.

Check digits

	John	Rachel	Together
For the year ended December 31, 2013:	**Using generic tax, CPP, and EI rates**		
Taxable employment income	86,490.00	39,480.00	
Net pay (take home pay)	59,565.29	30,555.66	
Net change in cash flow			1,368
As at December 31, 2013:			
Assets			460,119
Liabilities			79,901
Car lease and buyout			12,042
Mortgage			65,757

3. **Current financial situation.** In order to provide Rachel and John with sound advice, your report should take into account the following and should provide the rationale and numerical analysis that support your answer:
   i. Are the Whitneys maximizing their RRSP contributions?

      > Hint: Calculate their RRSP contribution room assuming their salaries have not changed from 2013.

      (Answer: yes)

   ii. Do they have enough emergency savings? (Answer: yes)
   iii. Do they have enough disability insurance? (Answer: yes)
   iv. Do they have enough life insurance? The answer is no. Use their present premiums to estimate the cost of the additional insurance. (Answer: about $1,311)

      > Hint: To estimate their life insurance requirements:
      > (a) How much do they need in total? PVA for 16 years at 3% real of take-home pay
      > (b) Subtract coverage at work and private in place to find out the amount they are short
      > (c) Round it to the closest $10,000 (should be at about $660,000 total — $300,000 for her, $360,000 for him)
      > (d) Now paying $185 for her for $100,000 — pro-rate
      > (e) Now paying $420 for him for $200,000 — pro-rate.

   v. Are there any obvious places in their cash flows where they are spending too much and should consider cutting back in order to meet their retirement objectives?
   vi. When will their mortgage be paid off? (Answer: June 30, 2023)

Part 2

4. **Annual budgets.** Prepare cash flow budgets for 2014, 2015–2019, 2020–2022, 2023 and 2024 to 2028 in order to see what the couple's available cash flows will be after they have paid off their present short-term debt. Prepare also the Statement of Financial Position for 2014, 2015, and 2016.

> Hint: You should round their current cash flows to the closest $100 when preparing the budgets — for example, heat and hydro were $2,957: round to $3,000. This approach helps remind everyone that these figures are only estimates. John and Rachel are prepared to skip their vacation in 2014 if they have to in order to pay off their credit cards. However, assume that they will spend about $1,200 on appliances and furniture in addition to $1,200 on home maintenance, which should give them a fairly large room for error. While the Cash Budget is prepared first, the Statement of Financial Position is shown first. Your Cash Budget will also show how much they can afford to deposit in RESPs and non-registered savings. Refer to **Margot and Craig's Statement of Cash Flows** for future years.

There is no correct answer. However, your cash flows should show that they will make RESP contributions and non-registered savings. Your answer will show something different than what follows, including retirement planning.

$2013		Actual 2013	Budget 2014	Budget 2015–2019	Budget 2020–2022	Budget 2023	Budget 2024–2028	In Retirement	
								First 20 years	**Last 17 years**
John — age		49	50	51–55	56–58	59	60–64		
Rachel — age		42	43	44–48	49–51	52	53–57		
Mark — age		11	12	13–17	18–20	21			
Virginia — age		8	9	10–14	15–17	18			
	n	0	1	5	3	1	5		
Revenue:									
John net pay		59,565	59,565	59,565	59,565	59,565	59,565		
Rachel net pay		30,556	30,556	30,556	30,556	30,556	30,556		
		90,121	90,121	90,121	90,121	90,121	90,121		
Shelter:								*House*	*Condo*
Mortgage		9,442	9,442	9,442	9,442	4,721	0	0	0
Savings:									
TFSA Financial Planning			500	500	500	500	500		
TFSA New car		0	0	4,200	4,200	4,200	4,200		
RESP contributions		2,000	????	????	????	????	????		
John RRSP contributions		3,720	3,720	3,720	3,720	3,720	3,720		
tax on contributions		(1,600)	(1,600)	(1,600)	(1,600)	(1,600)	(1,600)		
Rachel RRSP contributions		2,520	2,520	2,520	2,520	2,520	2,520		
tax on contributions		(882)	(882)	(882)	(882)	(882)	(882)		
		5,758	????	????	????	????	????		
Net increase/(decrease)		1,368	????	????	????	????	????		
TFSA long-term investing			0	????	????	????	????		
Invest in Balanced Funds		0	0	????	????	????	????		
Net after non-registered investment		1,369	????	????	????	????	????		
Retirement spending needed with cushion								????	????

Note: The excess cash flow after their non-registered investments *must* be reflected in the change in cash. Refer to the budgets for Margot and Craig in Chapter 1.

5. **Education funding.** Construct a timeline of education-spending requirements and provide them with a savings strategy, including the CESG that will enable them to meet their goal for their children's education. Use a return of 4.545% for this fund.

6. **Retirement planning.** This is Rachel and John's first look at a retirement plan. Will they be able to save enough to meet their retirement objectives or do they need to revisit some of their assumptions and plans? Refer to Example 10 in Chapter 2, Laura and Stephen to refresh your memory on the steps involved.

   Conventional wisdom states that retirees need 60% to 70% of their pre-retirement income after they retire. Prepare a retirement budget for John and Rachel for both the 20 years before John dies and the 17 years after John dies. Make some reasonable assumptions. The following are some of the choices they can make. You do not need to use them, and you can make different choices.

   i. Rachel will sell the house and move into a condo after John dies.
   ii. After John dies, Rachel will give up the car and take taxis, or the train and rent cars as needed.
   iii. They will both enroll in classes and take up new hobbies in retirement.
   iv. They will not go on great cruises but will want to have enough to visit their children if they do not live close by.
   v. Medical costs may very well increase; like many people, they will take more vitamins and other supplements.
   vi. They now read *The Globe and Mail;* might they subscribe to more newspapers, perhaps buy more books in retirement (or just use the library more)?
   vii. Will they still need life and disability insurance?

   > Hint: Do not use the 60%–70% estimate. See Chapter 1, **"Margot and Craig's Statement of Cash Flows,"** which includes their budget for future years as well as an estimate of retirement spending.

   John and Rachel are not real people, but they could be. The author has made assumptions about their preferences. You, the student, can now make some of your own assumptions. Be sure to state them and make the budget numbers realistic. If they can effectively income-split in retirement, what percentage of their gross pre-retirement income do they need in retirement? (Answer: Should be around 45% to 50% before John dies and 30 to 35% after he dies.)

   > Hint: John's DBPP is non-indexed. Assume Rachel collects 60% of it after John dies. In addition you will have to estimate the amount of John's DCPP. Again, assume Rachel collects 60% of it after John dies. First, calculate the value of the DCPP at retirement. This will provide an indexed annuity — discount it using the real rate of return. To find out how much each receives each year from the DCPP, you must solve the following equation:

   Estimate of DCPP annual indexed income

   (a) Find the value at retirement of John's DCPP, which grows at a nominal rate of 8% before retirement.

   (b) Using this as the present value at retirement, solve for PMT in the following equation, using the factors for $1 for PVIFA and PVIF.

   > Hint: For a review of calculating the factors for $1 for PVIFA and PVIF, see Appendix 1A, Future Value Interest Factor (FVIF), page 36 and see (c) below.

Rachel's age	42	58–77	78–94		dies @ 95
John's age	49	65–84			dies @ 85
	n	20	17		

$$\text{PVA} = \text{PMT}(\text{PVIFA}_{20,\ 3.9409\%}) + 0.6\text{PMT}(\text{PVIFA}_{17,\ 3.9409\%})(\text{PVIF}_{20,\ 3.9409\%})$$
$$\text{PMT} = 25{,}395$$

(c)   Calculate the factors to use in (b):

	PMT BOY	FV	n	k real	PVIFA	PVIF
$(\text{PVIFA}_{20,\ 3.9409\%})$	$1		20	3.9409%		
$(\text{PVIFA}_{17,\ 3.9409\%})$	$1		17	3.9409%		
$(\text{PVIF}_{20,\ 3.9409\%})$		$1	20	3.9409%		

Calculate where they stand at retirement using their RRSPs and all pensions but without their Tax-Free Savings Account and without the Balanced Fund. Show the result in a table similar to the table in Question 8, Chapter 8.

7. **Investment planning.** Outline an investment strategy that will give them a well-diversified investment portfolio for both their registered and non-registered assets, based on the outcome of the retirement plan and your recommendations from above. To implement your strategy, you are going to refer them to a colleague who is licensed to sell securities. In general, what types of securities should they be buying to meet their objectives? Since you are not licensed to sell securities, you cannot recommend specific investments. However, you can recommend categories and levels of acceptable risk and provide them with some examples of securities that would meet their objectives and risk-tolerance.

8. **Contingency plans.** Evaluate a range of "what if" retirement-planning scenarios in order to assess "best-case" and "worst-case" scenarios. For example, what if one of them becomes disabled, dies, or loses their job? These should be brief, general considerations, not a detailed plan.

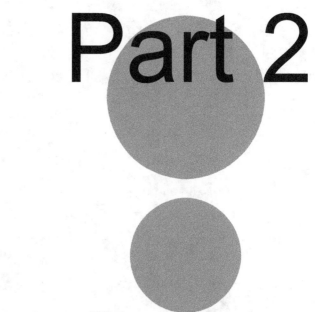

Part 2

Estate Planning

8

Introduction to Estate Planning

Learning Objectives

A.   Understand the issues involved in estate planning.

B.   Know what decisions have to be faced at the time of retirement.

C.   Follow Margot and Craig as they accumulate an estate.

D.   Look at alternatives for drawing down their retirement assets.

It is the beginning of 2038 and Craig and Margot are 67 and 68 years old. Margot has just retired while Craig has been retired for seven years. Over the years, they have been to see Francesca several times to look at their retirement plan. Saving for a satisfying and recreation-filled retirement was not too difficult. In fact, they are pleasantly surprised that they are far ahead of the financial position they envisioned when they first went to see Francesca 24 years ago. (Since Francesca enjoys her work so much, she continues to work on a part-time basis with the clients she has had for many years, but is also accepting no new clients.)

Craig and Margot go to see Francesca again. A year ago, when they last visited her, she suggested they might want to start thinking about estate planning issues. While they were aware that they might have an estate to leave to their children, they did not want to focus on it until they were certain of their own retirement. Always professional, Francesca has, of course, already ensured that they have dealt with some important issues. Both Margot and Craig have had wills and powers of attorney in place for many years.

INTRODUCTION

Estate planning is an ongoing process arising from changes throughout one's life. Events such as marriage, acquiring assets alone or with another, divorce, having dependent children, and premature death or disability necessitate regular assessment of issues such as wills and powers of attorney for both personal property and personal care. Assets acquired and businesses built become more urgent as estate planning issues as retirement approaches. Trusts, probate, and the final tax return concern one's death.

The act of retiring brings on decisions about using retirement savings in a way that minimizes taxes both during retirement and at death. This chapter looks in detail at Margot and Craig's building of a sizable estate. It explores three options for using their retirement savings to maximize the estate they leave their daughters.

A. ESTATE PLANNING ISSUES

As they sit down, Craig laughs. "This is certainly interesting. I realize we have managed to accumulate a lot more than we expected, but how complicated can our estate planning issues be? After all, we are not Bill Gates. We won't have millions to give away when we die."

"Well," Francesca replies, "the issues can get quite complex. For one thing, you might have more than you imagine, depending on how long you live and what you eventually inherit from your parents. Besides, estate planning is much more than just who gets how much when you die.

"Let's look at some examples from your own lives that you have mentioned over the years. Let's start with your mother, Margot. Any surprises there?"

Indeed! Margot was astounded to find that when her mother, **Gloria**, died, she did not have a will. She explains the circumstances to Francesca.

Wills

Gloria lived in Nova Scotia. She died in 2025. She lived fairly modestly and ran a **bed and breakfast** for a few years. Her home was quite small, so it was a very modest operation, but it was enough to supplement her government incomes. As a result, her retirement, or semi-retirement, was quite pleasant. However, Gloria died without a will, assuming she would leave a fairly modest estate and that everything would be divided equally between Margot and Margot's brother, Bob.

However, her estate turned out to be not-so-modest. Her rather small, three-bedroom house sold for an astounding $350,000 because it is located in beautiful downtown Lunenburg. Even after paying the tax on the capital gain (because part of the house was used as a business), the estate was larger than either Margot or Bob expected. Since Gloria **died intestate** (she did not have a will), the process took longer than it could have because someone had to be appointed to administer the estate. Fortunately, there were no problems between Margot and Bob. But what if Margot had died just before Gloria? Would any of the inheritance have gone to Margot's children? Gloria did not leave clear instructions, and things could have gone wrong.

Francesca comments, "Fortunately, there were no problems between you and your brother. Friends and family are not always as equitable as you and Bob were. Everyone assumes they can be fair when required, but it is surprising how differently people define 'fair and equitable.'"

"Oh," says Craig laughing. "There was a real mess in my cousins' family when their mother died just few months ago.

"My Aunt Hilda had a daughter, Janette, who lived across the country from Aunt Hilda, and a son, Bill, who lived in the same town. When Aunt Hilda died, Janette thought she should have the beautiful earrings because she had helped Aunt Hilda financially from time to time in the last few years of her life. Bill's wife, Marie, did not agree. She thought she deserved Aunt Hilda's diamond earrings because

> she had put up with Aunt Hilda's daily phone calls, ranting about the latest indignity she had suffered at the hands of Canada Post, *The Globe and Mail*, or the charity that kept bugging her about the pledge she had made several months ago."

In a case like this, both Janette and Marie had better hope that Aunt Hilda left a will, or neither one might get the earrings. Besides, who other than Aunt Hilda can really decide which of the two is more deserving?

Probate

> "What on earth is involved in the probate process?" Margot asks. "When my Aunt Helen died, the executor got a fair amount of money. What did she do to earn it? And what are probate fees? They sound like an estate tax, but I know that we do not have estate taxes in Canada."
>
> Francesca starts to answer Margot's questions with some general statements about probate.

Probate is the process of the provincial court validating a will and the authority of the executor who carries out the instructions of the will. The probate process is not always a big deal. But there is quite a long list of things the **executor** has to do: stop newspaper and magazine subscriptions, make sure that all the bank accounts are found and closed, sell the deceased's property (including the home), file the final tax return, pay final taxes due, distribute the assets, etc. Also, it is important to pick an executor who is competent. Sometimes people get sentimental and name an executor who is a close friend or family member but has no expertise in the issues involved in fulfilling the duties of an executor. This can lead to some real problems if the executor has to first learn what to do and what all the issues are; the learning curve can be even steeper if the estate is in another province.

Power of Attorney

> Francesca continues the discussion with the issue of power of attorney.

People often have a **power of attorney** to give another person the power to run their financial affairs when they are not able to do so themselves. However, the attorney may not be able to or may not want, to do the job when required. If there is no alternate person named, an application must be made to the courts to have an attorney appointed. In the meantime, nothing gets done — bills don't get paid, investment decisions cannot be made, etc.

In addition, people often do not realize that they may need a power of attorney for both their financial affairs and their personal care if they are not able to make decisions.

> "I know all about that," says Craig, nodding his head. "We had a real mess in my family not long ago. This story is not quite so funny

since it involves me." Craig has the good graces to look embarrassed.

Craig's mother died ten years ago and his father, **Hank**, is still going strong. However, Hank was in a car accident a few years ago. He had signed a power of attorney many years earlier, giving his wife and his friend, Jack, power of attorney. Unfortunately, by the time of the accident, Craig's mother had died and Jack had moved to Newfoundland. Craig's parents lived in Alberta, while Margot and Craig live in Kitchener, Ontario. Hank was unconscious in the hospital for a couple of weeks. Then he had to spend several months in a rehabilitation hospital with a broken leg and two broken arms. It was several weeks before Craig could have an Alberta lawyer granted power of attorney. Meanwhile, Craig had to fly out a couple of times and pay the bills out of his own pocket. He was reimbursed when the new power of attorney came into effect but the situation created a lot of trouble and anxiety for Craig.

Trusts

Craig then goes on to describe a new development in his family.

"And now," says Craig, "my father has a new girlfriend if you can call someone who is 62 a girlfriend. Anyway, **Brigid** is very nice. We like her a lot. And she makes my father happy, and he is no longer lonely. Brigid is divorced and has a son, **Steve**, who is physically handicapped. My father is 83. I don't want to seem greedy but my father is worth a lot — really a lot. Brigid is a lot younger and will probably outlive him. It's not so much for us, but I would like to make sure that my daughters get some of his money." Craig laughs. He is still embarrassed about talking to his father about his possible inheritance.

Francesca assures Craig that many children find it difficult to talk to their parents about how much they might inherit, or whether they will inherit at all, in the situation Craig has described. Craig explains a further complication.

Craig's older sister, **Joyce**, is not married and is a doctor in Vancouver. She has no children and doesn't much care whether or not she inherits anything. So she cannot be counted on to talk to **Hank**, their father. Craig's other sister, **Eileen**, was a nurse before she got married and had two sets of twins. Her husband, **Dwayne**, makes a decent living as a general repairman in Regina. But neither of them has a pension, and they certainly would be interested in part of the inheritance. They would also like to do some travelling since they couldn't afford to when they were bringing up the children. Unfortunately, both of them are worse than Craig when it comes to talking to Hank about money — quite possibly because they could really use it.

Francesca suggests that a trust might be a way to handle the situation. **Trusts** can be used to hold assets and distribute income for long periods of time, even indefinitely, subject to the 21-year rule, which requires a deemed disposition of assets in trusts except for spousal and common-law partner trusts. A deemed disposition means the property is considered to have been sold for tax purposes even if a sale has not taken place.

If Hank leaves his assets in a **trust** when he dies, he could look after Brigid while she is still alive but in a way that Hank's grandchildren could also benefit, if not now, then later. As for Eileen and

Dwayne, they could get money from a trust before Brigid dies. If they don't get anything until Brigid dies, they might be too old to travel — they could easily be in their late 70s by then. There are many ways of setting up a trust. The person setting up the trust can continue to control their assets after death as well as the income earned by those assets as long as they are in the trust.

Final Tax Return

> "I hear taxes really do end, and you know what they say: There are only three things in life you can be certain of: birth, death and taxes," says Margot. "My cousin was telling me about filing her father's final tax return and the effects of the final taxes on his RRSP, which everyone knew was being left to his grandson when he died."

When Margot's **Uncle Harry** died, he left his RRSPs to his grandson, **Pete**, who was 26 at the time. There was about $150,000 in the RRSPs, and Pete was shocked to find out that he would not get all of it — there was income tax to pay. Since Pete, the beneficiary of the RRSP, was not a spouse or financially dependent child or grandchild, the tax on the RRSP had to be paid before the money in the RRSP could be paid out to him. There were no other assets in Uncle Harry's estate that the executor could sell to pay the tax on the RRSP and, since the CRA will not sign off on the estate until all taxes on it are paid, Pete had to borrow the money and pay it back after he received the inheritance.

> "What is an **optional return**?" Margot asks. "I heard about it from a friend. Does it mean there are things that don't have to be reported on the final tax return?"

There are some types of income that can go on the final return or can be reported on a separate tax return (three separate optional returns, actually). The purpose of this approach is to reduce the total tax payable at death by reporting some of the income on separate returns. Each return is subject to personal tax rates and, because Canada has a progressive tax system, this separate reporting can reduce the total tax. Also, each return can claim the basic personal amount as a non-refundable tax credit, which also reduces the total tax payable.

Summary of Estate Planning Issues

As illustrated in the examples provided by Margot and Craig, above, estate planning deals with issues that must be confronted in order to ensure that one's assets are dispersed both according to one's wishes and in the most tax-efficient manner possible given the family's circumstances. While most issues can wait until retirement for detailed consideration, some issues, such as wills and powers of attorney (which safeguard your dependants and assets should you die before reaching retirement), need to be dealt with long before retirement. Though irrelevant to Margot and Craig but critical to many Canadians who are involved in small businesses or the ownership of investments, there are tax issues to consider long before retirement when planning to pass on or sell a family business. These issues, as well as other estate-related issues, will be discussed in detail in Chapters 8 to 12.

However, central to estate planning is maximizing one's after-tax estate. Chapter 7 presented alternatives for receiving tax-sheltered retirement savings. In addition, for retirees who have non-tax-sheltered savings, decisions also have to be made about how much retirement income should come from registered plans, which are fully taxable when received, and how much should come from non-sheltered savings, which are not fully taxable when received because taxes have already been paid on the annual income and on the funds invested. The goal of drawing down (using) retirement savings is to balance withdrawals from both registered and non-registered savings in a way that minimizes taxes in both the short run (i.e., to maximize disposable income) and the long run (i.e., to leave behind the maximum possible after-tax estate).

The rest of this chapter will focus on how to build an estate and the ways to maximize it through a detailed illustration of Craig and Margot's saving strategy between the time we met them at ages 43 and 44 in 2014 (Chapter 1), and their resulting financial position in 2038, when they are both fully retired at ages 67 and 68. Here, they will take their first serious look at ways to maximize their estate.

B. PLANNING *AT* RETIREMENT

At retirement, people face various decisions. These decisions include:

- How to structure the income from registered plans (this topic was covered in Chapter 7); decisions must be made about:
  - how much flexibility to retain
  - how much control over investments to retain, as opposed to certainty of income
  - how to structure annuities, which provide a large degree of certainty for the annuitant. These structure questions include allowing for inflation and survivor benefits.
  - how long one might live
    - for how long do the savings have to provide income, and
    - how much should be withdrawn annually to minimize overall taxes

- How much of an estate will there be to leave, who will receive the estate, and in what form; decisions must be made about:
  - a family cottage
  - donations before and after death
  - how to distribute various registered and non-registered assets in a fair and equitable manner (these are discussed in Chapters 9 to 12)

- How best to draw down assets in order to minimize taxes before and at death (this issue is discussed in this chapter)

Some of these decisions can be revisited several times, while others once made, cannot be changed. For instance, money in a RRIF or a LRIF can be left in these funds or can be used to buy an annuity, while money in a LIF must be used to purchase a life annuity at age 80. Most annuities, once purchased, cannot be reversed. One can change the beneficiary of a will unless the beneficiary is irrevocable, which is the case with certain donations made before death.

Factors Affecting Planning *at* Retirement

Like planning *for* retirement, there are factors — both controllable and non-controllable — that affect planning *at* retirement. Some of these factors were discussed in Chapter 2, and they continue to affect one's planning at retirement.

As discussed in Chapter 2, the following are considered to be **uncontrollable** factors:

- Life expectancy
- Rate of inflation
- Rate of return on assets
- Income tax rates.

On the other hand, the **controllable** factors are:

- Retirement spending
- Retirement date
- Savings — registered and non-registered
- Drawing down registered and non-registered savings and the tax implications
- Size of estate.

Many of these factors are interconnected. The amount of savings affects the amount available to spend in retirement as well as the retirement date. How to draw down retirement savings — registered savings versus non-registered savings — is, to some extent, dictated by the CRA, which requires that an RRSP be transferred to buy an annuity or into a RRIF by the end of the year the retiree turns 71. An annuity provides regular, taxable income that is more or less fixed for its life while, a RRIF has a minimum required annual withdrawal. These factors affect the amount of an estate one can leave for one's children. Presumably, most people assume children should be lucky to receive anything at all, especially if the retirees received little or nothing from their parents. Nonetheless, it is a consideration that can affect retirement spending.

A detailed look at Margot and Craig in both 2031 and 2038 will show how these factors interconnect and affect planning at retirement. At both points in time, Margot and Craig made decisions based on the following assumptions:

- Margot and Craig will live to their mid-90s (considering his father's overall health, Craig now believes he can live past his 80s — longer than he originally thought when they first started their retirement planning).
- Rates of returns must be realistic and based on historical rates adjusted for inflation.
- Income tax rates will not change in real terms.
- Planning will be done in real dollars since inflation varies and cannot be accurately predicted.
- All dollars are $2013, so a comparison can be made with Margot and Craig's original plans (alternatively, the original dollars and rates of returns projected could be increased to reflect inflation between 2014 and 2038).

To help keep things clear, let's summarize their ages at various points in time.

Ages of Margot and Craig

Beginning of Year	Event	Craig	Margot
2014	Begin retirement planning	43	44
2028	Craig contemplates retiring at age 60?	57	58
2031	Craig retires	60	61
2038	Margot retires	67	68
2066	Both die	95	96

C. MARGOT AND CRAIG: ACCUMULATING ASSETS

With Francesca's guidance, Margot and Craig started saving systematically for retirement in 2014. Although they have been reviewing their plan over the years and knew they were on track with their retirement savings plans, they have not paid attention to how much they accumulated and the estate they will be able to leave to their daughters. Now at the beginning of 2038, Craig has been retired for seven years and Margot has just retired, and they are ready to take their first serious look at the ways in which they can maximize their estate.

To do so, they will first review their saving strategy and the resulting financial position as of 2031, which they looked at in detail in 2028, when Craig explored his option of early retirement, and today, in 2038, as Margot contemplates her retirement. After seeing the value of the retirement assets they have accumulated, they will look at options for drawing down their retirement assets to maximize the after-tax estate without affecting their retirement.

Margot and Craig at 2028

In 2014, when Craig and Margot began planning for retirement, they were focused on saving enough both to put their children through university for undergraduate degrees and to have a comfortable retirement. They have been able to save more than enough to accomplish these goals. In fact, Craig was able to retire at age 60 in 2031. We will find out how this came to be through a detailed analysis by Francesca in 2028 of Margot and Craig's expected financial position in 2031 when they turn to her for advice in determining whether Craig could retire at age 60 in 2031 while Margot continued to work.

Overview of the Process

"Can we stop for a minute" Craig asks, "and have a bit of a review of everything that has happened so far and an overview of where we are going. I'm feeling a bit overwhelmed with all the steps although everything makes sense as we go through it."

"Of course," replies Francesca, "let me sketch out something that shows the steps we've taken so far and then I'll provide an overview of where we are going. This will become especially important since I am about to show you 31 tables building to a sizeable estate when you die, in 2066."

The Retirement Planning Process

Francesca starts with a table that outlines the steps in the retirement planning process. This topic was covered when we looked at:

• Craig and Margot in Chapter 1 and again in Chapter 8 as they are just beginning their retirement
• Laura and Stephen in Example 10 in Chapter 2 where it is shown that it doesn't matter if you plan before or after tax, you end up in the same place.

The Retirement Planning Process	Schedule	Ch. 8 Table
Step 1 Gather Current Financial Information	Ch 1, p.11	

Step 2 Prepare Statements to Reflect Current Financial Positions
    1. Calculate the take-home pay or after-tax income in order to have the Revenue for the Statement of Cash Flows
    2. Prepare the Statement of Cash Flows second
    3. Prepare the Statement of Financial Position third
  • Present the Statement of Financial Position before the Statement of Cash Flows followed by the detailed calculations of take-home pay or after-tax income
	Ch 2, p.88 Craig
	
	Ch 3, p. 142 Margot
	Ch 1, pp. 17, 19	

Step 3 Quantify Short- and Long-term Goals	Ch 1, p. 18	

Step 4 Prepare Short-term Budgets and Estimate Retirement Spending
  • See the explanation just before the Budgets for the Statement of Financial Position in Chapter 1 to see how the Statement of Cash Flows affects the Statement of Financial Position
  • Review Retirement Spending
	Ch1, pp. 22, 24
	
	Ch 8, p. 336	

Step 5 Calculate Required Retirement Savings
  • Retirement Income Needed — present value of annual needs
    • Step 1. Calculate before-tax income needed for each person
      • Prepare a Schedule of Rates of Return
    • Step 2. Draw the timeline for retirement income
    • Step 3. Calculate PV of retirement income, before and after tax
  • Retirement Income in Place
    • Step 4. Value at retirement of:
      • Government pensions
      • Indexed and non-indexed registered pension plans
      • Planned RRSP savings
      • Retirement Income to Save = Surplus or Deficit
	Ch 1, p 24
	Ch 1, p 26
	Ch 2, p 83
	Ch 2, p 83
	Ch 2, p 83
	Ch 1, p 27–28
	Ch 2, p 85
		
		8.1
		8.2
		8.3
		8.3
		
		8.4, 5
		8.6, 7
		8.8
		8.16, 17, 18

Step 6 Monitoring Their Progress	Ch 1, p. 28	

Semi-Retirement — Margot Works While Craig is Retired

Francesca explains that, after reviewing the Retirement Planning Process and their position in 2031, she will walk them through the result of Margot working for seven years after Craig retires at the beginning of 2031. During this time, while Craig is drawing on his retirement income, Margot is earning income and continues to contribute to her RRSP. Their spending patterns do not change a great deal from their planned retirement spending and, as a result, they generate a surplus that they invest in Mutual Funds. In addition, Margot inherited money when her mother died and this money is also part of her non-registered savings. Since the non-registered investments were made out of after-tax dollars, they are not 100% taxable when she draws on the funds. As explained in Chapter 6, pension sharing for tax purposes came into effect in 2007 so Margot and Craig do not have to concern themselves a great deal with whether or not they have saved so they can be taxed equally in retirement. Nonetheless, Francesca takes a look at the retirement cash flows that each of them will generate since they cannot share the tax on non-registered investments that are in Margot's name. And lastly, she calculates the minimize required RRIF withdrawals from each of their RRIFs.

Semi-Retirement — Margot Works While Craig is Retired	Table
Margot's Non-Registered Investments	
• Interest rates	8.9
• Adjusted Cost Base at 2031	8.10
• Market Value at 2031	8.11
• Capital gains tax	8.14
• Tax on Margot's non-registered assets	
• if sold in 2031	8.15
• if sold in 2038 and 2066	8.19
Effect of Margot's Employment Income After Craig Retires	
• PV of her cash flows at 2031	8.12
• Their combined cash flows from the beginning of 2031 to the end of 2037 when Margot retires	8.13
PV of Retirement Cash Flows at 2031	
• Surplus / (Deficit) before Margot's income	8.16
• PV of retirement needs	8.17
• minus Margot's net cash flows	
• minus retirement income in place	
• PV of Retirement Income of Margot and Craig separately	8.18
• Summary of retirement assets at the beginning of 2031 when Craig retires and the beginning of 2038 when Margot retires	8.20
PV of Retirement Cash Flows at 2038	
• Income from CPP, OAS, and RRIFs	8.21
• Minimum required withdrawals from their RRIFS	8.22, 23

Their Estate in 2066

Lastly, Francesca takes a look at three ways they can draw down their retirement assets — non-registered first, registered first and both at the same time. These calculations are only three of the many thousands of ways these assets can be drawn down and re-invested. We cannot look at very many options without a computer programme designed to run the numbers quickly. But we can take a look at the results of various approaches in order to see that it can and does make a difference to the amount of their after-tax estate.

And finally, Francesca points out that an estate worth $2 million in 2066 stated in $2013 is over $6 million in $2066 when inflation of only 2% a year is added. However, she want to make sure that Craig and Margot understand that the $6 million doesn't reflect the same purchasing power, that it isn't real, since $4 million of it is due to inflation and does not increase the actual buying power. This was addressed in Table 2.2 and is repeated here since many financial institutions and planners add inflation to their calculations and then produce graphs showing a huge increase in the value of their clients' assets without making it clear what the actual increase in purchasing power is.

Their Estate in 2066		Table
Scenario 1	**Draw Down Non-Registered Assets First**	
	• Estate After Tax	8.24
	• Annual After-Tax Income from Non-Registered Assets and the Value in 2066	8.25
	• Tax on Registered Assets in 2066	8.26
Scenario 2	**Draw Down Registered Assets First**	
	• Estate After Tax	8.27
	• Draw Down RRIFs and Invest After-tax Proceeds in Fixed Income Securities and the Value in 2066	8.28
	• Tax on Non-Registered Assets in 2066	8.29
Scenario 3	**Draw Down Both Registered and Non-Registered Assets by 2066**	
	• Estate After Tax	8.30
	Summary of the Three Scenarios	8.31

The Year 2028: Craig is 57 and Margot is 58

After working for more than 30 years, Craig is not sure he can stand to work for another 8 years until he turns 65. His firm cannot offer him part-time work. In fact, sometimes when they are working on a big project, he still works evenings and weekends. Like other people he knows who stayed in the same profession all their working lives, Craig is tired of the grind. All those books to read! All those hikes to take! All those trails to cycle! And he has developed an interest in cooking that he would like to pursue by taking some cooking classes. Of course, he can go to cooking classes at night. But, like others his age, Craig doesn't have the stamina he used to have, even though he is healthy and fit.

Margot still works part-time as an engineer for a consulting firm. Some months she works a lot. Some months things are slower. She is not tired of the grind yet because she hasn't experienced it in the way Craig has — she stayed home for a few years when the children were young. Margot thinks she can continue working until age 68.

They want to explore the possibility of Craig retiring in 2031, at age 60, while Margot continues to work part-time until age 68. If that is not feasible, could Craig possibly retire at 62? At 63?

To decide whether or not Craig can retire at age 60, Francesca needs to estimate the couple's retirement position in 2031 and how it will come to be by calculating the present value in 2031 of:

1. Their annual retirement spending required before and after tax
2. Their annual government pensions
3. Craig's DBPP and DCPP annual pension income
4. Their retirement savings, both registered and non-registered
5. Margot's employment income at age 61 to 68 and its effect on their non-registered savings
6. The amount of retirement savings they need and the amount they have in place, taking into account Margot's income and RRSP savings
7. Income splitting: who is receiving the retirement income based on their savings pattern to date

To keep things simple, we will assume that the analysis in 2028 of Margot and Craig's *expected* financial picture for 2031 is also their *actual* financial picture in 2031.

> Note: In this case, Margot continues to work part-time for seven years after Craig retires. In reality, many, if not most, couples retire at the same time. Having Margot continue to work complicates the example but not by much — as you will see. Working part-time before full retirement is a growing trend that will likely continue to increase as life expectancy continues to increase. Semi-retirement is a viable and desirable option for many people.

It is important that students understand each step of this example in order to understand the approach that is taken. As stated earlier, in working life, one would use a retirement planning package. Nonetheless, it is important to understand the process so that students can think through various retirement scenarios for themselves — not the least of which is when to use which tax rate and which discount rate.

1. Retirement Spending

With Francesca's guidance, Margot and Craig determine:

(a) How much they need after tax each year in retirement (Statement of Expected Retirement Spending)

(b) How much they need before tax each year (Table 8.1)

(c) The present value (PV) of their before-tax retirement income (Table 8.3); the rates of return for this and other calculations are shown in Table 8.2.

1a. Annual Retirement Income

The original estimate that Margot and Craig did with Francesca (in Chapter 1) is more or less accurate. However, they have changed as people in the past few years. As mentioned above, Craig has developed an interest in cooking. Margot thought she would grow old and garden. But after taking a couple of botanical drawing and watercolour courses at the University of Waterloo, she now wants to spend her spare time in the Zen-like concentration of very precise botanical painting.

Instead of the universal health care they used to enjoy, government cutbacks in the national medicare plan have made it necessary to spend more on health care. Government-funded health care is now means-tested, with low income seniors getting a tax credit that is inversely proportional to their income.

They now have three delightful grandchildren. After raising their own children, they were not prepared for the joy that grandchildren can bring — and you can hand them back to their parents at the end of the day. As a result, they are thinking that they might spend less time travelling to exotic places and more time interacting with their grandchildren. This is part of Craig's motive for thinking it might be a fine idea if his father puts the family cottage in a trust for everyone to enjoy, suspecting there may be tax implications (the tax implications of Craig's speculations will be discussed in Chapter 12).

They have also decided that they do not need to save for a new car out of their annual cash flows. They have saved more than they need. They will just take funds out of their RRIFs as they need them — split between them, of course, and over two years to minimize taxes.

The following Statement of Expected Retirement Spending shows how their assumptions have changed from 2014, when they took their first look at their spending, to now, in 2028, as they review it again.

Margot and Craig
Statement of Expected Retirement Spending
in $2013

	Estimate at	
	2014	2028
Shelter:		
Mortgage	0	0
Mortgage insurance	0	0
Hydro, gas, etc.	3,500	4,000
House insurance	700	600
Realty taxes	3,000	3,500
Maintenance	1,500	1,500
	8,700	9,600
Car:		
Insurance	1,500	1,500
Gas	2,000	2,000
Maintenance, licence	1,500	1,500
	5,000	5,000
Food, wine, beer	12,300	12,300
Other:		
Books, newspapers	1,400	1,500
Classes and supplies	0	2,000
Clothes	1,500	1,500
Computer — misc.	400	400
Dog and cat	1,600	1,000
Donations	5,000	5,000
Family activities	1,500	1,500
Garden	1,000	500
Gifts	5,000	5,000
Insurance — life, disability	0	0
Medical	0	5,000
Telephone	1,500	1,500
	18,900	24,900
Total cash out	44,900	51,800
Net cash flow	(44,900)	(51,800)
Discretionary:		
Vacation	5,000	5,000
Appliances, furniture	1,000	1,000
	6,000	6,000
Net increase/(decrease)	(50,900)	(57,800)

In 2028, they estimate they will need $57,800 after tax — $6,900 a year more than their estimate 14 years ago. Just to be on the safe side, they are going to go with an estimate of $64,000 per year, or $32,000 after tax each.

1b. Annual Retirement Income before Tax

Their annual retirement spending after tax is used to calculate their required annual retirement income before tax. As in Chapter 1, this calculation uses trial and error, and only the final numbers are presented here.

Table 8.1 Annual Before-tax Retirement Income

		Average	Marginal
Taxable Income		38,000.00	100.00
Federal tax			
15%	39,500	5,700.00	15.00
Non-refundable tax credits			
Basic personal amount	*10,000*		
Pension amount	*2,000*		
	12,000		
× *15%*		1,800.00	
Basic federal tax		3,900.00	
Provincial tax			
8%	38,000	3,040.00	8.00
Non-refundable tax credit			
Basic personal amount	*9,000*		
Pension amount	*1,100*		
	10,100		
× *8%*		808.00	
Basic federal tax (BFT)		2,232.00	
Total tax		6,132.00	23.00
Income after tax each		31,868.00	77.00
Income after tax total		63,736	
Average tax rate		**16.14%**	
Marginal tax rate			**23.00%**

Gross income of $38,000 each will provide $31,850 after tax each, or $63,700 together. These average and marginal tax rates will be used several times in this illustration.

1c. Present Value (PV) of Before-tax Retirement Income

Before calculating the present value of Margot and Craig's before-tax retirement income, we need to know their assumptions about rates of return. The tax rates used in **Table 8.1** are from Chapter 3, where Margot's take-home pay was calculated. However, as can be expected, their assumptions about rates of return are no longer the same as they were in 2014 (in Chapter 1). The stock market turmoil in 2002 and 2013 made them very nervous. As a result, they began to invest more conservatively than they had planned. Their funds are invested in balanced and fixed-income mutual funds. The returns were not what they might have received had they invested in stocks for the past 14 years but they feel, even now, that they made the right decision for them. In addition, the Bank of Canada continued its emphasis on keeping inflation low — it averaged 2% during the 14-year time period instead of the 3% Craig and Margot had used in their initial estimate. Table 8.2 shows their actual past returns and their new estimated future returns both before and after tax.

Table 8.2 Rates of Return, Nominal and Real, Before and After Tax

Retirement:	Before		During	K real
	Both	Margot	Both	Calculation
k nominal	7.00%		6.00%	
inflation	2.00%		2.00%	
k real	**4.90%**		**3.92%**	*(1.06 ÷ 1.02) – 1*
Marginal tax rate		35.00%	23.00%	
k real after tax		3.19%	3.02%	*3.92% (1 – 0.2300)*
Marginal rate on dividends		5.85%	5.85%	
Average tax rate		21.02%	**16.14%**	
k real after tax		3.87%	3.29%	*3.92% (1 – 0.1614)*
k nominal after tax			5.03%	*6.00% (1 – 0.1614)*

Note: The correct calculation of the real after-tax rate of return beginning with the nominal rate of return is:

1. Take out the tax
2. Take out the inflation.

However, we are always starting with real dollars and so have started with the real rate of return. As a result, for the after-tax rate of return, tax is taken off the real rate.

Calculations are done on a calculator at this point to ensure that students understand what is going on. When they become practitioners, students will be using computer programs for the calculations.

Using a real before-tax discount rate of 3.92%, the present value of their before-tax income in 2031, when Craig is age 60, is $1,489,965. They are working with before-tax cash flows. The taxes and after-tax cash flows are given only to show the complete calculations and to indicate the appropriate tax rate.

Table 8.3 PV of Retirement Income Required in 2031

Years:	2031–2035	2036, 2037	2038–2066			
Margot's age	61–65	66, 67	68–96	dies @ 96		
Craig's age	60–64	65, 66	67–95	dies @ 95		
n =	5	2	28			

Need in retirement					Tax @avg	
PVA @ beginning of 2031	n	k real	*$ BOY	Before tax	16.14%	After tax
	35	3.92%	76,000	**1,489,965**	240,433	1,249,532

*$ BOY 76,000 = $38,000 each at the beginning of the year

2. Government Pensions

Since these estimates are in $2013, Francesca uses the generic rates shown in Chapter 3 for income from the Canada Pension Plan ($11,500 for the full pension at age 65) and Old Age Security ($6,400). They agree that the future of OAS is uncertain and so will use only 50% of the generic rate.

Although Margot can start collecting OAS at age 65 even though she is still working, they decide she will not begin to collect it until she retires and since they are using only 50% of OAS, they are not going to adjust the OAS to reflect that Margot begins to take it after age 65. And their retirement income is such that their OAS will not be clawed back. With these things in mind, Francesca calculates the present value of expected income from the CPP and OAS for both Margot and Craig. There are two ways to calculate these values (as shown in Tables 8.4 and 8.5), and both show that the present value (PV) of expected government pensions at 2031 if Craig retires at age 60 is $430,447 before tax.

As was illustrated in Chapter 2, it doesn't matter if the discounting is done before or after tax as long as the before-tax discount rate is used. Again, the real discount rate in retirement of 3.92% is used.

Table 8.4 PV of Government Pension Benefits in 2031

Years:	2031–2035	2036, 2037	2038–2066	Before tax	Tax @avg 16.14%	After tax
Indexed taxable income	T_0–T_4	T_5, T_6	T_7–T_{35}			
Margot's age	60–65	66, 67	68–96	Dies @ 96		
Craig's age	60–64	65, 66	67–95	Dies @ 95		
n=	5	2	28			

Table 8.4 Continued.

Years:	2031–2035	2036, 2037	2038–2066	Before tax	Tax @avg 16.14%	After tax
CPP — Margot			13,432	*11,500 × 116.8%*		
CPP — Craig	7,360	7,360	7,360	*11,500 × 64%*		
OAS — Margot			3,200			
OAS — Craig		3,200	3,200			
BOY cash flows	7,360	10,560	27,192			
n =	5	2	28			
k real =	3.92%	3.92%	3.92%			
PVA @ BOY:	**2028**	**2036**	**2038**			
PVA =	34,125	22,722	475,158			
PV @ 2031 BOY	34,125	17,096	362,993	**414,214**	66,841	347,373

Table 8.5 Alternate Calculation of PV of Government Pension Benefits at 2031

	n	k real	$ BOY	Before tax	Tax @avg 16.14%	After tax
Margot — CPP	28	3.92%	13,432			
	7	3.92%	234,713	179,307	28,935	150,373
Margot — OAS	28	3.92%	3,200			
	7	3.92%	55,917	42,718	6,893	35,824
Craig — CPP	35	3.92%	7,360	144,291	23,284	121,007
Craig — OAS	30	3.92%	3,200			
	5	3.92%	58,056	47,898	7,729	40,169
				414,214	66,841	347,373

3. Craig's Pension Income from Registered Pension Plans

Craig's company started the pension plan only 14 years ago. He can get his pension without a penalty when he retires if he is within 10 years of the normal retirement age (NRA) of 65 and has either:

- 30 years of service
- a factor of 85

Since he has been with his current employer for only 24 years, he cannot take early retirement at 60. When his company started the pension plan, the employees were not given the option of buying back prior years of service. However, the years that the company did not have a pension plan do count when calculating when the employee can retire with an unreduced pension. At the present time, Craig is within 10 years of the NRA of 65 and has:

- 24 years of service
- a factor of 81 (24 years of service + 57 years old)

In three years, he will have:

- 27 years of service
- a factor of 87 (27 years of service + 60 years old)

If Craig retires at age 60, his pension will be $26,520 (2% × $78,000 × 17 years). Craig's company does not have a mandatory retirement policy at age 65 because mandatory retirement has been outlawed in his province, so he could continue to work until he is 67 and retire at the same time as Margot. Regardless of when he retires, he cannot collect OAS until he is 65. If he collects it at age 65 and continues to work, most of the OAS will be clawed back. Hank, Craig's father, is still going strong at 83, so Craig thinks he will live to collect his pension for a long time.

As we learned in Chapter 1, Craig worked for another company for nine years, and left his pension there. He can collect a non-indexed pension of $10,800 per year if he retires at 65, or $8,100 per year if he retires at 60. He has checked with his old employer to find out exactly how much he will get if he works to age 62 or 67. With this information, along with the calculations she made earlier, Francesca is able to calculate what his income will be at different Retirement ages.

Table 8.6 Craig's Retirement Income at Different Retirement Ages

Age	60	62	65	67
DBPP	30,600	34,200	39,600	43,200
CPP	7,360	9,016	11,500	13,432
Total indexed	37,960	43,216	51,100	56,632
Non-indexed pension	8,100	9,180	10,800	11,880
	46,060	52,396	61,900	68,512

Francesca also shows the couple the present value of Craig's before-tax pensions in 2031 — $724,389, if he retires at 60 and lives to age 95. The indexed pension is discounted at the real rate of return while the non-indexed pension is discounted at the nominal rate of return to reflect the loss due to inflation.

Table 8.7 PV of Craig's DBPP and DCPP in 2031

	n	k	$ BOY	Before tax	Tax @ avg 16.14%	After tax
Indexed taxable income		k_{real}				
DBPP (2% × $90,000) × 17 years	35	3.92%	30,600	599,907	96,806	503,101
Non-indexed taxable income		$k_{nominal}$				
DCPP	35	6.00%	8,100	124,482	20,087	104,394
				724,389	116,894	607,495

4. Retirement Savings

Francesca will now calculate the estimated value of Margot and Craig's retirement savings at 2031, the earliest Craig can retire. She will calculate:

(a)   Their RRSP balances in 2031 (Table 8.8)

(b)   The value of their non-registered savings at 2031 (Table 8.11).

4a. RRSPs in 2031

Based on their initial estimate with Francesca (in Chapter 1), Margot and Craig have been saving close to the money they planned to save and, as a result, they will have $600,000 in their RRSPs when Margot is 61 and Craig is 60.

Most of their savings are in Margot's RRSP. Since pension sharing was introduced in 2007, Craig and Margot do not have to concern themselves as much as before with whose name their savings are in. Nonetheless, since Craig has two pensions, they have decided to save as much as possible in Margot's name. It can still be an issue if all savings and investments are in one person's name as only pension income can be shared.

As shown in Chapter 6, during 2015 to 2019, they were able to contribute $25,000 a year, using up their $63,600 of unused contribution room ($35,600 for Craig and $28,000 for Margot). Beginning in 2020, Margot began to contribute $10,500 per year, approximately 18% of her $58,200 net income, to her RRSP, and $14,500 to non-registered mutual funds, while Craig continued to contribute to the spousal RRSP to use up his unused contribution room.

Table 8.8 shows how these annual RRSP contributions will turn into $613,064 in their combined RRSPs at the beginning of 2031, when Craig is 60 and would like to retire. All savings are done at the end of the year, and the tax rate is their estimated average retirement tax rate of 16.14%, as shown in Table 8.1. (Note: For future reference, this table also contains the present value of Margot's RRSP contributions during the years she continues to work while Craig is retired.)

Table 8.8 Value of RRSPs at the Beginning of 2031

	n	k real	$ EOY	Before tax	Tax @ avg 16.14%	After tax
RRSP balance at end of 2013						
FV — Craig	17	4.90%	59,700	134,678	21,733	112,945
FV — Margot	17	4.90%	39,000	87,980	14,197	73,783
Margot's Contributions						
FV of 2014 contribution	16	4.90%	4,000	8,602	1,388	7,214
2015–2019 contributions	5	4.90%	25,000			
FVA @ end of 2019			137,871			
FV @ end of 2030	11	4.90%	137,871	233,395	37,663	195,732
FVA of 2020–2030 contributions	11	4.90%	10,500	148,409	23,949	124,461
Total at 2031 BOY				**613,064**	98,929	514,135
PVA of 2031–2037 contributions	7	4.90%	10,500	60,973	9,839	51,134
Total for Margot and Craig				674,038	108,768	565,269
Craig				134,678	21,733	112,945
Margot				539,360	87,036	452,324

4b. Non-Registered Savings in 2031

In 2014, when Francesca first looked at their financials, Craig owned some preferred shares. The shares were sold several years ago so the family could go south on vacation together (before the girls got to an age when they would not travel to a resort with their parents). Beginning in 2020, Margot was contributing the maximum possible to RRSPs. As a result, she was able to save $14,500 per year in non-registered investments. In addition, Margot inherited $150,000 from her mother, who died in 2025. Margot and Craig had decided on a goal of a before tax 4.9% real rate of return (7.0% nominal) before retirement. They looked for an investment that would pay some dividends and also grow in value each year.

Their conservative equity fund pays dividends of 1.5% real before tax (1.41% after her marginal tax on dividends of 5.85%). Margot has the dividends reinvested automatically so the investment (adjusted cost base) in the fund is growing by an after-tax rate of 1.41%. In addition the shares are increasing in price by 3.4% real rate of return. Thus, the market value of the fund is growing by 4.86% [(1.0141 × 1.034) − 1] per year before retirement. When she sells units of the fund, the capital gain will be the difference between:

• the adjusted cost base, which is growing by 1.41%
• the market value, which is growing by 4.86% before retirement.

Table 8.9 summarizes these rates of return.

Table 8.9 Real Interest Rates for Margot's Non-Registered Investments

	Before tax	Tax	After tax
Both investments pay a dividend of	**1.50%**	*5.85%*	**1.41%**

	Before	After
re: *Margot's retirement:*		
Goals for rates of return (from Table 8.2)	4.90%	3.92%
less dividend before tax	1.50%	1.50%
Both investments will grow each year by	**3.40%**	**2.42%**
× after-tax dividend (growth rate in ACB)	1.41%	1.41%
= growth rate in market value	**4.86%**	**3.87%**
Calculation of 4.86%	*(1.034 × 1.0141) − 1*	
Calculation of 3.87%	*(1.0242 × 1.0141) − 1*	

Tax on dividends is payable when dividends are earned, not when they are received. Thus, Margot is reinvesting the dividends after tax. Francesca now calculates the value of the amount she invested between 2020 and 2030. Francesca points out to Margot that, as the dividends are invested, they increase the amount of the base on which dividends are paid; i.e., the investment is being compounded.

Table 8.10 Value of the Adjusted Cost Base (ACB) of Margot's Non-Registered Savings at the Beginning of 2031

	n	k real	$ EOY	Before tax
Margot non-registered savings	11	1.41%	14,500	171,254
Gloria's estate at end of 2030	5	1.41%	150,000	160,895
				332,149

Each unit of Margot's investment is growing by 3.4%. Since she is reinvesting the dividends, her investment is growing by 4.86% and is expected to reach a total market value in 2031 of $394,712, as shown in the following table.

Table 8.11 Market Value of Margot's Non-Registered Savings at the Beginning of 2031

	n	k real	$ EOY	Before tax
Margot non-registered savings	11	4.86%	14,500	204,522
Gloria's estate	5	4.86%	150,000	190,190
				394,712

"Since Margot has paid tax on the dividends, does that mean there is no more tax to pay on these non-registered savings?" asks Craig innocently.

Francesca knows that Craig is perfectly aware of the tax on capital gains and says, "Let's leave that for the moment. Since Margot is still working part-time, let's see what effect this has on your required retirement savings."

5. Margot's Income from Employment from 2031 to 2038, Inclusive, and Its Effect on Required Retirement Savings

Francesca will now look at the effects of Margot continuing to work for seven years after Craig retires. She will calculate:

(a) The present value of the income she will continue to earn as well as the RRSP contributions she can make because she has earned income (Table 8.12)

(b) Their cash flows during the seven years; we will see that they have enough not only to finance what their desired retirement income, but extra money to invest in non-registered mutual funds (Table 8.13)

(c) The present value in 2031 of the capital gains tax on these mutual funds in 2031, assuming they are sold in 2038 (Table 8.14)

(d) The tax on their total non-registered assets (Table 8.15)

5a. The Effect on Required Retirement Savings of Margot's Income from 2031 to 2037

Since the OAS is subject to the clawback, Margot has decided not to collect the OAS until she stops working even though she is well below the maximum clawback level. Because she is still earning income, if there is enough cash flow, she will continue to contribute to her RRSP, which generates a reduction in taxes for her at her marginal rate.

Using Margot's cash flows as shown in Chapter 3, the present value of her before-tax income from age 61 to age 68 is $343,774.

Table 8.12 PV at 2031 of Margot's Cash Flow from 2031 to 2037

	n	k real	$ EOY	Before tax	Tax, CPP	After tax
Margot's net income (Ch. 3)	7	4.90%	59,200	**343,774**	97,687	246,087
RRSP contributions, 2031–2037 (Ch. 6)	7	4.90%	10,500	(60,973)		(60,973)
Tax savings on RRSP contributions		*a marginal rate of 23.00%*		14,024		14,024
				296,824	97,687	199,137

5b. Margot and Craig's Combined Cash Flows, 2031 to 2037

When Francesca puts all the numbers together, they are pleasantly surprised to learn that, if Margot continues to work as much as she did before Craig retired, they will be able to invest even more in mutual funds.

Thus far, they have assumed they would consume all their income during the seven years while Margot is still working after Craig retires. Let's take a closer look at those cash flows to see how much after-tax funds are available at the end of the year to invest in mutual funds.

If Margot continues to work three days a week while Craig takes cooking classes, they will have more funds than they need even with Margot making annual deposits to her RRSP. Notice that Craig's non-indexed DCPP is *decreasing* each year because of inflation — the purchasing power of the DCPP in 2032 will be *2% less* than in 2031 because inflation is 2%. In addition, the excess funds are being invested in the same non-registered investments, so they grow at the same rate.

Table 8.13 Excess Cash Flows, 2031 to 2037, and More Non-Registered Investments

	2031	2032	2033	2034	2035	2036	2037
	T_0	T_1	T_2	T_3	T_4	T_5	T_6
Indexed income							
Craig CPP	7,360	7,360	7,360	7,360	7,360	7,360	7,360
Craig OAS						3,200	3,200
Craig DBPP	30,600	30,600	30,600	30,600	30,600	30,600	30,600
Craig's tax @ average rate	–6,126	–6,126	–6,126	–6,126	–6,126	–6,126	–6,126
$BOY	31,834	31,834	31,834	31,834	31,834	34,518	54,518
Margot — net income after tax, CPP	42,378	42,378	42,378	42,378	42,378	42,378	42,378
RRSP contributions after tax	–8,085	–8,085	–8,085	–8,085	–8,085	–8,085	–8,085
$EOY	34,293	34,293	34,293	34,293	34,293	34,293	34,293
Non-indexed income							
Craig DCPP	8,100	7,941	7,785	7,633	7,483	7,336	7,193
Tax @ average rate	–1,307	–1,281	–1,256	–1,232	–1,208	–1,184	–1,161
$BOY	6,793	6,660	6,529	6,401	6,276	6,153	6,032
Total income	72,920	72,787	72,656	72,528	72,403	74,963	74,843
Total needed before cushion	57,800	57,800	57,800	57,800	57,800	57,800	57,800
Excess is invested in mutual funds	15,120	14,987	14,856	14,728	14,603	17,163	17,043
Growth in investment @ 1.41%		30,320	45,605	60,977	76,441	94,684	**113,064**
Growth in fund @ 4.86%		30,842	47,198	64,221	81,946	103,094	**125,150**

5c. The Value in 2031 of the Investment of Margot and Craig's Excess Income

Now Francesca will calculate the capital gains tax on the mutual funds. She will calculate this amount for the value of the mutual funds in both 2038 and the present value, in 2031. Francesca warns Margot and Craig that this calculation is going to produce something rather odd — a capital loss and thus a negative tax. This occurs because the market value is discounted at a higher rate than the growth in the cost of the investments.

Table 8.14 Capital Gains Tax on Investments Made from 2031 to 2038

	n	k	FV @ 2038	PV @ 2031
FV/PV (Table 8.13)	7	4.86%	125,150	89,762
Investment (Table 8.13)	7	1.41%	113,064	102,492
Capital gain			12,086	–12,730
Taxable capital gain			6,043	–6,365
Marginal tax rate			23.00%	23.00%
Tax @ date of FV / PV			**1,390**	**–1,464**

5d. Tax and Tax Rate on Non-Registered Savings in 2031

Taxes on the non-registered savings are calculated differently from taxes on registered savings. The mutual funds are growing at an after-tax rate of return. The calculation of the tax on the capital gain in retirement assumes that the mutual funds are withdrawn over time (i.e., not as a lump sum) in order to minimize taxes on the capital gain by keeping the taxable amount below the next tax bracket.

Table 8.15 Tax on Non-Registered Assets at 2031

| | Tables 8.10 and 8.11 | | | Table 8.14 | |
| | *a* | *b* | *c = a + b* | *d* | *e = c + d* |
	Margot	**Gloria**		**M Funds**	**Total 2031**
Adjusted cost base	171,254	160,895	332,149	102,492	434,641
Market value of investments	204,522	190,190	394,712	89,762	484,474
Capital gain	33,268	29,295	62,563	−12,730	49,833
Taxable capital gain	16,634	14,647	31,281	−6,365	24,917
Marginal rate in retirement	*23.00%*	*23.00%*		*23.00%*	
Tax @ marginal rate	3,826	3,369	7,195	−1,464	5,731
Marginal tax rate on FV					1.18%

Assumes investment is not withdrawn in a lump sum

It will be illustrated later that the tax and the tax rate on this investment grow as the value of the investment grows, since the increase is a capital gain.

6. Total Retirement Savings in 2031

Now Francesca will put all the information together to see where they stand. She will do this in *two ways*, which will produce the same result:

(a) Add the present value of Margot's earned income during the first seven years of Craig's retirement to the surplus resulting from the net of the present value at 2031 of:
   i. total retirement income needed, and
   ii. total retirement income available.
This makes it easier to calculate the effect if Margot decides to retire earlier than age 68 (Table 8.16).

(b) Deduct Margot's 2031 to 2038 income from total retirement income needed at 2031. Then deduct all available retirement income. This shows more clearly the effect on their retirement needs of Margot's continuing to work and, thus, not consuming any retirement assets (Table 8.17).

6a. Total Retirement Cash Flows Deducting Margot's Earned Income at the End

Francesca begins with the present value of their retirement income. Then she deducts government and employer-sponsored registered pensions. After deducting their RRSP balances at 2031, she deducts Margot's earned income, the increase in the RRSP balance, and the effect of the RRSP contributions after tax for the seven years while Craig is retired. This presentation of their position shows the effect of Margot continuing to work part-time for seven years after Craig retires and allows them to see what assets they would have even if Margot decided to retire earlier than 2038.

Table 8.16 Value at 2031$_{BOY}$ of Total Retirement Cash Flows from 2031 to 2066

	Table		Before tax	Tax 16.14%	After tax
Need in retirement	8.3		1,489,965	240,433	1,249,532
Have in place:					
Government pensions — CPP, OAS	8.4, 5		414,214	66,841	347,373
Craig's DBPP (2% × $90,000) × 17 years	8.7		599,907	94,806	503,101
Craig's DCPP	8.7		124,482	20,087	104,394
		a	1,138,603	183,735	954,869
Savings needed			351,362	56,699	294,663
Savings to draw on:					
Margot's RRSPs at 2031	8.8		613,064	98,929	514,135
Margot's Non-registered savings 2020–2030	8.15		394,712	7,195	387,517
		b	1,007,776	106,124	901,652
Surplus/(Deficit) before Margot's income			656,414	49,425	606,989
Margot's cash flows, 2031–2037					
Net income after tax	8.12		343,774	97,687	246,087
PV of RRSP, 2031–2037	8.8		60,973	9,839	51,134
PV of RRSP contributions	8.12		−60,973		−60,973
Tax saved on RRSP contributions	8.12		14,024		14,024
Non-registered savings, 2013 to 2037	8.15		89,762	−1,464	91,226
		c	447,560	106,062	341,498
			1,103,974	155,488	948,487
Total present value of all retirement income and Margot's income	a+b+c		2,593,940	See Table 8.18	

6b. Total Retirement Cash Flows Deducting Margot's Earned Income from Retirement Income Needed

We can look at this scenario in a different way. Since Margot is still working, she is not consuming retirement assets. Thus, her income reduces the amount of "Retirement Income Required" (Table 8.3). This can be done using the information already obtained. Table 8.17 shows, in one line, the effect on their required retirement income of Margot continuing to work from 2031 to 2038.

Table 8.17 Value at 2031 of Total Retirement Cash Flows, 2031 to 2066

	Table	Before tax	Tax 16.14%	After tax
Need in retirement				
PVA @ beginning of 2031	8.3	1,489,965	240,433	1,249,532
Less PVA Margot's net income 2031-2037				
after RRSP contributions	8.12	296,824	97,687	199,137
		1,193,141	142,746	1,050,395
Retirement income in place				
Government pensions	8.4	414,214	66,841	347,373
DBPP indexed taxable	8.7	599,907	96,806	503,101
DCPP non-indexed taxable	8.7	124,482	20,087	104,394
RRSPs	8.8	674,038	108,768	565,269
Non-registered savings	8.15	484,474	5,731	478,744
		2,297,115	298,234	1,998,881
Surplus (deficit)		**1,103,974**	155,488	948,487

It appears that Craig will be able to retire at 60. Even if Margot changes her mind and decides to retire earlier than 68 or work less than the three days a week she does now, there should be no difficulty with his retirement date.

7. Income Splitting and Pension Sharing

Pension sharing, introduced in 2007, means it is no longer as necessary to have saved in such a way as to ensure that Margot and Craig are paying the same amount of tax. However, since income from non-registered income savings cannot be shared, Francesca wants to see how much income each of them will have in retirement.

To find out, Francesca begins by providing a summary of their retirement assets as of 2031 based on the information worked out earlier. However, this time, she summarizes the assets according to the income each of them will receive.

Table 8.18 PV at 2031 of Retirement Income of Each

	Table	Before tax		Tax 16.14%	After tax
Margot					
CPP	8.5	179,307		28,935	150,373
OAS	8.5	42,718		6,893	35,824
		214,656	8.6%	35,828	186,197
RRSPs	8.8	539,360		87,036	452,324
Mutual funds	8.15	484,474		5,731	478,744
		1,023,834	39.5%	92,766	931,068
Income 2031–2037 net of RRSP contributions	8.12	296,824	12.7%	97,687	199,137
		1,320,658		190,454	1,130,205
		1,542,683	**59.5%**	226,281	1,316,402
Craig					
CPP	8.5	144,291		23,284	121,007
OAS	8.5	47,898		7,729	40,169
		192,190	7.4%	31,013	161,176
DBPP	8.7	599,907		96,806	503,101
DCPP	8.7	124,482		20,087	104,394
RRSPs	8.8	134,678		21,733	112,945
		859,067	33.1%	138,626	720,440
		1,051,256	**40.5%**	169,640	881,617
Total Margot and Craig		**2,593,940**	100.0%	395,921	2,198,018
Retirement income needed	8.3	1,489,965		240,433	1,249,532
Surplus (deficit)		**1,103,974**		155,488	948,487

Table 8.18 shows that, utilizing the savings strategy presented thus far, there will be more savings in Margot's name by 2031. A significant amount is the mutual funds investment that will be taxed at a much lower rate than their RRSPs, government pensions, and Craig's RPPs and they can utilize line 116 on the T1 General — Elected split-pension amount — to make sure they are paying the same income taxes.

However, between 2014 and 2028, Francesca would have reviewed their progress regularly and recommended appropriate adjustment to their saving strategy. In fact, Margot and Craig have gone to see her every year or two, as their financial position changed or as new issues arose, and Francesca would have regularly checked to see:

• How much each of them would have in retirement assets at 2030, their original planned retirement date.

- How much retirement income each of them will bring in each year of retirement.

As a result, she would have regularly made adjustments to their saving pattern by reallocating their retirement savings to Craig for non-registered savings and to a spousal RRSP for Margot. We will assume that this reallocation has taken place, although we will not actually move the balances in the savings (to make it easier to follow). Consequently, their retirement income is evenly split between them and they have the same average and marginal tax rates.

Margot and Craig at the Beginning of 2038

In 2028, Margot and Craig reviewed their financial picture to determine whether or not Craig could retire at 60. He could and did. It is now 2038, and Margot is retiring shortly. They are going to start drawing down their retirement assets, including transferring their RRSPs to RRIFs. As they have done in the past, they come to Francesca for advice.

The Year 2038: Craig is 67 and Margot is 68

Although Craig happily took his retirement in 2031, Margot continued to work until 2038. As a result, their retirement assets at 2031 did not start to shrink because of Margot's income and the seven years of compounding. However, do they have enough assets to support a comfortable retirement now that they have both retired? What is the best way for Margot and Craig to draw down their assets? To answer all these questions, Francesca now needs to look closely at:

1. the value in 2038 of their retirement assets (Table 8.20)
2. how much income each of them will have in retirement from sources they cannot reallocate (Table 8.21)

1. Value of Retirement Assets in 2038

Francesca needs to bring Margot and Craig's schedule of retirement assets at 2031 up-to-date. But first she looks at the tax implications of their non-registered investments at 2038.

Table 8.19 Tax on Non-Registered Assets

			Table 8.15	
Assume all sold in:			**2038**	**2066**
Growth in investment (ACB)		Value @	**2031**	**2038**
			434,641	479,472
		k =	1.41%	1.41%
		n =	7	28
	(1)	FV =	476,472	710,060
Growth in market value		Value @	**2031**	**2038**
			484,474	675,469
		k =	4.86%	3.87%
		n =	7	28
	(2)	FV =	675,469	1,954,774
Capital gain	(2) – (1)		195,996	1,244,714
Taxable capital gain			97,998	622,357
Marginal rate			*35.00%*	*35.00%*
Tax @ marginal rate			34,299	217,825
Marginal tax rate on FV			*5.08%*	*11.14%*
Assumes investment is not withdrawn in a lump sum				

The non-registered assets are their only source of retirement income that is not taxed at their average rate. All other sources — government pensions, the registered pension plans, and RRIFs — are taxed in full in the year received. Because Margot and Craig would like to get an idea of what their estate will be when they die, Francesca will also calculate the tax on their non-registered assets in 2066, based on an assumption that they did not use any of these assets. Francesca simplifies the calculation by assuming the mutual funds are not sold in a lump sum but rather over time so she can use their marginal tax rate. Later she will look at the tax implications of selling the assets all at once when they die (Table 8.29).

Now that Francesca has worked out the value of the non-registered assets, she can provide Margot and Craig an up-to-date schedule of retirement assets. And their financial position at the beginning of 2038?

Table 8.20 Retirement Assets at 2038

PV of retirement income		@ 2031				@ 2038		
Margot	k	PMT		Table	n	Before tax	Tax	After tax
Government pensions	3.92%	16,080	222,025	8.5	PVA	28	290,631	46,899	243,732
RRSPs @ 2031	4.90%	n/a	478,387	8.8	FV	7	668,751	107,915	560,835
RRSP contributions, 2031–2037	4.90%	10,500	60,973	8.8	FVA	7	85,236	13,754	71,482
Non-registered savings	4.86%	Varies	484,474	8.15	FV	7	675,469	34,299	641,169
			1,245,859				1,720,086	202,868	1,517,219
Net income less RRSP contributions			296,824	8.12			0	0	0
			1,542,683				1,720,086	202,868	1,517,219
Craig									
Government pensions	3.92%	11,250	192,190	8.5	PVA	28	184,527	29,777	154,750
DBPP	3.92%	26,520	599,907	8.7	PVA	28	534,710	86,285	448,425
DCPP	6.00%	8,100	124,482	8.7	PVA	28	115,105	18,574	96,531
RRSPs @2031	4.90%	n/a	134,678	8.8	FV	7	188,270	30,381	157,889
			1,051,256				1,022,613	165,017	857,595
			2,593,940				**2,742,699**	367,885	2,374,814
Summary									
Government pensions			414,214	8.4			475,158		
RPP			724,389	8.6			649,815		
RRSPs			674,038	8.8			942,257	to Table 8.24	
Non-registered			484,474	8.15			675,469	to Table 8.24	
Margot's income			296,824	8.12			0		
			2,593,940				**2,742,699**		

Craig and Margot are astounded to see that things have worked out as planned 10 years ago when they set up their retirement plan. Why are they astounded? While they have always received good advice from Francesca, including referrals to other professionals as required, somehow they never thought they would actually accumulate so much. (And as a reminder to students: These numbers are in $2013 or 2013 purchasing power. In reality, when increased with inflation, the numbers would be much larger.)

> Craig is amazed. "We are closer to Bill Gates than I ever imagined possible," he says, laughing. "Who would have dreamed that we could ever be worth so much!"

How did they end up with so much in assets? In 2028, when they were looking at their retirement needs, they had planned for 35 years of retirement for both of them even though Margot continued to work for seven years. This is a very conservative approach. In Table 8.16, we saw that they had a surplus of $656,414 in retirement assets in 2031 before including Margot's income from working. This means that she could have stopped working earlier if she changed her mind about continuing to work. Since she continued to work, only Craig was using their retirement assets during those seven years. Furthermore, they were able to save more in non-registered assets.

2. How Much Income Does Each Receive?

Francesca will now show Craig and Margot how much income they will have each year and who receives it. Based on the schedule of retirement assets that Francesca provided, Margot and Craig do not have to use any of their non-registered savings to finance their retirement. Thus, Francesca will use only their government pensions, Craig's registered pension plan income, and the minimum required withdrawals from their RRIFs. The CPP, OAS, and the RPPs are a given, and there is no changing who receives them, although they can share their CPP and RPP income if it makes sense.

Table 8.21 Income from CPP, OAS, RPPs, and Minimum Required Withdrawals from RRIFs, 2038–2066

	n	k	Annual PMT BOY	Before tax	Tax 16.14%	After tax
Craig						
CPP, OAS	28	3.92%	10,560	184,527	29,777	154,750
DBPP	28	3.92%	30,600	534,710	86,285	448,425
DCPP	28	6.00%	8,100	115,105	18,574	96,531
			49,260	834,343	134,637	699,706
RRIF — minimum required		average	10,139	180,212	29,081	151,131
			59,399	**1,014,555**	**163,717**	**850,838**
Margot						
CPP, OAS	28	3.92%	16,632	290,631	46,899	243,732
RRIF — minimum required		average	40,377	726,997	117,314	609,683
			57,009	**1,017,628**	**164,213**	**853,415**
Total	28	**3.93%**	116,408	2,032,183	327,930	1,704,253
Tax @ average tax rate			18,785			
After-tax total			97,624			
Annual spending after tax			62,800			
Annual surplus after tax			**34,824**			

RRIF minimum required annual income is the average of the minimum required withdrawals; see Tables 8.22 and 8.23.

The real rate of return of **3.93%** is not an actual rate of return for any one asset: it is calculated from the PVA and annual payments.

Tables 8.22 and 8.23 show the minimum required withdrawals from their RRIFs, but not the calculation, which was already covered in Chapter 7. They decide they will make the minimum required withdrawals starting when Margot retires rather than waiting until the year after they each turn 71.

Table 8.22 Margot's Minimum Required RRIF Withdrawals

Age	Balance BOY	Required withdrawal		Balance after withdrawal	Interest @ 3.92%	Balance EOY	PV in 2038 of withdrawals @ 3.92%
		Formula	$BOY				
68	0					753,987	
68	753,987	**0.0455**	34,272	719,715	28,224	747,939	34,272
69	747,939	**0.0476**	35,616	712,323	27,934	740,257	34,272
70	740,257	**0.0500**	37,013	703,244	27,578	730,822	34,272
71	730,822	0.0738	53,935	676,888	26,545	703,432	48,056
72	703,432	0.0748	52,617	650,816	25,522	676,338	45,113
73	676,338	0.0759	51,334	625,004	24,510	649,514	42,352
80	493,052	0.0875	43,142	449,910	17,644	467,553	27,191
90	242,298	0.1362	33,001	209,297	8,208	217,504	14,158
96	99,053	0.2000	19,811	79,243	3,108	82,350	6,747
Total			1,130,567				726,997
Average/year			**40,377**				25,964

Table 8.23 Craig's Minimum Required RRIF Withdrawals

Age	Balance BOY	Required withdrawal		Balance after withdrawal	Interest @ 3.92%	Balance EOY	PV in 2038 of withdrawals @ 3.92%
		Formula	$BOY				
67	0					188,270	
67	188,270	**0.0435**	8,186	180,084	7,062	187,146	8,186
68	187,146	**0.0455**	8,507	178,640	7,005	185,645	8,186
69	185,645	**0.0476**	8,840	176,805	6,934	183,738	8,186
70	183,738	**0.0500**	9,187	174,552	6,845	181,397	8,186
71	181,397	0.0738	13,387	168,010	6,589	174,598	11,478
72	174,598	0.0748	13,060	161,538	6,335	167,873	10,775
73	167,873	0.0759	12,742	155,132	6,084	161,215	10,116
80	122,380	0.0875	10,708	111,672	4,379	116,051	6,494
90	60,140	0.1362	8,191	51,949	2,037	53,987	3,382
95	29,573	0.2000	5,915	23,658	928	24,586	2,014
Total			283,885				180,212
Average/year			**10,139**				6,436

Not only do Margot and Craig not have to use any of their non-registered savings, they do not have to withdraw more than the minimum required amount from their RRIFs. In fact, they have an excess, which they can spend, give to their children now (with no tax consequences once they have paid the income tax), or reinvest.

Without going through the calculations, we will assume that Margot and Craig saved appropriately in order to be able to split their income in the most efficient manner possible to minimize income taxes, as shown in the following:

Top Generic Federal Tax Bracket		
Maximum combined income	Maximum income each	Tax rate in top bracket
79,000	39,500	15%
158,000	79,000	22%
254,000	127,000	26%
> 254,000	> 127,000	29%

Now it is time to look at the options for drawing down their assets.

D. DRAWING DOWN RETIREMENT ASSETS

Conventional wisdom on this topic varies from expert to expert. Generally, the idea is to defer the use of tax-sheltered income as long as possible in order to defer taxes as long as possible. Thus, assets at retirement should be drawn down in the following order to achieve this goal:

1. lower-income spouse non-registered assets (the lower-income spouse will pay less tax on annual retirement income)
2. higher-income spouse non-registered assets
3. lower-income spouse registered assets
4. higher-income spouse registered assets (allowing the assets to accumulate on a tax-deferred basis as long as possible)

There are three challenges to this approach:

• registered assets must begin to be withdrawn the year after the retiree turns 71
• non-registered assets are subject to tax only on the capital gain. If the retiree dies before drawing down all the registered assets, the tax on the final return can be very high
• assets remaining in registered plans when the surviving spouse dies can be subject to a high rate of tax when the final tax return is filed

As of this writing, there is no model that calculates the optimal draw down of retirement assets to minimize both taxes during retirement and taxes on the final tax return. This issue is addressed in the software called *How to Avoid Outliving Your Money*, written by Moshe Milevsky, and distributed by Captus Press (www.captus.com). Since the focus of the software is on asset allocation and retirement cash flows, it is beyond the scope of this book. We, however, will see why the issue of taxation at death is important, with its effects illustrated in Margot and Craig's case.

According to Francesca's calculations, Margot and Craig will leave quite a large estate when they die since they have far more than they need to finance the retirement they want. While there is no estate tax in Canada, there is a "deemed" disposition of all assets when the surviving spouse dies, meaning that the CRA considers the assets to have been sold at the date of death, usually generating taxable capital gains. This topic is covered in Chapter 11.

There are an infinite number of possibilities for drawing down retirement assets. It is not possible to know the best scenario without a computer model to find it. Margot and Craig have some flexibility because they have saved more than they need. In fact, with the income from CPP, OAS, RPPs, and minimum required withdrawals from their RRIFs, they have $34,824 more annual income after tax than they believe they will need (Table 8.21). Francesca wants to illustrate the consequences of various courses of action, so she will look at only three possibilities:

1. They draw down all their non-registered assets by the anticipated date of their death and take the minimum required withdrawals from their RRIFs, leaving the balance of the RRIFs to be taxed at their death.
2. They draw down all their registered assets by the anticipated date of their death, leaving the non-registered assets to be taxed at their death.
3. They draw down all of their registered *and* non-registered assets by the anticipated date of death, reinvesting the unused balance in fixed-income investments.

Francesca assumes that they will reinvest any excess funds in fixed-income securities earning a taxable real return of 3% a year, 2.31% after tax [3.00% (1 – 0.2300)], which will not be subject to tax when they die. This is quite a conservative return, given that Margot and Craig expect to be retired for nearly 30 years. However, they have decided they don't want to risk their daughters' inheritance. They could, of course, choose to give money to their children while they are younger and probably could use it. They can think about that later; for now, their daughters will have to wait.

Before showing Margot and Craig the impact on their estate under the three different draw-down scenarios, Francesca restates the value of their retirement assets at 2038, which was shown in Table 8.20.

Government pensions	475,158
RPP	649,815
RRSPs	942,257
Non-registered	675,469
Margot's income	0
	2,742,699

She also tells them they will look at only the annual surplus that is reinvested and the final balance from the RRIFs and non-registered assets.

Scenario 1. Draw Down Non-Registered Assets First

For Scenario 1, Francesca assumes:

1. The balance in the RRIFs continues to grow at a before-tax real return of 3.92% and is fully taxable when Margot and Craig die.
2. The non-registered assets are drawn down evenly over the 28 years. At each withdrawal, a capital gain is generated, 50% of which is taxable at their marginal rate of 23.00%. To calculate the capital gain, the cost is amortized on a straight-line basis over 28 years.
3. The annual surplus after tax are invested in fixed-income securities that earn an annual after-tax rate of return of 2.31%. These securities do not generate a capital gain when Craig and Margot die — they are Guaranteed Investment Certificates (GICs) on which interest income is taxable each year as it is earned.
4. All withdrawals begin in 2038 when they are both retired, whether they need the money or not (this is to simplify the calculations).

Table 8.24 summarizes their retirement savings and estate after tax in both 2066, when they die, and the value of it in 2038 when they are both retired. The present value in 2038 of their after-tax 2066 estate using this draw-down strategy is $1,493,672. Their assets at 2038 are from Table 8.20. Margot has $82,350 in her RRIF when she dies (Table 8.22), while Craig has $24,586 (Table 8.23).

Table 8.24 Estate After Tax from Drawing Down Non-Registered Savings First

	Assets @ 2038	Estate @ 2066			Estate @ 2038
		Estate	Tax*	Net	
Registered/RRIFS	942,257	128,626	42,224	86,402	
Non-registered	675,469	0	0	0	
Fixed-income securities from:					
RRIFs		0	0	0	
Non-registered		1,394,876	0	1,394,876	28 n
Annual surplus after tax		1,349,864	0	1,349,864	2.31% k
	1,617,726	2,873,366	42,224	2,831,142	**1,493,672**

*Tax is calculated in Table 8.26. Assets are from Table 8.20.

Table 8.25 calculates the annual after-tax income from the non-registered plans (Table 8.19) that are invested in fixed-income securities. These funds are withdrawn at the end of the year and reinvested immediately, growing to $1,394,876. The after-tax annual surplus income of $34,824 shown in Table 8.21 will also be invested in fixed-income securities and grows to $1,349,864 by the time Margot and Craig die. As stated in assumption 3 above, neither of these amounts will generate a capital gain when they die.

Table 8.25 Annual After-Tax Income from Non-Registered Assets and the Value in 2066

		n	k	PMT_{BOY}
Market value in 2038 (*Table 8.19*)	675,469	28	3.78%	38,436
Cost — straight-line amortization (*Table 8.19*)	479,472	28	divide	17,124
Capital gain				21,312
Taxable capital gain				10,656
Marginal tax rate				23.00%
Tax				2,451
Annual income after tax				35,985

Reinvest in fixed income	n	PMT_{EOY}	$k_{after\ tax}$	FVA 2056
Income after tax	28	35,985	2.31%	**1,394,876**
Annual Surplus after tax (Table 8.21)	28	34,824	2.31%	**1,349,864**

The RRIFs are taxable when the surviving spouse dies. When the first spouse dies, there is a tax-deferred spousal rollover of the deceased's registered plans, which is covered in Chapter 11. Francesca has calculated the tax for Margot and Craig's dying at the same time and also at different times, which is more likely (even though she is assuming they both die in 2066, albeit not at the same moment). As stated earlier, the assets were saved so as to keep the taxable income of Craig and Margot equal.

Table 8.26 Tax on Registered Assets in 2066

		Both die in 2066			Surviving spouse
		Margot	**Craig**	**Total**	
RRIF — Margot		49,527	49,527	99,053	
RRIF — Craig		14,786	14,786	29,573	
		64,313	64,313	128,626	128,626
Federal tax					
15%	39,500	5,925	5,925	11,850	5,925
22%	39,500	5,459	5,459	10,918	8,690
26%	48,000				12,903
29%	127,000				
		11,384	11,384	22,768	27,518

Table 8.26 Continued.

		Both die in 2066			Surviving spouse
		Margot	Craig	Total	
Non-refundable tax credits	10,000	1,500	1,500	3,000	1,500
Basic federal tax (BFT)		9,884	9,884	19,768	26,018
Provincial tax					
8%	38,000	3,040	3,040	6,080	3,040
13%	38,000	3,421	3,421	6,841	4,940
17%	76,000				8,946
		6,461	6,461	12,921	16,926
Non-refundable tax credits	9,000	720	720	1,440	720
Basic provincial tax (PBT)		5,741	5,741	11,481	16,206
Total tax		15,625	15,625	31,249	42,224
Average tax rate		*24.29%*	*24.29%*	*24.29%*	*32.83%*

Scenario 2. Draw Down Registered Assets First

In this scenario, Francesca shows the results of drawing down Margot and Craig's RRIFs in full and paying the tax each year. Again, the proceeds after tax are invested in fixed-income securities. With this draw-down strategy, the present value in 2038 of their after-tax estate is $1,785,343, as shown in Table 8.27. The value of the non-registered estate can be found in Table 8.19.

Table 8.27 Estate After Tax from Drawing Down Registered Savings First

	Assets @ 2038	Estate @ 2066			Estate @ 2038
		Estate	Tax*	Net	
Registered	942,257	0	0	0	
Non-registered	675,469	1,954,774	100,141	1,854,634	
Fixed income securities from:					
RRIFs		214,020	34,536	179,484	
Non-registered		0	0	0	28 n
Annual surplus after tax		1,349,864	0	1,349,864	2.31% k
	1,617,726	3,518,658	134,677	3,383,982	**1,785,343**

*Tax is calculated in Table 8.29.

Francesca goes on to show them how much of the estate is the result of drawing down all their RRIFs before 2066 and investing the after-tax proceeds in fixed-income securities.

Table 8.28 Draw Down RRIFs and Invest After-tax Proceeds in Fixed Income Securities and the Value in 2066

	PVA 2038	n	k	PMT EOY	n	k	FVA 2066
RRIFs @ 2038	942,257	28	3.92%	56,037			
less minimum withdrawals				50,516			
Additional withdrawals (surplus)				5,521	28	2.31%	**214,020**
Marginal tax rate			*16.14%*				
Tax				891	28	2.31%	34,536
Additional withdrawals after tax				4,630	28	2.31%	**179,484**
Annual Surplus after tax				34,824	28	2.31%	**1,349,864**

In addition, Francesca shows them her calculation of the taxes, $269,389 (Table 8.29), on the non-registered assets that have continued to grow at 4.86% (Table 8.19). She also points out that the tax calculation is different from the tax shown in Table 8.19. Here she is showing the actual tax payable because there is a deemed disposition at death. In the earlier calculations (Table 8.14 and Table 8.15) the marginal tax rate was used since the assumption was that the assets would be drawn down over time, triggering tax at the marginal rate.

Table 8.29 Tax on Non-Registered Assets in 2066

Market value in 2066	1,954,774	from Table 8.19			
Investment in 2066	710,060	from Table 8.19			
Capital gain	1,244,714				
Taxable capital gain	622,357				

Tax on capital gain		Margot	Craig	Total	Survivor
Taxable capital gain		311,179	311,179	622,357	622,357
Federal tax					
16%	39,500	5,925	5,925	11,850	5,925
22%	39,500	8,690	8,690	17,380	8,690
26%	48,000	12,480	12,480	24,960	12,480
29%	127,000	53,412	53,412	106,824	143,654
		80,507	80,507	161,014	170,749
Non-refundable tax credits	10,000	1,500	1,500	3,000	1,500
Basic federal tax (BFT)		79,007	79,007	158,014	169,249
Provincial Tax					
8%	38,000	3,040	3,040	6,080	3,040
13%	38,000	4,940	4,940	9,880	4,940
17%	76,000	39,980	39,980	79,961	92,881
		47,960	47,960	95,921	100,861
Non-refundable tax credits	9,000	720	720	1,440	720
Basic provincial tax (BPT)		47,240	47,240	94,481	100,141
Total tax		126,247	126,247	252,494	269,389
Average tax rate		*40.57%*	*40.57%*	*40.57%*	*43.29%*

Scenario 3. Draw Down Both Registered and Non-Registered Assets by 2066

After considering drawing down registered and non-registered assets separately, Francesca now shows Craig and Margot the effects of drawing down all their assets before they die, which means there will be no taxable retirement assets when they die. Since all the numbers have already been calculated in the last two scenarios, Francesca needs only to put them together.

Table 8.30 Estate After Tax after Drawing Down All Retirement Assets by 2066

	Assets @ 2038	Estate @ 2066			Estate @ 2038
		Estate	Tax	Net	
Registered	942,257	0	0	0	
Non-registered	675,469	0	0	0	
Fixed income securities from:					
RRIFs		214,020	0	214,020	
non-registered		1,394,876	0	1,394,876	28 n
annual surplus after tax		1,349,864	0	1,349,864	2.31% k
	1,617,726	2,958,760	0	2,958,760	**1,561,002**

Finding the Best Draw-Down Strategy: Comparing the Scenarios

Now that they have looked at all three scenarios, which of the three strategies will provide Margot and Craig with both a comfortable retirement and the largest estate for their daughters? Francesca prepares a summary that compares the three options.

"Let's also put 2% inflation into the numbers," says Francesca. "Since we have been working in $2013, we'll have to add 53 years of inflation. I'll show you that calculation in a minute."

Table 8.31 Summary of the Three Scenarios

After-tax estate in:	$2013			$2066	$ Inflation
	@ 2066	PV @ 2038		@ 2066	in $2066
1. Draw down non-registered assets first	2,831,142	1,493,672	inflation = 2.00%	8,086,690	5,255,548
2. Draw down registered assets first	3,383,982	1,785,343	n = 53	9,665,784	6,281,803
3. Draw down all savings by 2066	2,958,760	1,561,002		8,451,209	5,492,449

The present value in 2038 of their after-tax estate was calculated using 2.31%, the after-tax return on fixed-income securities.

For example, for Scenario 1 (Table 8.24):
$$PV = \$2,831,142 \ (PVIF_{28, \ 2.31\%}) = \$1,493,672$$

The value in 2066 of their after-tax estate in $2066 was calculated by adding inflation of 2% for 53 years (2066 – 2013), since all the numbers used are in $2013.

Again, for Scenario 1:
$$FV = \$2,831,142 \ (FVIF_{53, \ 2\%}) = \$8,086,690$$

In this example, their estate of $8,086,690 includes $5,2551548 of inflation when inflation of 2% per year is added to the amount in $2013. This $5 million is not an increase in purchasing power. The purchasing power of their estate in $2013 is just under $3 million. This was demonstrated in Table 2.2 and shows why we prefer to use $real so as to not mislead our clients about how much their assets are truly growing.

From the summary Francesca prepares, Margot and Craig can see that drawing down non-registered assets first is not the best strategy for them. In fact, for them, it is the worst option, reinforcing that conventional wisdom is not always appropriate. Margot and Craig are fairly middle-class people who make a good, but not great, income. Of course, we have not taken into account possible changes to their ability to save $14,500 a year in non-registered assets — they might have divorced, they might have decided to send one or more of their daughters to private school (they are very smart, after all), or either Margot or Craig might have become disabled for a while. These events would change their financial picture rather dramatically.

Students who wish to become financial planners on an hourly, fee-for-service basis need to understand the limitations of formulae and rules of thumb for determining what is right for their clients. There are legal limitations to conventional wisdom — for example, RRIFs must be set up at a certain age and there is a minimum required withdrawal from them.

In the near future, a model will be developed for optimizing the draw down of assets. In the meantime, the student needs to be aware of the limitations of conventional wisdom. Analyses needs to be done before making recommendations.

SUMMARY

The fundamental issues in estate planning involve planning for assets at death or planning for becoming incapacitated so that the assets are managed and passed on to beneficiaries according to one's wishes but and as tax-efficient a manner as possible. These issues are handled though wills, powers of attorney, and trusts and include probate and the final tax return.

In this chapter, we have shown in some detail how Margot and Craig accumulated a sizable estate. Without a computer and using only a calculator, the calculations are time consuming but not exceedingly difficult, with the advantage of allowing students to understand the assumptions behind the results obtained. This is important because students need to develop an ability to mentally predict an outcome and to question the results if the outcome seems too far off from what is expected.

We worked through the numbers for Margot and Craig since Craig retired seven years before Margot, who continued to work part-time. We saw the results as Margot continued to earn income and therefore make RRSP contributions even after Craig retired. Understanding the implications of this way of retiring will become even more important in the future as an increasing number of people begin their retirements on a part-time basis for the first few years.

MARGOT AND CRAIG

After buying their house at the top of the market and watching housing prices fall, Margot and Craig are pleasantly surprised to find that their retirement will be comfortable in the sense that they will be able to do what they enjoy doing. As it turns out, they will also be able to leave their children a substantial inheritance.

Margot and Craig have considered buying Hank's cottage, but they haven't made a decision. Clearly, they can afford to buy it. But do they want to? Do they want to inherit part of it with all the grief that can come with trying to share ownership and use of a recreational property? Should the cottage go into a family trust?

KEY TERMS

Conventional wisdom

Final tax return

Inter vivos trust

Optional tax return

Power of attorney

Probate

Probate fees

Testamentary trust

Will

PROBLEMS

These problems ask the student to do some of the calculation from the case, changing some of the assumptions as follows:

- Margot retires at age 66, and Craig retires at age 65, at the beginning of 2036.
- Their rate of return before retirement is 6%, and after retirement is 4.5%, when inflation is 1.5%.
- They will die at ages 96 and 95, respectively, the same as in the case.

Year	Event	Craig	Margot
2014	Begin retirement planning	43	44
2036	Both retire at the same time	65	66
2066	Both die	95	96

1. If Margot and Craig together need $80,000 a year after tax, how much do they need each before tax? What are their average and marginal tax rates? (Answer: $50,500, 20.60%, 35.00%)

2. Prepare a table like Table 8.2 that includes all the relevant rates of return.

	Retirement:	
	Before	**During**
k nominal	6.00%	4.50%
inflation	1.50%	1.50%
k real	4.4335%	2.9557%
Marginal tax rate — Margot	35.00%	35.00%
k real after tax	n/a	????
Average tax rate	n/a	20.60%
k real after tax	n/a	????
k nominal after tax	n/a	????

3. Craig and Margot need $50,500 each before tax. What is the present value at retirement of their retirement needs before and after tax.? (Answer: $2,049,886, $1,627,650)

4. What is the present value of their government pension benefits before and after tax? ($616,305, $489,359).

5. What is the present value before and after tax of Craig's pension income?

> Hint: Check the amount of his pension — he is retiring later than in the case.

(Answer: $987,554, $784,138)

6. Margot makes RRSP contributions to her RRSP of $10,500 for 16 years from 2020 to 2035. What is the value at retirement of Margot and Craig's RRSPs? (Answer: $776,980, $616,937)

RRSP Balances and Contributions (Table 8.8)

	n	$ EOY
Balance @ end of 2013		
Craig	22	59,700
Margot	22	39,000
Deposits:		
2014 deposit	21	4,000
2015–2019 contributions	5	25,000
FVA @ end of 2019		
FV @ end of 2035	16	
FVA — 2020–2035 contributions	16	10,500
Total at 2036$_{BOY}$		

7. What is the after-tax value at retirement of Margot's non-registered assets assuming she continues to save $14,500 from 2020 to 2035 inclusive (16 years)?

Tables 8.9, 10, 11, 12	k real	Values @ retirement		
Tax on non-registered investments		Margot	Gloria	Total
		2020–2035	2025	
n =		16	11	
PMT =		14,500		
PV =			150,000	
Investment (ACB) at 2036$_{BOY}$	1.41%			
Market value at 2036$_{BOY}$	4.86%			
Capital gain				
Taxable capital gain				
Marginal rate in retirement				
Tax @ marginal rate				
Value at retirement after tax		330,824	244,797	575,621
Marginal tax rate on FV				2.76%

8. What is the present value at retirement of all their retirement income from government pensions, Craig's RPPs, RRSPs and non-registered savings before and after tax?

Answer:

	Problem	Before tax	Tax Rate	Tax	After tax
Need in retirement	#3	2,049,886	20.5980%	422,236	1,627,650
Have in place:					
Government pensions	#4	616,305	20.5980%	126,947	489,359
Craig's DBPP	#5	803,718	20.5980%	165,550	638,168
Craig's DCPP	#5	183,836	20.5980%	37,867	145,970
		1,603,860		330,363	1,273,496
Savings needed		446,027		91,873	354,154
Savings to draw on					
RRSPs	#6	776,980	20.5980%	160,042	616,937
Non-registered savings	#7	591,973	2.7623%	16,352	575,621
		1,368,952		176,394	1,192,558
Surplus / (deficit)		**922,926**		**84,522**	**838,404**

9. Ignoring pension splitting, how much retirement income before tax will each of them receive if the minimum required withdrawal from their RRIFs averages $7,283 for Craig and is $29,229 for Margot a year? (Answer: Craig $72,383, Margot $44,895). What is their surplus after tax each year? (Answer: $13,121)

9

Family Law and Power of Attorney

Learning Objectives

A. Understand family law:
    • Know the jurisdiction for various aspects of family law
    • Be aware of support obligations for children, spouses, and parents and the way support payments are taxed
    • Understand the legislation regarding division of property in divorce.

B. Understand power of attorney:
    • Know the two types and purpose of each.

During one of the sessions she has with Margot and Craig, Francesca goes over the basics of family law and the legal obligations people have to their spouses and dependent children — many of which Margot and Craig (probably most of us) may be unaware of. Her purpose is to provide them with background information so that they can begin to organize their own estate.

When Margot and Craig first went to see Francesca in 2004, they had both types of power of attorney that they filled out from a kit provided free by the Ontario Ministry of the Attorney General. However, since there are possible pitfalls if a power of attorney is not made out carefully enough, especially for a couple with dependent children, Francesca suggested that they consult a lawyer — which they did. They know it's not a good idea to write their own wills or use a kit to do so, but their wills needed to be reviewed and updated. At that time, Francesca referred them to one of the three lawyers to whom she refers client when they need legal counsel. Each of the three has expertise in different areas of the law, and Francesca chooses the most appropriate one for each referral.

INTRODUCTION

Family law is both a specific area of law and a general term. Family law is a provincial responsibility and refers specifically to the division of property and support obligations when a marriage breaks down. As shown in Table 9.3, the legislation is called by different names in different provinces and territories — *Family Law Act, Matrimonial Property Act*, Family Relations Law, etc. However, the term is also used more broadly to cover the financial implications of cohabiting and having children. Family law affects retirement planning because, while one does not like to imagine it, an untimely death or long illness of a major breadwinner can upset the best-made plans. And divorces do happen, even to couples who are currently getting along just fine. Although we may never be faced with such unfortunate events, we should be aware of their implications when making plans.

In this chapter, we will look at those aspects of family law that cover the rights of spouses and children who are financially dependent on the taxpayer. These include issues that arise in a divorce, such as the division of matrimonial property, support obligations, the splitting of pension credits and benefits, and the failure of one party to live up to obligations established in the divorce. In some provinces, family law also covers support obligations for a child resulting from a one-night stand. There are financial and legal obligations after death, and dependants can obtain an order against an estate to override a will if they are not adequately provided for in a will. Since family law is primarily under provincial jurisdiction, arrangements can be affected if you move from one province to another.

We look first at the family law that affects estate planning. In this chapter we then go on to look at the two types of powers of attorney. One is for personal care if the grantor, the person who appoints the attorney, is not able to make his or her own personal-care decisions because he or she is physically or mentally incapacitated. The other is for property and is intended to be used primarily if the grantor becomes unable to manage his or her financial affairs.

A. FAMILY LAW
Jurisdiction

Obligations for family relationships fall under several federal and provincial jurisdictions. The federal government has jurisdiction over marriage and divorce, while the provinces have control over the administration of marriage and property and family-support laws. In addition, the federal Income Tax Act recognizes the rights of opposite-sex and same-sex partners, which are not necessarily recognized under other legislation. The Modernization of Benefits and Obligations Act under Bill C-23 was passed into law on July 31, 2000 and came into effect by sections between 2001 and 2003. It gives same-sex, common-law partners the same tax benefits and subjects them to the same obligations as married couples and opposite-sex, common-law couples. It includes such things as the spousal rollover of RRSPs, spousal RRSP contributions, and claiming the spousal amount and other tax credits on personal tax returns. Table 9.1 provides the jurisdiction for relevant legislation.

Table 9.1 Jurisdictions for Family Law

	Federal	Provincial
Marriage	A person cannot marry someone who is lineally related (i.e., a person cannot marry their father or mother, daughter or son, grandparents or grandchildren). In addition, one cannot marry one's brother or sister.	• additional prohibitions (e.g., first cousins cannot marry in some provinces) • who can perform the ceremony • number of witnesses required • age requirements • registration of the marriage • mental competency requirements
Definition of spouse	**Income Tax Act:** Common-law partners, either same-sex or opposite-sex, are treated the same as married partners. Persons of either sex must have: • lived together for at least 12 months, or • be living together in a conjugal relationship and have a child together.	Legally married, or: • have lived together for some predetermined period of time (e.g., for three years), or • are living together in a relationship of some permanence and have a natural or adopted child Some provinces also recognize common-law relationships under other legislation, such as Workers' Compensation. Several jurisdictions now recognize same-sex marriages.

Table 9.1 Continued.

	Federal	Provincial
Annulment		Children resulting from a voided or voidable marriage have the same rights as children from a valid marriage. **Void marriages** are treated as marriages that never happened. **Voidable marriages** have a fatal flaw but are recognized until and unless someone brings the flaw to the attention of a court. These are described further after this table.
Separation	Income attribution rules cease to apply — a separation agreement is not required. Parties are living separately and independently even if in the same dwelling.	
Divorce	**Divorce Act:** A breakdown of marriage has occurred if: • the spouses are living separately and have done so for one year before the divorce proceedings, or • one spouse has committed adultery since the marriage, or • one spouse has subjected the other to mental or physical cruelty which is intolerable.	**Provincial Courts of Competent Jurisdiction** are empowered to administer the divorce in the province where either spouse lived for one year before the initiation of the divorce proceedings. Provincial courts must be satisfied that support for children has been established before a divorce can be granted under the Divorce Act.
Spousal support	Divorce Act	Most provinces include common-law relationships.
Child support	Divorce Act	A child born from a one-night stand does not automatically result in a common-law partnership although the father may be obliged to pay child support.
Parental support		Child might be required to support parent(s).
Division of property		Provincial legislation.

Void and Voidable Marriages

Void marriages have a fatal flaw and are not valid regardless of the position of the spouses and are treated as if the marriage never happened. Void marriages include marriage of a child younger than age seven; marriage where one of the spouses is already married; and marriage between closely-related people, including adoption or where there was a mistake concerning the identity of one partner. Provincial legislation provides the legal minimum age for marriage; and, generally, marriage of males below the age of 15 and females below 12 are void.

Voidable marriages are valid even though there is a fatal flaw, until and unless someone brings the flaw to the attention of a court. This can occur if someone was so intoxicated during the ceremony that consent was not possible or if someone was forced into marriage or if one of the spouses was misled as to the nature of the ceremony because, for instance, the ceremony was in a language he or she did not understand. Marriages have to be consummated by sexual intercourse and are voidable if one partner is impotent. Impotence includes an aversion to sexual intercourse. Even one act of consummation removes this as grounds for voiding a marriage.

Marriages of convenience for social assistance, immigration, or tax purposes are not voidable on these grounds alone because courts do not care about the motive for marrying. **Religious annulments** are not recognized in the legal system.

A child from a void marriage who would have been legitimate had the marriage been valid is considered legitimate. A child from a voidable marriage is legitimate if conceived before the marriage was annulled. These provisions mean that these children have succession rights as legitimate children.

Support Obligations

Child support and spousal support are legal obligations at both the federal and provincial levels. A parent has a legal obligation to support minor children and older children who are, for instance, disabled. One may also choose to support one's grandchildren, although there is no legal obligation to do so. However, once begun, there are implications, particularly in connection with the Income Tax Act. There is generally no obligation to support parents and grandparents, although some provinces require children to support parents and/or grandparents who supported them when they were young. One does not have a legal obligation to support siblings and their children.

We will look at the following financial support obligations:

- Child support
- Spousal support
- Parental support

We will also look at the issues that arise from these obligations:

- Taxation of support payments
- Enforcing support payments
- Mediation

Child Support

Child support guidelines are covered both federally and provincially, depending on the marital status of the couple.

Federal

The **federal Divorce Act** contains **Child Support Guidelines** that outline rules for determining child support when a couple is divorcing. These rules take into account:

- the type of custody
- the number of financially dependent children
- the income of both parents, and
- the province or territory in which the parents live.

These guidelines apply only if the parents are getting a divorce. Provincial guidelines come into play if the parents are separated but not divorcing or were never married. A court can award a different amount if, for instance, there are special or extraordinary expenses, the parents share custody, or the paying parent has support obligations from a prior relationship.

There are three types of **custody** arrangements:

1. **Shared custody**: Each parent has physical custody of or access to the child or children for at least 40% of the time in a year
2. **Sole custody**: The child or children resides less than 40% of the time in a year with the paying parent

3. **Split custody**: The children are divided between the parents — that is, a child or some children live with one parent, some with the other. Each parent calculates how much they must contribute to the other for the support of the child or children who live with the other. The parent who is required to pay the higher amount then pays the difference to the other

The federal guidelines are specific as to the amount to be paid. For instance, if the paying parent lives in Nova Scotia, has an income from employment, self-employment, and income from investments of $82,000 a year, and has two dependent children who live most of the time with the other parent, the paying parent must pay $1,132 a month in child support, or $1,475 for three children. The federal guidelines cover income up to $150,000. For income levels above this amount, a percentage of the additional income is generally allocated. In this Nova Scotia scenario, if the paying person earns $160,000, the amount is $1,913 plus $112 (1.12% of income over $150,000) for two children (see Department of Justice, Federal Child Support Guidelines Simplified Tables, by province).

Each parent's contribution is treated separately regardless of the income of the custodial parent. **Income** includes all sources of income before tax. The goal is to ensure that the children participate in any increases or decreases in the income level of each parent in the same way they would if the parents were still living together.

The federal guidelines contain schedules for each province to take into account the differing provincial and territorial tax rates. In addition, many provinces and territories have their own provincial guidelines that are used in place of federal guidelines if both parents live in the same province. If the parents live in different provinces or territories, the federal guideline for the province of the paying parent is used. If one parent lives outside of Canada, the federal guidelines will be used for the province in which the Canadian resident lives.

The federal guidelines do not include amounts for additional child-related expenses that can be added to support payments. These additional costs include child care costs, uninsured medical costs over $200, special education needs, and costs for extracurricular activities. Generally, both parents are expected to participate in paying for these additional expenses.

Provincial

Provincial child support laws tend to provide only guidelines for how to determine the amount each spouse should pay by taking into account reasonable living costs (accommodation, food, clothing, etc.) and the ability of each parent to pay. Natural parents have an obligation that overrides the obligation of a subsequent spouse. However, if the natural parent fails in their obligation, a step-parent is expected to meet the obligation. These laws apply when the parents are divorcing and the province of residence has guidelines. They also apply when the parents are separating but were not married.

Many provincial courts rely on a variation of the Paras Formula, which resulted from a 1971 child support court proceeding (*Paras v. Paras*). In this proceeding, the amount needed to support and educate a child is determined, and this amount is then allocated between the parents according to their ability to pay. There may be an adjustment whereby a basic subsistence allowance is subtracted from each parent's income before the allocation is made.

Most provincial legislation does not impose a deadline for the application for support, meaning the application can be made at any time, even if the parent making the application is slow to act.

Spousal Support

Spousal support (also called *alimony* or *spousal maintenance*) can ensue when a marriage breaks down. The amount depends on the needs of each spouse and on their income and resources, and is separate and distinct from child support. Spousal support, as indicated in Table 9.1, also falls under both federal and provincial jurisdictions.

Federal

A claim for spousal support can be made at the time of the divorce petition or after the divorce. The federal Canada Divorce Act, Section 15.2, aims to reduce economic hardship for one spouse arising from a divorce while promoting the self-sufficiency of both spouses. Priority is given to child support. A spousal support order will take into account:

- length of time the spouses lived together
- functions performed by each spouse during cohabitation
- any support agreement already in place.

The Divorce Act goes on to state that an order for support should:

- recognize any economic advantages or disadvantages to the spouses arising from the marriage or its breakdown
- apportion between the spouses any financial consequences arising from the care of any child of the marriage over and above any obligations for the support of any child of the marriage. This means that, since child support takes precedence, spousal support may be suspended if child support payments exhaust the financial resources of the paying parent
- relieve any economic hardship of either spouse arising from the breakdown of the marriage
- insofar as practicable, promote the economic self-sufficiency of each spouse within a reasonable period of time.

The division of family assets is covered by provincial legislation.

Provincial

Provincial laws often, but not always, apply to common-law, opposite-sex relationships as well as to married couples. There is often a deadline by which the claim for spousal support must be made: for instance, in some provinces the claim must be made within two or three years of the time the couple separated.

Periodic spousal support payments (payments made at regular time intervals — monthly, quarterly, annually) are taxable to the receiving spouse and tax-deductible to the paying spouse. This is commonly known as the **inclusions/deduction rule**. These payments are called an **allowance** by the CRA and reflect a specific amount to be paid on a regular basis, not to exceed annual payments. The recipient must be able to use the payments as they wish. Payments that are tax-deductible under this rule are not eligible for a tax credit.

Parental Support

Although looking after an elderly parent is increasingly common these days, given longer lives and better health treatment, it is done most often as a moral obligation.

Federal

There is no federal law requiring a person to take care of a parent.

Provincial

Several provinces require children to support the parent(s) if the parent is in need *and* provided care and support when the child was young. The amount of the support payment takes into account both the parent's and the child's ability to pay as well as other support payment obligations in effect.

Taxation of Support Payments

Table 9.2 summarizes the taxation of support payments.

Table 9.2 Taxation of Support Payments

As of May 1, 1997	Payments received	Payments made
Child support	Not taxable	Not tax deductible
Spousal support payments • Periodic* • Lump sum	 Taxable Not taxable	 Tax deductible Not tax deductible
Combined payments**	Not taxable	Not tax deductible
Parental support = a gift	Not taxable	Not tax deductible

*There must be a written agreement or a court order for the payments to be tax-deductible.

**Combined payments are considered to be child support.

If the total payments in a year are less than the written agreement states, the payments are considered to be child support for tax purposes.

The following three examples demonstrate the taxation of support payments. Example 1 illustrates the effect when support payments are not defined as child or spousal payments; Example 2, when an amount, $1,500, is named as spousal support; and Example 3, when the payment is made in a lump sum.

Example 1   Andrea is a doctor and makes about $175,000 per year. Mark is a child-care worker making $29,000 per year. When they divorced, they worked out their own support agreement. They don't know much about law and tax, but they pride themselves on their innate fairness. Because Andrea works very long hours sometimes, Mark has custody of their two young children. Andrea agreed to pay Mark $4,000 per month in support.

Because their agreement does not stipulate what kind of support payments Andrea agreed to make, they will be considered child support. As a result, Andrea cannot deduct them and Mark does not have to declare them as income.

Example 2   Assuming that Andrea and Mark have agreed in writing that $2,500 per month is child support and $1,500 per month is spousal support, Andrea will be able to deduct the $1,500 per month in spousal support while Mark must add the same amount to his taxable income.

Example 3   Before going ahead with the agreement in Example 2, Andrea accepted a job with Doctors Without Borders. Because her income is going to be next to nothing for the next three years, she sold some of her investments that had been earnings 10% per year and gave Mark $130,000 [48,000 (PVIFA$_{10\%, 3}$)] in a lump sum. This amount is not tax deductible for Andrea and is not taxable to Mark, even though it was 5/8 child support and 3/8 spousal support because it is a lump sum.

Legal fees to establish or change support payments are not tax deductible, but legal fees to enforce a support order are deductible for the recipient.

Enforcing Support Payments

The purpose of support payments is either to help support a child or to ensure that a spouse does not suffer economic hardship after a divorce. Provinces are becoming increasingly adamant about enforcing support payments awards. These enforcement methods include:

- garnishing wages, whereby the employer of the payor deducts the amount from the payor's pay and remits it to a central agency
- charging interest
- setting up data banks to track "deadbeat" parents
- seizing assets or placing liens on assets
- authorizing the arrest of the deadbeat parent
- suspending licences, such as a driver's license

An obligation to support is not cancelled by **bankruptcy**. Nor can these obligations be avoided through death. A court can override a will that fails to take into account the needs of dependants. These dependants can include children, spouses, common-law spouses, and parents.

Alternative Dispute Resolution to Avoid Court in a Divorce

Going to court to obtain a divorce is both stressful and expensive — legal fees can rise rapidly. Even if court proceedings have begun, the proceedings can be stayed or stopped by a family law judge. There are four ways to avoid court.

1. Mediation
2. Negotiation
3. Collaboration, and
4. Arbitration.

Avoiding court is called Alternative Dispute Resolution. The Department of Justice of Canada has a website that provides information by province; it also provides links to provincial and territorial websites. This information can be found at:

- Canada — Department of Justice — Programs and Initiatives — Child Support — Links to Related Sites
  - Provincial and territorial governments
    - Inventory of Government-based Family Justice Services
  - Government of Canada — Parenting after Divorce
  - Other sites — Lawyer Referral Services

Mediation

Mediation involves the divorcing spouses meeting with a mediator to discuss the issues with the goal of resolving them. The mediator is a neutral third party paid for by the spouses. Mediation is offered when couples are separating and is sometimes required by provincial jurisdictions. The goal of mediation is to provide co-operative, non-adversarial conflict resolution relating to family issues such as separation and divorce and child welfare. Legal aid is generally available to low-income families to facilitate a divorce.

Negotiation

Negotiation is the process of discussing the issues arising from the divorce with the goal of resolving them. Each party has to be ready to compromise and modify the original positions. It can be done between spouses or between the spouses' lawyers.

Collaboration

In collaborative family law, if the negotiation process breaks down, both spouses must get new lawyers for litigation — the lawyers lose their clients. The result is that there are strong financial incentives for everyone to try to resolve the issues without going to court.

Arbitration

In arbitration, an arbitrator makes a binding decision about the issues. The arbitrator is a neutral third party, usually a senior family law lawyer. This process is much like a private court and has the advantage of being quick and private.

Division of Property

During a marriage, each spouse is entitled to manage their own assets as they wish without the consent of the other spouse. This right is illustrated in Example 4.

Example 4   Mary bought 300 shares of Redberry just before its first fall. John, her husband, thinks Redberry will come back and that she should keep the shares. Mary wants to sell them and does not need John's permission to do so since the shares are in her name.

When a marriage breaks down, certain assets are divided. Division of property when a marriage ends is covered by provincial and territorial legislation. We will examine:

- Property to be divided
- Property exempt from division
- Contracts
- Joint tenancy and tenancy in common
- Equalization payments

Different provinces have different names and definitions for assets that are part of a marriage. These names include *community property, family property, matrimonial property* and *net family assets*. Table 9.3 lists the relevant legislation for each province. There is a separate Family Law Act for support and custodial issues in jurisdictions where there is an Act for the disposition of property.

Table 9.3 Legislation for Division of Property

Alberta	Matrimonial Property Act, R.S.A. 1980 as amended
British Columbia	Family Relations Act, R.S.B.C. 1979 as amended, Part 3 — Matrimonial Property
Manitoba	The Marital Property Act, R.S.M. 1987 as amended
New Brunswick	Marital Property Act, S.N.B. 1980 as amended
Newfoundland	Family Law Act, R.S. Newfoundland 1990 as amended, Part II — Matrimonial Assets
Northwest Territories	Family Law Act, S.N.W.T. 1997
Nunavut	Family Law Act (Nunavut)
Nova Scotia	Matrimonial Property Act, R.S.N.S. 1989
Ontario	Family Law Act, R.S.O. 1990, Part I — Family Property
Prince Edward Island	Family Law Act, S.P.E.I. 1995 as amended, Part I — Family Property
Quebec	Quebec Civil Code, Book Two (The Family), Chapter IV (Effects of Marriage), Section III (Family Patrimony)
Saskatchewan	Matrimonial Property Act, 1997 — Distribution of Matrimonial Property
Yukon	Family Property and Support Act, R.S.Y. 1986 as amended, Part I — Family Assets

Common-Law Couples

While the CRA defines spouse to include opposite- and same-sex partners, provincial intestate and succession laws (the laws that apply when there is no will) generally apply only to married spouses. The definition of common-law is not the same in all jurisdictions. Most require that you have lived together in a conjugal relationship for:

• at least two or three years or
• one year if the couple has a biological or adopted child.

Table 9.4 Property Rights of Common-Law Couples

	Definition of Common-Law	Property Rights
AB	An **Adult Independent Relationship AIR** includes the cohabitation requirement and also that the couple have entered into the AIR agreement. The couple needs to be committed financially but is not necessarily conjugal.	None. Only married couples are entitled to a division of family property under family property legislation
BC	Has met the conjugal relationship criteria	None. Only married couples
MB	Must register the relationship under the *Vital Statistics Act* or have met the conjugal relationship criteria	Same as married couples
NB	Has met the conjugal relationship criteria	None. Only married couples
NL	Has met the conjugal relationship criteria	None. Only married couples
NT/NU	Has met the conjugal relationship criteria	Same as married couples
NS	Must register their partnership as a Domestic Partnership under the *Vital Statistics Act* to receive property rights	Same as married couples
ON	Has met the conjugal relationship criteria	None. Only married couples
PE	Has met the conjugal relationship criteria	None. Only married couples
QC	Must enter into a Civil Union to receive property rights. *De facto* couples are not registered as a Civil Union	Same as married couples. Have no property rights
SK	Has met the conjugal relationship criteria	Same as married couples
YT	Definition varies by statute	None. Only married couples

Source: Christine Van Cauwenberghe, Wealth Planning Strategies for Canadians 2012, pp. 56–75

In the absence of division or property rights, a person in a common-law relationship can file a lawsuit claiming that the other partner, the owner of the property, enjoyed an unjust enrichment and the non-owner should be awarded some amount, likely much less than 50%, for having made a contribution such as sharing mortgage payments or providing child care services in the relationship.

Legislated property rights often means that a common-law partner of either sex is treated like a spouse with regard to succession rights if one spouse dies without a will (covered in Chapter 10). When there are no legislated property rights for common-law partners in either opposite-sex or same-sex relationships, these couples must use:

- Wills
- Cohabitation agreements
- Designated beneficiaries
- Power of attorney
- Joint tenants with rights of survivorship
- Living trust

Each of these items will be discussed in this and later chapters.

Property to Be Divided

In most jurisdictions, the legislation applies only to property acquired *after* the marriage except for the matrimonial home. In addition, it might also apply to the increase in value of assets that were acquired before the marriage as well as to the income earned from these assets. In other jurisdictions, such as Nova Scotia, it applies to all family property including assets that were acquired before the marriage unless the asset is specifically excluded by domestic contract.

Community property or **family assets** to be divided include:

- the **matrimonial home,** whether it was bought before or after the marriage. Matrimonial home, as defined in the Family Law Act of Ontario, for example, is every property in which a person has an interest and was, at the time of separation, ordinarily occupied by the person and the spouse as their family residence. It is subject to special rules in most jurisdictions as outlined in the next section.
- benefits under a **registered pension plan.** The non-member spouse is entitled to a maximum of 50% of the commuted value of the benefits accrued during the relationship. The commuted value can be:
  1. used to purchase a deferred annuity for the non-member spouse
  2. transferred to an RPP for the non-member spouse
  3. transferred to a locked-in RRSP for the non-member spouse
  4. used to provide the non-member spouse with pension income.
- CPP retirement benefits credits, also based on the period of marriage or cohabitation. The division is mandatory (but not automatic). The unadjusted pensionable earnings of both spouses for the time they lived together are split, with each getting half of the other's
- RRSPs and RRIFs that are divided can be transferred directly to the ex-spouse's RRSP or RRIF and are thus not subject to taxation at the time of the transfer
- the cash surrender value of a life insurance policy

Business assets are generally excluded from division but are not excluded in Alberta and Manitoba if the assets were acquired during the marriage. In addition, in some provinces investments in shares are family property to be divided, in most provinces they are not considered to be family assets.

Matrimonial Home

There can be more than one matrimonial home where the couple normally resides. They can, for instance, have a home in the city, and a cottage or a boat, where they normally reside for part of the year. In most jurisdictions, the right to posses the matrimonial home is not based on ownership. In other words, in all provinces except Alberta, B.C. and Quebec, both parties in a marriage can apply to the courts to have the right to remain in the matrimonial home regardless of whose name is on the deed. This means neither party can sell or mortgage the house without the written consent of the other spouse.

Furthermore, the right to live in the matrimonial home is not the same as the right to share in the value of the home, that is, family assets might be shareable regardless of when they were acquired and who acquired it.

- In Newfoundland, Ontario and Saskatchewan, the entire value of the matrimonial home will be shared from the time of the marriage.
- In British Columbia and Nova Scotia, all family assets are divided.
- In Manitoba nd New Brunswick, assets acquired "in contemplation of marriage" can be shareable.
- In addition, some jurisdictions deem assets acquired while living common-law are shareable.

Example 5 illustrates such a situation using the matrimonial home a couple has been sharing since getting married.

Example 5   When Rod and Janine married, Janine owned a house that she had purchased seven years earlier for $80,000. At the time of the marriage the house was worth about $100,000. Fifteen years after they were married, they divorced. The house was worth about $190,000 when they separate. During their marriage, they both worked and shared their living costs. When they divorced, the house was still owned by Janine. However, Rod was entitled to 50% of the $190,000 value of the house at the time of their separation.

Exclusions from Division of Property

Although most of the assets accumulated during the marriage are to be divided, some types of property are exempt from division. These exemptions include:

- Proceeds from life insurance policies received by one spouse named as a designated beneficiary
- Proceeds from gifts and inheritances
- Damages from personal injury awards, such as accident awards
- Business property in which the non-owning spouse did not participate in the business
- Anything that the couple have agreed by domestic contract to be excluded from division
- The value of assets at the time of the marriage except for the matrimonial home.

If the proceeds from any of these exempted properties were invested in the matrimonial home or used to pay down a mortgage on the matrimonial home, they are not exempt from division. In Ontario, the onus of proving an exclusion from property to be divided is on the person claiming the exclusion.

Contracts

There are several types of contracts that can protect one's own assets in the event of the end of a relationship or death. Two types of contracts are made before marriage or cohabitation:

- **Marriage contract:** A contract that stipulates the rights and obligations of both spouses during and at the end of a marriage.
- **Cohabitation agreement**: An agreement between common-law partners that specifies the rights and obligations of each spouse.

One type of contract occurs after the couple has separated:

- **Separation agreement**: An agreement voluntarily agreed to by both spouses spelling out the terms under which they will live apart. It may include division of property and child and spousal support.

Tenants in Common and Joint Tenants

In addition to contracts, both married and common-law partners can use joint ownership to safeguard their assets. There are two types of joint ownership of property: tenants in common and joint tenants. Property under joint ownership can include the matrimonial home, investments in financial assets, the family cottage and other family assets.

Tenancy in Common

In this scenario, each party has an undivided interest in the whole, meaning that each tenant does not own a separate part of the property unless it has been divided. For instance, every unit owner in a condominium owns all the hallways, stairways, and entrance lobbies.

The interest in the property of each owner does not have to be equal. Each owner may deal with their share as they wish without permission of other owners; i.e., each can sell his or her share without the permission of the others. But the most important feature is: There is no **right of survivorship**. Upon the death of one owner, the deceased's portion is transferred according to a will or intestacy rules (if there is no will). While these assets under a tenancy in common can be transferred to a common-law partner by a will, a will is a public document, and a same-sex couple who is not "out" may find this prospect intrusive. In addition, a will can easily be changed — a spouse or partner may assume they will inherit should the other die but there is no guarantee. And in these times of blended families and second marriages, formal or informal, it has happened that, even after 30 years of living together, the deceased has decided to leave their share to children from a former union, much to the surprise and dismay of the surviving partner. Because the assets have to pass through the estate, they are subject to probate fees.

Joint Tenants (or Joint Tenants with Rights of Survivorship)

The tenants own the property equally, and neither can sell their share without the permission of other tenant(s). The most important feature of joint tenancy is the **right of survivorship**, which gives the surviving tenants the automatic right to the deceased's share of the whole property held in joint tenancy. This means that when one joint tenant dies, the others automatically receive the deceased's share — a joint tenant cannot pass their interest to another person through a will. This arrangement makes the asset a non-estate asset and not subject to probate and probate fees.

There are, however, tax implications if the joint tenancy is created through a transfer of title from sole owner to joint tenancy. In this case, there is a deemed disposition for tax purposes (although a principal residence is exempt from capital gains tax). If the joint tenants are not spouses, when one dies there is a deemed disposition, which can trigger a capital gain. This could happen if a mother and daughter together own a cottage that is not the principal residence of either. If the transfer from sole owner to joint tenancy is to a minor child, the child's 50% interest is deemed to have been made at fair market value and, unless it is the principal residence, is subject to tax on the taxable portion of the capital gain.

There are four requirements to forming a joint tenancy:

1. **Unity of possession:** each co-owner must be entitled to possess the entire property.
2. **Unity of interest:** each co-owner must have an equal interest in the property.
3. **Unity of time:** all co-owners must have received their interests in the property at the same time.
4. **Unity of title:** all co-owners receive their interests in the property the same way (from the same document) — for example, by will or by transfer of deed.

Example 6 applies these four requirements.

Example 6   When Janine and Rod married, Janine transferred 50% of the ownership of her house to Rod. They agreed to own the house as joint tenants and met the four requirements. They have:

1. Unity of possession: if one of them dies, the other will automatically receive ownership of the entire property — each has the right to occupy the entire house.
2. Unity of interest: they both own 50% of the entire house.
3. Unity of time: they both received their 50% share of the house at the same time, when title was transferred.
4. Unity of title: both receive their 50% ownership through a transfer of title by Janine.

Equalization Payments

Equalization payments under family law put both spouses in an equal financial position after a divorce or separation. The spouse with the lower **net family property** will receive one-half of the difference in the values of both spouses' net family property. Net family property is the value of RRSPs, pensions, shareholdings, and other items of value minus debts and contingent liabilities, such as the cost of disposing of any assets and tax payable. The list of property exempt from division stated above is also exempt here. The value of net family property on the valuation date, generally the fair market value, minus the value at the time of the marriage is the value used to calculate the equalization payment. The valuation date is the date the spouses separate with no prospect that they will resume cohabitation — the date a divorce is granted, the marriage is declared null, or the day before one of the spouses dies. For example, in Ontario, when a spouse dies, if the net family property of the deceased spouse is greater than the net family property of the surviving spouse, the surviving spouse is entitled to half the difference between them.

The calculations and valuations for equalization payments can be complex and there are many exceptions, so it is important to consult a lawyer who is knowledgeable about family law in the relevant province or territory.

B. POWER OF ATTORNEY

A **power of attorney** authorizes a person (a friend, a relative, a lawyer, an accountant), or a corporation — for example, a trust company — to manage one's affairs when one is not able to do so. This authorized person is called an **attorney**, a **proxy**, or an **agent**. This attorney is not necessarily a lawyer. The person who appoints the attorney is called the **principal** or the **grantor** (or **donor** in some provinces).

There are two types of powers of attorney:

• A **power of attorney for property** covers financial affairs only. One can also have a power of attorney at a bank, which covers only the assets at that bank.
• A **power of attorney for personal care** (or **representation agreement** or **health care directive**) covers personal and health care and appoints someone to have guardianship of a person — that is, to make personal care decisions for you if you are not able to do so. Personal-care decisions are decisions relating to aspects of daily life that maintain your health and well-being. This form of power of attorney is also known as a **living will,** although that is not accurate unless it also dictates your wishes if, for instance, you are in a coma from which you will not recover or it contains a "do not resuscitate" directive, if that is your wish.

A power of attorney can be limited:

• in time — for instance, while you are on a vacation or a business trip
• in scope — for instance, to manage only a certain bank account or to only pay bills.

Someone who has your power of attorney cannot make or sign your will.

A power of attorney takes effect when it is signed. To safeguard your assets, you can leave it with a trusted third party or add a condition as to when it is to come into effect. A **contingent power of attorney** or **springing power of attorney** takes effect only when some specified event happens. This means that one can set up a power of attorney that is not valid until the principal is unable to manage their own affairs due to either physical or mental impairment — that is, they have become incapacitated. An **enduring power of attorney** or **continuing power of attorney** remains in effect even if the principal is no longer legally competent, although the grantor must have been competent when the power of attorney was set up.

A power of attorney normally ends when you die, although it may be terminated in other ways. The principal can revoke the power of attorney in writing at any time as long as they are competent. It is also terminated if the attorney dies.

Anyone can be named your attorney as long as the person has reached the age of majority as defined in each province and is able to understand the responsibilities involved. Most people choose their husband, wife, friend, or other family member. You can also appoint more than one person for one responsibility or for different functions. If you do, you must specify in the power of attorney whether they will act together or individually (e.g., whether both signatures are required for writing cheques?). If only one person is named, there should be an alternate named who can take over if the first is unable or unwilling to fulfill the obligation. Remember the problems that arose when Craig's father was in an accident and his appointed power of attorney had moved away? Craig and Margot, having named each other as their power of attorney, also have their siblings as backups in case they become incapacitated at that same time.

A power of attorney may be more important than a will for single people because it is far more likely that you will be incapacitated than die. If you die without a will and have no children or spouse, your assets will go to your immediate family (a topic to be covered in the next chapter). But if you are young and do not have a power of attorney in place, who will manage your affairs if you are incapacitated for a long period of time?

> Francesca asks about Margot and Craig's daughters; because the couple is still quite young, they perhaps cannot envision that they might be unable to manage their own affairs. Francesca relates the following example about her nephew.

Example 7   Francesca has a beloved nephew, Robbie. As far as Francesca is concerned, Robbie walks on water, although she is only too aware of his shortcomings. Last Thanksgiving, Robbie, age 24, ran a red light on his motorcycle and hit a car. No one in the car was injured, but Robbie was thrown over the car and hit a cement wall. He was taken to hospital in another city that has better medical facilities than the hospital in the small city where he lives. He had an operation to replace his aorta that night. Despite the odds, he survived. It has been six months since the accident. Robbie is in a rehabilitation hospital because he still cannot walk — and may never walk.

Robbie rents an apartment in a small building that his father, Jake, owns. Shortly before the accident, Jake's common-law relationship ended and he moved in with Robbie. When Robbie's VISA bill came in, Jake couldn't pay it out of Robbie's bank account because only Robbie has signing authority. Robbie has a job with disability benefits. Who had the authority to apply for disability income, since Robbie was semi-conscious for several weeks?

Robbie's VISA bill was only $150, and Jake paid it. He asked Alice, Robbie's mother, if it was alright for him to keep the $150 that was in Robbie's wallet to compensate himself.

> "These are not life-threatening decisions in the context of Robbie's medical problems," says Francesca, "but it added unnecessary stress and anxiety at a time when no one needed it." If Robbie had a power of attorney in place, Jake, or whoever was named, could have taken immediate control of Robbie's finance affairs."

In fact, Jake had to apply to the Office of the Public Guardian and Trustee (part of the Department of Justice, Ministry of the Attorney General in most provinces and territories) to obtain Robbie's power of attorney.

Your attorney has significant power, so be sure to choose somebody you trust. The power of attorney for property requires decisions that are mostly financial matters — choose someone who is comfortable with that. This is not a time to choose someone for sentimental reasons. Make sure that the named attorneys know what you want and what you expect from them. Most important: Make sure the person is willing to be your attorney.

Powers of attorney are entitled to fees, although close family members may not ask for compensation. If you choose a trust company as your attorney, ask the trust company how much it will charge you. You can also name a Public Guardian and Trustee (a government official) in your province or territory; there are also fees for their services.

Samples of Power of Attorney

A power of attorney from a kit or pre-printed form may be adequate if you are single and have no financial dependants. However, if you have dependent children, it is important that provisions be made for them should you and your spouse both become incapacitated, or if one of you dies and the other is incapacitated, or if there is no spouse. In these instances, a power of attorney must be drawn up by a lawyer to ensure that it covers all eventualities. Many people keep the name of the executor of their will and the guardian for their children up-to-date but forget the power of attorney.

The samples below of the two types of power of attorney are for Ontario. You may prefer to use a sample from your own province or territory. Forms can be obtained from your Member of Provincial Parliament (MPP) and on the website for provinces and territories. You can also provide additional information, such as:

- a list of documents and items to make known
- the location of these documents and items
- a list of family advisors, including your spiritual advisor, doctor, lawyer, insurance agent, power of attorney, bank, trustee, and employer
- funeral arrangements desired and perhaps in place and paid for

Ontario Powers of Attorney

In Ontario, power of attorney laws are contained in the *Substitute Decisions Act, 1992*. Under this Act, the provincial government is a substitute decision-maker of the last resort only for people who have no one else, or who have not designated anyone else, to make decisions on their behalf. If there is no power of attorney, a family member or friend may apply to be appointed as guardian.

The Office of the Public Guardian and Trustee in the Ontario Ministry of the Attorney General produces a booklet with instructions for setting up the two kinds of power of attorney shown below.

The forms and directions reproduced are taken from the kit provided by the Ontario Ministry of the Attorney General. They are used here to illustrate the kinds of decisions that need to be made and are not intended to replace either the full kit for a relatively straightforward power of attorney for property or the services of a lawyer for more complex needs. The forms have additional instructions that are part of the kit, included for clarification.

Continuing Power of Attorney for Property (Ontario)

1. I, _____ revoke any previous continuing power of attorney

    (Print or type your full name here.)

    for property made by me and **APPOINT**:_____

    _____ to be my attorney(s) for property.

    (Print or type the name of the person or persons you appoint here.)

    > You must be 18 years of age or more and mentally capable of giving a continuing power of attorney for property. This means that you:
    > * Know what property you have and its approximate value
    > * Are aware of your obligations to those people who depend on you financially
    > * Know what authority your attorney will have
    > * Know that your attorney must account for all the decisions he or she makes about your property
    > * Know that, if you are capable, you may cancel your power of attorney
    > * Understand that unless your attorney manages your property prudently, its value may decline
    > * Understand that there is always the possibility that your attorney could misuse the authority
    >
    > Many trust companies are prepared to act as attorney and charge a fee for this service.

2. If you have named more than one attorney and you want them to have the authority to act separately, insert the words "jointly and severally" here:_____

    (This space may be left blank.)

    > You can name more than one person or one person and a substitute or backup if your first choice resigns, gets sick, or dies. If you appoint more than one attorney, the law requires them to make decision together unless you specifically authorize them to act separately by putting it in writing on this form. If one is sick or away, the other is not free to act. On the other hand, each can serve as a backup for the other. You should make clear how disagreements get resolved or else they may have to go to court and have the judge decide. If you do not write "jointly and severally," your attorneys will have to make your financial decisions <u>together</u> at <u>all</u> times.

3. If the person(s) I have appointed, or any one of them, cannot or will not be my attorney because of refusal, resignation, death, mental incapacity, or removal by the Court, I SUBSTITUTE: *(This space may be left blank.)*

_____

to act as my attorney for property with the same authority as the person he or she is replacing.

> Again, if you appoint more than one substitute attorney, they would have to make decision together unless you indicate otherwise by writing "jointly and severally" after their names.

4. I AUTHORIZE my attorney(s) for property to do on my behalf anything in respect of property that I could do if capable of managing property, except make a will, subject to the law and to any conditions or restrictions contained in this document. I confirm that he or she may do so even if I am mentally incapable.

> If you want to limit the powers of your attorney(s), you can do so in part 5. This part makes it clear that you want your attorney to be able to act if you become mentally incapable of making financial decisions. See also part 6.

5. CONDITIONS AND RESTRICTIONS
Attach, sign, and date additional pages if required. *(This part may be left blank.)*

_____

6. DATE OF EFFECTIVENESS
Unless otherwise stated in this document, this continuing power of attorney will come into effect on the date it is signed and witnessed.

> You can leave this document in a safe place or with a trusted third person, such as a lawyer or an accountant with written instructions as to when it may be released to the person you have appointed.
> Alternatively, in part 5, you can state that the document comes into effect on a certain date or when something specific happens. If you are not very specific about this, your attorney may have to pay an assessor to judge your mental capacity.

7. COMPENSATION
Unless otherwise stated in this document, I authorize my attorney(s) to take annual compensation from my property in accordance with the fee scale prescribed by regulation for the compensation of attorneys for property made pursuant to Section 90 of the *Substitute Decisions Act, 1992.*

> The rates permitted to guardians and attorneys of property are 2.5% on monies received and paid out and 2/5 of 1% on the average annual value of the assets.

8. **SIGNATURE:** _____ DATE:_____
   (Sign your name in the presence of two witnesses.)
   ADDRESS: _____
   (Insert your full current address here.)
   _____

9. **WITNESS SIGNATURE:**
   [Note: The following people cannot be witnesses: the attorney or his or her spouse or partner; the spouse, partner, or child of the person making the document, or someone that the person treats as his or her child; a person whose property is under guardianship or who has a guardian of the person; a person under the age of 18.]

Witness #1: *Signature:* _____ *Print Name:*_____

Address: _____

_____ *Date:* _____

Witness #2: *Signature:* _____ *Print Name:* _____

Address: _____

_____ *Date:* _____

Additional guidelines are provided regarding:
- What to do if the person making this document cannot read
- What to do with this form after it is signed
- How to revoke this Power of Attorney.

Power of Attorney for Personal Care (Ontario)

Additional instructions are provided similar to those outlined in the Power of Attorney for Property.

1. I, _____ revoke any previous power of attorney for personal
   (Print or type your full name here.)
   care made by me and **APPOINT:** _____
   (Print or type the name of the person or persons you appoint here.)

   _____

   to be my attorney(s) for personal care in accordance with the *Substitute Decisions Act, 1992.*

   [**Note:** A person who provides health care, residential, social, training, or support services to the person giving this power of attorney for compensation may not act as his or her attorney unless that person is also his or her spouse, partner, or relative.]

2. If you have named more than one attorney and you want them to have the authority to act separately, insert the words "jointly and severally" here:

_____

(This space may be left blank.)

3. If the person(s) I have appointed, or any one of them, cannot or will not be my attorney because of refusal, resignation, death, mental incapacity, or removal by the Court, **I SUBSTITUTE:**

_____

(This space may be left blank)

to act as my attorney for personal care in the same manner and subject to the same authority as the person he or she is replacing.

4. I give my attorney(s) the **AUTHORITY** to make any personal care decision for me that I am mentally incapable of making for myself, including the giving or refusing of consent to any matter to which the *Health Care Consent Act, 1996* applies, subject to the *Substitute Decisions Act, 1992* and any instructions, conditions, or restrictions contained in this form.

5. INSTRUCTIONS, CONDITIONS and RESTRICTIONS
   Attach, sign, and date additional pages if required. *(This part may be left blank.)*

_____

_____

_____

6. **SIGNATURE:** _____ **DATE:** _____
   (Sign your name in the presence of two witnesses.)

   ADDRESS: _____
   (Insert your current address here.)

7. **WITNESS SIGNATURES**

   [Note: The following people cannot be witnesses: the attorney or his or her spouse or partner; the spouse, partner, or child of the person making the document, or someone that the person treats as his or her child; a person whose property is under guardianship or who has a guardian of the person; a person under the age of 18.]

Witness #1: *Signature:* _____ *Print Name:* _____

Address: _____

_____ *Date:* _____

Witness #2: *Signature:* _____ *Print Name:* _____

Address: _____

_____ *Date:* _____

SUMMARY

The federal Divorce Act sets out child support obligations in the event of a divorce or breakdown of a common-law relationship when children are involved. These guidelines are specific as to the amount to be paid by province or territory and are dependent on the income of the parents and the type of custody. Spousal support is also covered by the Divorce Act, and the Income Tax Act governs taxation of these support payments. The division of family assets is covered by provincial legislation. Some property is exempt from division, and property can be owned jointly to facilitate the transfer of ownership.

Powers of attorney for property and for personal care are covered by provincial legislation. They stipulate who controls your financial affairs if you are unable to do so and who will make decisions about your health care if you are incapacitated.

MARGOT AND CRAIG

"Well," says Craig, "I certainly wish I had known all this before dad had his accident. I would have made sure that he had alternates in place."

Craig continues: "I don't wish Steve any harm and it is rather reassuring to know that if dad left him out completely, Steve could go to court and probably get the same financial support he had before my father died. But at least he can't get it all. There should be something for the girls after all. Now all I have to do is talk to dad."

SOURCES

- Federal Child Support Guidelines, Department of Justice, Canada, Child Support, Simplified Tables: <www.canada.justice.gc.ca>
- Ontario Ministry of the Attorney General, Office of The Public Guardian and Trustee, Powers of Attorney, (Toronto: Queen's Printer for Ontario, 1996). ISSN 0-7778-2574-0.
- Van Cauwenberghe, Christine. *Wealth Planning Strategies for Canadians*, Carswell, 2012

KEY TERMS

Agent	Matrimonial property
Alternative dispute resolution	Mediation
Arbitration	Negotiation
Ascendants	Net family assets
Attorney	Parental support
Child support	Power of attorney
Child Support Guidelines	Power of attorney for personal care
Cohabitation agreement	Power of attorney for property
Collaboration	Principal
Collateral relatives	Provincial Courts of Competent Jurisdiction
Community property	Proxy
Contingent power of attorney	Religious annulment
Continuing power of attorney	Right of survivorship

Custody: shared, sole, split

Descendants

Divorce Act

Enduring power of attorney

Equalization payments

Family Law

Family property

Grantor

Health care directive

Joint tenants

Living will

Marriage contract

Marriage of convenience

Matrimonial home

Separation agreement

Shared custody

Sole custody

Split custody

Spousal support

Springing power of attorney

Support payments

Tenants in common

Unity of interest

Unity of possession

Unity of time

Unity of title

Unjust enrichment

QUESTIONS

Family Law

1. Indicate whether each of the following is governed by federal or provincial legislation.
    (a) A woman cannot marry her brother.
    (b) The minimum age a person can get married.
    (c) Common-law partners receive the same tax treatment.
    (d) Children born from a voided marriage have the same rights as children from valid marriages.
    (e) A couple can be separated although living in the same dwelling.
    (f) The definition of marriage breakdown is contained in what Act?
    (g) Spousal support is covered.
    (h) Child support is covered.
    (i) Parental support is covered.
    (j) Division of property is covered.

2. John's son is 25 years old and disabled. Is John required to support his son?

3. What are the names of the following types of custody?
    (a) Anne lives with her father, and Jeff lives with his mother.
    (b) Anne and Jeff spend every Wednesday night and every other weekend with their mother. Their father has what kind of custody?
    (c) Anne and Jeff spend one week with their mother and one week with their father, who both live in the same block.

4. Andrea has sole custody of her son, Max. If Max wants to play hockey, can his father be required to help pay for this activity?

5. Debbie and Mark divorced last year after 35 years of marriage. Debbie ran the household and raised their four children — the last one moved out only two years ago. Debbie has not worked outside of the home for money since before their marriage. Can Debbie reasonably expect to receive any spousal support from Mark?

6. Diane and Jason divorced last year after 35 years of marriage. They both worked — Diane as an economist, Jason as an accountant. They both contributed to the domestic help they

needed to run their household. Can Diane reasonably expect to receive any spousal support from Jason?

7. When Barry and Joanne had their two children, they agreed that Barry would stay home with the children for a few years. When the youngest was six, Barry and Joanne divorced, and agreed that Barry would have custody of the children, as Joanne's job required her to travel a great deal. Joanne makes $120,000 a year, while Barry makes $23,000 teaching part-time. Joanne agreed to pay Barry $1,800 a month in spousal support, and $1,500 a month in child support. Assuming they have no other tax deductions, what is their taxable income in each of the following circumstances?

   (a) They write their own agreement and state only that Joanne will pay $3,300 a month.
   (b) The courts award Barry $1,800 a month in spousal support and $1,500 in child support.
   (d) They write their own agreement that Joanne will pay Barry $1,800 a month in spousal support and $1,500 in child support.
   (e) Joanne is paying $1,800 a month in spousal support and $1,500 in child support as per their written agreement in part c. Barry runs into financial difficulties, and Joanne gives him an extra $5,000.
   (e) The court order states that Joanne pays $1,800 a month in spousal support and $1,500 in child support. For the last six months of the current year, she paid a total of $2,800 a month.
   (f) Joanne is paying $1,800 a month in spousal support and $1,500 in child support. However, she got behind on several months payments, and Barry had to go to court to get her to pay. Joanne paid all that was due, but Barry incurred legal expenses of $3,500.
   (g) Joanne pays $1,500 in child support, but paid Barry a $200,000 lump-sum instead of paying monthly support payments.

   Answer:

	Barry	Joanne
(a)	23,000	120,000
(b)	44,600	98,400
(c)	44,600	98,400
(d)	44,600	98,400
(e)	33,800	109,200
(f)	41,100	98,400
(g)	23,000	120,000

8. Does it ever happen that an adult child must support his or her:
   (a) Parents?
   (b) Sisters and brothers?

9. While the *Income Tax Act* makes provision for common-law partners, provincial intestate and succession laws do not. In each of the following, what would be appropriate alternative methods to protect the property rights of opposite and same-sex partners?
   (a) Justin and Steve live together as a family in a house that Justin owned before they got together. They have been living together for 23 years.
   (b) Steve has a life insurance policy that now has his estate as the beneficiary.
   (c) Justin has developed multiple sclerosis and is slowly losing his ability to move. He can live a long time, and can well afford to pay for daily help to come in to help with his health care. Justin is concerned about what will happen to his investments when he can

no longer sign a document or speak clearly — he could live for several years in this condition.

10. Marty was ordered by the court to pay Ellen $56,000 of the $135,000 in his RRSP. Neither Marty nor Ellen has any unused RRSP contribution room. What are the tax consequences of this direct transfer from Marty's RRSP to Ellen's RRSP?

11. Which of the following are properties that are exempt from division in a divorce? If they must divide the asset, what is the value to be divided?
    (a) Ellen's house was worth $35,000 when she and Marty got married and he moved in. When they divorced, the house was worth $255,000.
    (b) Marty was in a car accident two years ago. Three months before they separated, he received a settlement of $95,000.
    (c) Ellen's grandfather died last year, leaving her $20,000.
    (d) Ellen's grandmother died two years ago, leaving her $15,000. She used the money to upgrade the kitchen.
    (e) Marty was the beneficiary on one of his father's life insurance policies. He received $68,000.

12. What is the difference between a marriage contract and a cohabitation agreement?

13. Steve and Tom are friends who own a house together. Tom died without a will. What happens to the ownership of the house:
    (a) If they own it as tenants in common?
    (b) If they own it as joint tenants with rights of survivorship?

14. What are the four criteria Steve and Tom must have met to own the house as joint tenants?

Power of Attorney

15. What is the name of the person who appoints a power of attorney?

16. Does the attorney have to be a lawyer?

17. What are two other names for the attorney?

18. What are the two kinds of power of attorney, and what do they cover?

19. What is another name for a power of attorney for personal care?

20. What are the names of a power of attorney that does not become effective until the principal becomes incapacitated?

21. If a person signs a power of attorney for property, can a friend who is the attorney use it immediately to take all the funds out of the grantor's bank account?

22. What can be done to prevent the person who has a power of attorney from taking over the financial affairs of the principal immediately?

23. Why would someone appoint more than one person to have power of attorney?

24. Is a person who has the power of attorney entitled to be paid?

10

Disposing of Estate Assets

Learning Objectives

A.   Understand the consequences of dying without a will.

B.   Know the types of wills and the general format and content of a will.

C.   Recognize the scope and limitations of the executor's duties.

D.   Identify ways of avoiding and reducing probate fees.

E.   Know the ways of buying out a deceased partner's or shareholder's portion of a business.

Margot and Craig made out wills when their first child was born and updated them with the birth of each of their other two daughters. However, 15 years ago, Margot and Craig were not sure if their parents had wills — and they were very reluctant to ask. Somehow this seemed just too personal to ask about. Francesca tells them that many people feel this way — they will talk about all kinds of personal matters but cannot bring themselves to talk about money and death with their family.

Since Gloria, Margot's mother, died without a will, they have some idea of the process of an intestate death. But there are many things they still don't know. Margot wants to know what a will could do for her brother, Bob, who is gay and living in a permanent relationship with Max. They have a house together and, while Margot does not want to pretend to be a financial planner, she would like to know enough to advise Bob on what the two men should be doing to protect their assets when one of them dies.

In addition, Margot's friend, Liz, was telling her about a real mess that was created when one of Liz's friends, Marge, predeceased her mother. When the mother died, Marge's children did not inherit Marge's share of her mother's estate, and Margot wonders if this is always how it happens. Francesca assures her that this is not how it has to happen, which is why wills need to be regularly updated to reflect changes in circumstances. In addition, while Francesca can tell Margot and Craig about wills, it is important to have a lawyer, who is an expert, draw up the will to make sure the estate is divided as one would wish if, for instance, one child should predecease the parents. Many people do not make a provision for this scenario, assuming the parents will die first.

INTRODUCTION

There are several ways to distribute one's assets after one's death. They include:

- distributing according to the provincial intestate laws
- distributing through a will
- naming beneficiaries on life insurance policies, pension plans, RRSPs, and RRIFs. When there is a named beneficiary, the assets can pass directly to the beneficiary without going through the estate, which means these assets are not subject to probate fees
- giving them away before death (Chapter 12)
- distributing through joint ownership of property (Chapter 9)
- setting up trusts (Chapter 12)

A. DYING WITHOUT A WILL — DYING INTESTATE

Dying without a will is called **dying intestate**. The provinces and territories have laws that dictate what happens to a person's assets if that person dies without a will. Spouses to whom one is legally married at the time of death will inherit, but in many jurisdictions common-law partners will receive nothing if there is no will. If divorced, the former spouse usually does not inherit. If separated, the former spouse may inherit, depending on the provincial legislation. In Ontario, for instance, they do inherit, even if there is a separation agreement.

Provincial legislation requires that there be an executor. If there is no will, no executor has been appointed. A provincial court will appoint an **administrator** (or **personal representative**) to administer the estate when:

- there is no will, or
- there is a will but the executor has died, or
- the executor is not willing or able to perform this function.

If no family member applies to act as administrator, the courts appoint a **Public Trustee/Official Administrator**, who will distribute the assets according to the formulas that follow.

All assets, whether distributed with or without a will, that go through the estate are subject to probate fees — a fee charged by each province or territory for validating the will — before being distributed to the beneficiaries. The probate process takes time and delays the distribution of assets, which could otherwise go directly to the beneficiaries. Some assets, such as life insurance policies, pension plans, RRSPs and RRIFs, can avoid probate fees if they are left directly to named beneficiaries. Other assets will usually be subject to probate fees; they are discussed later in this chapter.

Intestate Rules

If a person dies intestate, their assets are distributed in accordance with the **intestate rules** of their province or territory, which dictate who the beneficiaries are and how much each receives. Intestate rules apply to the residue of the estate after taxes, bills, fees, and expenses have been paid. If you die intestate and are survived by:

- a spouse and no relatives, everything goes to the spouse
- a spouse and relatives, everything goes to the spouse except in Quebec where:
  - two-thirds goes to the spouse
  - one-third is divided among parents or brothers and sisters
- a child or children but no spouse, everything goes to the child or children **per stirpes** (defined below)

- no spouse or children, everything goes to the next of kin usually in the following order:
  - parents
  - brothers and sisters per stirpes if no parents
  - nieces and nephews if no parents, brothers and sisters
  - other relatives according to their closeness in Table 10.2, "Table of Consanguinity"
  - the government if no surviving relatives

If there is a surviving spouse and a child or children, the spouse receives an amount first, which is called the **preferential share**. The remaining amount, which is called the **distributive share**, is divided according to the formula in Table 10.1, "Intestate Rules". The preferential share is the amount, if any, listed on the first line for each province or territory as "Spouse: 1st $xx,xxx" in the table.

If a child predeceases a parent, what happens to the deceased's shares if there is no will or up-to-date will to specify this? Will the deceased's share go to the children of the deceased or will the other beneficiaries split the deceased's share? There are two possibilities:

1. **Per stirpes:** "For each person descended from a family branch". The children of a deceased beneficiary share equally the deceased beneficiary's portion. It is more common than per capita — that is, in most provinces and territories, if there is no will, the children of a deceased child will share equally the deceased child's share.
2. **Per capita:** "Divided equally among all people". Each beneficiary or child who is still alive receives the same amount; the children of a deceased child receive nothing.

Example 1 shows the difference between distributing one's estate per stirpes and per capita.

Example 1   Laura died intestate with an estate of $450,000 after taxes. Laura is survived by her:

- husband Jim
- daughter Karen, who has one child.

Laura was predeceased by her:
- daughter Sarah, who had three children
- son Tom, who had two children

A **per stirpes** estate in Nova Scotia will be divided up as follows:

1. Jim, her husband, gets the first $50,000 as preferential share
2. The remaining distributive share, $400,000, is divided:
    - Jim gets one-third of the $400,000 ($133,333)
    - The children or their heirs share the remaining distributive share which is $266,667:
      - Karen gets one-third, or $88,889
      - Sarah's three children divide up Sarah's share and get $29,630 each
      - Tom's two children divide up Tom's shares and get $44,444 each

A **per capita** estate in Nova Scotia will be divided up as follows:

1. Jim, her husband, gets the first $50,000 as preferential share
2. The remaining distributive share, $400,000, is divided:
    - Jim gets one-third of the $400,000 ($133,333)
    - The surviving children share the remaining distributive share which is $266,667:
      - Karen gets $266,667 since she is the only surviving child.

- Sarah's three children get nothing.
- Tom's two children get nothing.

Per stirpes and per capita rules also apply when there is a will that is not updated when a child dies before a parent. Example 2 illustrates a negative effect of not making it clear in a will how to distribute the inheritance of a deceased child who dies after the will was written but before the parent dies.

Example 2   **Yvonne** died suddenly at the age of 48. She was survived by her husband, **Mike**, and their daughter and son. A few months later, Yvonne's mother, a widow, died. She was survived by a son, **Stan**, and daughter **Maggie**. As it turned out, Yvonne's mother left a large estate consisting of investments in rental property, shares, and a cottage. The six grandchildren, Yvonne's two children, Stan's three children, and Maggie's child, were each left $50,000 in the will. The balance of the estate is to be split between the children.

Stan, Yvonne's brother, is the executor and insists that the real property is worth $500,000. Mike, Yvonne's husband, believes the two properties are worth much more than $500,000. He is sure the rental property is worth something like $800,000, while the cottage might be worth $200,000. The investments are probably another $300,000. While Mike did not expect to inherit anything himself, he is upset that Stan is insisting that Mike's children will not inherit Yvonne's share of the inheritance, which, Mike estimates, is worth over $1 million in total. Mike is convinced that his mother-in-law would have wanted Yvonne's share to go to his and Yvonne's children, and he has made an appointment with a lawyer because he wants to contest the will on behalf of his children. In addition, he does not trust the accuracy of the evaluations Stan is putting forward.

If the estate is divided per stirpes, Yvonne's two children will inherit her one-third share. If the estate is divided per capita, Yvonne's brother and sister will share the estate equally and Yvonne's children will receive nothing except the $50,000 each that was bequeathed to them in the will.

Table 10.1 shows the intestate rules for all the provinces and territories. Example 3 shows the distribution of an estate of someone who died intestate leaving a surviving spouse, two surviving children, one deceased child and six grandchildren. The amount each receives from the estate, according to each province, is provided in the right-hand column of Table 10.1.

Example 3   The estate is $500,000 in proceeds after expenses from a life insurance policy that had the estate named as the beneficiary and a matrimonial home, owned jointly by the deceased and the surviving spouse. Because the home is owned jointly, the surviving spouse now owns it. How much of the $500,000 insurance proceeds do each of the heirs inherit? There is a surviving spouse with three adult children from this marriage, one of the whom has died. All three adult children have two children. Only the two children from the deceased child will inherit per stirpes. How much does each heir inherit?

In Table 10.1, "Spouse" indicates how much the surviving spouse will receive, "Children" indicates how much *each* of the surviving children will receive, and "Grandchildren" refers to how much *each* of the grandchildren (the children of the deceased child) will receive.

Table 10.1 Intestate Rules

	Spouse and 1 child	Spouse and children		$500,000
AB	Spouse: 1st $40,000 Rest split equally*	Spouse: 1st $40,000 Rest: 1/3 to spouse, 2/3 to children	Spouse Children Grandchildren	193,334 102,222 51,111
BC	Spouse: 1st $65,000 + household furniture and a life interest in the family home. Rest split equally*	Spouse: $65,000 + household Rest: 1/3 to spouse, 2/3 to children	Spouse Children Grandchildren	210,000 96,667 48,333
MB	Spouse gets 100% if all of the children are the children of the surviving spouse. If some of the children are not the children of the surviving spouse: Spouse: greater of $50,000 or 1/2 of estate. Rest: 1/2 to spouse, 1/2 to children		Spouse Children Grandchildren	500,000 0 0
NB	Spouse: marital property Rest split equally	Spouse: marital property Rest: 1/3 to spouse, 2/3 to children	Spouse Children Grandchildren	166,666 111,111 55,556
NL	Split equally	1/3 to spouse 2/3 to children	Spouse Children Grandchildren	166,666 111,111 55,556
NT	Spouse: 1st $50,000 Rest: split equally	Spouse: 1st $50,000 Rest: 1/3 to spouse, 2/3 to children	Spouse Children Grandchildren	200,000 100,000 50,000
NS	Spouse: 1st $50,000 Rest split equally	Spouse: 1st $50,000 Rest: 1/3 to spouse, 2/3 to children	Spouse Children Grandchildren	200,000 100,000 50,000
NU	Spouse: 1st $50,000 Rest: split equally	Spouse: 1st $50,000 Rest: 1/3 to spouse, 2/3 to children	Spouse Children Grandchildren	200,000 100,000 50,000
ON	Spouse: 1st $200,000 Rest: split equally	Spouse: 1st $200,000 Rest: 1/3 to spouse, 2/3 to children	Spouse Children Grandchildren	300,000 66,667 33,333
PE	Split equally	1/3 to spouse 2/3 to children	Spouse Children Grandchildren	166,666 111,111 55,556
QC	1/3 to spouse 2/3 to child	1/3 to spouse 2/3 to children	Spouse Children Grandchildren	166,666 111,111 55,556
SK	Spouse: 1st $100,000 Rest: split equally	Spouse: 1st $100,000 Rest: 1/3 to spouse, 2/3 to children	Spouse Children Grandchildren	233,334 88,889 44,444
YT	Spouse: 1st $75,000 Rest: split equally	Spouse: 1st $75,000 Rest: 1/3 to spouse, 2/3 to children	Spouse Children Grandchildren	216,667 94,444 47,222

*In this table, "split equally" means the spouse and child will each receive 50% of the distributive share per stirpes.

Generally, children of a deceased child will inherit per stirpes, as in the above example.

Dying Intestate with No Close Relatives

In this case, provincial legislation dictates who can inherit. The *Ontario Succession Law Reform Act*, R.S.O. 1990, c.S.26, states "degrees of kindred shall be computed by counting upward from the deceased to the nearest common ancestor and then downward to the relative, and the kindred of the half-blood shall inherit equally with those of the whole-blood in the same degree".

Consanguinity is the relationship of individuals by blood. The following Table of Consanguinity shows the relationship of ascendants and descendants. The **direct line is shown in bold** and the numbers indicate the closeness of the relationship. This table is used to distribute intestate assets if there is no next of kin after nieces and nephews.

Descendants are one's biological and adopted children (also called *issue*), grandchildren, and great-grandchildren. They are the first to inherit according to intestate rules. **Ascendants** are one's direct parents, grandparents, etc. They will inherit if a person dies intestate without descendants. **Collateral** relatives include brothers and sisters and their children. They may inherit if a person dies without a will and without surviving ascendants and descendants.

The direct line are relatives one is not allowed to marry under federal legislation. Some provinces prohibit the marriage of collateral relatives. The names in Table 10.2 refer to the names used in Example 4.

Table 10.2 Table of Consanguinity

				4. Great-Great Grandparents	
			3. Great-Grand mothers/fathers	5. Great-grand aunt/uncle	
		2. Grandmother /father	4. Great aunt/uncle *(Great-uncle Alfred)*	6. 1st cousins twice removed	
	1. Mother/Father	3. Aunt/Uncle	5. 1st cousins once removed *(Mary)*	7. 2nd cousins once removed	
YOU *(Anne)*	2. Sisters/Brothers	4. First cousins *(Kay)*	6. 2nd cousins *(Jacob)*	8. 3rd cousins	
1. Children	3. Nieces/Nephews	5. 1st cousins once removed *(Judy)*	7. 2nd cousin once removed	9. 3rd cousin once removed	
2. Grandchildren	4. Grand-nieces/ nephews	6. 1st cousins twice removed	8. 2nd cousin twice removed	10. 3rd cousin twice removed	

Note: There are several other versions of this table. The relationships remain the same but the names of the relationships are different.

Example 4 illustrates the relatedness of people using the Table of Consanguinity.

Example 4   Anne has a Great-uncle Alfred. Alfred's daughter, Mary, is Anne's first cousin once removed. Alfred's grandson, Jacob, is Anne's second cousin.

Anne also has a first cousin, Kay. Kay's daughter, Judy, is therefore Anne's first cousin once removed.

Example 5 illustrates how these relationships are used to divide up an estate.

Example 5   Marshall died intestate leaving no spouse, no parents, and no children who would be his closest blood or adopted relatives, no siblings, no grandchildren, or grandparents, who all share the second degree of consanguinity. He did have relatives who were distantly related. He left an estate of $800,000 after taxes and probate fees. His nearest relatives can inherit. If he has nieces and nephews or aunts and uncles, they could inherit as they share the same degree of consanguinity.

Common-law Spouses

Although the rights of common-law spouses, opposite-sex and same-sex, have advanced in recent years, in many provinces and territories, they do *not* have automatic rights to property under intestate laws. However, in some jurisdictions, they do have property rights as was outlined in Table 9.4, "Property Rights of Common-Law Couples". If they or their children were financially dependent on the deceased, they might have rights to the matrimonial home or financial support, depending on their province of residence.

Example 6 demonstrates the distribution of an estate when the will had not been updated to reflect a new common-law relationship.

Example 6   John and Mark started living together in 2008 as same-sex spouses. In 2012, Mark, as his sister's named guardian of her daughter, was declared guardian of Lucia, age seven, when Mark's sister was killed in a car accident. John had been married to Stella many years before he met Mark. At the time that John made out his will, he was undecided whether he should leave his assets to Stella or to his estate. After consulting with a lawyer, he left his assets to Stella, assuming she would look after their son, James.

When James was four, John and Stella separated. Three years later, John started a same-sex relationship with Mark, which continued until John's untimely death of an unexpected heart attack in 2014. John had not made a new will.

When John and Stella separated, John signed over his share of the matrimonial home. He had $75,000 in investments, which he kept. He and Mark bought a home in 2010. Mark was not "good with money", so could contribute only some very fine paintings and furniture to their new home. John made the entire down payment, although they owned the home as joint tenants.

The home purchase with Mark was a very good investment for John. At the time of his death, the house was worth $400,000, although they had paid only $250,000 for it four years earlier. John also had $100,000 in investments when he died. He had a life insurance policy that he had taken out taken out in the early years of his marriage to Stella, worth $500,000. Again, John forgot that he had made Stella the beneficiary on the insurance policy — he had been vacillating between making Stella or his estate the beneficiary.

After Lucia came to live with them, Mark quit his rather low-paying job to stay home and look after the household and Lucia. To what is Mark entitled when John died?

- They owned the house jointly, so Mark gets the house (and the mortgage).
- Mark does not have automatic rights to the investments, although, since he and Lucia were financially dependent on John, he can go to court and probably get title to the investments.
- Mark is not entitled to the insurance policy. John had not made out a subsequent will, so Stella, the named beneficiary, is entitled to the proceeds from the life insurance policy. Will Stella see the light and "give" Mark some of the proceeds? Certainly she is not obligated to do so. She may decide that it is only fair that she and Mark share the life insurance proceeds since both she and Mark have a young child to support. But she is not

obligated to share anything — she is the named beneficiary. Stella will no longer receive support payments from John. Might she feel some bitterness from the divorce, which could prevent her from "doing the right thing"? Quite possibly. In that case, Mark will receive nothing from the insurance.

B. WILLS

Wills make it possible for the deceased to decide:

• who will administer the estate
• who the beneficiaries will be and how much each receives, and when
• who will manage any assets that may remain in the estate for, perhaps, years

The will is the mechanism for giving clear title to heirs. It can facilitate tax planning, and business succession, and can provide for minor children and dependent spouses. Intestacy laws can divide up an estate but cannot ensure that a dependent spouse has enough of the estate to pay the bills since the assets of children who inherit through these laws are automatically put into a trust until the children reach the age of majority. Wills can ensure that grandchildren inherit a deceased child's portion if that was the intention or assumption of the deceased.

By definition, all estate assets go into a testamentary trust at death and remain there until the estate is distributed. Testamentary trusts receive their instructions from the wording in the will. Without a will, the deceased does not control who manages that trust.

Property Covered by a Will

Wills deal with property the deceased owned at the time of death, but not:

• property held in joint tenancy since this property is transferred automatically to the other joint tenant(s). Property held as tenants in common is covered by wills
• assets with named beneficiaries, such as life insurance policies, pension plans, RRSPs, and RRIFs. A will overrides a named beneficiary at a financial institution for an RRSP, RRIF, pension plan, or a life insurance policy, if the will was written later
• business assets governed by a shareholders' agreement or buy-sell agreement
• income from a trust where the trust agreement says the income stops on your death
• assets covered in a written marriage contract or a cohabitation agreement

The public and media have access to the details of any will. Margot's brother, Bob, may want to keep the details of his private life private since homosexuality still carries a stigma in many communities. Bob and his partner may prefer to use other methods to pass on their assets to the survivor when one of them dies. These other methods include designating beneficiaries on RRSPs, RRIFs, pension plans, and insurance policies, as well as owning their family assets and perhaps financial investments as joint tenants.

Alternate beneficiaries should also be named in case the named beneficiary has died. A newer will automatically overrides an older will. Assets on which there is a named beneficiary are not subject to probate fees because the assets never become part of the estate. Only the estate is subject to probate fees. In addition, since these assets can go directly to the beneficiary without going through the estate, the beneficiaries can receive the assets more quickly. If the beneficiary of an RRSP or RRIF is not the spouse, there is no **spousal rollover** (the assets pass to the spouse on a tax-deferred basis), and the deceased must pay the taxes owed on the final tax return. If there are not enough assets to pay the taxes, the beneficiary will have to pay the tax before the CRA will issue a tax-clearance certificate, which allows the executor to distribute the estate.

In all jurisdictions except Quebec, marriage automatically revokes all prior wills but entering into a common-law relationship generally does not revoke all prior wills (unless the union is registered as outlined in Chapter 9). In British Columbia, Nova Scotia, Ontario, Prince Edward Island, Quebec and Saskatchewan, divorce automatically revokes a prior will, but separation does not automatically revoke a will. At separation, a new will is needed. In addition, a spouse cannot be written out of a will unless there is a marriage contract stating otherwise. Everyone else except the surviving spouse and financially dependent children can be written out of a will. Example 7 shows how an estranged adult child can be written out of a will.

Example 7   Joseph has not seen his eldest daughter, Camille, for 15 years. At the last family get-together, Joseph and Camille had a big argument. Joseph thought it was just another of their disagreements, but Camille apparently felt differently. At first she refused to return his phone calls. The last he heard, she had moved to the other side of the country.

Now Joseph, a widower, has cancer. He knows he can be opinionated, but his other daughter, Laura, still sees him and appears to be friendly. Joseph was a construction worker who was not able to save much but was able to pay off the family home in only 12 years. He expected to have a modest retirement, perhaps finishing the basement to rent out. The house is now worth about $250,000.

Joseph wants to sell his house so that he can give Laura the proceeds in cash. Well, not cash exactly. He wants to open a savings account for Laura and put the proceeds into this account. He knows there is no probate or capital gains on cash on hand. Bank accounts are part of the deceased's assets and are subject to probate, while interest income is taxed annually and generates no capital gain that would have to be dealt with on the final tax return. However, he is concerned that Camille will show up and demand a share of the proceeds. His concern is that she will contest the will in court, and, while his lawyer assures him she could not win such a claim, the situation would cause Laura a lot of anguish.

Joseph's lawyer assures him that Camille has no right to any of his money, but, if it will put his mind at rest, he could leave Camille $5,000 so she can't go to court and claim she was left out completely. Camille has not been financially dependent on Joseph for 25 years. She has no claim to his estate.

Types of Wills

There are three types of wills:

1. A **holograph will** is a will that is handwritten by the person making the will. It must be signed and dated but no witnesses are required and is not valid in some provinces. If the **testator** (the one making out the will) has typed out a will or filled in the blanks on a pre-printed will, it is not considered a holograph will and will have to be witnessed to be valid.
2. A **form will** is a pre-printed form either from a kit or off the Internet. It must be witnessed by two people who are not beneficiaries since it is not handwritten.
3. A **formal will** is drawn up by a lawyer and is signed and witnessed in the presence of the lawyer.

A will should be drawn up by a lawyer. Since a will is a legal document, it is important that the wording is correct and clearly states the client's wishes. For instance, a will could leave all the estate to "my issue". The intention might be that all children should share in the estate. But what if one of the children has died? Is it intended that the deceased's share go to that child's children, or to the other surviving children? What if the client has remarried and the new spouse has children? Does "my issue" include them?

Format of a Will

All wills have common elements. In addition to the standard clauses and format (numbers 1. to 4., below), a will can include other clauses to deal with different aspects of the estate (part 5, below).

1. Identify **testator** (the person making the will, also called the **grantor**)

    This is the last will and testament of me, Margot Jane Daniels, of the city of Kitchener, Ontario.

2. Revoke (make invalid) all previous wills and **codicils** (formal amendments to a will that are also witnessed).

    I revoke all former wills and other testamentary dispositions made by me.

3. Appoint the **executor**, who fulfills the instructions in your will.

    I appoint my cousin, Donald John Daniels, to be the executor and trustee of this my will, provided that if Donald John Daniels shall have predeceased me or shall survive me but die before the trusts hereof shall have terminated or shall refuse or be unable to act or to continue to act as such executor and trustee, then I appoint my friend, Judy Jane Doe, to be the executor (executrix) and trustee of this my will in the place and stead of Donald John Daniels. I hereinafter refer to my executor and trustee for the time being as my "trustee."

4. Leave all your property to the executor in trust:

    I give all my property wheresoever situate, including property over which I may have a general power of appointment, to my trustee upon the following trusts, namely:

    (a) Authorize your debts to be paid or else creditors will place claims against the estate. If the will does not authorize the executor to pay any outstanding debts, the creditors will place claims against the estate and delay the process of distributing the assets.
    To pay out of and charge to the capital of my general estate my just debts, funeral, and testamentary expenses.

    (b) Specific bequests (i.e., who gets what):
    -   *To deliver to my cousin, Charlotte Daniels, my diamond earrings and all my clothes* (specific personal property is a **bequest**)
    -   *To deliver to my friend, Francesca Clark, all my CDs and Beethoven piano music.*
    -   *To pay to my friend, Rachel Robertson, the sum of ten thousand dollars ($10,000) that she might take a trip* (cash is a **legacy**)
    -   *To pay to the World Wildlife Fund the sum of five thousand dollars ($5,000) for its general purposes* (a **donation**)
    -   *If my husband, Craig Stewart, survives me by 30 days, to pay, transfer, and assign the **residue of my estate** for his use absolutely.* Dealing with the residue is called the **residuary clause**. The reference to 30 days is called a **common disaster clause**. Its purpose is twofold:
        i.   to avoid double probate fees by designating another beneficiary if Margot and Craig should die within 30 days of each other.
        ii. to determine whether it is Craig's will or Margot's will that dictates the distribution of their assets. Margot's will might say: *"If my husband, Craig Stewart, does not survive me by 30 days, to pay, transfer, and assign the residue of my estate as follows: ..."*. Margot might decide to leave part of her estate to a close friend or relative to compensate them for serving as surrogate parents for their children.

    The time period that a person must survive to benefit from the estate, 30 days, is called a **survival clause**. Craig will receive the residue of Margot's estate — he will receive everything that is left after the debts are paid and specific bequests have been distributed.

Rather than leave Craig the residue of her estate, Margot could leave Craig the use of the property for his lifetime (Craig would have a **life interest** and would be the **life tenant**) and then give it to the children, who would then have a **capital interest**. This measure would ensure that the children inherit Margot's estate if Craig should remarry after her death.

There should also be a clause stating what happens to her estate if Craig does not survive her by 30 days, as there would also be the need to set up trusts and guardians for their children.

5. Testimonium and Attestation
   Formally confirms that Margot has read and understood the contents in the will and signed with witnesses that were present at the time she signed the will. When and where the will was signed is also to be listed.

6. Additional clauses to a will can give the executor the power to deal with:
   - the terms of any trusts that are set up through the will
   - the management of investments or other assets in the estate without the approval of the court
   - the appointing of **guardians** of minor children and **trustees** or guardians of property that minor children inherit
   - compensation for administering the estate (the executor is entitled to compensation whether or not this is stated in the will)
   - **alternate beneficiaries** — other people named as beneficiaries in case the original beneficiaries are not alive
   - funeral instructions. It is important that the family and executor are aware of any special wishes, such as cost, location of burial (or if cremation is preferred, a funeral or a memorial service), and whether or not the funeral arrangements have been made and/or prepaid
   - organ donations.

In addition, an **encroachment clause** gives the executor the power to give additional funds to a **life interest beneficiary** or a **capital interest beneficiary** (the one who inherits the capital after the life interest beneficiary dies) for special circumstances or needs.

There might be a clause covering a loan made to a beneficiary — is the loan forgiven (the recipient does not have to repay it) or does the amount of the loan reduce the bequest? **Ademption by advancement** means a bequest to a beneficiary is reduced by gifts made before death unless there is a clause against ademption by advancement. Without this clause, the gift will be considered a loan to be recovered when the estate is divided up. This clause addresses the issue of property identified in a will that cannot be given to a beneficiary because it does not belong to the deceased at the time of death. The property may have been destroyed, sold, or given away between the time of the will and the time of death. Example 8 illustrates ademption by advancement.

Example 8   Joanne, a 53-year-old widow, was killed in a car accident. She had a will that essentially left everything (about $300,000) divided equally between her two children, Stuart and Maggie. Joanne had paid for Maggie's university education. Stuart did not go to university — he became a Master Gardener and now runs a gardening business, which is just getting off the ground but shows every sign of success.

A year before she died, Joanne loaned $40,000 to Stuart to set up his business — buy the equipment, a small van, a computer for designing and invoicing. It was understood that Stuart would pay back the $40,000 when he was able — or maybe not. Mostly, it would depend on whether or not Joanne needed the money.

After Joanne's death, the executor had to ask Stuart either to pay back the money or have the $40,000 taken out of his share of the estate. The executor, a close family friend, understood Joanne's intentions, but her will did not include a clause against ademption by advancement. As a result, Stuart received $130,000 while Maggie received $170,000. Maggie did not "do the right thing" — she did not give Stuart $20,000 to even out the distribution. The bad feelings between Maggie and Stuart continue to this day.

Sometimes **partial intestacy** arises because there is no residue clause in the will — a will makes specific bequests but there are assets remaining after those bequests. Without a residue clause, these assets will be distributed according to provincial intestacy laws.

A **mirror will** is a will where each spouse leaves everything to the other and then to the children when both are deceased. If both spouses die at the same time, in some provinces there are Survivorship Acts that may state the younger is presumed to have survived the older. This can be important if one spouse had children from a prior marriage who inherit if the current spouse dies first. The other spouse may leave all the assets to their favourite charity. Who died first becomes critical. With an additional clause, the result may adhere more closely to both grantors' wishes.

C. EXECUTOR

An **executor** is a person who is appointed by a grantor to administer and implement the terms of the will. If an executor is not named, the courts will appoint one who cannot act until appointed — another good reason why a lawyer should draw up the will. A lawyer will make sure all necessary information is included. The executor, be it a person or a trust company, might hire an **agent for the executor** to administer the estate and/or provide advice.

Responsibilities of the Executor

The executor has the following responsibilities:

1. Arrange the funeral
2. Contact relevant government departments to:
   - apply for probate and pay probate fees
   - cancel CPP and OAS income and apply for survivor benefits
3. File the final tax return (covered in Chapter 11) and get a tax-clearance certificate that certifies that all taxes, CPP, EI, the interest and penalties have been paid to the CRA or that security for payment has been accepted
4. Act as the trustee and manage the assets of the estate. The estate is a testamentary trust until the assets are distributed. The assets could earn income while in the trust. In addition, the trustee, if given the authority, can invest the assets. The executor also needs to:
   - transfer any joint accounts to the surviving spouse and close any other bank accounts
   - transfer or roll over RRSPs and RRIFs
   - confer with the spouse about an election to make a contribution to a spousal RRSP if there is unused contribution room
   - complete claims for life insurance
   - arrange for sale of real estate, if required
   - redirect mail and cancel subscriptions
5. Pay the debts of the estate and get receipts
6. Distribute the assets according to the will. The trustee must act with an even hand and consider the best interests of all beneficiaries if there are any decisions to be made.

It is important to choose an executor who can and is willing to perform these functions. An alternate executor should also be named in case the first is not available or is unable to perform the duties.

The estate is tied up—no assets can be distributed—until all legal requirements have been met. An incompetent executor, regardless of how competent they might be in other areas of life, can be detrimental to the estate. They can, for instance, destroy a business by failing to act, as shown in Example 9.

Example 9   Jane was named executor by her brother, John. Very competent in her own field, she was diagnosed with cancer a few months after John died. As a result, she did not proceed to execute the will and the business that John and his wife had worked so hard to build failed to survive. This was a second marriage for John. His children from his previous marriage were well looked after, but the current spouse was dependent on the business and could not continue until the estate was settled.

Location of Documents — Virtual Shoebox

The executor must be able to find all relevant documents. The Canadian Life and Health Insurance Association has a tool for keeping track of personal and household documents. It is a 25-page pfd file called Virtual Shoebox and can be found at www.clhia.ca Home > For Consumers > Virtual Shoebox.

Compensation for the Executor

The executor is entitled to compensation, whether or not it is stipulated in the will. Compensation is often in the range of:

- 2 1/2% of original estate assets, plus
- 1 to 2 1/2% of capital distributed
- up to 5% of the estate income

If the estate of the deceased is worth $400,000 (not all that difficult to attain in a large city where real estate prices are high), the executor could collect $14,000 to $20,000 (3 1/2% to 5% of $400,000).

D. PROBATE

Probate is the process of the provincial court validating the will and the authority of the executor. Probate protects banks and insurance companies who will be transferring property to beneficiaries. Before they transfer assets, these parties want assurances that they are acting according to the latest will, that the items named in the will actually belong to the deceased, and that they are acting on the instructions of the correct executor.

Letters of probate, documents produced by the provincial court confirming the validity of a will, grant the authority of the executor. If the deceased died intestate, if the will is not valid, if there is a will but no named executor, or if the executor has died, **letters of administration** are issued appointing an administrator, who might be someone from the public trustee's office or a spouse or relative. This person then deals with the administration of the estate.

Probate is not required if the estate is straightforward and/or small, consisting perhaps of only a joint or small bank account. In this case **a letter of indemnity** or a copy of the will may suffice to indemnify a financial institution against any possible loss. Any assets that are registered (for example, a mortgage registered with a bank, or a home or car registered in a provincial registry) require that the will be probated.

Probate Fees

Probate fees are usually charged only in the province in which the deceased lived at the time of death. However, ownership of assets in a second province require a second probate (called **resealing**) sometimes with additional probate fees. In most jurisdictions, probate fees are charged on the **net assets – total market value** of the **estate assets minus** only a **registered mortgage,** but some provinces, such as B.C. and Manitoba, charge probate fees on the gross estate (all real estate and property) regardless of where it is located. When these assets are transferred from the surviving spouse to the next generation, probate fees are charged again. However, if an asset is held jointly, probate fees are charged only on the death of the second spouse.

Probate fees are not tax-deductible. All probate fees and taxes owed are paid from the estate before the estate is distributed. **Table 10.3** lists the probate fees charged in all provinces and territories and shows the calculation of probate fees for an estate of $500,000.

In 1998, the Supreme Court of Canada ruled that probate fees in Ontario were unconstitutional. The Court ruled that if the revenue collected was much greater than the cost of providing compulsory service, the fee should be considered a tax and, as such, must be established in legislation. Some provinces revised their probate fee schedule to reflect this decision. The following table reflects these revisions.

Table 10.3 Probate Fees by Province and Territory, 2013

Province/Territory	Fee schedule		Fee on $500,000	
AB	If the estate is < $10,000	$ 25		
	> $10,000 and < 25,000	$100		
	> $25,000 and < 125,000	$200		
	> $125,000 and < 250,000	$300		
	> $250,000	$400		$400
BC	Filing fee for estates > $25,000	$208	208	
	On the first 25,000	$ 0		
	$25,001 to 50,000	$6/$1,000 (0.6%)	150	
	> $50,000	$14/$1,000 (1.4%)	6,300	$6,658
MB	On the first $10,000 or less	$70	70	
	On the amount >$10,000	$7/$1,000 (0.7%)	3,430	$3,500
NB	If the estate is $5,000 or less	$25		
	> $5,000 and < $10,000	$50		
	> $10,000 and < $15,000	$75		
	> $15,000 and < $20,000	$100		
	> $20,000	$5/$1,000 or portion (0.5%)		$2,500
NL	On the first $1,000	$60	60	
	>$1,000	$0.50/$1,000 (0.5%)	2,495	$2,555
NT	Same as Alberta			$400
NS	If the estate is $10,000 or less	$78.54		
	> $10,000 and < $25,000	$197.48		
	> $25,000 and < $50,000	$328.65		
	> $50,000 and < $100,000	$920.07		
	If the estate is > $100,000			
	On the first $100,000	$902.07	920	
	> $100,000	$15.53 per $1,000 or portion (1.553%)	6,212	$7,132

Table 10.3 Continued.

Provinces/Territory	Fee schedule		Fee on $500,000	
NU	Same as Alberta			
ON	If the estate is $1,000 or less	$0		
	If the estate is > $1,000	$100		
	On the first $50,000	$5 / $1,000 (0.5%)	250	
	> $50,000	$15/$1,000 (1.5%)	6,750	$7,000
PE	If the estate is $10,000 or less	$50		
	$10,001–$25,000	$100		
	$25,001–$50,000	$200		
	$50,001–$100,000	$400		
	If the estate is > $100,000			
	On the first $100,000	$400	400	
	> $100,000	$4 / $1,000 or portion (0.4%)	1,600	$2,000
QC	No probate fee. Court filing charge	$99		$99
SK		$7/$1,000 (0.7%)		$3,500
YT	On the first $25,000	$0		
	> $25,000	$140		$140

Minimizing Probate Fees

Probate fees are charged on assets going through the estate. Example 10 shows the effects on two beneficiaries when one inherits assets that are not subject to probate and income tax, while the other's inheritance is subject to both.

Example 10   Bea died. Her son, Pete, was the named beneficiary on her $80,000 life insurance policy, while her daughter, Leanne, was to receive the investments, which were also worth $80,000. There were $17,000 taxes, payable on the sale of the investments, and the probate fees were $1,120. On the other hand, there is no tax on the proceeds of the insurance policy, and because Pete was named the beneficiary instead of the estate, there are no probate fees for Pete either.

As a result, Pete received $80,000 while Leanne received $61,880 ($80,000 – $17,000 – $1,120). Income taxes and probate fees must be paid by the estate before the estate can be distributed.

As probate fees are charged only on assets going through the estate, the proceeds of an insurance policy with a named beneficiary would be paid directly to the beneficiary and not go through the estate; therefore, the proceeds would not be subject to probate. If, however, the estate is the named beneficiary, the proceeds are subject to probate and cannot be paid to a beneficiary named in the will until the entire estate is settled.

An asset that is not part of the estate — that is, it is not controlled by a will and is not subject to probate — is called a **non-estate asset**. Probate fees are reduced by using:

1. Named beneficiaries
2. Joint ownership
3. Multiple wills

4. Trusts
5. Gifting before death.

Named Beneficiaries

Name a beneficiary on life insurance policies and pension plans including RRSP and RRIFs and the assets will pass directly to the beneficiary without probate. The beneficiary of a RRIF or other annuity is called a **successor annuitant**.

Joint Ownership

Have a joint owner on investments, if appropriate. However, joint ownership with a child may expose you to their marriage and creditor problems. Also, when a transfer is made other than to the spouse, there is a "deemed disposition" with tax consequences.

- **Joint tenants** (with right of survivorship): The deceased's interest is automatically transferred to the surviving owner and is not handled by a will, although this isn't useful if both spouses die at the same time. There cannot be a joint tenant on RRSPs and RRIFs.
- **Tenancy in common**: The assets are transferred according to the will and are therefore estate assets.

Multiple Wills

In some jurisdictions, probate fees are very high and can be reduced by having more than one will and there are some circumstances where this is appropriate. Multiple wills are valid in Ontario but not in Nova Scotia and Manitoba. In other jurisdictions, they may not have been put to the test enough for there to be a legal ruling on their validity.

If a person owns shares in a private corporation such as a family business, the shareholders will likely not require probate to validate ownership. In this case, the assets of the corporation can be dealt with in a separate will that will not be probated. In addition, if a person's personal assets include paintings or jewellery and the beneficiary is a friend or relative, the beneficiary may not need court-approval to know that the asset is coming from the deceased. These assets will need to be fairly valuable to justify having a separate will.

Each will can have its own executor and should mention the existence of the other will(s).

Trusts

Probate fees are charged on assets going into a **spousal testamentary trust** but not when the assets come out of this trust to children or other beneficiaries in accordance with the instructions in the trust agreement. There are no probate fees on an **inter vivos (living) trust** since the deceased does not own it at the time of death. However, the probate fees need to be more than the cost of administering the trust to make the trust worthwhile. Trusts are discussed in detail in Chapters 12.

Gifting Before Death

Assets that will be bequeathed on your death can be given away before death, thereby avoiding probate at death since the deceased no longer owns the asset. There is no tax on cash given away. However, some assets, such as investments and the family cottage, might give rise to a taxable capital gain at the time of the transfer so it is important to understand the possible tax implications of the transfer before it is made.

Assets Located in the United States

All real property and personal assets (e.g., corporate stocks, bonds, and government debt) normally located in the United States, regardless of where they were purchased or where they were physically located at the time of death, are called **U.S. situs assets** (situs literally means the place where some-thing exists or originates — that is, the place where an asset is to be located in law). American law require foreign owners of American property to pay tax on their American estate that is above the value of a certain exempt amount on U.S. situs assets when they die. This topic is covered in Chapter 12, under the heading "E. Assets in the United States".

E. BUSINESS ASSETS

Succession planning for owner/managers of small businesses is more complex than simply stating one's wishes in a will or setting up a trust because there are business partners and other shareholders to con-sider. In addition, the business may employ some family members but also others who, nonetheless, should participate in inheriting some portion of the net assets in the future.

Partnerships and Private Corporations

Businesses having more than one owner, either as a partnership or as a private corporation, should decide, in advance of an untimely death of an owner, both how the business will continue and how the surviving owners will buy out the deceased's share of the business. Two methods are available.

1. A **buy-sell agreement** is an agreement that stipulates that the remaining owners or shareholders can buy the share(s) of a deceased owner or shareholder when one partner or shareholder dies. The price can be fixed or determined according to a formula.

2. A **share redemption plan** is an agreement whereby the corporation itself buys back the shares of the deceased, again either at a fixed price or using a formula.

For both plans, the remaining owners, shareholders, or the corporation must be able to finance the purchase of the deceased's share(s). There are several ways to provide this financing. The business could:

1. Have a sinking fund whereby some portion of profits are set aside in a special account every year. However, sinking funds can take a few years to acquire the necessary funds and are exposed to creditor claims should the business experience financial difficulty.

2. Sell assets. This would, presumably, not be in the best interest of the remaining partners.

3. Take out a bank loan. Depending on the leveraged position of the business, this could hamper the future ability of the business to continue operations.

4. Have a life insurance policy on each of the partners or shareholders. The policy premiums can be paid by:

(a) All partners or shareholders in proportion to the interest each partner or shareholder holds in the business. Each policy would be payable to the other partners or shareholders in proportion to their share of the ownership of the business. This makes it more fair for owners who own a smaller portion of the business. However, it does not deal with the issue of the health and relative age of each partner or shareholder since the premium on an insurance policy for an older shareholder will be higher than that for a younger shareholder.

(b) The partnership or corporation could make the payments. The policy could be payable to:

    i.   each shareholder, who can then purchase the share(s) of the deceased, or

    ii.   the corporation, which can then buy the shares in a share redemption plan.

This method reduces profits, leaving less funds to be paid out as dividends. In effect, all partners or shareholders pay equally.

As illustrated in **Annuities** in Chapter 7, the face value of an insurance policy is not taxable.

Family Businesses and Estate Freezes

Family businesses may also want to take advantage of an **estate freeze**. An estate freeze can be enacted for personal assets but is more likely to be useful in a family business. An **estate freeze** locks in the value of shares of an owner of a business. There are several ways to enact an estate freeze:

1. Sell or give the assets to the beneficiaries. This immediately leads to a capital gain on the actual or deemed disposition. If the transfer is made at less-than-fair-market value, income attribution rules will be applied. In addition, the owner no longer controls the assets.

2. Transfer the assets into an inter vivos trust with the owner having a life interest in the assets and the children being named as capital beneficiaries. This option generates an immediate capital gain on the deemed disposition of the assets

3. Create a holding company. The owner of the company (Operating Company or Opco) sets up a holding company (Holdco) and transfers the voting, common shares of Opco to Holdco in exchange for voting, non-participating, non-cumulative preferred shares equal in value to the fair market value of the shares of Opco. Holdco issues new, non-voting common shares either to the children or to a trust, with the children as beneficiaries. Growth in Holdco accrues to the new common shares. In addition, at the owner's death, the $800,000 lifetime capital gains exemption can be used to reduce the amount of the taxable capital gain. An example showing the tax consequences of this approach is provided at the end of Chapter 11.

SUMMARY

Wills are the mechanism for distributing personal assets according to one's wishes. Because wills are not mandatory, each province and territory has intestate rules that apply when a person dies without a will. There are also rules that dictate the hierarchy in the degree of relatedness of close relatives to indicate who inherit first when someone dies intestate. Wills can vary a great deal but all wills have some common elements, such as naming the grantor, revoking all former wills, naming an executor, and stating how estate assets are to be distributed among the beneficiaries. Because the executor has many responsibilities, it is important to appoint an executor who is competent and willing. Unless specifically set up otherwise, the assets of a deceased are distributed through an estate, and all assets in an estate are subject to probate to verify the will and the authority of the executor. The assets of small businesses require special attention so that they are distributed according to the wishes of the deceased when the business carries on after the death of a partner or shareholder.

MARGOT AND CRAIG

Craig shakes his head. "I wish I had known all this a year ago before my aunt died. She made me executor of her will. I remember her asking me nine or ten years ago at a family picnic if I would agree to this. I didn't think much about it at the time so I agreed. Then she died. Her estate is worth only about $300,000 — just her house in Swift Current, Saskatchewan, some really fine furniture, and priceless books. But it is taking a lot of my time. And sure, I can be paid for all this work; but she left her estate to the Regina Humane Society, and I feel bad taking anything out of it. But, it is a lot of work. I'm an architect — I feel like I don't really know what I am doing. So much for family picnics!"

SOURCES

Foster, Sandra E. (2000) *You Can't Take It With You*, 3rd edition (Toronto: John Wiley & Sons Canada Limited).

Gray, Douglas and John Budd, (2000) *The Canadian Guide to Will and Estate Planning* (Toronto: McGraw-Hill Ryerson Limited).

Ho, Kwok and Chris Robinson, (2000) *Personal Financial Planning*, 3rd edition (Toronto: Captus Press Inc.).

Van Cauwenberghe, Christine. (2012) *Wealth Planning Strategies for Canadians*, Carswell, ON.

Various websites, including: www.taxtips.ca/willsandestates/probatesfees.htm

KEY TERMS

Ademption by advancement	Legacy
Administrator	Letters of indemnity
Agent for the executor	Letters probate
Alternate beneficiaries	Life interest
Beneficiaries	Life interest beneficiary
Beneficiaries, named	Life tenant
Bequest	Mirror will
Buy-sell agreements	Multiple wills
Capital interest	Official Administrator
Capital interest beneficiary	Partial intestacy
Codicils	Per capita
Collateral relatives	Per stirpes
Common disaster clause	Personal representative
Consanguinity	Preferential share
Direct line	Probate

Distributive share
Donation
Encroachment clause
Estate freeze
Executor
Executrix
Form will
Formal will
Grantor
Guardians
Holograph will
Intestate
Intestate rules
Joint tenants

Probate fees
Public Trustee
Resealing
Residuary clause
Residue of the estate
Share redemption plan
Situs assets
Spousal rollover
Successor annuitant
Survival clause
Tenants in common
Testator
Trustee

QUESTIONS AND PROBLEMS

1. Helen died intestate. Her estate, which did not include marital property, was worth $127,000. She leaves behind her a spouse and one surviving child. Her other child died, leaving behind a widow and four children. The surviving child has one child. How much do her spouse, child and each grandchild get in each province and territory (or just in the province or territory where you live) using both per stirpes rules and per capita rules?

Answer

	Per stirpes			Per capita		
	Spouse	**Child**	**Grandchild**	**Spouse**	**Child**	**Grandchild**
AB	69,000	29,000	7,250	69,000	58,000	0
BC	85,667	20,667	5,167	85,667	41,333	0
MB.	127,000	0	0	127,000	0	0
NB	42,333	42,333	10,583	42,333	84,667	0
NL	42,333	42,333	10,583	42,333	84,667	0
NT	75,667	25,667	6,417	75,667	51,333	0
NS	75,667	25,667	6,417	75,667	51,333	0
NU	75,667	25,667	6,417	75,667	51,333	0
ON	127,000	0	0	127,000	0	0
PE	42,333	42,333	10,583	42,333	84,667	0
QC	42,333	42,333	10,583	42,333	84,667	0
SK	109,000	9,000	2,250	109,000	18,000	0
YU	92,333	17,333	4,333	92,333	34,667	0

2. What if Helen's only relatives were Claire, the daughter of her first cousin, and Joe, the son of her niece? How much would each inherit using the Table of Consanguinity? (Answer: Claire: $0, Joe $127,000)

3. What is your relationship to the following relatives of your first cousin's:
   (a) Children
   (b) Grandchildren

4. You and Jerry have the same grandmother but are not siblings. What is Jerry's relationship to you? If you are a woman and Jerry is a man, can you marry?

5. Many people believe that if a couple live together long enough (however long that might be) both partners are obligated to split assets such as the matrimonial home and pensions in the

same way that these assets would be divided if they were married. Is this true in every province and territory?

6. What property does not have to be included in a will for the asset to bypass a will?

7. When Kate died intestate, she left two children. Her estate comprised a $75,000 life insurance policy on which her son was the named beneficiary. In addition, she owned a house with a market value of $150,000 as a joint tenant with her daughter. What is the value of the inheritance that each child will receive? (Answer: Son inherits $75,000, daughter gets her mother's half of the house valued at $75,000)

8. Just before she died, Kate had a falling out with her son, and changed the beneficiary on the insurance policy to her estate. What is the value of the inheritance each of her children receives if the probate fees are $1,000? (Answer: $37,000 each, and the daughter gets her mother's half of the house)

9. Joe and Samantha separated, and Samantha moved in with Tim. Two years later, Samantha died without updating her will. In her will, she left her RRSPs worth $80,000 to Joe. To how much is Tim entitled? (Answer: $0)

10. Mary Jo, in her will, left the following to her friends. What is each of the gifts called?
    (a) $10,000 to the Halifax Humane Society
    (b) $10,000 to her friend, Alexis, to take a trip
    (c) Her clothes and jewellery to her sister, Alanis.

11. Mary Jo left the use of her house to her second husband, Terry, and the house itself to her children from her first marriage.
    (a) What is Terry's share called?
    (b) What are her children's share called?

12. Alan died on June 12, leaving his entire estate to his wife Camilla, Camilla's daughter, and his son. He had lent his son $60,000 to buy a condo. Before he died, Alan liquidated his investments and paid the tax, giving him $300,000. It was his wish to leave $100,000 to each. He had not updated his will making an ademption against advancement. How much did each of them get? (Answer: Camilla $120,000, Camilla's daughter $120,000, son $60,000)

13. Roger was leaving for two months in the Azores with the three children. Gail planned to follow two weeks later for three weeks — she could not leave her business for two months. Before Roger left, Gail got a sample will off the Internet, and made mirror wills for both of them.
    (a) What is a mirror will?
    (b) They had two neighbours, Mildred and Carole, witness them. Are the wills valid?
    (c) If Roger witnessed Gail's will along with Mildred, is Gail's will valid? Why or why not?
    (d) Should Gail have included a common disaster clause (referring only to this summer's vacation)?

14. Stewart agreed to be the executor of his aunt's estate, which was worth $230,000, all of it distributed in her will.
    (a) What is the range of compensation Stewart can expect for being the executor? (Answer: $8,050 to $11,500)
    (b) If the estate was worth $750,000 and was going to bring in income of $63,000 a year, what compensation could Stewart expect? Assume no assets are distributed. (Answer: $21,900)
    (c) Is it Stewart's responsibility to do the following?
        i. Cancel her subscription to *Canadian Geographic*
        ii. Decided who will take her cats

iii. File her final tax return

iv. Track down and close out all her bank accounts

v. Cancel her CPP and OAS

vi. Decide who gets her prized antique Samovar

vii. Pay her final hydro bill

viii. Pay himself

Problems

15. Frank left everything to his estate, which was worth $1,150,000.

    (a) What are the probate fees for each province and territory (or just the province or territory in which you live)?

    (b) If Frank left the $300,000 RRIF to his spouse; the insurance policy with a face value of $150,000 to his daughter; his cottage, worth $170,000, in an inter vivos trust (not subject to probate); the matrimonial home, worth $300,000, owned as a joint tenant with his wife; and his $230,000 of non-registered investments owned jointly with his son, what would the probate fees be?

	(a)	(b)
AB	400	0
BC	15,758	0
MN	8,050	0
NB	5,750	0
NL	5,810	0
NT	400	0
NS	17,227	0
NU	400	0
OT	16,750	0
PE.	4,600	0
QC	99	0
SK	8,050	0
YU	140	0

16. Once upon a time there were three partners. Tom, age 57, had an impressive M.B.A. and years of banking experience. Gary, age 33, was the sales person — he could sell anything to anybody and have them thanking him after he was done. Zoe, age 45, can administer anything — there isn't a mess that Zoe can't sort out in short order. They are partners in a business supplying support to entrepreneurs. They supply working capital, keep the books, provide monthly financial reports and feedback on their progress, and manage their sales efforts. One of Zoe's friends died suddenly, and they are now thinking about the need for life insurance on each of them. While none would be easy to replace, they feel that they don't need the added burden of struggling to survive while they test out replacements. They have decided they need $500,000 of life insurance on each of them.

    They have contacted you, their financial planner, for advice. The annual premiums are quite different. Tom: $2,200, Gary: $440 and Zoe, who smokes: $1,100. They want your advice on the equitable way to handle this. What are the pros and cons if:

    (a) the company pays

    (b) they each pay for their own, or

    (c) they pay for each other

    To whom should the policies be payable — pros and cons?

11

Taxation Issues

Learning Objectives

A. Know the tax implications of disposing of assets owned for personal use.

B. Know the tax implications of disposing of assets used to earn income.

C. Understand how the tax rules are different if the transfer is made to a spouse.

D. Know the tax implications of selling or transferring assets before death to family members at less than the fair market value.

E. Know the tax implications of deemed dispositions at death.

F. Be able to use the capital gains exemption and estate freeze to minimize the tax on certain transfers of capital property.

G. Understand the required and optional tax returns to be filed after death.

Craig and Margot are completely lost when it comes to taxes beyond their own basic income tax returns. They know that Gloria paid a lot of tax on capital gains that was probably not worth the capital cost allowance tax deductions that she took on the income from her bed-and-breakfast. But hindsight is 20/20. If Gloria's house had not increased in value so much, the deductions might well have been worth it.

Margot had not thought of her mother as a business woman operating a business. To Margot, Gloria was just making a few extra dollars taking in boarders! Who could have guessed the bed-and-breakfast would have such tax repercussions? What about their friend, Lily, who lives in a little town just outside of Stratford, Ontario. Lily gives piano lessons. Is she a business person also? Are there tax consequences to what Lily does?

Margot and Craig realize that they have been pretty naive about what a business is and how changes in the value of the assets affect the tax return. They know lots of people who run small businesses. Many of these businesses are quite small — intended to supplement other income. Certainly Margot and Craig understand about taxes on income, and even on business income. But Margot is still shaking her head over the tax on the capital gain her mother had to pay on her little house in Lunenburg.

Margot's university roommate, Kathy, married a farmer. They have a farm outside of Peterborough, where they grow bedding plants for nurseries. Margot had always viewed this activity as just a way of life. But she is beginning to understand that this way of life can bring with it a very large amount of capital assets. Margot is curious. What are the tax implications when Kathy and her husband retire and pass on the farm to their only son? How will their only daughter feel about this circumstance if the farm is worth so much and her brother gets it cheaply or for nothing?

Craig is remembering a year ago when he had to deal with his aunt's estate. He hired an accountant to help him with the tax returns. Optional returns? Who knew? "What are these about?" asks Craig.

INTRODUCTION

The Canada Revenue Agency (CRA) has rules in place to ensure that the disposition of capital property is not done in such a way as to deprive the Agency of tax revenue. There are two mechanisms for enacting this goal on the part of the CRA.

One mechanism is the **deemed disposition** of assets — in circumstances that will be described shortly, the asset is *deemed* to have been disposed of, usually at the fair market value, even if it has not *actually* been disposed of. This action leads to a deemed capital gain or loss for the taxpayer.

The second mechanism operates via **income attribution** rules, whereby the transfer of the property is deemed to have been an attempt to reduce taxes on the income earned by the assets by transferring the income to a lower-income spouse or minor child. The income is "attributed" to the transferor — the person who originally owned the property.

Estate planning involves transferring assets to one's intended beneficiaries. Sometimes this involves gifts or transfers while still alive while other times, it involves transfers at death. Either way, the tax implications are *usually* the same. In this chapter, we will review tax rules associated with the disposition of capital property owned for both personal use and for producing income.

Deemed Dispositions

There are tax implications with any disposition — actual or deemed. Traditionally, we think that the disposition of an asset occurs only when the asset is sold to a third party or when a property is involuntarily disposed of, such as fire, theft or expropriation. However, a disposition for tax purposes can also occur even if a sale or actual disposition did not take place. This is called a **deemed disposition.** The CRA dictates that there has been a deemed disposition:

- for most **inter vivos gifts/transfers** to another person and/or trust while the owner of the property is still alive
- on the **day of the death of the taxpayer**
- with a **change of use** from personal use to income-producing or vice versa
- when emigrating

For these situations, the proceeds of disposition (POD) is usually deemed to be the **fair market value (FMV).**

We examine these situations in this chapter as well as Chapter 12, "Trusts" where we look at the tax implications of transfers to trusts.

Capital Assets

A capital asset is an asset that you own for long-term benefit and is most commonly thought of as an asset producing either:

- business income, or

• property income such as dividends, interest, royalties and rental income.

The disposition of these income-producing assets often gives rise to capital gains and losses. However, some personal assets can also give rise to capital gains and losses.

Capital gains and losses are recognized for tax purposes only when there is an actual or deemed disposition. The capital gain / (loss) is based on the proceeds of disposition (POD) minus the cost or adjusted cost base of the asset.

Proceeds of Disposition (POD)

For **actual dispositions**, the POD is generally the selling price of the asset. When the asset has been traded for another, the POD is equal to the FMV of the asset received. If the asset is lost, stolen or destroyed, the POD is the insurance proceeds.

For **deemed dispositions**, the POD is usually equal to the FMV of the asset on the date of deemed disposition. The only exception to this rule is when the asset has been transferred to a spouse. In this instance, the transfer automatically occurs with POD equal to the transferor's tax value — the undepreciated capital cost (UCC) for depreciable assets defined in section B. Disposition of Assets Used to Earn Income or adjusted cost base (ACB) defined in the next paragraph. This transfer to a spouse is called a Spousal Rollover and the rules are defined in the section C. Transfer of Assets to Spouse.

Adjusted Cost Base (ACB)

The **adjusted cost base (ACB)** of an asset can include:

+   original cost
+   acquisition, legal, accounting, engineering, appraisal costs, etc.
+/–   share of partnership profits and losses
–   government grants or subsidies
+   costs incurred that cannot be deducted — for example, interest on vacant land waiting to be developed
+   elections made on the demise of the $100,000 Lifetime Capital Gains Exemption
+   superficial losses arising from the purchase of property identical to a property that has been sold
+   interest and property taxes on land not deducted as an expense
+   the discount on a bond if it is included in income

The adjusted cost base does not include disposal costs.

Some property expenses are not deductible as either current or capital expenditures — these costs are not part of the ACB. They include:

• land transfer taxes
• principal payments
• income tax penalties
• value of the taxpayer's labour

Capital Gains

A **capital gain** results when the proceeds minus the selling costs and minus ACB is positive. The taxable portion of the capital gain is currently 50% of the capital gain and is called the **taxable capital gain**. The 50% is called the **inclusion rate**.[1]

There cannot be a capital gain on:

- eligible capital expenditures (intangible assets) except for qualified farm property
- gains on inventory
- unpaid interest on bonds sold between coupon dates
- insurance policies
- certain types of cultural property sold to certain cultural institutions
- resource properties
- the interest of a beneficiary under a qualifying environmental trust

Capital Losses

A **capital loss** occurs when the proceeds minus the selling costs and minus the original cost or the ACB is negative. The deductible portion is called an **allowable capital loss**.

Net taxable capital gains for the current year are:

- taxable capital gains, minus
- allowable capital losses

Net allowable capital losses for the current year are:

- allowable capital losses, minus
- taxable capital gains

Allowable capital losses can be deducted *only* from taxable capital gains. The taxpayer is not obligated to deduct the allowable capital loss. If allowable capital losses are to be deducted, they *must* be deducted from taxable capital gains in the *current year*. If the current year's allowable capital losses are greater than the current year's taxable capital gains, the unused allowable capital loss is converted to a **net capital loss** and can be deducted as described in the next paragraph.

A *net* capital loss can be deducted *only* from *net* taxable capital gains (except for allowable business investments losses [ABILs], which are not covered in this course). A net capital loss can be carried:

- back three years, and
- forward indefinitely

Example 1 shows how a capital loss is generated and converted to a net capital loss.

Example 1   Joanne finally gave up on her cousin's business — a high-tech start-up that, after five years, shows no signs of going anywhere. She had invested $8,000, and her cousin can now offer her only $2,000 for her shares, generating a capital loss of $6,000. In the past three years and in the current year, Joanne has not disposed of any other capital assets, so she cannot deduct her allowable capital loss of $3,000. Her allowable capital loss, now called a *net capital loss*, can be deducted against future taxable capital gains.

---

1   When capital gains tax was introduced on January 1, 1972, the inclusion rate was set at 50%. Until then, the inclusion rate was, in effect, 0% since there was no tax on capital gains. On January 1, 1988, it became 66.67%, on January 1, 1990, 75%, February 28, 2000, 66.67% and on October 18, 2000, it became the current 50%.

Suppose that three years ago, Joanne sold some other shares generating a capital gain of $4,000 and a taxable capital gain of $2,000. She can now re-file her tax return from three years ago, deducting $2,000 of her current allowable capital loss from the taxable capital gain. In this case, she would now have a net capital loss of $1,000 to be deducted from future taxable capital gains.

There are two other types of capital losses: "personal-use property" and "listed personal property" which are discussed in the next section.

Table 11.1 Summary of Types of Capital Property

Business Property		
Capital Property		
• machinery, truck, building • shares in another company	• bought for long-term use • generates income	• **can** generate a taxable capital gain or allowable capital loss
Business Property		
• inventory, accounts receivable	• not long-term • generates business income/(loss) and cash flow	• no capital gain or loss
Personal Property		
Capital Property		
• Personal-Use Property (PUP): house, cottage, car, furniture, big-screen TV, home theatre system	• bought for long-term use • often consumed through use	• usually no taxable capital gain • no allowable capital loss
• Listed Personal Property (LLP): paintings, stamp collections, jewellery, pianos, boat, high-end sound systems	• bought for long-term use and enjoyment • usually not consumed through use and enjoyment	• **can** have a taxable capital gain or allowable loss
Non-capital Property		
• food, prescriptions, laundry detergent	• expenditures to be consumed	

A. DISPOSITION OF ASSETS OWNED FOR PERSONAL USE

Many transfers of capital property occur while the owner is still alive. Assets owned for personal use can be sold at their fair market value (FMV) but they can also be sold for less than the FMV or they can be given away. There are two types of personal assets that can give rise to a capital gain or loss. The difference between them is the tax treatment of capital losses that might arise upon their disposal.

> *The deemed proceeds to the seller* is the greater of the FMV or the actual proceeds.
> The *cost to the buyer* is the lower of the FMV or the actual proceeds.

Personal-Use Property (PUP)

This is property owned for pleasure and enjoyment, such as a house, a cottage, a grand piano, a boat, furniture, a personal computer or a high-end sound system. This property may be consumed and wear out. When these assets are sold or disposed of:

• Gains are taxable in the same way as other capital gains, subject to the $1,000 rule described below

• Losses are *not deductible* even against other personal-use capital gains; i.e., the loss is assumed to be nil. While no capital cost allowance has been taken, the loss is assumed to arise from the use of the asset. An exception to this rule is *Listed Personal Property*, described below

Example 2 illustrates the tax effects of selling personal-use property both below and above the FMV.

Example 2   Anne has decided to sell her old recreational vehicle (RV) because she seldom uses it. Her brother and sister use it a lot, and Anne thinks one of them should buy it. Her brother has helped with upkeep, fixing this and that, and he and his wife helped paint the outside of the RV last year. So Anne would be willing to sell it to him at less than the fair market value. Anne's sister, on the other hand, has been using it for years and has never contributed a dime or flexed a muscle to help with the upkeep. So Anne has no qualms about asking her to pay more than the fair market value. Because the RV is old and in very good condition, the fair market value is greater than the cost.

	Her brother	Her sister	Her brother	Her sister
Cost	50,000	50,000	50,000	50,000
FMV	60,000	**60,000**	43,000	**43,000**
Selling price = Anne's *actual* proceeds	**55,000**	67,000	**43,000**	58,000
Anne's *deemed* proceeds = greater of FMV or actual proceeds	60,000	67,000	43,000	58,000
Anne's capital gain / (loss)	10,000	17,000	(7,000)	8,000
Anne's taxable capital gain	5,000	8,500		4,000
Anne's allowable capital loss			0	
Sibling's cost = lower of FMV or actual proceeds	**55,000**	**60,000**	**43,000**	**43,000**

If Anne sold the RV for a fair market value of $43,000, she would *not* be able to claim an allowable capital loss of $3,500, 50% of $7,000 (50,000 cost – 43,000 FMV) because she cannot claim an allowable capital loss on this type of personal-use property, even though she will have a taxable capital gain if she sells it for more than her cost of $50,000.

Cottages

Cottages are considered personal-use property (unless they are the principal residence). Therefore, Anne could not claim an allowable capital loss on a cottage.

Grand Pianos and Antiques

Grand pianos or antiques, which may or may not decrease in value, are personal-use property. As such, they are subject to capital gains but there is no allowable capital loss since, despite a gain or loss in their value, these items are for personal use. A grand piano owned by a professional musician is a business-use asset, however, that can be depreciated for tax purposes. A piano store owns pianos as inventory.

$1,000 Floor Rule

The CRA bulletin IT332R provides a $1,000 floor rule to eliminate calculations on small amounts:

- If the ACB is less than $1,000, the deemed ACB is $1,000, or
  - deemed ACB is *the greater of*:
    - actual ACB, and
    - $1,000
- If the proceeds are less than $1,000, the deemed proceeds are $1,000, or
  - deemed proceeds is *the greater of*:
    - actual proceeds, and
    - $1,000.

Table 11.2 $1,000 Floor Rule

• If ACB < $1,000, deemed ACB = $1,000	• $1,000 = minimum ACB
• If Proceeds < $1,000, deemed proceeds = $1,000	• $1,000 = minimum Proceeds

Example 3 illustrates the $1,000 floor rule on personal-use property.

Example 3 After many years of playing with a trio on Sunday afternoons, John, who made his living as a librarian, sold his flute when the other two members of the trio moved to another city. In the first scenario below, the original cost of the flute was $1,500 and John sold it for $600. In the second scenario, John bought the flute for $700 and sold it for $1,200.

	Scenario 1			Scenario 2		
	Actual	Deemed	Use	Actual	Deemed	Use
Cost	1,500	1,000	1,500	700	**1,000**	1,000
Proceeds	600	**1,000**	1,000	**1,200**	1,000	1,200
Capital gain						200
Non-deductible loss			500			

Since the flute is personal-use property, John cannot deduct the $500 capital loss and must declare the $200 capital gain. If this sale occurred after John's death, the $500 in the first scenario is not deductible, but 50% of the $200 gain in the second scenario would be added to his final tax return, along with any other capital gains he might have.

Listed Personal Property (LPP)

Listed personal property (LPP) is defined in Section 54 of the Income Tax Act and includes prints, etchings, drawings, paintings, sculptures or similar works of art, jewellery, rare folios, rare books, rare manuscripts, stamps, and coins. They face the same $1,000 rule for the adjusted cost base and the proceeds. After using the $1,000 floor rule, capital losses can be applied against capital gains from other listed personal property, carried back three years and forward seven years.

Example 4 illustrates the sale of listed personal property using the same numbers as in Example 4.

Example 4 John sold his flute music but in two different years. He sold the first batch in 2011 and the rest of it in 2013. Some of the music had become rare.

	2011			2013		
	Actual	Deemed	Use	Actual	Deemed	Use
Cost	1,500	1,000	1,500	700	**1,000**	1,000
Proceeds	600	**1,000**	1,000	**1,200**	1,000	1,200
Capital gain						200
Loss deductible against gains			500			

John can carry the $500 capital loss from LPP back three years or forward seven years to be applied against future capital gains. In 2013, he can apply $200 (of the $500 capital loss) against the $200 capital gain. He will not be able to deduct the balance, $300, of the 2011 capital loss until he generates $300 of capital gain from listed personal property.

Personal Real Estate

There are special rules for real property — your home, your cottage — since there is a tax exemption for the capital gain on your principal residence. If you own a vacation property such as a cottage, you can choose which to call your principal residence and it is not dependent on how much of the time you actually live there.

Principal Residence Exemption

A principal residence is the residence that is owned by the taxpayer and/or spouse and in which the taxpayer and/or spouse and/or child or children normally live or live for a portion of the year. The predominate use of the principal residence is personal rather than to produce business or rental income. The final decision on which home, a house or condo in the city perhaps or a cottage in the country, is the principal residence can wait until the first one is sold and then the decision is based on which one has experienced the largest increase in price or FMV.

A house or cottage that is not the principal residence is personal-use property, and the taxpayer may have a taxable capital gain when the property is disposed of. However, the taxpayer will not be able to deduct an allowable capital loss on the sale of that home.

Before 1982, a taxpayer and spouse could each designate the house or the cottage as the principal residence. Since December 31, 1981, only one residence can be claimed as the principal residence for the family unit. The **principal residence exemption** provides a tax exemption on the capital gain on the principal residence. The tax on capital gains was introduced to Canadians on January 1, 1972. The amount of capital gain that is *exempt* is:

$$\frac{N1 + 1}{N2} \times \text{capital gain realized}$$

N1: # of full or part years designated as principal residence after 1971
N2: # of full or partial years owned since 1971

N1 + 1 cannot be greater than N2.

Example 5 illustrates the use of the principal residence exemption being allocated between a house and a cottage.

Example 5   Stan and Liz bought their house on May 12, 1965 for $40,000. On **Valuation Day (V-day) December 31, 1971**, their home had an estimated market value of $48,000 — an increase of approximately 3% a year. On April 17, 1976, they bought a cottage for $15,000. The cottage was a bit of a wreck when they bought it but they were able to renovate and winterize it in 1982 for $30,000. Until 1982, Stan designated the cottage as his principal residence, while Liz designated the house as such. On October 27, 2013, they sold the house to rent an apartment because they had semi-retired and were spending a lot of time at the cottage. They got $595,000 for the house. Cottage prices had been going up dramatically — the cottage was worth an estimated $475,000 when they sold the house.

Should they have claimed the capital gains exemption on the house or the cottage in 2013 when they sold the house? They should claim the exemption on the house, since it had the larger capital gain for each year of ownership after 1971 (N2) at the time of the sale of the house.

	House	Cottage
Purchase date	May 12, 1965	April 17, 1976
Purchase price	40,000	15,000
V-day value — Dec 31, 1971	48,000	n/a
Renovations — 1982		30,000
ACB		45,000
Proceeds from sale Oct 27, 2013	595,000	
FMV in 2013		475,000
Capital gain as at 2013	547,000	430,000
N2	42	38
Capital gain/N2 (Note 1)	13,024	11,316
N1 before January 1, 1982	10	6
N1 for 1982–2013	32	32
N1 — Total maximum possible	42	38
Designated N1 (Note 2)	41	1
Exempt portion: (N1+1)/N2	100.00%	5.26%

Note 1: The capital gain per years owned dictates which one is the starting point for allocating the principal residence — the largest capital gain per year of ownership.

Note 2: Allocating all 42 years of ownership of the house wastes one year of exemption since you cannot exempt more than 100% of the capital gain on one residence. Allocating one year to the cottage will maximize the exemption.

B. DISPOSITION OF ASSETS USED TO EARN INCOME

Many individuals own capital property with the expectation that they will immediately, or in the future, earn income from that property. In most instances, they would like to transfer ownership of all or part of that property, usually by selling at some point in the future.

Non-Depreciable Capital Property

This type of property includes assets that do not wear out or become used up. Both individuals and individuals operating a business can have a capital gain or loss on non-depreciable property because both can own property whose purpose is to earn income. Example 6 shows the calculation of a net capital loss, which occurs when one asset is sold at a profit and one is sold at a loss that is greater than the profit on the other asset.

Example 6   Katie bought Nortel and Bombardier Inc. shares when her friend, Joanne, bought her shares. Katie doesn't know much about investing and decided to do what Joanne did in the mistaken belief that Joanne was an expert. When Joanne died, Katie panicked and sold all her shares.

	ACB	Proceeds	Capital gain/loss	Taxable capital gain/ (allowable capital loss)
Nortel	7,000	1,500	(5,500)	(2,750)
Bombardier	2,000	5,000	3,000	1,500
Net capital loss				(1,250)

Katie has a capital gain on her Bombardier shares and a capital loss on her Nortel shares. Her net allowable loss for the year is $1,250. She could, if she had unused taxable capital gains from prior years, apply this loss against those gains by refiling her prior tax returns. But Katie has no unused taxable capital gains, so all she can do is carry this loss forward, converting her net allowable loss into a net capital loss, until she has a taxable capital gain sometime in the future.

Depreciable Capital Property

The disposition of depreciable property can lead to a **capital gain, recapture** or a **terminal loss** (but not a capital loss) for an individual operating a business, including a farm. Because it is income-producing property, the tax department allows you to deduct the capital cost as a business expense over several years.

- The **capital cost** is the acquisition cost at the time the asset is purchased and it is the basis for CCA.
- **Capital cost allowance (CCA)** is the tax deduction permitted on a **class** of depreciable capital assets. The Income Tax Act specifies the classes and the maximum amount (percentage) of CCA that can be taken each year.
- **Undepreciated capital cost (UCC)** is the capital cost of the asset less minus accumulated CCA for that class.

The capital cost is usually the same as the ACB at the time the asset is purchased. The capital cost is the acquisition cost and it goes into the CCA pool. The ACB is the basis for calculating the capital gain or loss and is sometimes different if the capital cost or the ACB is adjusted to reflected advanced tax rules. It is not mandatory to deduct CCA in a given tax year if it produces a non-deductible loss.

Craig chuckle. "I thought I was doing pretty well until now with this tax stuff. I've had some investing profits and losses over the years so I have been following everything you have said so far. But this idea of CCA is new to me. Can you show me how it works?"

"Yes," says Francesca. "Let me show you how the CCA and UCC is calculated for the next example. Lily's grand piano would be in Class 8 (20%), "Machinery and Equipment not included in another class, furniture, photocopiers, and facsimile machines". The 20% means that each year, the maximum amount of CCA Lilly can claim as a tax deduction is 20% of the prior year's ending balance in her Class 8. The **half-year rule** dictates that you can take only 50% of the CCA on any new assets acquired during the year. This has the effect of assuming all assets are owned for one-half of the year regardless of when they were bought.

Table 11.3 Calculation of Capital Cost Allowance — Class 8, 20% declining balance

Year	UCC_{BOY}	Addition (+) Dispositions (–)	UCC after +/- = base for CCA	CCA	UCC_{EOY}
1	0.00	25,000.00	25,000.00	2,500.00	22,500.00
2	22,500.00	0.00	22,500.00	4,500.00	18,000.00
3	18,000.00	0.00	18,000.00	3,600.00	14,400.00
4	14,400.00	0.00	14,400.00	2,880.00	11,520.00
5	11,520.00	0.00	11,520.00	2,304.00	9,216.00
6	9,216.00	0.00	9,216.00	1,843.20	7,372.80
7	7,372.80	0.00	7,372.80	1,474.56	5,898.24
8	5,898.24	0.00	5,898.24	1,179.65	4,718.59
9	4,718.59	0.00	4,718.59	943.72	3,774.87
				21,225.13	

Example 7 calculates capital gain, recapture, and a terminal loss on the sale of a business asset for three different proceeds.

Example 7   Lily lives in Tavistock, Ontario, and has been a piano teacher for many years.
There are several community public schools in Oxford County that are too small to have their own music teacher. So Lily travels around the county in her van to provide music classes to students in four of these schools. She spends an afternoon a week in each school, giving classes for which she receives a salary and a T-4 each year. After school and on Saturdays, Lily gives private piano lessons at the school and in her home.

Lily is thinking of selling her grand piano and buying a good upright piano. It won't be the same as her grand, but she is tired of having it take up so much room. She put an ad in a national newspaper in order to get as much as she can for the piano. The following illustrates the tax implications three different proceeds for her piano.

Capital cost / ACB	25,000	25,000	25,000
CCA taken to date	21,225	21,225	21,225
UCC	3,775	3,775	3,775
Proceeds	**–3,000**	**–18,000**	**–30,000**
Balance to account for	775	–14,225	–26,225
Capital gain: Proceeds > cost and 50% is taxable income	0	0	5,000
UCC pool just before disposition	3,775	3,775	3,775
Lower of cost or proceeds	–3,000	–18,000	–25,000
Balance in UCC pool after disposition	775	–14,225	–21,225
Recapture 100% = taxable income		14,225	21,225
Terminal loss 100% = tax deduction	–775		
UCC after accounting for balance	0	0	0

"And how do you come up with these numbers for capital gain, recapture and terminal loss," Craig asks.

Francesca provides him with the following explanation. "Let's use the same format to show the possible balances in the UCC for each amount of proceeds and then let's figure out the implication of each possible outcome."

"Step one is to check to see if there is a capital gain, that is, did you receive more for the asset than the original cost. This does not occur frequently but can happen with some depreciable assets such as buildings. The amount of the capital gain cannot be taken out of the **UCC pool** because this excess of proceeds over cost was never in the pool.

In this example, the proceeds of $30,000 are $5,000 more than the capital cost. This $5,000 is the amount of the capital gain."

"Step two is to account for the balance in the UCC pool after the proceeds are subtracted from it."

Table 11.4A Balance in the UCC Pool after Recording the Lower of Cost or Proceeds

Year	UCC_BOY	Addition (+) Dispositions (–)	UCC after +/- = base for CCA	CCA	UCC_EOY
10	3,774.87	–3,000.00	774.87		
10	3,774.87	–18,000.00	–14,225.13		
10	3,774.87	–25,000.00	–21,225.13		

* to a maximum of the capital cost.

Table 11.4A Accounting for the Balance in the UCC Pool after Recording the Lower of Cost or Proceeds

Step 1	Is there a capital gain? Are the proceeds > the ACB?			
	Proceeds	3,000	18,000	30,000
	less ACB	25,000	25,000	25,000
	Capital gain – 50% is taxable income	no	no	5,000
Step 2	Balance in UCC pool after taking out lower of cost or proceeds	775	–14,225	–21,225
	Recapture = 100% taxable income		14,225	21,225
	• If the balance is negative			
	• too much CCA has been taken			
	• the balance is 100% taxable			
	• May not be the last asset in the class.			
	Terminal Loss = 100% tax deductible	–775		
	• If the balance is positive AND			
	• If there are no more assets in the pool			
	• not enough CCA has been taken			
	• the balance is 100% tax deductible.			
	UCC pool balance	0	0	0

Summary

Capital gain: Proceeds are greater than the original cost = proceeds minus original cost or ACB

Recapture: Proceeds are greater than the UCC = lesser of capital cost / ACB and proceeds minus UCC — *effectively a result of too much CCA taken.* The disposition of this asset may leave other assets in the pool, that is, it is not necessarily the last asset in the class.

Terminal loss: Proceeds are less than the UCC — *effectively a result of too little CCA taken.* It has to be the last asset in the class.

Capital loss: Occurs *only* with non-depreciable assets. All assets owned for personal use are non-depreciable.

Sale of Land and a Building

If the **sale of land and building** results in a terminal loss on the building and a capital gain on the land, the proceeds are redistributed to reduce or eliminate the terminal loss and reduce the capital gain. The effect is to increase taxable income. This scenario is illustrated in Example 8.

Example 8   Many years ago, Lily and her husband, Sam, bought a small apartment build-ing in Stratford. They have not spent much on the upkeep, so the building needs a lot of repairs and renovating. Sam wants to sell it so they can both be free to travel. They sold the land and building for $270,000 – $210,000 for the land and $60,000 for the building.

The following table illustrates both their initial capital gain and terminal loss and the revised calculation.

	Land	Building	Total
Cost	80,000	100,000	180,000
UCC		75,000	75,000
Original calculation			
Proceeds	210,000	60,000	270,000
Capital gain	130,000		130,000
Terminal loss		(15,000)	(15,000)
Income	65,000	(15,000)	**50,000**
Revised calculation			
Proceeds	195,000	75,000	270,000
Capital gain	115,000		115,000
Terminal loss		0	0
Income	57,500	0	**57,500**

Even if they are sold in different years, another provision in the Income Tax Act leads to the same result (although normally the land and building cannot be sold separately in different years). Each rental property over $50,000 acquired after 1971 must be in a separate class to force the recognition of the recapture as each is sold (unless the asset was replaced by another asset; in this case, recognition of the recapture is deferred). The $800,000 capital gains exemption on qualified investments is discussed later in this chapter.

Personal Real Estate and Change in Use of Property

Converting Non-Income-Producing Property into Income-Producing Property

Sometimes at retirement, retirees will decide to live in a cottage and rent out the city home. In this instance, the cottage may become the principal residence. Or a family may move to another city for a few years to pursue a job opportunity. They may buy or rent in the other city and, in either case, rent out their original residence for the duration of the stay in the other city. A taxpayer can move out of their primary residence for up to four years and rent it out and have it remain the principal residence as long as the taxpayer:

• remains in Canada
• does not designate some other property as a principal residence
• files a "**no change of use**" with CRA, and

• does not claim any CCA on the residence while it is being rented out.

If the residence is rented out longer than four years, the "no change of use" election remains (unless revoked) but the principal residence exemption ends, that is, if it is rented out for longer than four years, the four years can still be exempt.

If the "no change of use" election is revoked, there is a deemed disposition and reacquisition at FMV of the residence on January 1 of the year the election was revoked. Claiming CCA automatically revokes the election. CCA claimed on a portion of the principal dwelling that is rented out can lead to a capital gain or loss and recapture or a terminal loss when it is sold on that portion of the residence on which CCA was claimed. Example 9 again shows the allocation of the principal residence exemption.

Example 9 Stan and Liz of Example 5 decided to move to their cottage in October 2004 and rent out their house in the city instead of selling it. In 2013, when they sold the house for $595,000, they also sold the cottage for $475,000 in order to buy a larger cottage with a better view of the lake. They can designate both the house and the cottage as the principal residence until the end of 1981. The cottage is the principal residence from 2004 to 2013. But what about the 23 years from 1982 to 2004? Since the house has the largest capital gain per year of ownership, it will be the exempt portion for the maximum possible number of years.

	House	Cottage	Total
Purchase date	May 12, 1965	April 17, 1976	
Purchase price	40,000	15,000	
V-day value — Dec 31, 1971	48,000	n/a	
Renovations — 1982		30,000	
ACB		45,000	
Proceeds from sale Oct. 27, 2013	595,000		
FMV in 2013		475,000	
Capital gain as at 2013	547,000	430,000	
N2	42	38	
Capital gain / N2 (Note 1)	13,024	11,316	
N1 before January 1, 1982	10	6	
N1 Maximum possible after January 1, 1982	23	32	977,000
N1 – Total maximum possible	33	38	80
Years house is rented out	9	0	
N2	42	38	
N1 – Total maximum possible	33		
N1 – "No Change of Use"	4		
N1 – Total	37	5	42
N1 + 1	38	6	
Exempt portion: (N1+1)/N2	90.48%	15.79%	
Capital gain — Exempt portion	494,905	67,895	562,799
Capital gain — 50% not taxable	26,048	181,053	207,100
Capital gain — 50% taxable	26,048	181,053	207,100
Capital gain — Total	547,000	430,000	977,000

Liz and Stan likely don't know the actual value of either property until they sell one of them. At that point, they have to get a reasonable estimate of the value of the property they have not sold so they can make a decision about which to declare as the principal residence.

To Take CCA or Not to Take CCA?

There is no way to predict the future FMV of a home. While owners of real property have rules of thumb, that is all they are — guidelines, not facts. If housing prices increase a great deal during the rental period, the taxpayer might be better off not taking CCA and therefore avoiding the recapture, which is taxed at full rates. This scenario is illustrated in Example 10.

Example 10   Liz and Stan deem the house their principal residence from 1982 to the end of 2004 (23 full or part years) because it had the larger increase in value. Since they are renting out their house beginning January 1, 2005, they claim CCA in order to minimize their income taxes on the rental income. When they begin renting out the house, they pay for an evaluation so they have a sound basis for their CCA calculation.

House	CCA taken	No CCA taken
FMV January 1, 2005 — estimate	450,000	450,000
less CCA* taken 2005–2012	118,612	0
UCC	331,388	450,000
less Proceeds	595,000	595,000
Total gain (Proceeds less UCC)	263,612	145,000
Total gain is comprised of:		
• Capital gain: 50% is taxable in 2013	145,000	145,000
• Recapture: 100% taxable in 2013	118,612	0
	263,612	145,000

*On FMV using 4% a year and the half-year rule (Income Tax, Regulations, Part XI, Capital Cost Allowance; Schedule II, Capital Cost Allowances). No CCA is taken in the year of disposal.

In this scenario, housing prices are rising (as they usually, but not always, are). As a result, when Liz and Stan sell the house, they sell it for more than the FMV on the date they started renting it out. This produces a capital gain of $145,000 ($595,000 – $450,000) whether or not they take CCA. The CCA taken produces recapture equal to the FMV on the date of the conversion minus the UCC ($450,000 – $331,388). The recapture is 100% taxable in the year it occurs.

And what happens to their total taxable capital gain if they take CCA (and therefore cannot elect a "No Change in Use")? Let's take the chart in Example 9 and eliminate these four years from N1 for the house. We will sell both the house and the cottage in 2013 as we did in Example 9 and will not use an evaluation for the house as shown in the prior chart but rather will use N1+1 and N2 to calculate the capital gain. As shown in the following table, we now have $3,416 (210,516 – 207,100) more in taxable capital gain in addition to the recapture that is equal to the CCA taken.

	House	Cottage	Total
Capital gain as at 2013	547,000	430,000	977,000
N2	42	38	80
N1 — Maximum possible for the house	33	9	42
N1 + 1	34	10	
Exempt portion: (N1+1)/N2	80.95%	26.32%	
Capital gain — Exempt portion	442,810	113,158	555,967
Capital gain — 50% not taxable	52,095	158,421	210,516
Capital gain — 50% taxable	52,095	158,421	210,516
Capital gain — Total	547,000	430,000	977,000

Were Liz and Stan better off taking the CCA over the eight years and reducing their taxable income in those years but then paying the tax on the recapture? It depends on the other income in those years and in the year of disposal. It also depends on future housing prices, which can fall and take a long time to recover their value. Unfortunately, these predictions usually cannot be accurately estimated in advance.

Converting Income-Producing Property into Non-Income-Producing Property

There is a deemed disposition at FMV and the property is deemed to have been immediately reacquired at FMV. However, the taxpayer can elect to call it the principal residence for up to four years prior to the year actually occupied if, during the four years, the taxpayer

* was a resident in Canada
* did not designate another residence as the principal residence, and
* did not take CCA

as outlined above.

Principal Residence of a Farm

The principal residence of a **farm** is also exempt from capital gains tax. There are two methods for calculating the capital gain on this type of principal residence:

1. Deduct $1,000 a year for each year after 1971 and deduct that total from the total capital gain.

2. Generally, only 1/2 hectare is deemed to be the land that belongs to the principal residence, although this depends on the area that is designated to be necessary to the use and enjoyment of the house. The value of the buildings is based on the market value of homes in the general area. A proportionate share of the land is assigned for the personal residence.

Eligible Capital Property

The CRA bulletin "T-4002 Business and Professional Income" defines **intangible assets** as property that does not physically exist but gives you a lasting economic benefit. These intangible assets must have been paid for and include:

* franchises and licences for an unlimited time
* goodwill
* incorporation or reorganization costs
* customer lists
* trademarks
* patents and patent rights

- milk quotas
- government rights

Excluded:

- debt payments, dividends paid, cost of shares, mortgages, etc.
- intangible assets that have a limited life are depreciable property, not eligible capital property. This includes franchises, patents, concessions and licences for a specified period of time.

This kind of property is called **eligible capital property** and the price paid to buy it is called an **eligible capital expenditure (ECE)**. There must be a separate account for each business operated by one person or corporation. The **cumulative eligible capital account (CEC account)** is a tax account that holds 75% of the cost of the eligible capital expenditure — that is, you cannot deduct the full cost of the eligible capital expenditure but you can deduct part of it. The 75% is called the **eligible capital value**. The CEC account is used to keep track of property bought and sold.

Using the declining-balance method, 7% of the net amount in the account can be taken as an amortization expense (called **annual allowance**) each year, but you do not have to take the full amount of the maximum annual allowance expense each year — you can deduct up to the 7% maximum allowance. There is **no half-year rule** for eligible capital property. The half-year rule for depreciable assets limits CCA to be calculated on 50% of net additions in the year of acquisition.

On the **disposal** of eligible capital property, 75% of the proceeds are deducted from the cumulative eligible capital account. If the pool balance at the end of the year is negative, the balance must be taken into income (like recapture). Qualified farming and fishing property has a combination of income and capital gains, as illustrated in Example 11.

Only individuals operating a business, including farming and fishing, can experience a business expense or a capital gain from eligible capital property. Example 11 illustrates the calculation of the annual deduction for cumulative eligible capital and the effects of a negative balance after disposition.

Example 11   Chloe, Lily's daughter, ran Lily's business for a couple of years after Lily retired. Then Chloe was offered a full-time teaching job at a local community college and decided to give up her business and part-time teaching. When Chloe took over Lily's business, she paid Lily $20,000 for the business. When Chloe sold the business two years later, she got $22,000 for it.

		Amortization	Buy/Sell	Balance EOY
Year 1 addition	Goodwill 75% × $20,000		15,000	15,000
Year 1 expense	7%	(1,050)		13,950
Year 2 expense	7%	(977)		12,973
Year 3 disposal	Sale 75% × 22,000		(16,500)	(3,527)

Treatment of **negative year-end balance of $3,527**:

Add to business income:

- An amount up to the amounts claimed (the recaptured CECA) 1,050 + 977 =   2,027
- Rest of the negative balance 1,500 (= 3,527 – 2,027) multiplied by 2/3* =   <u>1,000</u>

Taxable income	**$3,027**
Non-taxable amount	<u>500</u>
Total negative balance	<u>**$3,527**</u>

* This has the effect of treating the recovery of the expense like recapture and also of including 50% of the entire capital gain in income (22,000 – 20,000), not just the 75% that is eligible for the annual amortization:

- Recaptured CECA   1,050 + 977 = $2,027
- Taxable capital gain at 50% inclusion rate (22,000 – 20,000) × 50% = 1,000
- Taxable income $3,027

Items such as milk quotas qualify as eligible capital farm property, and an interest in a fishing licence qualifies as eligible capital fishing property. This permits the individual to report a gain from disposition as a capital gain rather than business income, and this gain is, therefore, eligible for the $750,000 capital gains exemption.

Table 11.5 Summary of the Categories of Income-Producing Capital Property

	Non-depreciable	Depreciable	Eligible capital property
	Land, shares, animals, trees	*Buildings, cars, computers*	*Goodwill*
Annual tax deduction	n/a	CCA	Annual Allowance
If sold for more than UCC or cost	Capital gain	Capital gain, recapture	Farms and fishing: Business income + capital gain Other: Business income
If sold for less than UCC or cost	Capital loss	Terminal loss	Business expense

C. TRANSFER OF ASSETS TO SPOUSE

Special rules apply when capital property is transferred to a spouse. A spouse includes a spouse, spousal trust, or ex-spouse as part of a divorce settlement.

Spousal Rollover

A person can transfer assets to their spouse at any time without triggering a capital gain (or loss). This is a spousal rollover (Income Tax Act section 73) and it applies to transfers while the transferor is alive (inter vivos transfers) or after death. The spousal rollover applies automatically unless the spouse or executor elects out of it.

Under the spousal rollover, the receiving spouse essentially steps into the tax shoes of the transferor, assuming their tax values — capital cost, UCC and ACB. The proceeds of disposition are deemed to be the tax value of the asset — the ACB for non-depreciable assets and the UCC for depreciable assets. As such, there is no tax implication at the time of the transfer.

Note: The same rollover provisions

1. Apply to transfers to financially dependent minor children or grandchildren, and
2. May trigger the Income Attribution Rules if the transferor is still alive. This is discussed in the next section "D. Non-arm's Length Transfers and Income Attribution."

Table 11.6 Spousal Rollover of Assets

Non-Depreciable Assets	Depreciable Assets
• These assets, such as shares and the family cottage, are transferred (roll over) at the ACB of the transferor	• These assets produce business or rental income (and are, therefore, not assets owned for personal use and enjoyment) and CCA can be taken on them.
• Deemed proceeds of disposition (POD) equals ACB	• Deemed proceeds of disposition (POD) equals UCC
• No capital gain or loss	• No capital gain, recapture or terminal loss.
• Recipient's ACB = Transferor's ACB	• Recipient's capital cost = Transferor's capital cost
	• Recipient's UCC = Transferor's UCC

Example 12A   Lily died unexpectedly at the age of 61. She had not yet retired. At the time of her death, Lily's business assets were a grand piano, a photocopier, and the van.

Lily's assets:	Piano	Copier	Van
Cost	25,000	4,000	35,000
CCA taken to date	21,225	1,620	20,422
UCC	3,775	2,380	14,578
FMV	30,000	1,200	20,000

Since the assets rollover to the spouse at the transferor's ACB or UCC, there is no tax consequence at the time of the transfer. However, any capital gain for the beneficiary is based on this original ACB or UCC.

Example 12B   When **Lily** died, she and her husband, **Sam**, had mirror wills — each left everything to the other and then to the children should they die at the same time. Sam's cost and UCC are the same as Lily's, since the assets are rolled over to him.

	Piano	Copier	Van
Lily's deemed proceeds = UCC	3,775	2,380	14,578
Recapture/(terminal loss)	0	0	0
Capital gain	0	0	0
Sam's cost = Lily's cost	25,000	4,000	35,000
Sam's UCC = Lily's UCC	3,775	2,380	14,578

Electing Out of the Spousal Rollover

There are situations when the transferor may not want the spousal rollover to apply. To do this, the taxpayer / executor must elect out of the automatic spousal rollover provision by **filing an election** to roll the assets over at FMV, that is, the deemed POD is the FMV.

The electing out can occur on a property by property basis, rolling over some at the UCC / ACB and some FMV. For instance, some shares could be transferred at ACB and others at FMV. Or some of Lily's assets can be transferred at UCC and others at FMV.

Table 11.7 Electing Out of Spousal Rollover of Assets

Non-Depreciable Assets	Depreciable Assets
Deemed POD = FMV	Deemed POD = FMV
Recipient's ACB = FMV	Recipient's capital cost = FMV

Example 13 Lily's executor decided to rollover Lily's piano and photocopier at their FMV to use up some tax losses Lily had incurred when she sold some shares during a market downturn.

	Elect Out	Elect Out	Roll Over	
Transfer at:	**FMV**	**FMV**	**UCC**	
	Piano	**Copier**	**Van**	**Taxable income**
Cost	25,000	4,000	35,000	
CCA taken to date	21,225	1,620	20,422	
UCC	3,775	2,380	14,578	
Lily's deemed proceeds = FMV	30,000	1,200	14,578	
Capital gain	5,000	0	0	2,500
Recapture / (terminal loss)	21,225	(1,180)	0	20,045
				22,545
Sam's cost	30,000	1,200	14,578	

The executor might also file this election if Sam is going to be facing some large tax issues in the future.

D. NON-ARM'S LENGTH TRANSFERS AND INCOME ATTRIBUTION

The deemed proceeds of disposition (POD) depends on the relationship of the person and the transfer price.

- Spousal rollover transfers occur at cost with no immediate tax consequences. This Income Tax Act (ITA) Section 73 provision also applies to financially dependent minor children and grandchildren. In addition, unless steps are taken as outlined below, income attribution rules will apply.
- If it was a gift,
  - the deemed POD is FMV, giving rise to recapture, a terminal loss, or a capital gain for the taxpayer, and
  - the recipient's ACB is the FMV.
- If it was sold for more or less than the FMV,
  - the deemed POD is FMV
  - the recipient's ACB is the actual price paid to a maximum of the FMV.

Table 11.8 Non-Arm's Length Transfers and Gifts that are Not Spousal Rollovers

Gifts	Sold for Less than or More than FMV*
Deemed POD = FMV	Deemed POD = FMV
Recipient's ACB = FMV	Recipient's ACB = actual price paid to a maximum of FMV

* Presumably this is a non-arm's length transaction because
  - the seller wouldn't sell it at arm's length for less than FMV, and
  - an arm's length buyer wouldn't pay more than FMV.

Example 14 illustrates the effects of disposing of a business asset by giving it to a charity or a relative or selling it below market value to a relative.

Example 14   Let's roll back the clock from Example 11. Lily has not yet retired. She is thinking of getting rid of her grand piano if she can find a good upright piano. Lily decides her options are to:
- give the piano to a charity,
- give the piano to her daughter,
- sell the piano to her daughter for *less* than the fair market value, or
- sell the piano to her daughter for *more* than the fair market value.

Presumably she would not sell the piano in an arm's length transaction for less than the fair market value.

	Give to charity	Give to daughter	Sell to daughter	Sell to daughter
	Arm's length	*Non-arm's length*	*Non-arm's length*	*Non-arm's length*
Actual Proceeds	= 0	= 0	< FMV	> FMV
Adjusted cost base (ACB)	25,000	25,000	25,000	25,000
CCA taken to date	21,225	21,225	21,225	21,225
UCC	3,375	21,225	21,225	3,775
FMV	**15,000**	**15,000**	15,000	15,000
Actual proceeds	**0**	**0**	8,000	18,000
Lily's deemed proceeds	15,000	15,000	15,000	18,000
Lily's recapture	11,225	11,429	11,429	14,225
Recipient's ACB	**15,000**	**15,000**	**8,000**	**15,000**
If the next sale of the asset is for more than the higher of the current FMV or actual proceeds, there will be double taxation on			7,000	3,000

For the first three scenarios having the same ACB, UCC, and FMV, Lily's deemed proceeds and Lily's recapture are the same. However, the buyer's ACB is *not* the same.
- If Lily gives the piano away in either an arm's length transaction (to a charity, for instance) or a non-arm's length transaction (to her daughter), Lily's actual proceeds are $0 and the recipient's ACB is equal to the FMV ($15,000).
- If Lily sells it in a non-arm's length transaction for less than the FMV ($8,000 in this example), this is the amount of the ACB for the buyer.
  - Note that this non-arm's length sale for less than FMV will result in **double taxation** on $7,000 if Chloe, the buyer, sells the asset for more than $15,000. Lily has already reported $11,225 (15,000 – 3,775) as recapture but Chloe's gain will start at the $8,000 she actually pays, not at the $15,000 that is Lily's deemed proceeds. The non-arm's length sale for more than the FMV will also result in double taxation since the buyer's ACB is the FMV, not the actual proceeds.

Income Attribution Rules

An individual might transfer title to another person with the aim of reducing or avoiding future income taxes. The CRA discourages this behaviour in a couple of ways.

1.   When a taxpayer disposes of property by way of a gift or inadequate consideration (the buyer paid less than the fair market value), there is a deemed disposition at the fair market value.

2. Reallocating income to lower income family members saves tax. **Income splitting** is the reallocation of income among family members to reduce the total amount of tax paid by the family unit by taking advantage of:
   - the fact that Canadians file individual tax returns — that is, they do not file as a family unit
   - Canada has progressive personal tax rates.

   However, this strategy is restricted by the income attribution rules.

Income Attribution Rules are the rules under the Income Tax Act that govern who pays the tax on income or capital gains when the property has been transferred (given) or sold at less than the fair market value. If the income arises from:

- loans made at low or no interest, and
- transfers and gifts at less than FMV

and is made to:

- a spouse, minor child, or other non-arm's length person, and
- these assets earn property income (which is defined in Table 11.6),

the income is attributed to the original taxpayer, which means the original owner pays the income tax on the income. Attribution does not apply to business income. Income attribution rules do not apply if interest is charged at a minimum of the prescribed rate set by CRA and the interest is paid within 30 days of the year-end. Income from limited partnerships is property income, not business income. The tax liability arising from attribution rules is the joint and several liability of both parties.

There is no income attribution after death.

Table 11.9 What Is Attributed to the Donor?

Transferred to:	Spouse, common-law partner, spousal trust	Related minor	Other non-arm's length
Method of Transfer:	All loans and gifts	All loans and gifts	Loans made to reduce or avoid tax. See Notes.
Type of income resulting from the transfer			
Property income Interest Dividends Rent income Business income earned by a specified member of a partnership	Yes	Yes while the child is < 18	Yes
Income on the attributed income	No	No	No
Property losses Rent income Business income earned by a specified member of a partnership	Yes	Yes while the child is < 18	No
Capital gains and losses	Yes (1)	No (2)	No
Business income and losses (rental income with services is business income)	No	No	No
Deemed proceeds ACB for new owner	ACB / UCC ACB / UCC	FMV FMV	FMV FMV

(1) In a Section 73(1) spousal rollover, when the spouse sells the property, the capital gain or loss is attributed to the donor. If the donor elects out of the automatic rollover and the property was sold at FMV, attribution rules do **not** apply.

(2) If an asset is transferred, the transfer is done at FMV and the capital gain at the time of the transfer is immediate. If the child sells it before turning 18, no further capital gains and losses are attributed.

Notes:

A **spouse** is a legal and common-law spouse.

Related minors include a child, niece, or nephew under the age of 18.

A **non-arm's length person** includes:

• related persons connected by blood, marriage, or adoption; i.e., spouse, direct descendants and their spouses, brothers and sisters (in-law) but not nieces and nephews

• unrelated but not at arm's length which may be indicated by a price below FMV or a transaction that does not reflect ordinary business dealings

Attribution rules do apply if the loan was made to or from a trust on behalf of one of the beneficiaries.

There is **no income attribution**:

• when there is a transfer to a spouse for the FMV, but the taxpayer must file an election to not have the spousal rollover provisions apply

• on **loans for value** where the interest rate is reasonable or more than the CRA prescribed rate currently 1%, and is paid consistently. Note that, if the prescribed rate is used, it remains the same forever even if the prescribed rate increases

• when the spouses are living apart (either separated or divorced), and both spouses agree to this

Attribution stops when:

• the taxpayer ceases to be a resident of Canada
• the taxpayer or designated person **dies**
• the related minor turns 18
• a marriage breaks down.

The same attribution rules apply to:

• substituted property
• transferred or loaned property acquired using a trust or something else
• loans and transfers to a trust.

Kiddie tax is the name given to the income tax on dividends paid from a private corporation to a child under the age of 18 who owns shares in a private corporation. These dividends are now taxed at the highest federal rate of 29% and the only tax credit permitted is the dividend tax credit — not even the basic personal amount can be used. It was created in Section 120.44 of the Income Tax Act to prevent high-income people from reducing taxes by issuing shares in a private corporation to their minor children and then declaring dividends on those shares. Before the kiddie tax was implemented, the dividends received by the minor child were then used to pay private school fees, camp fees or fees for extracurricular activities.

E.   DEEMED DISPOSITIONS AT DEATH

In the previous sections, we have looked at the tax implications associated with the disposition of personal, financial and business assets. In all cases, the taxpayer was still alive at the time of the transfer. With these rules in minds, we examine the tax implications when the taxpayer has died.

When a taxpayer dies, there is a deemed disposition of all their assets. The deemed proceeds of disposition (POD) depends on who is the beneficiary of each asset. Generally, POD is deemed to be the FMV at the time of death. The exception to this rule occurs when the beneficiary is the surviving spouse (or financially dependent child or grandchild). Then, the spousal rollover rules apply and the assets are deemed to be transferred with no tax implications unless the executor elects out of these automatic spousal rollover provisions.

Table 11.10 Deemed Proceeds of Disposition for Deceased and Cost for Beneficiary

Beneficiary	Spouse / Spousal Trust*	Non-Spouse — Child, Grandchild, Friend, Charity
Personal Assets • House, cottage car, painting, antiques	Spousal rollover at ACB unless executor elects out. Then transferred at FMV	Deemed disposition at FMV (Principal residence exemption is available to the deceased in the year of death)
Non-registered Financial Assets • Shares, Bonds, Mutual Funds, GICs	Spousal rollover	Deemed disposition at FMV
TFSA	Technically, it is a spousal rollover, unless executor elects out. But any capital gain is never taxed so it doesn't matter	Deemed disposition at FMV, but any capital gain is never taxed in TFSA so it doesn't matter
Registered Financial Assets • RRSP, DPSP, RRIF, LRIF	Spousal rollover, at ACB, to spouse's RRSP/RRIF/LRIF (remains registered upon transfer)	Deemed disposition at FMV. Upon transfer, the entire FMV is taken out of the registered fund so 100% of the FMV at the time of death is taxable in the year of death
Depreciable Assets	Spousal rollover. Recipient assumes the capital cost, UCC and CCA balance of deceased.	Deemed disposition at FMV Recipient assumes capital cost of the deceased, with difference between capital cost and FMV = deemed CCA.
Eligible Capital Property	Spousal rollover. Recipient assumes the eligible capital expenditure (ECE) and Cumulative Eligible Capital (CEC) balance of the deceased.	Deemed disposition at CEC balance, as long as beneficiary carries on business. Note that this is not at FMV. (Why? It could impair the business' ability to continue if burdened with a tax liability on high FMV of goodwill and other ECE assets.)

* Also applies to a financially dependent minor child or grandchild.

Now let's re-visit Example 13 and have Lily leave her business assets to her daughter Chloe instead of her husband, Sam. It doesn't matter whether Lily leaves her assets to her daughter Chloe or her friend, Annette — the tax implications for both Lily and the beneficiary are the same.

Example 15   Lily was still working when she died and left her business assets to her daughter, Chloe, who also gives piano lessons. Chloe is going to apply for her mother's job at the four schools and thus would continue to use the assets as business assets.
- Lily's deemed proceeds equal the FMV at death
- Chloe's UCC equals FMV at death
- Chloe's cost is *the greater of*:
  - actual cost ($0 in this scenario), and
  - the FMV

FMV/Capital cost	>	≤	≤	
	Piano	Copier	Van	Taxable income
Cost	25,000	4,000	35,000	
CCA taken to date	21,225	1,620	20,422	
UCC	3,775	2,380	14,578	
Lily's deemed proceeds = FMV	30,000	1,200	20,000	
Lily's actual proceeds	**0**	**0**	**0**	
Capital gain	5,000	0	0	2,500
Recapture/(terminal loss)	21,429	(1,180)	5,422	25,671
				27,967
Chloe's costs = UCC = FMV	30,000	1,200	20,000	
Chloe's deemed capital cost *			35,000	
Chloe's deemed CCA *			15,000	

* This happens only when the FMV is greater than the UCC but less than the capital cost. Theoretically, Chloe could sell the van the next day for $22,500. In this case, the FMV for the transfer should have been $22,500, not $20,000 and the recapture would have been $7,922, not $5,422. By deeming the UCC to be $20,000 (35,000 − 15,000), her $2,500 gain is recapture and not a capital gain.

Lily is very generous to Chloe. Not only has Chloe paid nothing for her mother's business assets, but Lily has also paid the tax on the deemed disposition at FMV. Perhaps Sam and Lily want to help Chloe out while she is still young.

If you are buying assets from an estate, you have to be careful because the non-arm's length transaction rules can apply if the actual proceeds is either more or less than the FMV as shown in Example 14. This would result in double taxation.

Net Capital Losses at Death

Taxable capital gains are reported on the final tax return of the deceased and the tax payable must be paid by the estate before CRA will release the assets to the beneficiary. Certain capital property is eligible for the principal residence exemption and/or the a lifetime capital gains exemption of $800,000

Earlier we stated that a net capital loss is any net allowable capital loss that is not deducted for the current year. A **net capital loss carryforward** at death is applied:

1. to net capital gains in the year of death
2. after deducting any **capital gains deduction** (covered as part of the "Final Tax Return" later in the chapter), to any other source of income in the year of death and the year before death

There are two ways to handle a **net capital loss, which occurs in the year of death**:

1. carry it back three years and apply it to realized taxable capital gains, **or**
2. + current net capital loss
   + any net capital loss carryforward outstanding
   − any capital gains deduction claimed

Special Rule
Any remaining balance can be applied to **any income** in:
• the year of death, **or**
• the year before death, **or**
• both years

Example 16 shows how the capital loss from Example 1 is deducted.

Example 16 When Joanne died unexpectedly in 2013, she owned shares in Rosebud Inc. and Bombardier Inc. She had left instructions in her will that the shares should be sold regardless of the price. In 2010, she sold the shares she owned in her cousin's high-tech start-up, realizing a capital loss of $6,000. She had no other assets that would give rise to a taxable capital gain or allowable capital loss.

	ACB	Proceeds	Capital gain/ (loss)	Taxable capital gain/ (allowable capital loss)
Net capital loss carryforward	(3,000)		(6,000)	(3,000)
Net capital loss in year of death:				
Rosebud Inc.	7,000	1,500	(5,500)	(2,750)
Bombardier Inc.	2,000	5,000	3,000	1,250
				(4,250)

Joanne's executor has two options.

Option 1. She could carry the $1,250 net capital loss in the year of death back three years — but Joanne has no capital gains in those three years against which she can deduct the net capital loss.

Option 2. Her executor can deduct the $4,250 total net capital loss against any other of her income:
• in the year of death,
• in the year before she died, or
• in both years.

	Description	$
add	current net capital loss	(1,250)
subtract	net capital loss carryforward	(3,000)
		(4,250)

Craig is seriously frowning now. "I've been following it all quite well I think," he says, "but it would help a lot if you could provide some kind of a summary for us." Francesca sketches out the following example for them.

Table 11.11 Taxation of Assets at Death

	ACB / Capital Cost	UCC	FMV	Widowed 50-year old, leaving assets to adult children		Married 50 year old, leaving assets to spouse	
				Amount that impacts taxable income		In general, there are no tax implications	
Personal Assets							
House	200,000		500,000	nil	• Designate as principal residence	nil	• No impact due to spousal rollover
Car	48,500		28,500	nil	• No capital loss on personal use asset	nil	• No cap loss on personal use asset
Financial Assets							
Bonds	2,000		2,000	nil	• Paid with after-tax dollars	nil	• No impact due to spousal rollover
Shares of Scotia	40,000		85,000	22,500	• Non depreciable	nil	• No impact due to spousal rollover
Shares of Blueberry	95,000		22,000	(36,500)	• Non depreciable • Note allowable capital loss can offset only taxable capital gain	nil	• No impact due to spousal rollover
Mutual fund	34,000		43,000	4,500	• Non depreciable	nil	• No impact due to spousal rollover
RRSP	225,000		400,000	400,000	• Full amount included in income of deceased	nil	• Full amount included in income of deceased
TFSA	18,000		26,000	nil	• Never taxable	nil	• Never taxable
Luxury Assets							
Antique table	500		2,200	600	• $1,000 rule for PUP	nil	• $1,000 rule for PUP
Bateman painting	400		2,400	700	• $1,000 rule for PUP • this is LPP	nil	• $1,000 rule for PUP • this is LPP
Coin set	1,350		350	(175)	• $1,000 rule for PUP • this is LPP • Loss for LPP can only be applied against gain on LPP	nil	• $1,000 rule for PUP • this is LPP • Loss for LPP can only be applied against gain on LPP
Business Assets							
Office furniture	42,000	29,400	25,000	4,400	• Terminal loss. • $4,400 remains in UCC class after all assets are deemed disposed	nil	• Deemed disposition at POD = UCC
Building	165,000	148,500	201,000	18,000 16,500	• Taxable capital gain • Recapture because took too much CCA on asset that increased in value	nil	• Deemed disposition at POD = UCC
Land	235,000		250,000	7,500		nil	• Deemed disposition at ACB

F. FINAL TAX RETURN

When a taxpayer dies, the executor must file a final tax return, also called a **terminal return** for the **terminal period**, which is January 1 of the year of death to the date of death. The deadline for filing is the later of six months after death or the normal filing date of April 30 for the year of death (or June 30 if the deceased carried on a business). In addition, there are **three optional**, or **elective, returns** that might be filed on behalf of the deceased. Optional returns can reduce taxes — there are more returns at lower tax rates. These three are returns for:

1. "Rights or Things" for amounts owing at the time of death that would have been included in taxable income; for example vacation pay, salary, commissions earned but unpaid at death, and investment income declared but unpaid.
2. "A Partner or Proprietor" for business income
3. "Income from a Testamentary Trust". This return is not the same as the T-3 Trust Income Tax and Information Return for income that remains in a testamentary trust at the end of the year. This return is discussed in Chapter 12.

CRA provides three charts that summarize these returns. An example follows Chart 3. The three charts are:

Chart 1:	Returns for the Year of Death
Chart 2:	Income reported on the T-3 Trust Income Tax and Information Return — discussed in Chapter 12
Chart 3:	Non-taxable Amounts

Chart 1 — Returns for the Year of Death

Total Income

		Three optional returns		
Line(s)	Final return	Return for rights or things	Return for a partner or proprietor	Return for income from a testamentary trust
101 to 146	• all income received before death • all income from deemed dispositions • all periodic payments (for example, rent, salary, and accrued interest)	• salary, commissions, and vacation pay owed and paid after death (Note 1) • retroactive salary adjustments owed and paid after death • CPP and EI arrears • accounts receivable, supplies, and inventory (Note 2) • uncashed matured bond coupons • bond interest earned before death • dividends declared before the date of death but not received • crops, livestock (Note 3) • work in progress (Note 4)	• income from the business, from the end of the business' fiscal period to the date of death	• income from the trust, from the end of the trust's fiscal period to the date of death

Deductions for Calculating Net Income

Line(s)	Final return	Rights or things	Partner/proprietor	Testamentary trust
207 to 232	• all deductions from lines 207 to 232 that are allowable	• generally, none of these deductions can be claimed	• same as for return for rights or things 70(2)	• same as for return for rights or things 70(2)
235	• social benefits repayments	• Note 5	• not applicable	• not applicable

Deductions for Calculating Taxable Income — Split Deductions (Note 6)

Line(s)	Final return	Rights or things	Partner/proprietor	Testamentary trust
248	• home-relocation loans	• Note 7	• not applicable	• not applicable
249	• security-options deductions	• Note 7	• not applicable	• not applicable
250	• other payments	• not applicable	• not applicable	• not applicable
251 to 255	• losses or other deductions	• no	• no	• no
256	• vow of perpetual poverty	• yes	• not applicable	• not applicable

Federal Non-refundable Tax Credits (Note 13)

Line(s)	Final return	Rights or things	Partner/proprietor	Testamentary trust
300 to 306	• all personal amounts	• yes — in full	• yes — in full	• yes — in full
315	• caregiver amount	• yes — in full	• yes — in full	• yes — in full

Federal Non-refundable Tax Credits (Note 13) — Split Amounts (Note 6)

Line(s)	Final return	Rights or things	Partner/proprietor	Testamentary trust
308	• CPP or QPP contributions	• Note 7	• not applicable	• not applicable
310	• CPP or QPP contributions on self-employed income	• not applicable	• yes	• not applicable
312	• EI premiums	• Note 7	• not applicable	• not applicable
314	• pension income amount	• Note 8	• not applicable	• Note 8
316	• disability amount	• yes	• yes	• yes
318	• disability amount transferred from a dependant	• yes	• yes	• yes
319	• interest on student loans	• yes	• yes	• yes

Federal Non-refundable Tax Credits (Note 13) — Split Amounts (Note 6) Continued.

Line(s)	Final return	Rights or things	Partner/Proprietor	Testamentary trust
323 to 324	• tuition and education	• yes	• yes	• yes
326	• amounts transferred from spouse or common-law partner	• no	• no	• no
330	• medical expenses	• Note 9	• Note 9	• Note 9
340	• charitable donations	• Note 10	• Note 10	• Note 10
342	• cultural and ecological gifts	• yes	• yes	• yes

Refund or Balance Owing

Line(s)	Final return	Rights or things	Partner/Proprietor	Testamentary trust
412	• investment tax credit	• no	• no	• no
422	• social benefits repayment	• Note 5	• not applicable	• not applicable
425	• dividend tax credits	• Note 11	• not applicable	• Note 11
427	• minimum tax carryover	• no	• no	• no
452	• refundable medical expense supplement (Note 12)	• no	• no	• no

Notes for Chart 1

1. Salary, commissions, and vacation pay are rights or things if both of these conditions are met:
    • The employer owed them to the deceased on the date of death; and
    • They are for a pay period that ended before the date of death.

2. Accounts receivable, supplies on hand, and inventory are rights or things if the deceased's business used the cash method.

3. This includes harvested farm crops and livestock that is not part of the basic herd. For more information, see *Interpretation Bulletins IT-234, Income of Deceased Persons — Farm Crops, and IT-427, Livestock of Farmers.*

4. "**Work in progress**" is a right or thing if the deceased was a sole proprietor and a professional (accountant, dentist, lawyer [in Quebec an advocate or notary], medical doctor, veterinarian, or chiropractor), who had elected to exclude work in progress when calculating his or her total income. For more information about rights or things, see *Interpretation Bulletin IT-212, Income of Deceased Persons — Rights or Things,* and its *Special Release.*

5. This amount can be claimed if OAS or EI benefits have been reported on this return.

6. Claims split between returns cannot be more than the total that could be allowed if you were only filing the final return.

7. This amount can be claimed if related employment income has been reported on this return.

8. This amount can be claimed if pension or annuity income has been reported on line 115 or line 129 of this return.

9. The medical expenses can be split between the returns. Allowable medical expenses have to be reduced by the lesser of $1,813 or 3% of the total net income reported on **all** the returns.

10. The amount that can be claimed is the **lesser** of the eligible amounts of charitable donations or 100% of the net income reported on this return. Also, the total charitable donations claimed on **all** the returns cannot exceed the eligible amount of charitable donations.

11. This amount can be claimed if dividend income has been reported on this return.

12. Use the deceased's net income from the final return and the spouse's or common-law partner's net income for the entire year to calculate this credit.

13. If the deceased was a resident of a province or territory other than Quebec, they may now also be able to claim provincial or territorial tax credits. See the provincial or territorial pages in the deceased's forms book.

Chart 2 — Income Reported on the *T3 Trust Income Tax and Information Return*

This chart is found in Chapter 12 in the section on trusts.

Chart 3 — Non-taxable Amounts

Do not report the following amounts on a T-1 final return for a deceased person or a T-3 return for a trust:

1. Retroactive adjustments to the following employment income when a collective agreement or other authorizing instrument has been signed *after* the date of death:
    - salary or wages (including overtime) from the end of the last pay period to the date of death
    - salary or wages (including overtime) for a pay period finished before the date of death but paid after death, and
    - payment for vacation leave earned but not taken.

2. Group term insurance, such as the federal government's supplementary death benefit.

There are certain amounts you cannot normally claim on an optional return. A partial list includes:

- registered pension plan deduction (line 207)
- registered retirement savings plan deduction (line 208)
- annual union, professional, or like dues (line 212)
- child care expenses (line 214)
- support payments made (line 220)
- amounts you transfer from a spouse or common-law partner (line 326).

Example 17   Cindy died on November 14, 2013. To minimize her taxes, her executor elected to file all the optional returns as well as the final return. The column on the right shows what the final return would have looked like if the executor had elected to file only one tax return. Cindy had a part-time job teaching in addition to income from her part-time business preparing and delivering gift baskets. The allocations have been made by her executor.

> **Note:** The numbers in the example for income and expenses to arrive at taxable income are "given" in the example, while the numbers from "Taxable income" to the end of the table are calculated by her executor, except for the amount of "Donations and Gifts" which are also "given".

The following table shows the calculation of the federal tax. Provincial tax would add to taxes payable and repeats the federal calculations using provincial rates.

Line		Final return	Rights or things	Partner/ proprietor	Testamentary trust	Total	All on final return
	Total income						
101	Employment income	40,000				40,000	40,000
120	Taxable dividends		5,000			5,000	5,000
121	Interest income				3,000	3,000	3,000
135	Business net income			45,000		45,000	45,000
		40,000	5,000	45,000	3,000	93,000	93,000
	Deductions for calculating net income						
207	RPP contributions	2,100				2,100	2,100
208	RRSP contributions	2,300				2,300	2,300
212	Union dues	350				350	350
		4,750	0	0	0	4,750	4,750
260	**Taxable income**	**35,250**	**5,000**	**45,000**	**3,000**	**88,250**	**88,250**
8	Federal tax using generic rates	5,288	750	7,135	450	13,623	17,020
	Federal non-refundable tax credits						
300	*Basic personal amount*	*10,000*	*10,000*	*10,000*	*10,000*		*10,000*
308	*CPP*	*2,104*					*2,104*
312	*EI*	*701*					*701*
335	*Total available*	*12,805*	*10,000*	*10,000*	*10,000*		*12,805*
348	*Tax credit (available × 15%)*	*1,921*	*1,500*	*1,500*	*1,500*	*6,421*	*1,921*
	Donations and gifts	2,600		11,400		14,000	14,000
349	Tax credit (covered in Chapter 12)	726		3,278	0	4,008	4,032
350	Total federal non-refundable tax credits (lines 348 + 349)	2,647	1,500	4,778	1,500	10,425	5,953
425	**Dividend tax credit**		948	0	0	948	948
	Total tax credits (lines 350 + 425)	2,647	2,448	4,778	1,500	11,373	6,901
	Federal tax minus tax credits	2,641	(1,698)	2,357	(1,050)	2,249	10,119
13	**Basic federal tax**	**2,641**	**0**	**2,357**	**0**	**6,253**	**10,119**

Notice in this example:

• All dividend income has been allocated to the Return for Rights or Things, and does not use up all the available tax credits (see "Federal tax minus tax credits" of negative $1,698). Since this is a result of non-refundable tax credits, this negative federal tax cannot be used. This is true also for Return for Income from a Testamentary Trust where, on the same line, $1,050 cannot be used.

• RRSP contributions are allocated to the final return even though the Return for a Partner or Proprietor could make better use of it.

• By filing four returns, federal tax is reduced from $17,020 to $13,623, and non-refundable tax credits are increased from $1,921 to $6,421.

• Donations have been allocated between the Final Return and the Return for a Partner or Proprietor to minimize total tax payable.

• Filing four separate returns instead of one reduces federal tax payable by 38%, from $10,119 to $6,253.

In the year of death, the tax credit for charitable donations can equal 100% of net income instead of the usual 75% of net income.

Filing deadlines are:

• for deceased persons and their spouses: the later of the normal filing date or six months after the date of death

• for trusts: 90 days after the trust's fiscal year-end.

G. CAPITAL GAINS EXEMPTION AND ESTATE FREEZE

A taxpayer may have a business in which his or her children and/or grandchildren participate. There are ways to minimize the tax on the capital gain arising from the transfer of the assets using the Capital Gains Exemption and special rollover provisions for farming and fishing. A Section 85 rollover provision can be used to enact an Estate Freeze whereby the current owner can maintain control and have an income while the next generation accepts the tax liability arising from growth in the value of the company shares after the freeze.

1. Capital Gains Exemption[2]

Up to $800,000 (formerly $750,000) of capital gain (or $400,000 of taxable capital gains) is exempt from tax on **qualified farm and fishing property** and shares in a **qualified small business corporation**. The **maximum deduction** is:

• the unused lifetime deduction adjusted for differing capital gain inclusion rates as outlined earlier,
• various gains limits, and
• deductions under the **Lifetime Capital Gains Exemption** of $100,000 for general property, which was discontinued on February 23, 1994.

Amounts of the capital gains exemption claimed are called **capital gains deduction.**

1a. Qualified Small Business Corporation

Shares in a qualified small business corporation are eligible for the capital gains exemption — up to $800,000 of capital gains (or $400,000 of taxable capital gains at a 50% inclusion rate). A qualified small business corporation must be a **Canadian-controlled private corporation (CCPC)**. That is:

• more than 90% of its assets are used in an active business carried on in Canada,
• it is owned by the taxpayer, spouse, or related parties, and
• during the previous 24 months:
  • was not owned by an unrelated person, and
  • more than 50% of the assets during that time were used to carry on an active business in Canada.

It includes shares of a holding company but does not include shares of public companies. The taxpayer can claim the deduction only against taxable capital gains from the sale of the shares.

1b. Qualified Farm Property

Qualified farm property is also eligible for the $800,000 capital gains exemption. It is property owned by an individual or spouse where farming is the primary source of revenue. The farm must have been used for farming:

• in the year of disposition, or
• for five years during the time this family owned it, and
• for farms bought after June 17, 1987, for the two years before disposition:
  • the gross revenue must be larger than income from all other sources, and
  • the property must have been used for farming.

---

2   The Capital Gains Exemption started at $500,000 in 1985 and applied to all assets owned by individuals in order to stimulate investment and, in 1988, was reduced to $100,000. In 1994, this general exemption was eliminated and was increased to $500,000 for capital gains from the disposition of the shares of qualified small business corporations and qualified farm property. It was increased to $750,000 in 2007 and to $800,000 in 2014.

Qualified farm property includes:

- **real property**, the land and buildings, but not the machinery, and
- **eligible capital property**; e.g., a milk quota

Farm property sold or given to a child, grandchild, or their spouse does not have to be used for farming after the transfer for the exemption to be used, although it must have been used for farming before the transfer. The deemed disposition is the actual proceeds as long as the actual proceeds are between the ACB or UCC and the FMV.

	Inter vivos or upon death
Non-depreciable	between FMV and ACB
Depreciable	between FMV and UCC
Eligible capital property	between FMV and 4/3 of the eligible capital value

The deemed proceeds and child's acquisition cost (assuming the FMV is greater than the ACB or UCC) are:

- FMV if the actual proceeds are greater than the FMV, and
- ACB or UCC if the actual proceeds are less than the ACB or UCC

If the taxpayer, deceased or still living, has unused capital gains exemption, the executor can elect deemed proceeds of between the ACB or UCC and the FMV. This action increases the child's ACB and decreases the capital gain when the child disposes of the property.

1c. Qualified Fishing Property

Qualified fishing property is also eligible for the $800,000 capital gains exemption. It includes **real property, fishing vessels, and eligible capital property** that has been used principally in a fishing business carried on in Canada. The individual, spouse or common-law partner, parent, child or grandchild had to have been actively employed in the fishing business regularly and continuously.

The valuation methods are the same as for qualified farming property.

2. Estate Freezes Using Rollovers

An estate freeze minimizes taxes on deemed dispositions at death by passing title to the assets at some time before death. However, the estate freeze usually leads to capital gains at the time of the freeze. These capital gains are, presumably, less than the capital gains would be at death many years later. In addition, income attribution rules will apply to income-producing property if the transfer is made for less than the fair market value. This topic was covered above. The transferor (the original owner) can use the lifetime capital gains exemption of $750,000. We will now discuss the ways to enact an estate freeze.

2a. Individuals

1. Transfer the assets to an inter vivos trust, which is covered in Chapter 12. The owner names themself the life beneficiary and the heirs are capital beneficiaries.
2. Sell or give the assets, as discussed above.

2b. Corporations

There are two ways that corporations can enact an estate freeze.

1. A **Section 85 Rollover**, also called a Holdco Estate Freeze, transfers the assets of an operating company, Opco, to a holding company, Holdco, freezing the value of the shares for the owner of Opco. Opco must be a qualified small business corporation as outlined earlier.
2. A **Section 86 Rollover** which is a Corporate Reorganization. The owner gives up common shares and receives preferred shares. New beneficiaries receive common shares and will receive the benefit of future increases in the value of the common shares.

Section 85 Rollover: A Holdco Estate Freeze

The owner of the shares of the operating business, (Opco) a qualified small business corporation, transfers Opco's shares to a holding company, Holdco. Because these shares have appreciated in value since the owner incorporated the business, this transfer will trigger a large capital gain and thus a large tax burden if the owner is deemed to have disposed of these shares at the FMV at the time of the transfer. To avoid this tax burden, the Income Tax Act (ITA) allows the owner to transfer these shares to Holdco under a Section 85 rollover provision.

To qualify for a Section 85 rollover, the owner of Opco transfers the shares of Opco to Holdco, in exchange for payment (consideration) that includes at least one share of Holdco. Payment can also include non-share consideration (cash or a promissory note from Holdco) in addition to the Holdco shares that are issued to the owner of the Opco shares. The transfer can occur at an **elected transfer price** (ETP) that is between the adjusted cost base (ACB) at the low end and the fair market value (FMV) at the high end. The ETP is the deemed proceeds of disposition for the owner of the Opco shares and the ACB for Holdco. Depending on the ETP selected by the taxpayer, this transfer can be made without triggering an immediate taxable capital gain. However, an ETP can also be selected that will trigger a capital gain if the owner of the Opco shares has an unused portion of the $800,000 Lifetime Capital Gains Exemption.

To enact the estate freeze,

1. Create a holding company, Holdco.
2. Transfer the original owner's common shares to Holdco using a Section 85 rollover, meaning the elected transfer price (ETP) can be between the ACB and the FMV. This ETP is:
   • the POD for the transferor. This POD is the basis for the tax implications of the deemed disposition.
   • the ACB of Holdco's preferred shares that will be issued to the Opco owner.
3. Holdco issues new common shares at a nominal price of $1.00 to the beneficiaries who are the children of the original owner. Since there are no assets in Holdco at this point, there is little value to acquire and the value of the future growth of the assets will accrue to these common shareholders.
4. The owner of the shares of Opco transfers the shares / assets into Holdco, and **must** receive at least one share of Holdco in return. This is the Section 85 Rollover. The shares will likely be preferred shares:
   • voting in order to maintain control for the present time
   • have a right to dividends. Since dividends on preferred shares are paid before dividends on common shares, the owner continues to receive income.
   • have the right of redemption at the issue value, which is the value at which the assets went into the holding company

In addition to at least one share, the consideration can include cash[3] or a promissory note that can be forgiven. If the non-cash consideration is more than the ACB of the shares, the value of this non-share consideration is the lower limit for the ETP. Conceptually, if I take $300 cash out and my ACB is $20, it does not make sense that I would be able to elect a transfer price of $20. I took $300 out in cash so that is my minimum proceeds.

The elected transfer price must be between the ACB and the FMV and both parties must agree to the price, which can be set to take advantage of the $800,000 capital gains exemption or set higher to use up any unused allowable capital losses.

The taxpayer and the corporation can jointly elect the proceeds to be any amount between:
- an **upper limit** of the FMV of the property, and
- a **lower limit**, which is the *greater* of:
  1. FMV of non-share consideration, and
  2. the *lesser* of:
     3. FMV of property, and
     4. ACB of property

  (*See numbering in following example.*)

Example 18   Mr. Smith incorporated his manufacturing company, Smithco Ltd in 1995. At that time, he invested $10,000 in exchange for 1,000 common shares. He is the only shareholder of Smithco Ltd which is a qualified small business corporation. Over the years, Smithco has been very successful and now, the 1,000 common shares have a FMV of $1,000,000. Mr. Smith has decided that it is time to execute an estate freeze and will be transferring 100% of his shares to a holding company (Holdco). His children will subscribe to the new common shares of Holdco and Mr. Smith will take back preferred voting shares of Holdco.

The following table shows the tax consequences of various transfer prices using a Section 85 rollover to transfer the shares of Smithco Ltd. to the holding company. The tax consequences depend on the amount and form of the "consideration" that Mr. Smith receives from Holdco. The following situations are illustrated:

1. Transfer all the shares to the beneficiaries at FMV without the Section 85 rollover.
2. Transfer under Section 85, taking consideration of 100 preferred shares only.
3. Transfer under Section 85, taking consideration of 100 preferred shares and cash of $25,000.
4. Transfer under Section 85, taking consideration of 100 preferred shares and cash of $400,000.

3   Holdco might have received cash from the children when it was incorporated. However, it is more likely that the non-share consideration would be a "note payable" that gives original owner the right to demand cash from Holdco as required.

		Without Section 85	Preferred Shares Only	Shares + $10,000 Cash	Shares + $400,000 Note
FMV of shares and property	1	1,000,000	1,000,000	1,000,000	1,000,000
ACB		10,000	10,000	10,000	10,000
Non share consideration	2		nil	25,000	400,000
Preferred shares issued			100 shares	100 shares	100 shares
Upper Limit = FMV of property	1		**1,000,000**	**1,000,000**	**1,000,000**
Lower Limit – greater of:					
• FMV of non-share consideration	2		nil	25,000	400,000
• Lesser of A and B	3				
• A. FMV of property	1		1,000,000	1,000,000	1,000,000
• B. ACB	4		10,000	10,000	10,000
Lower limit (greater of 2 or 3)			**10,000**	**25,000**	**400,000**
Range of possible elected or deemed value:					
Lower limit = minimum elected transfer price (ETP)			10,000	25,000	400,000
Upper limit = FMV			1,000,000	1,000,000	1,000,000
Deemed Proceeds of Disposition (ETP)		1,000,000	10,000	25,000	400,000
ACB		10,000	10,000	10,000	10,000
Capital gain / (loss): Deemed ETP minus ACB		990,000	0	15,000	390,000

In this table, the ETP was the minimum within the range. The taxpayer can choose any value for ETP between the lower limit and the upper limit. Therefore, they can "choose" to trigger a capital gain through the ETP that they select.

In scenario #2, there would be no tax implications if the transferor selected an ETP equal to the lower limit. If Mr. Smith has not used any of his lifetime capital gains exemption, he would likely select an ETP of $810,000 so that he could trigger a capital gain of $800,000 that would then be offset by the $800,000 Lifetime Capital Gains Exemption.

The ETP of $400,000 in scenario #4 will trigger a capital gain of $390,000 because the taxpayer opted to take back non-share consideration (that is, cash or notes payable) of $400,000 that is $390,000 in excess of his original $10,000 ACB of the shares.

The concept is simple enough, but a tax expert is needed to be sure of the implications.

Section 86 Rollover: Corporate Reorganization

Section 86 allows a tax-free exchange of all of the shares of one class for consideration that includes all of the shares of another class of capital stock of the corporation. The owner of the common shares exchanges all of them for redeemable, voting preferred shares having attributes similar to those in the prior section. At this point, the original common shares are redeemed by the corporation. Then, new common shares are issued to the beneficiaries (children) or to a trust for the beneficiary at a nominal value, usually $1 each. Any increase in value of the corporation after the new issue of common shares will increase only the value of the common shares. This will effectively pass the "growth" to the common shareholders (the children), and control is maintained by the original owner (the parent). This Section 86 rollover provision can defer the tax until the owner dies. Again, this is a simple concept with complex implications requiring input from a tax expert.

2c. Farms

Special rollover provisions are aimed at encouraging more young people to stay on farms. These provisions also reflect an increase in the value of farmland and farm quotas. The tax on capital gains on farm property can be postponed if the property is transferred to a child who has been using the farm mainly for farming. Property that can take advantage of this rollover provision include farmland, depreciable property, and eligible capital property. No capital gain is reported until the child sells the property. If the property is continuously transferred to the next generation, the capital gain can be deferred indefinitely.

2d. Fishing Property

Fishing property (land, depreciable property, and eligible capital property) that has been used principally in a fishing business can be transferred to a child or grandchild without triggering a taxable capital gain. The individual's proceeds and the child's cost are set at the individual's costs allowing the child to assume the individual's tax position. Special rules to minimize capital gains tax similar to those for farming will apply if the individual actually receives proceeds.

SUMMARY

This chapter illustrates tax issues that individuals face when they dispose of capital property both before and after death. The tax consequences depend on the use of the asset, the amount paid, the relationship of that price to the fair market value, and the relationship of the person who received it to the person disposing of the asset.

When a taxpayer dies, the executor must file a final tax return and pay final taxes due. There are optional returns available that can reduce the amount of taxes payable on the deceased's final return.

> Both Margot and Craig are feeling completely overwhelmed. They are beginning to understand why top tax advisors cost so much. They have seen only the very top of the tip of the tax iceberg — who can remember all this information?
>
> Nonetheless, they will hang on to the examples and are feeling good about their new knowledge of some of the issues that affect many of their friends.

SOURCES

Canada Revenue Agency: <www.cra-arc.gc.ca>
- T4011 Preparing Returns for Deceased Persons 2007
  - Chapter 3 — Optional returns
  - Appendix

Canadian Income Tax Act with Regulations, 86th ed., 2008, (Toronto: CCH Canada Limited).

Beam, Robert E. F.C.A., Stanley N. Laiken, PhD., and James J. Barnett F.C.A. *Introduction to Federal Income Taxation in Canada, 2008–2009, 29th edition* (Toronto: CCH Canada Limited).

KEY TERMS

$1,000 Floor Rule	Loans for value
Adjusted Cost Base (ACB)	Net allowable capital loss
Allowable capital loss	Net capital loss
Annual allowance	Net taxable capital gain
Canadian-controlled private corporation (CCPC)	Non-depreciable capital property
Capital cost	Optional returns

Capital Cost Allowance (CCA)
Capital gain
Capital gains exemption
Capital loss
Change of use
Corporate reorganization
Cumulative eligible capital account (CEC account)
Deemed disposition
Depreciable capital property
Elected Transfer Price (ETP)
Eligible capital expenditure (ECE)
Eligible capital property
Eligible capital value
Estate Freeze
Fair Market Value (FMV)
Final tax return
Half-year rule
Holdco Estate Freeze
Income attribution
Inter vivos transfer
Kiddie tax
Listed personal property (LPP)

Personal-use property (PUP)
Principal residence exemption
Proceeds of disposition (POD)
Qualified farm property
Qualified fishing property
Qualified small business corporation
Qualified small business property
Recapture
Return for a partner or proprietor
Return for income from a testamentary trust
Return for rights or things
Rollover, farms
Rollover, fishing property
Section 73 rollover
Section 85 rollover
Section 86 rollover
Spousal rollover
Taxable capital gain
Terminal loss
Terminal return
UCC pool
Undepreciated Capital Cost (UCC)

QUESTIONS AND PROBLEMS

Deemed Dispositions and Capital Losses

1. Name four events that result in a deemed disposition.

2. If the proceeds of disposition (POD) for actual dispositions is the selling price of the asset, how is the POD determined for deemed dispositions where there is no actual sale?

3. Mike bought a piece of land on which he plans to build several townhouses. He is in the process of finalizing the building plans and getting appropriate municipal approvals. In the meantime, he is paying the mortgage, principal, and interest, on the land. He cannot deduct the interest portion because he has no income at this point. Can he add the interest cost to the cost of the land? (Answer: Yes)

4. When Carlton bought his factory, he paid land transfer tax of $12,000. Is this added to the capital cost of the land or building? (Answer: Not expensed and not capitalized)

Capital Gains and Losses

5. Define "inclusion rate." What is the current rate?

6. If a net allowable capital loss cannot be used in the current year:
   (a) What is it called?
   (b) For how many years can you carry it back to be deducted from capital gains?
   (c) For how many years can you carry it forward?

Personal-use Property (PUP)

7. What is the primary purpose of personal-use property? Does it ever wear out?

8. With regard to the sale of personal-use property in general,
   (a) Are capital gains taxable? (Answer: Yes)
   (b) Are capital losses tax deductible? (Answer: No)

9. Deirdre sold her piano to her sister, Diane. Deirdre paid $40,000 for the piano in 1989, and sold it in 2008 when the market value was $60,000. For each of the following:
   (a) What are Deirdre's deemed or actual proceeds, and what is Diane's deemed or actual cost?
   (b) What is Deirdre's taxable capital gain or allowable capital loss, assuming the piano was not used for Deirdre to earn income?

	Actual selling price	Deirdre proceeds	Diane cost	Taxable capital gain
i.	50,000			
ii.	60,000			
iii.	70,000			

(Answer: Deirdre's proceeds $60,000, $60,000, $70,000; Diane's cost $50,000, $60,000, $60,000; Taxable capital gain: $10,000, $10,000, $15,000)

10. What is the purpose of the $1,000 Floor Rule?

11. Fred sold his violin to buy a better one to play with his friends in an amateur string quartet. For each of the following, what is his taxable capital gain or allowable capital loss?

	Cost	Proceeds
(a)	900	1,200
(b)	3,500	1,900
(c)	10,000	15,000
(d)	1,500	600
(e)	200	800

(Answer: (a) $100, (b) $0, (c) $2,500, (d) $0, (e) $0.)

Listed Personal Property (LPP)

12. How can you know if your asset is personal-use property (PUP) or listed personal property (LPP)?

13. With regards to deducting capital losses arising from the disposition of listed personal property
   (a) Against what can the allowable capital loss be deducted?
   (b) For how many years can the allowable loss can be carried
      i. Back?
      ii. Forward?

14. Arthur has a coin collection. In the past few years, he has been buying and selling a few coins. What is his taxable capital gain or allowable capital loss on each of the following sales and when can he deduct the loss? Use a 50% inclusion rate.

Year	Cost	Proceeds	Taxable gain/ (allowable loss)	Carryforward $	Declare/claim	
					Amount	Year
2010	1,000	1,300				
2011	1,000	2,500				
2012	4,500	1,000				
2013						
2014						

(Answer: Declare gain of $150 in 2010 and $750 in 2011. Claim allowable capital loss, and apply against prior two gains. Carry forward $850 remaining allowable capital loss for seven years.)

Personal Real Estate — Principal Residence Exemption

15. The principal residence exemption is based on N1, the number of full or part years the home is designated as the principal residence since 1971. How many full or part years did the Morrison's own their home if the bought it on Oct 17, 2009 and sold it on May 12, 2013? (Answer: 5 years)

16. If the Morrison's also owned a cottage, what is the maximum number of years they would allocate to the house as their principal residence? (Answer: Four years)

Disposition of Non-Depreciable Capital Property Used to Earn Income

17. Jennifer sold the holdings of three shares. What is her capital gain or loss for each and in total? What is her total net taxable capital gain or net allowable capital loss for each and the total?

	(a)	(b)	(c)	Total
Cost	16,500	16,500	16,500	
Proceeds	21,000	1,000	9,500	
Capital gain				
Capital loss				
Net taxable gain or allowable loss				

(Answer: Total allowable loss = $9,000)

Disposition of Depreciable Capital Property Used to Earn Income

18. Suzanne bought a van for $40,000 for her highly-successful catering business. The van falls into class 10 which has a CCA rate of 30% based on a declining balance.
    (a) Using the half-year rule, how much CCA cans Suzanne deduct in the first year? (Answer: $6,000)
    (b) What is the balance in the UCC pool at the end of Year 1? (Answer: 34,000)
    (c) How much CCA can she deduct in year 2? (Answer: $10,000)

19. Jenny runs a gardening business. She has a small van that she bought used for $16,500. She is now going to sell the van, and use her brother's van for a couple of years while he is working in Australia. For each of the following, what is her recapture, terminal loss, and/or capital gain? (Ignore that some of the proceeds are far-fetched.)

	(a)	(b)	(c)
Cost	16,500	16,500	16,500
UCC	6,872	6,872	6,872
Proceeds	21,000	1,000	9,500
Recapture			
Terminal loss			
Capital gain			

(Answer: (a) recapture $9,628, capital gain $4,500, (b) terminal loss $5,872, (c) recapture $2,628)

Sale of Land and Building

20. Mark just sold a building he had owned for a few years. He received $200,000 for the land and $60,000 for the building. He paid $200,000 — $100,000 for the land and $100,000 for the building. His UCC on the building was $70,000 at the time of the sale.
    (a) What is his taxable income before reallocating the proceeds (Answer: $40,000)
    (b) What is his taxable income after reallocating the proceeds (Answer: $45,000)

Personal Real Estate and Change in Use of Property

21. Tom has just been offered a promotion that require he and his family to move to Vancouver for three years. Tom and Marsha plan to rent out their house and to live in it again at the end of the three years when they return to Toronto. If they want to avoid paying capital gains tax on their home for the three years they rent it out, what are the four criteria they must meet?

22. Melvyn bought his house in 1980 for $47,000. He promptly spent $30,000 renovating it. In 1987, he bought a cottage for $20,000. In 2001, he moved into the cottage to work full-time. He kept the house in the city for weekend visits. He sold them both in 2008 — the house for $195,000 and the cottage for $135,000.
    (a) For how many years can he declare both the cottage and the house as his principal residence? (Answer: None)
    (b) The exempt portion is N1 +1, so either the cottage or the house should be declared his principal residence for at least 1 year. What is his taxable capital gain on each if:
        i.   he declares the house as his principal residence for 28 years and the cottage as his principal residence for 1 year (Answer: $52,273), and
        ii. he declares the house as his principal residence for 8 years and the cottage as his principal residence for 21 years? (Answer: $40,690)

Eligible Capital Property and Capital Gain on Disposal of Assets Used to Earn Income

23. Wilhelm bought the farm next to his father's in 2000 for $480,000. After eight years of farming, he sold everything for $650,000 (in year nine). After buying the farm, he bought equipment that cost $55,000.

	2000 FMV	2008 FMV	2008 UCC
Land	150,000	200,000	n/a
Buildings	70,000	90,000	51,549
House	80,000	100,000	n/a
Cows	40,000	55,000	n/a
Equipment	40,000	15,000	2,800
New equipment — cost		60,000	12,245
Milk quota	100,000	130,000	Calculate
	480,000	650,000	

(a) Calculate the ending balance in the eligible capital property account after the sale. (Answer: –$55,531)

(b) What is Wilhelm's total gain on the sale of the farm including both recapture and capital gain? Ignore that some land is exempt because the house sits on it. (Answer: $218,937)

(c) What is Wilhelm's taxable income for 2008 without the $750,000 capital gains exemption? (Answer: $166,437) *Note: The capital gains exemption was $750,000 in 2008. It became $800,000 in 2014.*

Income Attribution and Spousal Rollover

24. Rod has just learned about joint tenancy. He wants to transfer 50% of his investments to his son, James, who is 14 years old. His shares cost him $10,000 over the years, and would now sell for $149,000. These shares pay him dividends of $7,000 a year.

(a) What is Rod's taxable capital gain when he makes the transfer? (Answer: $34,750)

(b) What will Rod's taxable dividend income be after the transfer? (Answer: $10,150)

(c) If Rod sells all the shares two years later for $175,000, what is the taxable capital gain for each of them? (Answer: Rod $41,250, Son $6,500)

(d) If Rod sells all the shares seven years later for $185,000, what is the taxable capital gain for each of them? (Answer: Rod $43,750, Son $9,000)

25. When he died, Rod owned shares for which he paid $10,000. Rod's wife, Annette, received 50% of the shares and James, age 14, received 50% of the shares when the fair market value was $149,000.

(a) What is Rod's taxable capital gain in the year of his death if the executor takes advantage of rollover provisions? (Answer: $34,750)

(b) If both Annette and James sell the shares seven years later for $185,000, what is the taxable capital gain for each of them? (Answer: Son $9,000, Annette $43,750)

Non-Arm's Length Transfers

26. What if Jenny of Question 19 gave the van to her church, a registered charity? Or to her sister? Or sold it to her sister for $6,500?

    (a)   Complete the following chart.

	Give to church	Give to sister	Sell to sister
Cost	16,500	16,500	16,500
UCC	6,872	6,872	6,872
FMV	8,000	8,000	8,000
Proceeds	0	0	6,500
Deemed proceeds			
Recapture			
Terminal loss			
Capital gain			
Recipient's ACB			

(Answer: Deemed proceeds: $8,000 for each. Recipient's ACB: $8,000, $8,000, $6,500)

    (b)   Which of the scenarios could lead to double taxation and how much capital gain would be taxed twice? (Answer: Scenario 3, $1,500)

Deemed Dispositions at Death

27. When John died, his wife, Anne inherited his RRSP which had a balance of $$240,000 when he died.

    (a)   How much of this is taxable to John's estate? (Answer: none)

    (b)   Anne died suddenly three months later, before she had withdrawn anything from John's RRSP. Their son, Bernie, is the designated beneficiary on the RRSP.

    i.   How much of the $240,000 is taxable to Anne's estate? (Answer: $240,000)

    ii.   If Anne's marginal tax rate is 30%, how much will Bernie receive? (Answer: $168,000)

28. When Claudette died, she wrote a will leaving $100,000 of her estate to her life partner, Stan, and the remaining $200,000 to be divided equally between her two children. Her estate comprised a life insurance policy for $100,000 with Stan as the named beneficiary, her principal residence with a net worth of $120,000 and RRSPs worth $80,000. She left the principal residence and the RRSPs to her estate, expecting that her two children would get $100,000 each. Using generic federal tax rates, no provincial taxes, and the probate fee schedule in Chapter 10, what does each of her children receive if Claudette lived in Manitoba (i.e., Manitoba probate fees)? (Answer: $92,613)

Net Capital Losses at Death

29. Marsha died in October 2013. She was expecting to have some very large capital gains in 2015 so had not applied the net allowable capital losses against taxable capital gains of earlier years. However, the assets she expected to generate the capital gain in 2015 were jointly owned. As a result, she had a net capital loss in the year of death. She was not eligible to use the capital gains exemption.

Year	Taxable income	Net taxable capital gains	Net allowable capital losses
2013	65,000		25,000
2012	80,000		
2011	80,000		15,000
2010	80,000		
2009	80,000	5,000	

(a) Could she have applied the $25,000 loss against the $5,000 gain? (Answer: No. Can carry back only three years)

(b) Could she have applied the $15,000 loss against the $5,000 gain? (Answer: Yes. Here, the executor will have to file an amended return for 2011)

(c) What is her net capital loss carryforward when she dies, assuming her executor filed an amended return for 2012? (Answer: $10,000)

(d) What is her total net capital loss to be deducted against any other source of income? (Answer: $35,000)

(e) Should she deduct the loss against 2013 income, 2012 income, or both? (Answer: Both)

(f) If she deducts the loss against both years' incomes, how should she allocate the loss to minimize taxes? (Answer: $10,000 to 2013, $25,000 to 2012 giving her taxable income each year of $55,000)

Final Return

30. When Liz died in 2014,
    (a) she had the following income in 2014:
        i. Salary $80,000
        ii. Vacation pay owed to her and received after her death $1,600
        iii. Net capital loss carryforward $7,000
        iv. Capital gains $140,000 from the disposition of shares in a qualified small business corporation
        v. Capital gain of $120,000 on the sale of her condo at a local ski resort; she did not own any other real property.
        vi. Her shares of partnership net income $60,000
        vii. Bank interest received of $540
        viii. Bond interest received of $1,600
        ix. Bond interest earned but not received $800
        x. Dividend income received from a trust set up by her grandfather $16,000. Trust income is covered in Chapter 12. Include this in the "Trust" column.
    (b) She paid CPP and EI premiums on her salary
    (c) She made donations of $14,000 before her death (Hint: Allocate to Final Return)
    (d) She had $300,000 of unused capital gains exemption

What is her federal tax payable on the final return and each of the optional returns using generic rates for taxes, CPP, and EI?

What would her federal tax payable have been if her executor had filed only one tax return?

	Final Return	Rights or things	Partner/ proprietor	Testamentary trust	Total	All on one return
Taxable Income	82,140	2,400	60,000	23,200	167,740	167,740
Basic federal tax	9,479	0	8,935	0	18,886	28,557

31. Suppose Wilhelm bought his father's farm in 2000 and that the farm is Qualified Farm Property.

	V-day	2000 UCC	2000 FMV	2000 actual proceeds	2000 deemed proceeds	Recapture/ business income	Capital gain
Land	40,000	n/a	150,000	100,000			
Buildings	20,000	9,000	70,000	50,000			
House	30,000	n/a	80,000	50,000			
Cows	2,000	n/a	40,000	50,000			
Equipment	3,000	700	40,000	0			
Milk quota	5,000	1,200	100,000	60,000			
			480,000	310,000	300,700	14,800	183,000

   (a) What are the deemed proceeds for Wilhelm's father? (Answer: $300,700)
   (b) If Wilhelm's father uses the capital gains exemption, what is his taxable capital gain? (Answer: $0)
   (c) What is Wilhelm's cost when he sells the farm? (Answer: Father's deemed proceeds)

32. Theresa wants to transfer her business to her children but she will continue to work there and withdraw funds as they take over the business. She will use a Section 85 rollover. When she started the business 30 years ago, she invested $5,000 which is now the ACB. She was recently offered $2 million for the business by a third party but she would rather have her children take it over. She has never used the $800,000 Lifetime Capital Gains exemption.
   (a) What is highest possible elected transfer price they could choose if they want to minimize Theresa's taxes now and the children's taxes later? (Answer: $2 million)
   (b) If she receives preferred shares and nothing else, what is the minimum ETP they could choose? (Answer: $5,000)
   (c) If she receives preferred share and $100,000 in cash that her children have invested, what is the minimum ETP? (Answer: $100,000)
   (d) If she receives preferred share, $100,000 in cash and a note payable for $700,000, what is the minimum ETP? (Answer: $800,000)

12

Trusts, Donating to Charity, and U.S. Assets

This chapter has been updated as of November 2015, courtesy of Carolyn Fallis of George Brown College.

Learning Objectives

A. Recognize the uses of trusts as well as their costs and limitations.

B. Understand the taxation of assets going into and coming out of trusts as well as the taxation of income earned by the trust.

C. Understand the various types of donations that can be made and the amount of tax credit they generate.

D. Understand using life insurance to pay the final taxes.

E. Have an overview of taxes required on assets held in the United States.

A.   TRUSTS

> Craig's father, Hank, owns a cottage in Muskoka in central Ontario. He and Craig's mother bought it many years ago when cottages were cheap and their children were young. It is a small cottage, not winterized, and right on the water. However, cottage prices have increased dramatically in the past few years so it is now worth about $220,000 even though it is nothing fancy. Hank and Brigid usually come to the cottage in the summer for the month of July, and the children and their families take turns visiting them.
>
> Hank wonders if he should be putting the cottage in a trust. He is not much interested in such matters so he asked Craig to investigate this for him. After all, Craig and his two siblings will inherit it eventually. Craig's father wants to know the benefits of putting the cottage in a trust. Can he avoid taxes by doing this? He likes the idea of that very much.

The Canada Revenue Agency (CRA) defines a **trust** as "a binding obligation, voluntarily undertaken, but enforceable by law when undertaken. It may be created by one of the following:

• a person (either verbally or in writing);

• a court order; or

• a statute."

There are two types of trusts:

1. **Inter vivos trusts**, which are set up while the **settlor**, or **grantor** (the person setting up the trust), is still alive

2. **Testamentary trusts**, which are set up automatically when a person dies — the deceased's assets are part of the estate. The assets remain as part of the estate until either

(a) the assets are distributed to the beneficiaries according to the will or using intestate rules,

or

(b) the assets are transferred to a new formal testamentary trust set up in the will and in which some or all of the estate assets are managed by a trustee until some point in the future.

Trusts are governed by provincial laws. A trust can have more than one settlor — more than one person can contribute to a trust. In addition, several trusts can have the same beneficiary. A trust can have several beneficiaries, whose benefit in a trust can vary. There are many different kinds of trusts, all of which have different uses.

Purpose of Trusts

Trusts can have many uses. Depending on the type of trust, they are useful for tax planning, reducing probate fees, managing the assets for underage children, protecting the assets from creditors, estate planning, preserving privacy (trusts are private whereas wills are a matter of public record), charitable giving, and controlling the use of and income from the assets after death. A trust can be used to:

- Provide income for a current spouse after death but preserve the capital for children from an earlier marriage. This also preserves the capital should the surviving spouse remarry.
- Reduce probate fees. Investments in a testamentary trust are subject to probate when the settlor dies. However, if the assets are left in the trust, the spouse can receive the income and, at the death of the second spouse, the assets are not subject to probate fees again.
- Enact an estate freeze.
- Make a charitable donation.
- Provide professional management for beneficiaries who cannot manage the assets themselves. Such beneficiaries include minor children, older children who are not ready to manage a large sum of money, and also infirm or disabled beneficiaries.

Setting Up a Trust

For a trust to be set up, three things must be clear. These three items are called the **Three Certainties**. There must be:

- **Certainty of Intent** — there must be a clear intention to create a trust
- **Certainty of Subject Matter** — it must be clear what assets are being transferred to the trust, and
- **Certainty of Objects** — it must be clear who the beneficiaries are and what type of beneficial interest each beneficiary has

The duties of the settlor are to:

- establish the trust when alive or in a will
- place assets and/or property in the trust, and
- set up the rules for operating and winding up the trust

The **trust agreement**, also called a **trust deed**, specifies the terms and conditions of the trust, including:

- the purpose of the trust
- the assets being transferred to the trust
- the beneficiaries, and what they will receive and when, and
- the names of the trustees and the power granted to these trustees

Example 1 shows how a trust can be set up to control the assets, even after death, to ensure that the assets are eventually distributed as the grantor wishes.

Example 1   Marcia, age 63, has inoperable cancer. In her will, Marcia instructed the trustee of her estate to sell her house and its remaining contents after her two children, Sandra and Jim, have received certain pieces of furniture and personal items of Marcia's. She estimates that her net worth will be about $600,000, including $100,000 of investments that are providing regular, steady dividends. Her estate will also include the commuted value of her pension, which after tax will be about $150,000.

Maricia does not like or trust Sandra's husband, Steve. Marcia knows that in a divorce, Steve would not be entitled to any of the inheritance unless Sandra and Steve invest it in the family home. However, Steve always seems to be off on one wild goose chase after another. Marcia is afraid that if Sandra inherits the money outright, Steve will persuade Sandra to "lend" him money, which he will squander. Sandra and Steve have no children and no plans to have children. Sandra is a high-school teacher earning a good salary.

Marcia adores Jim's wife, Janet, and their twins, Carole and Christie. But Jim is very difficult and demanding. While Janet does not say much, Marcia would not be surprised if the marriage ended in divorce. Marcia wants to ensure that some of the inheritance is used to support Janet, Carole, and Christie.

Marcia sets up a formal testamentary trust that will come into effect when she dies. All of her assets will be transferred to the trust and held there until Carole and Christie are 25 years old. Both of Marcia's children will receive annual income from the trust although Jim's will be paid to Janet because a) she is in a lower tax bracket and b) Marcia thinks Jim and Janet may separate, and Marcia wants to give Janet additional financial support. Jim is a corporate lawyer, and Marcia feels he will always be in a sound financial position. (The exact nature of the disposition of the income and assets will continue later in this chapter.)

Costs of Trusts

Trusts incur costs to set up, administer, and wind up. These costs are tax deductible in the calculation of the trust's taxable income. These costs include:

- Legal costs involved in setting up the trust. The legal fees might cost $1,000 for a straightforward trust. Temporary testamentary trusts are set up automatically when the settlor dies, so the cost of setting them up is part of the cost of a will.
- Ongoing administration. This might be 0.5% of the assets plus perhaps 5% of the income earned by the trust. If the trust has assets of $100,000 earning income of $8,000 a year, this fee might be $900 a year [$400 (5% × $8,000) + $500 (0.5% × $100,000)]. The administration fees on large trusts can probably be negotiated but will still be significant.
- Final distribution fees. This fee is based on the value of the assets and the amount of paperwork involved.
- Filing annual tax returns and paying the income tax on any income received by the trust that remains in the trust at the end of the year. The cost of filing the return might be $400.

As a very general rule of thumb, it is not worth setting up a trust unless it will hold assets of at least $150,000. The person setting up the trust must have a very clear intention in mind other than attempting to avoid taxes. Trusts do not avoid taxation. However, there may be reasons why a settlor wishes to set up a trust with less assets. In the event of bankruptcy, assets in trusts cannot be seized by creditors.

Beneficiaries

A beneficiary is someone who benefits from a trust. A person has a **beneficial interest in a trust** if that person has a right to receive income or capital from a trust at some time. There are several types of beneficiaries, which allows the settlor to control their assets even after death.

- An **income beneficiary** receives income from the trust. This income is added to any other income, making it taxable at the beneficiary's marginal rate. If the income from the trust is the only source of income, it is taxed at the beneficiary's average tax rate. There can be a tax advantage to the beneficiary in that a trust may be taxed a higher rate than the beneficiary. This can be advantageous to a beneficiary who has a life interest but not a capital interest.
- A **capital beneficiary** receives capital (property and/or assets)
- A beneficiary can receive income and capital. The income can be left to compound in the trust or can be paid out all or in part as it is earned. The capital, once paid out, no longer earns income in the trust. It can be paid out immediately or later, in a lump sum or in smaller amounts, either as per the settlor's directions or at the trustee's discretion, depending on the powers assigned to the trustee in the trust agreement.
- A **life interest** is the right to use the asset for a specified time period (usually the beneficiary's life). The beneficiary is a **life tenant**.
- A **remainder beneficiary** is a capital beneficiary where there is a life interest beneficiary. A **remainder interest** is a capital interest that does not come into effect until the person having a life interest dies.
- **The 21-year rule** states that, except for spousal trusts, trusts must report a deemed disposition on assets in the trust, recognizing capital gains and paying tax on the taxable portion of the gain every 21 years. This ensures that assets cannot avoid tax forever by being held in a trust. Spousal and common-law trusts are exempt from this rule. The date of the deemed disposition is the date the spouse or common-law partner dies.
- **Exempt beneficiaries** were eliminated for taxation years after 1998. They were designated direct relatives who were exempt from the 21-year rule (as spouses still are). Using exempt beneficiaries, the recognition of accrued capital gains under the 21-year rule was deferred until the last exempt beneficiary died.
- **Preferred beneficiaries** could be named until 1996. As a result, although the income was not paid out to them, the income was taxed as if it were in the hands of the beneficiary. If the beneficiary had little or no income, the income would be taxed at a very low rate and remain inside the trust to grow. In 1996, the preferred beneficiary was eliminated.

Example 2 illustrates capital beneficiaries.

Example 2   Marcia from Example 1 has decided that all the assets should remain in the trust and only the income earned each year will be paid out. When the twins are 25 years old, the capital is to be paid out 1/3 to Sandra, 1/3 to Jim, 1/6 to Carole, and 1/6 to Christie. Sandra, Jim, Carole, and Christie are **capital beneficiaries**.

In the trust agreement, Marcia names her good friend, Andrea, as one of the trustees whose function is to manage the investments. Andrea and Marcia discussed the types of investments that would be appropriate. The other trustee has been granted the duty of reviewing the investments annually. Marcia and Andrea estimate that the trust should generate approximately an 8% before tax rate of return per year. Some of the income is in the form of dividends, some is interest, and there will be capital gains and losses along the way. However, in general, they think the trust will generate income of $45,000 to $50,000 a year. Marcia wants the annual income to be used as follows:

1. $5,000 to an RESP for Carole and $5,000 for Christie for ten years at which point the maximum contributions to the RESPs have been reached. The twins are now four years

old. When the RESPs have reached their maximum contributions, the same amount will be paid to each of the twins for spending money.

2. An after-tax amount equal to the annual rate of inflation will remain in the trust to guarantee the purchasing power of the trust. This is an estimated $12,000 ($600,000 × 2% inflation) per year in interest income.

3. Jim and Sandra will each receive the balance divided equally between them, although Jim's share will be paid to Janet, as indicated above. Marcia stipulated that if Janet dies before the twins are 25 years old, the income is to be paid to Jim.

Types of Trusts

There are several types of trusts depending on the purpose of each. Some terms are merely generic definitions.

Commercial vs. Personal Trusts

- **Commercial trust:** A trust that is not a personal trust; i.e., the beneficiary has received his interest by paying something for it. Some mutual funds are set up as unit trusts. A person obtains rights to the benefits by paying for the units.
  - **Mutual fund trust:** A trust whose only undertaking is the investing of its funds in property (not real property) and/or acquiring, maintaining, leasing, or managing real property that is capital property of the trust.
  - **Segregated fund trust:** Also called an **Insurance segregated fund trust**, it is an inter vivos trust that is a related segregated fund of a life insurer for life insurance policies. The fund's property is trust property, the fund's income is trust income, and the life insurer is the trustee.
- **Personal trust:** No beneficiary has attained interest by paying for it; i.e., it is either a testamentary trust or inter vivos trust in which no beneficial interest was acquired by payments made by the trust or to a person who contributed to a trust. The person or related person who creates an inter vivos trust may acquire an interest in it without the trust losing its status as a personal trust.

Discretionary vs. Non-discretionary

- **Discretionary trust:** The trustee has been granted the right to use their own discretion to distribute the income and the capital. A trustee can have full discretion or only partial discretion. A trustee having:
  - **mere power** can distribute some or all of the income and capital to some or all of the beneficiaries when and if the trustee wishes.
  - **trust power** must distribute the income and/or capital but the trustee uses their own discretion as to how to divide the income and/or capital amongst the beneficiaries.
- **Non-discretionary trust:** The trust agreement outlines the duties and responsibilities in detail. If the trust agreement does not specify the duties and does not specify that the trustee has the discretion to act, the duties and responsibilities are prescribed by law.

Irrevocable vs. Revocable

- **Irrevocable trust:** A trust that cannot be dissolved or revoked once it is set up. The assets are vested indefeasibly or are locked in — the terms of the trust cannot be changed except with the expressed permission of the beneficiary. The beneficiary has an absolute right to the property.
- **Revocable trust:** A trust that can be dissolved or revoked at the discretion of the settlor.

Special Inter Vivos Trusts

There are two kinds of inter vivos trusts whose goals are to minimize probate fees. They can also be used as alternatives to a power of attorney since the trustees can manage the assets if the person setting up the trust is no longer able to do so. Both of these are inter vivos trusts and, therefore, have personal tax implications. Since they are inter vivos trusts, any income left in the trust is taxed at the highest personal tax rate. They are special because there is no tax on the deemed disposition of the assets when they are transferred into the trust.

- **Alter ego trust**: A trust designed for single people. It is an inter vivos trust created by a person age 65 or older. The settlor is entitled to receive all of the income from the trust during their lifetime and is the only person who can receive income or use the income and capital of the trust during his or her lifetime. The tax on the taxable capital gain on assets transferred into the trust can be deferred until the death of the settlor, using the rollover provisions at which time there is a deemed disposition of the assets and the taxable capital gain is included in the deceased's terminal return.

- **Joint Partner Trust — joint spousal trust** and **joint common-law partner trust**: These trusts are for legally married spouses and common-law partners, both of the opposite sex and same sex. It is created by the grantor, who is 65 years old or older at the time the trust is established. Only the grantor and spouse can receive income or use the income and capital of the trust until both die. This type of trust is also called a **joint and last survivor trust** since the tax on the taxable capital gain on assets transferred into the trust is deferred until the death of the second partner. The capital gain is included in the terminal return of the second partner.

In-Trust Account for Education Funding

In-trust account: It is a trust account for minor or incapacitated children (a spendthrift trust is an in-trust account). If the beneficiaries are underage, an inheritance must be held in a trust (unless the courts decide otherwise) until the child reaches the age of majority, even if there is a spouse. Often the children do not inherit when only one spouse dies. If there is a will, the assets are often inherited by the surviving spouse.

Before the introduction of the CESG, many people preferred to use an in-trust account to save for their child's education. While the beneficiary is a minor, there is income attribution on dividend and interest income earned (but not on capital gains if the trust is irrevocable; i.e., if the contributor and the trustee are different people). Unlike the RESP, earned income retains its beneficial characteristics; i.e., only 50% of capital gains are taxable and Canadian dividends receive the dividend tax credit. There are two major differences between the RESP and an In-Trust account:

- The RESP must be used for the child's education while, at the age of majority, the funds in an in-trust account belong to the beneficiary who may use the funds for any purpose whatsoever.

- There is no tax implication to withdrawing the funds from the In-Trust account as there is no change in beneficial ownership — the funds belong to the child whereas, with an RESP, unused CESG received and income earned on it must be returned and any remaining unused income from the contributions is returned to the contributor, not the beneficiary, and is subject to tax at the marginal rate as well as an additional 20% unless the subscriber has adequate unused RRSP contribution room.

Henson Trust and Providing for Disabled Children

- Henson Trust: Also called an **absolute discretionary trust**, it is a trust designed to benefit disabled people. It protects the right of the disabled person to collect government benefits and entitlements when they accumulate considerable assets, often by inheriting them. The trustee has absolute discretion in deciding whether to pay out funds to the beneficiary, and how much. This means that the assets do not belong to the beneficiary and thus cannot be used to deny means-tested government benefits. It can be set up as either an inter vivos trust or a testamentary trust. (See B. Trusts and Taxation. Qualified Disability Trusts — QDT.) If the latter, the trust can provide income tax relief by being taxed at a lower marginal rate than if the beneficiary's total assets were considered. If the beneficiary is capable of managing their own money and is not receiving social assistance payments, a Henson Trust takes all control away and gives it to someone else, forcing the beneficiary to ask for funds as required.

- This trust can supplement an RDSP. It has no eligibility criteria, no contribution limits, can have residual beneficiaries and no restrictions on the timing of payments from it.

- If the beneficiary qualifies for the Disability Tax Credit (a requirement for the RDSP), the trustees can use a "Preferred Beneficiary" election and attribute the trust income to the beneficiary without the trust actually paying out the income. The trust income thus can use the personal amount and other tax credit that are otherwise not allowed for trusts. This can lead to considerable tax savings if the trust is an inter vivos trust, otherwise taxable at the highest personal tax rate.

Other Types of Trusts

- **Communal organization**: An inter vivos trust for a congregation whose members live and work together and follow the same religious practices and beliefs. The congregation does not permit its members to own property and operates a business to support them. It must allocate its income to its members to avoid paying income taxes at the top personal rate. See Information Circular 78-5R3.

- **Deemed resident trust:** A trust that is resident in another country but either:
  - the assets were transferred in by a Canadian resident who has a beneficial interest in the trust, or who is related to someone who has a beneficial interest, or
  - the beneficiary acquired an interest in the trust by buying it or by receiving it as a gift or inheritance.

- **Express trust**: A trust established deliberately; i.e., an inter vivos trust or through a will. An example of a trust that is *not* an express trust is a trust set up when both parents die before the children reach the age of majority. This trust is set up automatically since the children are minors. The assets are placed in a trust until they reach the age of majority (age 18 or 19 in most jurisdictions). An express trust is set up in order to defer taxes on assets going into the trust. (The assets go into the trust at fair market value but future increases will not be taxed until the assets are sold by the beneficiary. Future taxes will be based on the cost of the assets when they entered the trust — the fair market value.)

- **Family trust**: A trust established for the benefit of family members — for example, underage children and children with special needs.

- **In-trust account**: It is a trust account for minor or incapacitated children (a spendthrift trust is an in-trust account). If the beneficiaries are underage, an inheritance must be held in a trust (unless the courts decide otherwise) until the child reaches the age of majority, even if there is a spouse. Often the children do not inherit when only one spouse dies. If there is a will, the assets are often inherited by the surviving spouse.

- **Master trust**: An inter vivos trust that meets all of the following criteria:
  - it was resident in Canada
  - its only undertaking was the investing of funds
  - it never borrowed money except for a term of 90 days or less (and was not part of a series of short-term loans or repayments)
  - it has never accepted deposits, and
  - each of the beneficiaries is a registered pension plan or a deferred profit sharing plan.

- **Non-profit organization:** An organization that operates exclusively for social welfare, civic improvement, pleasure, recreation, or any other reason except profit. It is exempt from tax as long as none of its income is paid or payable for the personal benefit of an owner, member or shareholder. If its main purpose is to provide services such as dining, recreational, or sporting facilities to its members, it is an inter vivos trust that pays tax only on income from property, including the capital gains from the disposal of property not used to provide the services.

- **Residual trust:** A charity or other beneficiary is the capital beneficiary while the donor/settlor keeps a life interest; i.e., the settlor receives the income from the trust but has donated the rights to the capital.

- **Retirement Compensation Arrangement (RCA):** It was described in Chapter 5.

- **Salary deferral arrangement:** It is a trust that holds funds for future payment of present services.

- **Specified investment flow-through trust (SIFT):** It is a trust that is not a real estate investment trust (REIT) and that invests in stock exchange listed or traded shares and holds one or more non-portfolio properties

- **Specified trust:** It includes trusts such as RESP, RPP, RRIF, RCA, DPSP, RRPS, master trust and others and is used by the Canada Revenue Agency to defined reporting requirements.

- **Spendthrift trust:** A trust that holds the assets and distributes the income for spendthrift or irresponsible beneficiaries. This kind of arrangement can be used to take care of individuals such as spouses and children while the settlor is absent on a business trip or vacation.

- **Spousal trust,** also referred to as a **spousal testamentary trust** (although it also applies to inter vivos spousal trusts) or a **qualifying spousal trust:** The assets can be transferred to the trust on a tax-deferred basis as long as the spouse is the only person who can receive the income or have use of the capital during the spouse's lifetime — the current (not former) spouse receives all of the income and no one else may receive income or use the capital while the spouse is still alive. This tax-deferred transfer is called a **spousal rollover.** It applies also to common-law partner trusts. This type of trust protects the assets for the benefit of capital beneficiaries should the surviving spouse enter a new relationship, remarry or experience diminished capacity in the future. Again, when the beneficiary of a spousal trust dies, the capital gain is included on their terminal return.
  - **Tainted spousal trust:** Someone other than the spouse receives income or has the right to receive income or use the assets. In this case, the tax-free rollover provisions cannot be used.

- **Voluntary trust:** A trust set up by oneself, transferring one's own assets to an irrevocable trust to protect the assets from one's own spendthrift ways.

Duties of the Trustee

The duties of a trustee can include:

- managing the assets according to the trust agreement and provincial legislation, including making investment decisions
- paying out income according to trust agreement guidelines or using their own discretion
- filing the income tax returns annually, and
- having the power to decide when to pay out capital or extra income, and how much

The trustee must:

- act in the best interests of all the beneficiaries and without conflict of interest. The relationship between the trustee and the beneficiaries sets up a fiduciary obligation for the trustee to act in the best interests of the beneficiaries even though the trustee controls the assets

- perform the duties with honesty, skill, and highest level of care, and
- perform the duties personally. Delegation is allowed, but the trustee is responsible to act in the best interests of the beneficiaries; i.e., to **act with an even hand**. The trustee can, therefore, use appraisers, tax experts, and lawyers as part of the trust team.

The trustee can be held personally responsible for any financial losses unless released from this consequence in the trust agreement, provided the trustee acts in good faith. Any accusers must prove a lack of due diligence.

B. TRUSTS AND TAXATION

Income earned by assets in a trust and not paid out to beneficiaries by the end of the taxation year are subject to income taxes at personal tax rates. The tax rates are:

- the top personal income tax rates for
  - inter vivos trusts and
  - **formal testamentary trusts** that are set up in the will using a trust agreement, and
- the applicable graduated personal income tax rates for the following testamentary trusts:
  - **graduated rate estates (GRE)** which are trusts that are set up automatically, without a trust agreement, when a person dies. These graduated rates are in effect during the time it takes to settle the estate for a maximum of 36 months after the date of death. If the estate is not settled at the end of 36 months, there is a deemed disposition of the remaining estate assets and the top personal income tax rates apply until the estate is settled, and
  - **qualified disability trusts (QDT)** in which the beneficiary is eligible for the disability tax credit. The graduated tax rates will continue to be in effect with no time limit as long as the beneficiary is eligible for the disability tax credit.

All assets transferred into a trust are deemed to have been disposed of for tax purposes at their fair market value, which becomes the trust's acquisition cost. In all but three instances, this may trigger a capital gain which is taxable. The three exceptions to this rule are assets transferred into:

- a spousal trust
- an alter ego trust and
- a joint spousal trust.

In all three cases, the assets are deemed to be transferred to the trust at their tax values, therefore no capital gains are realized at the time of the transfer.

Trust Tax Returns

Trusts must file annual tax returns using the T-3 Trust Return. Information on filing this return is found under the heading "Sources" at the end of the chapter. Only income received by the trust and not paid out to beneficiaries is taxable. In general, the income remaining in an inter vivos trust and a formal testamentary trust is taxed at the highest rates — 29% federal tax and without the non-refundable tax credits. Tax credits are available for donations as well as the dividend tax credit on dividends received from taxable Canadian corporations.

Total income includes:

- taxable capital gains
- pension income
- actual amount of dividends received from taxable Canadian corporations

- foreign investment income
- net business, farming, fishing, and rental income, and
- deemed realizations

Deductions to reduce total income include:

- carrying charges
- trustees fees
- Allowable Investment Businesses Losses (ABILs), which we will not cover
- taxable benefits:
  - upkeep, maintenance, and costs for property occupied or used by a beneficiary
  - value of other benefits to a beneficiary
- amounts paid or payable to beneficiaries

The 45% gross up on dividends received but not paid out is then added to arrive at **taxable income**. The following income is also included in total income.

Income Splitting Using Trusts

Income that is taxed within a trust is not taxable again when it is paid to the beneficiary; i.e., the beneficiary receives the funds tax free. This can be a useful income-splitting device for the graduated rate estate and the qualified disability testamentary trusts whereby the beneficiary and the trust split the taxes on income being paid to the beneficiary.

Chart 2 — Income reported on the T3 Trust Income Tax and Information Return

Report the following amounts on line 19 of the *T3 Trust Income Tax and Information Return* for the year in which you receive the income. If the income is received in a year after the year of death, report it on the T3 return for that subsequent year.

Type of income	Information slip
1. Severance pay received because of death. As this is a death benefit, up to $10,000 may be non-taxable.	T-4A, Box 28
2. Future adjustments to severance pay regardless of when the collective agreement was signed.	T-4A, Box 28
3. Refund of pension contributions payable because of death.	T-4A, Box 18
4. Guaranteed minimum pension payment (this is not a death benefit).	T-4A, Box 18
5. Deferred profit-sharing plan payment.	T-4A, Box 18
6. CPP or QPP death benefit, if not reported by the recipient.	T-4A(P), Box 18

There is a **minimum tax payable** on trust income that is not from a mutual fund trust, a segregated fund trust, a spousal/common-law partner trust or a master trust. The calculation of the minimum tax is similar to the calculation of minimum tax for individuals. The minimum-tax calculation adds back into income items such as the non-taxable portion of capital gains, losses created by the CCA and limited partnership losses.

Taxation of various kinds of trusts is covered on the following pages.

Trusts — General

	Testamentary trusts	Inter vivos trusts
Uses	• Provide privacy • Protect assets from creditors and lawsuits • Avoid second probate fees • Manage the assets of minors of incapacitated adults • Provide income for surviving spouse while preserving assets for children should the spouse remarry • Provide income for current spouse while preserving assets for children from a former marriage.	• Provide privacy • Protect assets from creditors and lawsuits • Not subject to probate fees • Give the use of property to a spouse and give the property to the children when the spouse dies • Donating to charity • Alternative to power of attorney • Estate freeze • Shelter assets before going into a nursing home.
Assets transferred	When the settlor dies	While settlor is alive
Who controls the assets	The trustee	The trustee
Probate fees	Yes; on assets going into the trust but not when they come out (e.g., on death of second spouse)	No
Revocable trust	n/a	Yes. It provides creditor protection for debts incurred after the trust was set up.
Irrevocable trust	n/a	Yes — is the default

Taxation of Trust Income

	Graduated rate estates/trust (GRE) and Qualified disability testamentary trust (QDT)	Inter vivos and formal testamentary trusts
Taxation year	Calendar year or any time in the first 12 months after the death of the settlor	Calendar year
Filing dates	No later than 90 days after the trust year-end. Use tax rates at the trust's year-end	Same as box on the left
Taxation of net income left in the trust	Paid by the trust at **applicable personal income tax rates**. Cannot use personal tax credits or non-refundable tax credits	Paid by the trust at **top personal income tax rate** unless the beneficiary is the spouse or under 18, in which case *income attribution* rules apply. Cannot use personal tax credits or non-refundable tax credits
Example 3 The trust holds assets that earned *interest income* of $20,000, of which $12,000 was paid out to one beneficiary, age 35	The trust pays tax on income of $8,000. The federal tax rate is **15%** The beneficiary will pay tax on $12,000 at their top marginal rate and will receive $6,800 ($8,000 x .85) non-taxable income (using only federal tax rates)	The trust pays tax on income of $8,000. The federal tax rate is **29%** The beneficiary will pay tax on $12,000 at their top marginal rate and will receive $5,680 ($8,000 x .71) non-taxable income

Taxation of income received from a trust, including dividend income	Paid by beneficiary at their marginal personal rate	*Income attribution rules* apply for income from spousal trusts and trusts set up for minor children — the settlor pays the tax
Example 4 The trust holds assets that earned *dividend income* of $20,000, of which $12,000 was paid out to one beneficiary, age 35	The trust pays tax on income of $11,600 ($8,000 × 1.45). The federal tax rate is **15%**. The beneficiary will pay tax on $17,400 at their marginal rate. Both can use the dividend tax credit	The trust pays tax on income of $11,600. The federal tax rate is **29%**. The beneficiary will pay tax on $17,400 at their marginal rate. Both can use the dividend tax credit
Taxation of *taxable capital gains* earned by the trust, some or all of which was paid out	Retain tax-preferred treatment both in the trust and when passed on to the beneficiary — the tax benefits flow through to the beneficiary	*Income attribution rules* apply for income from spousal trusts but not to trusts established for minor children — the settlor pays the tax
Capital cost allowance	Does not flow through to beneficiaries	Same as box on the left
Example 5 The trust holds assets that earned $20,000 *net rental income before CCA* of $5,000, of which $12,000 was paid out to one beneficiary, age 35	The trust will pay tax on $3,000 ($20,000 − $12,000 − $5,000). The beneficiary will pay tax on $12,000 at their marginal rate	Same as box on left. If the beneficiary is a spouse or minor child, income attribution rules apply.

Taxation on Capital Gains of Trust Assets

	Qualified disability testamentary trusts (QDT)	Inter vivos and formal testamentary trusts
21-year rule	At least every 21 years, the trust must report a "deemed disposition" of the assets at their fair market value and pay the capital gains tax. If there is not enough cash, the trust will have to sell some of the assets to pay the tax. There are several exceptions, including spousal trusts. *See T4013 T-3 Guide and Return, p. 26*	Same as box on the left

1. Spousal Trusts

Taxation of Capital Gain on:	Graduated rate estates (GRE) and Qualified disability trusts (QDT)	Inter vivos and formal testamentary trusts
Assets going into a spousal trust: *"Section 73 rollover," Section 73 of the Income Tax Act*	None = a spousal rollover – assets are transferred in at UCC. Settlor may elect to recognize a capital gain to make use of unused allowable capital losses. No capital gain is realized until the spouse or spousal trust *disposes* of the property	Same as box on left. The spouse must be entitled to receive all the income from the trust before the settlor's death and is the only one who can receive capital payments during their lifetime. See "tainted spousal trust"
Example 6 Martin transferred the family cottage into a spousal trust — his spouse is much younger than he. The cottage cost $35,000 and now has a FMV of $225,000	Cost for trust = $35,000. No capital gain must be recognized although the asset can be transferred at any value between $35,000 and $225,000 to use up capital losses	Same as box on the left

Assets in a spousal trust being transferred to:		
• the spouse	None until sold = a spousal rollover	None = a spousal rollover
Example 7 Martin's wife, Alma, had the title transferred to her when the FMV was $260,000	Alma's taxable capital gain = $0	Same as box on the left
Example 8 Three years after title passed to her, Alma sold the cottage for $294,000	Alma's taxable capital gain = $129,500 [50% × ($294,000 − 35,000)]	If transferred after Martin's death: Same as box on left. If transferred before Martins' death: Martin has a taxable capital gain of $129,500
• Someone other than the spouse whether the spouse is still alive or is deceased	Transferred at FMV. The tax is paid by the *trust* based on the last adjusted cost base established when the assets entered the trust. If there is not enough cash, CRA will "ask" the beneficiary to pay the tax.	Same as box on the left
Example 9 Alma had the title transferred to her son when the FMV was $260,000	Alma's taxable capital gain = $0 Trust's taxable capital gain = $112,500 [50% × (260,000 − 35,000)]. If the trust has no cash to pay the tax, Alma's son must pay the tax before title can pass to him.	Same as box on the left

2. Non-Spousal Trusts

Taxation of Capital Gain on:	Graduated rate estates (GRE) and Qualified disability trusts (QDT)	Inter vivos and formal testamentary trusts
Assets going into a non-spousal trust: *Section 69 of the Income Tax Act*	Tax arising from deemed disposition is paid on the settlor's final tax return − cost = FMV just before death of settlor	Tax arising from deemed disposition is paid by settlor when the assets enter the trust, except for Alter Ego Trusts and Joint Partner Trusts
Example 10 Martin transferred the family cottage into a trust for his son, age 35. The cottage cost $35,000 and now has a FMV of $225,000	Martin owes taxes on the taxable capital gain of $95,000 [50% × ($225,000 − $35,000)]	Same as box on the left
Assets coming out of a non-spousal trust; i.e., when title passes to the beneficiary who is not the spouse	Is a rollover when title passes — no taxes are due. Taxes are paid when the asset is *sold* by beneficiary based on the ACB established when the asset went into the trust	Same as box on the left
Example 11 Martin's son, Grant, had the title transferred to him when the FMV was $260,000	Grant's taxable capital gain = $0	Same as box on the left
Example 12 Three years after title passed to him, Grant sold the cottage for $294,000	Grant's taxable capital gain = $34,500 [50% × ($294,000 − 225,000)]	Same as box on left regardless of whether or not Martin is still alive

C. DONATING TO CHARITY

Craig's father has always loved dogs. Sometimes they had three or four dogs in their home waiting to find someone who could take them. Hank is considering making a large donation to the Edmonton Humane Society, but he would like to know what his options are. He has several assets he could donate but would donating cash give him a better tax receipt? Craig promises to look into the issue and get back to him.

The federal government encourages donations to charities by providing tax credits that are deducted from federal taxes payable. The provinces and territories follow the lead of the federal government and also provide tax credits. These tax credits are mainly at the top tax rate, so even if a taxpayer is in the 22% or 26% tax bracket, most of the federal tax credit is at 29% (the first $200 receives a federal tax credit of 15%).

Charitable giving to registered charities is a way for taxpayers to make a financial contribution to a worthy cause of their choice. The charity must be registered, meaning it meets certain criteria as being a non-profit organization whose goal is to provide a service to people in need. If no one made charitable donations and the causes were worthy, the federal government would have to decide which charity would get how much money. In many instances, the federal and provincial governments make these decisions through various funding mechanisms. But charitable giving shifts the decision-making responsibility to the taxpayer who is making the donation.

A **charitable gift** is a voluntary transfer of property to a registered charity for which the donor receives no benefit or a benefit of nominal value in return. A **benefit of nominal value** means that the value of the benefit is less than 10% of the value of the gift, to a maximum value of $50. If a taxpayer gives $1,000 to a registered charity and receives a benefit of:

- a discount card that gives the taxpayer a 10% discount every time a book is purchased. There is no way to know how many books will be bought, so there is no way to put a value on the benefit. No tax receipt can be issued.
- meeting Wayne Gretzky. There is no way to put a value on this benefit, so no tax receipt can be issued.
- a book worth $37. The charity can issue a tax receipt.

Tax receipts could be issued for the first two even though a value could not be established — there is value even if it cannot be substantiated.

Generally, the value of the donation is reduced by any **advantage** the donor receives. If you donate $1,000 to a registered charity that, in return gives you a ticket to a show worth $100, your advantage is $100 and the amount eligible for the donation and gifts tax credit is $900 ($1,000 – $100).

A **gift in kind** is any gift other than cash or personal services. It includes capital property, depreciable property, personal-use property, a licence, a share, and inventory of a business. The charity issues a tax receipt for the fair market value (FMV) of the gift on the date it was donated.

The **federal tax credit** is deducted from federal tax payable. For 2013, it is:

- 15% of first $200
- 29% of amounts over $200

The **maximum deductible donation (donation limit)** for the current year is:

- prior to 1997: 20% of net income for the current year
- after 1996: 75% of net income for the current year

• in the **year of death** and in the prior year, the limit is 100% of net income for the individual

"Net income" (line 236) is "Total income" (line 150) minus RRSP and pension contributions, support payments, etc.

An **unused gift** is that portion of the gift that has not been claimed for tax purposes. Unused gifts can be **carried forward for five years**. This means that the taxpayer has six years to take the tax credit on the donation. The taxpayer can claim an amount or portion of an amount only once and must claim the oldest gifts first.

Types of Gifts and the Tax Credit Available

Auctions

If a gift is donated to be sold in the auction, a tax receipt is issued for the fair market value of the gift. No tax receipt is issued if an item is purchased at a fundraising auction — not even if the price paid exceeds the FMV.

Example 13	Cindy gave a set of dishes to her church for its annual fundraising auction. She received a tax receipt for $50 — the FMV of the dishes.

At the auction Cindy bought some patio chairs for $30 each. She could have bought the same thing at Canadian Tire for $15 each, but she wanted to help out her church. She will get no tax receipt for the chairs.

Business Inventory

If a business makes a donation out of its inventory — for example, blankets from The Bay or tires from Canadian Tire — an official tax receipt for the FMV is issued but the business must include the FMV of the gift in income. For a business, the revenue and the tax deduction will offset each other. Gifts of cash or non-inventory items receive normal tax benefits.

By Businesses

Any benefit received from the gift must be of nominal value. If the business:

• pays $2,000 for advertising space in the charity's magazine, there is no gift
• gives $2,000, which is acknowledged in the charity's newsletter, there is a gift

Canadian Cultural Property

These gifts include paintings, sculptures, books, and manuscripts. The donor can claim up to **100%** of net income for gifts:

• of cultural property that have been certified by the Canadian Cultural Property Export Review Board (CCPERB) as being of outstanding significance and national importance, and
• made to Canadian institutions and public authorities that have been designated by the Minister of Canadian Heritage to ensure that the property is properly collected, preserved, and made accessible to the public for research or display purposes

The value of the tax receipt is the FMV of the gift. There is no capital gain resulting from the gift but you can deduct capital losses on the property within the usual limits.

Contributions of Services

An official receipt cannot be given for volunteered services even if it is the donor's regular line of work. But if the charity pays for the work and the donor returns all or part of the income as a donation, a tax receipt for the cash donation is issued and the payment for the work is part of the donor's income.

Ecological Gifts

These are gifts of land that have been designated by the Minister of the Environment as being ecologically sensitive and deserving of conservation and protection. The tax credit can be up to **100%** of income. The gift can be to:

- a registered charity
- a Canadian municipality, or
- after 1996, to the federal government or to a province

Any restrictions on the use of the property must be respected by current and future landowners. For a donation for an easement, covenant, or servitude, the value of the official tax receipts is *the greater of*:

- the FMV of the restriction if this can be determined, and
- the reduction in FMV of the land due to the restriction

Example 14   Carole owns a large piece of land that has been in her family for generations. Carole agreed to have an easement registered on the property in the name of a registered charity designated by the Minister of the Environment. The easement prevents development of the land for housing or commercial use, although it can be developed somewhat as a public or private park.

A year ago Carole was offered $5 million for the land by a developer who was interested in building townhouses on it. With the easement, the local municipality is willing to pay her $500,000 to turn it into a public park. The value of the tax receipt is $4.5 million.

Governments

For gifts to the federal government or a province or their agent, the donor can claim up to **100%** of net income if the donation was made or the donor entered into a written agreement to make the gift before February 19, 1997. Otherwise, the maximum is 75% of net income.

Tickets

1. Tickets for lotteries, draws, or raffles are not gifts.
2. Tickets to fundraising dinners, balls, concerts, shows, or like events can provide a tax receipt. A **like event** is a service or consumable good that must be used by/on a particular date because after that date it has no value. Tickets to a concert are a like event but goods bought at an auction are not. The value of the tax receipt is:
   - the ticket price of fundraising or like event less
   - the FMV of the food or entertainment.

The cost to the charity to put on the event is *not* included in the FMV.

Example 15   Philip works for a large hospital foundation that puts on four fundraising dinner-dances per year. Philip makes $60,000 per year. The tickets to these events cost $300 each, while the food and entertainment cost $97 per person. The hospital can issue a tax receipt for $203 ($300 – $97).

If the event included a lottery to win a car, there is no gift at all — that is, no official receipts can be issued. This situation can be avoided by selling the two tickets — one for the dinner-dance and one for the lottery.

Capital Property
1. Buildings and Equipment

If the donated value is greater than the UCC, there is **recapture** (the amount by which the lesser of the Cost/Adjusted Cost Base or FMV exceeds the UCC). The taxpayer can increase the donation limit by 25% of the recapture in the year of the gift for gifts after 1996. In addition, the donation limit is also increased by 25% of the taxable capital gain. The donation limit cannot exceed the net income for the year.

Example 16   Elsa had a very successful clothing store. When she decided to sell the business in May 2013, she also decided to donate the land and building to the Winnipeg Humane Society. The following table deals only with the building which Elsa owned.

Elsa's 2013 income		70,000
Cost of building	150,000	
UCC	50,000	
FMV	325,000	
Recapture (Cost – UCC)	100,000	100,000
Capital gain (FMV – Cost)	175,000	87,500
Taxable income		**257,500**
Maximum available for tax credit in 2013		

75% of taxable income	75%	257,500	193,125
25% of recapture	25%	100,000	25,000
25% of taxable capital gain	25%	87,500	21,875
			240,000
Tax credit	15%	200	30
	29%	239,800	69,542
			69,572

The total amount she can deduct is $325,000, the fair market value of the gift. In 2013, she can deduct $240,000 of the $325,000. The remaining amount of donation can be claimed in each of the next five years, up to 75% of each year's income.

If her income from investments in the next five years is $70,000 per year, she can deduct:

Year	Taxable income		Amount deducted	Tax credit
2013	257,500	from above	240,000	69,574
2014	70,000	75% of income	52,500	15,199
2015	70,000	balance of FMV	32,500	9,399
			325,000	94,172

2. Non-depreciable Capital Property

The value of the donation is the FMV of the assets being donated. An amount less than the FMV but more than the ACB can be designated as the value to reduce the amount of the capital gain. If the FMV is less than the ACB, the deemed proceeds are the FMV resulting in a capital loss.

This property was bought for investment purposes or to earn income. (The donation of publicly traded securities has a special deduction that we will deal with in the next section.) The donor is deemed to have disposed of it at FMV. This action can lead to a capital gain, of which 50% is taxed at regular rates. As with the building in the prior example, the standard donation limit of 75% of net income is increased by adding 25% of the taxable capital gain resulting from the donation for gifts after 1996.

Example 17   Elsa donated the land. We will first show the calculation as if she had not donated the building.

Elsa's 2013 income			70,000
Cost of land		150,000	
FMV		320,000	
Capital gain		170,000	85,000
Taxable income			**155,000**
Maximum available for tax credit in 2013			
75% of taxable income	75%	155,000	116,250
25% of taxable capital gain	25%	85,000	21,250
			137,500
Tax credit	15%	200	30
	29%	137,300	39,817
			39,847

The total amount she can deduct is $320,000. In 2013, she can deduct $137,500 of the $320,000. The remaining amount of donation can be claimed in each of the next five years, up to 75% of each year's income.

But Elsa did not donate the land and building separately. Let's look at the donations together and the limitations imposed on her deductions by her income. Combining Examples 16 and 17, her 2013 taxable income and donation tax credits are as follows:

Elsa's 2013 income			70,000
Recapture on building		100,000	100,000
Capital gain on building		175,000	87,500
Capital gain on land		170,000	85,000
Taxable income			**342,500**
Maximum available for tax credit in 2013			
75% of taxable income		342,500	256,875
25% of recapture		100,000	25,000
25% of taxable capital gain on building		87,500	21,875
25% of taxable capital gain on land		85,000	21,250
			281,875
Tax credit	15%	200	30
	29%	281,675	81,686
			81,716

Let's look at the effect of the donation on Elsa's taxes in 2013 and 2014, both with and without the donation. Let's assume she continues to earn $70,000 a year.

In 2014, Elsa has negative basic federal tax. That's fine, but when will she get to deduct it? The short answer is that she won't (if her income continues to be $70,000) because the donations and gifts tax credit is part of the non-refundable tax credits. Let's review her status.

		2013		2014	
		With gift	**Without gift**	**With gift**	**Without gift**
Income before donation		70,000	70,000	70,000	70,000
Recapture on building		100,000			
Taxable capital gain — building		87,500			
Taxable capital gain — land		85,000			
Taxable income		**342,500**	70,000	70,000	70,000
Federal tax					
15%	39,500	5,925	5,925	5,925	5,925
22%	39,500	8,690	6,710	6,710	6,710
26%	48,000	12,480			
29%	127,000	62,495	0	0	0
		89,590	12,635	12,635	12,635
Non-refundable tax credit	10,000	1,500	1,500	1,500	1,500
Subtotal		88,090	11,135	11,135	11,135
Donation tax credit		81,716	0	15,197	0
Basic federal tax		6,374	11,135	(4,062)	11,135

	Taxable income	Donation limit	Tax credit based on 75% of income	Actual tax credit possible
2013	342,500	281,875	81,716	81,716
2014	70,000	52,500	15,197	11,135
2015	70,000	52,500	15,197	11,135
2016	70,000	52,500	15,197	11,135
2017	70,000	52,500	15,197	11,135
2018	70,000	52,500	15,197	11,135
		544,375	157,701	137,391
Total value of donation		645,000		
Amount not claimed		100,625		

In the five years following the donation, Elsa can deduct only 75% of her net income. This means she will not be able to deduct $100,625. But the tax credit produces negative net income, which she will not be able to use. In reality, people who make large donations like this one have incomes much higher than $70,000 a year, so this is not a problem for high-income donors. It does, however, show the way the tax credit is limited both in terms of the annual deduction limit and the five-year limit.

3. Publicly Traded Shares and Stock Options

Donations of this type, other than those to a private foundation, have an inclusion rate of 0% if you received no advantage. An **advantage**, proceeds of some kind, reduce the amount that has no inclusion rate. This eligibility applies to:

• a share, debt obligation, or right listed on a designated stock exchange
• a share of capital stock of a mutual fund corporation
• a unit of a mutual fund trust
• an interest in a related segregated fund trust
• a prescribed debt obligation, such as a government savings bond, and
• ecologically sensitive land (including a covenant, an easement, or in the case of land in Quebec, a real servitude)

Non-qualifying Securities

There is **no** tax receipt if the securities are:

* not on a prescribed stock exchange (which are listed in RC4142E but are not listed here)
* shares in a business controlled by the donor
* debts or obligations between:
  * the donor and a company controlled by the donor, or
  * between the donor and someone else who is related to the donor

Ways to Make a Charitable Donation

There are many ways to make a donation. Donations can even be made which allow the donor to enjoy the gifted property before death. The ways to make a donation are:

1. Through a will (see Chapter 10, "**Format of a Will**," 4b).
2. Making a donation before death, as illustrated in the above examples.
3. Transferring the assets to an inter vivos trust (described above). The donor can continue to enjoy the benefits of the donation by giving the donor a life interest and making the charity the capital beneficiary. The gift must be irrevocable. The value of donation is the capital at the time it is transferred into the trust reduced by the present value of the life interest.

Example 18   Marsha has been a devoted piano teacher all of her working life. She wants to make a donation of $200,000 to the Royal Conservatory of Music but she counts on the $10,000 annual income she receives from the $200,000. At the time, the CRA long-term prescribed interest rate was 6%. Based on mortality tables approved by CRA, Marsha can expect to live another 14 years. The value of the donation is:

$$PV = \$200,000(PVIF_{6\%,\ 14}) = \$88,460$$

Marsha can claim a tax credit of $25,625.40 [($200 × 15%) + ($88,260 × 29%)]. In the current year, Marsha can claim the tax credit for up to 75% of her net income. She can carry the tax credit forward for five years.

> This approach can be useful if a person wishes to donate their principal residence but continue to live in it until death. Any future capital appreciation accrues to the charity (and is, therefore, also an **estate freeze**, described in Chapter 11). Since charities do not pay tax, there will be no tax on any future capital appreciation if and when the charity sells the asset. This type of donation is not permitted for certified cultural property.
>
> In addition, since the assets are in a trust, there are no probate fees payable when the donor dies.

4. The donor may be able to make the charity the beneficiary on a life insurance policy.
   (a) For a term life policy, the value of the annual donation is the annual amount of the premiums paid. Either the donor or the charity can make the payments. If the premiums are not paid, the policy will lapse.
   (b) The value of the donation for a whole-life policy is the cash surrender value (CSV) of the policy as long as future premiums are not paid out of the CSV (in which case, there is no donation). The donor is deemed to have disposed of the policy. If the adjusted cost base of the policy (premiums paid minus dividends received) is less than the CSV, the difference is

taxable income to the donor. The tax credit for the donation will partially offset the tax on the deemed income.

To receive a donation receipt, the beneficiary designation must be irrevocable.

5.   The donor can make a donation and receive an annuity, either term certain or for life (covered in Chapter 7). For this donation to benefit the charity, the donor must die before the value of the annuity consumes the value of the amount donated. The value of the donation receipt is:

the amount of the donation − (annuity payments × life expectancy at the time of donation)

If there is interest included in the annuity payment, the interest is taxable income to the donor.

The charity might buy an annuity contract from an insurance company to reduce its risk exposure and administrative costs. Any outstanding annuity payments at the time of the donor's death would be paid to the charity.

D.   LIFE INSURANCE TO PAY FINAL TAXES

Chapter 10 discussed buy-sell agreements. The best way to finance these is using life insurance policies. This is a very general discussion of a topic more appropriately covered in an insurance course.

Should seniors have life insurance to pay the taxes due on the final return? The face value of an insurance policy is not taxed when it is received as a lump sum — that is, it is not taxed as an annuity, where the interest portion is taxed. There are many types of insurance policies. **Whole-life policies** have a savings component, which means the premiums are higher, since some of the premium is invested. This does not meet the requirement of having a policy to pay the taxes on the final return. **Term insurance** is much cheaper and would meet the need, but it is for a definite time period — 10 years, 20 years — and it is possible to outlive the policy and defeat the purpose.

Term-to-100, joint and last survivor policy is term insurance that continues until the second person to die is 100 years old. For a healthy couple in their early 70s, such a policy could cost $6,000 a year for a face value of $250,000, which covers the taxes on a taxable estate of $636,000. Another type of term-to-100 policy pays when the first spouse dies, but it costs almost double. If the second-to-die lives for 20 years after the policy is taken out, the premiums would be $120,000 to $200,000 over the 20 years for a policy with a face value of $250,000, which will pay from the day the policy is taken out.

E. ASSETS IN THE UNITED STATES

Some Canadians own real estate in United States.[1] There are two classes of Canadians living in the U.S. Both classes are:

• not American citizens and
• living in the U.S., and are either:
   • a **non-resident alien** who does not intend to remain there permanently, or
   • an **American resident** who plans to live there permanently

---

1   We are dealing with only the United States as many Canadians own property in the U.S. A tax specialist knowledgeable about taxation in other countries is needed for property owned outside of Canada in other countries, including the United States.

Rental Income

If non-resident aliens rent out their American home while they return to Canada, the American Internal Revenue Service requires that:

- 30% of the gross rents be withheld and remitted to them. The taxpayer files Form 1040 NR, U.S. Non-Resident Alien Income Tax Return once. The rental agent then files the returns for the withholding tax on the gross rental income, or
- The taxpayer can elect to file Form 1040 NR, U.S. Non-Resident Alien Income Tax Return every year and treat the property as a U.S. business activity. This enables the non-resident alien to be taxed at the same rates as American citizens.

U.S. Estate Taxes

All assets normally located in the U.S. are part of a U.S. taxable estate, with some exceptions. This includes American real estate as well as shares in American companies even if held in a Canadian brokerage account including RRSPs and TFSAs. However, there is a **unified tax credit**, which effectively means that there is no tax on up to the first $5,250,000 for 2013 on estates for U.S. residents and resident aliens. As shown in the following table, in the past, the amount of the exemption was much lower and the tax rate was much higher. As a result, it was rather easy for Canadians who owned a home, cottage and some investments in Canada in addition to an American vacation home to find themselves owing U.S. estate tax as well as tax on the deemed disposition of their taxable Canadian assets.

Table 12.1 U.S. Estate and Gift Tax Rates and Unified Credit Exemption Amount

Year	Exemption equivalent	Top tax rate
2001	$675,000	55%
2002	$1,000,000	50%
2003	$1,000,000	49%
2004	$1,500,000	48%
2005	$1,500,000	47%
2006	$2,000,000	46%
2007	$2,000,000	45%
2008	$2,000,000	45%
2009	$3,500,000	45$
2010*	$5,000,000 or $0	35% or 0%
2011	$5,000,000	35%
2012	$5,120,000	35%
2013	$5,250,000	35%

* In 2001, under President Bush, the estate tax was scheduled to be phased out in 2010. However, a change in government resulted in a change in the schedule. For 2010, the estate of those who died in 2010 can be taxed using the $5,000,000 estate exemption and a 35% tax rate or $0 exemption and 0% tax rate coupled with some carryover rules.

For Canadians, the assets are still subject to Canadian capital gains tax on the deemed disposition. This leads to double taxation if the estate is greater than $5,250,000 U.S. in 2013. The formula for the unified tax credit is:

$$\frac{\text{Gross U.S. estate}}{\text{Gross worldwide estate}} \times \text{U.S. exemption}$$

Example 19   Sherry and Kevin own a condo in Arizona worth $900,000 U.S. They also own a house in Canada worth C$1,600,000, a cottage worth C$650,000, non-registered investments of C$2,850,000 and RRIFs worth a total of C$1,400,000. They were planning to sell the condo but died in an automobile accident before they could sell it. The exchange rate was $1Cdn = $0.95U.S. How much of their estate is subject to U.S. estate tax?

The exemption for 2013 is:

$$\frac{\$900,000 \text{ U.S.}}{\$900,000 \text{U.S.} + 0.95(\$1,600,000 + 650,000 + 2,850,000 + 1,400,000)} \times \$5,250,000$$

$$= \frac{\$900,000 \text{ U.S.}}{\$7,075,000 \text{ U.S.}} \times \$5,250,000 = \textbf{\$667,845 U.S.}$$

Since their condo is worth $900,000, they owe U.S. estate tax on $232,155 U.S. ($900,000 – $667,845)

And the Canadian tax? They will have a taxable capital gain on the deemed disposition of their cottage. They will also owe income tax on the balance in their RRIF.

SUMMARY

The two types of trusts — testamentary trusts, which own assets after the death of the owner, and inter vivos trusts, which own assets that the former owner has transferred while still alive — serve many purposes, such as facilitating tax planning, reducing probate fees, managing assets for underage children, protecting assets from creditors, facilitating estate planning, preserving privacy, facilitating charitable giving, and controlling the use of and income from the assets after death. There are many types of trusts as well as many types of beneficiaries.

Donating to charity both while alive and after death is encouraged through the income tax system. Rules are in place to prevent misuse while still promoting philanthropic activities.

Life insurance can be purchased to pay these final taxes due. Assets owned and situated in other countries require special handling to reflect tax laws in other countries. We looked briefly at American estate taxes.

In addition, Craig will report all this information about trusts to his father. Craig is not sure he sees any benefit to a trust of any kind for the family cottage. Craig knows for sure that he does not want to get stuck with any tax bill for a cottage he will use only two or three weeks a year. As a matter of fact, Craig would prefer that his father sell the cottage now and join Craig and Margot at the family resort he and Margot take their daughters to every summer — with lots of different activities for each member of the family. Margot agrees. They camp at the resort, but they can also take advantage of the restaurant. Margot likes to get a break from cooking at least once a day. And Craig does not relish the idea of another property to look after.

If Craig's father sells the cottage now and pays the tax, this is one less thing Craig has to think about. And he can avoid the possibility of future conflicts with his siblings over the cottage.

Craig is feeling quite overwhelmed about charitable donations. He had no idea there were so many options available or that the tax benefits could be so large. Then again, Craig's assets are quite modest by some standards. There are a lot of people who have money to give and appreciate a tax break for being willing to give something back to their community by making substantial donations.

SOURCES

Canada Revenue Agency: <www.cra-arc.gc.ca>
- IT-288 Gifts of Capital Properties to a Charity and Others.
- P113(E) Rev. 07 Gifts and Income Tax
- RC4142E Tax Advantages of Donating to Charity
- T4013(E) Rev. 07 T3 Guide and Trust Income Tax and Information Return, Chapter 3 and Appendix

KEY TERMS

Absolute discretionary trust	Like event
Advantage	Master trust
Alter ego trust	Maximum deductible donation
American resident	Mere power
Auction, gift to	Mutual fund trust
Beneficial interest in a trust	Non-depreciable capital property, gift of
Beneficiary	Non-discretionary trust
Benefit of nominal value	Non-profit organizations
Business inventory, gift of	Non-qualifying securities, gift of
Buildings and equipment, gift of	Non-resident alien
Canadian cultural property, gift of	Personal trust
Capital beneficiary	Preferred beneficiary
Capital property, gift of	Publicly traded shares and stock options, gift of
Certainty of Intent	Qualifying spousal trust
Certainty of Objects	Remainder beneficiary
Certainty of Subject Matter	Remainder interest
Charitable gift	Residual trust
Commercial trust	Revocable trust
Common-law partner trust	Salary deferral arrangement
Communal organization	Segregated fund trust
Contribution of services, gift of	Specified investment flow-through trust
Deemed resident trust	Specified trust
Discretionary trust	Spendthrift trust
Donation limit	Spousal trust
Ecological gift	Spousal roll-over
Even hand	Spousal testamentary trust
Exempt beneficiary	Spousal trust
Express trust	Tainted spousal trust
Family trust	Term insurance
Federal tax credit	Term-to-100 insurance
Gift by businesses	Testamentary trust

Gift in kind	Three Certainties
Governments, gifts to	Tickets, gift
Henson trust	Trust agreement
Holding company	Trust deed
Income beneficiary	Trust power
Insurance segregated fund trust	Trust tax return
Inter vivos trust	Trustee
In-trust account	21-year rule
Irrevocable trust	Unified tax credit
Joint common-law partner trust	Unused gift
Joint spousal trust	Voluntary trust
Life interest	Whole life insurance
Life tenant	

QUESTIONS AND PROBLEMS
Trusts

1. Alan wants to set up a trust for his nephew, Rodney. He wants Rodney to receive $20,000 a year from the trust. In addition, Rodney will receive the capital when he turns 50. Alan thinks he may cash in some of his investments to finance the trust. Or he may start a sort of sinking fund, and put the funds into the trust over a period of a few years. Alan has not met all the criteria for setting up a trust. What criteria has he failed to meet?

2. Finally, Alan decided that Rodney should have an income for life, but that the capital would remain in the trust until Rodney's death, at which point the assets would be transferred to Rodney's daughter, Lucille.
   (a) What kind of beneficiary is Rodney?
   (b) What kind of beneficiary is Lucille?

3. In his will, Maurice set up a spousal trust for his wife, Françoise. The trust gave her the use of their ski chalet as long as she is alive. When Françoise dies, the title to the chalet will pass to their son, Steve. Shortly after Maurice's death, Steve quit his job at the local library to write the book he has always wanted to write. To save money, he gave up his apartment and moved into the chalet for two years. What are the tax consequences for Françoise of this move by Steve?

4. Assume Steve did not move in and the spousal rollover provisions that applied in the prior question. When Francoise dies, will there be probate fees charged on the assets in the trust?

5. When he died, Jacob's father set up a formal trust with Jacob, age 42, as the beneficiary. The trust earns dividend income of $45,000 a year of which $35,000 is paid to Jacob. However, for the first three years, the funds remain in a graduated rate estate. In these three years:
   (a) What is the trust's taxable income? (Answer: $14,500)
   (b) How much federal tax will the trust pay? (Answer: $2,175)
   (c) What is Jacob's federal taxable income from the trust? (Answer: $50,750)

6. From the prior question (question 5), the formal trust was set up immediately after the father's death.
   (a) What is the trust's taxable income? (Answer: No change $14,500)
   (b) How much federal tax will the trust pay? (Answer: $4,205)
   (c) What is Jacob's federal taxable income from the trust? (Answer: No change $50,750)

7. From the prior question (question 5), if Jacob's father were still alive when the trust was set up:
   (a) What is the trust's taxable income? (Answer: No change $14,500)
   (b) How much federal tax will the trust pay? (Answer: $4,205)
   (c) What is Jacob's federal taxable income from the trust? (Answer: No change $50,750)

8. Ken's spouse, Marta, owned a cottage when they got married. She had paid $17,000 for it. When she died, the cottage was worth $42,000. In her will, she transferred the cottage to a trust for Ken, assuming he would transfer it to their son, Keith after Ken's death. After Marta died, Ken kept the cottage for a few years. Then he had the title transferred to him when the fair market value was $89,000. Four years after that, Ken sold the cottage for $93,000.
   (a) What was Marta's taxable capital gain when she died? (Answer: $0)
   (b) When Ken took ownership of the cottage, what was his taxable capital gain? (Answer: $0)
   (c) When Ken sold the cottage, what was his taxable capital gain? (Answer: $38,000)

9. Ken's spouse, Marta, owned a cottage when they got married. She had paid $17,000 for it. When she died, the cottage was worth $42,000. In her will, she arranged for the cottage to be transferred to a trust to be set up for their son, Keith. He could transfer the title whenever he wanted. After Marta died, Keith kept the cottage for a few years. Then he had the title transferred to him when the fair market value was $89,000. Four years after that, Keith sold the cottage for $93.000.
   (a) What is Marta's taxable capital gain when she died? (Answer: $12,500)
   (b) When Keith took ownership of the cottage, what was his taxable capital gain? (Answer: $0)
   (c) When Keith sold the cottage for $93,000, what was his taxable capital gain? (Answer: $25,500)

Donating to Charities

10. John made a donation of $150 to his favourite non-profit television station. In return, he got a membership gift of a coffee mug that reads: "She who must be obeyed" (spoken frequently by one of his favourite mystery characters). Will he receive a tax receipt? Why or why not?

11. Arthur's salary in the current year is $35,000.
    (a) What is the maximum donation he can deduct in the current year? (Answer: $26,250)
    (b) If he makes the donation from part (a):
        i. How much will his tax credit be? (Answer: $7,584.50)
        ii. How much is his federal tax after taking the donation tax credit? (Answer: $0)
        iii. How much cannot be deducted in the current year? (Answer: $3,834.50) What is this as a percentage of his total donation? (Answer: 50.56%)
    (c) What happens to the unused tax credit? Does he lose it? What happens to it?
    (d) Re-do this question assuming Arthur's salary is $85,000 and he makes a donation of $63,750. (Answer: $18,459.50, $0, $3,784.50, 20.50%)

12. If Arthur died in the current year, what is the maximum donation claim he could make if his salary is $35,000? (Answer: $35,000)

13. Darwin, our beloved piano teacher, decided to donate half of his vast collection of music to a foundation that provides music camps for children in the summer.
    (a) If Darwin's annual income is $37,000, and he donates music having a fair market value of $35,000, how much of the donation can he deduct in the year of the donation? Assume he wrote off the music as he bought it since each piece of music has a low cost. As a result, the FMV is all capital gain. (Answer: $27,750)
    (b) If Darwin's taxable income is $37,000, how much federal tax does he owe? (Answer: $0)

(c) How much tax credit can he use from the donation in the current year? (Answer: $4,050.00)

(d) How much tax credit can he carry forward? (Answer: $3,969.50)

14. In 1996, Carlita signed a pledge card promising to make a donation of $1,500 a year to the NDP party of Canada. If her income is $18,000, what is the maximum she can deduct in the current year? (Answer: $18,000) What is the maximum amount of the donation she can claim in the current year if she made the pledge in 1998? (Answer: $13,500)

15. Annabelle has a consulting business organizing fund-raisers for non-profit organizations. She charges $55 an hour, and an event usually takes about 350 hours to organize. The last fund-raiser she organized charged $80 per person and sold 400 tickets. The cost for the food and speaker was $41 per person. What is the value per person of the tax receipt that charity can issue? (Answer: $39)

16. Alexis bought an expensive vase at a fundraising luncheon. She saw the same vase last week in The Bay. It cost $92.00 at The Bay. She paid $125 for it at the auction. What is the value of the tax receipt she will receive? (Answer: $0)

17. Max builds wrought-iron garden fences and trellises. He recently decided to retire. He decided to donate his equipment to a local community college. The equipment cost $95,000 and now has a UCC of $38,000. The equipment has a fair market value of $50,000. Max's income in the year he retired was $75,000. How much is his tax credit? (Answer: $14,472.00)

18. Darwin died four years after the donation in Question 12. In his will, he stated that his studio would go to his wife, and his grand piano and the rest of his music to the foundation for the children's music camp. His piano cost $25,000, and had a UCC of $5,900. At the time of his death, the piano had an FMV of $45,000. The second half of the music had an FMV of $35,000 (with a cost of $0 since he wrote it off as he bought it). The year of his death, Darwin's income was $42,000. What is the value of his tax credit? (Answer: $23,172.00)

Life Insurance

19. Ads on television tell seniors to take out life insurance to pay the taxes due on the family cottage when the children inherit. The ads go on to say that the children can pay the premiums. If there are two children who are 35 and 37, both teachers with good but not large incomes, both married with young children to educate and mortgages, why might the children not agree with the ads?

U.S. Assets

20. Michael and Janice, both age 58, died at the same time, driving back from their home in Florida. They had come to hate the Canadian winters, so they lived in Florida from the beginning of January to mid-May each year. They have four children and eight grandchildren in Canada as well as a small house and their registered and non-registered investments. Their house in Florida has a value of $1,300,000 U.S., while their Canadian home has a value of C$1,550,000. Their RRIFs total C$950,000, while their non-registered assets are worth C$1,700,000. Using an exchange rate of $1 Canadian = $.95 U.S., and assuming they died in 2013:

(a) What is the value of their estate before all taxes in Canadian dollars? (Answer: $5,568,421)

(b) On how much will they owe U.S. estate tax? (Answer: $9,830)

Part 3

Appendices

Acronyms, Tax Rates and Time Value of Money Formula

Chapter numbers are in brackets.

ACRONYMS

ACB	Adjusted Cost Base (11)		LIRA	Locked-in retirement account (7)
ACESPG	Alberta Centennial Education Savings Plan Grant (6)		LLP	Lifelong Learning Plan (6)
			LOC	Letter of Credit (5)
AIP	Accumulated income payments (6) re RESP		LRIF	Locked-in retirement fund (7)
APR	Annual percentage rate (1A)		LRSP	Locked-in RRSP (7)
AVC	Additional voluntary contributions (4)		NCBS	National Child Benefit Supplement (6)
BFT	Basic federal tax (2)		NRA	Normal retirement age (4)
CANSIM	Canada Socio-Economic Information Management System (7)		NRTxCr	Non-refundable tax credits (2)
			OAS	Old Age Security (3)
CAP	Capital Accumulation Plan (5)		PA	Pension adjustment (5)
CCA	Capital Cost Allowance (11)		PAR	Pension adjustment reversal (5)
CCPC	Canadian Controlled Private Corporation (2)		POA	Power of Attorney (9)
CCTB	Canada Child Tax Benefit (6)		PRIF	Prescribed Retirement Income Fund (7)
CDSB	Canada Disability Savings Plan (6)		PSPA	Past service pension adjustment (5)
CDSG	Canada Disability Savings Grant (6)		PV	Present value (1, 1A)
CLB	Canada Learning Bond (6)		PVA	Present value of an annuity (1, 1A)
CDB	Child Disability Benefit (6)		PVIF	Present value interest factor (1A)
CRA	Canada Revenue Agency (2) <www.cra.gc.ca>		PVIFA	Present value interest factor of an annuity (1A)
CEC	Cumulative Eligible Capital (11)		r	Correlation Coefficient (2A)
CESG	Canada Education Savings Grant (6)		RDSP	Registered Disability Savings Plan (6)
CPP	Canada Pension Plan (3)		RESP	Registered education savings plan (6)
CV	Coefficient of Variation (2a)		RLIF	Restricted Life Income Fund (7)
DBPP	Defined benefit pension plan (4)		RLSP	Restricted Locked-in Savings Plan (7)
DCPP	Defined contribution pension plan (4)		RPP	Registered pension plan (4)
DPSP	Deferred profit sharing plan (5)		RRIF	Registered retirement income fund (7)
E (k)	Expected return (2A)		RRSP	Registered retirement savings plan (4)
EAP	Educational assistance payments (6) re RESP		SERP	Supplemental employee retirement plan (5)
EAR	Effective annual rate (1A)		SMERS	Specified multi-employer plan (5)
FMV	Fair market value (6)		SRA	Specified retirement arrangement (5)
FV	Future value (1A)		SRA	Supplemental retirement arrangement (5)
FVA	Future value of an annuity (1A)		SWP	Systematic withdrawal plan (SWP) (7)
FVIF	Future value interest factor (1A)		TFSA	Tax Free Savings Account (6)
FVIFA	Future value interest factor of an annuity (1A)		TONI	Tax on net income (2)
GIS	Guaranteed Income Supplement (3)		TSX	Toronto Stock Exchange (2A)
HBP	Home Buyers' Plan (6)		TVM	Time value of money, TVM (1A)
HPR	Holding period return (2)		UCC	Undepreciated Capital Cost (11)
$(k_{real; AT})$	Real rate of return after tax (2)		WITB	Working Income Tax Benefit (6)
$(k_{nominal; AT})$	Nominal rate of return after tax (2)		YBE	Year's Basic Exemption, CPP (3)
LIF	Life income fund (7)		YMPE	Year's Maximum Pensionable Earnings, CPP (3)

GLOSSARY OF TAX AND TIME VALUE OF MONEY TERMS

Amortization period (1A):   The length of time over which a loan is to be repaid.

Amortization table (1A):   A table that shows the amount of interest and principal in each of the payments in a stream of payments.

Annual percentage rate, APR (1A):   The annual interest rate stated without compounding, regardless of the frequency of the compounding. It is always the rate stated.

Annuity due (1A):   The regular equal payments that are made at the beginning of the period. See Ordinary annuity.

APR (1A):   See Annual percentage rate.

Average tax rate (2): Total tax payable divided by the income *received*. It is useful when comparing before- and after-tax income at various levels of income both before and after retirement as well as when comparing tax rates in different provinces, territories, and countries.

Basic federal tax, BFT (2): The amount of federal tax payable after deducting some tax credits from federal tax payable. These deductions include non-refundable tax credits and the dividend tax credit.

Basic personal amount (2): A flat amount, which everyone filing a tax return is entitled to include as part of amounts available for the non-refundable tax credit. For 2013, the federal amount was $11,038 which means that anyone whose taxable income is less than $11,038 will not pay federal tax on it.

Calculating tax (2): See the end of this glossary.

Calculating time value of money (1A): See the end of this glossary.

Capital gain (2): The excess of the fair market value over the adjusted cost base or undepreciated capital cost. Only a part of capital gains are subject to tax. At the present time, the inclusion rate that is subject to tax is 50%; i.e., 50% of the capital gain is the taxable capital gain.

Capital loss (11): The excess of the adjusted cost base or undepreciated capital cost over the fair market value. Only a part of capital loss is deductible against taxable capital gains. At the present time, the inclusion rate that is subject to tax is 50%; i.e., 50% of the capital loss is the allowable capital loss.

CRA (2): Canada Revenue Agency <www.cra.gc.ca>

Compounding (1A): The calculation of interest on an amount that includes unpaid interest from prior periods.

Cost of capital (1A): The value of interest and/or dividends on invested funds. The APR.

Default risk (1A): The risk that a borrower will not repay the loan. It increases the cost of borrowing.

Discount rate (1A): The APR. It is used when calculating the present value.

Dividend tax credit (2): A tax credit that reduces both federal and provincial taxes payable. The tax credit equals:
- For Type A "Eligible" Dividends from Canadian public Companies
  - 18.9655% of taxable dividends (the grossed up amount is 145% of dividends received)
- For Type B "Ineligible" Dividends from most Canadian Controlled Private Corporations (CCPC)
  - 2/3 of the gross up (25% of dividends received), or
  - 1/6 or 16.67% of the dividends received, or
  - 1 ÷ 7½ or 13.33% of the grossed-up amount (125% of the dividends received).

Dividends (2): Payments to shareholders who own shares in corporations. Unlike interest, which is deducted before tax is calculated, dividends are paid out of after-tax income.

EAR (1A): See Effective annual rate.

Effective annual rate, EAR (1A): The annual interest rate compounded to include the effects of calculating interest more frequently than once a year.

Future value (1A): See FV.

Future value of an annuity (1A): See FVA.

Future value interest factor (1A): See FVIF.

FV, future value (1A):   The value at some time in the future of one amount of money today. See FVIF for an example.

FVA, future value of an annuity (1A):   The value in the future of a series of equal payments made at the same, regular interval. See FVIFA for an example.

FVIF, future value interest factor (1A):   The value in the future of $1.00 today where today is the present value, PV. The FVIF for 5 years at an interest rate of 4% is $1.00 ($FVIF_{5,\ 4\%}$) = 1.21665. The FVIF multiplied times the amount in the present equals the future value. If the present value is $100: FV = $100 ($FVIF_{5,\ 4\%}$) = $100 \times 1.21665 = $121.67.

FVIFA, future value interest factor of an annuity (1A):   The value in the future of $1.00 paid or received at regular intervals. The FVIFA for 5 annual payments made at the end of each year at an interest rate of 4% is $1.00 ($FVIFA_{5,\ 4\%}$) = 5.41632. The FVIFA multiplied times the annual payments equals the future value. If the payments are $100: FVA = $100 ($FVIFA_{5,\ 4\%}$) = $100 \times 5.41632 = $541.63. The total amount actually paid over the 5 years is $500 and the equivalent if paid in a lump sum in 5 years is $541.63. Alternatively, $100 saved at the end of each of 5 years earning 4% will accumulate to $541.63 at the end of 5 years.

Gross-up (2):   Dividends from public Canadian corporations are increased or grossed-up by 25% to arrive at taxable dividends. The 45% increase is the gross-up. See Dividend tax credit.

Grossed-up (2):   Taxable dividends are 145% of dividends received. The 145% is the grossed-up amount. See Dividend tax credit.

Holding period return, HPR (1A):   The rate of return for the length of time an investment is held.

HPR (1A):   See Holding period return.

Hurdle rate (1A):   The rate of return required to make an investment beneficial.

Inclusion rate (2):   The portion of a capital gain that is taxable, or the portion of a capital loss that is deductible from taxable capital gains.

Interest income (2):   Added to income to arrive at taxable income. Interest expense is deducted by a corporation before tax is calculated, so there is no special tax concession for interest income in the Income Tax Act.

Marginal tax rate (2):   The tax on the next $1.00 of income. Since the tax rate will be at the highest rate that the income is currently paying, the marginal tax rate is extremely useful for estimating after-tax income on any additional income. Since the additional income could take the taxpayer into the next tax bracket, the marginal rate can be relied on to provide only an estimate of after tax-income.

Net income (2):   Some tax deductions are subtracted from Total Income to arrive at Net Income on the personal tax return. These deductions include RRSP contributions, RPP contributions, child care expenses and union dues.

Nominal interest rate (1A):   The APR. It includes inflation.

Non-refundable tax credits (2):   Tax credits which reduce tax payable but which will not be paid to the taxpayer if the amount of tax minus these tax credits is negative.

Opportunity cost (1A):   The cost to an investor of income lost on an alterative investment. The APR.

Ordinary annuity (1A):   The regular equal payments that are made at the end of the period. See Annuity due.

Perpetuity (1A):   A capital amount that pays interest forever; i.e., the capital is never used up.

Present value (1A):   See PV.

Present value of an annuity (1A):   See PVA.

Present value interest factor (1A):   See PVIF.

Progressive tax system (2):   Higher amounts of taxable income are taxed at higher rates. For all tax-payers, the first amount is taxable at the lowest rate. For those having income greater than the lowest tax bracket, the portion above the lowest bracket is taxed at the next, higher rate.

Pure interest rate (1A):   Interest rates that reflect only the cost to borrow, the time value of money, with no additions for risk.

PV, present value (1A):   The value now of some future amount of money. See PVIF for an example.

PVA, present value of an annuity (1A):   The value now of a series of equal payments made at the same, regular interval in the future. See PVIFA for an example.

PVIF, present value interest factor (1A):   The value now of $1.00 in the future. The PVIF for 5 years at an interest rate of 4% is $1.00 ($PVIF_{5,\,4\%}$) = .82193. The PVIF multiplied times the amount in the future equals the value today. If the future value is $100: PV = $100 ($PVIF_{5,\,4\%}$) = $100 × .82193 = $82.19.

PVIFA, present value interest factor of an annuity (1A):   The value now of $1.00 paid or received at regular intervals. The PVIFA for 5 annual payments made at the end of each year at an interest rate of 4% is $1.00 ($PVIFA_{5,\,4\%}$) = 4.45182. The PVIFA multiplied times the annual payments equals the present value. If the payments are $100: PVA = $100 ($PVIFA_{5,\,4\%}$) = $100 × 4.45182 = $445.18. The total amount actually paid over the 5 years is $500, and the equivalent if paid in a lump sum today is $445.18.

Real interest rate (1A):
   • see risk free rate , or
   • the interest the interest rate without inflation

Required rate of return (1A):   The rate of return required to compensate an investor for a given level of risk. The APR.

Risk-free interest rate (1A):   The interest rate without any adjustments for risk, also called pure or real interest rate, typically is 2 to 4%.

Simple interest (1A):   The calculation of interest based on an amount that does not include prior, unpaid interest. It is almost never used.

Stated rate (1A):   The APR.

Surtax (2):   An additional tax that is intended to be short term, although a surtax can last for several years. Sometimes the surtax applies to all income; sometimes it applies only to higher levels of income. It can be calculated either as a percentage of income or as a percentage of federal or provincial tax.

Tax credits (2):   Are deducted from taxes payable.

Tax deferral (2):   Taxes are paid later.

Tax deductions (2):   Are deducted from taxable income.

Tax on net income, TONI (2):   Provincial and territorial taxes are calculated on taxable income in the same manner as federal tax.

Tax on tax (2): Provincial and territorial taxes used to be calculated as a percentage of Basic federal tax.

Tax savings (2): Taxes which are never payable.

Taxable dividends (2): Dividends received from a taxable Canadian corporation are grossed up 45% to arrive at taxable dividends; i.e., taxable dividends are 145% of dividends received. Dividends received from corporations other than taxable Canadian corporations are taxed like interest income, and the dividend tax credit may not be used.

Taxable income (2): On a personal tax return, after deducting some rather specialized deductions from net income, one arrives at the amount of income on which tax is calculated.

TONI (2): Tax on net income; i.e., federal, provincial, and territorial taxes are calculated on taxable income.

Term, mortgage (1A): The period of time for which the interest rate is locked in.

Term to maturity (1A): The length of time before a debt instrument has to be repaid.

Time value of money, TVM (1A): The change in value of a money due to a change in time.

Total income (2): The first section of a personal tax returns adds all taxable income to arrive at Total income.

Type A "Eligible" dividends: See Dividend tax credit.

Type B "Ineligible" dividends: See Dividend tax credit.

DISCOUNTING AND COMPOUNDING CASH FLOWS

Cash Flows: (2)

Discount or compound:	Using a discount/interest rate that is:
Nominal cash flows (e.g., non-indexed income) Real cash flows (e.g., indexed income)	Nominal Real

Income from Investments: (2)

Discount or compound dividends, interest and capital gains that are:	Using a discount/interest rate that is:
Before tax After tax	Before tax After tax

Retirement Cash Flows: (2)

Discount or compound retirement cash flows that are:	Using a discount/interest rate that is:
Before tax After tax	Before tax Before tax

RATES OF RETURN
Coefficient Correlation (r): (2A)

		Nominal				Real		
		Bonds	TSE	S&P		Bonds	TSE	S&P
1950–1999	50 years	T-bills	0.31	–0.14	–0.05	T-bills	0.52	–0.07	0.13
		Bond		0.07	0.36	Bonds		0.15	0.43
		TSE			0.73	TSE			0.75

Coefficient of Variation (CV): (2A)

Standard deviation (σ) ÷ Mean (k)

1990–1999	k_{real}	σ	CV
T-bills	4.4%	1.7%	0.39
Bonds	10.3%	10.4%	1.01
TSE	9.4%	15.2%	1.62

Expected Return (E(k)): (2A)

	% in portfolio	k_{real}	σ
Bonds	30%	10.3%	10.4%
TSE	70%	9.4%	15.2%

$$E(k) = wt_1\ E(r_1) + wt_2\ E(r_2)$$
$$= (.3 \times 10.3\%) + (.7 \times 9.4\%)$$
$$= \mathbf{9.7\%}$$

Nominal After-tax Rate of Return ($k_{nominal\ AT}$): (2A)

marginal tax rate = 48%

return × (1 – marginal tax rate)

interest income of 6%: $[(.06 \times (1 - .48)] = 3.12\%$

capital gain of 6%: $[(.06 \times (1 - \{.48 \times .5\})] = 4.56\%$

Real Rate of Return Before Tax: (2)

$k_{nominal} = 7.0\%$

$k_{inflation} = 3.5\%$

$$k_{real} = \left(\frac{1 + \text{nominal rate}}{1 + \text{inflation rate}}\right) - 1 = \frac{(1.07)}{(1.035)} - 1 = 3.38\%$$

Real Rate of Return After Tax ($k_{real;\ AT}$): (2)

$k_{Inflation} = 3\%$
marginal tax rate $= 48\%$

Using	$k_{real,AT} = \dfrac{1+k_{nom}(1-T)}{1+i} - 1$
interest income of 6%:	$k_{real,AT} = \dfrac{1+[0.06(1-0.48)]}{1.03} - 1 = 1.165\%$
capital gain of 6%:	$k_{real,AT} = \dfrac{1+[0.06(1-0.24)]}{1.03} - 1 = 1.515\%$

Standard Deviation of a Portfolio (σ): (2A)

$r = .43$

$$\sigma = [wt_1^2\sigma_1^2 + wt_2^2\sigma_2^2 + 2wt_1wt_2r_{1,2}\sigma_1\sigma_2]^{1/2}$$
$$= [(.3 \times .3 \times .104 \times .104) + (.7 \times .7 \times .152 \times .152) + (2 \times .3 \times .7 \times .32 \times .104 \times .152)]^{1/2}$$
$$= [.00097344 + .01132096 + .002124595]^{1/2}$$
$$= .014418995^{1/2}$$
$$= .120079 = \mathbf{12.0\%}$$

PERSONAL INCOME TAXES
Generic Tax Rates Used

Federal tax			
	15% of the first $39,500 of taxable income	on the first	39,500
	22% of the amount above $39,500 up to $79,000	on the next	39,500
	26% of the amount above $79,000 up to $127,000	on the next	48,000
	29% of the amount over $127,000	over	127,000
− less Non-refundable tax credit (NRTxCr)	15% of the eligible amount, which includes the basic personal amount of $10,000		
= Basic federal tax (BFT)	Federal tax less NRTxCr less dividend tax credit		
Provincial tax			
+	8% of the first $38,000 of taxable income	on the first	38,000
+	13% of the amount above $38,000 up to $76,000	on the next	38,000
+	17% of the amount over $76,000	over	76,000
− less Non-refundable tax credit (NRTxCr)	8% of the eligible amount which includes the basic personal amount of $9,000		
= Total tax			
Tax Rate	Total tax divided by Income **Received**		

Tax Calculation (using Table 2.3)

$ Received:		Interest		Dividends		Capital Gains	
		Average	Marginal	Average	Marginal	Average	Marginal
Interest		70,000	100.00				
Dividends				70,000	100.00		
Capital gains						70,000	100.00
Taxable income		70,000	100.00	101,500	145.00	35,000	50.00
Federal tax:							
15% on the first	35,900	5,925.00		5,925.00		5,250.00	7.50
22% on the next	35,900	6,710.00	22.00	8,690.00			
26% on the next	48,000			5,850.00	37.70		
29% over	127,000						
Total federal tax:		12,635.00	22.00	20,465.00	37.70	5,250.00	7.50
Dividend Tax Credit				19,249.98	27.50		
NRTxCr* — 15% of	10,000	1,500.00		1,500.00		1,500.00	
Basic federal tax (BFT)		**11,135.00**	**22.00**	**(284.98)**	**10.20**	**3,750.00**	**7.50**
Provincial tax							
8% on the first	38,000	3,040.00		3,040.00		2,800.00	4.00
13% on the next	38,000	4,160.00	13.00	4,940.00			
17% over	76,000			4,335.00	24.65		
Total provincial tax		7,200.00	13.00	12,315.00	24.65	2,800.00	4.00
Dividend Tax Credit				12,180.00	17.40		
NRTxCr* — 8% of	9,000	720.00		720.00		720.00	
Basic provincial tax (BPT)		**6,480.00**	**13.00**	**(585.00)**	**7.25**	**2,080.00**	**4.00**
Total Tax		**17,615.00**	**35.00**	**(869.98)**	**17.45**	**5,830.00**	**11.50**
Average tax rate		*25.16%*		*−1.24%*		*8.33%*	
Marginal tax rate			*35.00%*		*17.45%*		*11.50%*

	Contribution Rates		Benefits	
Canada Pension Plan (CPP)	2013	Generic	2013	Generic
YMPE	51,100	**46,000**		
YBE	3,500	3,500		
Rate	4.95%	4.95%		
Maximum payable	2,356.20	2,103.75	12,150	**11,500**
Old Age Security (OAS)	n/a	n/a	6,552.84	**6,400**
Employment Insurance (EI)				
Maximum insurable	47,400	**43,300**		
Rate	1.88%	1.62%		
Maximum amount	891.12	701.46		

TIME VALUE OF MONEY (TVM)
TVM Formula

FV =	$PV\,(FVIF_{n,\,k})$	The future value of one amount of money.
FVA =	$PMT\,(FVIFA_{n,\,k})$	The future value of a series of equal payments made at the end of the same, regular interval (an ordinary annuity).
PV =	$FV\,(PVIF_{n,\,k})$	The present value (now at T_0) of one amount of money.
PVA =	$PMT\,(PVIFA_{n,\,k})$	The present value of a series of equal payments made at the end of the same, regular interval (an ordinary* annuity).

*When the payments are made at the beginning of the period, it is called an **annuity due**.

TVM Acronyms

One amount of money:		Annuities:	
FV	Future Value	FVA	Future Value
PV	Present Value	PVA	Present Value
n	Number of *compounding periods*	n	Number of *payments**
i	Nominal interest rate	i	Nominal interest rate
k	Interest rate per *compounding period*	k	Interest rate per *payment** period
EAR	Effective annual rate	EAR	Effective annual rate
		PMT	Amount of regular payment
		*assumes PMT is at the *end* of the period	

TVM Calculations

1. Draw the timeline including:
   - the dates
   - the "time" i.e., T_1, T_2, ... T_n
   - amount(s) of money
   - the interest rates if it changes during the time of the timeline
2. Write down what is given, i.e PV, FV, PVA, FVA, PMT, n and i.
3. Write the appropriate equation from above; i.e., the formula for PV, FV, PVA or FVA.
4. Convert n and i to reflect the appropriate compounding if required.
5. Write the equation with the numbers.
6. Solve for the unknown.

TVM Rules

#	Rule
1.	The interest rate given is always the APR i.e., compounded annually, unless stated otherwise.
2.	The future value annuity formula includes the assumption that the payments are made at the end of each period. Thus, the last payment is not compounded.
3.	When you have used the formula, make sure you know where you are in time.
4.	The present value annuity formula assumes the payments are made at the end of each period. The first payment is discounted one period.
5.	Always convert the interest rate to match the compounding or payment period.
6.	To get the monthly rate from the: • APR, divide the APR by 12: 9% APR ÷ 12 = .75% per month • EAR, add 1 to the EAR, take the 12th root, subtract 1 $(1.0938)^{1/12} - 1 = .75\%$ per month
7.	To get from a monthly rate to an: • APR, multiply by 12: .75% × 12 = 9.00% • EAR, add 1, raise it to the 12th power, subtract 1. $(1.0075)^{12} - 1 = 9.38\%$
8.	The formula for taking inflation out of a nominal return is: $$\frac{(1+\text{nominal rate})}{(1+\text{inflation rate})} - 1 = \text{real rate}$$
9.	To put inflation back into a real rate: nominal rate = (1 + real rate) × (1 + inflation rate) − 1
10.	Discount or compound • after-tax income *from investments* using after-tax discount rates • before-tax income *from investments* using before-tax discount rates.

Glossary of Retirement
Planning Terms

Chapter numbers are in brackets.

A

Accumulated income payments (AIP), RESP (6): Payments of the income earned on RESP contributions. They are paid to the contributor, if alive, and if the beneficiary does not use the RESP. These payments are subject to regular tax plus a special tax, which is waived in some circumstances.

Actively managed (3): Investment management whereby investments are deliberately chosen with some goal in mind.

Additional voluntary contributions AVC, DCPP (4): Additional contributions that can be made to a defined contribution pension plan to increase the retirement benefit. Members of a DBPP may be able to buy back earlier years of service for pension benefits for which they were not previously eligible. These are voluntary contributions but are not additional voluntary contributions.

Alberta Centennial Education Savings Plan Grant (ACESPG), RESP (6): Available to children born after 2005.

Allowance, OAS (3): Available to seniors whose spouse or partner receives the OAS pension, who are 60 to 64 years of age and who meet citizenship and residency requirements.

Allowance for the survivor, OAS (3): Available to seniors whose spouse or partner has died, who are 60 to 64 years of age and who meet citizenship and residency requirements.

Annual contribution, CPP (3): The amount that the employer and employee each pay to the Canada Pension Plan.

Annuitant (7): The one to whom the annuity is paid or the owner of an RRSP.

Annuity (7): A contract to make regular, periodic payments made by a financial institution to the annuitant.
- Annuity certain: See Guaranteed-term annuity.
- Cashable annuity can be cashed in to buy another annuity if interest rates increase.
- Contingent annuity pays until the second spouse dies.
- Deferred annuity is an annuity where the first payment is made at least one year in the future.
- Fixed-term annuity: See Guaranteed term annuity.
- Fixed-annuity pays the same amount for life.
- Guaranteed term annuity pays for a minimum number of years or to a specific age.
- Immediate annuity begins to pay one time period after the annuity is purchased.
- Income-reducing annuities decrease the payment to the surviving spouse when the annuitant dies.
- Indexed annuity payments increase each year by either a fixed amount or by an amount linked to the CPI
- Integrated annuity pays less when the annuitant begins to receive the CPP pension.
- Joint-and-survivor annuities are payable until the second death.
- Joint-and-survivor, guaranteed 5, 10, or 15 years pay a guaranteed number of years and to the estate if the annuitant dies before the payments stop.
- Life annuity pays for only the life of the annuitant. It is sold only by insurance companies.
- Prescribed annuity payments are calculated based on life expectancy but the taxable interest in each payment is a fixed percentage based on the total amount of interest paid over the life of the contract.

- Reducing annuity: See Integrated annuity.
- Term-certain annuity: See Guaranteed term annuity.
- Variable annuity pays out based on the investment return.

Asset classes (2A): Different kinds of (investment) assets.

Assignment:
- CPP (3): Spouses over age 60 can elect to pool their CPP retirement benefit in proportion to the length of time they have lived together compared with their contributory period. Also called pension sharing.
- RPP (4): No amount of pension benefits may be used as collateral for a loan.

Average rate of return (2A): The rate of return over a given number of time periods.

B

Beneficiary, RESP (6): The person who receives the capital and income when she or he attends a qualifying institution.

Benefit earned, DBPP (5): The portion of a member's pension that is considered to have accrued during the year in a defined benefit plan. Multiply the plan's formula for the lifetime benefit by the member's pensionable earnings. It is the lowest of:
1. the plan formula
2. 2% of earnings up to $134,833 of earnings for 2013
3. The defined benefit limit, which is the greater of:
   (a) the overriding provision, and
   (b) the dollar limit for 1990 to 1994 inclusive.

Best earnings, DBPP (5): The benefit received is based on the best 3 perhaps, or 5 perhaps years of service. The pension benefit is: *x% × the best # of years of earnings × # of years of service*

Bracket creep (2): Moving into a higher tax bracket when salary increases to compensate for inflation but the tax brackets do not increase.

C

Canada Disability Savings Bond (CDSB) (6): Available to low-income families for beneficiaries who qualify for the disability tax credit.

Canada Disability Savings Grant (CDSG) (6): Matches contributions to a Registered Disability Savings Plan.

Canada Education Savings Grant (CESG), RESP (5): A grant paid to RESPs on behalf of the beneficiary. The grant is 20% of the contribution to an annual maximum of $500, with additional amounts available to low-income families, and a total maximum of $7,200.

Canada Learning Bond (CLB), RESP (6): Available to low-income families.

Capital Accumulation Plan (5): A tax-assisted investment or savings plan that allows members to make their own investment decisions from not less than two options.

CANSIM (Canada Socio-Economic Information Management System) (6): Rate used to calculate minimum withdrawals from LIFs.

Career average earnings, DBPP (4): The benefit received is based on the average earnings during the period of service. The pension benefit is: $x\%$ × *career average earnings* × *# of years of service.*

Carrier (6): An insurance company, or a Canadian trust company or institution, that is licensed to carry on an annuities business.

Cash profit sharing plan (5): In effect, a bonus.

Cashable annuity (6): See Annuity.

CRA designated (6): Rates designated by CRA which determine the minimum withdrawal from a RRIF.

Children's benefit, CPP (2, 3):
- Disability — paid to the children of people receiving the CPP disability benefit
- Survivor — paid to the children of deceased CPP contributors.

Clawback, OAS (3): A special tax of 15% of OAS benefits received. This tax is applied to OAS income when taxable income is over some threshold amount ($70,954 for 2013, $68,000 generic). At a salary of $110,667 generic the OAS is totally clawed back.

Coefficient of variation (2A): Measures the relatives risk of invested assets, i.e., the amount of risk per unit of return, calculated by dividing the standard deviation by the mean (average) return.

Commutation payment (4): A lump sum payment to a pension plan member. The amount is equal to the present value of the expected future pension payments.

Commuted value, RPP (7): See Commutation payment.

Connected person (5): A person who is closely connected to the corporation or a related corporation. Closely connected could mean the person owns at least 10% of the shares of the employer, or the person does not deal at arm's length with the employer.

Contingent annuity (7): See Annuity.

Contribution, annual, CPP (3): The amount paid by the employer and employee into the Canada Pension Plan each year.

Contribution holiday, DBPP (4): Employer and employee contributions are reduced or suspended, since the contributions are made out an excess surplus.

Contribution limit:
- RESP (6): No annual maximum, lifetime total is $50,000.
- RRSP (4): The maximum a taxpayer can contribute to an RRSP each year. It includes current year contribution room and unused contribution room from prior years.

Contribution rate, CPP (3): The percentage applied to CPP pensionable earnings to arrive at the employee and employer's annual contributions to the Canada Pension Plan.

Contribution room, RRSP (5): The new amount one can contribute to an RRSP in a year. It does not include unused contribution room which is contribution room from prior years not used.

Contributory period, CPP (3): Contributions based on earned income begin at the 18th birthday and continue until retirement, between the ages of 60 to 70.

Contributory plan, RPP (4): A registered pension plan to which the employees makes contributions.

Correlation coefficient (2A): Indicates how two invested assets react, relative to each other, to changes in the market. Positively correlated assets move together although perhaps not perfectly, so (+1). Negatively correlated assets move in opposite directions, although perhaps not perfectly, so (− 1).

Credit splitting, CPP (3): Spouses who are separating pool and divide their CPP pension credits equally between them. It is mandatory but not automatic.

D

Death benefit:
- CPP (3) is a one-time payment to a maximum of $2,500.
- RPP (4): A payment made if the member dies before retirement. The maximum amount of the payments is the greater of contributions plus income, and the accrued entitlement.

Deferred annuity (7): See Annuity.

Deferred compensation, RPP (4): A pension is considered to be deferred compensation for services rendered.

Deferred profit sharing plan (DPSP) (5): A defined contribution plan whose contributions vary since they are made out of profits. Maximum contributions are the lesser of ½ of the money purchase limit and 18% of salary before the DPSP.

Defined benefit limit (DBPP) (5): The greater of:
  1. the overriding provision, and
  2. the dollar limit.

Defined benefit pension plan (DBPP) (4): Defines the amount of pension the employee will receive. The investment risk is borne by the employer, who must ensure that the pension fund has enough funds to pay the future pension liability.

Defined contribution pension plan, DCPP (4): Technically, a defined contribution plan covers both a money purchase plan and a deferred contribution plan whereby the amount of the pension is based on contributions and the earnings from the investment of the contributions. Thus, the investment risk is borne by the employee. Money purchase plan is the name for the registered pension plan as opposed to the deferred profit sharing plan. However, in general usage, DCPP refers to the pension plan while DPSP refers to the deferred profit sharing plan. Canada Revenue Agency uses the technically correct terms, money purchase plan (MPP) and deferred profit sharing plan (DPSP).

Demutualization (7): The name given to the process of an insurance company issuing shares to its policyholders in an amount equal to the value of the shares in order to change the structure of the company. If this is taken as cash, it is a taxable dividend income when deceived. If taken as shares, there will likely be a capital gain when the shares are sold. The adjusted cost base of the shares is zero.

Dependants' pension benefits, RPP (4): Pension benefits may be paid to dependants when he retiree dies after retiring.

Designated educational institution, LLP (6): A university, college, or other educational institution that qualifies for the education tax credit in the non-refundable portion of the tax return.

Disability benefit, CPP (3):
  - A benefit paid to CPP contributors who have a severe and prolonged disability, have made contributions to the CPP, and are under age 65. At age 65, it is converted to the regular CPP pension benefit.
  - Children of disabled contributor benefit, paid to dependant children of contributors who are receiving CPP disability benefits.

Disabled, CPP (3): The disability must be "severe and prolonged". "Severe" means the condition prevents the contributor from working regularly at any job. "Prolonged" means the condition is long term and may result in death.

Dollar limit, DBPP (5): One-ninth of the money purchase limit for 1990 to 1994 and after 2004.

Double dipping, RPP (5): An employee can obtain extra RRSP contribution in the year an employer sets up a pension plan since RRSP contribution limits are based on prior year's income.

E

Early retirement:
- CPP (3): To qualify, the contributor must have substantially stopped working meaning their annual earned income is less than the maximum CPP retirement benefit.
- RPP (4): Early retirement can be taken if the employee has a minimum number of pension credits. The benefit can be reduced (with a penalty) or unreduced (without a penalty). See also Normal retirement age
  - with a penalty, RPP (4): The retiree's pension is reduced by some percentage for every year the employee is short of all or some of: normal retirement age, years of service, and/or the qualifying factor
  - without a penalty, RPP (4): The retiree may not meet all the criteria for retirement (age, years of service, and qualifying factor) but the plan permits early retirement if one or more of the qualifications are met.

Earned income:
- CPP (3) includes salaried income, self-employed net income, and commissions.
- RPP (4): See Prescribed income.
- RRSP (6) includes employment income, commissions, net income/loss from a business or real property, taxable support payments received but not investment income, royalty income, net research grants, and employment insurance benefits.

Educational assistance payments, RESP (6): The income on the contributions, the grant, and the income earned by the grant. They are payable to the beneficiaries and are taxable to the recipient.

Eligible earnings, RPP (4): Include salaries, wages, bonuses, vacation pay, honorariums, commissions, taxable allowances, taxable benefits, and director's and officers' fees.

Eligible service, RPP (4): Generally, only employment income from an employer carrying on all or part of its business in Canada. See also Prescribed compensation.

Eligibility, RPP (4) defines who can and who cannot participate in an RPP. Essentially, only employees may participate.

Employee profit sharing plans (EPSP) (5): Extra contributions paid to a trustee to manage. The plan can be registered with the CRA, in which case the employer contributions are tax deductible. Employees can make contributions that are not tax deductible.

Employer-sponsored pension plans (4): Registered pension plans that are organized by employers. Other types are government administered plans and individual plans (RRSPs).

Employment insurance premiums (EI) (3): EI premiums are 1.62% of salary for 2013 to a maximum salary of $43,300; the generic rate used in this text is 1.62% of maximum insurable earnings of $43,300. They are included with amounts eligible for non-refundable tax credits.

Excess amount, RRIF (7): An amount withdrawn from a RRIF above the minimum required amount. The excess amount is subject to withholding tax.

Excess earnings approach (4): In a DBPP, a supplementary pension benefit can be based on, for instance, the Consumer Price Index or if the fund has generated excess earnings, which are defined in the plan.

Excess surplus, DBPP (4): The plan has generated income that produces a surplus greater than a certain minimum required level of surplus. The amount over the required minimum surplus is the excess surplus.

F

Family plans, RESP (6): Can have more than one beneficiary as long as the beneficiaries are related by blood or adoption.

Final Earnings, DBPP (5): The benefit received is based on the last 3 (perhaps), or last 5 (perhaps) years of service. The pension benefit is: *x% × the best # of years of earnings × # of years of service.*

Financially dependant child or grandchild (6) Someone who is financially dependant on the taxpayer, and the child's net income is less than a defined amount.

First time buyer, HBP (6): Someone who, with or without a spouse and during the period beginning 4 years before the year of the withdrawal and ending 31 days before the withdrawal has not owned a home that was occupied as a principal residence.

Fixed-term annuity (7): See Annuity.

Flat benefit, DBPP (5): The benefit received is a flat rate per year or month of service. The pension benefit is: *$x / year or month × # of years of service.*

Foreign pension plan (4): RPPs for foreign employees working outside of Canada for Canadian employers.

Forfeited amounts, DCPP, DPSP (5): Benefits to which a former member has no right because the member quit working for the employer before the benefits were vested.

Full pension:
- OAS (3): The maximum pension based on meeting residency requirements.
- RPP (4): See Unreduced pension.

Full retirement benefit, CPP (3): The maximum amount one can receive at age 65.

G

Government-administered pension plans (4): Include CPP, OAS, and GIS.

Group plans, RESP (6): Plans that pool investments and beneficiaries by age.

Guaranteed Income Supplement (GIS) (3): Paid to low-income seniors based on the residency requirements for the OAS and annual taxable income.

Guaranteed number of years (4): For a DCPP, the maximum number of years that can be guaranteed when paid as a life annuity is the lesser of 15 years, or the date of retirement to the day before the member's 86th birthday.

Guaranteed term annuity (7): See Annuity.

H, I

Home Buyers' Plan (HBP), RRSP (6): Allows first-time home buyers to borrow up to $25,000 from their RRSP. This loan is interest free and must be repaid over no more than 15 years.

Immediate annuity (7): See Annuity.

Income attribution for spousal RRSPs (6) and spousal RRIFs (7): See Spousal RRSP and Spousal RRIF.

Income attribution rules (6): See Income attribution rules in Estate Planning Glossary.

Income-reducing annuity (7): See Annuity.

Indexed (2): Refers to amounts which increase each year usually based on the change in the consumer price index.

Indexed annuity (7): See Annuity.

Individual pension plan IPP (5): A defined benefit pension plan for connected persons. It is paid for by the employer.

Individual plans (6): A type of RESP where there is only one beneficiary.

Integrated annuity (7): See Annuity.

Integrated pension plan, DBPP (5): An employer-sponsored pension plan that is integrated with the Canada Pension; i.e., the contributions are less on earnings up to the Year's Maximum Pensionable Earnings and higher on earnings above the YMPE. When received, the pension formula is lower for the earnings up to the YMPE and is higher above the YMPE.

J, L

Joint-and-survivor annuity(7): See Annuity.

Joint-and-survivor, guaranteed 5, 10, or 15 years (7): See Annuity.

LIF and LRIP unlocking (6): Allows holders to transfer funds to plans that may not be locked-in or that have maximums.

Life annuity (7): See Annuity.

Life benefit (4): The benefit is received until death.

Life expectancy (2): The number of years one can expect to live.

Life Income Fund LIF (7): A RRIF that restricts the maximum as well as the minimum withdrawals. At age 80, the balance must be used to purchase a life annuity.

Lifelong Learning Plan (LLP), RRSP (6):   Permits taxpayers and their spouses to borrow up to $10,000 a year to a maximum of $20,000 to return to school. The loan is interest free and must be repaid in not more than 10 years.

Locked-in Retirement Account (LIRA) (7)   Along with locked-in RRSP LRSP (6), holds funds until the funds are transferred to another vehicle to pay retirement income.

Locked-in Retirement Income Funds (LRIF) (7):   In Alberta and Saskatchewan, the LRIF is available and, like a LIF, it has maximum and minimum withdrawal rules. The maximum relates to the plan's earnings, not its age. However, an annuity can be purchased at any time (or not purchased at all).

Locked-in RRSP LRSP (7):   See Locked-in Retirement Account.

Longevity (2):   See Life expectancy.

M

Matured RRSP (6):   Paying out retirement income to the annuitant or a beneficiary if the annuitant has died.

Maximum benefit (3):
- CPP is $12,150 for 2013 and the generic rate is $11,500.
- GIS is $8,885 for 2013 and the generic rate is $7,900.
- OAS is $6,553 for 2013 and the generic rate is $6,400.

Maximum pensionable earnings, RPP (4):   The maximum amount of eligible earnings on which pension contributions can be made.

Maximum withdrawals, LIF and LRIF (7):   The maximum one can withdraw based on a formula provided by CRA.

Means tested (3):   The GIS benefit is means-tested, meaning it is reduced as income increases over a specified amount.

Minimum withdrawals from RRIF, LIF, and LRIF (7):   Tax-sheltered savings encourage taxpayers to save for their retirement by sheltering deposits to registered plans from taxes. Since these plans are intended to be consumed in retirement, there are minimum required withdrawals which are taxable.
- Minimum withdrawals from a RRIF are based on:
  1. the age (in whole numbers) of the individual or the individual's spouse at the beginning of the year (or the age they would have been had they been alive at the beginning of the year), and
  2. the fair market value of the RRIF at the beginning of the year.
  Withdrawals from the RRIF must start the year after the RRIF was established.

Money purchase limit (5):   The maximum contributions to all pension plans (RPP + RRSP + DPSP) in any year.

Money purchase plan (MPP) (4):   See Defined contribution pension plan.

Multi-employer plan (MEP) (5):   A pension plan with several employers.

N

Named beneficiary, RESP (6): Can be changed under certain circumstances.

New contribution room, RRSP (6): The RRSP contribution room for the current year.

Nominal dollars (1): The value of future dollars, including inflation.

Nominal rate of return (2): Rates of return calculated over a period of time that include inflation.

Non-contributory pension plans, RPP (3): Registered pension plans to which the employee does not make contributions.

Non-indexed (2): Annual amounts are not increased to reflect inflation.

Non-qualifying RRIF (7): Set up after 1992. See end of handout for minimum withdrawal requirements. See also qualifying RRIF.

Non-sheltered savings (6): Retirement savings which are not in registered pension plans; i.e., the contributions are not tax deductible, and the annual income is subject to tax.

Normal retirement age (NRA), RPP (4): The age when a member of a pension plan is entitled to receive a full, unreduced retirement benefit assuming enough years of service. See also Early retirement.

O

Old Age Security Pension (OAS) (3): OAS is based on the number of years of residency in Canada.

Old Age Security Program (3): Includes the OAS pension and the GIS pension.

Original subscriber, RESP (6): The first subscriber to an RESP. After 1997, the original subscriber can be replaced only if the original dies or the new subscriber if the (former) spouse or common-law partner of the original subscriber and the rights were obtained under a divorce decree or a written agreement dividing the property upon separation.

Overcontributions to:
- **RESPs (6):** Contributions over the $50,000 lifetime maximum are subject to a penalty of 1% a month pro-rated between contributors if there are more than one.
- **RRSPs (6):** Contributions over $2,000 more than the contribution limit are subject to a penalty of 1% per month. The $2,000 can be carried forward to future years, but only one amount of $2,000 is permitted.

Overriding provision, DBPP (5): See Benefit earned.

P

Partial pension, OAS (3): A reduced OAS pension available to people who have lived in Canada after the age of 18 but have not lived in Canada long enough to qualify for the full OAS pension.

Passively invested (3): Investment management that replicates the TSE 300 stock composite index and a world market index.

Past service pension adjustment (PSPA), DBPP (5): Arises out of benefit improvements for events related to periods of past service after 1989:
- benefits are improved retroactively;
- an additional period of past service is credited to the member; or
- there is a retroactive change to the way a member's benefits are determined.
  A PSPA is equal to the additional pension credits that would have been included in the member's PA if the upgraded benefits or additional service had actually been provided in those previous years.

Pay-as-you-go, CPP (3): See Steady state financing

Pension adjustment PA, RPP (4,5): The total of a member's pension credits from all plans in which the member's employer participates in the year. The PA reduces the amount that a member can contribute to an RRSP in the following year.

Pension adjustment offset (5): Part of the pension credit formula. The offset is $600 after 1996 and $1,000 before 1997.

Pension adjustment reversal PAR, RPP (5): Restores an individual's RRSP room in situations where the individual terminates membership in a registered pension plan or a deferred profit sharing plan and receives an amount that is less than the accumulated PAs and PSPAs that have been calculated in respect of the benefit.

Pension assignment, CPP (3): See Assignment, CPP. Also called pension sharing.

Pension credit, RPP (5): A measure of the value of the benefit the member earned or accrued during the calendar year. RRSPs do not generate pension credits. The pension credit for:
- a defined contribution plan and a deferred profit sharing plan equals the total contributions.
- a defined benefit pension plan equals the pension credit formula.
- pension credit formula, DBPP (5) is (9 × benefit earned) — PA offset.

Pension credits, CPP (3): The CPP retirement benefits earned based on pensionable earnings and contributions made over the years.

Pension formula (5): The formula that states how much pension will be paid in a defined benefit pension plan.

Pension income amount, taxation (3): A federal tax credit for certain retirement income. The credit is 16% of $1,000 of eligible income and is part of the non-refundable tax credits.

Pension income splitting (5): Allows spouses to split up to one-half of pension income for tax purposes.

Pension sharing, CPP (3): See Assignment, CPP. Also called pension assignment.

Pensionable earnings, CPP (3): The maximum amount of earnings on which a contribution to the CPP is made (after subtracting the year's basic exemption — YBE). See yearly maximum pensionable earnings — YMPE.

Portable, RPP (4): An employee can transfer the pension to another pension plan or to a locked-in RRSP.

Prescribed amount, RPP (5): The reduction in allowable pension contributions for a connected person in the year a pension plan is set up. The prescribed amount is the lesser of 18% of 1990 RRSP earned income and $11,500.

Prescribed annuity (7): See Annuity.

Prescribed compensation, RPP (4):   Types of compensation that are eligible for RPP contributions during periods of reduced service.

Prescribed Retirement Income Funds (PRIF) (6):   Replaces (in Saskatchewan) or supplement (In Manitoba) LIFs and LRIFs.

Promoter, RESP (6):   The financial institution to which the RESP contributions are made.

Q

Qualifying educational institution, RESP (6):   A college, university, or other designated education institution in Canada or outside Canada if the program is a post-secondary school program and lasts at least 13 weeks, or is an educational institution in Canada that is certified by the Minister of Human Resources Development as offering non-credit courses to develop or improve skills of an occupation.

Qualifying educational program
- LLP (6) is a full time program which last 3 months or more and the students is in class or work at least 10 hours a week. Courses or work include lectures, practical training, labs and research but does not include study time.
- RESP (6) is a full time program which last 3 weeks or more, requires the student to be in class at least 10 hours a week and is not part of the student's employment.

Qualifying factor, RPP (4):   The number which may be required to receive an unreduced pension. It is age plus # of years of qualifying service.

Qualifying home, HBP (6):   Located in Canada, it is a single family dwelling, a semi-detached home, a townhouse, a mobile home, a condominium unit, a share of the equity in a co-op, an apartments in a duplex, triplex fourplex or an apartment building.

Qualifying RRIF (7):   Set up 1992 or earlier and has had no property or funds transferred to it since the end of 1992. It has different withdrawal rules than a non-qualifying RRIF. See also non-qualifying RRIF.

R

Real dollars (1):   Amounts in the future calculated without inflation.

Real rate of return (1):   Rates of return calculated over a period of time which do not include inflation.

Reasonable minimum pension (4):   An employee must receive, for example, at least $300 a month pension after 10 years of service.

Reduced pension, RPP (4):   See Early retirement with a penalty.

Reducing annuity (7):   See Annuity.

Refund of premiums, RRSP (7):   The payout to a beneficiary of a matured RRSP when the annuitant dies if the beneficiary is a spouse or financially dependent child. The amount can be rolled over to the beneficiary's RRSP without affecting the contribution room of the beneficiary.

Registered Disability Savings Plan (RDSP) (6):   Defers tax on income until the beneficiary receives an assistance payment.

Registered education savings plan RESP (6):   A plan sponsored by the federal government to provide an incentive to save for children's education. Contributions are not tax deductible and are not taxed when withdrawn. The income is taxable to the beneficiary when withdrawn.

Registered funds (1):   Tax-sheltered savings; i.e., they are tax deductible when contributed, fully taxable when withdrawn and the income is not taxed while the funds are in the registered plan.

Registered Retirement Income Fund RRIF (7):   The proceeds of an RRSP received no later than the year in which one turns 69. It can also receive funds from an RPP if the RPP permits and from another RRIF. It is used to provide retirement income directly, as a lump sum or via an annuity. It is subject to minimum withdrawal requirements.

Restricted Locked-in Savings Plan (RLSP) (7):   Receives funds from a RLIF for unlocking.

Retirement benefits, CPP (3):   Pension benefits paid from the CPP program.

Retiring allowance, RRSP (6):   An amount received by an employee after termination of employment. In some circumstances, a retiring allowance will give the taxpayer additional RRSP contribution room.

Reverse Mortgage, <www.chip.ca> Canadian Home Income Plan (7):   A combination of a loan against the equity in the home and an annuity paid to the homeowner.

Risk/return tradeoff (14):   The more risk one is willing to accept, the higher the expected return.

RRSP contribution limit (4,5):   See Contribution limit.

RRSP contribution room (5):   See Contribution room.

RRSP contributions (5):   Limited to 18% of earned income to a 2013 maximum of $24,270.

RRSP maximum dollar limit (5):   The lesser of 18% of prior year's earnings or the money purchase limit for the prior year.

S

Self-directed RRSP (6):   An RRSP where the taxpayer pays a fixed fee per year to be able to choose investments not ordinarily offered by the financial institution.

SERP (5):   See Supplemental employee retirement plans.

Severance pay, RRSP (6):   An amount received by an employee to terminate their employment. In some circumstances, severance pay will give the taxpayer additional RRSP contribution room.

Sheltered savings (6):   Savings intended for retirement in registered funds, which grow before tax.

Significant shareholder (4):   A shareholder who, alone or with a parent, spouse or child, owns or has a direct or indirect beneficial interest in 10% or more of the voting shares of a corporation.

SMEPP (5):   See Specified multi-employer plans.

Specified multi-employer plan SMEPP (5):   An RPP offered by a group of employers.

Specified (or supplemental) retirement arrangement SRA (5):   See Supplemental retirement arrangement.

Spousal rollover, RRSP (6): Allows the transfer of a deceased's RRSP to a surviving spousal or financially dependant child or grandchild without taxation at the time of the transfer.

Spousal RRIF (7): The same attribution rules apply to spousal RRIFs as to Spousal RRSPs except that it applies only to the excess amount, which is any amount withdrawn above the minimum required amount

Spousal RRSP (7): An RRSP in the name of the spouse. The total RRSP contributions to one's own plan and to a spousal plan must not exceed the taxpayer's total contribution limit. The funds must remain in the RRSP for two years before being withdrawn or the funds are taxed in the hands of the original contributor (called income attribution).

Spouse, RRSP (6): Includes a married partner, opposite-sex partners, and same-sex partners with whom the contributor is living.

SRA (5): See Supplemental retirement arrangement.

Standard deviation (2A): A measure of risk.

Statement of Contributions, CPP (3): Details all the benefits currently available based on contributions paid to date.

Steady-State Financing, CPP (3): The contribution rate for the CPP that will lead to a 20% reserve. Up to half of the CPP portfolio will be more actively managed to assist in reaching the goal of not increasing the contribution rate past 4.95%. See also Actively managed, Passively managed.

Subscriber, RESP (6): The person who makes the contributions.

Substantially stopped working, CPP (3): A contributor may take the CPP early if he or she is between the ages of 60 and 65 and annual earnings are less than the amount payable at age 65.

Supplemental employee retirement plans (SERP) (5): An additional RPP, either defined contribution or defined benefit, for high income earners.

Supplemental retirement arrangement (SRA), DBPP (5): Permits pension benefits over the legislated maximum. It applies only to DBPP since there are no maximums for DCPP.

Supplementary pension benefit, DBPP (4): Additional benefit received to reflect increases in the cost of living.

Surplus, DBPP (4): A surplus in a pension plan occurs when the income and increase in market values produce assets minus liabilities over and above that which is required to pay the future liability for pensions.

Survivor benefits, CPP (3):
- Lump-sum death benefit paid to the estate of the contributor,
- Survivor benefit payable to the surviving spouse of a deceased contributor,
- Children of deceased contributor paid to minor children of a deceased contributor, or to the child's age 25 if the child is still in school.

Systematic Withdrawal Plan (SWP) (7): Enables investors to liquidate small portions of their units from a non-registered mutual fund portfolio on a regular basis. The capital remains invested in growth equities while income is received from selling small portions of the units. These small portions are made up of some of the after-tax capital invested as well as unrealized capital gains. The withdrawals can be altered or discontinued at any time.

T

Tax credit (2): A reduction of tax payable.

Tax deduction (2): A reduction of taxable income.

Tax-Free Savings Account (TFSA) (6): A savings plan available to everyone over the age of 18. The income is never taxed, and borrowed funds can be replaced without using new contribution room.

Term certain annuity (7): See Annuity.

Threshold amount, OAS (3): The amount of taxable income at which a tax of 15% of OAS is applied.

U

Unlocking (7): The ability of the holder of a LIF or LRIF to transfer the funds to a plan with different or no locking-in provisions.

Unmatured RRSP (6): An RRSP that is not yet paying out retirement income.

Unreduced pension, RPP (4): See Early retirement without a penalty.

Unused contribution room (5): See Contribution room.

V, W, Y

Variable annuity (7): See Annuity.

Vesting, RPP (4): Refers to the point in time when the employer's contributions become the property of the employee. In federal plans, this happens no later than two years after the date of employment.

Voluntary contributions, RPP (4): See Additional voluntary contributions.

Withholding tax (6): Applies to RRSP withdrawals and to the excess amount of RRIF withdrawals. The amount withheld is 10% on the first $5,000 or less, 20% of $5,001 to $15,000, and 30% on amounts over $15,000.

Yearly maximum pensionable earnings (YMPE), CPP (3): The maximum amount of earned income on which one pays CPP contributions.

Year's basic exemption (YBE), CPP (3): The first amount of earned income on which no one pays CPP contributions. It has been $3,500 since 1996.

Glossary of Estate Planning Terms

Chapter numbers are in brackets.

A

Ademption by advancement (10): A bequest to a beneficiary is reduced by gifts made before death unless there is a clause against ademption by advancement.

Adjusted cost base (ACB). (11): The cost of an asset adjusted to reflect other costs which have been capitalized, i.e., not expensed as they occurred. These other costs include items such as acquisition costs, installation expenses, and government grants.

Adjusted net capital loss (11): The amount of a net capital loss adjusted to reflect the current capital gains inclusion rate of 50%.

Administrator (10): Appointed by the courts to administer the estate when there is no will or living executor, or the executor is not willing or able to perform this function. Also called a personal representative and is similar to an executor.

Agent, power of attorney (9): See Attorney.

Agent for the executor (10): A person or trust company hired by the named executor to administer the estate and/or provide advice.

Allowable capital loss (11): Fifty percent of the loss.

Allowance (9): Specific periodic spousal or child support payments, which the recipients can use at they see fit.

Alter ego trust (12): Designed for single people. Tax on assets transferred into the trust is deferred until the death of the settlor.

Alternate beneficiary (10): Another person named as beneficiary in case the original is not alive.

An even hand (12): The trustee must consider the best interests of all beneficiaries.

Annulment (9): The marriage is not valid; i.e., it is void or voidable.

Arbitration (9): A process whereby both parties to a divorce make their cases to a neutral third party, the arbitrator, who makes a binding decision.

Ascendant (9): Parents, grandparents, etc. See Consanguinity.

Attorney (9): A proxy or agent who manages one's affairs under a power of attorney and is not necessarily a lawyer.

Attribution rules (11): See Income attribution rules.

Auctions (12): See Gifts, charitable.

B

Beneficiary, named (10): The person or organization who benefits. Assets in an RRSP, RRIF, or life insurance policy can pass directly to them without going through the estate. A named beneficiary in a will overrides a named beneficiary at a financial institution if the will was written later.

Beneficial interest in a trust (12):   The person has a right to receive income or capital from a trust at some time.

Benefit of nominal value (12):   A charitable gift means that the value of the benefit is less than 10% of the value of the gift to a maximum value of $50.

Bequest (10):   To make a gift of personal property in a will to a person or organization.

Breakdown of marriage (9):   See Divorce Act.

Business inventory (12):   See Gifts, charitable.

Buildings and equipment (12):   See Gifts, charitable.

Buy-sell agreements (10):   An agreement to purchase the share(s) of a partnership or corporation when one partner dies at a fixed price or according to a formula.

C

Canadian cultural property (12):   See Gifts, charitable.

Capital beneficiary (12):   Entitled to receive capital held by a trust.

Capital Cost Allowance (CCA) (11):   The amortization of the cost for tax purposes. There is none in the year of death.

Capital gain (11):   Deemed or actual net proceeds less adjusted cost base.

Capital gains exemption (11):   Up to $800,000 for shares of qualified small business corporations.

Capital interest (10):   The beneficiary who receives the capital from an estate but may not be the beneficiary who has the right to use the capital during the life tenant's lifetime.

Capital interest beneficiary (10):   The one who inherits the capital after the life interest beneficiary dies.

Capital loss (11):   Adjusted cost base less deemed or actual proceeds. It does not apply to not depreciable property.

Capital property (11):   Owned assets that are depreciable, non-depreciable, or eligible capital property.

Capital property, gifts (12)   See Gifts, charitable.

C.C.A. (11):   See Capital Cost Allowance.

C.R.A. (11):   Canada Revenue Agency.

Certainty (12):   For a trust to be set up, three things must be clear:
- Intent — there must be a clear intention to create a trust
- Subject Matter — what assets are being transferred
- Objects — who the beneficiaries are.

Certainty of Intent (12):   See Certainty.

Certainty of Objects (12):   See Certainty.

Certainty of Subject Matter (12):   See Certainty.

Charitable gift (12):   Donation of money or other assets to a registered charity. See Gifts, charitable.

517

Child-related expenses (9): They are added to support payments, e.g., child care-costs, uninsured medical costs over $200, special education needs, costs for extracurricular activities.

Child Support Guidelines (9): They are federal (although there are also provincial guidelines) and determine how child-support matters are determined under the Divorce Act. They take into account income levels of both parents, number of children, type of custody, and province of residence.

Claim (9): An application for spousal support. There are 2 types: a corollary claim is made at the same time as the divorce petition while a statement of claim is made after the divorce.

Clearance certificate (10): It certifies that all taxes, CPP, EI, and interest and penalties have been paid to the CRA, or security for payment has been accepted.

Codicil (10): A formal amendment to a will, which must also be witnessed.

Cohabitation agreement (9): An agreement between common-law spouses that specifies the rights and obligations of each spouse.

Collaboration Family Law (9): Requires both spouses to get new lawyers if the process breaks down and the spouses go to court.

Collateral heirs (10): Brothers, sisters, and their heirs. See Consanguinity.

Collateral relatives (10): A common ancestor but in a different line such as cousins, aunts and uncles. There is no statutory obligation to support them. See Consanguinity.

Commercial trust (12): Not a personal trust; i.e., the beneficiary has received his interest by paying something for it. See also Mutual fund trust and Segregated fund trust.

Common disaster clause (10): An extreme contingency clause that names an alternate beneficiary if the original beneficiary dies at the same time as the testator. It usually is between spouses. One can also stipulate that a beneficiary must survive by 30 days to avoid double probate. See Survival clause.

Common-law partner trust (12): See Spousal trust.

Common-law spouses (10): They do not have automatic property rights under intestate laws.

Communal organization (12): An intro vivos trust for congregations who live and work together communally.

Community property (9): See Matrimonial property.

Consanguinity (10): The relationship of individuals by blood. The Table of Consanguinity determines who inherits if there are no close surviving relatives.

Constructive trust (12): A non-titleholder volunteered a financial contribution that cost him financially. The contribution directly caused the asset to increase in value.

Contingent power of attorney (9): Takes effect when some event happens. It is also called a springing power of attorney.

Continuing power of attorney (9): See Enduring power of attorney.

Contribution of services (12): See Gifts, charitable.

Corollary claim (9): See Claim.

Court of competent jurisdiction (9): The court in each province that is designated by the federal *Divorce Act* to hear divorce proceedings.

Corporate insurance (10): Insurance on the shareholder's life payable either to the other shareholders or to the corporation to redeem the shares.

Cross-insurance (10): Each partner or shareholder buys enough insurance on the partners' lives to buy that share if and when that partner dies.

Crown gifts (12): Gifts to Her Majesty for Canada or a province or a Crown agency controlled by a provincial ministry.

Cultural gifts (12): See Gifts, charitable.

Cumulative eligible capital account (11) is a notional account that holds 75% of the cost of eligible capital. Amortization expense can be taken annually — the amount is 7% on a declining-balance basis.

Custody (9): See Sole, Shared and Split custody.

D

Deemed allowable capital loss (11): Fifty percent of the deemed capital loss.

Deemed disposition (11): Property is considered sold even if a sale did not take place. For instance, a cottage, mutual funds, stocks, or any asset other than cash given to an adult child leads to a deemed disposition at fair market value.

Deemed proceeds (11): Fair market value (FMV).

Deemed resident trust (12): An offshore trust that is deemed to be resident in Canada for tax purposes under certain circumstances.

Deemed taxable capital gain (11): Fifty percent of the deemed capital gain.

Depreciable property (11): Property which wears out or becomes obsolete.

Descendants (9): Biological and adopted children and all their descendants. See Consanguinity.

Designated beneficiary (10): Named beneficiary who can therefore receive life insurance proceeds, survivor benefits from a pensions plan and RRSP/RRIFs without probate; i.e., the funds are not part of the estate.

Direct line (10): One's parents, grandparents, great-grandparents, etc. and one's children, grandchildren, etc.

Disaster clause, joint (10): See Common disaster clause.

Discretionary trust (12): Trustee has the power to distribute the income and property as he sees fit. See Mere power and Trust power.

Distributive share (10): What remains after the preferential share of an intestate's estate.

Divorce Act (9): A federal act. Breakdown of marriage has occurred when the couple has lived separate and apart for at least one year and were living separate and apart at the commencement of the divorce proceedings, or one spouse has committed adultery or subjected the other spouse to physical or mental cruelty

Domestic contracts (9): A marriage contract for those legally married, a cohabitation contract for common-law and same-sex couples, and separation agreements for all three.

Donation (10): A gift to a registered charity.

E

Ecological gifts (12): See Gifts, charitable.

Elective returns (11): See Optional returns.

Eligible capital expenditures (11): Intangible assets that have been paid for, such as goodwill or a trademark.

Encroachment clause (10): Gives the executor power to give added funds to a life interest beneficiary.

Enduring power of attorney (9): Allows a power of attorney to survive even if the grantor is no longer legally competent . The grantor must have been competent when the power of attorney was set up. Also called continuing power of attorney.

Equal share per capita (10): See Per capita.

Equal shares per stirpes (10): See Per stirpes.

Equalization payment (9): Upon separation, the lower-income spouse is entitled to half of the difference between the net family properties of both spouses. It can also apply to a deceased spouse.

Estate freeze (10, 11): To minimize taxes at death by transferring the assets now by selling or gifting the assets, transferring them to an inter vivos trust, creating a new holding company, or reorganizing the share structure of the existing corporation.

Executor (10): The person who executes a will. If an executor is not named, the courts will appointed one who cannot act until appointed. The responsibilities of an executor include arranging the funeral, acting as the trustee, and managing the assets of the estate (which is a testamentary trust until the assets are distributed), paying the debts of the estate, filing the final tax return and obtaining a tax clearance certificate, and distributing the assets according to the will. The executor is entitled to compensation.

Executrix (10): See Executor

Exempt beneficiary (12): One used to be able to defer accrued capital gains under the 21-year rule by designating direct relatives as exempt. The gain was deferred until the last exempt beneficiary died.

Express trust (12): Trust established deliberately, i.e., inter vivos trust or through a will.

Extreme contingency clause (10): See Common disaster clause.

F

Family Law (9): Its coverage includes division of matrimonial property (including the family home, pension credits, and benefits), and the failure of one party to live up to obligations established in the divorce. In some provinces, it also covers support obligations for a child resulting from a one-night stand. There are financial and legal obligations after death and dependants can obtain an order against the estate which overrides a will. Family law is under provincial jurisdiction and is affected if you move to another province. It includes equalization payments.

Family property (9): See Matrimonial property.

Family trust (12): A trust established for the benefit of family members.

Farm property (11): It can transfer to the next generation before death to be actively farmed by them. The deemed disposition is at the lesser of cost or FMV. See Rollover special.

Fiduciary (12): The relationship between the trustee and the beneficiaries whereby the trustee acts in the best interests of the beneficiaries.

Final tax return (8, 11): A tax return filed for a deceased for the year in which death occurred.

First deemed disposition date for trusts (12):
- spousal inter vivos and testamentary trusts — the date of death of the spouse or beneficiary
- pre-1972 spousal trusts — the later of January 1, 1993 and the date of the spouse's death
- the rest — later of January 1, 1993 and 21 years from the date the trust was established.

FMV (11): Fair market value

Form will (10) A will from a kit or the Internet and requires two witnesses.

Formal will (10) A will drawn up by a lawyer and is witnessed in the presence of a the lawyer.

G

Garnishing wages (9): Having the employer of the payor deduct the amount from the payor's pay and remit it to a central agency.

Gift by businesses (12): See Gifts, charitable

Gifts, charitable (12): Ownership is voluntarily transferred to a registered charity, and the donor receives no benefit in return. If there is a benefit to the donor, the benefit must be of nominal value; i.e., the Fair Market Value (FMV) of the benefit is less than 10% of the amount of the gift and the benefit is not more than $50. Also, one must be able to establish the FMV of the benefit. FMV does not include commissions and sales taxes.

- Auctions: No tax receipt is issued if an item is purchased at a fundraising auction — not even if the price paid exceeds the FMV.
- Buildings and equipment: If the donated value is greater than the UCC, there is recapture (the amount by which the FMV exceeds the UCC). The taxpayer can increase the donation limit by 25% of the recapture in the year of the gift for gifts after 1996.
- Businesses: If the donor receives promotional or advertising services in return for the gift, there is no gift, e.g., if the donor pays $2,000 for advertising space in the charity's magazine, there is no gift. If, however, the donor gives $2,000, which is acknowledged in the charity's newsletter, there is a gift.
- Contributions of services: An official receipt cannot be given for volunteered services even if it is the donor's regular line of work. But if the charity pays for the work and the donor returns all or part of the income as a donation, a tax receipt for the cash donation is issued and the payment for the work is part of the donor's income.
- Cultural property, Canadian: Includes paintings, sculptures, books, and manuscripts that have been certified by the Canadian Cultural Property Export Review Board. This applies to gifts made to Canadian institutions and public authorities that have been designated by the Minister of Canadian Heritage to ensure that the property is properly collected, preserved, and made accessible to the public for research or display purposes. Can claim up to 100% of your net income. There is no capital gain resulting from the gift but you can deduct capital losses on the property within the usual limits.

- Ecological gifts are gifts to a registered charity that have been designated by the Minister of the Environment, or to a Canadian municipality or, after 1996, to the federal government or to a province. The taxpayer can claim a tax credit or deduction of up to 100% of your net income.
- Government, federal or a province or their agent: The donor can claim up to 100% of net income if the donation was made or the donor entered into a written agreement to make the gift before February 19, 1997. Otherwise the 75% rule applies; i.e., the maximum is 75% of net income.
- In kind refers to property other than cash or personal services. It includes capital property, depreciable property, personal-use property, a licence, a share, and inventory of a business. The charity issues a tax receipt for the FMV of the gift on the date it was donated.
- Inventory, e.g., a computer from a computer store, food from a grocery store: Gifts of cash or non-inventory items receive normal tax benefits. Gifts from inventory result in an official tax receipt but the business must include the FMV of the gift in income. For a business, these offset each other.
- Non-depreciable capital property was bought for investment purposes or to earn income. The donor is deemed to have disposed of it at FMV. This can lead to a capital gain of which 50% is taxed at regular rates. The standard donation limit of 75% is increased by adding 25% of the taxable capital gain resulting from the gift for gifts after 1996.
- Securities:
  - Publicly traded securities (for donations made or agreed to after October 18, 2000): The inclusion is 0% of the capital gain (instead of the usual 50%) if there is no "advantage".
  - Non-qualifying securities: There is no tax receipt if the securities are not on a prescribed stock exchange (which are listed in RC4142E but are not listed here), are shares in a business controlled by the donor, or are debts or obligations between the donor and a company controlled by the donor or between the donor and someone else who is related to the donor.
- Tickets:
  - Fund-raising dinners, balls, concerts, shows, or like events: The gift is the difference between the ticket price of fund-raising or like event, and the FMV of the food or entertainment. The cost to the charity to put on the event is *not* included in the FMV.
  - Lotteries, draws, or raffles are not gifts. If the above event included a lottery to win a car, there is no gift at all; i.e., no official receipts can be issued. This can be avoided by selling the 2 tickets — one for the dinner-dance, one for the lottery.
  - Gift in kind (12) See Gifts, charitable.

Gifts (11):   See Attribution rules.

Governments, gifts to (12):   See Gifts, charitable.

Grantor:
  - Power of attorney (9) is the one who assigns the power of attorney. Also called Principal.
  - Will (10) is the one who makes the will. Also called Testator.

Guardian (9, 10):   A person who takes responsibility for a minor child until the child reaches the age of majority.

Guardianship of estate (9, 10):   Management of an estate.

Guardianship of person (9, 10):   Personal care decisions.

H

Health care directive (9):   See Power of attorney for personal care.

Henson Trust (12):   Either a testamentary trust or an inter vivos trust set up for the benefit of a disabled person.

Holograph will (10):   A will that is handwritten by the person making the will. It must be signed and dated but no witnesses are required. It is not valid in some provinces.

I

Inclusion rate (11):   The rate applied to a capital gain to calculate how much of the gain is taxable.

Inclusions/deduction rule (9):   Periodic spousal support payments (or allowance) are taxable to the receiving spouse and tax-deductible to the paying spouse. See Taxation of support payments.

Income attribution rules (11):   The rules under the *Income Tax Act* that govern who pays the tax on income or capital gains when property has been transferred (given) to a spouse or minor child. Income attribution rules do not apply if interest is charged at the proscribed rate and the interest is paid within 30 days of the year-end.
- Minors: The assets are transferred at FMV, which is the ACB for the minor. Income attributes to the transferor end in the year the minor turns 18.
- Spouses or former spouses: attribution rules do not apply when separated if both agree to this. These rules also do not apply if the spouse earns property income from the asset but do apply for business income earned.

Gift to:	Interest	Dividend	Capital Gains
Spouse	Giver	Giver	Giver
Spousal trust	Giver	Giver	Giver
Child < 18	Giver	Giver	Giver if sold before the child turns 19
Grandchild <18	Giver	Giver	Same as box above.
Child > 18	Child	Child	Child
Grandchild >18	Grandchild	Grandchild	Grandchild

Income beneficiary (12):   A beneficiary who is entitled to receive income earned by a trust.

Inter vivos transfers (11):   A transfer of assets while the original owner is still alive.

Inter vivos trust (12):   A trust established while still alive.

Intestacy or intestate rules (10):   The provincial legal rules that apply if a person dies without a will.

Intestate (10):   A person who dies without a will.

In-trust account (12):   A trust account for minor children.

Inventory (12):   See Gifts, charitable.

Irrevocable trust (12):   A trust that cannot be revoked or dissolved once it is set up.

Issue (10):   See Descendants.

J

Joint disaster (10): See Common disaster clause.

Joint spousal trust (12): A joint spousal trust is for all spouses both married and common-law, opposite sex and same sex. The tax on the assets transferred into the trust is deferred until after the death of the second spouse.

Joint tenants (9): Tenants that own equally and each cannot sell without the permission of the other. Upon the death of one, the other automatically receives the deceased's share; i.e., the property does not go through the estate and is not, therefore, subject to probate. An asset which is a non-estate asset means joint tenants with rights of survivorship. If there is a transfer from sole owner to joint tenancy, there is a deemed disposition for tax purposes.

L

Legacy (10): Cash left to a beneficiary in a will.

Letters of indemnity (10): May be provided to a financial institution if there is only one. It is an alternative to probating a will.

Letters probate (10): Documents produced by the provincial court confirming the validity of a will and granting the authority of the executor.

Life interest (10): It permits the use of the property for the life of the person who receives the life interest. The beneficiary is also called a life tenant.

Life tenant (10): Entitled to a life interest in the capital property.

Like event (12): Services or consumable good that must be used by/on a particular date, e.g., a concert is a like event but an auction is not.

Lineally related (10): One cannot marry parents, grandparents, children, and grandchildren.

Listed personal property (11): This list is defined in section 54 of the Income Tax Act. If an asset is not listed there, it is not listed personal property. Taxable capital gains are taxed as regular income and allowable losses can be applied against taxable gains and carried back three years and forward seven years.

Living trust (12): See Inter vivos trust.

Living will (9): See Power of attorney for personal care.

Loanback (12): An attempt to get tax credits by transferring funds to a charity and then borrowing the funds back. A tax credit may not be received.

M

Marital home (9): See Matrimonial home.

Marriage contract (9): A contract that stipulates the rights and obligations of both spouses during and at the end of a marriage.

Marriage of convenience (9): A marriage made for social assistance, immigration, or tax purposes.

Master trust (12): An inter vivos trust that is resident in Canada whose only activity is investing funds, does not have any debt longer than 90 days, has never accepted deposits and the beneficiaries area registered pension plan or a deferred profit sharing plan.

Matrimonial home (9): The dwelling normally inhabited by the family. It is also called the marital home or the family home.

Matrimonial property (9): Assets associated with the marriage that will be divided when the marriage breaks down. It does not include property inherited after the marriage unless it was invested in the marital home; damages received for personal injury, etc.; proceeds of a life insurance policy; anything excluded by domestic contracts; the value of assets at the time of marriage; and business, assets. Also called community property, family property and net family assets.

Mediation (9): The intervention by a third party to bring about an agreement between people who are separating or divorcing. Legal aid is available in some provinces to low-income families.

Mere power (12): The discretionary power of the trustee to distribute trust income or property to some or all of the beneficiaries only if he wants to. See also Trust power.

Mirror will (10): A will where each spouse leaves everything to the other and then to the children when both are deceased.

Mutual fund trust (12): A trust whose only undertaking is investing its funds in property but not real property.

N

Named beneficiary (10): A designated beneficiary. See Beneficiary, named.

Negotiation (9): A process of discussing issues arising from a divorce until compromises are reached.

Net allowable capital loss (11): Total deemed and actual allowable capital losses less total deemed and actual taxable capital gain. On the final tax return these losses can be deducted from all other income and can be carried back 1 year OR carried back 3 years against prior capital gains.

Net capital loss (11): Allowable capital losses minus taxable capital gains.

Net family property or assets (9): See Matrimonial property.

Net taxable capital gains (11): Total deemed and actual taxable capital gains less total deemed and actual allowable capital losses.

Non-arm's length transactions (11): Transactions between people who are related or people who do not have separate economic interests.

Non-depreciable property (11): Property that does not wear out or become obsolete, such as land or trees.

Non-depreciable property, donations (12) See Gifts, charitable.

Non-discretionary trust (12): The trust agreement states the duties and responsibilities in detail, and the trustee cannot act independently unless the trust agreement specifically states this.

Non-estate asset (10): An asset that is not part of the estate, is not controlled by a will and is not subject to probate.

Non-family assets (9): Business assets and property. They are subject to division only to the extent that each spouse contributed to their acquisition and/or operation.

Non-qualifying securities (12)   See Gifts, charitable.

Non-profit organization (12):   A type of trust that pays no taxes.

Non-resident alien (12):   A non-U.S. citizen who is living in the U.S. but does not intend to remain there permanently.

O, P

Official administrator (10):   See Public Trustee.

Optional returns (11):   Can be filed for the year of death. The three optional returns are rights and things, business income as a sole proprietor or partner, and income from a testamentary trust. See Final tax return

Paras formula (9):   A 1971 child support proceeding. The amount needed to support and educate a child is determined. This amount is then allocated between the parents according to their ability to pay.

Partial intestacy (10):   A will makes specific bequests but there are assets remaining after those bequests.

Per capita (10):   Divided equally among all people. Each beneficiary or child who is still alive receives the same amount and the children of a deceased child receive nothing.

Per stirpes (10):   For each person descended from a family branch. The children of a deceased beneficiary share equally the deceased beneficiary's portion. It is more common than per capita.

Personal care decisions (10):   Decisions relating to aspects of daily life which maintain your health and well-being.

Personal representative (10):   See Administrator.

Personal trust (12):   No beneficiary has attained his interest by paying for it.

Personal-use property (11):   Depreciable property owned for pleasure and enjoyment, such as a boat. Taxable capital gains are subject to regular tax but capital losses are not deductible against any kind of income.

Planned giving (12):   Making charitable donations as part of estate planning.

Post-mortem control (10):   The deceased can control the disposition of property after death through a beneficiary designation or a will.

Power of attorney (8, 9):   It takes effect when signed unless it states differently. One can leave the document with a trusted 3rd party or have a springing or contingent power of attorney.
  • At a bank: Covers only the assets at that bank.
  • Enduring or Continuing: Continues after the grantor becomes legally incapacitated.
  • Financial: Covers financial affairs.
  • For personal care (9): Covers personal and health care. Also called a living will or health care directive.
  • For property (9): Covers financial affairs only.

Precatory trust (12):   Property transferred from a trust in the hope that the beneficiary will feel morally obligated to handle it in a certain way.

Preferential share (10):   The first portion of an intestate's estate, which is set aside for the surviving spouse.

Preferred beneficiary (12):   A Canadian resident who is the spouse, former spouse, great/grand/child or spouse of them. Until 1996, one could make elections about them that allowed reduction of taxes

Principal, power of attorney (9):   See Grantor.

Principal residence exemption (11):   A tax exemption on the capital on the principal residence.

Probate (8, 10):   The process of the provincial court validating the will and the authority of the executor. It not required if the estate is straightforward.

Probate fees (8, 10):   Fees charged by the province in which the deceased lived when at the time of death. Ownership of assets in a second province required a second probate (called resealing) but more probate fees are not charged.

Probate bond (10):   Similar to an insurance premium to provide security to a financial institution and avoid probate.

Provincial Courts of Competent Jurisdiction (9):   Administers divorce in the province where either spouse lived for one year before the initiation of the divorce proceedings.

Proxy (9):   See Attorney.

Proxy directive (9):   In a power of attorney for personal care, a provision to appoint a specific person to make health care decisions.

Public charge (9):   Under the guardianship of the province.

Public trustee (9, 10):   A person appointed by a provincial court if no family member applies to act as administrator for a person who has died intestate. The public trustee will distribute the assets in accordance with provincial instate laws.

Publicly traded securities (12)   See Gifts, charitable.

Q

Qualifying farm property (11):   Is eligible for the $800,000 capital gains exemption. The farm must have been used for farming in the year of disposition or for five years during the time the family owned it, and for farms bought after June 17, 1987, for the two years before disposition, the gross revenue must be larger than the income from all other sources and the property must have been used for farming.

Qualified fishing property (11):   Property that is eligible for the $800,000 capital gains exemptions for the transfer of real property, fishing vessels, and eligible capital expenditures.

Qualified small business corporation (11):   Up to $800,000 of capital gains (or $400,000 of taxable capital gain at a 50% inclusion rate) on these shares can be exempt from income tax if the corporation is a Canadian-controlled private corporation (CCPC): resident in Canada, private corporation, not controlled by non-residents ro public corporations, not listed on a Canadian and 25 foreign stock exchanges, and substantially all (more than 90%) of the value of the assets must be used in an active business carried on primarily in Canada. Shares or debt in such small business corporations can qualify as such assets. In addition, it was owned by the taxpayer, taxpayer's spouse, or a related person which, in the two years prior to being sold, was not owned by anyone else, and during the two years, more than 50% of the corporate assets must have been used primarily in an active business carried on in Canada or invested in other small business corporations. Income Tax Act 110.6(1)

Qualifying spousal trust (12): See Spousal trust.

R

Recapture (11): Deemed or actual proceeds less undepreciated capital cost UCC

Reinsurance gift annuity (12): An annuity given by a charity whereby the insurance company guarantees the payments even if the annuitant lives longer than expected.

Related minor (11): A person less than 18 years of age who is not at arm's length; i.e., is a parent or child and is a niece or nephew.

Related minor income attribution rule (11): See Income attribution rules

Related persons (10): Persons related by blood, marriage or adoption.

Remainder beneficiary (12): A capital beneficiary where there is a life interest.

Remainder interest (12): A capital interest that does not come into effect until the person having a life interest dies.

Resealing (10): The process of probating a will in a second province where the deceased had assets. Generally there is no cost for the second probate.

Residual trust (12): A charity is the capital beneficiary while the donor keeps a life interest.

Residuary clause (10): Gives the residue of an estate to a beneficiary.

Residuary estate (10): What remains after the debts are paid and specific bequests have be distributed.

Residue (10): See Residuary estate.

Residue of the estate (10): Assets that are not specifically provided for in an estate. See Residuary estate.

Return for a partner or proprietor (11): An optional return for the terminal period, which includes business income as a sole proprietor or partner.

Return for income from a testamentary trust (11): An optional return for the terminal period, which includes income from a testamentary trust.

Return for rights or things (11): An optional return for the terminal period which includes amounts receivable at the date of death, such as vacation pay or commissions.

Revocable trust (12): A trust that can be dissolved or revoked at the discretion of the settlor.

Revoke a will (10): Make a will invalid.

Right of survivorship (9): The automatic right to property held in joint tenancy.

Rollover, farms (11): Allows farming property to be transferred to a child or grandchild without reporting a capital gain.

Rollover, fishing (11): Allows fishing property to be transferred to a child or grandchild without reporting a capital gain.

Rollover, spousal (10):   See Spousal rollover.

Rollover, special (11):   A qualified farm property in Canada is eligible for a special rollover which defers the capital gain. See Qualifying farm property.

S

Securities (11):   See Gifts, charitable.

Section 85 rollover (11):   A provision that defers the recognition of a capital gain when assets are transferred to a corporation.

Section 86 rollover (11):   Allows the tax-free exchange of all of the shares of one class for the shares of another class.

Segregated fund trust (12):   An inter vivos trust that holds the investment funds of a life insurance policy. The life insurer is the trustee.

Self-insured gift annuity (12):   An annuity offered by a charity whereby the charity guarantees the payments even if the annuitant lives longer than expected.

Separation (9):   Both parties have lived separately and independently even if in the same dwelling.

Separation agreement (9):   An agreement to which both spouses voluntarily agree which includes the terms under which they will live apart. It may include division of property, and child and spousal support.

Separation as to bed and board (9):   Separated and no longer living together.

Settlor (12):   One who establishes an inter vivos trust.

Settlor, trust, duties of (12):   Someone who places assets/property in the trust, sets up rules for operating and winding up the trust, establishes trust when alive or in will.

Share-redemption plan (10):   The corporation must purchase the shares of the deceased either at a fixed price or using a formula.

Shared custody (9):   Each parent has physical custody or access at least 40% of the time in a year.

Situs assets (10):   All real and personal assets normally located in the U.S. regardless of where they were purchased or where they were at the time of death.

Sole custody (9):   The child resides less than 40% of the time in a year with the paying parent.

Specified investment flow-through trust (SIFT) (12):   A trust that invests in stock-exchange listed shares.

Specified trust (12):   The name for a group of trusts such as RESPs and RPPs to define reporting requirements.

Spendthrift trust (12):   A trust designed to protect the assets from a beneficiary who might be irresponsible.

Split custody (9):   The children are divided between the parents; i.e., a child or some children live with one parent, some with the other. Each parent calculates how much he/she must contribute to the other for the support of the child or children living with the other. Then the parent who is required to pay the higher amount pays the difference to the other.

Spousal common law partner trust: (12)   See Spousal Trust.

Spousal order (9):   An order to pay support. It will take into account number of years they lived together and functions each performed.

Spousal rollover (10):   The deceased's assets are transferred to the surviving spouse at the deceased's adjusted cost base. The capital gain is deferred until the death of the surviving spouse. Section 73 rollover.

Spousal testamentary trust (12):   See Spousal trust.

Spousal trust (12):   The current, not former, living spouse is the only one who can receive the income or use the capital. It applies also to common-law spouses.

Spouse (11):   Generally, under provincial Family Law Act, a spouse is a man and woman who are legally married or a man and woman who have lived together for at least 3 years or in a relationship of some permanence and have natural or adopted child. Under the Income Tax Act, a spouse is a couple who are legally married or a couple who have lived together for at least 12 months or a couple who live together and have a child together.

Springing power of attorney (9):   See Contingent power of attorney.

Statement of claim (9):   See Claim.

Successor annuitant (10):   The beneficiary of a RRIF or other annuity.

Superficial loss rule (11):   A spouse cannot transfer assets to a spouse being divorced (but who is not yet divorced) and claim a capital loss. A capital loss can be claimed if the property is transferred after a divorce and the FMV is less than the ACB.

Support payments (9):   The parent's financial obligations to the children are treated separately; i.e., the paying parent pays according to his/her income without reference to the income of the custodial parent. Federal and provincial governments provide tables as guidelines. See also Taxation of support payments.

Survival clause (10):   The amount of time a beneficiary must survive the testator in a common disaster clause.

Survivorship Acts (10):   In some provinces, if both die at the same time, the younger is presumed to have survived the older.

T

Table of Consanguinity (10):   A table that shows the closeness of relatives. It is used to determine who inherits if there are no close surviving relatives.

Tainted spousal trust (12):   Someone other than the spouse receives income or has the right to receive income or use the assets. In this case, the tax-free rollover provisions cannot be used.

Tax clearance certificate (10):   See Clearance certificate.

Taxable capital gain (11):   That portion of a capital gain that is taxable.

Taxation of support payments (9): As of May 1, 1997:

	Payments received	Payments made
Child support including combined payments	Not taxable	Not tax deductible
Spousal support payments		
Periodic*	Taxable	Tax deductible
Lump sum	Not taxable	Not tax deductible
Parental support = a gift	Not taxable	Not tax deductible

*There must be a written agreement or a court order for the payments to be tax-deductible. If the total payments in a year are less than the written agreement states, the payments are considered to be child support for tax purposes. Legal fees to establish or change support payments are not tax deductible but legal fees to enforce a support order are deductible for the recipient.

Tenancy in common (9): Each has an undivided interest in the whole, each can sell without permission of the other. Upon the death of one, that portion is transferred in the will or according to intestacy rules and is subject to probate.

Term insurance (12): Temporary insurance with no savings component. See also Whole life insurance.

Terminal loss (11): UCC less deemed or actual proceeds.

Terminal period (11): January 1 of the year of death to the date of death.

Terminal return (11): See Final tax return.

Testamentary debts (10): Debts due immediately before death or upon death.

Testamentary trust (8, 12): A trust established after death. All estate assets are automatically in a testamentary trust until distributed to the beneficiaries.

Testacy (10): A testate estate; i.e., an estate left through a will.

Testator or testatrix (10): The man or woman who writes a will. Also called a grantor.

Three certainties (12): They are needed to establish a trust i.e., intent, content, and objects. See Certainties.

Tickets (12): See Gifts, charitable.

Total gifts (12): The sum of allowable charitable, crown, and cultural gifts. It is used to calculate the federal tax credit and is subject to the limits related to net income for each category.

Trust (12): See Alter ego trust, Commercial trust, Constructive trust, Discretionary trust, Express trust, Family trust, Inter vivos trust, Irrevocable trust, Joint spousal trust, Master trust, Mutual fund trust, Non-discretionary trust, Personal trust, Qualifying spousal trust, Residual trust, Revocable trust, Segregated fund trust, Spendthrift trust, Spousal (testamentary) trust, Tainted spousal trust, Testamentary trust, and Voluntary trust.

Trust agreement (12): See Trust deed.

Trust, costs (12): Include setting up (or is included in the cost of the will); legal, ongoing administration, and final distribution fees; and filing the annual tax return

Trust deed (12): Describes the terms and conditions of the trust.

Trust indenture (12): See Trust deed.

Trust power (12): Discretionary power of the trustee to distribute income or assets as he or she sees fit while being required to distribute the income or capital. See also Mere power.

Trust tax return (12): T3 Trust Income Tax and Information Return

Trustee, estate (10): The executor or executrix of an estate; i.e., the personal representative who holds title to property in a testamentary trust. See Executor for a list of duties. A trustee can also be the guardian of property for minor children who are beneficiaries in a will.

Trustee, trust (12):
• duties can include managing the assets, filing the income tax returns annually, following the trust agreement, managing and controlling the property, having discretionary investment powers, having the power to decide what and when to pay out capital or extra income.
• obligations are to act in the best interests of all the beneficiaries, perform the duties with honesty, skill and highest level of care, perform the duties personally; i.e., not delegate them, and act without conflict of interest. The trustee can be held personally responsible for any financial losses unless released in the trust agreement

21-year Rule (12): Except for spousal trusts, trusts must recognize capital gains every 21 years.

U

UCC (11): See Undepreciated capital cost.

Undepreciated capital cost (11): Adjusted cost base minus capital cost allowance.

Underage beneficiaries (10): An inheritance must be held in a trust (unless the courts decide otherwise) until the child reaches the age of majority even if there is a spouse.

Unity (9): To form a joint tenancy, there are four requirements:
1. Unity of possession; i.e., each co-owner must be entitled to possess the entire property.
2. Unity of interest; i.e., each co-owner has an equal interest in the property.
3. Unity of time; i.e., all co-owners receive their interest at the same time.
4. Unity of title; i.e., all receive their interest the same way; by will or by transfer of deed.

Unified tax credit (12): Effectively means there is no tax on the first amount of the estate for U.S. residents and resident aliens. For Canadians, the assets are still subject to Canadian capital gains tax on the deemed disposition. This leads to double taxation if estate is greater than the amount.

Unused gift (12): The amount of a donation that is not yet used for the tax credit.

U.S. resident (12): A non-U.S. citizen who lives there and plans to live there permanently. See also Resident alien.

U.S. taxable estate (11): All U.S. situs assets (assets normally located in the US) are part of a U.S. taxable estate except for exempt assets and deductions for estate settlements and non-recourse mortgages.

V

Valuation day (V-day) (11): December 31, 1971; prior to that date, there was capital gains tax.

Vested indefeasibly (12): Locked-in; i.e., the terms of the trust cannot be changed.

Void ab initio (9): Void from the beginning; i.e., can seek an annulment in any jurisdiction.

Voidable marriage (9): Due to facts that arise after the ceremony. The marriage must be voided in the jurisdiction where the husband lives.

Voluntary trust (12):   Transferring one's own assets to an irrevocable trust to protect the assets from one's own spendthrift ways.

W

Ways to distribute assets (10):   1. provincial intestate laws, 2. named beneficiaries on life insurance policies, pension plans, RRSPs and RRIFs, 3. giving them away before you die, 4. joint ownership of property, and 5. through your will.

Whole life insurance (12):   Permanent insurance which provides both insurance and a savings component.

Will format (10):   Identify testator, revoke all previous wills, appoint the executor, authorize your debts to be paid to prevent creditors from placing claims against the estate, specify who gets what and guardians for minor children.

Wills, forms (10):   See Form will, Formal will, Holograph will,

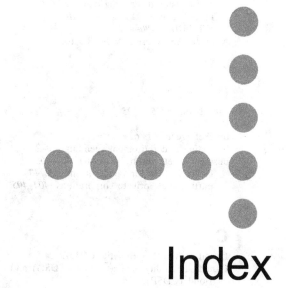

Index

W